How to access the supplemental web resource

We are pleased to provide access to a web resource that supplements your book, *Lesson Planning for Middle School Physical Education*. This resource offers printable versions of all lesson plans found in the book, along with a lesson plan template.

Accessing the web resource is easy!
Follow these steps if you purchased a new book:

1. Visit **www.HumanKinetics.com/LessonPlanningForMiddleSchoolPhysical Education**.

2. Click the <u>first edition</u> link next to the book cover.

3. Click the Sign In link on the left or top of the page. If you do not have an account with Human Kinetics, you will be prompted to create one.

4. If the online product you purchased does not appear in the Ancillary Items box on the left of the page, click the Enter Key Code option in that box. Enter the key code that is printed at the right, including all hyphens. Click the Submit button to unlock your online product.

5. After you have entered your key code the first time, you will never have to enter it again to access this product. Once unlocked, a link to your product will permanently appear in the menu on the left. For future visits, all you need to do is sign in to the textbook's website and follow the link that appears in the left menu!

→ Click the Need Help? button on the textbook's website if you need assistance along the way.

For technical support, send an e-mail to:

support@hkusa.com . . . . U.S. and international customers
info@hkcanada.com . . . . Canadian customers
academic@hkeurope.com . . . . European customers
keycodesupport@hkaustralia.com . . . . . Australian and New Zealand customers

Product: Lesson Planning for Middle School Physical Education web resource

Key code: LPMSCE-RX9SP3-OSG

HUMAN KINETICS WEB RESOURCE

This unique code allows you access to the web resource.

Access is provided if you have purchased a new book. Once submitted, the code may not be entered for any other user.

HUMAN KINETICS
The Information Leader in Physical Activity & Health

03-2017

Lesson Planning for Middle School Physical Education

Meeting the National Standards & Grade-Level Outcomes

Robert J. Doan, PhD
University of Southern Mississippi

Lynn Couturier MacDonald, DPE
State University of New York College at Cortland

Stevie Chepko, EdD
Independent Consultant and Researcher

Editors

SHAPE America SOCIETY OF HEALTH AND PHYSICAL EDUCATORS®

health. moves. minds.

HUMAN KINETICS

Library of Congress Cataloging-in-Publication Data

Names: Doan, Robert J., editor | MacDonald, Lynn C., editor. | Chepko, Stevie, editor.
Title: Lesson planning for middle school physical education / Robert Doan, PhD, Lynn MacDonald, DPE, Stevie Chepko, EdD.
Description: Champaign, IL : Human Kinetics, [2017] | Includes bibliographical references.
Identifiers: LCCN 2016029850 | ISBN 9781492513902 (print)
Subjects: LCSH: Physical education and training--Study and teaching (Middle school)--United States. | Lesson planning--United States.
Classification: LCC GV365 .D63 2017 | DDC 613.70712--dc23 LC record available at https://lccn.loc.gov/2016029850

ISBN: 978-1-4925-1390-2 (print)

Acquisitions Editors: Ray Vallese and Scott Wikgren; **SHAPE America Editor:** Joe McGavin; **Senior Developmental Editor:** Bethany J. Bentley; **Managing Editors:** B. Rego and Kirsten E. Keller; **Associate Managing Editors:** Carly S. O'Connor and Anna Lan Seaman; **Copyeditor:** Patricia L. MacDonald; **Permissions Manager:** Dalene Reeder; **Graphic Designer:** Dawn Sills; **Cover Designer:** Keith Blomberg; **Photograph (cover):** © Human Kinetics; **Photographs (interior):** © Human Kinetics, unless otherwise noted; p. 13 © fishwork/iStock/Getty Images; p. 203 © Rich Legg/Getty Images; p. 295 © Alex Potemkin/iStock/Getty Images; p. 391 © Image Source/Digital Vision/Getty Images; p. 483 © gbh007/iStock/Getty Images; **Photo Asset Manager:** Laura Fitch; **Photo Production Manager:** Jason Allen; **Senior Art Manager:** Kelly Hendren; **Illustrations:** © Human Kinetics; **Printer:** Sheridan Books

SHAPE America – Society of Health and Physical Educators
1900 Association Drive
Reston, VA 20191
800-213-7193
www.shapeamerica.org

Printed in the United States of America   10 9 8 7 6 5 4 3 2 1

The paper in this book is certified under a sustainable forestry program.

Human Kinetics
Website: www.HumanKinetics.com

United States: Human Kinetics
P.O. Box 5076
Champaign, IL 61825-5076
800-747-4457
e-mail: info@hkusa.com

Canada: Human Kinetics
475 Devonshire Road Unit 100
Windsor, ON N8Y 2L5
800-465-7301 (in Canada only)
e-mail: info@hkcanada.com

Europe: Human Kinetics
107 Bradford Road
Stanningley
Leeds LS28 6AT, United Kingdom
+44 (0) 113 255 5665
e-mail: hk@hkeurope.com

Australia: Human Kinetics
57A Price Avenue
Lower Mitcham, South Australia 5062
08 8372 0999
e-mail: info@hkaustralia.com

New Zealand: Human Kinetics
P.O. Box 80
Mitcham Shopping Centre, South Australia 5062
0800 222 062
e-mail: info@hknewzealand.com

E6629

Contents

Preface

This book is designed to complement *National Standards & Grade-Level Outcomes for K-12 Physical Education* (SHAPE America, 2014) and to help you develop and implement lesson plans that will help your students attain those outcomes. SHAPE America's National Standards and Grade-Level Outcomes are intended to produce physically literate individuals; that is, young adults who have "the knowledge, skills and confidence to enjoy a lifetime of healthful physical activity" (p. 11). As a physical education teacher, you are positioned ideally to help students become physically literate. You can educate the *whole* person by providing learning experiences in the psychomotor, cognitive, and affective learning domains. This holistic education requires a high-quality physical education program, in which students demonstrate content mastery in all three learning domains through formal assessment. The National Standards and Grade-Level Outcomes delineate the grade-specific content that students should learn and master. At the same time, the outcomes provide a structure for you to use in developing meaningful learning experiences for your students.

The lesson plans in this book have been contributed predominantly by practitioners who are experienced in teaching middle school–level physical education content that is driven by the National Standards and Grade-Level Outcomes. Each lesson plan addresses specific Grade-Level Outcomes; provides deliberate, progressive practice tasks; integrates appropriate assessments to evaluate and monitor student progress; and includes resources, references, equipment lists, and student assignments, as appropriate. You can implement the lesson plans in this book as they are, but they will be more effective if you modify them to meet the needs of your students. In fact, these lesson plans are intended to be used as models for creating your own lessons and learning activities, as well as providing a framework for the curriculum development process.

HOW TO USE THIS BOOK

The content in this book is divided into two parts: Part I, Planning for Student Success in the Middle Grades (Chapters 1 through 3), and Part II, Lesson Plans for Middle School Physical Education (Chapters 4 through 11). Part II of the book corresponds with and expands upon Chapter 4 in *National Standards & Grade-Level Outcomes for K-12 Physical Education* (SHAPE America, 2014), which explores the Grade-Level Outcomes for middle school.

As you might assume, the Grade-Level Outcomes devoted to middle school students are quite different from those devoted to elementary or high school students and are predicated on the differences in their developmental levels. The emphasis in middle school is on learning to apply foundational skills and knowledge, which students acquired in elementary school, to a variety of physical activities and environments (Gallahue et al., 2012). By adolescence, students have the cognitive ability to understand and integrate abstract concepts, which makes middle school an appropriate time for teaching game tactics, problem solving, and performance strategies. More information about developmental considerations specific to middle school students appears in Chapter 3.

As noted, Chapters 4 through 11 contain lesson plans, arranged in modules (instructional units) of eight lessons each. These chapters are organized by category of activity rather than by national standard. While it is possible to teach a lesson or module on a particular standard, it's more realistic to integrate the appropriate outcomes under various standards within the activity being taught. For example, you can teach Standard 4 outcomes, which center on personal and social responsibility, during lessons on games or fitness or dance, etc. For more information on embedding outcomes within lessons, see Chapter 2.

While this book contains a wide variety of modules and lesson plans, it does not include all possible activities that you might want to teach in your physical education program. You can think of these lesson plans as models for developing your own when teaching new or different activities. An accompanying web resource includes an editable lesson plan template as well as all lesson plans in PDF format for easy printing and easy accessibility from a computer or tablet. Visit www.HumanKinetics.com/LessonPlanningForMiddleSchoolPhysicalEducation.

Many resources are available to help you increase your content knowledge in new activities, including conferences, books, activity-specific websites, and movement-oriented applications. We hope that you will exercise your passion for lifelong learning to extend the materials offered in this book into new areas for your students and your own professional development.

eBook
available at
HumanKinetics.com

SHAPE AMERICA'S COMMITMENT: 50 MILLION STRONG BY 2029

Approximately 50 million students are enrolled currently in America's elementary and secondary schools (grades preK through 12). SHAPE America is leading the effort to ensure that by the time today's youngest students graduate from high school in 2029, all of America's young people are empowered to lead healthy and active lives through effective health and physical education programs. To learn more about 50 Million Strong by 2029, visit www.shapeamerica.org.

PART I

Planning
for Student Success
in the Middle Grades

CHAPTER 1

The Importance of Teaching for Student Learning in the Middle Grades

National Standards & Grade-Level Outcomes for K-12 Physical Education (SHAPE America, 2014) provides important guidance for middle school teachers to enable student learning. In fact, the book's underlying premise is that student learning is the essence of physical education. Students at any grade level cannot attain the National Standards and Grade-Level Outcomes without learning taking place, and student learning cannot take place without effective lessons, learning experiences, and assessments.

As physical educators, we believe that physical education is a critical component of student development and the overall school curriculum. We can support that belief, however, only if we take an educational approach, as opposed to a recreational or a public health approach, in our physical education programs (Ennis, 2011, pp. 11-12). In the educational approach, student learning is the primary instructional goal. Simply keeping students "busy, happy and good" (Placek, 1983) will not lead to their becoming physically literate individuals, as prescribed in *National Standards & Grade-Level Outcomes for K-12 Physical Education*. Also, without instruction and learning, physical education diverges from schools' core mission (Ennis, 2011, p. 16) and can be marginalized too easily. With accountability measures on the rise in public education, physical educators must be prepared to both articulate and demonstrate what students have learned in physical education. If we are not able to provide evidence of student learning, the credibility of our subject area and our position in schools could be jeopardized.

FACTORS THAT INFLUENCE STUDENT LEARNING

Many factors influence student learning and the subsequent development of physical literacy, including elements such as student engagement, motor skills competency, gender differences, and instructional environment (SHAPE America, 2014). Student engagement refers to the level of personal involvement in the learning activity: in other words, the degree to which a student is engrossed physically, cognitively, and/or socially in the learning experience. A passive bystander in a soccer game is not necessarily "engaged," even though that student might technically be "participating" in the activity. The list that follows summarizes what researchers have determined will affect student engagement in any subject area. For more detail about each point, please review the studies under each topic area in the reference list.

Students are more likely to engage in an activity if

- they believe that they have the skills to succeed in the activity;
- the learning activity is interesting; and
- the learning experience provides a socially supportive and inclusive climate.

Having the Skills to Succeed in an Activity

Skill competency and perceived competency are *both* critical for student engagement and learning. When students believe that they have the skills to participate successfully in an activity, they approach it with more interest and confidence, and they are more willing to put effort into the task. When students do *not* believe they have the skills to participate successfully in an activity, they are less willing to put themselves at risk of possible negative social comparisons with their peers and, accordingly, are less likely to engage in the activity (Garn, Cothran, & Jenkins, 2011; Ommundsen, 2006). Those social comparisons often occur in activities in which students perform individually while other students observe (e.g., batting in softball) or in competitive games.

Skill competency and perceived competency are just as important for students to *continue* participating in a physical activity and in fitness as they are for students to engage initially. Researchers have found that kindergarten children who are proficient in motor skills are more physically active than those children who are not as proficient (Kambas et al., 2012); that skillful children are more likely to be fit and physically active as adolescents than are less-skilled children (Barnett et al., 2008a; Barnett et al., 2008b); and that a positive relationship exists between motor skill competence and health-related fitness in young adults (Stodden, Langendorfer, & Roberton, 2009). In other studies, skillful middle school students were found to be more active and more effective during game play than less-skilled students (Bernstein, Phillips, & Silverman, 2011). The less-skilled students often were excluded from game play, resulting in their developing negative attitudes toward it. In general, game play led to fewer skill practice opportunities, lower levels of perceived competence, and a lack of engagement for less-skilled students. Stodden et al. (2008) hypothesized that as children mature, the relationship between motor competence and physical activity strengthens. In that model, those who are not skillful are less likely than skillful peers to participate and, therefore, they become less fit, leading to a "negative spiral of disengagement" (p. 296).

The development of competence, then, is a key strategy for promoting long-term physical activity and fitness. Indeed, "SHAPE America considers the development of motor skill competence to be the highest priority in the Grade-Level Outcomes" (SHAPE America, 2014, p. 9). The fundamental movement patterns form the foundation for physical activity, and those skills require instruction and practice from qualified teachers and coaches (Strong et al., 2005, p. 736). As a physical education teacher, you play a critical role in ensuring that all of your students develop motor skill competence through the progressive and sequential development of learning experiences and high-quality lesson plans.

Offering Learning Activities That Are Interesting

Students' interest in any particular activity is influenced by their individual interests, their situational interest, choice, and challenge. Individual interest is a relatively stable construct and depends on each student's personal characteristics and experiences. Situational interest is more variable and is influenced by the learning environment. As a teacher, you can increase situational interest by manipulating the level of cognitive demand or challenge (Chen & Darst, 2001; Smith & St. Pierre, 2009) and by providing choices to students. It's essential, then, to design learning experiences that require exploration, problem solving, and/or higher levels of thinking (e.g., applying skills to a new situation, synthesizing knowledge from different areas) in order to increase the likelihood that the activities you present to your students will interest them and engage them in learning. If your lesson activities are too basic or are mindlessly repetitive, students will be bored and will check out mentally. An activity has to contain enough challenge to hold your students' attention and motivate them to apply effort to the practice tasks.

Providing choice in the instructional experiences is essential to attracting and maintaining student interest, as well as appealing to students' sense of autonomy (Bryan et al., 2013; Ntoumanis et al., 2004). By being allowed to make some choices, students can invest a bit of themselves in the task at hand. This can be as simple as allowing students to pick their own partners or pieces of equipment. You also can offer students more complex choices, such as choosing between game play and additional practice tasks, or selecting a practice task from among several of varying difficulty (differentiated instruction). By creating an instructional environment that supports student choices, all students can engage in the lesson in a way that challenges them and leads to success.

Providing a Socially Supportive and Inclusive Instructional Climate

Most students prefer to engage in physical education when the instructional environment is inclusive and feels supportive (relatedness) (Zhang et al., 2011). To be inclusive, the learning experiences should be welcoming to students of all ability levels (differentiated instruction) and should accommodate a variety of student interests. Often—especially for less-skilled students—a curriculum that is oriented toward competitive team sports does not feel inclusive or supportive. A competitive instructional environment allows highly skilled students to dominate, reducing practice opportunities for other students and increasing their chances of being embarrassed (Bernstein, Phillips, & Silverman, 2011; Hill & Hannon,

2008). Less-skilled students prefer cooperative and noncompetitive activities that allow them to participate on more even footing.

Beginning with adolescence, gender preferences become an important consideration for inclusiveness. Substantial evidence suggests that adolescent girls are dissatisfied with the traditional physical education curriculum. With the exception of those who are highly skilled, most adolescent girls prefer activities such as dance, fitness, and cooperative activities to traditional team sports (Grieser et al., 2006; Hannon & Ratcliffe, 2005). In addition, girls are more likely than boys to perceive the physical education environment as a barrier to participation, indicating that sweating as well as showering and changing clothes in a locker room discourage their involvement in class (Couturier, Chepko, & Coughlin, 2007; Xu & Liu, 2013). Given that girls' physical activity levels are lower than boys' in general, and that those activity levels drop off further in adolescence, teachers must attend to gender differences and preferences in planning learning experiences for their students. The curriculum that you design must have the potential to engage *all* students, regardless of skill level, gender, or personal interest.

THE INSTRUCTIONAL ENVIRONMENT

Ultimately, your challenge is to create an environment that maximizes student engagement and skill development. To accomplish that, you will need to create a mastery climate for instruction, one that emphasizes

- skill acquisition,
- effort,
- individual improvement, and
- assessment of student performance.

Skill Acquisition

Mastery climates reflect effective learning experiences, with progressive, sequential practice tasks as the core of the lesson plan and instructional unit. You must plan the learning tasks in a way that affords students the maximum number of practice opportunities possible, because acquiring skill requires repetition. You can employ many strategies for maximizing practice opportunities, such as providing enough equipment for everyone to participate at once, modifying the task environment or conditions, and using small-sided games to increase the number of touches for each student. The practice tasks should resemble the performance context, but simplified at first, followed by gradual increases in complexity. For example, if the skill is shooting in a soccer game, practicing by shooting without a defender will not transfer to the performance condition (game). Instead, you could plan the practice task to include a passive defender whom the shooter must recognize and avoid by using fakes and dodges. After the shooter encounters some success, you change the task so that the defender is semi-active; that is, the defender may move but may not take the ball from the shooter. Eventually, the defender becomes fully active. In such a series of practice tasks, the learning experiences always reflect the conditions of performance but become increasingly complex. For more examples and information about planning deliberate practice tasks, see Chapter 7 of *National Standards & Grade-Level Outcomes for K-12 Physical Education* (SHAPE America, 2014).

Effort

We physical educators often focus on making activities fun, but fun doesn't necessarily lead to learning and competency. Your students simply cannot improve their skills without effort and practice; they have to *work* at it. Grit, or persistence, is essential for acquiring skill and attaining long-term goals such as physical literacy (Duckworth et al., 2007). It's all about repetition, repetition, repetition. In fact, becoming an expert performer at anything requires more than 10,000 hours of deliberate practice, although some people can establish basic competence with as few as 50 hours of training (Ericsson, 2006). Obviously, you don't have enough class time for students to reach expert levels of performance, but basic competence is within reach and should be the goal. You also can foster a mastery climate by emphasizing and rewarding effort and persistence among your students.

Individual Improvement

Focusing on improvement rather than competition is another element of a mastery climate (Garn, Ware, & Solmon, 2011; Stuart et al., 2005). A competitive environment inevitably yields losers as well as winners, but when the lesson focuses on improvement, all students can succeed. For a focus on individual improvement to be effective in a mastery climate, you will need to plan differentiated instruction for students of all ability levels. Each practice task will need modifications to simplify it, or make it more complex, depending on your students' skill levels. Practice tasks should be challenging but achievable. It helps if students realize that they probably won't have a lot of success at the beginning and that they should expect some failure. Your assessments will help you identify individual students' areas of weakness, which you must communicate to each of them, along with how they can improve. With a focus on improvement, students are less concerned about how their performance compares to that of other students, and physical education becomes a more positive, supportive climate for learning.

Assessment of Student Performance

Implementing a mastery-oriented instructional climate isn't possible without assessment. You will need to conduct frequent formal and informal assessments to measure student improvement and mastery of the content. Assessment should occur before instruction to establish what students already know and can do. This pre-assessment establishes your baseline for planning and implementing instruction. You also should integrate assessment throughout the instructional unit to measure progress between lessons (formative assessment) as well as cumulative learning at the end of the unit (summative assessment). As the teacher, you are engaged in a cycle of assessing, analyzing the results, and applying your analysis through corrective feedback or modification of learning experiences. For more information about assessments, see Chapter 8 of *National Standards & Grade-Level Outcomes for K-12 Physical Education* (SHAPE America, 2014).

Physical literacy–driven physical education is all about student learning, and you are the key to delivering the experiences that lead to that student learning. Fortunately, many of the variables that influence student learning are within your control because *you* shape the learning environment (Subramanian, 2009). By keeping your focus on what students are learning, and by using the National Standards and Grade-Level Outcomes as guideposts, you can help students become physically literate and physically active for a lifetime.

HOW THE GRADE-LEVEL OUTCOMES ARE CODED

As you dig deeper into the Grade-Level Outcomes for middle school, you will see that each outcome has a number code. The code signifies the National Standard, level, and grade with which each outcome is associated. As an example, S1.M3.7 refers to Standard 1, Middle School Outcome 3, Grade 7 (SHAPE America, 2014, p. 12). You will find this coding helpful in identifying the relationship between standards and outcomes, as well as locating particular outcomes within each grade level.

UNDERSTANDING THE SCOPE AND SEQUENCE FOR K-12 PHYSICAL EDUCATION

To help you develop your own lessons, this book replicates a table from *National Standards & Grade-Level Outcomes for K-12 Physical Education* that details a scope and sequence of instruction for all grade levels, not just middle school (see table 1.1). The table is designed to give you a quick visual representation of when to teach the skills and content specified in the Grade-Level Outcomes. Each skill is coded with "E" for "emerging," "M" for "maturing," and "A" for "applying" (SHAPE America, 2014, p. 65). Emerging indicates when skills and knowledge should be introduced and practiced. Maturing indicates when students should be able to demonstrate the critical elements of the skills or knowledge while continuing to refine them. Applying indicates when students should be able to demonstrate the critical elements of the skill or knowledge in a variety of physical activity settings. The scope and sequence table also provides a framework for a continuum of instruction and learning from the earliest grades through high school graduation, so that you and your colleagues at other grade levels can ensure that everyone is on the same page for curriculum development.

TABLE 1.1

Standard 1. Motor skills & movement patterns

	Kindergarten	Grade 1	Grade 2	Grade 3	Grade 4	Grade 5	Grade 6	Grade 7	Grade 8	High School
Hopping	E	M	A	→						→
Galloping	E	M	A	→						→
Running	E	→	M	A	→					→
Sliding	E	M	A	→						→
Skipping	E	→	M	A	→					→
Leaping		E	→	M	A	→				→
Jumping & landing	E	→		M	A	→				→
• Spring & step					E	M	A	→		→
• Jump stop							E	M	A	→
• Jump rope	E	→		M	A	→	i	i	i	i
Balance	E	→		M	→	A	→			→
Weight transfer			E	M	→		A	→		→
Rolling	E	→				M	A	→		→
Curling & stretching	E	→	M	→		A	→			→
Twisting & bending		E	M	→		A	→			→
Throwing										
• Underhand	E	→	M	→			A	→		→
• Overhand	E	→				M	A	→		→
Catching	E	→			M	A	→			→
Dribbling/ball control										
• Hands	E	→			M	A	→			→
• Feet		E	→			M	A	→		→
• With implement				E	→	M	A	→		→
Kicking	E	→			M	→	A	→		→
Volleying										
• Underhand	E	→			M	A	→			→
• Overhead					E	→	ii	ii	ii	ii
• Set								E	→	M
Striking—with short implement	E	→			M	A	→			→
• Fore/backhand							E	→	M	A
Striking—with long implement			E	→		M	A	→		→
• Fore/backhand								E	→	M
Combining locomotors & manipulatives					E	→	M	→	A	→
Combining jumping, landing, locomotors & manipulatives						E	M	A	→	→
Combining balance & weight transfers			E	→		M	→	A	→	→

iJump rope becomes a fitness activity after grade 5 and is absorbed into Standard 3. Engages in fitness activities.

iiOverhead volley becomes a specialized skill for volleyball—setting—that begins being taught in middle school.

(continued)

(continued)

	Kindergarten	Grade 1	Grade 2	Grade 3	Grade 4	Grade 5	Grade 6	Grade 7	Grade 8	High School
Serving										
• Underhand							E	M	A	→
• Overhand							E	→	→	M
Shooting on goal						E	→	→	M	*
Passing & receiving										
• Hands						E	→	M	→	*
• Feet					E		→	→	M	*
• With implement							E	→	M	*
• Forearm pass							E	→	M	A
• Lead pass						E	→	M	→	*
• Give & go							E	M	→	*
Offensive skills										
• Pivots							E	M	A	*
• Fakes							E	→	M	*
• Jab step							E	→	M	*
• Screen									E	*
Defensive skills										
• Drop step							E	→	M	*
• Defensive or athletic stance							E	→	M	*

*Teaching team sports skills is not recommended at the high school level.

Standard 2. Concepts & strategies

	Kindergarten	Grade 1	Grade 2	Grade 3	Grade 4	Grade 5	Grade 6	Grade 7	Grade 8	High School
Movement concepts, principles & knowledge	E	→			M	→	A	→		→
Strategies & tactics				E	→		M	→	A	→
Communication (games)							E	→	M	A
Creating space (invasion)										
• Varying pathways, speed, direction							E	M	A	*
• Varying type of pass							E	M	A	*
• Selecting appropriate offensive tactics with object							E	→	M	*
• Selecting appropriate offensive tactics without object							E	→	M	*
• Using width & length of the field/court							E	→	M	*
• Playing with one player up (e.g., 2v1)							E	→	M	*
Reducing space (invasion)										
• Changing size & shape of the defender's body							E	M	A	*
• Changing angle to gain competitive advantage							E	→	M	*
• Denying the pass/player progress							E	→		*
• Playing with one player down (e.g., 1v2)							E	→		*
Transition (invasion)							E	M	A	*
Creating space (net/wall)										
• Varying force, angle and/or direction to gain competitive advantage							E	→	M	A
• Using offensive tactic/shot to move opponent out of position							E	→		M
Reducing space (net/wall)										
• Returning to home position							E	→	M	A
• Shifting to reduce angle for return							E	→		M
Target										
• Selecting appropriate shot/club							E	→	M	A
• Applying blocking strategy							E	→		M
• Varying speed & trajectory							E	→	M	A
Fielding/striking										
• Applying offensive strategies								E	→	*
• Reducing open spaces							E	→	M	*

*Teaching team sports skills is not recommended at the high school level.

(continued)

(continued)

Standard 3. Health-enhancing level of fitness & physical activity

	Kindergarten	Grade 1	Grade 2	Grade 3	Grade 4	Grade 5	Grade 6	Grade 7	Grade 8	High School
Physical activity knowledge	E					M			A	→
Engages in physical activity	E					M				A
Fitness knowledge	E					M				A
Assessment & program planning				E		M			A	→
Nutrition	E							M		A
Stress management							E			M

Standard 4. Responsible personal & social behavior

	Kindergarten	Grade 1	Grade 2	Grade 3	Grade 4	Grade 5	Grade 6	Grade 7	Grade 8	High School
Demonstrating personal responsibility	E			M			A			→
Accepting feedback	E			M			A			→
Working with others	E			M			A			→
Following rules & etiquette			E			M		A		→
Safety	E		M			A				→

Standard 5. Recognizes the value of physical activity

	Kindergarten	Grade 1	Grade 2	Grade 3	Grade 4	Grade 5	Grade 6	Grade 7	Grade 8	High School
For health			E				M			A
For challenge			E				M			A
For self-expression/enjoyment	E					M				A
For social interaction				E			M			A

CHAPTER 2

Teaching to Standards: Planning Middle School Lessons Using the Outcomes

Planning effective lessons is a challenge that integrates an understanding of your students, your mastery of the content, and your application of sound pedagogical skills and instructional strategies. *National Standards & Grade-Level Outcomes for K-12 Physical Education* (SHAPE America, 2014) is a tool that makes this process somewhat easier by providing a structure—a scope and sequence—to use when developing your lesson content and your curriculum. This chapter focuses on the process of planning lessons for modules, sometimes called units, for middle school physical education that align with SHAPE America's National Standards and Grade-Level Outcomes. This process will include three components:

1. Planning for the module
2. Planning for individual lessons
3. Planning for embedded outcomes

One note before we continue: Each module in the book contains eight lessons, as recommended in *National Standards & Grade-Level Outcomes for K-12 Physical Education* (SHAPE America, 2014), and are designed to fit a 50-minute time block.

PLANNING FOR THE MODULE

Before planning your lessons, consider what your intended outcomes are for the module and how that module fits within the context of your middle school curriculum. In general, your students can attain the relevant Grade-Level Outcomes through a variety of learning activities, so it's important to consider how the outcomes that you select will address their needs and interests. How do the outcomes build on the skills that your students learned and the knowledge that they acquired in elementary school and earlier in middle school? How do the learning activities fit with the geographical opportunities available to your students, to their cultural backgrounds, and to the gender preferences of students within each class? Don't forget to factor in any constraints that you might have, such as limitations on the number of lessons that you can teach and the amount of time that you have to teach each lesson, as well as the facilities and equipment that you have at your disposal.

Once you have determined which outcomes to include in your module, and what constraints that you and your class will face, you can create a block plan, which lists the outcomes and objectives for each individual lesson in your module (see table 2.1). One of the many techniques that you can use to create your block plan is "backward mapping," which is simply a process by which you start at the end point (in this case, the outcomes for the module) and work your way back to the first lesson to determine what students should know and be able to do at each step along the way. Figure 2.1 illustrates what using backward mapping to create a block plan would look like.

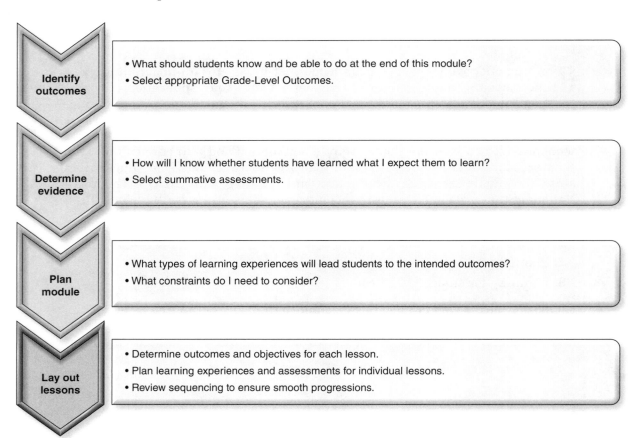

Identify outcomes
- What should students know and be able to do at the end of this module?
- Select appropriate Grade-Level Outcomes.

Determine evidence
- How will I know whether students have learned what I expect them to learn?
- Select summative assessments.

Plan module
- What types of learning experiences will lead students to the intended outcomes?
- What constraints do I need to consider?

Lay out lessons
- Determine outcomes and objectives for each lesson.
- Plan learning experiences and assessments for individual lessons.
- Review sequencing to ensure smooth progressions.

FIGURE 2.1 Backward mapping for module block plans.

After selecting the outcomes that you want your students to have attained by the end of the module, determine what summative assessment(s) you will use to measure students' progress toward those outcomes. It's essential that you know how you will evaluate student learning before designing the learning activities. By determining first how you will determine student learning, you can align the instructional activities closely with the assessment. Once you've selected or created the assessment, you can move on to thinking about the types of learning experiences that fit into the context of your learning environment. Finally, you will want to lay out the number of lessons and specify the outcomes and objectives for each lesson plan. You also might want to include formative assessments in your block plan. See figure 2.2 for an example.

A simple chart with boxes for each lesson can help you create an outline for the entire module that will allow you to check off all the important concepts and skills that the lessons in the module will cover. Knowing that students usually don't get enough practice time in one class period to master the skills or knowledge addressed in most lessons on the middle school level, you should expect to address the same outcomes for multiple lessons and, most likely, multiple modules throughout the year. In table 2.1, you will see that the outcomes are repeated, even though the lesson objectives change. The practice tasks will change, as well. Once you have completed an outline of the outcomes and objectives, you can design the learning activities and formative assessments that you want to include in each lesson.

The process of planning modules is important for assuring effective learning experiences for students, but once you've planned your modules, you will need to

Identify outcomes
- Executes consistently (at least 70% of the time) a legal underhand serve for distance and accuracy for net or wall games such as badminton, volleyball, or pickleball. (S1.M12.8)

Determine evidence
- Select summative assessments.
- Select Volleyball Skills test (serving). The test is designed to reward points for distance and accuracy in volleyball.

Plan module
- Select instructional task with which to teach the underhand volleyball serve correctly (toss, weight transfer, contact, follow through), and how to serve for distance and accuracy.
- This process might cover multiple years (6th to 8th grades).

Lay out lessons
- Students will toss volleyball the correct height and drop to spot in front of them correctly 80% of the time (6th grade).
- Students will serve the volleyball over the net 70% of the time during practice (7th grade).
- Students practice serving for accuracy while not sacrificing speed during serving drills (8th grade).

FIGURE 2.2 Example of backward mapping for a volleyball module block plan.

TABLE 2.1 Sample Middle School Block Plan for Badminton

Lesson Plan #	Grade-Level Outcomes Addressed	Lesson Objectives
1	**Striking** Strikes with a mature overhand pattern in a dynamic environment for net/wall games such as volleyball, handball, badminton or tennis. (S1.M13.7) **Forehand & backhand** Demonstrates the mature form of forehand and backhand strokes with a long-handled implement in net games such as badminton or tennis. (S1.M14.7)	**The learner will:** • demonstrate the ability to perform both the V-grip and thumb grip. • demonstrate the ability to perform the forehand clear shot by completing three of five attempts successfully during the grids practice task. • demonstrate the ability to perform the backhand clear shot by completing three of five attempts successfully during the grids practice task.
2	**Striking** Strikes with a mature overhand pattern in a dynamic environment for net/wall games such as volleyball, handball, badminton or tennis. (S1.M13.7) **Forehand & backhand** Demonstrates the mature form of forehand and backhand strokes with a long-handled implement in net games such as badminton or tennis. (S1.M14.7)	**The learner will:** • demonstrate the ability to perform the drop-shot movement pattern during the mimic-with-teacher task. • perform basic offensive and defensive strategies during the clear-rally practice task. • select offensive shots, including serves, based on the opponent's location during the grid extension activity.
3	**Striking** Strikes with a mature overhand pattern in a dynamic environment for net/wall games such as volleyball, handball, badminton or tennis. (S1.M13.7) **Creating space through variation** Creates open space in net/wall games with a long-handled implement by varying force and direction, and by moving opponent from side to side. (S2.M7.7) **Using tactics & shots** Reduces offensive options for opponents by returning to mid-court position. (S2.M8.6)	**The learner will:** • perform clear shots correctly during the uncontrolled environment practice task. • perform basic offensive strategies of moving an opponent from side to side during the practice task. • demonstrate basic defensive strategies by returning to mid-court or home base after hitting clear shots in the practice task.
4	**Serving** Performs a legal underhand serve with control for net/wall games such as badminton, volleyball or pickleball. (S1.M12.6) **Serving** Executes consistently (at least 70% of the time) a legal underhand serve to a predetermined target for net/wall games such as badminton, volleyball or pickleball. (S1.M12.7)	**The learner will:** • demonstrate the ability to perform the long serve by completing three of five attempts successfully during the grids practice task. • demonstrate the ability to perform the short serve by completing three of five attempts successfully during the grids practice task. • perform short and long serves with at least 70 percent accuracy during the hoop practice task.

Lesson Plan #	Grade-Level Outcomes Addressed	Lesson Objectives
5	**Serving** Performs a legal underhand serve with control for net/wall games such as badminton, volleyball or pickleball. (S1.M12.6) **Striking** Strikes with a mature overhand pattern in a non-dynamic environment for net/wall games such as volleyball, handball, badminton or tennis. (S1.M13.6) **Creating space through variation** Creates open space in net/wall games with either a long- or short-handled implement by varying force or direction, or by moving opponent from side to side and/or forward and back. (S2.M7.8) **Using tactics & shots** Selects offensive shot based on opponent's location (hit where opponent is not). **(**S2.M8.7)	**The learner will:** • demonstrate the ability to perform the drop shot movement pattern during the mimic-with-teacher task. • perform basic offensive and defensive strategies during the clear-rally practice task. • select offensive shots, including serves, based on the opponent's location during a grid extension activity.
6	**Serving** Performs a legal underhand serve with control for net/wall games such as badminton, volleyball or pickleball. (S1.M12.6) **Striking** Strikes with a mature overhand pattern in a dynamic environment for net/wall games such as volleyball, handball, badminton or tennis. (S1.M13.7) **Creating space through variation** Creates open space in net/wall games with either a long- or short-handled implement by varying force or direction, or by moving opponent from side to side and/or forward and back. (S2.M7.8) **Using tactics & shots** Reduces offensive options for opponents by returning to mid-court position. (S2.M8.6)	**The learner will:** • demonstrate the ability to perform the smash shot by completing three of five attempts successfully during the grids practice task. • perform basic offensive and defensive strategies during a clear-rally practice task. • reduce offensive options for opponents by returning to mid-court position during modified game play.
7	**Striking** Performs a legal underhand serve with control for net/wall games such as badminton, volleyball or pickleball. (S1.M12.6) **Creating space through variation** Creates open space in net/wall games with either a long- or short-handled implement by varying force or direction, or by moving opponent from side to side and/or forward and back. (S2.M7.8) **Using tactics & shots** Selects offensive shot based on opponent's location (hit where opponent is not). (S2.M8.7)	**The learner will:** • demonstrate the ability to perform the smash or block by completing three of five attempts successfully during the grids practice task. • perform basic offensive and defensive strategies in modified game play. • apply the rules and strategies of doubles.
8	**Forehand & backhand** Demonstrates the mature form of forehand and backhand strokes with a short- or long-handled implement with power and accuracy in net games such as pickleball, tennis, badminton or paddle ball. (S1.M14.8)	**The learner will:** • perform a variety of badminton skills during game play. ***Note: Assess student skills and use of strategies during game play.***

remain flexible. Your students will progress at different rates, and even the best plans will need to be adjusted to meet student needs.

PLANNING FOR INDIVIDUAL LESSONS

A comprehensive yet flexible lesson plan template is an important tool for developing your lessons. All of the lessons included in this book were developed from a common template, although some lessons might contain slight variations, depending on the lesson content. That template appears in the web resource.

We also offer some guidance on what is meant by each heading in the template so that you will understand the various sections in the same way that those who contributed the lesson plans to this book understood them. We realize that we could have included many other headings in this template, but we tried to reduce the template to just those elements that are critical for addressing students' attainment of the Grade-Level Outcomes. Therefore, it will be up to you to include other elements such as warm-ups, cool-downs, instant activities, and routines. Finally, we hope that you will find this template to be user-friendly and adaptable to your needs. Of course, you might already have a lesson plan format that you prefer, so feel free to continue to use it when developing your own lessons and modules.

SETTING UP THE LESSON

The top portion of the lesson plan template establishes the framework for the instructional tasks that will follow. Within the five text boxes at the top, list the outcomes that you've targeted, the lesson's objectives, the materials and equipment you will need, and how you will introduce the lesson. Select the outcomes from table 3.1. Consider them to be longer-term objectives for the module or curriculum, as they are designed to be met by the end of the grade level. It's likely that you will address the same outcomes in several modules throughout the year so as to provide students with enough learning and practice opportunities to attain them. Each individual lesson and learning activity should move students closer to the selected outcomes. The Lesson Objectives section is where you will write the objectives that align with the outcomes that you've selected and will lead students to attain the outcomes. While it's usually a good idea to include the task, situation, and criteria when writing lesson objectives, most of the objectives in the lessons in this book have been simplified and might not include all of those components. The criteria should be set locally, based on student ability,

TABLE 2.2 Sample Lesson Objectives Aligned With a Grade-Level Outcome

Grade-Level Outcomes	Lesson Objectives
Assessment and program planning Designs and implements a program of remediation for 2 areas of weakness based on the results of health-related fitness assessment. (S3.M15.7)	**The learner will:** • design a program of remediation for two areas of weakness based on the results of his or her Fitnessgram report. • include as part of the program physical activity that results in attaining either a minimum health standard or an optimal functioning level. • implement the program once it has been designed.

experience, and pre-assessment data. Table 2.2 contains an example from the Physical Activity & Fitness Program Design module for grade 7 in Chapter 11.

The Equipment and Materials and Introduction sections in the lesson plan template are there to help you list all of the instructional materials that you will need for each lesson and help you prepare to introduce the lesson. Your Introduction of the lesson should capture students' attention and outline what they will learn in the lesson. You also can include an instant activity in your Introduction to start the lesson. Try to think of ways to link the content in each lesson to what students have learned previously or connect it somehow with their interests. Here is an example of these sections from a badminton lesson plan in Chapter 6:

Equipment/Materials

- Yarn balls and shuttles—at least 5 for every 2 students
- Badminton rackets and long-handled lollipop paddles—1 per child
- 4 cones for grids—4 cones for every 2 students
- Tape for targets on wall
- Pedometers

Introduction

Today, we begin our module on striking with a long implement, using the sport of badminton to do so. We will start with grips, forehand clears, and backhand clears. Throughout the unit, we will progress to more advanced motor skills such as smashes and drop shots, as well as learning the rules and basic tactics for succeeding in game play.

EMBEDDED OUTCOME: S3.M16.6. Show a badminton video clip to pique students' interest.

We also will continue tracking our physical activity with this module. It will be interesting to see how our step-count goals are different with badminton. Track your step count for each lesson, and track your physical activity outside of class, as well.

Note: Once you have completed this portion of the lesson plan, you will have a clear direction for planning your instructional tasks.

Instructional Plan

This section of the lesson plan is where you will specify each learning task for the lesson as well as the progressions associated with it. Under the Instructional Task heading, list the lesson's "big ideas," also thought of as the main skills, concepts, and behaviors that students are expected to learn. Use the Practice Task section to indicate *how* students will learn the skills in each instructional task. You will notice that the Practice Task section carries a note that reads, "Add as many as appropriate." That is to encourage you to think about multiple practice tasks related to the original one. Remember, you want students to master the task, and that doesn't happen if you offer one practice task and then move on to the next lesson or skill. To master any skill, students will need a carefully planned sequence of deliberate practice tasks.

The Extensions and Refinements headings within the Practice Task section reinforces the need for this type of planning. The progression should move from a simplified version of the task to a more complex version. You can think of this as moving students from a controlled practice environment to a less-controlled environment or modifying the initial practice task to be easier or more difficult. In the end, you might place only a few practice tasks in the lesson, but each might have several extensions or refinements. Here is an example from a badminton lesson plan in Chapter 6:

Within the Practice Task section, you also will see a note about *Guiding Questions for Students*. Sometimes, practice tasks lend themselves to guided exploration, and if you want to use that approach, this heading encourages you to plan for it. Here are some examples of guiding questions that could emanate from a badminton lesson:

What did you change about your movement to send the shuttlecock to the back of the court? To the front of the court? Did you use smaller or larger movements? How does the length of the movement affect the distance that the shuttlecock travels?

Asking students questions like those helps engage them cognitively in the activity and helps them draw connections to concepts that they have learned in other activities. Placing *guiding questions* within your practice tasks will help

Instructional Task	Practice Tasks *[Add as many as appropriate.]*
Forehand & backhand strike in grids	Teaching in grids, assign tasks from the controlled environment, moving toward an uncontrolled environment.
	As you call out commands, students practice each task 5 times and then switch with partners. Partners must cooperate by making good tosses. Partners also should encourage each other.
	Task 1. *Toss the yarn ball to the midsection of your partner's forearm side for 5 hits.*
	Same task with backhand.
	Task 2. *Toss the yarn ball so that your partner has to take a quick step to the forearm side to hit the shuttle.*
	Same task with backhand (step toward backhand side).
	Task 3. *Toss the yarn ball so that your partner has to take a quick step forward and hit a forearm shot.*
	Same task with backhand.
	Task 4. *Toss the yarn ball so that your partner has to take a quick step back while still hitting a forearm shot.*
	Same task with backhand.
	Extension:
	We now will move into a more game-like or uncontrolled setting. The partner tossing now should toss the ball using any of the previous commands. Make sure you still toss at the midsection and still use only the forehand or backhand shot. Switch after 5 tosses.
	Repeat this extension until many have had success.

enhance the learning experience for students. The same is true for embedded outcomes. Place an embedded outcome next to the practice task in which you expect to have the opportunity to address it. That reminds you to teach to the outcome when you reach that particular practice task. For example, while having students practice forehand clears in badminton, you might choose to include peer assessments, integrating (embedding) an outcome from under Standard 4 about delivering feedback:

Provides corrective feedback to a peer, using teacher-generated guidelines, and incorporating appropriate tone and other communication skills. (S4.M3.7)

The Instructional Plan area also includes a heading for Student Choices/Differentiation. The content in this section should look different from the Extension/Refinement(s) in the Practice Task section. This is where you indicate how students will be able to participate in the practice tasks at their own levels. The following examples help illustrate student choices:

- *Provide a variety of throwing objects for student choice and differentiation.*
- *Toss can begin from 3 to 5 feet (1 to 1.5 m) away with lower trajectory. Encourage students to discuss the distance that they feel will best help them learn.*
- *Instead of having the performer move, allow the tosser to move so that the tosses come from different angles.*

Other possibilities include modifying the size of grids or practice areas, altering the speed of the movements, grouping by ability, and encouraging students to stay with an earlier progression rather than moving to a more difficult one. Although you won't always make use of this heading, planning for differentiation is an important tool for creating a mastery environment that is inclusive of all ability levels.

The final heading in the instructional planning area is What to Look For, which should force you to think about the critical elements of the task or skill during the lesson's planning phase. These elements form the basis of the corrective feedback that you will provide during the lesson to help students improve their performance. This heading also should cause you to consider how you evaluate student performance during the practice task, including the critical elements associated with the skills or concepts. The practitioners who contributed the lesson plans in this book did not include these critical elements because most teachers have developed their own unique ways of providing those elements through teaching cues and key phrases. In addition, these cues are readily available online and often include video clips related to correct technique or concepts. In many cases, the lesson plan contributors listed resources through which to find this type of information.

The rest of the instructional plan includes assessments, resources, closure, reflection, and homework. Because assessment is the key to evaluating student progress and learning, it is essential that you plan for it in each lesson, even if it is to be informal assessment, formative assessment, or both. You should formally assess students against the outcomes for each module (summative assessment) at least once, and ideally, you would pre-assess students' knowledge and abilities before planning the lessons. Many types of assessments are available to teachers, including exit slips, checks for understanding, peer assessments, analytic rubrics, written tests, fitness tests, and portfolios. If you are using a published assessment (e.g., *PE Metrics,* Fitnessgram), make sure that you are familiar with the testing protocols before trying to use it in class. Also, students should have the opportunity to practice assessments and protocols before they are scored or graded. For more information on creating and using assessments, see Chapter 8 of *National Standards & Grade-Level Outcomes for K-12 Physical Education* (SHAPE America, 2014).

The Resources section in the lesson plan is there for you to list any materials that might enhance student learning and could include any websites, books, handouts, visual aids, DVDs, etc., that you used to help prepare the lesson plan or that you want to bring to the attention of interested students. The Closure section is there to help you think about how to pull the various tasks within the lesson together and focus students on what they learned. It also gives you an opportunity to preview the next lesson in the module. Pre-planning some initial questions is a good way to focus students on the important aspects of the day's lesson, as this example from Lesson 1 in the Badminton Module in Chapter 6 illustrates:

- What types of grips did you learn today?
- Name three critical features of the forehand clear.
- Name three critical features of the backhand clear.
- Give some examples of cooperation in today's class.
- Keep practicing the skills at home, if you can. In the next lesson, we will learn the overhead and underhand clear shots.

While the Closure section pulls it together for the students, the Reflection section is there to pull it together for *you*. It provides an opportunity for you to evaluate student progress at the end of the lesson and to consider what you might want to do differently (or the same) the next time you teach the lesson. This example from Lesson 1 in the Badminton Module in Chapter 6 provides some guiding questions to consider after teaching:

- Do students strike the shuttle so that it travels forward instead of mostly upward?
- Are they able to transfer the striking movement pattern with the long implement, making sure that they complete the strike with a follow-through?
- Are students getting enough practice hits throughout the lesson?

The questions are aligned closely with the outcomes and objectives targeted in the lesson, and your assessment of how well students attained those outcomes and objectives might cause you to consider adjusting your next lesson. If students are not "getting it," you might need to take a step back in your progressions before moving on to new content.

The final component of the instructional plan is the Homework section. As with other subject areas, homework can play a vital role in reinforcing skills and knowledge acquired in physical education classes. It also can encourage students to adopt desirable behaviors outside of the school day, such as being physically active in formal or informal activity settings, keeping a physical activity log, and investigating community-based opportunities for active recreation, to name a few. By setting up homework as an expectation, you can extend the reach of physical education beyond your classroom and into the family and community.

Sample Homework

- Striking (with hand, short implement, or long implement) will help support what you are learning in physical education class. It doesn't matter what piece of equipment or ball you use, as long as you practice the movement pattern and eye–hand coordination.

■ Also, take home the worksheet with pictures of the grips and the critical features of the forehand and backhand clear. Also, review the grips and instructional videos that are posted to the school's physical education website.

EMBEDDED OUTCOME: S3.M16.6. Remind students to record physical education step counts, daily physical activity time, and reflections in personal log after each lesson in the module.

OPTIMIZING LEARNING THROUGH EMBEDDED OUTCOMES

During your planning, it's important to think about other Grade-Level Outcomes that students might work toward while concentrating on the primary outcomes that you've targeted in the lesson. We call these "other" outcomes *embedded outcomes*. Embedded outcomes are secondary outcomes related to the primary content of the lesson that require deliberate planning for instruction (Holt/Hale, 2016, p.18; SHAPE America, 2014, p. 41). They differ from "teachable moments" because they don't just happen; you have to plan for—and teach—these secondary outcomes as part of each lesson. For example, you can embed an outcome on responsibility and respect from under Standard 4 while teaching a skill-based lesson on creating open space in soccer (Standard 1). The choice of which outcomes to embed in your lessons depends on the content and types of practice tasks that you plan for teaching the primary outcomes. The Embedded Outcomes section appears in the template to remind you to plan for these outcomes as you develop the instructional tasks.

Embedding outcomes can play an important role in helping students become physically literate individuals. *National Standards & Grade-Level Outcomes for K-12 Physical Education* (SHAPE America, 2014) presents 203 outcomes for the middle grades alone. Even if your students had physical education every day of the school year, you would be hard-pressed to plan individual lessons for all 203 outcomes. In fact, doing so is probably not a good idea. Teaching to every outcome separately would obscure the connections between and among different skills and knowledge, leading to compartmentalization of physical education content. While the outcomes are organized by standard, the content cannot be taught without considering the context in which it takes place. For example, students can pursue and appreciate the challenge (Standard 5) of orienteering, but they also must have specialized skills such as reading a compass (Standard 1), and must exhibit responsible personal and social behaviors (Standard 4) to participate in a team treasure hunt. The process of integrating or "embedding" outcomes from different standards in lesson plans is the focus of the remainder of this chapter.

Embedded outcomes are rooted in the learning or practice task by the very nature or challenge of the learning experience. You should not think of these outcomes as by-products or incidental to the primary objective or task, but rather as opportunities to meet more than one outcome during the learning or practice task. These opportunities are part of everyday school practice, and you should exploit them to optimize learning.

While teaching for skill development or refinement, you have opportunities to embed outcomes from both the cognitive and affective domains into motor competency learning experiences. For example, during practice tasks designed to increase both skill and tactical competency for invasion game play, you can embed affective objectives specific to cooperation and communication without sacrificing skill and tactical practice time. The meeting of the affective domain objective is embedded in the practice task and is integral to the success of the skill and tactical practice task. Without cooperation and communication, teammates will not succeed in the primary practice tasks of passing, receiving, and applying invasion game tactics. However, one must not assume that students will learn cooperation and communication skills just because you have planned a passing and receiving practice task. You have to *teach* to those outcomes and provide feedback on them in the context of the passing and receiving tasks.

The use of grids for teaching students to apply the fundamental skills of passing and receiving (Outcome S1.M4.6) while practicing the tactics of executing a cut and a give and go (Outcome S2.M2.6) off a pass illustrates the embedded outcome approach. Once the passer makes the lead pass to a receiver, the passer executes a give and go and becomes the receiver. The nature of the practice task requires students to throw to a spot to which the receiver is moving and for the receiver to provide a target for the passer (while moving to another corner of the grid). The passer must make a quality pass (give) to the receiver and move immediately (go) to a corner to receive a return pass from the receiver. The success of the practice task depends on the ability of the two students to cooperate with each other (Outcome S4.M5.6) and make effective passes and cuts. The design of the learning experience will enhance skill and tactical competency, but it also can help students understand the importance of cooperation and how their success depends on one another. That can happen only if you take the time to teach to the embedded outcome (in this case, cooperation) intrinsic to the task.

Mastery Environment and Embedded Outcomes

The key to embedding outcomes is creating a mastery environment, in which students seek to improve their skills based on the required skill or competency. For example, two partnered students pass, receive, and cut for 45 seconds while two other students record the number of passes completed in those 45 seconds. The two recorders then become passers and receivers for 45 seconds and have the number of their completed passes recorded. The original two partners repeat the practice task and try to increase the number of completed passes in the same 45-second period. In a mastery environment, students try to improve upon their best performances. The focus is on personal improvement and not on defeating an opponent. This emphasis on a mastery environment allows physical educators to provide feedback on the skills required for the practice task (passing and receiving) while incorporating tactics important for successful game play (throwing lead passes, using a give and go, making straight-line cuts) and taking the opportunity to teach to the embedded outcome of cooperation.

After the group has completed two cycles of the practice task, you can ask students to identify why their scores improved (or why they didn't). The students could brainstorm on ways to improve their scores, which could include ideas such as making better passes or cuts, or simply working together more productively by improving communication. You should capitalize on opportunities to teach to these embedded objectives during various practice tasks. For each practice task you plan for a lesson, ask yourself, "What else can I teach in conjunction with this task?"

Because teachers often have students working with a partner or on small-sided teams, cooperation, sportsmanship, and communication might be obvious choices for embedding outcomes into skill competency learning experiences. But you have many other opportunities to embed outcomes into practice tasks, as well. While teaching a module (unit) in dance (Outcome S1.M1.7), you could embed cognitive outcomes related to basic mechanical principles (Outcome S2.M12.7). Students can explore these principles by executing turns or changing their centers of gravity. Different forms of dance provide opportunities for teaching about dance as a means of self-expression (Outcome S5.M5.7), as well as a means of inclusion (Outcome S4.M1.7). The latter is particularly true in partner or social dance. If you teach to these embedded outcomes through dance, students will begin to understand simple biomechanical concepts and apply them to their own movements. They also can improve their interpersonal skills and begin to appreciate the value of movement, leading to more competent and physically literate students. Below is an example from the Badminton Module in Chapter 6.

Modified doubles game using strategies:

- Using a foam ball and no rackets, students play a game of doubles badminton, focusing on the type of shots and shot placement that they should use in badminton.
- Students should practice side-by-side defense, as well as front-and-back defense.
- Embedded outcome: This is a great opportunity to teach students Outcome S5.M6.6: Demonstrates respect for self and others in activities and games by following the rules, encouraging others and playing in the spirit of the game or activity. Be sure to point out examples of these behaviors and provide feedback to students on them. Also, ask students for examples of these behaviors during closure.

The examples that we've offered so far have involved embedding cognitive or affective outcomes into motor competency tasks, but embedding can also work in the other direction. When teaching a sequence of learning experiences with the primary focus on problem solving (Outcome S4.M5.7) or critical thinking (e.g., adventure education), you will have many opportunities for sharing skill cues with participants that address components of motor competency (Standard 1). If the primary focus of the lesson is learning to vary the placement, force, and timing of a return shot in a net or wall game to prevent the opponent from returning the shot (Outcome S2.M8.8), it's easy to find ways to provide students with feedback on their skill competency (Outcome S1.M14.8). How students execute the forehand and backhand strike will have a direct impact on the effectiveness of their game tactics and shot strategy.

Implementing Embedded Outcomes

Using embedded outcomes also can increase practice and activity time during a lesson. Because you don't have to plan separate learning activities for every outcome, you can use instruction and management time more efficiently. One practice task, or a sequence of practice tasks, can address more than one outcome, leaving more time for practice attempts and moderate to vigorous activity. As noted earlier, though, these opportunities require careful planning before the lesson, as well as attention to delivery during the lesson, to be effective. It's also critical that you assess embedded outcomes at some point during the module to track student progress, just as you would for other outcomes. These assessments don't have to be complex. You can use checks for understanding and exit slips for many types of embedded outcomes. Peer assessments also can be very effective, as can other, more formal forms of assessment, such as rubrics and checklists.

The modules in this book include embedded outcomes from multiple standards to take advantage of opportunities presented by the content. You can see an example of this in the Badminton Module in Chapter 6, in which most lessons address primary outcomes from under Standards 1 and 2, but also include embedded outcomes from under Standards 4 and 5. Another approach to embedding outcomes is to select one standard as a theme for the entire module. For example, the Badminton Module could just as easily incorporate outcomes from Standard 3 only, because the intent is to illustrate how badminton contributes to fitness and physical activity knowledge and skills. Each approach has its advantages and disadvantages. Pulling embedded outcomes from multiple standards allows you a great deal of flexibility because you can choose from many outcomes. However, it may be difficult to track students' acquisition of these embedded outcomes across the grade level if you haven't created a pattern for including them. Conversely, identifying a theme for the module simplifies your assessment and monitoring of outcomes across the year, but using outcomes from only one standard might be more difficult to align with some of your lesson content. Either approach can work, but you should decide what makes the most sense for the content that you are teaching.

Embedding outcomes is not about changing what we do, but about leveraging our teaching effectiveness through careful planning and maximizing the opportunities available to us in every lesson. Thinking about embedding outcomes will help you integrate the skills, knowledge, and behaviors from the five National Standards for K-12 Physical Education in a meaningful way for your students. In the end, a physically literate individual experiences physical literacy in a multi-dimensional way, not one standard at a time. So, as you plan or reflect on your lessons, remember to ask yourself, "What more can I teach through this learning experience?"

SUMMARY

Everything we've covered in this chapter comes down to planning. Careful and thorough planning for the module before instruction begins will help you ensure a comprehensive and effective learning experience for your students. Without a doubt, the first time you teach a module, the planning phase will be labor-intensive. Backward-mapping the module and developing your block plan takes time, as does developing individual lessons and embedding outcomes. However, a good structure will allow you to see gaps in your instructional plan before you even begin teaching it. With a strong framework in place, you will be able to more easily refine and improve your lessons as you move through the module, as well as when you re-teach it in the future.

CHAPTER 3

Meeting the National Standards and Grade-Level Outcomes in Middle School

As a middle school physical education teacher, you are building on the foundation laid by teachers who used the Grade-Level Outcomes for elementary school to further students' progress toward physical literacy. To implement the Grade-Level Outcomes for middle school in your lessons and curricula effectively, you will need to familiarize yourself with their content and structure, as well as how they differ from the Grade-Level Outcomes for both elementary school and high school. The first part of this chapter focuses on the developmental characteristics of students in the middle school years and how those characteristics are evident within the outcomes for middle school. The second part of the chapter focuses on the structure of the outcomes across the grade levels. The end of the chapter includes a table of the Grade-Level Outcomes for middle school (table 3.1), for your reference. You can find more information about the outcomes in Chapter 4 of *National Standards & Grade-Level Outcomes for K-12 Physical Education* (SHAPE America, 2014).

DEVELOPMENTAL CHARACTERISTICS OF MIDDLE SCHOOL STUDENTS

The middle school years are a time of rapid developmental change. After relatively steady growth and development during the elementary school years, students enter puberty with all its irregular adjustments in height, weight, and secondary sex characteristics. Middle school students are not necessarily excited about all of the changes they are experiencing. Sudden growth spurts can make students feel uncoordinated, as if they've lost control of their bodies. The development of secondary sex characteristics, in particular, can make students feel uncomfortable or embarrassed, especially if they are one of the first (or last) in their class to experience these changes. Along with these physical changes come important advancements in cognitive development, such as increased ability for abstract thought and problem solving (Haibach, Reid, & Collier, 2011). At the same time, peer-group beliefs and interests begin to exert a greater influence on many students than those of their families or teachers.

Diverging Interests and Preferences

The emergence of secondary sex characteristics in middle school means that students' bodies change in ways that influence physical performance characteristics. Because girls typically enter puberty a year or two before boys, they might be taller and heavier than boys in middle school and might have an advantage in certain types of activities. By the end of middle school, however, most girls will lose those advantages, and boys will begin to exert an edge over girls in activities that favor speed, strength, power, and size (SHAPE America, 2014, p. 40). In addition to these physical differences, middle school boys and girls begin to diverge in their physical activity preferences. Girls are more likely to prefer dance, fitness, and cooperative activities, while boys generally prefer competitive or physically challenging activities (Couturier, Chepko, & Coughlin, 2007). Girls also tend to perceive sweating as well as showering and changing clothes in a locker room as greater barriers to participating in physical education and other physical activities than boys do. During middle school, many girls find single-sex physical education environments to be more inviting, leading to higher levels of participation (Derry, 2002). The exception to that tendency is highly skilled and athletic girls who are comfortable in the coeducational physical education environment.

Declining Physical Activity Levels

Unfortunately, physical activity among both girls *and* boys tends to decline during the middle school years, which coincides with the onset of puberty (Yli-Piipari et al., 2012). This drop-off in physical activity is more serious for girls, because they tend to exhibit lower levels of physical activity throughout childhood and adolescence than boys to start with. It's important, therefore, to find ways of engaging both middle school–age girls and boys in physical activity to combat this downward trend. The Grade-Level Outcomes for middle school address that by promoting a curriculum that includes activities that are appealing to girls, such as dance and fitness activities, within a broader range of activities designed to engage all students, regardless of ability or skill. Both dance and fitness provide a counterbalance to the competitive games and sports preferred by many boys (Eime et al., 2013; Hill & Hannon, 2008).

The curriculum is intended to be delivered through a mastery-oriented instruction environment, which focuses on self-improvement, student choice, cognitive challenge, carefully designed practice tasks and progressions, and maximized practice opportunities. This type of instruction environment promotes skill development and appeals to modestly skilled students in physical education classes. For more information on mastery climates, see Chapter 1 of this book and Chapter 7 of *National Standards & Grade-Level Outcomes for K-12 Physical Education*

(SHAPE America, 2014). You can find additional resources on the developmental factors that influence middle school physical education in the Topic Area References at the end of this book.

Connecting the Changes of Adolescence to the Outcomes

The physical, social, and cognitive changes associated with puberty form the basis of the application stage of motor development, which serves as the framework for the Grade-Level Outcomes for middle school (Gallahue, Ozmun, & Goodway, 2012). In the applying stage of acquiring a new skill, middle school students are able to integrate and apply the foundational skills and knowledge that they acquired in elementary school in new ways that are specific to organized games, sports, and physical activities. At the same time, new intellectual capabilities mean that middle school–age students are ready to learn and apply strategies, tactics, and performance concepts, as well as to engage in problem-solving activities and goal setting. Consequently, the emphasis within the Grade-Level Outcomes shifts from acquiring fundamental motor skills and movement patterns at the elementary level to applying knowledge and skills at the middle school level.

Middle school students are ready developmentally to take on the challenge of implementing game strategies with sport-specific skills. As a result, you will notice a focus on teaching tactics in invasion, fielding and striking, and target and net or wall games in the outcomes for middle school. Offensive and defensive skills are taught in conjunction with related conceptual knowledge, such as identifying and creating open space, closing or reducing space, and playing in advantage situations, capitalizing on the synergy between outcomes in Standards 1 and 2.

You will see the same focus on integrating concepts in the outcomes for dance, outdoor, individual-performance, and fitness activities. An emphasis on students' cognitive abilities also is evident in the problem-solving and goal-setting outcomes that you can address in activities such as group initiatives, adventure activities, and fitness program planning (SHAPE America, 2014, pp. 42-46). The outcomes for middle school also tap into the importance of respecting and cooperating with peers by including many opportunities for small-sided games, peer assessments, and cooperative activities that emphasize inclusive, socially responsible behavior (Standard 4).

STRUCTURE OF THE GRADE-LEVEL OUTCOMES

The Grade-Level Outcomes for middle school are similar in structure to the outcomes for elementary school in that they are organized by grade level: in this case, grades 6, 7, and 8. They are designed with the assumption that middle school students have attained the Grade-Level Outcomes for elementary school and are ready to move on to more applied skills. (If you find that most of your students are not ready, you will need to back up a bit and work on those outcomes that students might not have attained in elementary school before you move ahead with more applied skills and knowledge.) Ideally, your school or district's curriculum is designed for continuity among elementary, middle, and high school, with student performance being monitored and passed along to the next level. However, if that is not the case, pre-assessment takes on an even more critical role in ascertaining student readiness for these more complex outcomes.

The outcomes for middle school also serve to help students transition to the more specialized knowledge and skills that they will learn at the high school level. These activities are organized into these categories: individual-performance activities; dance and rhythms; fitness activities; outdoor pursuits; aquatics; and games and sports. While the categories for the high school outcomes are the same, the emphasis is somewhat different at each level. The breadth of the outcomes for middle school allows students to explore many new types of activities that they will develop further and refine in high school, while the outcomes for high school students offer less breadth in the types of activities addressed but explore those activities in more depth. The activity categories are used to group the modules, with multiple modules for each content category. Please note that many activities could be listed under more than one category, depending on what the emphasis is intended to be. For example, a module on orienteering could be an outdoor pursuit or a fitness activity or both.

The most important aspect of the outcomes for middle school is the progressions across the grade levels. The modules are designed to demonstrate sequential progressions, no matter the grade level. As the teacher, you should assess student progress and stick with the progressions until students have become competent in the skills and knowledge. When students are more advanced, or when they perform behind the indicated grade level, use extensions and refinements to optimize student learning.

Remember that the outcomes are designed to be mastered by the end of the grade level and not in any one module. Generally, you will teach several modules in a year—or at least across the three years of middle school—that address particular outcomes. Ultimately, students should attain the outcomes before moving on to high school.

The middle school modules are intended to be at least eight lessons long, with lesson plans designed for 50-minute time blocks. If your classes are of a different length, please adjust the lesson content accordingly. At times, the content described for the lesson might seem too much for a 50-minute class because your students need more practice. Knowing your students and accommodating their needs is more important than following the module in lockstep. You can carry over the content to the next lesson, and you can always consider extending the duration of the module. You also might find that, for some lessons, only your most advanced students will use some of the extensions. The progressions in the lessons promote the use of differentiated instruction to facilitate optimal learning for all students.

GRADE-LEVEL OUTCOMES FOR MIDDLE SCHOOL (GRADES 6-8)

By the end of grade 8, students should be able to do the following:

- Apply tactics and strategies to modified game play.
- Demonstrate fundamental movement skills in a variety of contexts.
- Design and implement a health-enhancing fitness program.
- Participate in self-selected physical activity.
- Cooperate with and encourage classmates.
- Accept individual differences and demonstrate inclusive behaviors.
- Engage in physical activity for enjoyment and self-expression.

Note: Swimming skills and water-safety activities should be taught if facilities permit.

TABLE 3.1 Middle School Outcomes (Grades 6-8)

By the end of Grade 8, the learner will apply tactics and strategies to modified game play; demonstrate fundamental movement skills in a variety of contexts; design and implement a health-enhancing fitness program; participate in self-selected physical activity; cooperate with and encourage classmates; accept individual differences and demonstrate inclusive behaviors; and engage in physical activity for enjoyment and self-expression. Notes: For operational definitions and examples of activity types, see the end of this table. Swimming skills and water-safety activities should be taught if facilities permit.

Standard 1	Grade 6	Grade 7	Grade 8
The physically literate individual demonstrates competency in a variety of motor skills and movement patterns.			
Dance & rhythms			
S1.M1	Demonstrates correct rhythm and pattern for one of the following dance forms: folk, social, creative, line or world dance. (S1.M1.6)	Demonstrates correct rhythm and pattern for a different dance form from among folk, social, creative, line and world dance. (S1.M1.7)	Exhibits command of rhythm and timing by creating a movement sequence to music as an individual or in a group. (S1.M1.8)
Games & sports: Invasion & field games			
S1.M2 Throwing	Throws with a mature pattern for distance or power appropriate to the practice task (e.g., distance = outfield to home plate; power = 2nd base to 1st base). (S1.M2.6)	Throws with a mature pattern for distance or power appropriate to the activity in a dynamic environment. (S1.M2.7)	Throws with a mature pattern for distance or power appropriate to the activity during small-sided game play. (S1.M2.8)
S1.M3 Catching	Catches with a mature pattern from a variety of trajectories using different objects in varying practice tasks. (S1.M3.6)	Catches with a mature pattern from a variety of trajectories using different objects in small-sided game play. (S1.M3.7)	Catches using an implement in a dynamic environment or modified game play. (S1.M3.8)
Games & sports: Invasion games			
S1.M4 Passing & receiving	Passes and receives with hands in combination with locomotor patterns of running and change of direction and speed with competency in invasion games such as basketball, flag football, speedball or team handball. (S1.M4.6)	Passes and receives with feet in combination with locomotor patterns of running and change of direction and speed with competency in invasion games such as soccer or speedball. (S1.M4.7)	Passes and receives with an implement in combination with locomotor patterns of running and change of direction, speed and/or level with competency in invasion games such as lacrosse or hockey (floor, field or ice). (S1.M4.8)
S1.M5 Passing & receiving	Throws, while stationary, a leading pass to a moving receiver. (S1.M5.6)	Throws, while moving, a leading pass to a moving receiver. (S1.M5.7)	Throws a lead pass to a moving partner off a dribble or pass. (S1.M5.8)
S1.M6 Offensive skills	Performs pivots, fakes and jab steps designed to create open space during practice tasks. (S1.M6.6)	Executes at least one of the following designed to create open space during small-sided game play: pivots, fakes, jab steps. (S1.M6.7)	Executes at least two of the following to create open space during modified game play: pivots, fakes, jab steps, screens. (S1.M6.8)
S1.M7 Offensive skills	Performs the following offensive skills without defensive pressure: pivots, give & go, fakes. (S1.M7.6)	Performs the following offensive skills with defensive pressure: pivots, give & go, fakes. (S1.M7.7)	Executes the following offensive skills during small-sided game play: pivots, give & go, fakes. (S1.M7.8)
S1.M8 Dribbling & ball control	Dribbles with preferred hand using a change of speed and direction in a variety of practice tasks. (S1.M8.6)	Dribbles with preferred and non-preferred hands using a change of speed and direction in a variety of practice tasks. (S1.M8.7)	Dribbles with preferred and non-preferred hands using a change of speed and direction in small-sided game play. (S1.M8.8)

(continued)

(continued)

Standard 1	Grade 6	Grade 7	Grade 8
S1.M9 Dribbling & ball control	Foot-dribbles or dribbles with an implement implement with control, changing speed and direction in a variety of practice tasks. (S1.M9.6)	Foot-dribbles or dribbles with an implement combined with passing in a variety of practice tasks. (S1.M9.7)	Foot-dribbles or dribbles with an implement with control, changing speed and direction during small-sided game play. (S1.M9.8)
S1.M10 Shooting on goal	Shoots on goal with power in a dynamic environment as appropriate to the activity. (S1.M10.6)	Shoots on goal with power and accuracy in small-sided game play. (S1.M10.7)	Shoots on goal with a long-handled implement for power and accuracy in modified invasion games such as hockey (floor, field, ice) or lacrosse. (S1.M10.8)
S1.M11 Defensive skills	Maintains defensive-ready position, with weight on balls of feet, arms extended and eyes on midsection of the offensive player. (S1.M11.6)	Slides in all directions while on defense without crossing feet. (S1.M11.7)	Drop-steps in the direction of the pass during player-to-player defense. (S1.M11.8)
Games & sports: Net & wall games			
S1.M12 Serving	Performs a legal underhand serve with control for net or wall games such as badminton, volleyball or pickleball. (S1.M12.6)	Executes consistently (at least 70% of the time) a legal underhand serve to a predetermined target for net or wall games such as badminton, volleyball or pickleball. (S1.M12.7)	Executes consistently (at least 70% of the time) a legal underhand serve for distance and accuracy for net or wall games such as badminton, volleyball or pickleball. (S1.M12.8)
S1.M13 Striking	Strikes with a mature overhand pattern in a nondynamic environment for net or wall games such as volleyball, handball, badminton or tennis. (S1.M13.6)	Strikes with a mature overhand pattern in a dynamic environment for net or wall games such as volleyball, handball, badminton or tennis. (S1.M13.7)	Strikes with a mature overhand pattern in a modified game for net or wall games such as volleyball, handball, badminton or tennis. (S1.M13.8)
S1.M14 Forehand & backhand	Demonstrates the mature form of the forehand and backhand strokes with a short-handled implement in net games such as paddle ball, pickleball or short-handled racket tennis. (S1.M14.6)	Demonstrates the mature form of forehand and backhand strokes with a long-handled implement in net games such as badminton or tennis. (S1.M14.7)	Demonstrates the mature form of forehand and backhand strokes with a short- or long-handled implement with power and accuracy in net games such as pickle- ball, tennis, badminton or paddle ball. (S1.M14.8)
S1.M15 Weight transfer	Transfers weight with correct timing for the striking pattern. (S1.M15.6)	Transfers weight with correct timing using low to high striking pattern with a short-handled implement on the forehand side. (S1.M15.7)	Transfers weight with correct timing using low to high striking pattern with a long-handled implement on the forehand and backhand sides. (S1.M15.8)
S1.M16 Volley	Forehand-volleys with a mature form and control using a short-handled implement. (S1.M16.6)	Forehand- and backhand-volleys with a mature form and control using a short-handled implement. (S1.M16.7)	Forehand- and backhand-volleys with a mature form and control using a short-handled implement during modified game play. (S1.M16.8)
S1.M17 Two-hand volley	Two-hand-volleys with control in a variety of practice tasks. (S1.M17.6)	Two-hand-volleys with control in a dynamic environment. (S1.M17.7)	Two-hand-volleys with control in a small-sided game. (S1.M17.8)

Standard 1	Grade 6	Grade 7	Grade 8
Games & sports: Target games			
S1.M18 Throwing	Demonstrates a mature pattern for a modified target game such as bowling, bocce or horseshoes. (S1.M18.6)	Executes consistently (70% of the time) a mature pattern for target games such as bowling, bocce or horseshoes. (S1.M18.7)	Performs consistently (70% of the time) a mature pattern with accuracy and control for one target game such as bowling or bocce. (S1.M18.8)
S1.M19 Striking	Strikes, with an implement, a stationary object for accuracy in activities such as croquet, shuffleboard or golf. (S1.M19.6)	Strikes, with an implement, a stationary object for accuracy and distance in activities such as croquet, shuffleboard or golf. (S1.M19.7)	Strikes, with an implement, a stationary object for accuracy and power in activities such as croquet, shuffleboard or golf. (S1.M19.8)
Games & sports: Fielding & striking games			
S1.M20 Throwing	Strikes a pitched ball with an implement with force in a variety of practice tasks. (S1.M20.6)	Strikes a pitched ball with an implement to open space in a variety of practice tasks. (S1.M20.7)	Strikes a pitched ball with an implement for power to open space in a variety of small-sided games. (S1.M20.8)
S1.M21 Catching	Catches, with a mature pattern, from different trajectories using a variety of objects in a varying practice tasks. (S1.M21.6)	Catches, with a mature pattern, from different trajectories using a variety of objects in small-sided game play. (S1.M21.7)	Catches, using an implement, from different trajectories and speeds in a dynamic environment or modified game play. (S1.M21.8)
Outdoor pursuits			
S1.M22 (See end of section for examples.)	Demonstrates correct technique for basic skills in one self-selected outdoor activity. (S1.M22.6)	Demonstrates correct technique for a variety of skills in one self-selected outdoor activity. (S1.M22.7)	Demonstrates correct technique for basic skills in at least two self-selected outdoor activities. (S1.M22.8)
Aquatics			
S1.M23	Preferably taught at elementary or secondary levels. However, availability of facilities might dictate when swimming and water safety are offered in the curriculum.		
Individual-performance activities			
S1.M24 (See end of section for examples.)	Demonstrates correct technique for basic skills in one self-selected individual-performance activity. (S1.M24.6)	Demonstrates correct technique for a variety of skills in one self-selected individual-performance activity. (S1.M24.7)	Demonstrates correct technique for basic skills in at least two self-selected individual-performance activities. (S1.M24.8)
Standard 2	Grade 6	Grade 7	Grade 8
The physically literate individual applies knowledge of concepts, principles, strategies and tactics related to movement and performance.			
Games & sports: Invasion games			
S2.M1 Creating space with movement	Creates open space by using locomotor movements (e.g., walking, running, jumping & landing) in combination with movement (e.g., varying pathways; change of speed, direction or pace). (S2.M1.6)	Reduces open space by using locomotor movements (e.g., walking, running, jumping & landing, changing size and shape of the body) in combination with movement concepts (e.g., reducing the angle in the space, reducing distance between player and goal). (S2.M1.7)	Opens and closes space during small-sided game play by combining locomotor movements with movement concepts. (S2.M1.8)

(continued)

(continued)

Standard 2	Grade 6	Grade 7	Grade 8
S2.M2 Creating space with offensive tactics	Executes at least one of the following offensive tactics to create open space: moves to open space without the ball; uses a variety of passes, pivots and fakes; give & go. (S2.M2.6)	Executes at least two of the following offensive tactics to create open space: moves to open space without the ball; uses a variety of passes, pivots and fakes; give & go. (S2.M2.7)	Executes at least three of the following offensive tactics to create open space: moves to create open space on and off the ball; uses a variety of passes, fakes and pathways; give & go. (S2.M2.8)
S2.M3 Creating space using width & length	Creates open space by using the width and length of the field or court on offense. (S2.M3.6)	Creates open space by staying spread on offense, and cutting and passing quickly. (S2.M3.7)	Creates open space by staying spread on offense, cutting and passing quickly, and using fakes off the ball. (S2.M3.8)
S2.M4 Reducing space by changing size & shape	Reduces open space on defense by making the body larger and reducing passing angles. (S2.M4.6)	Reduces open space on defense by staying close to the opponent as he or she nears the goal. (S2.M4.7)	Reduces open space on defense by staying on the goal side of the offensive player and reducing the distance to him or her (third-party perspective). (S2.M4.8)
S2.M5 Reducing space using denial	Reduces open space by not allowing the catch (denial) or by allowing the catch but not the return pass. (S2.M5.6)	Reduces open space by not allowing the catch (denial) or anticipating the speed of the object and person for the purpose of interception or deflection. (S2.M5.7)	Reduces open space by not allowing the catch (denial) and anticipating the speed of the object and person for the purpose of interception or deflection. (S2.M5.8)
S2.M6 Transitions	Transitions from offense to defense or defense to offense by recovering quickly. (S2.M6.6)	Transitions from offense to defense or defense to offense by recovering quickly and communicating with teammates. (S2.M6.7)	Transitions from offense to defense or defense to offense by recovering quickly, communicating with teammates and capitalizing on an advantage. (S2.M6.8)
Games & sports: Net & wall games			
S2.M7 Creating space through variation	Creates open space in net and wall games with a short-handled implement by varying force and direction. (S2.M7.6)	Creates open space in net and wall games with a long-handled implement by varying force and direction, and by moving opponent from side to side. (S2.M7.7)	Creates open space in net and wall games with either a long- or short-handled implement by varying force or direction, or by moving opponent from side to side and/or forward and back. (S2.M7.8)
S2.M8 Using tactics & shots	Reduces offensive options for opponents by returning to mid-court position. (S2.M8.6)	Selects offensive shot based on opponent's location (hit where opponent is not). (S2.M8.7)	Varies placement, force and timing of return to prevent anticipation by opponent. (S2.M8.8)
Games & sports: Target games			
S2.M9 Shot selection	Selects appropriate shot and/or club based on location of the object in relation to the target. (S2.M9.6)	Varies the speed and/or trajectory of the shot based on location of the object in relation to the target. (S2.M9.7)	Varies the speed, force and trajectory of the shot based on location of the object in relation to the target. (S2.M9.8)
Games & sports: Fielding & striking games			
S2.M10 Offensive strategies	Identifies open spaces and attempts to strike object into that space. (S2.M10.6)	Uses a variety of shots (e.g., slap & run, bunt, line drive, high arc) to hit to open space. (S2.M10.7)	Identifies sacrifice situations and attempts to advance a teammate. (S2.M10.8)
S2.M11 Reducing space	Identifies the correct defensive play based on the situation (e.g., number of outs). (S2.M11.6)	Selects the correct defensive play based on the situation (e.g., number of outs). (S2.M11.7)	Reduces open spaces in the field by working with teammates to maximize coverage. (S2.M11.8)

Standard 2	Grade 6	Grade 7	Grade 8
Individual-performance activities, dance & rhythms			
S2.M12 Movement concepts	Varies application of force during dance or gymnastic activities. (S2.M12.6)	Identifies and applies Newton's laws of motion to various dance or movement activities. (S2.M12.7)	Describes and applies mechanical advantage(s) for a variety of movement patterns. (S2.M12.8)
Outdoor pursuits			
S2.M13 Movement concepts	Makes appropriate decisions based on the weather, level of difficulty due to conditions or ability to ensure safety of self and others. (S2.M13.6)	Analyzes the situation and makes adjustments to ensure the safety of self and others. (S2.M13.7)	Implements safe protocols in self-selected outdoor activities. (S2.M13.8)
Standard 3	Grade 6	Grade 7	Grade 8
The physically literate individual demonstrates the knowledge and skills to achieve and maintain a health-enhancing level of physical activity and fitness.			
Physical activity knowledge			
S3.M1	Is able to identify three influences on physical activity (e.g., school, family and peers; community and built environment; policy). (S3.M1.6)	Identifies barriers related to maintaining a physically active lifestyle and seeks solutions for eliminating those barriers. (S3.M1.7)	Develops a plan to address one of the barriers within one's family, school or community to maintaining a physically active lifestyle. (S3.M1.8)
Engages in physical activity			
S3.M2	Participates in self-selected physical activity outside of physical education class. (S3.M2.6)	Participates in a physical activity two or more times a week outside of physical education class. (S3.M2.7)	Participates in physical activity three or more times a week outside of physical education class. (S3.M2.8)
S3.M3	Participates in a variety of aerobic fitness activities such as cardio-kick, step aerobics and aerobic dance. (S3.M3.6)	Participates in a variety of strength- and endurance-fitness activities such as Pilates, resistance training, bodyweight training and light free-weight training. (S3.M3.7)	Participates in a variety of self-selected aerobic-fitness activities outside of school such as walking, jogging, biking, skating, dancing and swimming. (S3.M3.8)
S3.M4	Participates in a variety of aerobic-fitness activities using technology such as Dance Dance Revolution® or Wii Fit®. (S3.M4.6)	Participates in a variety of strength- and endurance-fitness activities such as weight or resistance training. (S3.M4.7)	Plans and implements a program of cross-training to include aerobic, strength and endurance, and flexibility training. (S3.M4.8)
S3.M5	Participates in a variety of lifetime recreational team sports, outdoor pursuits or dance activities. (S3.M5.6)	Participates in a variety of lifetime dual and individual sports, martial arts or aquatic activities. (S3.M5.7)	Participates in a self-selected lifetime sport, dance, aquatic or outdoor activity outside of the school day. (S3.M5.8)
S3.M6	Participates in moderate to vigorous aerobic physical activity that includes intermittent or continuous aerobic physical activity of both moderate and vigorous intensity for at least 60 minutes per day. (S3.M6.6)	Participates in moderate to vigorous muscle- and bone-strengthening physical activity at least three times a week. (S3.M6.7)	Participates in moderate to vigorous aerobic and/or muscle- and bone-strengthening physical activity for at least 60 minutes per day at least five times a week. (S3.M6.8)
S3.M7 Fitness knowledge	Identifies the components of skill-related fitness. (S3.M7.6)	Distinguishes between health-related and skill-related fitness.[i] (S3.M7.7)	Compares and contrasts health-related fitness components.[ii] (S3.M7.8)

(continued)

(continued)

Standard 3	Grade 6	Grade 7	Grade 8
Fitness knowledge			
S3.M8	Sets and monitors a self-selected physical activity goal for aerobic and/or muscle- and bone-strengthening activity based on current fitness level. (S3.M8.6)	Adjusts physical activity based on quantity of exercise needed for a minimal health standard and/or optimal functioning based on current fitness level. (S3.M8.7)	Uses available technology to self-monitor quantity of exercise needed for a minimal health standard and/or optimal functioning based on current fitness level. (S3.M8.8)
S3.M9	Employs correct techniques and methods of stretching.[iii] (S3.M9.6)	Describes and demonstrates the difference between dynamic and static stretches.[iv] (S3.M9.7)	Employs a variety of appropriate static stretching techniques for all major muscle groups. (S3.M9.8)
S3.M10	Differentiates between aerobic and anaerobic capacity, and between muscular strength and endurance. (S3.M10.6)	Describes the role of exercise and nutrition in weight management. (S3.M10.7)	Describes the role of flexibility in injury prevention. (S3.M10.8)
S3.M11	Identifies each of the components of the overload principle (FITT formula: frequency, intensity, time, type) for different types of physical activity (aerobic, muscular fitness and flexibility). (S3.M11.6)	Describes overload principle (FITT formula) for different types of physical activity, the training principles on which the formula is based and how the formula and principles affect fitness.[v] (S3.M11.7)	Uses the overload principle (FITT formula) in preparing a personal workout.[vi] (S3.M11.8)
S3.M12	Describes the role of warm-ups and cool-downs before and after physical activity. (S3.M12.6)	Designs a warm-up and cool-down regimen for a self-selected physical activity. (S3.M12.7)	Designs and implements a warm-up and cool-down regimen for a self-selected physical activity. (S3.M12.8)
S3.M13	Defines resting heart rate and describes its relationship to aerobic fitness and the Borg Rating of Perceived Exertion (RPE) Scale.[vii] (S3.M13.6)	Defines how the RPE Scale can be used to determine the perception of the work effort or intensity of exercise. (S3.M13.7)	Defines how the RPE Scale can be used to adjust workout intensity during physical activity. (S3.M13.8)
S3.M14	Identifies major muscles used in selected physical activities.[viii] (S3.M14.6)	Describes how muscles pull on bones to create movement in pairs by relaxing and contracting.[ix] (S3.M14.7)	Explains how body systems interact with one another (e.g., blood transports nutrients from the digestive system, oxygen from the respiratory system) during physical activity.[x] (S3.M14.8)
Assessment & program planning			
S3.M15	Designs and implements a program of remediation for any areas of weakness based on the results of health-related fitness assessment. (S3.M15.6)	Designs and implements a program of remediation for two areas of weakness based on the results of health-related fitness assessment. (S3.M15.7)	Designs and implements a program of remediation for three areas of weakness based on the results of health-related fitness assessment. (S3.M15.8)
S3.M16	Maintains a physical activity log for at least two weeks and reflects on activity levels as documented in the log. (S3.M16.6)	Maintains a physical activity and nutrition log for at least two weeks and reflects on activity levels and nutrition as documented in the log. (S3.M16.7)	Designs and implements a program to improve levels of health-related fitness and nutrition. (S3.M16.8)

Standard 3	Grade 6	Grade 7	Grade 8
Nutrition			
S3.M17	Identifies foods within each of the basic food groups and selects appropriate servings and portions for his or her age and physical activity levels.[xi] (S3.M17.6)	Develops strategies for balancing healthy food, snacks and water intake, along with daily physical activity.[xii] (S3.M17.7)	Describes the relationship between poor nutrition and health risk factors.[xiii] (S3.M17.8)
Stress management			
S3.M18	Identifies positive and negative results of stress and appropriate ways of dealing with each.[xiv] (S3.M18.6)	Practices strategies for dealing with stress, such as deep breathing, guided visualization and aerobic exercise.[xv] (S3.M18.7)	Demonstrates basic movements used in other stress-reducing activities such as yoga and tai chi. (S3.M18.8)

Standard 4	Grade 6	Grade 7	Grade 8
The physically literate individual exhibits responsible personal and social behavior that respects self and others.			
Personal responsibility			
S4.M1	Exhibits personal responsibility by using appropriate etiquette, demonstrating respect for facilities and exhibiting safe behaviors. (S4.M1.6)	Exhibits responsible social behaviors by cooperating with classmates, demonstrating inclusive behaviors and supporting classmates. (S4.M1.7)	Accepts responsibility for improving one's own levels of physical activity and fitness. (S4.M1.8)
S4.M2	Identifies and uses appropriate strategies to self-reinforce positive fitness behaviors, such as positive self-talk. (S4.M2.6)	Demonstrates both intrinsic and extrinsic motivation by selecting opportunities to participate in physical activity outside of class. (S4.M2.7)	Uses effective self-monitoring skills to incorporate opportunities for physical activity in and outside of school. (S4.M2.8)
Accepting feedback			
S4.M3	Demonstrates self-responsibility by implementing specific corrective feedback to improve performance. (S4.M3.6)	Provides corrective feedback to a peer, using teacher-generated guidelines, and incorporating appropriate tone and other communication skills. (S4.M3.7)	Provides encouragement and feedback to peers without prompting from the teacher. (S4.M3.8)
Working with others			
S4.M4	Accepts differences among classmates in physical development, maturation and varying skill levels by providing encouragement and positive feedback. (S4.M4.6)	Demonstrates cooperation skills by establishing rules and guidelines for resolving conflicts. (S4.M4.7)	Responds appropriately to participants' ethical and unethical behavior during physical activity by using rules and guidelines for resolving conflicts. (S4.M4.8)
S4.M5	Cooperates with a small group of classmates during adventure activities, game play or team-building activities. (S4.M5.6)	Problem-solves with a small group of classmates during adventure activities, small-group initiatives or game play. (S4.M5.7)	Cooperates with multiple classmates on problem-solving initiatives including adventure activities, large-group initiatives and game play. (S4.M5.8)

(continued)

(continued)

Standard 4	Grade 6	Grade 7	Grade 8
Rules & etiquette			
S4.M6	Identifies the rules and etiquette for physical activities/games and dance activities. (S4.M6.6)	Demonstrates knowledge of rules and etiquette by self-officiating modified physical activities and games or following parameters to create or modify a dance. (S4.M6.7)	Applies rules and etiquette by acting as an official for modified physical activities and games and creating dance routines within a given set of parameters. (S4.M6.8)
Safety			
S4.M7	Uses physical activity and fitness equipment appropriately and safely, with the teacher's guidance. (S4.M7.6)	Independently uses physical activity and exercise equipment appropriately and safely. (S4.M7.7)	Independently uses physical activity and fitness equipment appropriately, and identifies specific safety concerns associated with the activity. (S4.M7.8)

Standard 5	Grade 6	Grade 7	Grade 8
The physically literate individual recognizes the value of physical activity for health, enjoyment, challenge, self-expression and/or social interaction.			
Health			
S5.M1	Describes how being physically active leads to a healthy body. (S5.M1.6)	Identifies different types of physical activities and describes how each exerts a positive effect on health. (S5.M1.7)	Identifies the 5 components of health-related fitness (muscular strength, muscular endurance, flexibility, cardiovascular endurance and body composition) and explains the connections between fitness and overall physical and mental health. (S5.M1.8)
S5.M2	Identifies components of physical activity that provide opportunities for reducing stress and for social interaction. (S5.M2.6)	Identifies positive mental and emotional aspects of participating in a variety of physical activities. (S5.M2.7)	Analyzes the empowering consequences of being physically active. (S5.M2.8)
Challenge			
S5.M3	Recognizes individual challenges and copes in a positive way, such as extending effort, asking for help or feedback and/or modifying the tasks. (S5.M3.6)	Generates positive strategies such as offering suggestions or assistance, leading or following others and providing possible solutions when faced with a group challenge. (S5.M3.7)	Develops a plan of action and makes appropriate decisions based on that plan when faced with an individual challenge. (S5.M3.8)
Self-expression & enjoyment			
S5.M4	Describes how moving competently in a physical activity setting creates enjoyment. (S5.M4.6)	Identifies why self-selected physical activities create enjoyment. (S5.M4.7)	Discusses how enjoyment could be increased in self-selected physical activities. (S5.M4.8)
S5.M5	Identifies how self-expression and physical activity are related. (S5.M5.6)	Explains the relationship between self-expression and lifelong enjoyment through physical activity. (S5.M5.7)	Identifies and participates in an enjoyable activity that prompts individual self-expression. (S5.M5.8)

Standard 5	Grade 6	Grade 7	Grade 8
Social interaction			
S5.M6	Demonstrates respect for self and others in activities and games by following the rules, encouraging others and playing in the spirit of the game or activity. (S5.M6.6)	Demonstrates the importance of social interaction by helping and encouraging others, avoiding trash talk and providing support to classmates. (S5.M6.7)	Demonstrates respect for self by asking for help and helping others in various physical activities. (S5.M6.8)

The foundation for this section comes from Griffin, L.L. & Butler, J.I. (2005). *Teaching games for understanding: Theory, research and practice.* Champaign, IL: Human Kinetics; Griffin, L.L., Mitchell, S.A., & Oslin, J.L. (2006). *Teaching sport concepts and skills: A tactical games approach.* Windsor, Ontario: Human Kinetics; and Rovegno, I. & Bandauer, D. (2013). *Elementary physical education: Curriculum and instruction.* Burlington, MA: Jones & Bartlett Publishing.

[i] SHAPE America. (2012). Instructional framework for fitness education in physical education [Guidance Document]. Reston, VA: Author. (p.16).

[ii] Ibid.

[iii] Ibid., p. 7.

[iv] Ibid.

[v] Ibid., p. 17.

[vi] Ibid.

[vii] Ibid., p. 14.

[viii] Ibid., p. 13.

[ix] Ibid.

[x] Ibid.

[xi] Ibid., p. 42.

[xii] Ibid., p. 45.

[xii] Ibid., p. 40.

[xiv] Ibid., p. 35.

[xv] Ibid.

OPERATIONAL DEFINITIONS OF ACTIVITY CATEGORIES

Outdoor pursuits: The outdoor environment is an important factor in student engagement in the activity. Activities might include recreational boating (e.g., kayaking, canoeing, sailing, rowing); hiking; backpacking; fishing; orienteering or geocaching; ice skating; skateboarding; snow or water skiing; snowboarding; snowshoeing; surfing; bouldering, traversing, or climbing; mountain biking; adventure activities; and ropes courses. The selection of activities depends on the environment-related opportunities within the geographical region.

Fitness activities: Activities with a focus on improving or maintaining fitness. Fitness activities might include yoga, Pilates, resistance training, spinning, running, fitness walking, fitness swimming, kickboxing, cardio kick, Zumba, and exergaming.

Dance and rhythmic activities: Activities that focus on dance or rhythms. Dance and rhythmic activities might include dance forms such as creative movement or dance, ballet, modern, ethnic or folk, hip hop, Latin, line, ballroom, social, and square.

Aquatics: Might include swimming, diving, synchronized swimming, and water polo.

Individual-performance activities: Might include gymnastics, figure skating, track and field, multi-sport events, in-line skating, wrestling, self-defense, and skateboarding.

Games and sports: Includes the games categories of invasion, net and wall, target, and fielding and striking.

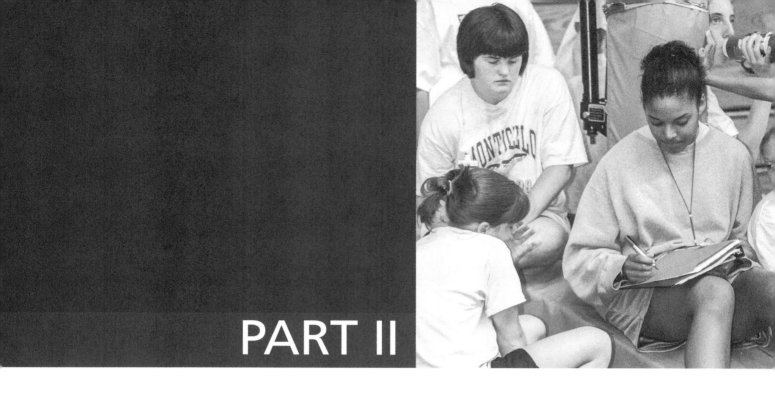

PART II

Lesson Plans for Middle School Physical Education

Applying Students' Skills and Knowledge to Dance and Rhythms

This chapter focuses on dance, which is an important content area for all ages in the physical education curriculum. Dance and rhythmic activities include, but are not limited to, dance forms such as creative movement, ballet, modern, ethnic or folk, hip hop, Latin, line, ballroom, social, and square (SHAPE America, 2014, p. 13). That gives teachers a wide array from which to choose the types of dances and rhythmic activities that best fit the needs of their students and the community. Also, many dances have steps and styles that students can apply to other dances or even to sports.

People of all ages have enjoyed rhythmic activities and dance for centuries, and children and young adults still love moving to music. Dance provides pleasure, as well as health benefits and opportunities for social interaction. It also can provide meaningful experiences in physical education and further your students' physical literacy.

Graham, Holt/Hale, and Parker (2010) assert that dance experiences in physical education class should give students:

- The ability to use their bodies to express feelings and attitudes about themselves and others;
- A sense of self-satisfaction that can be derived from effectively using one's body as an instrument of expression;
- Enjoyment and appreciation of dance as a worthwhile experience for all, not for just a few;
- An appreciation of dance as an art medium that can have value for both the participant and the spectator; and
- The ability to interpret and move to different rhythms. (p. 602)

Dance and rhythmic activities are a natural choice for addressing SHAPE America's National Standards for K-12 Physical Education and their accompanying Grade-Level Outcomes (SHAPE America, 2013), especially the outcomes under Standard 5, which focus on overall health, challenging activities, self-expression and enjoyment, and social interaction. Depending on your curricular goals, the lessons here also provide opportunities to address Standard 3 (physical activity and fitness knowledge) and Standard 4 (responsible personal and social behaviors).

This chapter contains two modules on dance and rhythmic activities. Each module demonstrates how to provide meaningful learning experiences using dance content to improve students' competency, overall health, and well-being. The modules also provide a strong model for teaching any form of dance that you or your students might choose.

The eight-lesson Social Dance Module begins with a lesson on basic waltz steps and progresses through different dance positions, turns, and transitions before moving on to basic swing dance steps. As in most dance lessons, the progressions in both the waltz and the swing dance lessons are similar (e.g., breaking the dance into eight-count steps, dancing without music, then adding music). Please note that, while the names of some dances and some of the moves might vary by region, the basic elements of the dances that are intended for student learning are the same.

The eight-lesson Folk Dance Module offers a variety of folk dances with the theme of taking students on a trip around the world. Students not only learn different dances, but they're also introduced to some of the culture and history behind those dances. That kind of immersive approach helps students create a dance portfolio that they can add to in the years to come.

For quick reference, each module begins with a block plan chart of the Grade-Level Outcomes that are addressed in each lesson. As you might expect, each lesson addresses Outcome S1.M1, which recommends that students be able to demonstrate correct rhythm and pattern in a dance form. As mentioned earlier, lessons in both dance modules also address outcomes under Standard 4, such as exhibiting personal responsibility by using appropriate etiquette (Outcome S4.M1.6), accepting differences among classmates (Outcome S4.M4.6), and implementing corrective feedback (Outcome S4.M3.6), as well as outcomes under Standard 5, such as describing how being physically active leads to a healthy body (Outcome S5.M1.6), identifying opportunities for reducing stress (Outcome S5.M2.6), and identifying how self-expression and physical activity are related (Outcome S5.M5.6).

SOCIAL DANCE MODULE

Lessons in this module were contributed by Robyn Davis, a physical educator and coach in Charlotte, VT.

Grade-Level Outcomes Addressed, by Lesson	Lessons							
	1	2	3	4	5	6	7	8
Standard 1. The physically literate individual demonstrates competency in a variety of motor skills and movement patterns.								
Demonstrates correct rhythm and pattern for one of the following dance forms: folk, social, creative, line or world dance. (S1.M1.6)	P	P	P	P	P	P	P	P
Exhibits command of rhythm and timing by creating a movement sequence to music as an individual or in a group. (S1.M1.8)				P				
Standard 2. The physically literate individual applies knowledge of concepts, principles, strategies and tactics related to movement and performance.								
Standard 3. The physically literate individual demonstrates the knowledge and skills to achieve and maintain a health-enhancing level of physical activity and fitness.								
Standard 4. The physically literate individual exhibits responsible personal and social behavior that respects self and others.								
Exhibits personal responsibility by using appropriate etiquette, demonstrating respect for facilities and exhibiting safe behaviors. (S4.M1.6)	P							
Demonstrates self-responsibility by implementing specific corrective feedback to improve performance. (S4.M3.6)	E		E	E			E	
Provides corrective feedback to a peer, using teacher-generated guidelines, and incorporating appropriate tone and other communication skills. (S4.M3.7)								E
Accepts differences among classmates in physical development, maturation and varying skill levels by providing encouragement and positive feedback. (S4.M4.6)		E		E	E			
Demonstrates knowledge of rules and etiquette by self-officiating modified physical activities and games or following parameters to create or modify a dance. (S4.M6.7)				P				
Standard 5. The physically literate individual recognizes the value of physical activity for health, enjoyment, challenge, self-expression and/or social interaction.								
Describes how being physically active leads to a healthy body. (S5.M1.6)				P				
Identifies components of physical activity that provide opportunities for reducing stress and for social interaction. (S5.M2.6)				E				
Describes how moving competently in a physical activity setting creates enjoyment. (S5.M4.6)							P	
Identifies how self-expression and physical activity are related. (S5.M5.6)							P	
Explains the relationship between self-expression and lifelong enjoyment through physical activity. (S5.M5.7)	P							

P = Primary; E = Embedded

LESSON 1: WALTZ BOX STEP

Grade-Level Outcomes

Primary Outcomes

Dance & rhythms: Demonstrates correct rhythm and pattern for one of the following dance forms: folk, social, creative, line or world dance. (S1.M1.6)

Personal responsibility: Exhibits personal responsibility by using appropriate etiquette, demonstrating respect for facilities and exhibiting safe behaviors. (S4.M1.6)

Self-expression & enjoyment: Explains the relationship between self-expression and lifelong enjoyment through physical activity. (S5.M5.7)

Embedded Outcome

Accepting feedback: Demonstrates self-responsibility by implementing specific corrective feedback to improve performance. (S4.M3.6)

Lesson Objectives

The learner will:

- perform the box step.
- perform the box step with a partner in practice position.
- demonstrate proper social dance etiquette by requesting and accepting invitations to dance.
- perform the box step with a partner in closed dance position.
- be able to explain the relationship between self-expression and lifelong enjoyment through physical activity.

Equipment and Materials

- Waltz music
- Music-playing device

Introduction

Today, we start our Social Dance Module. Dances are found in cultures all over the world as people celebrate, share traditions, and communicate. We begin with the waltz, first learning the box step, then progressing to different dance positions, turns, and additional waltz steps. After the waltz, we'll learn basic swing dance.

Show a video of several social dances to pique students' interest.

Instructional Task: Why We Dance

■ **PRACTICE TASK**

Discuss with students why people dance.

Guiding questions for students:

- What is self-expression?
- In what ways can people use dance for self-expression?
- What physical activities can people do throughout their lifetimes?
- Can dance be one of those?

Extension

In partners or small groups, have students come up with different dances or dance activities that they could enjoy throughout their lifetimes.

Student Choices/Differentiation

- Participate in teacher- or student-led discussions.
- Students choose partner.
- Watch a teacher-created PowerPoint, if needed.

What to Look For

Students can explain the relationship between self-expression and lifelong enjoyment through physical activity.

Instructional Task: Basic Waltz Box Step

■ PRACTICE TASK

Students perform the box step.

Students are either in a line side by side or a scattered formation facing the teacher.

Demonstrate without music, first facing students, then with back to students:

1. Left foot steps forward.
2. Sidestep to the right with the right foot.
3. Bring left foot to rest next to the right foot.
4. Step back with the right foot.
5. Sidestep to the left with the left foot.
6. Bring right foot to rest next to the left foot.

The box step is the same for both partners.

Imagine a box taped on the floor; your feet step on each corner of the box and glide over the sides of the box. The box is completed with two counts of three: Lead with the left foot, forward three counts; then, lead with the right foot, backward three counts to complete the box.

Count slowly while demonstrating a full box step, your back to the class. Then, prompt students to follow: Ready? And, forward-2-3, back-2-3.

Extensions

- After students repeat four to six times, turn to face students and repeat counts without demonstration. Students practice as long as necessary.
- Students repeat dance steps with music.
- Post dance and movement vocabulary in the classroom or gymnasium as reinforcement and a learning aid for visual learners.

Refinements

- Students may include the rise and fall. On count one, the step is normal step with the heel; counts two and three are taken with a slight lift on the toes.
- Students might need prompting for left–right steps. You can do that from behind students by tapping the appropriate shoulder or back of leg to initiate correct movement.

Student Choices/Differentiation

Students may review a video clip to help visualize the box step.

What to Look For

- The waltz is a smooth dance. Steps are evenly paced and not rushed.
- Students demonstrate steps with rhythmic acuity.
- Students perform correct steps in order.

Instructional Task: Dance Etiquette

■ PRACTICE TASK

Working in partners, students practice dance etiquette.

Throughout the module, we have leaders and followers for the two dancers in partner dances. In the case of mixed-sex couples, the male traditionally takes the lead and the female follows. To avoid the stress and embarrassment caused when trying to create mixed-sex couples when members of one sex outnumber the other, we recommend pairing students as leaders and followers rather than as girls and boys. The leader is responsible for guiding the couple and initiating transitions to different dance steps and, in improvised dances, for choosing the dance steps to perform.

Leaders stand in a line with their backs toward the wall. Followers stand in front of the leaders, facing the wall. Any student without a partner practices independently.

We practice appropriate dance etiquette each time we dance. We alternate "leader's request" and "follower's request." Today, we'll start with follower's request. Followers look their partners in the eye and ask, "Would you like to dance?," "May I have this dance?," or another appropriate request. Leaders should maintain eye contact and respond, "Yes," "Yes, thank you," or another appropriate acceptance. In class, your response to the request must always be appropriate and affirmative.

At the end of each dance, partners again make eye contact and say, "Thank you," "Thanks for the dance," or another appropriate response.

Have partners practice requesting and accepting.

Extensions

- Rotate partners; have one group stay in place while the other rotates down the line.
- On a small sheet of paper, partners write at least one thing they liked about how their partners requested or accepted.

Refinement

Do not allow students to be sarcastic during this activity.

Student Choices/Differentiation

- Students may use cue cards, if needed.
- If possible, the line of students should allow enough room between students to prevent physical contact during the practice session and enable students to focus on verbal interaction with their partners.

What to Look For

- Students demonstrate respectful and appropriate behaviors.
- Students speak with a strong and confident voice.
- Students use appropriate facial expressions.

Instructional Task: Box Step in Practice Position

■ PRACTICE TASK

Working in partners, students practice the box step in practice position.

Demonstration: Have two students demonstrate as you coach them.

Leaders stand with their backs to the wall; followers stand in front of them, facing the wall. Students without partners stand in the appropriate line and practice footwork independently.

Determine who (leader or follower) makes the dance request.

Practice position: Leaders extend the arms slightly at waist level with palms facing upward. Followers place their hands palm down in their partners' hands.

In the waltz, the dance usually starts with the leader stepping forward and the follower stepping back.

On your count, the leaders initiate the box step by stepping forward on the left foot at the same time the followers step back on their right, and they continue to complete the box step. *Ready? And 1-2-3, 1-2-3.*

Partners repeat the box step four to six times.

Extension

After thanking their partners, followers rotate to new partners and repeat the practice sequence.

Refinement

Encourage students to talk to one another to problem-solve length of steps, rhythm, and footwork.

Student Choices/Differentiation

Students working alone can either work independently or stand behind another student to shadow the movements.

What to Look For

- Students mirror each other's steps.
- Steps are smooth and slow.
- Students use the dance request process each time they change partners.

Instructional Task: Box Step in Closed Dance Position

■ PRACTICE TASK

Working in partners, students practice the box step in closed dance position.

Demonstration: Have two students demonstrate as you coach them.

Partners request and accept the dance.

Partners should face each other with shoulders parallel. Leaders extend their left arms to the side, palms facing up; followers rest their right hands in leaders' palms between the thumb and forefinger, and leaders close their hands lightly around followers' hands. These hands should be at eye level of the shorter partner. Leaders then place their right hands on their partners' backs, fingers together on the shoulder blade. Leaders' arms should be away from their bodies, with elbows pointing to the side. Followers rest their left arms on the leaders' arms, with palms on leaders' right shoulders. Partners should be slightly offset to the left to avoid stepping on each other. This is the closed dance position.

With you counting, partners initiate box step together in closed position. Repeat four to six times before rotating partners.

Refinement

If students are looking at their feet as they dance, encourage them to look over their partners' right shoulders.

Student Choices/Differentiation

Students can continue in the practice position and slowly progress to the closed position.

What to Look For

At this point, it's okay for students to look at their feet as they dance. However, as they become more skilled, encourage them to look over their partners' right shoulder.

Instructional Task:
Box Step, Closed Dance Position With Music

■ PRACTICE TASK

Students practice with partners to music.

Waltz music is in 3/4 time. Choose a slow waltz to begin when practicing, usually less than 90 beats per minute.

Music suggestions:

"Rainbow Connection" by the Carpenters

"Moon River" by Henry Mancini

"Could I Have This Dance" by Anne Murray

"Wallflower Waltz" by k.d. lang

With music playing, students rotate, request the dance, and assume the closed dance position. To ensure students are accurately hearing the rhythm pattern, count aloud: *1-2-3, 1-2-3, 1-2-3, 1-2-3. Ready? And 1-2-3, 1-2-3* . . .

Repeat six to eight times; partners thank each other.

Extension

Repeat, students rotating to new partners.

Refinement

Stop activity and review steps, dance requests, body position, and so on, as needed.

EMBEDDED OUTCOME: S4.M3.6. Encourage students to talk to each other to problem-solve footwork, dance positioning, and cooperation during dance pattern, and to accept each other's feedback.

Student Choices/Differentiation

Students may practice the sequence by themselves if needed.

What to Look For

- Students use the correct footwork.
- Students work together.
- Students maintain a smooth flow of dance.

Formal and Informal Assessments

Informal and partner feedback

Closure

- How many counts of three make a full box step?
- Who steps forward first to start the box step?
- When performing the box step, both the leaders and the followers always step forward on which foot?
- Where should you be looking while you dance the waltz?

Reflection

- Did students have enough time in practice position?
- Were all students treated respectfully?
- Did students rotate and participate with a large portion of their classmates?

Homework

Practice your dance etiquette by asking a parent or guardian to dance. It can be to any song, but I would love it if you taught someone the dance that you learned today.

Resources

Harris, J., Pittman, A., Waller, M., & Dark, C. (2008). *Dance a while: Handbook for folk, square, contra, and social dance.* Boston: Allyn & Bacon.

Kassing, G. (2014). *Discovering dance.* Champaign, IL: Human Kinetics.

Wright, J. (2013). *Social dance: Steps to success.* 3rd ed. Champaign, IL: Human Kinetics.

Internet keyword search: "waltz box step," "learning to waltz," "closed dance position," "waltz dance music"

LESSON 2: WALTZ BOX TURN

Grade-Level Outcomes

Primary Outcome

Dance & rhythms: Demonstrates correct rhythm and pattern for one of the following dance forms: folk, social, creative, line or world dance. (S1.M1.6)

Embedded Outcome

Working with others: Accepts differences among classmates in physical development, maturation and varying skill levels by providing encouragement and positive feedback. (S4.M4.6)

Lesson Objectives

The learner will:

- perform the box turn.
- perform the box turn with a partner in practice position.
- perform the box turn with a partner in closed dance position.
- perform a dance phrase by combining the box step and the box turn.

Equipment and Materials

- Waltz music
- Music-playing device

Introduction

Who had success teaching your parent or guardian the box step? Who practiced proper etiquette? Today, we will learn another waltz step called the box turn. The box turn is a challenging step, but as you continue to practice, you will become more skilled at this step.

Instructional Task:
Review Box Step With Partner in Closed Position

■ PRACTICE TASK

Working in partners, students perform the box step in closed position.

Today, followers stand in a line with their backs toward the wall, and leaders stand in front of them, facing the wall. Students without partners extend the line without partners and practice alone.

Today it is leader's request, as the music begins.

Count aloud: *1-2-3, 1-2-3. Ready? And 1-2-3, 1-2-3.*

Continue counting for four to six box steps as a review, then let students attempt to find the rhythmic pattern in the music. Stop and restart the group with a count if the class is not successful in finding the pattern.

Extension

Rotate partners every 90 seconds. Spend as much time as needed to have at least 80 percent of the class successful.

Refinements

- Students should begin to include the rise and fall; on count one, the step is normal step with the heel; counts two and three are taken with a slight lift on the toes.
- Prompt students to maintain good posture and focus their sight line over their partners' right shoulder.

Student Choices/Differentiation

Students can review video clips.

What to Look For

- The waltz is a smooth dance.
- The steps are evenly paced and not rushed.
- Students demonstrate steps with rhythmic acuity and proper form.

Instructional Task: Box Turn

■ PRACTICE TASK

Students are in a line side by side facing the teacher.
Demonstrate without music, first facing students, then with back to students.

1. Left foot steps forward.
2. Right foot steps forward as both feet quarter-pivot to the left.
3. Left foot closes and rests next to the right foot.
4. Right foot steps back.
5. Left foot steps back as both feet quarter-pivot to the left.
6. Bring your right foot to rest next to the left foot.

The box turn is the same for both partners.

Teacher cues: *Forward, forward pivot, together, back, back pivot, together.* A complete box turn would be four quarter turns to the left so the performer begins and ends facing front.

Continue individual practice until 80 percent of students are successful.

Extension

Add music to the steps.

Refinement

Students might need prompting for left–right. You can do that from behind by tapping the appropriate shoulder or back of leg to initiate correct movement.

Student Choices/Differentiation

- Watch video clips of the box turn.
- Practice turns at slower pace.

What to Look for

- Students pivot quarter turn to left. They should face each wall for a complete turn.
- Steps are smooth and rhythmic.

Instructional Task:
Box Turn With Partner in Practice Position

■ PRACTICE TASK

Working in partners, students practice one segment of the box turn in practice position.

Followers stand with their back toward the wall; leaders stand in front of them. Extra students without partners stand in the appropriate line and practice footwork alone.

Partners request and accept the dance.

Students assume practice position.

On your count, leaders initiate the box turn by stepping back on the right foot at the same time the followers step forward on the left, and they continue to complete one part of the box turn. *Ready? And 1-2-3.*

Partners repeat the single box turn segment six to eight times before thanking their partners. Leaders rotate to a new partner. Continue this practice until 80 percent of student partners are successful.

Extensions

- Partners repeat four segments of the box turn to complete a full turn.
- Rotate every 3 minutes, repeating the sequence with a new partner.

Student Choices/Differentiation

- Review video clips of the box turn.
- Practice turns at slower pace.

What to Look For

- Partners help each other.
- Partners move together.
- Students show confidence in their dance requests.

Instructional Task: Box Turn in Closed Dance Position

■ PRACTICE TASK

Working in partners, students practice the box turn in closed dance position.

Followers stand with their backs to the wall; leaders stand in front of them. Students without partners stand in the appropriate line and practice footwork independently.

Partners request and accept the dance.

Partners assume the closed dance position. Partners should be slightly offset to the left to avoid stepping on each other.

On your count, partners initiate the box turn together in closed position. Repeat six to eight times before leaders rotate to a new partner.

Refinement

Students can silently repeat to themselves "forward, forward, together, back, back, together" to keep steps flowing and smooth.

Student Choices/Differentiation

If class is struggling with this turn, go back to practice position for a few more times until students are ready to move forward and confident with the footwork.

What to Look For

- Partners work and move together.
- The turns are small quarter turns rather than larger strides.

Instructional Task: Combining the Box Step and the Box Turn

■ PRACTICE TASK

Partners combine the box step and the box turn to create a dance phrase.

Demonstration: Ask one set of partners to demonstrate a full box step and a full box turn. Count aloud during the demonstration six counts of three: complete box step (two counts of three) and complete box turn (four counts of three).

Partners practice the dance phrase.

Rotate partners every 3 minutes.

Extension

Students can challenge themselves by extending the phrase and repeating it two to four times.

Student Choices/Differentiation

- Watch video clips of the box turn.
- Practice turns at slower pace.

What to Look For

Students focus on moving from the box step to the box turn smoothly, without hesitation.

Instructional Task:
Combining the Box Step and Box Turn to Music

■ PRACTICE TASK

Students practice a combination dance phrase with partners and music.

Start the music as students rotate down the line. One student requests, and the partner assumes the closed dance position. Students initiate the dance phrase independently.

After 3 minutes, partners thank each other, rotate, and begin again with new partners.

Refinement

Transitions should be smooth from one dance step to another.

EMBEDDED OUTCOME: S4.M4.6. Use the rotation of partners to reinforce the importance of students' accepting differences and encouraging each other. Provide feedback to recognize students who support and encourage one another.

Student Choices/Differentiation

If students are struggling as to when to begin, you can count the rhythmic pattern aloud: *1-2-3, 1-2-3.*

What to Look For

- Students perform the dance steps in rhythm with the music.
- Students provide encouragement to others.
- Students move with purpose, according to the dance.

Formal and Informal Assessments

- Informal
- Self-assessment homework activity

Closure

- What part of the box turn is most difficult for you?
- Was there a teaching hint that you and one of your partners found helpful?
- If you didn't get it today, stay with it and we will practice again next class!

Reflection

- Are most students keeping up or is the pace a bit fast for the group?
- Have some students learned the skills enough to be student leaders and peer coaches?

Homework

Self-assessment activity: Please describe how you feel in relation to the dance activities. Are you comfortable with the steps without music? Do you feel confident when music is added? Are you excited to work with partners or do you prefer to work alone? How does it feel when someone encourages you? Have you encouraged others? Why or why not?

Resources

Harris, J., Pittman, A., Waller, M., & Dark, C. (2008). *Dance a while: Handbook for folk, square, contra, and social dance*. Boston: Allyn & Bacon.

Kassing, G. (2014). *Discovering dance*. Champaign, IL: Human Kinetics.

Wright, J. (2013). *Social dance: Steps to success*. 3rd ed. Champaign, IL: Human Kinetics.

Internet keyword search: "waltz left box turn," "waltz reverse turn," "waltz music list"

LESSON 3: WALTZ UNDERARM TURN

Grade-Level Outcomes

Primary Outcome

Dance & rhythms: Demonstrates correct rhythm and pattern for one of the following dance forms: folk, social, creative, line or world dance. (S1.M1.6)

Embedded Outcome

Accepting feedback: Demonstrates self-responsibility by implementing specific corrective feedback to improve performance. (S4.M3.6)

Lesson Objectives

The learner will:

- perform the box turn.
- perform the underarm box turn with a partner in practice position.
- perform the underarm box turn with a partner in closed dance position.
- perform a dance phrase by combining the box step and the underarm box turn.

Equipment and Materials

- Waltz music
- Music-playing device

Introduction

Please turn in your homework assignment. Who wants to share something from your self-assessments? (Share how you felt when you first started dancing.) Today, we will begin with a review of the box step and the box turn. Then, we will add a new step, the underarm turn, and combine them for some dance phrases.

Instructional Task: Review Box Step and Box Turn

■ PRACTICE TASK

Working in partners, students perform the box turn and a short dance.

Today, the leaders will stand in a line with their backs to the wall, and the followers will stand in front of them, facing the wall. Students without partners will extend the line without partners and will practice independently.

We will start with a full box step, then a full box turn, and then repeat that pattern. Let's walk through it in closed dance position without the music.

Count aloud: *1-2-3, ready and box-2-3, box-2-3, turn-2-3, turn-2-3, turn-2-3, turn-2-3, box-2-3, box-2-3, turn-2-3, turn-2-3, turn-2-3, turn-2-3.*

Continue counting this pattern until 80 percent of students/partners are successful.

Extension

Today is followers' request. When the music starts, followers request the dance, leaders accept, and you begin your dance phrase and repeat it.

Partners move to an open space and execute a dance phrase. Rotate partners every 2 minutes.

You have been moving and dancing in a defined space; it's time to move into open space. Rotate partners and remember who your new partner is. Leaders can continue to stand in a line; followers, come stand as a group off to the side. It is still followers' request today. When the music starts, followers walk over to their partners and request the dance. Leaders accept and together you find an open space in the gymnasium and repeat the same dance phrase (box step, box turn, repeat) that we have been practicing.

Refinement

Stop and restart the group with a count if the class is not successful in finding the rhythmic pattern.

EMBEDDED OUTCOME: S4.M3.6. Partners should talk and engage in peer coaching to create a successful partnership. Encourage students to provide feedback to and accept it from their partners, and to implement it to improve performance.

Student Choices/Differentiation

- Choose starting partner.
- Review video clip.
- Some partners might need cuing and counting to stay with the rhythmic pattern.

What to Look For

- Partners use correct form for the closed dance position.
- Students dance without looking at their feet.
- Box turns are a complete turn.
- Partners are staying in their own space rather than traveling around the floor.

Instructional Task: Underarm Turn

■ PRACTICE TASK

Working in partners, students practice the underarm turn.

Leaders stand with their backs to the wall; followers stand in front of them. Students without partners stand in the appropriate line and practice footwork independently.

Partners rotate and followers request the dance.

Partners assume the closed dance position.

Partners should be slightly offset to the left to avoid stepping on each other.

Partners initiate a basic box step: leader stepping back on right foot, follower stepping forward on left foot. After the first count of three (half of a box step), the leader raises his left hand, holding the follower's right hand above their heads. With his right hand on the follower's shoulder blade, he gently prompts the follower to perform a three-step turn to her right under their raised hands. This is an underarm turn.

Student Choices/Differentiation

- Review video clip that incorporates the turn.
- Choose partner.

What to Look For

- Partners stay with the count before and during the turn.
- Leaders remember to prompt partners to turn.

Instructional Task:
Dance Phrase That Incorporates the Underarm Turn

■ PRACTICE TASK

Demonstration: Have two students demonstrate as you coach them.

Students combine steps for a dance phrase.

Leaders stand with their backs toward the wall; followers stand in front of them. Extra students without partners stand in the appropriate line and practice footwork alone.

Partners rotate and followers request the dance.

Partners assume the closed dance position.

Students dance two full box steps, one full box turn, a half box step, and one underarm turn; they continue to repeat this dance phrase.

Extension

Rotate partners every 2 minutes.

Refinement

It is important to note that when the follower comes out of the turn, the leader should immediately initiate the closed dance position and move into a box step.

Student Choices/Differentiation

- Students may stop to find rhythmic pattern or to discuss with partner the phrase sequence.
- Students may practice in practice position until they are confident with the sequence.

What to Look For

- Students show correct posture and alignment in the closed dance position.
- Students are rhythmically accurate in their steps.
- Students incorporate the rise and fall.

Formal and Informal Assessments

- Informal assessments
- Exit slip: List as many critical elements from the dances as you can.

Closure

- Which of the steps are you finding most challenging?
- How were the transitions from step to step working for you and your partners?
- Are you finding some of the music choices easier than others when trying to identify the rhythmic patterns?

Reflection

- Are students working respectfully with each other?
- Are students without partners practicing footwork?

Homework

Practice your steps at home.

Write down a few ways that social dance can lead to a healthy body. Bring your list to the next class.

Resources

Harris, J., Pittman, A., Waller, M., & Dark, C. (2008). *Dance a while: Handbook for folk, square, contra, and social dance.* Boston: Allyn & Bacon.

Kassing, G. (2014). *Discovering dance.* Champaign, IL: Human Kinetics.

Wright, J. (2013). *Social dance: Steps to success.* 3rd ed. Champaign, IL: Human Kinetics.

Internet keyword search: "waltz underarm swing," "beginning waltz"

LESSON 4: WALTZ HESITATION STEP AND STUDENT-CREATED DANCE

Grade-Level Outcomes

Primary Outcomes

Dance & rhythms: Demonstrates correct rhythm and pattern for one of the following dance forms: folk, social, creative, line or world dance. (S1.M1.6)

Dance & rhythms: Exhibits command of rhythm and timing by creating a movement sequence to music as an individual or in a group. (S1.M1.8)

Health: Describes how being physically active leads to a healthy body. (S5.M1.6)

Embedded Outcomes

Accepting feedback: Demonstrates self-responsibility by implementing specific corrective feedback to improve performance. (S4.M3.6)

Health: Identifies components of physical activity that provide opportunities for reducing stress and for social interaction. (S5.M2.6)

Lesson Objectives

The learner will:

- perform the hesitation step.
- discuss how dance can contribute to a healthy body.
- work cooperatively in a small group.
- create and perform a dance phrase.

Equipment and Materials

- Waltz music
- Music-playing device
- Pencils
- Paper

Introduction

Today, we are going to learn another waltz step called the hesitation step. After we learn the hesitation, you are going to create your own dance phrase with a partner. First, let's review your homework from last class.

Instructional Task: Dance and Health Discussion

■ PRACTICE TASK

Lead discussion on how dance can contribute to a healthy body.

Guiding questions for students:

- How can dance make you healthier?
- What happens to your heart rate and breathing when you are dancing?
- What components of health-related fitness are involved?

Extension

EMBEDDED OUTCOME: S5.M2.6. Prompt students to think beyond the physical components of health to include wellness factors, such as social support and stress reduction.

Student Choices/Differentiation

- Students can share with a partner instead of the whole class.
- Students can write ideas down on poster paper.

What to Look For

- Students offer relevant suggestions.
- Everyone is contributing to the discussion.

Instructional Task: Hesitation Step

▦ PRACTICE TASK

Working in partners, students perform the hesitation step in closed position without music.

Have two students demonstrate as you coach them.

Partners request and accept the dance.

Partners are in closed position.

The hesitation step is one step that is taken in three counts. On the first count, the leader steps forward with the left foot as the follower steps back with the right foot. On counts two and three, the leader then slowly drags the right foot to close as the follower drags the left foot to close. This is repeated in reverse as the leader steps back and the follower steps forward.

The hesitation also can be performed to the side, as the leader steps left with the left foot at the same time that the follower steps right with the right foot.

Students perform a box step and two hesitations forward and back.

Extension

Add music.

Student Choices/Differentiation

- Watch video clip with hesitation step.
- Choose partner.

What to Look For

- Students perform the step and maintain the rise and fall.
- Students display proper body positon.

Instructional Task: Creating a Dance Phrase

▦ PRACTICE TASK

Working in groups of two or three, students create and perform a dance phrase incorporating the box step, box turn, underarm turn, and both forward-and-back hesitations and side-to-side hesitations.

Students build a pattern of steps to create a dance phrase.

Extension

Once students have written their phrases, partners should practice until they are confident with the phrase.

Refinement

Remind students that they can choose from among many options and combinations. For example, they could do two box steps, an underarm turn, a forward-and-back hesitation, two box steps, a side-to-side hesitation, and two box turns.

Student Choices/Differentiation

Students who find remembering the sequence challenging could simplify by doing one box step between each of the other steps.

What to Look For

- All partners contribute to the creation of the dance phrase.
- All components are included in each group's pattern.

Instructional Task: Student-Created Dance Phrase

■ PRACTICE TASK

Students perform their dance phrases.

Divide the groups in half.

Half of the students in each group watch their classmates perform. The other half request and accept the dance and move to an open space on the floor to perform their dance phrases for the duration of the selected music.

The groups then switch.

Extension

Using a checklist, have peers evaluate at least one dance phrase while they are observing. During a break, students share feedback from the checklist.

EMBEDDED OUTCOME: S4.M3.6. Using the peer checklist feedback, students work on improving performance of their dance phrases.

Student Choices/Differentiation

Students can write down their phrases and post them on the wall for reference.

What to Look For

- Transitions between dance steps are clean and smooth.
- Students incorporate all dance steps into the phrase.
- Students use appropriate audience behaviors.

Formal and Informal Assessments

- Peer assessment: Students use a checklist to determine whether their peers are performing dance steps correctly, are using proper etiquette, and are on rhythm with their dance partners.
- Students create their own dance.

Closure

- What did you see that your classmates did well when you were observing them?
- Did you see any interesting or unique sequences?
- Did you notice proper closed dance position?
- Did you observe partners who incorporated the rise and fall in their waltz?

Next class, we'll be moving on to swing dance. Take a few minutes to look at some video clips of this type of dance before coming to class.

Reflection

- Do students understand the waltz as a smooth dance?
- Did students give appropriate feedback and use dance vocabulary when responding?

Homework

Review video clips of east coast swing dance on school website or Internet.

Resources

Harris, J., Pittman, A., Waller, M., & Dark, C. (2008). *Dance a while: Handbook for folk, square, contra, and social dance.* Boston: Allyn & Bacon.

Kassing, G. (2014). *Discovering dance.* Champaign, IL: Human Kinetics.

Wright, J. (2013). *Social dance: Steps to success.* 3rd ed. Champaign, IL: Human Kinetics.

Internet keyword search: "dance vocabulary," "waltz for beginners"

LESSON 5: EAST COAST SWING

Grade-Level Outcomes

Primary Outcomes

Dance & rhythms: Demonstrates correct rhythm and pattern for one of the following dance forms: folk, social, creative, line or world dance. (S1.M1.6)

Rules & etiquette: Demonstrates knowledge of rules and etiquette by self-officiating modified physical activities and games or following parameters to create or modify a dance. (S4.M6.7)

Embedded Outcome

Working with others: Accepts differences among classmates in physical development, maturation and varying skill levels by providing encouragement and positive feedback. (S4.M4.6)

Lesson Objectives

The learner will:

- perform the rock step.
- perform the triple step.
- perform the basic swing dance step.
- demonstrate the open-facing two-hand-hold dance position.
- perform a basic swing step with a partner.
- demonstrate proper social dance etiquette by performing a skit.

Equipment and Materials

- Swing dance music
- Music-playing device
- Poly spots or tape

Introduction

Today, we will begin a new dance form called swing dance. There are many different types of swing dance; we will learn the east coast swing. We will begin with the two basic components for swing dance: the rock step and the triple step. Today, we will learn the basic swing dance step and work with partners.

Show video of swing dance to provide a visual for students.

Instructional Task: Basic Rock Step

■ PRACTICE TASK

Students perform the rock step.

Students stand in two lines side by side facing each other: leaders with their backs to the wall, followers across from them, facing the wall.

In swing dance, partners mirror movements. Leaders always rock back on the left foot while followers always rock back on the right foot.

Demonstrate with back to the leaders:

1. Left foot steps behind, with weight transferred to the ball of the left foot.
2. Weight then is transferred to right foot, with a small step forward.

Demonstrate with back to the followers:

1. Right foot steps behind, with weight transferred to the ball of the right foot.
2. Weight then is transferred to left foot, with a small step forward.

Repeat "rock step" or "1-2" as students practice, with the weight transfer happening on each word. Practice continues as long as necessary.

Student Choices/Differentiation

- Show video of rock step pattern.
- Slow speed of practice.
- Choose leader or follower role.

What to Look For

- Students transfer weight with each step.
- Backward step is on the ball of the foot.
- Steps for the rock step are small.

Instructional Task: Swing Dance Triple Step

▪ PRACTICE TASK

Students perform the triple step.

Students are in two parallel lines facing each other: leaders with their backs to the wall, followers across from them, facing the wall. Leaders and followers continue to mirror each other's movements.

The triple step is a three-step sequence done in two counts. Each of the steps is a small step. The first step is on count one; the second and third steps are quick on the half count and count two. The cue is "one and two." Steps two and three are taken on the ball of the foot, with weight transferred with each step.

We will practice a triple step to one side.

Demonstrate with back to the leaders:

1. Left foot takes a small side step to the left, followed by right foot and left again. With each step, weight should be transferred from one foot to the next.
2. (Count slowly while demonstrating to the left.)
3. Prompt leaders: *Leaders go to the left first, as I count the steps. Ready? One and two.*

Demonstrate with back to the followers:

1. Right foot takes a small side step to the right, followed by left foot and right again. With each step, weight is transferred from one foot to the next.
2. (Count slowly while demonstrating to the right.)
3. Prompt followers: *We go to the right first. Ready? One and two.*

Repeat with both groups.

Students next combine two triple steps, first in one direction followed by one in the opposite direction. Leaders begin going left and followers begin to the right.

Teacher cues: *Ready? One and two, one and two.*

Cue students and continue practice as long as necessary.

Extension

Post dance and movement vocabulary in the classroom or gymnasium as reinforcement and a learning aid for visual learners.

Refinements

- Take the second and third steps on the ball of the foot, almost as if limping on the second step.
- Students may incorporate a slight lean of the torso in the direction of the dance.
- Some students might need a visual prompt for steps. Poly spots or pieces of tape on the floor can help. Cues for poly spots could be *Red, yellow, red. Green, blue, green.* Tape can be colored or numbered (1, 2, 3, 4, 5, 6) for steps.

Student Choices/Differentiation

- Show video of triple step pattern.
- Slow speed of practice.
- Choose leader or follower role.

What to Look For

- Students demonstrate rhythmic acuity.
- Students transfer weight with each step.
- Students combine the two triple steps together without pause in between.

Instructional Task: Basic Swing Step

■ PRACTICE TASK

Students combine the triple step and the rock step for a complete basic swing step.

Students stand in two parallel lines facing each other: leaders with their backs to the wall, followers across from them, facing the wall.

Leaders and followers continue to mirror each other's movements.

Leaders begin to the left, followers to the right.

Demonstrate with back to leaders, and repeat demonstration in the opposite direction with back to followers.

Prompt students: *Ready? One and two, one and two, rock step.*

Repeat, with prompts, as long as necessary.

Student Choices/Differentiation

- Show video of basic swing step.
- Slow speed of practice.
- Choose leader or follower role.

What to Look For

- Steps are rhythmically accurate.
- Students transfer weight with each step.
- Students combine the two triple steps without pause in between.

Instructional Task: Rock Step in Open-Facing Two-Hand-Hold Position With Partner

■ PRACTICE TASK

Students practice with partners.

Partners request and accept the dance.

Swing dance is performed in many different dance positions. We will use the open-facing two-hand-hold dance position. It is similar to the practice position that we used in the waltz.

Leaders extend their arms slightly below waist level, palms facing upwards in a relaxed position. Followers place their hands palm down in their partners' hands.

We start by working on the rock step with a partner. Remember, leaders always rock back on the left foot, while followers rock back on the right foot.

As partners step back on the initial step, leaders open their left hands to drop the followers' right hands. Partners maintain contact: leaders' right hands and followers' left.

On the step forward of the rock step, partners rejoin hands for the dance position.

Partners practice the rock step independently.

Refinements

- Students talk to each other to problem-solve step length, rhythm, and footwork.
- Students may have a slight turn of the torso toward their respective free hands on the back step of the rock, turning back to face their partners on the forward step.
- For added style, the free hand and non-weight-bearing knee may be slightly elevated on the back step, as partners use their connected hands as a counterbalance point.
- As partners step forward, the leader's left foot and the follower's right foot should not come to rest, as this step initiates the triple step.

EMBEDDED OUTCOME: S4.M4.6. While students are talking to each other about the mechanics of the dance, they also should provide positive feedback and encouragement to their partners.

Student Choices/Differentiation

- Students working alone can work independently on either the leader's or follower's footwork or technique.
- Some students might find it helpful to stand behind a classmate and shadow his movements.

What to Look For

- Partners work together, mirroring each other's dance steps.
- Students hold the full-count steps for a full count and the half-count steps for just a half.
- This is not a traveling step; students might begin to shuffle step from side to side, as opposed to taking small steps in place.

Instructional Task: Basic Swing Dance Step in Two-Hand-Hold Open Position

■ PRACTICE TASK

Students practice the basic swing dance step.

The basic swing dance step is a rock step and two triple steps.

Demonstration: Two students demonstrate as you cue them.

We begin with the rock step, followed by two triple steps, and continue to repeat the pattern. Leaders step back on their left, followers step back on their right. As you take the second step forward, rejoin hands and move into two triple steps, leaders to the left and followers to the right.

Teacher cues: *Ready? And rock step. One and two, one and two, rock step. One and two, one and two, rock step.*

Extension

Repeat, rotating to a new partner.

Student Choices/Differentiation

- Choose partner.
- Choose leader or follower role.
- Slow speed of sequence.
- Review video of basic swing dance step.

What to Look For

- Partners work together.
- Partners are rhythmically accurate with the music.
- Steps are smooth and are not marching steps.
- Students are able to sustain the rhythm and pattern.

Instructional Task: Basic Swing Step With Music

■ PRACTICE TASK

Students practice with partners to music.

The swing dance music we are using is in 4/4 time. This offers a wide variety of music to choose from. With students new to swing dance, consider using music with fewer than 140 beats per minute. Suggestions:

"Ability to Swing" by Patti Austin

"Love Shack" by the B-52s

"Mercy" by Duffy

"Right as Rain" by Adele

Extensions

- With music playing, students rotate, request the dance, and assume the two-hand-hold open dance position. To assist students in finding the rhythmic pattern, count aloud: *Rock step. One and two, one and two, rock Step. One and two, one and two, rock step.*
- As students gain confidence in the pattern and the music, stop your verbal count. You can use rhythm sticks to reinforce the rhythm, as needed, throughout the class.
- Rotate partners every 2 minutes.
- Encourage partners to look at each other when swing dancing. It is a social dance, and there is a lot of partner communication.

Refinement

Make sure that students have smooth transitions.

Student Choices/Differentiation

- Choose partner.
- Choose leader or follower role.
- Slow speed of sequence.
- Review video of basic swing dance step.

What to Look For

- Students' footwork is correct.
- Partners work together.
- Partners maintain a smooth flow of dance.
- Partners maintain their space instead of drifting side to side.

Instructional Task: Etiquette

■ PRACTICE TASK

We have been dancing for a while now. In small groups, demonstrate your dance etiquette skills by creating a short skit on proper and improper dance etiquette.

Extension

Peer assessment checklist on skits

Student Choices/Differentiation

- Show students an example each of proper and improper etiquette.
- Have students choose from a list of etiquette choices.

What to Look For

- Students demonstrate knowledge of dance etiquette through well-planned skits.
- Students work well in groups, and skits are creative.

Formal and Informal Assessments

Peer assessment checklist on proper and improper dance etiquette, group work, and creativity

Closure

- What is another way that we could count the triple steps in basic?
- Can you feel you and your partner leading each other with your hands in the triple steps? Is that helpful?
- What level of energy did you feel when performing this dance?

Reflection

- Did students understand the difference between a full count and a half count in the triple step?
- Are students without partners participating?
- Were all students treated respectfully?
- Did students get to rotate and participate with a large portion of their classmates?

Homework

Students can practice the basic swing step at home.

Students can interview parents, grandparents, neighbors, friends, relatives: Did you ever learn to swing dance?

Resources

Harris, J., Pittman, A., Waller, M., & Dark, C. (2008). *Dance a while: Handbook for folk, square, contra, and social dance.* Boston: Allyn & Bacon.

Kassing, G. (2014). *Discovering dance.* Champaign, IL: Human Kinetics.

Wright, J. (2013). *Social dance: Steps to success.* 3rd ed. Champaign, IL: Human Kinetics.

Internet keyword search: "basic triple step," "east coast swing," "learning to swing dance"

LESSON 6: SWING STEP DANCE CREATION

Grade-Level Outcomes

Primary Outcome

Dance & rhythms: Demonstrates correct rhythm and pattern for one of the following dance forms: folk, social, creative, line or world dance. (S1.M1.6)

Embedded Outcome

Working with others: Accepts differences among classmates in physical development, maturation and varying skill levels by providing encouragement and positive feedback. (S4.M4.6)

Lesson Objectives

The learner will:

- perform a single turn.
- perform an underarm turn.
- demonstrate the open-facing two-hand-hold dance position.
- perform a basic swing step with a partner.
- review proper social dance etiquette by requesting and accepting invitations to dance.

Equipment and Materials

- Swing dance music
- Music-playing device
- Rhythm sticks
- Poly spots

Introduction

Today, we will begin with a review of the basic swing step. Then, we will expand our swing dance knowledge by learning some turns and practicing some combinations to create dance phrases. Did anyone interview someone who enjoys social dances?

Instructional Task: Review Basic Swing Step

■ PRACTICE TASK

Students perform the basic swing step.

Students extend and accept the invitation to dance. Students without partners find a space to practice independently.

Let's start with the basic swing step all together. We'll do two triple steps and one rock step and repeat that short phrase. Ready? One and two, one and two, rock step. One and two, one and two, rock step.

Repeat four to six times and rotate partners.

New partners extend and accept an invitation to dance.

As music begins, partners move together to an open space on the floor and begin the basic swing step independently.

Refinements

- Encourage students to learn both the leader's and follower's footwork to be more versatile.
- Encourage partners to stop and restart if they feel they are not rhythmically accurate with their footwork.
- Use rhythm sticks as necessary to help students with rhythmic pattern.

Student Choices/Differentiation

- Watch a video of swing dance combinations.
- Choose partner.

What to Look For

- Students are able to create dance phrases independently.
- Students incorporate torso lean and knee-hand lift for style.
- Partners maintain their dance space and don't wander the dance floor.

Instructional Task:
Short Dance Phrase With Basic Step and Single Turn

■ PRACTICE TASK

Partners learn the single turn.

Note: Because this instructional task involves combining dance steps and movements, teacher instructions to students are numbered to make them easier to follow.

1. We will begin with the turn first and add the footwork later.

Choose two students to demonstrate as you coach partners through a follower's single turn.

Partners begin in open-facing two-hand-hold dance position.

To leaders: *After a rock step, instead of resuming dance position, initiate the follower's single turn. Still holding your partner's left hand, gently guide both of your hands across the midline in front of your bodies and then release hands. When your partner completes the turn, extend your right hand to hold your partner's left, and repeat the rock step.*

To followers: *After a rock step, instead of resuming dance position, follow your joined hands to the right and complete a full turn. After you turn 360 degrees, extend your left hand to your partner and perform a rock step.*

Allow partners to practice at their own pace.

Repeat as many times as necessary for students to gain skill in this single turn.

Refinement

Students should walk slowly through this practice.

2. Now, we will add the footwork. We are still keeping the rhythmic step pattern and will practice this first without partners.

To leaders: *As you complete the rock step with a forward step on your right, guide your partner into a turn while you do a triple step to the left, followed by a triple step to the right, finishing with a rock step.*

Stand with your back to the leaders and cue slowly for leaders to shadow: *Rock step, guide follower's hand* (said at the cadence for the triple step), *one and two, rock step; one and two, rock step.*

Repeat as many times as necessary.

To followers: *As you complete the rock step with a forward step on the left, begin the triple step to the right, turning as you step, followed by a triple step leading with your left and continuing your turn, finishing with a rock step.*

Stand with your back to the followers and cue slowly for followers to shadow: *Rock step, one and turn* (said at the cadence for the triple step), *turn and two, rock step.*

Repeat as many times as necessary.

EMBEDDED OUTCOME: S4.M4.6. While you work with one group, students in the other group can work on peer assessment and coaching, using a checklist or rubric. If practical, use a device to record performance. Students should focus on providing corrective feedback in a supportive manner.

3. Single-turn with partners. Remember to extend your hand to your partner after the single turn to complete your final rock step.

Cue slowly for students to practice: *Rock step. One and two, one and two, rock step.*

4. Practice a short dance phrase with music. Remember, the basic step is two triple steps and a rock step. The pattern will be two basics and a single turn. Repeat that pattern until we rotate partners.

Refinement

In learning a new task, practicing each component of the skill separately and then combining them and adding music last will minimize the number of variables students need to navigate.

Student Choices/Differentiation

- Leaders can perform the single turn.
- Students can practice forward triple steps, alternating the right and left lead.
- Review video of basic step and turn.
- Choose partner.

What to Look For

- Followers turn in place.
- Leaders guide gently and don't push or force turns.
- Leaders maintain rhythm of triple steps and reach out for followers' hands after turns.
- Followers complete two triple steps forward to complete the turn.

Instructional Task: Underarm Turn

■ PRACTICE TASK

Leaders stand with their backs to the wall; followers stand in front of them. Students without partners stand in the appropriate line and practice footwork independently.

Partners assume the open-facing two-hand-hold dance position.

1. We will walk through the underarm turn and then add the footwork.

To leaders: *Drop your right hand and release the follower's left hand, at the same time raising your left hand, joined with the follower's right hand, above your heads. Keep these hands joined loosely as your partner turns under the raised hands.*

To followers: *As you drop your left hand down, raise your right hand, joined with the leader's left hand above your heads. Walk forward, turning under the raised hands.*

2. Now, we add the footwork.

To leaders: *As you drop your right hand, begin the basic step, triple step to the left, triple step to the right; as your partner completes the underarm turn, you simultaneously perform the rock step.*

To followers: *As your left hand is released, begin a forward triple step on your right, followed by a forward triple step on your left as you turn under the arch of raised hands. Your turn should be completed at the end of your second triple step, and you simultaneously perform your rock step with your partner.*

Practice this as many times as necessary to master footwork.

Add music.

Student Choices/Differentiation

- Leaders can perform the underarm turn.
- Choose partner.
- Review video of underarm turn.

What to Look For

- Partners keep the same rhythmic pattern together.
- Each rock step can be accentuated with the free hand lifted into the air.
- At this point, students should not be looking at their feet the entire time they are dancing.

Instructional Task: Perform a Dance Phrase That Incorporates the Single Turn and the Underarm Turn

▨ PRACTICE TASK

Students combine steps for a dance phrase.

Demonstration: Have two students demonstrate as you coach them.

Partners begin in open-facing two-hand-hold position.

Students dance two basic swing steps, one follower's single turn, two basic swing steps, and one follower's underarm turn. Partners continue to repeat this pattern.

Count aloud: *One and two, one and two, rock step. One and two, one and two, rock step.*

As students find the rhythmic pattern, stop verbal cues.

Refinements

- Rhythm sticks can be helpful for students to identify the rhythmic patterns.
- Rotate partners every 2 minutes.

Student Choices/Differentiation

- Encourage students to stop and talk about rhythm and footwork, as necessary.
- Students who find the pattern challenging might need to review again at a walking pace.
- Choose partner.

What to Look For

- Students are rhythmically accurate with the music.
- The steps are smooth and are not marching steps.
- Students are able to sustain the rhythm and pattern.
- Leaders lead followers out of the turns by gently guiding them into the rock step.

Formal and Informal Assessments

- Peer assessment
- Homework assignment

Closure

- Swing dance is an energetic and free-flowing dance form. Did any of you begin to add some of your own flair? What would be examples of that, keeping with the steps and rhythm that we have learned?
- Swing has no specific etiquette or form that tells you where you should direct your line of sight. Where do you look when you are dancing?

Reflection

- Do students dance with the music and understand the rhythm of swing dance?
- Is my music selection appropriate?

- Are students without partners participating?
- Were all students treated respectfully?
- Did students get to rotate and participate with a large portion of their classmates?

Homework

Write a reflection about how dance can contribute to self-expression and enjoyment. Due next class.

Resources

Harris, J., Pittman, A., Waller, M., & Dark, C. (2008). *Dance a while: Handbook for folk, square, contra, and social dance.* Boston: Allyn & Bacon.

Kassing, G. (2014). *Discovering dance.* Champaign, IL: Human Kinetics.

Wright, J. (2013). *Social dance: Steps to success.* 3rd ed. Champaign, IL: Human Kinetics.

Internet keyword search: "swing dance turns," "swing dance combinations," "swing dance underarm turn," "history of swing dance"

LESSON 7: SWING DANCE BARREL ROLL

Grade-Level Outcomes

Primary Outcomes

Dance & rhythms: Demonstrates correct rhythm and pattern for one of the following dance forms: folk, social, creative, line or world dance. (S1.M1.6)

Self-expression & enjoyment: Describes how moving competently in a physical activity setting creates enjoyment. (S5.M4.6)

Self-expression & enjoyment: Identifies how self-expression and physical activity are related. (S5.M5.6)

Embedded Outcome

Accepting feedback: Demonstrates self-responsibility by implementing specific corrective feedback to improve performance. (S4.M3.6)

Lesson Objectives

The learner will:

- review the basic swing step, the single turn, and the underarm turn in combination.
- perform the barrel roll with a partner.
- perform a double face loop with a partner.
- perform a combination dance phrase.
- identify how self-expression and physical activity are related.
- describe how moving competently in a physical activity setting creates enjoyment.

Equipment and Materials

- Swing dance music
- Music-playing device
- Rhythm sticks
- Poster paper and markers

Introduction

Today, we will review our swing dance skills and add some new moves and turns, including the barrel roll and double face loop. Both of these moves represent the fun and energetic style of swing dance. First, let's talk about your homework assignment.

Instructional Task: Homework Review

▧ PRACTICE TASK

Lead a brief discussion about the homework.

Guiding questions for students:

- How can social dance offer opportunities for enjoyment?
- In what ways can you find self-expression in dance?
- What other benefits does dance offer as a physical activity?

Student Choices/Differentiation

- Students may share with a partner instead of the entire class.
- Students may write ideas on poster paper.

What to Look For

- Students are offering relevant suggestions.
- Everyone is contributing.

Instructional Task: Review Basic Swing Step, Single Turn, and Follower's Underarm Turn

▦ PRACTICE TASK

Working in partners, students perform a dance phrase.

Students request and accept the dance.

Let's review our swing dance steps thus far. The pattern we will start with is basic, single turn, basic, and follower's underarm turn. Let's walk through the pattern without music.

Count aloud: *Ready? One and two, triple step, rock step, one and two, one and two, rock step, one and two, one and two, rock step.*

Repeat as necessary for review.

Have half of the class stand and observe while the other half dances the pattern with music. Use rhythm sticks or clap to help students find rhythmic patterns.

After the dance, observers can provide feedback.

Guiding questions for students:

- What did you notice about transitioning from the basic steps to some of the turns?
- What extra style additions did you observe?
- As you observed the group, did people seem to dance with the rhythm of the music?

Have groups switch and repeat the process.

Refinement

Encourage students to talk to one another, verbalize the pattern, and count aloud as needed as they dance.

Student Choices/Differentiation

Review video of basic swing step, single turn, and underarm turn.

What to Look For

- Both leaders and followers maintain footwork during turns.
- Leaders guide followers gently through turns.

Instructional Task: Barrel Roll

▦ PRACTICE TASK

Students choose new partners.

Performing the barrel roll requires cooperation and trust between partners. When executing the barrel roll, partners need to move together in unison, because their movements are mirrored.

Choose one set of partners to coach though a demonstration.

We will walk slowly through this move.

From the open-facing two-hand-hold position, leaders lift their left hands, joined with followers' right hands, into the air. At the same time, leaders cross the right hand, joined with followers' left, at waist level in front of partners to the left. As hands are moving, partners follow hands and turn until they are back to back, with both hands in the air above their heads. Partners continue to "roll" all the way around, hands joined, until they are back to the starting position.

Count aloud or use rhythm sticks as partners practice.

Extension

The timing for the barrel roll should start as a slow roll to two counts of three, or two triple steps counts, exiting into a rock step. As students become more proficient, they may choose to do the barrel rolls more quickly in one count of three or to do two consecutive barrel rolls in two counts of three.

Refinement

The barrel roll can be performed turning to either the right or left.

Student Choices/Differentiation

- Review a video clip of the barrel roll.
- Partners may release one or both hands, if necessary, to complete the move successfully.
- Add stylization at the end of the barrel roll as partners face each other with a surprised or happy expression.

What to Look For

- Students are moving respectfully with partners.
- Students are moving smoothly into the triple step after completing the turn.

Instructional Task: Double Face Loop

▨ PRACTICE TASK

Students choose new partners.

The double face loop is another swing dance move performed for visual impact. Let's walk through this and break the move into four parts. Then, we can add the footwork.

Beginning in open-facing two-hand hold, partners step forward slightly to their left so that they are standing side by side facing opposite directions. At this point partners are standing right hip to right hip, each with their own left hands in front of them, joined with partners' right hands.

The second move is for partners to lift both joined hands into the air above head height.

Next, keeping hands joined and remaining side by side, partners guide their left hands, along with partners' right, behind their own heads. Partners are now standing side by side, arms crossed and resting briefly behind their heads.

Practice and refine as necessary.

Last, each partner opens the left hand; right hands are on the back of the partners' head or neck area. Partners then pivot toward each other, stepping back slightly while sliding their right hands along partners' right arms until they join right hands.

Practice and refine as necessary.

Now, let's combine these four parts into two parts. First, from open-facing two-hand hold, as you move forward to the side-by-side position, lift your joined hands into the air at the same time.

Second, lower your hands behind your heads and, without pause, slide apart.

Allow practice until students are comfortable with this skill.

Let's add the footwork. Instead of stepping forward to be side by side with your partner, triple-step forward, raising your joined hands into the air. Let's practice that a few times. Followers lead with the right foot, leaders with the left.

Next, as you drop hands and slide, you should perform another triple step. Followers start with the left, leaders with the right. You now join hands in a right-hand-to-right-hand grip and will conclude with a rock step. After completing the rock step, change hands to the open-facing two-hand hold.

Note: Although the follower usually extends the left hand for the rock step, in this move, the follower performs the rock step with a right-hand-to-right-hand grip.

Use rhythm sticks as students practice and refine this skill.

Students choose new partners.

Refinements

- The forward diagonal triple step should be slightly forward, with small steps, so that partners stay in dance position.
- As partners guide their left hands behind their own heads, they need to allow their right hands to be guided behind their partners' heads.

Student Choices/Differentiation

- Review video clip of double face loop.
- Slow down practice as needed.

What to Look For

- Students remain within arm's reach throughout, not sliding past the right-hand-to-right-hand grip.
- Partners maintain footwork throughout the move.
- Partners transition smoothly in and out of the move.
- Leaders guide followers' hand exchange after the rock step to open-facing two-hand hold.

Instructional Task: Perform a Dance Phrase That Incorporates the Barrel Roll and the Double Face Loop

■ PRACTICE TASK

Students rotate partners and request and accept the dance.

The pattern is two basics, one barrel roll, two basics, and a double face loop.

Allow students to walk through the pattern two or three times, counting aloud before adding music.

Count, clap, or use rhythm sticks to reinforce step patterns.

Extension

Set up a video-recording station in one corner. As students become comfortable with the pattern, they rotate to the station to be recorded. Students replay the video and critique their own performances, then they write down areas for improvement.

EMBEDDED OUTCOME: S4.M3.6. Continue to practice, implementing corrective feedback from the video station.

Student Choices/Differentiation

Students can walk through the pattern for additional repetitions as needed.

What to Look For

- Partners maintain rhythm.
- Partners enter and exit moves smoothly.

Formal and Informal Assessments

Peer assessment

Closure

- Both of these moves required a lot of trust and cooperation between partners. How did that work for you? What specific feedback did you give or receive?
- Are you getting the feel of swing dance?
- Who will show me a favorite dance move?

Reflection

- Can I post examples of swing dance combinations on the website?
- Were all students treated respectfully?
- Were students able to rotate and participate with a large portion of their classmates?

Homework

Keep practicing your footwork and timing at home.

There are many musical choices for swing dance. Keeping in mind the school guidelines for music and lyrics, students may bring suggestions for music to be used in class, and the class can discuss what it was like to perform to the music.

Review for a quiz on terminology next class.

Resources

Harris, J., Pittman, A., Waller, M., & Dark, C. (2008). *Dance a while: Handbook for folk, square, contra, and social dance.* Boston: Allyn & Bacon.

Kassing, G. (2014). *Discovering dance.* Champaign, IL: Human Kinetics.

Wright, J. (2013). *Social dance: Steps to success.* 3rd ed. Champaign, IL: Human Kinetics.

Internet search terms: "swing dance barrel roll," "swing dance double face loop"

LESSON 8: PRESENTATION DAY

Grade-Level Outcomes

Primary Outcome

Dance & rhythms: Demonstrates correct rhythm and pattern for one of the following dance forms: folk, social, creative, line or world dance. (S1.M1.6)

Embedded Outcome

Accepting feedback: Provides corrective feedback to a peer, using teacher-generated guidelines, and incorporating appropriate tone and other communication skills. (S4.M3.7)

Lesson Objectives

The learner will:

- review and perform the basic swing step, single turn, follower's underarm turn, leader's underarm turn, barrel roll, and double face loop in various combinations.
- work cooperatively in a self-directed learning activity.
- create an original dance phrase.
- perform this original dance phrase.
- demonstrate appropriate audience behavior while observing a dance performance.

Equipment and Materials

- Cards with short (two or three moves) dance phrases for you to read aloud
- Swing dance music
- Music-playing device
- Swing dance videos or printed directions for swing dance moves
- Paper and pencils

Introduction

After our quiz today, you will have the opportunity to explore some self-directed learning to acquire a new swing dance skill. You then will combine your new learning with the moves we have practiced to create a swing dance combination.

Instructional Task: Quiz

■ PRACTICE TASK

Teacher-generated quiz on terminology and dance steps

Student Choices/Differentiation

Allow extra time if needed or give in a take-home format.

What to Look For

- Students can identify the differences between the waltz and swing dances.
- Students know the names of the steps.
- Students can identify proper dance etiquette.

Instructional Task: Review Basic Swing Step, Single Turn, Follower's Underarm Turn, Leader's Underarm Turn, Barrel Roll, and Double Face Loop

▣ PRACTICE TASK

Working in partners, students perform a short dance phrase as requested aloud by the teacher.

Students request and accept the dance.

Verbalize a short dance phrase (e.g., "basic, barrel roll, single turn, repeat"). Give students a short time to discuss and practice with partners.

When music begins, students perform the dance phrase.

Repeat with different dance phrases.

Students should rotate partners with each new dance.

Refinement

Encourage students to talk to each other during the brief practice. At this point, they should not be counting aloud during the dance. Steps should be automatic.

Student Choices/Differentiation

- Choose partner.
- Review video clips of step combinations.

What to Look For

- Students maintain footwork, with proper weight change for each step.
- Partners move in unison, with focus and concentration on the dance and their partners.
- Students transition smoothly from one move to the next while maintaining footwork.
- Students use correct rhythm and pattern.

Instructional Task: Students Select a Swing Dance Move to Learn

▣ PRACTICE TASK

Working in small groups of two to four, students observe and review teacher-selected videos or instructional diagrams of new swing dance moves.

The groups that you are in are going to be your performance groups. Today, your group will look at some swing dance moves that we have not done before. Your group selects one new move, and together, you learn and practice that move.

Once you have learned that move, your group incorporates it into a dance phrase that includes at least four other moves that we have learned in class. Try several different combinations before you determine your phrase. You should write down your dance sequence as a reminder for your practice sessions.

The dance that you create will be shared with the class, and we will have the opportunity to celebrate your work.

Play swing dance music as students work together and practice.

Allow as much time as necessary for groups to complete this work.

Extension

You can extend student learning into homework. You could post videos and instructional materials on the school's website, share or post them in classrooms, and make them available during other times throughout the day (recess, study hall, after school).

Student Choices/Differentiation

- Students should acknowledge skill challenges of partners in their group and work accordingly.
- Assignment may be altered to include fewer moves in the combination, or alternating each move with a basic step, as needed.
- Groups may choose to learn more than one new move.
- Students might need to post their written dance phrase on the wall as a reminder of the sequence as they practice.

What to Look For

- All group members participate in the process.
- Group members take turns listening and offering input.
- Students work together in a supportive way to learn the new dance move.
- Dance phrases are written using appropriate dance vocabulary.

Instructional Task: Presentation of Dance

■ PRACTICE TASK

Students perform their original dance phrase for classmates.

Divide the class in half, with one half performing while the other half is the audience. After audience feedback, groups switch.

Before beginning, remind students of expectations for performers and guiding questions for the audience to consider.

Performers

- As music starts, leaders request the dance, followers accept; partners move together to an open space on the floor and begin their dance, repeating their phrase until the music ends.
- Students focus on the dance and their partners throughout the performance.
- Dance should be performed with energy and confidence.

EMBEDDED OUTCOME: S4.M3.7 Students provide corrective feedback to peers using the following prompts.

Audience

- Which group executed its dance with particular skill and style? Describe what you observed.
- What did you see that was unique?
- Which group performed with observable positive energy and enthusiasm?

Make sure that students are using appropriate tone and other communication skills.

Extension

Before students perform, go over peer and teacher formal assessment.

Refinement

If possible, record student performances so they can view their dance for self-assessment.

Student Choices/Differentiation

Students can teach other groups their dance phrase.

What to Look For

- Students create sequences that combine four previously learned swing steps with new learning.
- All students in each group are able to perform the dance sequence.
- Students maintain focus on the dance and partners during the performance.
- Students interact with partners in a positive and supportive way while dancing.
- Audience members demonstrate appropriate behavior, watching and discussing the performance in a constructive and supportive way.

Formal and Informal Assessments

Peer assessments and formal presentation assessments

Closure

- How did you choose your moves?
- How did you choose the order of your moves?
- Were some moves bigger than others?
- Was there a different speed or force of movement for some of the moves?

This is our last social dance lesson for this module. I hope you feel more confident in your dance steps and have come to appreciate what a great lifelong physical activity this is.

Reflection

- What specific moves did the students do well? Which moves might I have spent more time teaching?
- Did students perform as expected?
- What would I change, add, or delete from this teaching progression?

Homework

Review the next module on the school's physical education website.

Resources

Harris, J., Pittman, A., Waller, M., & Dark, C. (2008). *Dance a while: Handbook for folk, square, contra, and social dance.* Boston: Allyn & Bacon.

Kassing, G. (2014). *Discovering dance.* Champaign, IL: Human Kinetics.

Wright, J. (2013). *Social dance: Steps to success.* 3rd ed. Champaign, IL: Human Kinetics.

Internet keyword search: "swing dance combinations," "swing dance moves," "east coast swing dance moves," "triple step swing dance moves"

FOLK DANCE MODULE

Lessons in this module were contributed by Colleen Buchanan, a lecturer at State University of New York College at Cortland who teaches a variety of dance, activity, and pedagogy courses. Previously, Colleen taught physical education in rural central New York.

Grade-Level Outcomes Addressed, by Lesson	Lessons							
	1	2	3	4	5	6	7	8
Standard 1. The physically literate individual demonstrates competency in a variety of motor skills and movement patterns.								
Demonstrates correct rhythm and pattern for a different dance form from among folk, social, creative, line and world dance. (S1.M1.7)	P	P	P	P	P	P	P	P
Standard 2. The physically literate individual applies knowledge of concepts, principles, strategies and tactics related to movement and performance.								
Standard 3. The physically literate individual demonstrates the knowledge and skills to achieve and maintain a health-enhancing level of physical activity and fitness.								
Describes how being physically active leads to a healthy body. (S5.M1.6)	P							
Identifies barriers related to maintaining a physically active lifestyle and seeks solutions for eliminating those barriers. (S3.M1.7)				E				
Participates in a self-selected lifetime sport, dance, aquatic or outdoor activity outside of the school day. (S3.M5.8)								E
Standard 4. The physically literate individual exhibits responsible personal and social behavior that respects self and others.								
Exhibits personal responsibility by using appropriate etiquette, demonstrating respect for facilities and exhibiting safe behaviors. (S4.M1.6)		E						
Exhibits responsible social behaviors by cooperating with classmates, demonstrating inclusive behaviors and supporting classmates. (S4.M1.7)	E							
Demonstrates self-responsibility by implementing specific corrective feedback to improve performance. (S4.M3.6)		E						
Provides corrective feedback to a peer, using teacher-generated guidelines, and incorporating appropriate tone and other communication skills. (S4.M3.7)	E							
Provides encouragement and feedback to peers without prompting from the teacher. (S4.M3.8)			E					
Accepts differences among classmates in physical development, maturation and varying skill levels by providing encouragement and positive feedback. (S4.M4.6)						E		
Cooperates with a small group of classmates during adventure activities, game play or team-building activities. (S4.M5.6)			E					
Standard 5. The physically literate individual recognizes the value of physical activity for health, enjoyment, challenge, self-expression and/or social interaction.								
Identifies components of physical activity that provide opportunities for reducing stress and for social interaction. (S5.M2.6)					E			
Recognizes individual challenges and copes in a positive way, such as extending effort, asking for help or feedback and/or modifying the tasks. (S5.M3.6)							E	
Describes how moving competently in a physical activity setting creates enjoyment. (S5.M4.6)						E		
Identifies how self-expression and physical activity are related. (S5.M5.6)						E		

P = Primary; E = Embedded

LESSON 1: ALUNELUL

Grade-Level Outcomes

Primary Outcomes

Dance & rhythms: Demonstrates correct rhythm and pattern for a different dance form from among folk, social, creative, line and world dance. (S1.M1.7)

Physical activity knowledge: Describes how being physically active leads to a healthy body. (S5.M1.6)

Embedded Outcomes

Personal responsibility: Exhibits responsible social behaviors by cooperating with classmates, demonstrating inclusive behaviors and supporting classmates. (S4.M1.7)

Accepting feedback: Provides corrective feedback to a peer, using teacher-generated guidelines, and incorporating appropriate tone and other communication skills. (S4.M3.7)

Lesson Objectives

The learner will:

- discuss ways in which dance can improve physical activity and lead to a healthy body.
- demonstrate rhythm identification using agility, coordination, and reaction time.
- demonstrate the difference between slow and quick rhythms and recite the cue for part 3 of the dance.
- perform the alunelul dance in lines and in small groups.

Equipment and Materials

- Music for alunelul
- Music-playing device

Introduction

Today, we start our Folk Dance Module, with dances from around the world. We travel today to Romania. In Romania, alunelul is a famous dance. The dance can be done at a variety of speeds. We will focus on a fast, athletic version.

Show students where Romania is on a map. Also, showing a video of other students performing the dance can stimulate students' interest before the lesson.

Show a video of several social dances to pique students' interest.

Instructional Task: Why We Dance

■ PRACTICE TASK

Lead a discussion with the students on why we should dance.

Guiding questions for students:

- Why do people like to dance?
- Why do we exercise?
- Where have you danced before?
- Do you find dancing enjoyable? Why or why not?
- Can dance contribute to increasing your physical activity?
- How does physical activity lead to a health body?

Extension

Distribute the pre-assessment rubric and describe the rubric before students start dancing so that they know what you are looking for. Throughout the lesson or at the end of the lesson, use the rubric to gauge students' dance ability.

Student Choices/Differentiation

- Show videos of people dancing.
- Students can work with partners or small groups before discussing the questions with the whole class.

What to Look For

- Students explore different forms of dance in their everyday lives.
- Students make a connection of dance leading to physical activity, which leads to a healthy body.

Instructional Task: Beginning Steps to Alunelul

■ PRACTICE TASK

Formation: two lines facing front

Perform the dance sequence without music until students master the footwork.

Part 1: Fives done while *leaping* (count to five, followed by two stomps)

> Count 1: Leap onto right foot (RF).
> Count 2: Leap onto left foot (LF) behind RF.
> Count 3: Leap onto RF.
> Count 4: Leap onto LF behind RF.
> Count 5: Leap onto RF.
> Stomp left foot in place two times.
>
> Repeat to the left, starting with LF.
> Repeat to the right, starting with RF.
> Repeat to the left, starting with LF.

Extensions

- Start slow, and increase speed as students start to master the dance moves.
- Add music for part 1.

Refinement

Students might benefit from a slow-motion cue: *Side, behind, side, behind, side, stomp, stomp.*
Cue while dancing:

> 1-2-3-4-5 stomp, stomp
> 1-2-3-4-5 stomp, stomp
> 1-2-3-4-5 stomp, stomp
> 1-2-3-4-5 stomp, stomp

or

> Right-2-3-4-5 stomp, stomp
> Left-2-3-4-5 stomp, stomp
> Right-2-3-4-5 stomp, stomp
> Left-2-3-4-5 stomp, stomp

Appropriate stride length: Don't let strides get too long so that students have enough control to execute the two stomps.

Student Choices/Differentiation

Have students recite the cue (not while dancing):

> 1-2-3-4-5 stomp, stomp
> 1-2-3-4-5 stomp, stomp
> 1-2-3-4-5 stomp, stomp
> 1-2-3-4-5 stomp, stomp

Let students watch a video of someone performing the steps to the dance.

What to Look For

- Students don't cross their feet in front, but to the back.
- Students maintain control during the dance.
- Students remember the steps of the dance.

Instructional Task: Part 2 of Dance

■ PRACTICE TASK

Part 2: Threes (count to three followed by one stomp)

As before, start slow, with no music.

> Count 1: Leap onto right foot (RF).
> Count 2: Leap onto left foot (LF) behind RF.
> Count 3: Leap onto RF.
> Stomp LF in place one time.
>
> Repeat to the left, starting with LF.
> Repeat to the right, starting with RF.
> Repeat to the left, starting with LF.

Extensions

- Speed up the steps.
- Add music.

Once students demonstrate mastery of part 2, combine parts 1 and 2, with no music. Start slow and increase speed.

Do parts 1 and 2 with music.

In pairs, have students perform each part for a partner for feedback.

EMBEDDED OUTCOME: S4.M3.7 Using teacher-generated guidelines of the correct steps and order, have students provide feedback, incorporating appropriate tone, to their peers.

Refinement

Slow-motion cue: *Side, behind, side, stomp, side, behind, side, stomp*

Cue while dancing:

> 1-2-3 stomp

or

> R-2-3 stomp
> L-2-3 stomp
> R-2-3 stomp
> L-2-3 stomp

Student Choices/Differentiation

- Have students recite the cue (not while dancing):

    1-2-3 stomp

    1-2-3 stomp

    1-2-3 stomp

    1-2-3 stomp

- Let students watch a video of someone performing the steps to the dance.
- To prevent over-traveling from side to side, have the students continue learning the dance with their hands joined behind their backs.

What to Look For

- Students perform steps correctly.
- Students stay on beat.

Instructional Task: Part 3 of Dance

■ **PRACTICE TASK**

Part 3: Ones

> Count 1: Leap onto RF.
>
> Count 2: Leap onto LF.
>
> Count 3: Leap onto RF.
>
> Stomp LF two times.

Cue

> 1-1-1 stomp, stomp

Or

> Leap, leap, leap, tap, tap
>
> Leap, leap, leap, tap, tap

Or

> Right, left, right, stomp, stomp
>
> Left, right, left, stomp, stomp

Or

> Slow, slow, slow, quick, quick
>
> Slow, slow, slow, quick, quick

Extensions

- Perform dance at higher speed.
- Add music.

Student Choices/Differentiation

Have students recite any of the cues.

What to Look For

- Leaps are controlled.
- Students don't travel side to side.
- Transitions are accurate from one part to the next.

Instructional Task: Perform Total Dance

■ PRACTICE TASK

Perform entire dance without music.
When students have mastered the steps without music, add music.

Extensions

- Once students have mastered the steps with the music, group students in twos or threes.
- Have students hold hands, with arms down.
- Once they've shown mastery in small groups, form a group circle, all dancers holding hands, arms down.
- Pre-assessment: Use a rubric to gauge students' dance and rhythm skills in a folk dance.

EMBEDDED OUTCOME: S4.M1.7. Encourage students to exhibit responsible social behaviors by cooperating with classmates instead of laughing at or making fun of each other.

Guiding questions for students:

- Why is it important to keep your strides short?
- When you start a part going to your right, which foot is free?

Student Choices/Differentiation

Students may practice steps to the side with or without music if needed.

What to Look For

- Students perform all steps correctly.
- Students work with group members appropriately.

Instructional Task: Dance Portfolio

■ PRACTICE TASK

Throughout the module, students create a portfolio of folk dances from around the world. Items to include:

- Dance steps
- History of the dance
- Pictures and information on the country or culture of where the dance was created
- Any additional information to enhance the portfolio

Extension

Pass out teacher-created rubrics and explain how students will be assessed on the portfolio.

Student Choices/Differentiation

- Let students see examples from previous students.
- Students can turn in a hard copy or an online portfolio.

What to Look For

- Students perform steps correctly.
- Students stay on beat.

Formal and Informal Assessments

Pre-assessment: Create a rubric that contains the following criteria: rhythm, footwork, pattern, and presentation of dance.

Portfolio assignment

Closure

- How many stomps do the fives get?
- What is the rhythm of the ones?
- What happens when your strides are too long?

Reflection

- Did I use the cues until mastery?
- How often did I have to jump in with verbal cues to help students keep going when they got off rhythm or footwork?
- Did I recognize when I needed to slow my verbal cues because some students were having difficulty in footwork or transitions?

Homework

There are many videos on the Internet. Find one of people dancing the alunelul dance and a different type of folk dance. Compare the dancers' traditional outfits. What similarities and differences did you find? Be prepared to discuss at the beginning of the next class.

Let's start adding to our dance portfolios. Research the alunelul dance and the culture and country in which the dance takes place. Show your family the alunelul dance!

Resources

Internet keyword search: "alunelul music," "alunelul dance steps," "folk dance," "portfolio"

LESSON 2: LIMBO ROCK

Grade-Level Outcomes

Primary Outcome

Dance & rhythms: Demonstrates correct rhythm and pattern for a different dance form from among folk, social, creative, line and world dance. (S1.M1.7)

Embedded Outcomes

Accepting feedback: Demonstrates self-responsibility by implementing specific corrective feedback to improve performance. (S4.M3.6)

Personal responsibility: Exhibits personal responsibility by using appropriate etiquette, demonstrating respect for facilities and exhibiting safe behaviors. (S4.M1.6)

Lesson Objectives

The learner will:
- demonstrate rhythm identification using agility, coordination, and reaction time.
- demonstrate the difference between slow and fast rhythms and recite the cue for part 3 of the dance.
- perform the limbo rock dance in his or her own personal space.

Equipment and Materials

- Music for limbo rock
- Music-playing device

Introduction

Today, we will continue our folk dance lessons from around the world. For homework, you were to compare two types of dances. What did you find? Who started gathering information for your portfolios? Today, we will travel to the Caribbean Islands.

Show students where the Caribbean is on a map, and mention popular foods or customs.

Instructional Task: Beginning Steps to Limbo Rock

■ **PRACTICE TASK**

Formation: two lines facing front

Perform the dance sequence without music until students master the footwork.

Part 1

Count 1: Left foot crosses the RF, weight placed on the LF.

Count 2: Transfer weight to RF (in place), still facing the right side slightly.

Count 3: Transfer weight to LF (to the back), still facing the right side slightly.

Count 4: Transfer weight to RF (in place).

Count 5: Transfer weight to LF (to the front).

Count 6: Transfer weight to RF (in place).

Count 7: Transfer weight to LF (back), turning to the left (half way), now facing the left side.

Count 8: Weight on LF, pause, and hold this beat.

Refinement

Students wil benefit from any of the cues until mastery.

Forward-2-3-4-5-6, turn, pause. Have students lift the foot during the pause to make sure they don't get ahead in the count.

or

Left, right, left, right, left, right, turn, pause, lift

Repeat to the left side, *starting with the right foot* crossing in front of the left foot.

Repeat to the right side, *starting with the left foot* crossing in front of the right foot.

Repeat to the left side, *starting with the right foot* crossing in front of the left foot.

This part is done pretty much in place. Students shouldn't travel. After the last set, students should end up facing the front for part 2 with the left foot free.

Extensions

- Start slow, and increase speed as students start to master the dance moves.
- Add music for part 1 once there is mastery in footwork.

Student Choices/Differentiation

- Have students recite the cue (not while dancing): 1-2-3-4-5-6, turn, pause, lift.
- Let students watch a video of someone performing the steps to the dance.

What to Look For

- Students stay in place and don't travel during this part.
- Students maintain control during the dance.
- Students remember the steps of the dance.

Instructional Task: Part 2 of Dance: Crossover Step

■ PRACTICE TASK

With the left foot free, begin a front crossover step to the right. This crossover step is a total of eight counts, but it's easier if counted *each time your foot crosses in front*, for a total of four counts.

Count 1: Cross LF in front of RF.

Count 2: Step to the side with RF.

Count 3: Cross LF in front of RF.

Count 4: Step onto RF.

Count 5: Cross LF in front of RF.

Count 6: Step onto RF.

Count 7: Cross LF in front of RF.

Count 8: Swing RF in prep for starting this going to the left.

Count 1: Cross RF in front of LF.

Count 2: Step to the side with LF.

Count 3: Cross RF in front of LF.

Count 4: Step onto LF.

Count 5: Cross RF in front of LF.

Count 6: Step onto LF.

Count 7: Cross RF in front of LF.

Count 8: Lift left foot in place.

As before, start slow with no music.

Extensions

- Speed up the steps.
- Add music.
- Once there is mastery in this part, go back and combine parts 1 and 2 together, with no music. Start slow and increase speed.
- Do parts 1 and 2 with music.
- Have students perform each part for a partner for feedback.

EMBEDDED OUTCOME: S4.M3.6. Emphasize with students the importance of using their peers' feedback to improve performance.

Student Choices/Differentiation

- Have students recite the cue (not while dancing):

  And cross, and 2 and 3 and 4, change

  And cross, and 2 and 3 and 4, lift

- Or *cuing for the foot as it crosses in front*:

  And left, left, left, left, change

  And right, right, right, right, lift

- Let students watch a video of someone performing the steps to the dance.
- To prevent over-traveling from side to side, have the students continue learning the dance with their hands joined behind their backs.

What to Look For

- Students perform steps correctly before moving on to part 3.
- Students stay on beat.
- Transitions are correct from one part to the next.

Instructional Task: Part 3 of Dance

■ PRACTICE TASK

With the left foot free and a "quick, quick, slow, pause" tempo:

Count 1: Step or leap to the front with LF

Count 2: Step or leap back in place onto the RF.

Count 3: Bring LF together with RF.

Count 4: Pause.

Count 5: Step or leap to the front with RF.

Count 6: Step or leap back into place onto the LF.

Count 7: Bring RF together with LF.

Count 8: Pause in place.

Cue

Front, back, together, pause, front, back, together, pause

or

Left, back, together, pause, right, back, together, pause

or

Quick, quick, slow, pause, quick, quick, slow, pause

Repeat dance from the top.

Extensions

- Once the students master part 3, slowly add all parts together, focusing on transitions.
- Perform dance with higher speed.
- Add music.

Student Choices/Differentiation

Have students recite any of the cues.

What to Look For

Leaps are executed with control, without a lot of distance forward or back.

Instructional Task: Perform Total Dance

■ PRACTICE TASK

Perform entire dance without music.

Extension

When students have mastery of the steps without music, add music.

EMBEDDED OUTCOME: S4.M1.6. Encourage students to exhibit personal responsibility by using appropriate etiquette, demonstrating respect for facilities, and exhibiting safe behaviors. Students should take the dance seriously and participate at a high level.

Guiding questions for students:

- What do I do on count eight of part 1?
- All three parts start with the same foot free. Which one?
- Can anyone identify why this is a Caribbean dance?

Student Choices/Differentiation

Students may practice steps to the side with or without music if needed.

What to Look For

- Students perform all steps correctly.
- Students maintain their own personal space for safety.

Teacher-created rubric: Social behaviors. Students can use a rubric to identify those who display appropriate personal responsibility during class.

Formal and Informal Assessments

Teacher-created rubric for students' social behaviors and feedback, with the following criteria:

Etiquette

Tone

Facial expressions

Choice of encouraging words

Closure

- On what count do you turn in part 1?
- What is the rhythm of part 3?
- Ask a question that was used in the introduction about popular foods.

Reflection

- Did I use the cues until mastery?
- How often did I have to jump in with verbal cues to help students keep going when they got off rhythm or footwork?
- Did I recognize when I needed to slow my verbal cues because some students were having difficulty in footwork or transitions?

Homework

Update your portfolio with the new dance we learned today. Start researching folk dance from Serbia, as we will travel there next class. Be prepared to discuss some of your findings.

Show your dance to as many friends as you can during recess!

Resources

Internet keyword search: "limbo rock music," "limbo rock dance steps," "folk dance"

LESSON 3: MILANOVO KOLO

Grade-Level Outcomes

Primary Outcome

Dance & rhythms: Demonstrates correct rhythm and pattern for a different dance form from among folk, social, creative, line and world dance. (S1.M1.7)

Embedded Outcomes

Accepting feedback: Provides encouragement and feedback to peers without prompting from the teacher. (S4.M3.8)

Working with others: Cooperates with a small group of classmates during adventure activities, game play or team-building activities. (S4.M5.6)

Lesson Objectives

The learner will:

- demonstrate rhythm identification using agility, coordination, and reaction time.
- perform Milanovo kolo individually in lines, small groups, and, ultimately, in a group circle holding hands.

Equipment and Materials

- Music for Milanovo kolo
- Music-playing device

Introduction

As I mentioned in our previous class, today we head for Serbia. What interesting facts did you find when you looked up Serbia? Who wants to show the video he or she found at home?

Teach students how to say "Hello" (Zdravo) and "Goodbye" (Vidimo se kasnije!) in Serbian.

Let's dance!

Instructional Task: Beginning Steps to Milanovo Kolo

▣ PRACTICE TASK

Formation: two lines facing front

Perform the dance sequence without music until students master the footwork.

Part 1

Start facing slightly to your right, right foot (RF) free:

> Count 1: Step with RF.
> Count 2: Hop with RF.
> Count 3: Step with LF.
> Count 4: Hop with LF.
> Count 5: Sidestep to the right with RF.
> Count 6: Step with LF, behind RF.

End with three small leaps in place (quick, quick, quick rhythm, or right, left, right).

The left foot is free to repeat sequence to the left. The right foot is free at the end of this sequence.

Refinement

Students will benefit from any of the cues until mastery.

Repeat to the left side, *starting with the right foot* crossing in front of the left foot.

Repeat to the right side, *starting with the left foot* crossing in front of the right foot.

Repeat to the left side, *starting with the right foot* crossing in front of the left foot.

This part is done pretty much in place. Students shouldn't travel. After the last set, students should end up facing the front for part 2 with the left foot free.

Extensions

- Start slow, and increase speed as students start to master the dance moves.
- Add music for part 1.

Student Choices/Differentiation

- Have students recite the cue (not while dancing):
    Right, hop, left, hop, side, behind, quick, quick, quick
    Left, hop, right, hop, side, behind, 1-2-3
- Let students watch a video of someone performing the steps to the dance.

What to Look For

- Students complete three steps or leaps in place so that they have the correct foot free to go to the other side (no taps in place).
- Students maintain control during the dance.
- Students remember the steps of the dance.
- Students transition cleanly from one part to the other.

Instructional Task: Part 2 of Dance

■ PRACTICE TASK

Part 2: Schottische (three walks followed by one hop)
One set = walk, walk, walk, hop
With the right foot free, two sets forward, two sets backward:

    Walk forward with RF, walk with LF.
    Walk with RF, hop with RF.
    Walk forward with LF, walk to RF, walk to LF, hop with LF.
    Walk back with RF, walk to LF, walk to RF, hop with RF.
    Walk back with LF, walk to RF, walk to LF, hop with LF.

Cue

    Walk, walk, walk, hop
    Walk, walk, walk, hop

Or

    Right-2-3-hop, left-2-3-hop
    Right-2-3-hop, left-2-3-hop

Or

    Forward-2-3-hop, forward-2-3-hop
    Back-2-3-hop, back-2-3-hop

Dance starts from part 1 again.

Extensions

- Speed up the steps.
- Add music.
- Once students show mastery in this part, combine parts 1 and 2, with no music. Start slow and increase speed.
- Do parts 1 and 2 with music.
- In pairs, have students perform each part for a partner for feedback.

EMBEDDED OUTCOME: S4.M3.8. Encourage students to provide feedback and encouragement to each other without prompting.

Student Choices/Differentiation

- Have students recite the cue (not while dancing).
- Let students watch a video of someone performing the steps to the dance.

What to Look For

- Students perform steps correctly.
- Students stay on beat.
- Students have the correct foot free at the end of a sequence, allowing for clean transitions.

Instructional Task: Perform Total Dance

■ PRACTICE TASK

Perform entire dance without music.
When students have mastered the steps without music, add music.

Extensions

- Once students show mastery with the music, group them into twos or threes.
- Have students hold hands with arms down.
- Once students show mastery in small groups, have them form a group circle, all dancers holding hands, arms down.

EMBEDDED OUTCOME: S4.M5.6. When students work in small groups, make sure students are cooperating with their classmates to learn the dance in the new formation.

Guiding questions for students:

- When you begin part 1 and part 2, which foot is free?
- Can you tap the quick, quick, quick part? (Answer: No, transfer your weight each time.)
- What makes this dance from Serbia?

Student Choices/Differentiation

Students may practice steps to the side with or without music, if needed.

What to Look For

- Students perform all steps correctly.
- Students work with group members appropriately.
- While dancing in a circle, students complete the schottische, moving forward safely so that they don't cause psychomotor or affective problems with the group.

Formal and Informal Assessments

Exit slip: Compare and contrast dances taught so far.

Closure

- Who can define *schottische*?
- Who can recite the cue for part 1?
- Why is it important to execute the schottische with control once we dance in a group circle?
- Who can say "Hello" (Zdravo) or "Goodbye" (Vidimo se kasnije!) in Serbian?

Reflection

- Did I use the cues until mastery?
- Did I jump in with the verbal cues to help students keep going when they got off rhythm or footwork?
- Did I recognize when I needed to slow my verbal cues because some students were having difficulty in footwork or transitions?
- Should I talk with their history teacher to see whether we can team up with classroom discussions about a particular country, while I teach a dance from that country?

Homework

Our next passport stamp will be Israel. See whether you can find out how to count 5-6-7-8 in Hebrew.

Keep adding to your folk dance portfolio.

Resources

Internet keyword search: "Milanovo kolo music," "Milanovo kolo dance steps," "folk dance"

LESSON 4: HORA

Grade-Level Outcomes

Primary Outcome

Dance & rhythms: Demonstrates correct rhythm and pattern for a different dance form from among folk, social, creative, line and world dance. (S1.M1.7)

Embedded Outcome

Physical activity knowledge: Identifies barriers related to maintaining a physically active lifestyle and seeks solutions for eliminating those barriers. (S3.M1.7)

Lesson Objectives

The learner will:

- demonstrate rhythm identification using agility, coordination, and reaction time.
- perform the hora individually in lines, small groups, and, ultimately, in a group circle holding hands.

Equipment and Materials

- Music for hora
- Music-playing device

Introduction

As I mentioned in our previous class, today we will head to Israel to learn the hora. The hora is a traditional Hebrew dance with several variations that is danced at Jewish celebrations. Did anyone find out how to count in Hebrew? Answer: hamesh (5), shesh (6), shera (7), shmone (8)

Teach students how to say "Hello" (Shalom) and "Goodbye" (Kol tuv) in Hebrew. You can make the lesson more challenging aerobically by, for example, adding leaping or elevation to the footwork, and the same is true for the other dances in this module.

Let's dance!

Instructional Task: Beginning Steps of the Hora

■ PRACTICE TASK

Formation: two lines facing front
Perform the dance sequence without music until students master the footwork.

Count 1: Step to your left, with LF.

Count 2: Step behind LF with RF.

Count 3: Step to your left, with LF.

Count 4: Hop with LF, and kick (RF).

Count 5: Step with the RF, hop and kick (LF).

This is the continuous pattern, starting at count 1.

Refinement

Cue while dancing:

Left, behind, side-hop and kick

Right hop and kick

Left, behind, side-hop and kick,

Right hop and kick

Extensions

- Start slow, and increase speed as students start to master the dance moves. Because students move to the left so much, they will run out of room eventually.
- In pairs, have students perform the dance for partner feedback.
- Speed up the steps.
- Add music.
- Once students have mastered the steps, have them form a circle and continue to use your cues, as students will not be mirroring you now.

Student Choices/Differentiation

- Have students recite the cue while not dancing.
- Let students watch a video of someone performing the steps to the dance.
- Some music variations will speed up as the dance goes along.

What to Look For

- Students complete three steps or leaps in place so that they have the correct foot free to go to the other side (i.e., no taps in place).
- Students maintain control during the dance.
- Students remember the steps of the dance.
- Students transition cleanly from one part to the other.

Instructional Task: Perform Total Dance

■ PRACTICE TASK

Perform entire dance without music. Perform dance in a circle, starting with right-hand palm up, left-hand palm down, and join hands as a group.

Extension

When students have mastery of the steps without music, add music.

Guiding questions for students:

- Which foot kicks first?
- What are some qualities of the dance that make it a dance from Israel?

EMBEDDED OUTCOME: S3.M1.7 Discuss with students barriers related to maintaining a physically active lifestyle.

Guiding questions for students:

- In the first lesson, we identified dance as a way to improve overall health. What barriers prevent people from dancing to improve fitness?
- How can we overcome these barriers?

Student Choices/Differentiation

Students may practice steps to the side with or without music, if needed.

What to Look For

- Students are performing all steps correctly.
- Students are working with group members appropriately.

Formal and Informal Assessments

Exit slip: What are some barriers related to maintaining a physically active lifestyle? What are solutions for eliminating these barriers?

Closure

- Who can count 5-6-7-8 in Hebrew?
- Who can recite the cue?
- Who can say "Hello" and "Goodbye" in Hebrew?

Reflection

- Did I use the cues until mastery?
- Did I jump in with the verbal cues to help students keep going when they got off rhythm or footwork?
- Did I recognize when I needed to slow my verbal cues because some students were having difficulty in footwork or transitions?
- Should I talk with the home and career teacher about baking a traditional cookie while I teach a dance from that country?

Homework

We will travel to England in our next class. See whether you can name the countries that make up Great Britain. Keep updating your portfolios!

Resources

Internet keyword search: "hora music," "hora dance steps," "folk dance"

LESSON 5: GREENSLEEVES

Grade-Level Outcomes

Primary Outcome

Dance & rhythms: Demonstrates correct rhythm and pattern for a different dance form from among folk, social, creative, line and world dance. (S1.M1.7)

Embedded Outcome

Health: Identifies components of physical activity that provide opportunities for reducing stress and for social interaction. (S5.M2.6)

Lesson Objectives

The learner will:

- demonstrate walking to the beat of the music, changing directions using agility, coordination, and reaction time.
- demonstrate smooth transitions.
- use academic language (line of dance, right- and left-hand stars)

Equipment and Materials

- Music for greensleeves
- Music-playing device

Introduction

Today, we will continue our folk dance lessons from around the world. As I mentioned in our previous class, we are going to Great Britain. Who found out what countries are in Great Britain? Answer: England, Scotland, and Wales.

Show students where Great Britain is on a map and the countries within it. Also, mention popular foods or customs.

Instructional Task: Beginning Steps to Greensleeves

▓ PRACTICE TASK

Formation: Students are in groups of two and are paired with other groups of two—one group in the front, the other group behind them, all groups facing the line of dance (LOD). LOD is all dancers in a circle, moving counterclockwise.

Traditionally, dancers are male and female couples, with the male on the left, but leaders and followers can be substituted for male and female.

Part 1: All dancers are holding hands at shoulder height, walking in LOD for 16 counts.

Cue

Walk-2-3-4-5-6-7-8
Walk-2-3-4-5-6-7-8

Refinement

Make sure students are starting with the correct foot.

Extension

Start slow, and increase speed as students start to master the dance moves.

Student Choices/Differentiation

Let students watch a video of the dance.

What to Look For

- Students walk to the beat.
- Students cooperate with others in their groups.
- Students maintain control during the dance.
- Students remember the steps of the dance.

Instructional Task: Part 2 of Dance: Right-Hand Star and Left-Hand Star

■ PRACTICE TASK

Working within the group in front or behind: Front group turns to face the back group, and all dancers put their right hands together in the center and walk clockwise for eight counts.

Repeat with left hands together in the center and walk counterclockwise for eight counts.

As before, start with no music.

Extensions

- Speed up the steps.
- Once students master this part, combine parts 1 and 2, with no music.
- In their groups of four, have one couple perform parts 1 and 2 for feedback. Reverse groups for feedback.

Student Choices/Differentiation

Have students recite the cue, focusing on efficient transitions in wording.

What to Look For

- Students travel enough so that when they complete the left-hand star, they are back to where they started the dance, facing LOD (same group in front or back).
- Students stay on beat.
- Transitions are efficient from one part to the next.

Instructional Task: Part 3 of Dance: Arches

■ PRACTICE TASK

This part is executed in counts of four, repeated three more times for a total of 16 counts.

The front couple get close to each other, continue to hold hands, and duck as they step back for four counts.

Simultaneously, the back couple separate, while raising joined hands high, and walk forward for four counts. The couple walk around the front group, while the front group go under the back group's raised arms.

Repeat, with front group going under and back group going over front group.

Cue

Arches-2-3-4
Change-2-3-4
Change-2-3-4
Change-2-3-4

Dancers should end up in their original starting positions.

Repeat dance from the top.

Extensions
- Master part 3, and slowly add all parts together, focusing on transitions.
- Perform dance at a higher speed.

Student Choices/Differentiation

Have students recite the counting so they understand that there are no pauses in this dance.

What to Look For
- The front group always goes under and the back group goes over in the arches.
- Students are working cooperatively so they don't bump into each other.

Instructional Task: Perform Total Dance

■ PRACTICE TASK

Perform entire dance without music.

When students have mastered the steps without music, add music.

Guiding questions for students:
- How many counts do you walk forward?
- Do you start with a left- or right-hand star?

EMBEDDED OUTCOME: S5.M2.6. Many people enjoy dancing because it reduces stress and lets them express how they feel. Discuss with students how dance provides these opportunities.

Student Choices/Differentiation

Students may practice steps to the side with or without music, if needed.

What to Look For
- Students perform all steps correctly.
- Students work cooperatively to execute the dance.

Formal and Informal Assessments

Exit slip: Identify three ways in which dance can lower stress and improve social interaction in life.

Closure
- What is the definition of LOD?
- Who did you execute the left- and right-hand star with?
- Ask a question that was used in the introduction about countries within Great Britain.

Reflection
- Did I use the cues until mastery?
- How often did I have to jump in with verbal cues to help students keep going when they got off rhythm or footwork?
- Did I recognize when I needed to slow my verbal cues because some students were having difficulty in footwork or transitions?

Homework

Gather as many friends together during recess and show your dance!

Next class, we will be in Germany. See whether you can learn three popular dishes from Germany, and maybe make one of them with the help of your parents or guardians. Be prepared to share what you find or make at the beginning of the next class.

Resources

Internet keyword search: "greensleeves music," "greensleeves dance steps," "folk dance"

LESSON 6: CLAP DANCE

Grade-Level Outcomes

Primary Outcome

Dance & rhythms: Demonstrates correct rhythm and pattern for a different dance form from among folk, social, creative, line and world dance. (S1.M1.7)

Embedded Outcomes

Working with others: Accepts differences among classmates in physical development, maturation and varying skill levels by providing encouragement and positive feedback. (S4.M4.6)

Self-expression & enjoyment: Describes how moving competently in a physical activity setting creates enjoyment. (S5.M4.6)

Lesson Objectives

The learner will:

- demonstrate clapping, galloping, and changing directions using correct rhythm, agility, coordination, and reaction time.
- demonstrate smooth transitions.
- become familiar with dance terms (e.g., line of dance, reverse line of dance).

Equipment and Materials

- Music for clap dance
- Music-playing device

Introduction

What country are we visiting today? What are some of the popular dishes that you found? Did anyone make a dish from Germany?

Show students where Germany is on a map and the country's flag. You could also work with the history teacher to pair this dance with discussion about historical and current German events in the classroom.

Instructional Task:
Beginning Steps to German Clap Dance

■ PRACTICE TASK

Formation: A double circle, facing a partner. Traditionally, the male is on the inside, with the female facing her partner. However, as long as students know who is the inside and outside person, pair students as appropriate.

Part 1

Count 1: Slap your thighs.
Count 2: Clap your hands.
Count 3: Clap your partner's right hand (to right hand).
Count 4: Slap your thighs.
Count 5: Clap your hands.
Count 6: Clap your partner's left hand (to left hand).
Count 7: Slap your thighs.
Count 8: Clap your hands.
Count 9: Clap your partner's hand with your right hand.

Count 10: Clap your partner's hand with your left hand.

Count 11: Slap your thighs.

Count 12: Clap your hands.

Count 13: Slap both your partner's hands.

Cue

Slap, clap, right

Slap, clap, left

Slap, clap, right, left

Slap, clap, together

Repeat the sequence, but instead of clapping with a partner, shake the index finger of that hand at your partner.

Cue

Slap, clap, shake (right)

Slap, clap, shake (left)

Slap, clap, shake, shake (right, left)

Slap, clap, shake (both hands)

Extensions

- Have students learn the clapping sequence without contact with their partners until you see that they have it. Then, add the physical contact.
- Start slow, and increase speed as students start to master the dance moves.

Student Choices/Differentiation

Have the students recite the clapping sequence as they do the dance.

What to Look For

- Students are respecting their partners by safely clapping with each other.
- Students are maintaining control during the dance.
- Students are remembering the correct clapping sequence.

Instructional Task: Part 2 of Dance

■ PRACTICE TASK

Part 2: Gallops in line of dance (LOD) with partner in loose ballroom hold

With the inside person's left foot and the outside person's right foot, gallop forward for seven counts.

On count eight, stop and prepare to repeat reverse line of dance (RLOD) clockwise (back where you just came from).

Stop on count eight again, to prepare galloping forward for another seven counts.

Stop on count eight, and inside person moves forward to the next person and gallops forward for a total of eight counts.

Cue

Gallop-2 & 3 & 4 & 5 & 6 & 7, stop

Back & 2 & 3 & 4 & 5 & 6 & 7, stop

Forward 2 & 3 & 4 & 5 & 6 & 7, stop

New partner 2 & 3 & 4 & 5 & 6 & 7, stop

Students repeat the dance from the top with their new partners.

Refinement

Make sure that students are using the correct footwork during transitions.

Extensions

- Speed up the steps
- Once students have mastered this part, combine parts 1 and 2, with no music.

EMBEDDED OUTCOME: S4.M4.6. Not all students are the same. Discuss with students how accepting differences among classmates in physical development, maturation, and varying skill levels by providing encouragement is important. Students also should use positive feedback to encourage others, when needed.

Student Choices/Differentiation

As students dance, have them help each other make smooth transitions (forward, back, forward, forward) by counting out the cue.

What to Look For

- Students stay on beat.
- Transitions are efficient from one part to the next.
- Students demonstrate respect for the partner every time they change to a new partner.

Instructional Task: Perform Total Dance

■ PRACTICE TASK

Perform entire dance without music.

When students have mastered the steps without music, add music.

Guiding questions for students:

- When you clap or point with your partner, which side is first?
- What are common elements of this song that make you think about Germany?

EMBEDDED OUTCOMES: S5.M4.6 AND S5.M5.6. Discuss with students how moving competently and with self-expression in dance are important tools for creating enjoyment and improving overall health.

Guiding questions for students:

- What are some things you are good at?
- Do you feel you can perform the skills correctly?
- In dance, when you know the steps and can perform the folk dance like the dancers from that particular culture, how does that make you feel? Do you feel enjoyment?
- Do you think people who dance (especially using folk dances) express themselves? How?
- How are self-expression and physical activity related?

Student Choices/Differentiation

Students may practice steps to the side with or without music, if needed.

What to Look For

- Students perform all steps correctly.
- Students work cooperatively with all partners to execute the dance.

Formal and Informal Assessments

Exit slip: With which folk dance that we've learned so far do you feel the most self-expression? Why? Which dance is the most fun for you? If your answer for both is the same dance, why do you think they are similar?

Closure

- What is the definition of RLOD?
- Once you join a new partner, for how many counts do you gallop forward?
- Who can point to Germany on the map?

Reflection

- Did I use the cues until mastery?
- How often did I have to jump in with verbal cues to help students keep going when they got off rhythm or footwork?
- Did I recognize when I needed to slow my verbal cues because some students were having difficulty in footwork or transitions?

Homework

The next country on our world tour is Norway. Be prepared to share something with the class that you found out about Norway on the Internet.

Keep updating your portfolios!

Discuss with parents or friends the importance of self-expression and enjoyment in improving overall health.

Get as many friends together during recess and show your dance!

Resources

Internet keyword search: "German clap dance music," "clap dance steps," "folk dance"

LESSON 7: NORWEGIAN MOUNTAIN MARCH

Grade-Level Outcomes

Primary Outcome

Dance & rhythms: Demonstrates correct rhythm and pattern for a different dance form from among folk, social, creative, line and world dance. (S1.M1.7)

Embedded Outcome

Challenge: Recognizes individual challenges and copes in a positive way, such as extending effort, asking for help or feedback and/or modifying the tasks. (S5.M3.6)

Lesson Objectives

The learner will:

- demonstrate correct rhythm and sequence.
- execute the correct number of sets as needed for each part of the dance.
- demonstrate patience while they learn the pattern of the dance.
- learn where the waltz originated.

Equipment and Materials

- Music for Norwegian mountain march
- Music-playing device
- Pieces of cloth or pinnies

Introduction

Does anyone know which body of water Norway is on? (Norwegian Sea) Who can point to it on the map? What did you find out about Norway in your research? This dance depicts a mountain guide leading two climbers up a mountain. As they travel up the mountain, the climbers' ropes get tangled and the guide goes back to help untangle them. They then can resume climbing up the mountain. The rhythm for this dance is the waltz. The waltz came from folk dances from Germany and Austria in the 18th century and is still very popular today.

Instructional Task:
Beginning Steps to the Norwegian Mountain March

■ PRACTICE TASK

Formation: Groups of three students forming a triangle (mountain guide in the front, two climbers behind making the other two corners of the triangle. Pieces of cloth or pinnies are used to connect the group together.

Each climber has a pinnie. The guide is the front point. In her right hand is a pinnie that connects her to climber 3 (with the climber's right hand).

In the guide's left hand is a pinnie that is held by climber 2. The two climbers in the back are connected by holding a pinnie in their inside hands.

    1 = guide

    2 = climber

    3 = climber

Part 1

Using the waltz rhythm and footwork, the group walks forward for a total of eight sets.

Down, up, up (LF, RF, LF)

Down, up, up (RF, LF, RF)

Down, up, up (LF, RF, LF)

Down, up, up (RF, LF, RF)

Down, up, up (LF, RF, LF)

Down, up, up (RF, LF, RF)

Down, up, up (LF, RF, LF)

Down, up, up (RF, LF, RF)

The following cue is very helpful for clarification in part 2:

Cue

1 up up

2 up up

3 up up

4 up up

5 up up

6 up up

7 up up

8 up up

Refinement

Make sure that students' waltz steps are smooth.

Student Choices/Differentiation

- This is a circle dance, but teach it with all students facing the front for clarification. Once there is mastery, move it to a circle with all groups facing LOD and the guide being the front point.
- Recite a few sets and see whether students can tell you how many you recited. For example:

  Down, up, up

  Down, up, up

  Down, up, up

  Down, up, up = 4 sets

- As they move forward, every time the guide steps on the "down" part, she looks back to check the safety of the climber, rotating looks back left and right.

What to Look For

- Students are maintaining their triangle form.
- Students are executing the correct down, up, up rhythm and footwork.
- Students are keeping the correct down, up, up sequence going uninterrupted. It doesn't matter if they start with the wrong foot.
- To help with part 2, have students move around in their own space using the footwork before gathering in their triangle. Have them go forward, go backward, and turn around.

Instructional Task: Part 2 of Dance

■ PRACTICE TASK

Part 2

All dancers continue the footwork without interruption. Each dancer has two sets to execute his or her solo turn.

The pattern is:

1. Climbers in the back raise their inside hands so that the guide can back up and go under their material.
2. The climber on the left turns toward his or her right arm, but passes under the guide's right arm and the other climber's left arm.
3. Climber 3 turns to the left, turning left under the left arm (and not passing anyone, and pretty much on his or her own spot).
4. The guide, now having both arms crossed, turns toward the arm that is on top. This opens up the group, but all dancers will need to adjust to face the LOD quickly to begin the dance again from the top.

Student Choices/Differentiation

- The goal for the group is to not get disconnected from its material, and not to get so tangled up that the dancers can't get out of the mess.
- Establish the part 2 pattern before adding footwork and solo sets.
- Once the pattern is established, each number (as indicated to the left under practice task) has two sets to execute his or her solo turn. When dancers aren't moving, they are continuing with waltz footwork in place.

What to Look For

- Students are staying on beat.
- Students are executing the footwork while on the spot when it isn't their turn to turn.

Instructional Task: Perform Total Dance

■ PRACTICE TASK

Perform entire dance without music.

When students have mastered the steps without music, add music.

Guiding questions for students:

- How many sets does each dancer have to execute during his or her turn?
- Why do you think it is called the Norwegian mountain march?

EMBEDDED OUTCOME: S5.M3.6. Help students with coping strategies such as extending effort, asking for help or feedback, or modifying the task.

The dance is related to mountain climbing. Whether we are climbing a mountain or studying for a difficult exam, life gives us many challenges.

What to Look For

- All dancers shift to face the LOD after the guide has untangled the group.
- Students work cooperatively with all partners to execute the dance.

Formal and Informal Assessments

Exit slip: Briefly describe a time when you coped in a positive way during a difficult challenge in physical activity.

Closure

- Who can recite two sets of the waltz?
- We know this dance is about mountain climbing, but what body of water is Norway located next to?
- In which countries did the waltz originate?

Reflection

- Did I use the cues until mastery?
- How often did I have to jump in with verbal cues to help students keep going when they got off rhythm or footwork?
- Are students finding successful ways to cope with challenges?
- Did I recognize when I needed to slow my verbal cues because some students were having difficulty in footwork or transitions?

Homework

The final stop next class will be back home in the United States. Try to find out when folk dancing started in the United States.

Talk to your grandparents to find out what countries they or their relatives came from, and share that with us next class.

Resources

Internet keyword search: "Norwegian mountain march music," "folk dance"

LESSON 8: PATTY CAKE POLKA

Grade-Level Outcomes

Primary Outcome

Dance & rhythms: Demonstrates correct rhythm and pattern for a different dance form from among folk, social, creative, line and world dance. (S1.M1.7)

Embedded Outcome

Engages in physical activity: Participates in a self-selected lifetime sport, dance, aquatic or outdoor activity outside of the school day. (S3.M5.8)

Lesson Objectives

The learner will:

- demonstrate rhythm identification using agility, coordination, and reaction time.
- work cooperatively with a variety of partners.
- perform the patty cake polka.

Equipment and Materials

- Music for patty cake polka
- Music-playing device

Introduction

Today, we end our world tour by coming back home to the United States. Folk dancing in the United States has a different history than in European countries. What did you find out? Today's dance goes back to the 19th century. This dance is a mixer, and you change partners throughout the dance. Many people enjoy polka dancing and continue to get physical activity each week by dancing. Let's learn the dance so that you can dance or teach the dance to your family members at the next family gathering.

Put a pin in the map or highlight it to show all the different countries from which the class learned dances.

Instructional Task: Beginning Steps to Patty Cake Polka

■ PRACTICE TASK

Formation: A double circle, males or leaders traditionally on the inside, females or followers outside, facing their partners. Partners are holding hands.

Part 1

Inside dancers execute part 1 with the left foot first, outside dancers with the right foot.

Inside dancers hop on the right foot, left heel comes forward, hop, left foot taps toes behind. Repeat again.

Inside dancers slide four times to their left.

Cue

Heel, toe, heel, toe, slide-2-3-4.

Heel, toe, heel, toe, slide-2-3-4.

Outside dancers do the same, except they start with their RF heel and toe, and slide to their right.

Repeat sequence; this time, inside dancers start with their right foot, and slide to their right.

Outside dancers start with their left foot and slide to their left.

Perform the dance sequence without music until students master the footwork.

Extensions

- Start slow, and increase speed as students start to master the dance moves.
- Add music for part 1 once students master the footwork.

Student Choices/Differentiation

- Have students recite the cue (not while dancing): heel and toe, heel and toe, slide-2-3-4.
- Master footwork individually before holding hands with a partner.

What to Look For

- Students maintain control during the dance.
- Students remember the steps of the dance.

Instructional Task: Part 2 of Dance

■ PRACTICE TASK

Part 2

Patty cake polka, in counts of three (1-2-3, 1-2-3, 1-2-3)

Partners slap right hands three times.

Partners slap left hands three times.

Partners slap both hands together three times.

Dancers slap their own thighs three times.

Cue (slow motion):

Right, right, right

Left, left, left

Together, together, together

Down, down, down

While dancing:

Right-2-3

Left-2-3

Together-2-3

Down-2-3

As before, start slow with no music.

Extensions

- Speed up the part to meet the speed of the music.
- Once students master this part, combine parts 1 and 2, with no music. Start slow and increase speed.
- In pairs, using a teacher-created checklist, have students perform each part for another couple for feedback.

Student Choices/Differentiation

Have students recite the cue (not while dancing):

Cue

Right, right, right

Left, left, left

Together, together, together

Down, down, down

What to Look For

- Students stay on beat.
- Students work with their partners and don't slap hands carelessly.
- Students don't speed up when they slap their thighs.

Instructional Task: Part 3 of Dance

■ PRACTICE TASK

Part 3

Skipping and changing partners for a total of eight counts

After executing the differentiation exercise, add the entire eight counts, with no skipping, just trying to get the sequence down.

Dancers make a right-elbow turn with their partners for four counts, ending where they started, inside or outside. Then, they walk to their new partners for four counts and join hands as if they were starting the dance from the top.

Once students master the steps, add the eight counts of skipping:

Four skips in a right-elbow turn with their partners

Four skips toward the new partners

Start dance from the top.

Cue

Skip & 2 & 3 & 4

New partner 6 & 7 & 8

Repeat dance from the top.

Extensions

- Master part 3, and slowly add all parts together, focusing on transitions.
- Perform dance at higher speed with your cues being the music.

Student Choices/Differentiation

- Have students face their partners, not hold hands.
- Have them point to the opposite person on their left. (Inside person points to an outside person; outside person points to the inside person.) Students pointing at each other are now partners. Have students walk toward their new partners, making sure that they're looking at each other. (The inside person is always an inside person. The outside person is always an outside person.)
- Repeat this sequence until you see a smooth transition from partner to partner.

What to Look For

- Students move to their left, toward their new partners.
- *Both* partners move or skip toward each other (one doesn't just move toward the other).

Instructional Task: Perform Total Dance

■ PRACTICE TASK

When students have mastered the steps without music, add music.

Guiding questions for students:

- How many counts do I skip with my partner while our right elbows are linked?
- If I am in inside person, do I stay an inside person during the entire dance?

Student Choices/Differentiation

Students may practice steps to the side with or without music.

What to Look For

- Students perform all steps correctly.
- Students maintain control in the slapping and clapping part and while turning their partners during the skips.
- Students are accepting of all new partners.

Instructional Task: End of Module Dance Assessment

■ **PRACTICE TASK**

Students may choose any dance from the Folk Dance Module. Students participate with classmates in the dance.

Students are evaluated using the rubric from Lesson 1, focusing on correct rhythm, footwork, pattern, and presentation of dance.

Student Choices/Differentiation

- Students choose dance to perform.
- If dance includes partners, students have a choice of which student to work with.

What to Look For

Students are able to perform steps correctly and have proper rhythm and presentation of the dance.

Formal and Informal Assessments

- Teacher-created rubric with the following criteria:
    - Rhythm
    - Footwork
    - Pattern
    - Presentation of dance
- Students' folk dance portfolios
- Peer checklist on dance steps
- Homework assignment

Closure

- If you are an outside person, with which foot do you start your heel and toe sequence?
- Do you move to your left or to your right to find your new partner?
- Please turn in your folk dance portfolios. How did you like the project? Did you learn anything from the experience? What was your favorite folk dance to research?

Reflection

- Did I use the cues until students mastered the skills?
- How often did I have to jump in with verbal cues to help students keep going when they got off rhythm or footwork?
- Did I recognize when I needed to slow my verbal cues because some students were having difficulty in footwork or transitions?

Homework

Write your reflections about all the countries that we visited, your favorite dances, and a favorite and unique thing that you learned about each country. Share these reflections with your history teacher.

EMBEDDED OUTCOME: S3.M5.8. Create a list of local and state dance opportunities in which students can participate. Encourage students to participate in at least one and to enjoy dancing with friends and family at least once a week.

Preview the next module on the school's physical education website.

Resources

Internet keyword search: "patty cake polka music," "patty cake polka dance steps," "folk dance"

CHAPTER 5

Applying Students' Skills and Knowledge to Invasion Games

This chapter focuses on invasion games, which is an important content area for middle school. Students in the middle grades have the cognitive ability to really understand and apply game strategies and tactics (SHAPE America, 2014). Fortunately, you have a multitude of options when choosing activities that will help students attain the Grade-Level Outcomes associated with middle school, including field hockey, flag football, soccer, basketball, ice hockey, lacrosse, ultimate, floor hockey, team handball, water polo, and even quidditch. Those sports share many commonalities in passing and receiving, offensive and defensive tactics, and creating and reducing space, which can be readily transferred from one sport to another.

This chapter contains modules for team handball, ultimate, and soccer. You can teach all three modules in a variety of environments without specialized equipment or facilities. The progressions that are offered can be used in teaching any invasion game. The Team Handball Module uses multiple sport skills from invasion sports (e.g., dribbling, passing, and shooting). It also has the advantage of using common skills, such as catching and throwing, so that students are able to focus on game tactics. The Ultimate Module involves many of the same tactics but uses a unique object to throw: a disc. The Soccer Module uses similar tactics and strategies but requires more specialized skills with the feet, such as dribbling and passing in a controlled manner while applying tactics in modified games. When teaching multiple modules of invasion games, it's important to help students make connections between similar skills and tactics within the modules. That should enhance student learning and help students progress toward becoming physically literate in invasion games.

You can increase the likelihood of skill transfer by incorporating transfer in actual practice tasks (Chepko & Doan, 2015). Using a grid formation, you can design lessons that allow students to practice a particular concept using a variety of equipment. The "give and go" is an example. Using discs, soccer balls, and team handballs, students can practice the give-and-go concept with each piece of equipment. After the practice session, discuss with students the similarities of the tactics in each invasion sport.

You also can enhance students' tactical success in modified or small-sided game play by creating advantage situations for the offense or defense. For example, placing students in a 2 v 1 situation will allow them to increase their success in the give and go substantially. After students experience some success, take away the advantage by having students work 2 v 2, which changes the practice task from a controlled to a less-controlled, more game-like environment. You also can manipulate small-sided games by adding a neutral or post player. For example, if you are teaching transitions from offense to defense or defense to offense, you can set up a 3 v 3 game, then create an advantage situation for the offense (4 v 3) by adding a neutral player who always plays offense, whichever side has the ball. That forces students on both teams to adapt quickly from advantage situations to disadvantage situations, and vice versa.

Another teaching tip: Place restrictions on defenders while players on offense are learning a new skill or concept, to add control to the practice task. You can tell defenders to be passive, semi-active, or active, for example. Passive defenders are allowed to move but may not intercept or steal the ball from the offense. This is most helpful when you want the offense to be aware of the defense but not experience a lot of 1 v 1 pressure, as when an offensive player is trying out a new move or a dodge. Semi-active defenders are allowed to move and intercept the ball but are not allowed to take it away from an offensive player's hands or feet. This is a good choice when the offense isn't experiencing a lot of success with a new tactic; it keeps the practice task game-like while fostering success for the offense. Once the offense is ready for full defensive pressure, turn your defenders loose by making them fully active to even the playing field and give the offense a game-situation test.

With many invasion sports, goalkeeping is an important and specialized skill. In the Soccer and Team Handball Modules, you will find practice progressions that teach the beginning skills of goalkeeping. With all goalkeeping tasks, we recommend giving students the option of playing keeper or not. All students should learn the physical and mental aspects of tending goal, but they should have the choice of either practicing goalkeeping or using the time to improve other skills.

For easy reference, each module begins with a block plan chart of the Grade-Level Outcomes that are addressed within each lesson. Each module incorporates multiple National Standards, although most of the outcomes addressed reside under Standard 1. For team handball, throwing (Outcome S1.M2) and catching (Outcome S1.M3) are the primary physical skills addressed, and reducing open space (Outcomes S2.M4 and S2.M5) is the tactical skill addressed. In the Ultimate Module, offensive skills (Outcomes S1.M6 and S1.M7) and creating open space on offense (Outcome S2.M3) are the primary skills addressed. The Soccer Module focuses on dribbling (Outcome S1.M.9), passing (Outcome S1.M4), and tactics related to open space (Outcomes S2.M2 and S2.M4). With all three modules, the main embedded Outcomes come from Standards 4 and 5: provides and receives feedback appropriately (Outcome S4.M3); identifies the rules and etiquette for the game (Outcome S4.M6); and demonstrates important social interaction skills (Outcome S5.M6). These modules are great references for improving skill transfer, as well as for teaching the skills of invasion games.

TEAM HANDBALL MODULE

Lessons in this module were contributed by Brad Rettig, a middle school physical education teacher in Lincoln, NE, Public Schools.

Grade-Level Outcomes Addressed, by Lesson	Lessons							
	1	2	3	4	5	6	7	8
Standard 1. The physically literate individual demonstrates competency in a variety of motor skills and movement patterns.								
Passes and receives with hands in combination with locomotor patterns of running and change of direction & speed with competency in invasion games such as basketball, flag football, speedball or team handball. (S1.M4.6)	P					P		
Throws a lead pass to a moving partner off a dribble or pass. (S1.M5.8)		P						
Performs pivots, fakes and jab steps designed to create open space during practice tasks. (S1.M6.6)			P					
Performs the following offensive skills without defensive pressure: pivot, give & go, and fakes. (S1.M7.6)			P					
Dribbles with dominant and non-dominant hands using a change of speed and direction in a variety of practice tasks. (S1.M8.7)		P						
Maintains defensive-ready position, with weight on balls of feet, arms extended and eyes on midsection of the offensive player. (S1.M11.6)	P							
Slides in all directions while on defense without crossing feet. (S1.M11.7)	P							
Standard 2. The physically literate individual applies knowledge of concepts, principles, strategies and tactics related to movement and performance.								
Creates open space by using locomotor movements (e.g., walking, running, jumping & landing) in combination with movement (e.g., varying pathways; change of speed, direction or pace). (S2.M1.6)				P				
Creates open space by staying spread on offense, and cutting and passing quickly. (S2.M3.7)			P			P		P
Reduces open space on defense by staying close to the opponent as he/she nears the goal. (S2.M4.7)								P
Reduces open space by not allowing the catch (denial) or anticipating the speed of the object and person for the purpose of interception or deflection. (S2.M5.7)					P			
Transitions from offense to defense or defense to offense by recovering quickly. (S2.M6.6)						P		P
Selects offensive shot based on opponent's location (hit where opponent is not). (S2.M8.7)							P	
Standard 3. The physically literate individual demonstrates the knowledge and skills to achieve and maintain a health-enhancing level of physical activity and fitness.								
Standard 4. The physically literate individual exhibits responsible personal and social behavior that respects self and others.								
Exhibits responsible social behaviors by cooperating with classmates, demonstrating inclusive behaviors and supporting classmates. (S4.M1.7)						E		
Provides corrective feedback to a peer, using teacher-generated guidelines, and incorporating appropriate tone and other communication skills. (S4.M3.7)	E							
Accepts differences among classmates in physical development, maturation and varying skill levels by providing encouragement and positive feedback. (S4.M4.6)						E		
Cooperates with a small group of classmates during adventure activities, game play or team-building activities. (S4.M5.6)			E	E				
Identifies the rules and etiquette for physical activities/games and dance activities. (S4.M6.6)					P			
Demonstrates knowledge of rules and etiquette by self-officiating modified physical activities and games or following parameters to create or modify a dance. (S4.M6.7)							P	P
Standard 5. The physically literate individual recognizes the value of physical activity for health, enjoyment, challenge, self-expression and/or social interaction.								
Generates positive strategies such as offering suggestions or assistance, leading or following others and providing possible solutions when faced with a group challenge. (S5.M3.7)							E	
Demonstrates the importance of social interaction by helping and encouraging others, avoiding trash talk and providing support to classmates. (S5.M6.7)		E						E

P = Primary; E = Embedded

LESSON 1: PASSING, CATCHING, AND REDUCING SPACE

Grade-Level Outcomes

Primary Outcomes

Passing & receiving: Passes and receives with hands in combination with locomotor patterns of running and change of direction & speed with competency in invasion games such as basketball, flag football, speedball or team handball. (S1.M4.6)

Defensive skills: Slides in all directions while on defense without crossing feet. (S1.M11.7)

Defensive skills: Maintains defensive-ready position, with weight on balls of feet, arms extended and eyes on midsection of the offensive player. (S1.M11.6)

Embedded Outcome

Accepting feedback: Provides corrective feedback to a peer, using teacher-generated guidelines, and incorporating appropriate tone and other communication skills. (S4.M3.7)

Lesson Objectives

The learner will:

- demonstrate the correct throwing techniques or mature pattern.
- demonstrate the correct catching techniques or mature pattern.
- apply defensive skills such as ready position and sliding.

Equipment and Materials

- 1 ball for every group, 5 or 6 in a group
- 4 poly spots or cones per group

Introduction

Today, we will begin our Team Handball Module. During this module, we will learn the rules and a variety of skills and strategies to help us succeed and have fun. Some of the skills, such as throwing, catching, and guarding, you might have learned while playing other sports such as basketball, ultimate, or football. You also might notice that some rules are the same as those of other games you might have played or learned. During today's lesson, we will see where your passing and receiving skill level is and check your basic understanding of the guarding position.

Show students a clip of what team handball is and how it's played.

Instructional Task:
Pre-assessment: Passing and Catching

■ PRACTICE TASK

Pre-assessment: Use the cues of a mature pattern for passing and catching. Use these as a checklist for the task and extensions.

In grids, students pass the ball back and forth in groups of three or four. Use this as a pre-assessment for throwing and catching.

Extensions

- Passer is moving.
- Receiver is moving.
- Both are moving.

- Vary the type of pass used.
- Vary the level of the receiver's target.
- Add a passive or semi-active defender.

Guiding questions for students:

- When have you thrown using this same motion?
- How is this throwing motion different from other throwing motions you have learned?
- In what activities have you used the same hand positions to catch the ball?

EMBEDDED OUTCOME: S4.M3.7 This is a great opportunity for students to provide feedback to one another using a checklist provided by the teacher. Emphasize how to provide appropriate feedback.

Student Choices/Differentiation

- Students start out 15 feet (4.6 m) apart and move back to 20 feet (6.1 m) or farther if they have the skill and space allows.
- Students who are not yet proficient stay with this instructional task with guided practice and feedback with regard to the cues.

What to Look For

Students use mature patterns for passing and catching.

Instructional Task: Passing to a Moving Target

■ PRACTICE TASK

Groups of 2 in grids of 10 × 10 yards or meters

One student is on one poly spot and will throw to another student who is moving to a different poly spot. The passer stays stationary and the receiver keeps receiving, throwing back to the passer and moving to a different poly spot. After 30 seconds, they switch roles.

Extensions

- Passer is also moving.
- Vary the types of passes used.
- Vary the height of the receiver's target.

Guiding questions for students:

- Why is it important to move around?
- When might one move be better than another for getting open?
- Where and when should you throw the ball to the person who is moving?

Student Choices/Differentiation

- Students choose the speed they use to make it easier to throw and catch.
- For groups who need more practice throwing and catching, have the person receiving run to a designated spot to get open.
- Stay with simple targets and chest passes.

What to Look For

- Students use mature patterns for throwing and catching.
- Students complete and catch the passes.
- Where is the passer throwing the ball in relation to the person catching it?
- Are students moving quickly or slowly?

Instructional Task:
Guarding a Person Using Defensive-Ready Position

■ PRACTICE TASK

Students spread out across the gym in defensive-ready position and practice sliding in all directions without crossing their feet.

Students then move in relation to you as if they are guarding you. If you move to your right, students slide to their left in defensive-ready position as if guarding you. If you move to your left, students slide to their right in defensive-ready position.

Extension

Move forward, backward, and diagonally, as students guard you. Then, increase the speed of your movements.

Refinement

Make sure that students are sliding in an athletic positon.

Student Choices/Differentiation

Students can stay on task until successful.

What to Look For

- Students are sliding, not crossing, their feet.
- Students stay on the balls of their feet.
- Students keep their arms extended.
- Students keep their eyes on your hips.

Instructional Task: Using the Defensive-Ready Position to Guard a Person Dribbling

■ PRACTICE TASK

In partners, have one student dribble across the gym at a moderate speed, changing hands and varying direction while the partner uses defensive-ready position and sliding to guard. Switch roles.

Extensions

- Repeat but allow students to dribble at a faster speed.
- Repeat, allowing defenders to use hands to deflect the ball.
- In small grids, one partner works on guarding person dribbling (1 v 1) for 20 seconds. Defender attempts to deflect ball. Switch roles.
- Play keep-away in a grid with 3 v 3, with one team remaining on defense for 30 seconds. Score a point each time the defense gets the ball. Switch roles.

Refinement

Make sure that defenders keep their eyes on the offensive player's hips and the ball.

Student Choices/Differentiation

- Modify speed if students have difficulty.
- If dribblers succeed, have them dribble with non-preferred hands or alternating hands.
- If defense is not successful in 3 v 3, remove one offensive player.

What to Look For

- Students are sliding, not crossing, their feet.
- Students stay on the balls of their feet.
- Students keep their arms extended.
- Students keep their eyes on your hips.

Formal and Informal Assessments

Pre-assessment: checklist for throwing and catching skills

Closure

- What are the cues for passing?
- What are the cues for catching?
- When on offense, why is it important to move around?
- Next class, we will add a different way to move the ball down the court.

Reflection

- How many students were able to pass with correct form?
- How many students were catching with correct form, and did this transfer over when running?
- Could the students throw accurately with correct form?
- Were they able to throw to a moving receiver?
- What happened when the person catching was guarded?
- Do we need to start the next class with catching on the move or adding a defender and catching on the move?

Homework

For students who are still working on catching or throwing to a moving target, provide them the cues and have them practice these during recess or at home before the next class.

Resources

USA Team Handball: www.teamusa.org

Internet keyword search: "team handball," "throwing and catching," "reducing open space"

LESSON 2: DRIBBLING AND OPEN SPACE

Grade-Level Outcomes

Primary Outcomes

Passing & receiving: Throws a lead pass to a moving partner off a dribble or pass. (S1.M5.8)

Dribbling/ball control: Dribbles with dominant and non-dominant hands using a change of speed and direction in a variety of practice tasks. (S1.M8.7)

Creating space using width & length: Creates open space by staying spread on offense, and cutting and passing quickly. (S2.M3.7)

Embedded Outcome

Social interaction: Demonstrates the importance of social interaction by helping and encouraging others, avoiding trash talk and providing support to classmates. (S5.M6.7)

Lesson Objectives

The learner will:

- practice dribbling with both the dominant and non-dominant hand during a variety of practice tasks.
- practice the lead pass off the dribble using correct form.
- demonstrate staying spread on offense.

Equipment and Materials

- Enough balls for every student
- 4 poly spots or cones per group

Introduction

Last class, we worked on a variety of skills, from passing and catching to closing space on defense. Today, we will build on the passing and catching skills by adding dribbling and offensive movements.

Prior-knowledge questions:

- Why is it important to move around when your team has the ball?
- How is standing or running beside a teammate helpful to the defense?
- How can dribbling help the offense?

Instructional Task: Dribbling

■ PRACTICE TASK

Each student practices dribbling with preferred hand in open space, looking up and avoiding others for 30 seconds.

- While running, students dribble with preferred hands.
- While running, students dribble with non-preferred hands.

Extensions

- Repeat, alternating hands.
- In groups of three with one ball, two students stand 5 yards or meters apart and are passive defenders (stationary and may not steal the ball). The remaining student dribbles around each passive defender, placing his body between the defender and the ball. Dribble for 30 seconds, then change roles.

- In a grid of 5 × 5 yards or meters with a partner, one person dribbles while the other acts as a semi-active defender (may move and deflect ball, but may not steal it). Dribble for 30 seconds, trying to maintain possession. Switch roles.

Refinement

Make sure that students look up when they dribble, not at the ball.

Student Choices/Differentiation

- Allow choice of ball size.
- Students choose speed of dribbling.
- If not successful, do not move on in progression.

What to Look For

- Are students using their fingers and not the palm of the hand to slap the ball?
- Is the ball coming up about waist high off the bounce?
- Are they in control of the ball or is the ball controlling the speed and direction they are going?
- Can they jog or run while dribbling or do they have to walk?

Instructional Task: Passing From a Dribble

▧ PRACTICE TASK

Partners are in a grid of 5 × 5 yards or meters. One student dribbles to a poly spot and passes to a stationary receiver at another poly spot. The receiver then dribbles to a poly spot and passes to her stationary partner. Continue for 30 seconds. Receiver must show target.

Extensions

- Repeat with both players moving from poly spot to poly spot. Receiver must show target.
- Repeat specifying a lead pass to the poly spot. Receiver must show target.
- Repeat with different types of passes (chest, bounce, and overhand throw). Receiver must show target.
- Repeat with a third player added to the grid who defends the passer. Passer should select a type of pass that will increase success. After 30 seconds, switch roles.
- Repeat with defender on receiver. Passer must throw lead pass to receiver.
- Repeat with a fourth player added to the grid to create 2 v 2. Defenders are semi-active.

Refinement

Make sure students are making accurate passes (even if they need to slow down to do so).

Student Choices/Differentiation

- Stay on task until successful. Don't add defenders until dribblers are ready.
- Students practice at half speed until they master the skill.

What to Look For

- Students can run and pass off the dribble.
- Students don't have to slow down or stop to control the ball before passing.
- Passes are accurate.
- Students select high-percentage passes.

Instructional Task:
Creating Open Space by Staying Spread

■ PRACTICE TASK

In grids, use poly spots or lines to establish three lanes. With 3 v 2, play keep-away for 30 seconds. Offensive players must stay in their lanes. Dribbling is not allowed. Defensive players may move anywhere in the grid but are semi-active.

Count the number of passes in which players receive the ball in their lanes.

Extensions

- Allow three dribbles.
- Allow both defenders to be fully active.
- Add a third defender.

EMBEDDED OUTCOME: S5.M6.7. Discuss constructive ways of supporting one another, providing examples of appropriate and inappropriate behavior. Be sure to reinforce these behaviors when students display them.

Student Choices/Differentiation

- Students choose speed of movement.
- Stay on progression until successful.

What to Look For

- Receivers move quickly to create open space.
- Receivers stay in their lanes.
- Students with the ball make a decision quickly and pass to a teammate.

Formal and Informal Assessments

- Informal assessment
- Exit slip: List two critical features each for dribbling and creating open space.

Closure

- How does dribbling help create space?
- Why should you move around when your team has the ball?
- When and why is it important to get rid of the ball quickly?

Reflection

- How many students cannot dribble while running?
- How many students are struggling to dribble with their non-preferred hand?
- Are students able to pass off the dribble, and are their passes accurate?
- Are students moving quickly and creating open space?

Homework

Review the school's physical education website for critical elements of passing, catching, offensive and defensive strategies, and dribbling.

Practice dribbling and passing to a wall or a friend.

Resources

Griffin, L., & Butler, J. (2004). *Teaching games for understanding: Theory, research and practice.* Champaign, IL: Human Kinetics.

Internet keyword search: "team handball strategies," "dribbling"

LESSON 3: CREATING SPACE

Grade-Level Outcomes

Primary Outcomes

Creating space with movement: Creates open space by using locomotor movements (e.g., walking, running, jumping & landing) in combination with movement (e.g., varying pathways; change of speed, direction or pace). (S2.M1.6)

Offensive skills: Performs pivots, fakes and jab steps designed to create open space during practice tasks. (S1.M6.6)

Offensive skills: Performs the following offensive skills without defensive pressure: pivot, give & go, and fakes. (S1.M7.6)

Embedded Outcome

Working with others: Cooperates with a small group of classmates during adventure activities, game play or team-building activities. (S4.M5.6)

Lesson Objectives

The learner will:

- demonstrate pivots, jab steps, and fakes to create space to throw when working with a partner.
- demonstrate and practice movement patterns such as slant, stop and go, curl or come back, or back-and-forth movements to get open.

Equipment and Materials

- Enough balls for each group of 4 to have 2
- Pre-determined markers for practice tasks
- Board or device to display rules

Introduction

Last class we practiced getting open by staying wide. Today, we will practice other ways of creating open space when you have a defender covering you, both with and without the ball.

Instructional Task:
Moving to Create Open Space Without the Ball

▦ PRACTICE TASK

Review different pathways for getting open (curl, slant, V, etc.). Set up grids with three students. One is a post passer at one corner; one is a receiver; and one is a semi-active defender (allows catch). Receiver shows a target for catch and passes back to post. Play for 30 seconds, then switch roles.

Direct students to use, among others:

- Curl
- Slant
- Give and go

Extensions

- Repeat with focus on stop or slow and go (change of speed) in combination with change in direction.
- Repeat with active defender on receiver.
- Repeat with post becoming active offensive player (2 v 1). Students must attempt to use give and go with semi-active defender. No dribbling permitted. Score a point for each successful give and go.
- Add second defender to create 2 v 2. No dribbling permitted. Score a point for each successful give and go.

Refinements

- Make sure students change speed.
- Receivers should try to make themselves big targets.
- Focus on making good passes.

Student Choices/Differentiation

- Receivers choose speed of movement.
- Allow students to stay on task until successful (more repetitions).

What to Look For

- Students use change of speed and direction effectively.
- Receivers make good targets.

Instructional Task: Creating Open Space With the Ball

■ PRACTICE TASK

Partners share one ball.

Player with ball practices jab step with partner as semi-active defender.

Switch after five attempts.

Extensions

- Repeat with pivots.
- Repeat with head or ball fake.
- Add third player who is a stationary receiver. Player with the ball must jab or pivot to create space with defender and then throw ball to stationary post.
- Repeat with ball handler dribbling three times with semi-active defender. On third dribble, ball handler jabs or pivots and then throws to post.
- Peer assessment: Have students record their peers performing any of the extension tasks.

Refinement

Make sure jab, pivot, or fake is quick and purposeful.

Guiding questions for students:

- What happens to the defender when you jab or fake?
- How does pivoting protect the ball?

Student Choices/Differentiation

- Receivers choose speed of movement and target for catch.
- Students can practice pivoting and taking jab step without the ball to simplify the task.
- Allow students to stay on task until successful (more repetitions).

What to Look For

- Jabs, pivots, and fakes are convincing.
- Players protect the ball during the dribble and the throw.

Instructional Task: Modified Game to Create Open Space

■ PRACTICE TASK

In grids, set up a player advantage situation (3 v 2 or 4 v 3). Play keep-away for 45 seconds with semi-active defenders. No dribbling allowed. Score a point for each completed give and go. Change roles.

Extra players keep score until they rotate in.

Extensions
- Repeat, permitting two dribbles.
- Repeat with active defenders.

Refinement
Make sure that students use quick movements on offense and defense.

Guiding questions for students:
- How does permitting the dribble affect play?
- What was the most difficult part of getting open?

EMBEDDED OUTCOME: S4.M5.6. Review importance of cooperating through communicating on offense. Provide keywords for students to use.

Student Choices/Differentiation
- Remove one defender until players are more successful.
- Have defensive player play at 50, 75, or 100 percent.

What to Look For
- Players can execute the give and go in a modified game.
- When dribbling is permitted, passing frequency does not diminish.
- Players communicate on offense.

Formal and Informal Assessments
- Informal assessment
- Peer assessment: critical elements of fakes, pivot, etc.

Closure
- What are some ways to create space when you have the ball? When you don't have the ball?
- How does your teammate know you are open and want the ball?
- Next class, we'll focus on helping the defense be successful in our games.

Reflection
- Review each practice task.
- Are most students able to create space when they have the ball?
- Can they create space to receive a ball?
- Are they communicating that they are open?

Homework
Optional: Watch a 3-minute clip of a team handball match. Count the number of times offensive players execute a give and go. Repeat for a jab step or pivot.

Using handout and physical education teachers' website, have students review rules of team handball for upcoming lessons.

Resources
USA Team Handball: www.teamusa.org

Internet keyword search: "creating open space for team handball," "offensive tactics in invasion sports"

LESSON 4: DEFENSIVE-READY POSITION AND RULES

Grade-Level Outcomes

Primary Outcomes

Reducing space using denial: Reduces open space by not allowing the catch (denial) or anticipating the speed of the object and person for the purpose of interception or deflection. (S2.M5.7)

Rules & etiquette: Identifies the rules and etiquette for physical activities/games and dance activities. (S4.M6.6)

Embedded Outcome

Working with others: Cooperates with a small group of classmates during adventure activities, game play or team-building activities. (S4.M5.6)

Lesson Objectives

The learner will:

- demonstrate and practice guarding a person to prevent him from receiving a pass, by using the body to deflect the pass or by preventing the person from being open for the pass.
- begin to learn and comprehend the rules of the game through discussion and demonstrations.

Equipment and Materials

- Enough balls for each set of partners
- Pre-determined markers for practice tasks
- Board or device to display rules

Introduction

In our past classes, we worked on helping the offensive team be successful by building skills and strategies to move the ball. For homework, you had the option to watch a 3-minute clip of a team handball match and count the number of times offensive players execute a give and go, jab step, or pivot. Did anyone do this? Can you share what you came up with?

Today, we will work on skills and strategies to help the defensive team. Specifically, we will focus on reducing open space and, hopefully, making scoring difficult.

Prior knowledge questions:

- When playing defense, what are you trying to do?
- When guarding someone, what can you do to help yourself be successful?
- Discuss how these skills are sport-specific and important for being successful. Discuss how these specific defensive skills differ and relate to health- and skill-related fitness.

Instructional Task: Reducing Open Space

■ **PRACTICE TASK**

Review or teach the defensive and denial positioning (triangle between ball, offensive player, and defender; hand in the passing lane).

In grids with groups of three, set up the passing and receiving drill with one defender in the grid. Start with defender denying the passing lane. Receiver moves to new cone with defender opening to the ball and positioning for denial at new cone. Continue for 30 seconds. Switch roles.

Extensions

- Repeat with passer attempting to make the pass. Count number of times defender blocks pass.
- Set up larger grid and repeat with 2 v 2.

Guiding questions for students:

- How did moving around make it easier for the passer to complete a pass?
- When defending, how did staying close to the receiver make it difficult to complete the pass?
- When passes were completed, what were the reasons?
- When passes were prevented from being completed, what were the reasons?

Student Choices/Differentiation

- Group by ability.
- Allow students to choose ball.

What to Look For

- Are students using the correct cues for passing and catching?
- On defense, are they staying close to the students catching?
- Where is the defender looking, and is this helping her or the person catching?

Instructional Task: Rules of Team Handball

■ PRACTICE TASK

Show students a video clip of a team handball game.

Using a board or device, display the rules for team handball and the rules incorporated for safety and facility restrictions. Show the lines and dimensions and what they mean.

Demonstrate the rules to show and teach students what they need to know to play the game.

Guiding questions for students:

- What sports have similar rules?
- Compare and contrast the differences in rules for similar games.
- What rules or playing areas should we modify so that we're able to play team handball at our school? Why are those modifications important?

Extension

Have students come up and perform skits of multiple rules of team handball.

EMBEDDED OUTCOME: S4.M5.6. Discuss with students important aspects of cooperating with group members when coming up with skits for the rules chosen.

Student Choices/Differentiation

- Provide skit topics, if needed.
- Show students an example of a skit.

What to Look For

- Do students have follow-up questions?
- After asking students to clarify, is their confusion a misunderstanding of the rules?
- Throughout the lessons, ensure that students implement the rules appropriately.
- Make sure that students understand the differences between the rules of similar games.
- Make sure that students understand the difference between the game's official rules and rules that you or the school have imposed to accommodate safety or space restrictions.

Instructional Task: Modified Game With Rules

■ PRACTICE TASK

Set up 4 v 4 games in grids. One team is on offense, the other on defense. The offense scores by successfully completing three passes.

The defense scores each time they create a turnover, but they return the ball to the offense (half-court formation). Switch roles after 1 minute. Students apply rules related to dribbling, passing, and defending.

Student Choices/Differentiation

- Add or delete players if needed.
- Students may choose to use this time to practice skills in isolation if needed.

What to Look For

- Are defenders staying close to their offensive player?
- Do defenders watch the ball while guarding?
- Can students apply the rules in the modified game?
- Can the offense get free under defensive pressure?

Formal and Informal Assessments

Exit slip: List three rules for team handball.

Closure

- Review the defensive-ready position and ask why this helps players be successful.
- Why is sliding a better choice than crossing your feet?
- Now that you have been guarded while dribbling, explain why being able to use both hands is important.
- What rules for handball are similar to those of games that you have played, and what rules are new to you?

Reflection

- Were students able to perform the defensive-ready position?
- Were students sliding in the defensive-ready position?
- How successful were students in dribbling with an active defender?
- Do you need to spend more time reviewing this?

Homework

Have students practice sliding in defensive-ready position.

Review rules and critical elements for team handball on the school's physical education website.

Resources

USA Team Handball: www.teamusa.org

Internet keyword search: "rules of team handball," "defensive-ready positon," "team handball"

LESSON 5: MODIFIED GAME AND TRANSITIONS

Grade-Level Outcomes

Primary Outcomes

Transitions: Transitions from offense to defense or defense to offense by recovering quickly. (S2.M6.6)

Creating space using width & length: Creates open space by staying spread on offense, and cutting and passing quickly. (S2.M3.7)

Reducing space by changing size & shape: Reduces open space on defense by staying close to the opponent as he/she nears the goal. (S2.M4.7)

Embedded Outcome

Personal responsibility: Exhibits responsible social behaviors by cooperating with classmates, demonstrating inclusive behaviors and supporting classmates. (S4.M1.7)

Lesson Objectives

The learner will:
- demonstrate transitions from offense to defense.
- demonstrate transitions from defense to offense.
- apply defensive strategies such as the ready position, staying close to opponent, and reducing space.
- apply tactics to create space, such as staying spread, cutting, and passing quickly.

Equipment and Materials
- Grids for half-court style of play
- The device or board you may need to review rules
- 1 ball per court

Introduction

Today, we will apply the skills that we have learned from passing off the dribble to throwing and catching. We also will apply the offensive strategies that we have learned to stay spread and moving to get open. On defense, we will apply the skills that we have learned to guard the offense, limiting their ability to move the ball and score. We also will learn about transitioning from offense to defense and defense to offense.

Instructional Task: Modified Game

■ PRACTICE TASK

Play 4 v 4 in half-court style. Students score by successfully catching a pass over the end line of their grid. When one team scores, the other team gets the ball. Review the rules of the game as needed. Students work together to self-officiate. Play for 4 minutes. Rotate groups to a different grid for one more round.

Guiding questions for students:
- How can you challenge the offense?
- How can you challenge the defense?
- What should you do when your team loses the ball?

Student Choices/Differentiation

- Group students by ability, if needed.
- Limit or eliminate dribbling.

What to Look For

- Can students answer the questions that you ask them?
- Is offensive and defensive play balanced?

Instructional Task: Transitions

■ PRACTICE TASK

In the same half-court setup, students perform a 3 v 3 drill.

There are two lines. One line is the defense and the other line is the offense. Each time this drill begins, the first three people in line take their positions. When it is over, they go to the end of the line opposite to where they were.

The defense wins or the drill ends when:

- the ball goes out of bounds;
- the offense scores;
- the defense steals the ball from the dribbler or intercepts a pass;
- the offensive player holds the ball for longer than 3 seconds;
- the offensive player takes more than 3 steps; or
- any other violation of the rules occurs that would cause the offense to lose possession of the ball.

Students rotate to next line.

Extension

The offense tries to score by hitting a pre-determined target.

Refinement

Stop the drill to refine dribbling, passing, other physical skills, or previously taught offensive and defensive tactics.

Student Choices/Differentiation

- Students can be organized by ability group.
- May add or subtract a player.

What to Look For

- Is the offense staying spread?
- Are they cutting and passing quickly?
- Are students dribbling with correct form, using both hands and changing speed and direction?
- Is the defense in the ready position staying close?
- Is the defense working to reduce the open space?
- Are students cooperative, supportive, and inclusive so that all can learn the skills?
- Are they applying the rules correctly?

Formal and Informal Assessments

Checklist (yes and no) for students applying the different types of offensive strategies during drill

Closure

- Discuss how getting open and moving around makes it harder for the defense.
- What helped make the defense successful?
- What helped make the offense more successful?
- How does including teammates, showing support, and cooperating help the team?

Reflection

- How well did students transition from offense to defense and defense to offense?
- Did students' performance suffer when students moved into game play?
- Are students cooperating?
- Did students implement the rules correctly?

Homework

Remind students to practice the skills they need to work on individually.

Have students review the rules and videos posted on the school's physical education website.

Resources

Dougherty, N.J. (Ed.) (2010). *Physical activity & sport for the secondary school student.* 6th ed. Reston, VA: National Association for Sport and Physical Education.

Internet keyword search: "team handball strategies," "transitions for invasion sports"

LESSON 6: GOALKEEPING, SHOOTING, AND MODIFIED GAME

Grade-Level Outcomes

Primary Outcomes

Using tactics & shots: Selects offensive shot based on opponent's location (hit where opponent is not). (S2.M8.7)

Passing & receiving: Passes and receives with hands in combination with locomotor patterns of running and change of direction & speed with competency in modified invasion games such as basketball, flag football, speedball or team handball. (S1.M4.6)

Rules & etiquette: Demonstrates knowledge of rules and etiquette by self-officiating modified physical activities and games or following parameters to create or modify a dance. (S4.M6.7)

Embedded Outcome

Working with others: Accepts differences among classmates in physical development, maturation and varying skill levels by providing encouragement and positive feedback. (S4.M4.6)

Lesson Objectives

The learner will:

- practice shooting on the goal and aiming for spaces.
- practice defending the goal and positioning defenders in the best place to block the shot.
- apply skills and strategies learned in small-sided games.

Equipment and Materials

- As many goals as you would need for the number of groups
- What you need to represent the goals
- 1 ball for each group
- Jerseys for teams
- Modified courts

Introduction

Last class, we learned the rules of team handball and practiced the skills and strategies. Today, we will play small-sided games to help build on these skills and implement the rules, as well. Before we play, we will work on shooting and shooting placement. We also will introduce goalkeeping skills.

Instructional Task: Shooting on Goal

■ PRACTICE TASK

Set up multiple stations with goal cages to practice shooting. Cages can be regulation or mini-cages. Rotate after set time (2 or 3 minutes).

Station 1: Hang two jump ropes to divide the cage into thirds. Students should aim for the right and left thirds, avoiding the center, where the keeper would normally be.

Station 2: Place a chair or other large object in the center of the goal to simulate the placement of the keeper.

Station 3: Hang or tape targets in each corner of the cage. These can be toys or other objects, so long as they are durable.

Students practice dribbling toward and shooting at the targets from 5 yards or meters out.

Extensions

- Repeat, with students adding a fake before the shot.
- Have students practice shooting with a defender on them.
- Repeat, with students receiving the ball from a post player and then shooting with a defender on them.

Refinement

Refine throwing skills, focusing on cues.

Student Choices/Differentiation

- Move the shooters to the left and right sides of the goal, making the target harder to hit.
- Don't add defender if shooter is having difficulty.

What to Look For

- Shooters should focus on speed, then through feedback (internal and external) work on accuracy.
- Are the shooters aiming for the open area of the goal?
- Are the shooters using correct throwing cues?
- Can they still get the shot off when there's a defender?

Instructional Task: Goalkeeping

■ PRACTICE TASK

Review basics of goalkeeping and the importance of stepping into the ball to cut down the angle.

With a modified ball (foam), have students work in partners. One throws as if shooting; the other steps into the ball and catches or deflects it.

Extensions

- Return to goal cages and remove targets. Repeat shooting sequences with modified ball and one student acting as a keeper.
- Repeat with regular ball but set parameters about shot location (not to head or body).

EMBEDDED OUTCOME: S4.M4.6 While working on goalkeeping skills, discuss with students how to be supportive of individual differences in skill, ability, and comfort level.

Student Choices/Differentiation

- If possible, increase or decrease the size of the goal based on each goalie's ability.
- Being a keeper should be a student's choice. Students should not be required to fill this position.

What to Look For

- Are goalies putting themselves between the goal and the shooter?
- Are goalies using their hands, feet, and legs to stop the ball?
- Do students understand the use of angles when they serve as goalkeeper?

Instructional Task: Implementing Skills and Rules During Small-Sided Games

■ PRACTICE TASK

In teams of 3 v 3, students play team handball for 3- or 4-minute games on a modified court. Start play with a throw-off.

While students are not playing, they should watch to see the rules in effect and to learn from what others are doing correctly or need to change.

Extensions

- Add a neutral player in the center of the court who can pass to either team. This forces teams to work on faster transitions.
- Have groups rotate so that one group is observing each court and using a game-play assessment of one of the teams.

Refinement

Make sure that students are transitioning from offense to defense or defense to offense by recovering quickly. .

Student Choices/Differentiation

- Pre-select who will guard whom throughout the games. That helps students who are still unsure of what to do on defense know who they need to prevent from receiving the ball and from scoring. It also will hold them accountable for guarding a person and for an assigned duty.
- Limit the number of steps or dribbles if the offensive team is dominating too much.

What to Look For

- How are students implementing the offensive skills?
- How are they implementing the defensive skills?
- Are they transitioning quickly and knowing what to do from offense to defense?

Formal and Informal Assessments

Peers use game-play assessment for team handball.

Closure

- Ask students what they learned from the games today.
- What did they notice as they were playing?
- What did they notice while they were watching?
- Inform students that they will be assessed on their knowledge of the rules and strategies during the next class.

Reflection

- Did students know the rules and did they follow them during the game?
- What skills were students missing that will need to be addressed?
- How were students working together as a team?
- Did students know what to do on offense and were they doing it?
- Did students know what to do on defense and were they doing it?

Homework

Review rules and strategies of the game.

Resources

USA Team Handball: www.teamusa.org

Internet keyword search: "goalkeeping," "team handball shooting," "game-play assessment invasion games"

LESSON 7: REVIEW SKILLS, MODIFIED GAMES, AND RULES TEST

Grade-Level Outcomes

Primary Outcome

Rules & etiquette: Demonstrates knowledge of rules and etiquette by self-officiating modified physical activities and games or following parameters to create or modify a dance. (S4.M6.7)

Embedded Outcome

Challenge: Generates positive strategies such as offering suggestions or assistance, leading or following others and providing possible solutions when faced with a group challenge. (S5.M3.7)

Lesson Objectives

The learner will:

- review and practice skills with classmates.
- review and practice offensive strategies to apply in modified game play.
- review and practice defensive strategies to apply in modified game play.
- follow rules and etiquette for a modified team handball game.

Equipment and Materials

- Modified courts
- Space with goal area for groups to practice
- Task cards with drills for students to practice as a team, which will focus on skills but also have them working together as a team and communicating
- Scrimmage vests

Introduction

Today, we will review and practice everything we have learned. We will start off today by practicing transitions in small-sided games. Working with your team, you will practice the skills and learn to communicate with one another, which will help you prepare for the last class. I will start assessing your game play during the small-sided games, and we'll end today with a quiz on the rules and strategies that you've been practicing.

Instructional Task: Stations

▨ PRACTICE TASK

Using the task cards from the different stations, explain the tasks that students will move through in this lesson.

Designate a certain amount of time for each or have groups spend as much time as they need so everyone gets to perform the skills two or three times and move on to the next task.

Station 1: Practicing goalkeeper skills and shooting on goal (one and then two shooters)

Station 2: Three teammates passing the ball down the court without dribbling or stepping with the ball, working on moving, passing, and using teammates

Station 3: Three on offense and two on defense working down the court by passing (no dribbling or stepping)

Station 4: Two on offense and three on defense, including goalie, working on communicating, applying skills, using strategies, and trying to score

Refinement

As you walk around observing the class, help students refine skills or concepts, as needed.

EMBEDDED OUTCOME: S5.M3.7 Discuss how to give positive feedback and suggestions and how to communicate in ways that support teammates.

Student Choices/Differentiation

- Students or groups should move at their own pace.
- Students should be goalie only if they choose to.
- Limit or add the number of steps or dribbles, if needed.
- Students should modify equipment, distance, or player personnel, as needed, throughout the stations.

What to Look For

- How are students working together?
- Are they applying the skills and strategies they learned? These would include:
  - Are they dribbling correctly?
  - How are they catching the ball?
  - Are they in the defensive-ready position when guarding?
  - Are they using different passes depending on how they are being guarded?
  - Are they staying spread on offense?
  - Are they moving around, making themselves more difficult to cover?
  - Are they talking to each other and providing feedback?

Instructional Task: Modified Game Play

■ PRACTICE TASK

Review rules and officiating with students before game play.

In teams of 4 v 4, students play team handball for 2-minute games on a modified court. A neutral post in the center of the court could be used. Post begins game with a throw-off. Rotate neutral player.

If students are not playing, they should be officiating.

Extensions

- Change to 5 v 5, removing the neutral player.
- Rotate teams to different courts once or twice. Evaluate game play of players.

Refinement

If players are crowding, make lanes. Wings stay in lanes unless another player switches with them.

Student Choices/Differentiation

- Players may choose to be goalkeepers.
- If defense struggles, limit steps or dribbles with the ball.

What to Look For

Use game-play assessment tool to begin evaluating skills and tactics during play.

Instructional Task: Quiz

■ PRACTICE TASK

Administer quiz on rules and strategies.

You can do this at the end of class or by using a station format, with a group rotating out of game play to take the test.

Student Choices/Differentiation

Provide test accommodations, as appropriate, to address student needs.

What to Look For

Students know basic rules and strategies of team handball.

Formal and Informal Assessments

- Quiz on rules and strategies
- Game-play assessment: team handball

Closure

- Review with students what you observed, specifically how they worked together as a team.
- Discuss what you observed with regard to moving around and getting open.
- Discuss what you observed with regard to guarding offensive players.

Reflection

From everything that you observed in the "What to Look For" section, what will you need to review or practice before students begin game play next class?

Homework

Review skills for game play.

Resources

USA Team Handball: www.teamusa.org

Internet keyword search: "offensive skills in team handball," "modifying team handball," "game-play assessment invasion games"

LESSON 8: ASSESSMENT REVIEW AND ROUND-ROBIN TOURNAMENT

Grade-Level Outcomes

Primary Outcomes

Transitions: Transitions from offense to defense or defense to offense by recovering quickly. (S2.M6.6)

Creating space using width & length: Creates open space by staying spread on offense, and cutting and passing quickly. (S2.M3.7)

Reducing space by changing size & shape: Reduces open space on defense by staying close to the opponent as he/she nears the goal. (S2.M4.7)

Embedded Outcome

Social interaction: Demonstrates the importance of social interaction by helping and encouraging others, avoiding trash talk and providing support to classmates. (S5.M6.7)

Lesson Objectives

The learner will:

- work with teammates to demonstrate skills learned in team handball.
- transition effectively during game play.
- apply offensive strategies learned to help move the ball, providing the opportunity to score.
- apply defensive strategies to limit opportunities for the opponent to score.

Equipment and Materials

- Several courts for modified games
- Scrimmage vests
- Game schedule for round-robin

Introduction

We're quickly going to review rules and strategies that you had trouble with on the quiz. Then, we'll put all our skills together in round-robin games of 5 v 5. I will continue to assess your game play during a round-robin tournament.

Instructional Task: Round-Robin Games

■ PRACTICE TASK

In grids of 30 × 20 yards or meters, students play team handball.

Use the same teams from the previous lesson. Students self-officiate while you assess game play. Rotate teams when time expires (5- to 6-minute rotations).

Extension

Students can officiate games while you complete the game-play assessment.

Refinements

- Make sure that students know who they are guarding.
- Stop the game, if needed, to reteach a rule or refine a skill.

EMBEDDED OUTCOME: S5.M6.7 This is a good opportunity to review the importance of encouraging and supporting teammates. Ask for examples of positive reinforcement during game play.

Student Choices/Differentiation
- Students can choose whom they want to guard and whether they want to be goalkeeper.
- Use game-play assessment tool to evaluate skills and tactics.

What to Look For
Students are officiating and applying rules correctly.

Instructional Task: Tactic Assessment

■ **PRACTICE TASK**
When not playing, students use a frequency-count worksheet to record the number of times a team performs a specified skill or tactic successfully (e.g., give and go, fake and shoot).

Student Choices/Differentiation
- Modify the task or assessment for students, as needed.
- This task can be done in pairs.

What to Look For
- Are students watching or not paying attention?
- Are students recording data correctly?

Formal and Informal Assessments
- Frequency-count recording sheet
- Game-play assessment: team handball

Closure
- Discuss how teams demonstrated sportsmanship and how they worked together.
- Explain and review rules that were not followed.
- Discuss how offenses worked well and what could be adjusted.
- Discuss how defenses looked, what went well, and what could be changed to help them be more successful.

Reflection
- From what you observed and discussed, what areas will you need to focus on the next time you teach an invasion game?
- What skills did students come in with that they might not need to spend as much time on?
- What offensive or defensive strategies need more time or tweaking for how they are taught?

Homework
Read a handout or watch a video clip from the class web page about the next module.

Resources
USA Team Handball: www.teamusa.org

Internet keyword search: "offensive and defensive tactics in team handball," "modifying team handball," "game-play assessment invasion games," "frequency counts in invasion sports"

ULTIMATE MODULE

Lessons in this module were contributed by Brad Rettig, a middle school physical education teacher in Lincoln, NE, Public Schools.

Grade-Level Outcomes Addressed, by Lesson	1	2	3	4	5	6	7	8
Standard 1. The physically literate individual demonstrates competency in a variety of motor skills and movement patterns.								
Throws with a mature pattern for distance or power appropriate to the practice task (e.g., distance = outfield to home plate; power = 2nd base to 1st base). (S1.M2.6)	P	P		P	P			
Catches with a mature pattern from a variety of trajectories using different objects in varying practice tasks. (S1.M3.6)	P	P						
Catches with a mature pattern from a variety of trajectories using different objects in small-sided game play. (S1.M3.7)							P	
Executes at least two of the following to create open space during modified game play: pivots, fakes, jab steps, screens. (S1.M6.8)							P	P
Maintains defensive-ready position, with weight on balls of feet, arms extended and eyes on midsection of the offensive player. (S1.M11.6)	P							
Slides in all directions while on defense without crossing feet. (S1.M11.7)	P							
Drop-steps in the direction of the pass during player-to-player defense. (S1.M11.8)		P						
Standard 2. The physically literate individual applies knowledge of concepts, principles, strategies and tactics related to movement and performance.								
Executes at least one of the following offensive tactics to create open space: moves to open space without the ball; uses a variety of passes, pivots and fakes; give & go. (S2.M2.6)				P				
Creates open space by using the width and length of the field/court on offense. (S2.M3.6)				P				
Creates open space by staying spread on offense, cutting and passing quickly, and using fakes off the ball. (S2.M3.8)							P	P
Reduces open space on defense by staying on the goal side of the offensive player and reducing the distance to him/her (third-party perspective). (S2.M4.8)							P	P
Reduces open space by not allowing the catch (denial) or by allowing the catch but not the return pass. (S2.M5.6)	P							
Reduces open space by not allowing the catch (denial) or anticipating the speed of the object and person for the purpose of interception or deflection. (S2.M5.8)		P						
Transitions from offense to defense or defense to offense by recovering quickly and communicating with teammates. (S2.M6.7)						P		
Transitions from offense to defense or defense to offense by recovering quickly, communicating with teammates and capitalizing on an advantage. (S2.M6.8)								P
Standard 3. The physically literate individual demonstrates the knowledge and skills to achieve and maintain a health-enhancing level of physical activity and fitness.								
Standard 4. The physically literate individual exhibits responsible personal and social behavior that respects self and others.								
Exhibits responsible social behaviors by cooperating with classmates, demonstrating inclusive behaviors and supporting classmates. (S4.M1.7)		E	E					
Demonstrates self-responsibility by implementing specific corrective feedback to improve performance. (S4.M3.6)	E							
Provides encouragement and feedback to peers without prompting from the teacher. (S4.M3.8)				E				
Accepts differences among classmates in physical development, maturation and varying skill levels by providing encouragement and positive feedback. (S4.M4.6)	E							
Responds appropriately to participants' ethical and unethical behavior during physical activity by using rules and guidelines for resolving conflicts. (S4.M4.8)						E		
Problem-solves with a small group of classmates during adventure activities, small-group initiatives or game play. (S4.M5.7)							P	
Demonstrates knowledge of rules and etiquette by self-officiating modified physical activities and games or following parameters to create or modify a dance. (S4.M6.7)							E	E
Standard 5. The physically literate individual recognizes the value of physical activity for health, enjoyment, challenge, self-expression and/or social interaction.								
Demonstrates the importance of social interaction by helping and encouraging others, avoiding trash talk and providing support to classmates. (S5.M6.7)						E		E
Demonstrates respect for self by asking for help and helping others in various physical activities. (S5.M6.8)				E				

P = Primary; E = Embedded

LESSON 1: THROWING AND CATCHING

Grade-Level Outcomes

Primary Outcomes

Throwing: Throws with a mature pattern for distance or power appropriate to the practice task (e.g., distance = outfield to home plate; power = 2nd base to 1st base). (S1.M2.6)

Catching: Catches with a mature pattern from a variety of trajectories using different objects in varying practice tasks. (S1.M3.6)

Embedded Outcomes

Accepting feedback: Demonstrates self-responsibility by implementing specific corrective feedback to improve performance. (S4.M3.6)

Working with others: Accepts differences among classmates in physical development, maturation and varying skill levels by providing encouragement and positive feedback. (S4.M4.6)

Lesson Objectives

The learner will:

- demonstrate the proper technique for a backhand throw.
- demonstrate the proper technique for catching a disc, using both the two- and one-hand catch.

Equipment and Materials

- 1 disc for every 2 students
- 1 hoop for every 2 students or as space allows; larger target for students who need it
- Recording device for every 2 students or as many as possible

Introduction

During this module, we will learn how to catch and throw a disc as well as play the exciting game of ultimate. Who has played ultimate with any type of equipment before? Do you know the names for any of the disc throws?

Show students a video of people playing ultimate disc and how to perform the backhand throw and one- and two-hand catch.

Instructional Task: Throwing and Catching (Stationary)

■ PRACTICE TASK

With a partner, students will practice throwing the disc back and forth about 7 yards or meters apart, working on the critical elements of the backhand throw and two-hand catch (sandwich) or one-hand catch.

Extensions

- Repeat with the thrower aiming a couple of steps to the receiver's right or left so the receiver must catch on the move.
- Repeat with the receiver varying the height of the target.
- In groups of four, have two of the students video-record the others. Using a checklist or rubric, have students evaluate how they are throwing and catching related to the critical elements.

EMBEDDED OUTCOME: S4.M3.6 Pass back peer evaluations. Have students review their evaluations and videos of throwing and catching. In groups, have students discuss how to implement the feedback from their evaluation sheets to improve their skill.

Student Choices/Differentiation

- The distance between the partners can be lengthened or shortened based on correct technique and how comfortable they are with catching.
- Students may catch with one or two hands.
- Students may use the foam or wire and fabric discs until they feel comfortable with catching and throwing.

What to Look For

- Are students performing with proper technique?
- Do they need to adjust the distance from where they are throwing?

Self-evaluation

Students should look for and adjust the following while watching their video of throwing and catching.

Throwing

- Do you have the proper grip?
- Are you sideways to the target?
- Are you bringing your arm level across your body?
- Is your non-throwing arm extended back and out of the way?
- Are you stepping toward the target as you bring your throwing arm across your body?
- Are you flicking your wrist?
- Are you releasing when your arm is extended toward the target?
- Are you following through?

Catching

- Two-hand catch
  - One hand on top and the other underneath the disc
  - Eyes on disc through the catch
- One-hand catch
  - Hand in a C shape with fingers on top and thumb under
  - Eyes on disc through the catch

Instructional Task: Throwing for Accuracy

■ PRACTICE TASK

In partners, students throw a disc through a hoop 10 to 15 feet (3 to 4.5 meters) away. Trading off throws, the partners try to make 20 through the hoop.

You can hang the hoop from the ceiling of the gym or trees outside.

Refinement

If students are sacrificing their technique for accuracy, move them closer to the hoop.

Extension

Repeat, varying the height of the hoop.

Guiding questions for students:

- Why is it important to release the disc when your arm is extended toward the target?
- How does flicking your wrist help the disc fly straight?

EMBEDDED OUTCOME: S4.M4.6. Discuss with students that classmates might have varying skill levels and physical development constraints, and that they should provide encouragement and positive feedback.

Student Choices/Differentiation

- If students are struggling to make 20 to end the game, drop the number to 10.
- Use different-sized targets.

What to Look For

- Are students standing sideways to the target?
- Are students releasing when the arm is extended toward the target?
- Are students stepping toward the target with the preferred leg?
- Where is the disc going?
- Are the wrist and hand in a position as if they are shaking hands on the release?

Formal and Informal Assessments

- Self-evaluation for throwing and catching
- Peer evaluation for throwing and catching

Closure

- Review with students what they observed with regard to their throwing and catching.
- What were you doing incorrectly while throwing?
- How did watching yourself affect your throwing by the end of class?
- Did you think you were doing something correctly, only to find out that you were not after watching the video of your throw?

Reflection

- How many students understood the grip and were able to follow the critical elements for throwing?
- How many students were still using the sandwich or pancake catch, compared to the one-hand catch?
- What percentage of students were struggling to catch or were afraid of the disc?

Homework

During recess or at home, practice throwing backhand. If possible, work on this with a partner to include catching.

Resources

Baccarini, M., & Booth, T. (2008). *Essential ultimate: Teaching, coaching, and playing.* Champaign, IL: Human Kinetics.

Dougherty, N.J. (Ed.) (2010). *Physical activity & sport for the secondary school student.* 6th ed. Reston, VA: National Association for Sport and Physical Education.

Parinella, J., & Zaslow, E. (2004). *Ultimate: Techniques & tactics.* Champaign, IL: Human Kinetics.

Internet keyword search: "disc throwing and catching techniques"

LESSON 2: THROWING AND CATCHING ON THE MOVE, PLUS DEFENSE

Grade-Level Outcomes

Primary Outcomes

Throwing: Throws with a mature pattern for distance or power appropriate to the practice task (e.g., distance = outfield to home plate; power = 2nd base to 1st base). **(S1.M2.6)**

Catching: Catches with a mature pattern from a variety of trajectories using different objects in varying practice tasks. (S1.M3.6)

Defensive skills: Maintains defensive-ready position, with weight on balls of feet, arms extended and eyes on midsection of the offensive player. (S1.M11.6)

Defensive skills: Slides in all directions while on defense without crossing feet. (S1.M11.7)

Reducing space using denial: Reduces open space by not allowing the catch (denial) or by allowing the catch but not the return pass. (S2.M5.6)

Embedded Outcome

Personal responsibility: Exhibits responsible social behaviors by cooperating with classmates, demonstrating inclusive behaviors and supporting classmates. (S4.M1.7)

Lesson Objectives

The learner will:

- demonstrate the correct elements of throwing for distance or power to students who are stationary and on the move.
- demonstrate the correct elements of catching two- and one-handed.
- maintain an appropriate ready position.
- slide in all directions while on defense.
- reduce space on defense by not allowing the catch.

Equipment and Materials

- 2 discs for every 2 people
- 20 more discs for disc frenzy
- Grids for disc frenzy

Introduction

Review the critical elements of throwing and catching. Ask students what they remember and how they can make their throws more powerful and accurate. Discuss with students what a grid area is and list the three instructional tasks for the day.

Instructional Task: Throwing and Catching on the Move

■ PRACTICE TASK

In grids of 15 × 15 yards or meters, three students practice throwing as well as receiving a pass on the run.

During this practice task, two group members run within the grid to receive a pass. After throwing the disc, the thrower then runs for a pass from the catcher. The thrower is stationary and the other two are always moving.

Extension

Guarding: The thrower is stationary, one person cuts and tries to receive a pass, and the other defends the person trying to catch the disc. Review and demonstrate defensive-ready position and sliding. Regardless of the outcome, everyone switches roles for the next throw and this process continues.

Guiding questions for students:

- While throwing to a person on the run, where should you be aiming?
- What critical elements do you need to focus on when throwing to a moving target?
- Why is it important to keep your eyes on the disc all the way through the catch?

Student Choices/Differentiation

- Group students by ability.
- If any students are struggling to throw and catch, place them together and have them start off stationary while throwing and catching.
- If students are struggling with a disc, have them throw a ball.

What to Look For

- Are students using correct technique while throwing to a moving student?
- Are students able to throw the disc accurately to a moving target?
- Are students able to catch the disc while running?
- Are students able to adjust to the throw to complete the catch?
- Are defenders staying in good defensive position?

Instructional Task: Denial Defense

▇ PRACTICE TASK

Teach defenders to be a point in a triangle, with the other points being the passer and the receiver. Make sure that defenders start in defensive-ready position, with weight on balls of feet, arms extended, and eyes on the midsection of the offensive player. Defenders need to see both the disc and the receiver. If the receiver moves to the other side, the defender should open to the disc while moving with the receiver so the disc can always be seen. Make sure that students are sliding and not crossing their feet.. Have two students pass back and forth, with a third student practicing being in the "triangle" position and opening up as the ball is passed.

Extensions

- Practice the previous throwing and catching task, with the focus on denying the catch to the receiver. The defenders must have their hands in the passing lanes.
- 2 v 2 in grids (45 seconds), with points awarded to the defense for a deflection or interception. Switch roles.

Student Choices/Differentiation

- Students practice at their own speed.
- Students choose their own groups.

What to Look For

- Are defenders opening to the disc when moving with the receiver?
- Are defenders sliding as they move?
- Are defenders maintaining their triangle between the passer and the receiver?

Instructional Task: Disc Frenzy

■ PRACTICE TASK

In a grid, create an area that has two end lines and a middle line like a basketball court. Each team has half of its members on its end of the court, within which they can move anywhere. The other half of the team is across the opposing team's end line. You can refer to that end as "jail." To be freed from jail, players must catch a disc thrown from a teammate. They then run to their area of the court and throw discs to other teammates still in jail.

Students may not go past the end line to guard a person in jail, but they may stay by the end line to deflect or intercept a pass (denial). Once all teammates are out of jail, the game starts over with new people in jail. Rotate teams.

Refinements

- Throwing the disc: Remind students to focus on the critical elements of throwing, practicing proper technique.
- Catching the disc: Students in jail should focus on the proper technique of catching either two- or one-handed.

Guiding questions for students:

- What are some things that worked in the game? What did not work?
- Did the disc go where you wanted it go?
- Did anyone have to make adjustments?

EMBEDDED OUTCOME: S4.M1.7 This practice task is a great way to discuss cooperation with classmates and include everyone on the team. The only way players can get out of jail is with help from their peers. Discuss with students ways to include everyone in the activity.

Student Choices/Differentiation

- Provide foam discs or fabric-based discs to aid in catching.
- Team sizes should allow for multiple touches and opportunities to throw, catch, and defend.

What to Look For

- Are students using correct form while throwing?
- Are students actively involved in the game, working on the skill of throwing and catching?
- Are students applying any type of tactics?

Formal and Informal Assessments

- Informal assessment
- Exit slip: List two or three critical elements of the disc throw and catch.

Closure

- With the class, discuss how catching on the move and throwing to a moving and guarded receiver went.
- How did you have to adjust your throwing to connect with a receiver on the move?
- As the receiver, what adjustments did you have to make to receive the pass on the move?
- How did adding a defender affect the way you threw the disc?
- In what ways did it change how you as the receiver moved around and caught the disc once a defender was added?

Reflection

- How are students doing with their catching while being defended or not being defended?
- How did students do with trying to deflect the disc down or intercept it?
- What defensive or offensive strategies did they seem to use, or did they use any?
- How did they work together as a team?
- What critical elements are students struggling with while throwing and catching?

Homework

During recess or at home practice throwing and catching, working on critical elements. Watch video clips of creative ways to catch and throw.

Resources

Baccarini, M., & Booth, T. (2008). *Essential ultimate: Teaching, coaching, and playing.* Champaign, IL: Human Kinetics.

Dougherty, N.J. (Ed.) (2010). *Physical activity & sport for the secondary school student.* 6th ed. Reston, VA: National Association for Sport and Physical Education.

Parinella, J. and Zaslow, E. (2004). *Ultimate: Techniques & tactics.* Champaign, IL: Human Kinetics.

LESSON 3: DEFENSE AND KEEP-AWAY

Grade-Level Outcomes

Primary Outcomes

Reduces open space by changing size & shape: Reduces open space by not allowing the catch (denial) and anticipating the speed of the object and person for the purpose of interception or deflection. (S2.M5.8)

Defensive skills: Drop-steps in the direction of the pass during player-to-player defense. (S1.M11.8)

Embedded Outcome

Personal responsibility: Exhibits responsible social behaviors by cooperating with classmates, demonstrating inclusive behaviors and supporting classmates. (S4.M1.7)

Lesson Objectives

The learner will:

- apply the different types of throws in a dynamic environment to complete the pass.
- apply defensive strategies to disrupt or intercept the pass.
- use a drop-step during player-to-player defense.

Equipment and Materials

- 1 disc for every 2 students
- Appropriate number of grids and size for 3 v 1 and 3 v 2
- Video-recording devices

Introduction

Today, we will practice defense, working on reducing open space and drop-stepping into the direction of the pass, and we will continue to improve at throwing and catching in game-like situations. We also will work on throwing, building up to the forehand, and, potentially, the overhand throw.

Instructional Task: 3 v 1 Keep-Away

■ PRACTICE TASK

In grids of 20 yards or meters, students play keep-away. Students with the disc may not run, and the defender should leave enough room for the student to throw.

A new student becomes defender when the disc hits the ground or is intercepted. If five consecutive catches occur, a new person becomes defender.

Discuss and demonstrate how to pivot in order to help move as the thrower and find the open person.

Extensions

- Repeat with 3 v 2.
- Repeat with 3 v 3.

Refinement

Demonstrate and discuss how watching the person throwing lets the defender know where to go so that she can drop-step into the direction of the pass.

Guiding questions for students:

- As a defender, what can you do to deflect the pass or disrupt the throw?
- What challenges are you experiencing with a defender?

- With only one defender, what strategies are you using to complete passes?
- Are there times when it is difficult to make a throw using only the backhand?

Extension

After guiding questions, have students practice the task again with the focus on reducing open space and defense-critical features.

EMBEDDED OUTCOME: S4.M1.7 During the 3 v 2 activity, students should exhibit responsible social behaviors by cooperating with classmates. Many keep-away games can be difficult for lower-skilled students. Make sure that students demonstrate inclusive behaviors and support classmates as they improve their skills.

Student Choices/Differentiation

- Different objects may be used, such as a ball.
- Reduce size of grid or number of students.

What to Look For

- Are students using correct form to throw when defended or hurried?
- Are defending students reducing the open space to deny the catch?

Instructional Task: Throwing

■ PRACTICE TASK

Partners practice the overhand and forehand throws.

Forehand

First: Practice the grip.

Second: Skeleton practice without the disc. (Skeleton practice means practicing the movement pattern without equipment.)

Third: Students pass with a partner.

Repeat with overhand throw.

Refinement

Make sure that students are using proper weight transfer on throws.

Extension

Record students throwing and catching. Partners offer feedback on their skill according to the critical-elements worksheet for assessment.

Guiding questions for students:

- How will these throws help during game situations?
- Did anyone have more success after focusing on weight transfer?

Student Choices/Differentiation

- For students who are still struggling with the backhand, have them practice throwing either to a stationary partner or to their partners on the move.
- For students who are proficient at the forehand throw, have them work on the overhand throw. Have students watch how this is performed and work together to break down the grip, transfer of weight, arm motion, and release. Then, have them practice.

What to Look For

- Students use proper grip, arm motion, and proper weight transfer (weight back and step forward).
- How many students are working on the forehand or overhand throw?

Video Analysis

Have students watch and give feedback on other students' performance, looking at the following critical features:

- Grip
- Transfer of weight back and then forward
- Step
- Arm motion
- Release

Instructional Task: 3 v 2 Keep-Away

■ PRACTICE TASK

In grids, students practice throwing, catching, and defending in open space.

Students use any of the three throws learned to provide an advantage based on the positioning of the two students in the middle.

Guiding questions for students:

- Where do you need to be looking to step in the middle of a pass to break it up?
- In 3 v 2, how can you work together to reduce open space?

Student Choices/Differentiation

Change grid size to increase or decrease difficulty. The size of the grid also will provide opportunity and challenges for throwing.

What to Look For

- While students throw, are they applying the critical elements of the throws?
- Are students not in the middle, moving continually to make themselves difficult to cover?
- What are students doing in the middle to intercept the disc or knock it down?

Formal and Informal Assessments

Using their peer videos, students identify the critical elements performed correctly and offer feedback to their partners.

Closure

- Discuss with students the three types of throws and why they can be helpful during game situations.
- Provide examples from the 3 v 2 when students reduced open space and deflected passes and what they did that made them successful.
- Ask students what they did to help them be successful.

Reflection

- Do students understand defensive strategies or are they just using physical abilities in the task?
- What is the skill level of passing and catching after three lessons?
- Are students showing appropriate personal responsibility during the keep-away game?

Homework

Read the rules of ultimate by reviewing the school's physical education website.

Continue practicing the different types of throws to a moving target and also receiving.

Resources

Baccarini, M., & Booth, T. (2008). *Essential ultimate: Teaching, coaching, and playing.* Champaign, IL: Human Kinetics.

Dougherty, N.J. (Ed.) (2010). *Physical activity & sport for the secondary school student.* 6th ed. Reston, VA: National Association for Sport and Physical Education.

Parinella, J., & Zaslow, E. (2004). *Ultimate: Techniques & tactics.* Champaign, IL: Human Kinetics.

Internet keyword search: "ultimate rules," "help with the rules of ultimate," "overhand throw," "forehand throw"

LESSON 4: DISC GOLF

Grade-Level Outcomes

Primary Outcomes

Throwing: Throws with a mature pattern for distance or power appropriate to the practice task (e.g., distance = outfield to home plate; power = 2nd base to 1st base). (S1.M2.6)

Creating space using width & length: Creates open space by using the width and length of the field/court on offense. (S2.M3.6)

Creating space with offensive tactics: Executes at least one of the following offensive tactics to create open space: moves to open space without the ball; uses a variety of passes, pivots and fakes; give & go. (S2.M2.6)

Embedded Outcomes

Accepting feedback: Provides encouragement and feedback to peers without prompting from the teacher. (S4.M3.8)

Social Interaction: Demonstrates respect for self by asking for help and helping others in various physical activates. (S5.M6.8)

Lesson Objectives

The learner will:

- demonstrate throwing with correct form for distance, power, and accuracy.
- create open space by using an offensive tactic as well as length and width of the field.

Equipment and Materials

- Discs
- Cones
- Long ropes or end line markers

Introduction

Last class, the homework was to read over the rules of ultimate. Ask students to explain what the rules are and discuss or clarify as a class.

Today, we will apply the different types of throws that we have learned in a modified game of ultimate, as well as with a defender guarding the pass. It is very important to continue to develop appropriate technique and accuracy to be successful in ultimate disc. We also will learn how to score in ultimate.

Have students demonstrate the different types of throws, and discuss the critical elements of each throw.

Instructional Task: Passing and Catching in Grids

■ PRACTICE TASK

In grids of 15 × 15 yards or meters, four passers are stationary while passing to their peers, who are on the move.

While throwing, the passers should use the three different types of throws, while receivers work to get open. Do this for a set time.

Refinements

- Make sure that students are practicing creating space (getting open) and receiving on the run.
- If students have difficulty getting open, review pivoting, faking, and change of speed and direction.

Extensions

- The activity can be extended to 2 v 2 in grids.
- Add a defender to the task.

EMBEDDED OUTCOME: S4.M3.8. Instruct both students to provide feedback to each other on throwing. The feedback should relate directly to the critical elements and should be encouraging in nature.

Student Choices/Differentiation

- Students may adjust the size of the grid to ensure accuracy.
- Higher-skilled students may make the grid larger to accommodate more difficult throws.

What to Look For

Students are using the critical elements of passing and catching.

Instructional Task: Defender on Passer

■ PRACTICE TASK

In grids of 15 × 15 yards or meters and groups of three, students focus on passing with a defender guarding the passer.

Begin with a passive defender standing in the way of the pass. Passer must bend, lean, or reach to pass the disc to a partner across from her.

Extensions

- Defender plays at 50 percent to 75 percent effort.
- Defender plays at 100 percent effort.
- Partner moves back and forth in the grid.
- Add a second defender to the guard passer.
- Apply pressure after offensive player catches the disc.

Refinements

- Students should snap their throws.
- Make sure that students are using jab steps and fakes, and changing their levels of the throw.

EMBEDDED OUTCOME: S5.M6.8. Discuss with students how playing defense at 50 percent or 75 percent effort can help the offense (especially with a defender playing close to the passer). Discuss how helping others or asking for help in physical activities is important for learning and living a healthy lifestyle.

Student Choices/Differentiation

- Students may choose how much effort defender uses to guard.
- Students can watch videos of throw techniques to help learn how to throw and to pass with a defender.

What to Look For

- Are students using different skills to get the pass off?
- Are students using correct form and making accurate passes?
- Are defenders being respectful?
- Are students encouraging one another or offering praise as they play?
- Are students asking for help as they play or encounter difficult situations?

Instructional Task: Scoring Over an End Line

▓ PRACTICE TASK

Discuss with students the differences in scoring in invasion games.

Guiding questions for students:

- How do we score in basketball? Soccer? Team handball? Ice hockey?
- How do we score in ultimate disc?

As you can see, not all invasion games are alike. In large grids, we are going to play 3 v 3 ultimate. The goal is to score over an end line.

Extensions

- Play 3 v 4.
- Play 4 v 3.

Refinements

- Make sure students are trying to get open across the end line.
- Students are moving within the grid (not going out of bounds).

Student Choices/Differentiation

- Make grids larger or smaller.
- Add more students or play with fewer.
- For less-skilled students, they can start with a ball and then progress to a disc.

What to Look For

- Students are getting open on opponents' side of the end line.
- Students are using quick cuts and verbal communication.
- Students are using the entire grid.

Formal and Informal Assessments

Assess students' throwing, catching, and tactic skills informally.

Closure

- Review the critical elements of throwing with students. Share with them what you observed while monitoring the class.
- Ask students what they learned with regard to throwing with an active defender guarding.
- What are some important things to consider when trying to score over an end line?

Reflection

- Did students have success with throwing with a defender guarding?
- What skills did students use to throw with a defender or to score over an end line? What skills do I need to review in the next lesson?
- How did students work together on giving one another feedback?

Homework

Does anyone know of a sport that uses discs similar to ultimate disc? (Answer: disc golf) Many athletes who play ultimate practice their throwing skills by playing disc golf. If you have a disc at home or during recess, play a game of disc golf to practice and improve throwing skills. You can assign different objects (tree, monkey bars, etc.) as targets (do not use younger siblings as targets). Practice throwing the disc to prepare for the throwing assessment next class. Use the critical elements and any video clips to learn and review from.

Resources

Baccarini, M., & Booth, T. (2008). *Essential ultimate: Teaching, coaching, and playing.* Champaign, IL: Human Kinetics.

Dougherty, N.J. (Ed.) (2010). *Physical activity & sport for the secondary school student.* 6th ed. Reston, VA: National Association for Sport and Physical Education.

Parinella, J., & Zaslow, E. (2004). *Ultimate: Techniques & tactics.* Champaign, IL: Human Kinetics.

Internet keyword search: "scoring in ultimate disc," "throwing with a defender guarding close"

LESSON 5: THROWING ASSESSMENT AND TRANSITIONS

Grade-Level Outcomes

Primary Outcomes

Throwing: Throws with a mature pattern for distance or power appropriate to the practice task (e.g., distance = outfield to home plate; power = 2nd base to 1st base). (S1.M2.6)

Transitioning: Transitions from offense to defense or defense to offense by recovering quickly and communicating with teammates. (S2.M6.7)

Embedded Outcome

Social interaction: Demonstrates the importance of social interaction by helping and encouraging others, avoiding trash talk and providing support to classmates. (S5.M6.7)

Lesson Objectives

The learner will:

- demonstrate the critical elements while throwing.
- apply the game rules while playing ultimate ball.
- apply transitional skills and knowledge during ultimate ball.

Equipment and Materials

- 3 discs for every group
- 4 targets at set distances for every group
- Grids for students to work on transition
- Enough fields for teams of 4 to play at the same time

Introduction

Did anyone practice throwing by playing disc golf? It is important to practice these skills with many different activities.

Explain to students that the first practice task will be an assessment. Briefly review the procedures for the assessment. Review the critical elements, as needed.

When the assessment is complete, we will play ultimate ball. This game applies the rules of ultimate but uses a ball. Through this activity, we will explore how the game is played and apply strategies you may know from other sports.

Instructional Task: Throwing for Accuracy Assessment and Throwing With a Defender to a Moving Target

■ PRACTICE TASK

Assessment 1

In groups of two or three, students throw discs at targets set at four distances. Each student throws three times.

Students are assessed on their ability to use the critical elements of the backhand throw, as well as their accuracy with the throw.

Assessment 2

In groups of four, students pass to a partner with defenders guarding.
Offensive players play at 100 percent effort; defensive players play at 75 percent.

Assessment 3

In groups of four, two students defend while two players pass. One defensive player guards the passer while the other defender covers a receiver.

Offensive player plays at 75 percent effort; defensive player plays at 100 percent.

Note: For assessments (especially assessments 2 and 3), group students by ability. Remind students that the purpose of the assessment is to measure offensive or defensive skills. Students should give an appropriate amount of effort to allow their peers to demonstrate their abilities on the assessment.

Extensions

- Challenge students by making the farthest target worth 4 points and the closest worth one.
- Challenge all players to play at 100 percent effort.

Refinement

Students should refer to the critical elements to adjust, if needed.

Student Choices/Differentiation

- Students can choose to throw at the different-distance targets.
- Students can choose their partners.
- If students are not successful, you can pull one player to create an advantage situation for the assessment.

What to Look For

Students are
- using proper throwing skills,
- passing and catching effectively with a defender, and
- using the defending skills assessment to evaluate ultimate skills.

Instructional Task: Transitioning

■ PRACTICE TASK

Students learn to transition from offense to defense by playing tag. Each student has a partner, and each partner has a number, either 1 or 2. Partners may tag only partners.

Within their grid of 15 × 15 yards or meters, partners start off facing each other. Call out either number 1 or 2 to be "it." That number then tries to tag the partner, who runs around within the grid to avoid being tagged. After 10 to 15 seconds, call the other number, forcing the partner running away to change roles by chasing (guarding) her partner, who now runs to open space. Continue to call out number 1 or 2, forcing partners to transition from offense to defense.

Refinement

Make sure that students maintain a low center of gravity when transitioning and use an explosive step to get back on defense or offense.

Guiding questions for students:

Discuss what it means to transition from offense to defense or defense to offense.

- Why is it important to transition?
- Why is it important to transition quickly?
- How is this like transitioning in ultimate or games such as basketball?

Discuss how to use the entire grid and move to open space.

- In this activity, did you use the entire grid?
- What is the benefit of using the entire grid in this activity?
- What is the benefit of using the entire space in invasion games (e.g., basketball, soccer, ultimate)?

Extensions

- Do the same activity, but now 2 v 2 or 3 v 3, with one group the 1s and the other group the 2s.
- Students choose to tag anyone in the grid. This provides students with a great opportunity to communicate with one another for transitional offense and defense.

Guiding questions for students:

- How was this task more difficult than 1 v 1?
- Was it easier in some instances? Why?
- Why was communication important?

Student Choices/Differentiation

- For different speeds, after a number has been called, the taggers may have to count to three or perform five jumping jacks before they can chase.
- If runners are tagged, you can have them wait until the next number is called or have them ask their partners questions that they have to answer related to ultimate or disc golf.

What to Look For

- Are students transitioning quickly from tagger to trying not to get tagged?
- Are they transitioning using a low center of gravity?
- Are they communicating well with teammates?

Instructional Task: Ultimate With a Ball

■ PRACTICE TASK

Students play ultimate with a ball to learn the game and apply rules without focusing on the skills of throwing and catching a disc.

With modified courts, each team should have three to five students.

Grid size is 20 × 10 yards or meters.

Students should focus on using quick transitions and appropriate communication with teammates during the game.

Refinements

- During the game, review rules to help students understand how the game is played.
- Make sure that students are using appropriate transitions during the game.

Extensions

- Repeat with a disc.
- Limit the number of steps allowed when a player has possession.

Guiding questions for students:

- Was the game easier with a ball than with a disc?
- Why is it important to transition quickly during the game?
- Who will share the successful communication strategies that you and your team used?

EMBEDDED OUTCOME: S5.M6.7. Talk with students about the importance of social interaction during invasion games. Some talking points include helping and encouraging others, avoiding trash talk, and providing support to classmates.

Student Choices/Differentiation

- Change the type of ball to allow for different skill levels.
- Adjust the size of the field to meet students' needs.
- Modify the rules to help students understand how the game is played.

What to Look For

- Do students know the rules and are they applying them?
- When on offense, are students trying to get open and using the whole field?
- Are students transitioning from offense to defense?
- While on defense, are students covering offensive players effectively and talking to their teammates?

Formal and Informal Assessments

Checklist or rubric for throwing for accuracy. The teacher-created assessment can assess process (critical elements) and product (how many targets the student hit).

Closure

- Discus with students how the ultimate ball games went.
- What did they learn while playing and what will they need to work on?
- Provide an overall evaluation of how students threw, based on the assessment.

Reflection

- How did the assessment go? What are students struggling with that needs to be practiced and retaught?
- Are students able to apply the rules of ultimate?
- How did the game go?
- What strategies were they using?

Homework

Review ultimate rules for the upcoming ultimate disc knowledge test.

Resources

Baccarini, M., & Booth, T. (2008). *Essential ultimate: Teaching, coaching, and playing.* Champaign, IL: Human Kinetics.

McManama, J., Hicks, L., & Urtel, M. (2010). *Physical education activity handbook.* 12th ed. San Francisco: Benjamin Cummings.

Parinella, J., & Zaslow, E. (2004). *Ultimate: Techniques & tactics.* Champaign, IL: Human Kinetics.

Internet keyword search: "ultimate rules," "transitions in ultimate," "transitions in invasion sports"

LESSON 6: OFFENSIVE AND DEFENSIVE TACTICS

Grade-Level Outcomes

Primary Outcomes

Offensive skills: Executes at least two of the following to create open space during modified game play: pivots, fakes, jab steps, screens. (S1.M6.8)

Reducing open space by changing size & shape: Reduces open space on defense by staying on the goal side of the offensive and reducing the distance to him/her (third-party perspective). (S2.M4.8)

Creating space using width & length: Creates open space by staying spread on offense, cutting and passing quickly, and using fakes off the ball. (S2.M3.8)

Embedded Outcome

Working with others: Responds appropriately to participants' ethical and unethical behavior during physical activity by using rules and guidelines for resolving conflicts. (S4.M4.8)

Lesson Objectives

The learner will:

- apply pivots, fakes, cutting maneuvers, quick passes, and screens to get open.
- explore defensive strategies to reduce the offense's ability to score.
- stay spread on offense while cutting and passing quickly.
- apply offensive and defensive strategies during a modified game of ultimate.

Equipment and Materials

- Grids of 20 × 10 yards or meters for every group
- 1 disc for each grid
- 1 set of jerseys for each field

Introduction

Today, we will practice the give and go to continue working on throwing to a moving target, catching on the run, and getting open. Our objective for the day is to play a modified game of ultimate and to learn and apply offensive and defensive strategies.

With student help, demonstrate and explain pivots, fakes, and screens as well as staying on the goal side of the offensive player.

Instructional Task: Offensive Skills With the Ball

■ PRACTICE TASK

In small grids, 2 v 1, have a student with the disc attempt to jab and pass to a receiver while defended. The defender may not take the disc from the passer but may intercept or deflect (semi-active). If successful, defender moves to receiver. Play for 30 to 45 seconds and then switch roles.

Extensions

- Repeat, but passer must use pivot before releasing the disc.
- Repeat, with passer adding a fake.
- Play 2 v 2. Award points for using a pivot or jab step.

Refinement

Make sure that students are using quick movements.

Student Choices/Differentiation

- Students may use a ball or disc for this task.
- Students may modify grid size to make task easier or more difficult.

What to Look For

- Are students making their jab steps convincing?
- Are students making accurate passes after making an offensive move?
- Are receivers using change of speed and direction to get open?
- Are receivers providing a good target for passers?

Instructional Task: Give and Go—Getting Open Activity

■ PRACTICE TASK

In grids, two or three students practice the give and go, working to all sides of the grid without dropping the disc.

Students practice until you stop to discuss what students are doing well or need help with.

Refinements

Stop every 2 or 3 minutes to discuss what you are seeing:

- Are students moving continually after the throw?
- Students should be using the entire field and staying spread, not running next to defenders.
- Are students exploding, or using sudden bursts, after the give?

Extensions

- Repeat, adding a semi-active defender.
- With an extra student in groups, students can record the performance and conduct a peer assessment using critical features.

Guiding questions for students:

- How does give and go relate to ultimate?
- Why is it important in ultimate to give and go?
- How does pivoting help with this activity? How will it help during a game?

Student Choices/Differentiation

- If a student is not moving a lot, put him with one person to encourage movement.
- To prompt students to move and throw, place cones out for students to move to and throw from.
- Students may use a ball or disc for this task.
- Students may modify grid size to make task easier or more difficult.

What to Look For

- Are students running to get open after the throw?
- Are students communicating to help them be successful?
- Are they using more than one type of throw?
- How proficient are they at throwing and catching?

Peer Assessment

Students use a teacher-created checklist for:

- Give and go
- Using pivots, fakes, and screens
- Staying on the goal side of the offensive player

Instructional Task: Defensive Skills

■ PRACTICE TASK

Set up 3 v 2 grids. Position defenders on the goal side of the offense, with the defender closest to the disc playing the passer and the off-disc defender dropping back on a diagonal.

Defenders adjust position when a pass is thrown. No steps allowed on offense. Offense scores when passer throws to a teammate over the goal line.

Refinement

Stop the action and reposition defenders until they grasp the concepts of playing on the goal side and on a diagonal.

Extensions

- Repeat with 3 v 3.
- Add bonus points for using a give and go.

Student Choices/Differentiation

- Play at half speed.
- Use a ball instead of a disc.

What to Look For

- Are students dropping to cover the passing lane?
- Can they adjust when they are one pass away? Two passes away?
- Are they communicating about which defender is covering the disc?

Instructional Task: Ultimate

■ PRACTICE TASK

In teams of four, students play a modified game of ultimate.

Refinements

- During the game, remind defenders to keep themselves between the offensive person and the goal line.
- During the game, highlight when students use pivots, fakes, and screens to get open.
- Make sure that students are using appropriate transitions.

Guiding questions for students:

- How can using a screen help the offense?
- Why does the defense want to stay between the offensive player and the goal line?

EMBEDDED OUTCOME: S4.M4.8. During the unofficiated games, remind students to resolve conflicts by using rules and guidelines designed by the class.

Student Choices/Differentiation

- Students may choose ball or disc.
- Adjust size of playing space to increase or decrease the difficulty.
- Group teams by ability.

What to Look For

- Do students know the rules?
- What skills and strategies need to be refined?
- Are they staying spread on offense?
- Are defenders staying between the offense and the goal line?
- Are they applying pivots and fakes?

Formal and Informal Assessments

Peer assessment: critical elements of the give and go as well as other offensive moves

Closure

- Have students demonstrate the offensive and defensive strategies applied today.
- Have students discuss how those strategies worked during the game, and how other strategies that were not used might have helped.

Reflection

- How did the ultimate game go with the disc?
- How are students working together on offense and defense?
- What strategies are they applying while playing?
- Are students understanding the concepts of the game?

Homework

Continue practicing catching for the skills assessment next class.

Because we worked on a couple of offensive and defensive tactics, draw up one offensive and one defensive play and be ready to share with the class tomorrow.

Resources

Baccarini, M., & Booth, T. (2008). *Essential ultimate: Teaching, coaching, and playing.* Champaign, IL: Human Kinetics.

Dougherty, N.J. (Ed.) (2010). *Physical activity & sport for the secondary school student.* 6th ed. Reston, VA: National Association for Sport and Physical Education.

Parinella, J., & Zaslow, E. (2004). *Ultimate: Techniques & tactics.* Champaign, IL: Human Kinetics.

Internet keyword search: "give and go," "offensive moves in ultimate"

LESSON 7: CATCHING ASSESSMENT AND PLANNING TACTICS

Grade-Level Outcomes

Primary Outcomes

Catching: Catches with a mature pattern from a variety of trajectories using different objects in small-sided game play. (S1.M3.7)

Working with others: Problem-solves with a small group of classmates during adventure activities, small-group initiatives or game play. (S4.M5.7)

Embedded Outcomes

Social interaction: Demonstrates the importance of social interaction by helping and encouraging others, avoiding trash talk and providing support to classmates. (S5.M6.7)

Rules & etiquette: Demonstrates knowledge of rules and etiquette by self-officiating modified physical activities and games or following parameters to create or modify a dance. (S4.M6.7)

Lesson Objectives

The learner will:
- demonstrate the ability to catch from a variety of trajectories.
- apply skills and rules learned during ultimate.
- work with others to develop simple plays and implement them during a modified game.

Equipment and Materials

- 1 disc and grid large enough for 3 v 1 catching assessment
- 1 grid for each team of 4 to practice and apply skills and strategies
- 1 set of jerseys for each field
- Enough fields for all students to play

Introduction

Today, we will assess your ability to catch a disc during 3 v 1 keep-away.

Discuss and show the critical elements and assessment to students, and explain how that will occur.

After the assessment, you will be placed in your ultimate teams and be given time to complete two offensive plans to use during your games.

Instructional Task:
Assess Catching During Small-Sided Game Play

■ PRACTICE TASK

During 3 v 1 keep-away, assess students' ability to catch from a variety of trajectories.

Extension

Play 3 v 2 keep-away.

Student Choices/Differentiation

If the defender is not allowing the receiver to make the catch, ask the defender to play at 50 percent effort. This would allow the receiver to move around but not have the pass intercepted or deflected.

What to Look For

Using the assessment rubric, check if students are able to catch from a variety of trajectories using the critical elements.

Instructional Task:
Practicing Communicating and Planning Strategies

■ PRACTICE TASK

During this practice time, student groups should work together on passing and receiving. Students should devise strategies appropriate for group members' abilities. Teams should design two plans:

- scoring quickly from midfield
- including screens to get open

Each group member must have a role in each plan.

Each member has to catch or throw the disc in at least one of the two plans.

Extension

If the two plans are developed and practiced, groups may create a third one.

Refinement

While developing plans, students should remember to create open space.

Guiding questions for students:

- How does having a plan help?
- Why is it important to involve everyone on your team?
- What will happen if one teammate chooses not to follow through with the plan?
- What will happen if a teammate doesn't play offense or defense?

EMBEDDED OUTCOME: S5.M6.7 Discuss the importance of social interaction as a team. Help students find ways to help and encourage others on their team.

Student Choices/Differentiation

- Have a couple of examples for students to review.
- Let students use the Internet to search for ideas.

What to Look For

- Do the plans include everyone?
- Do the plans include scoring quickly from midfield and using screens?
- Are all students involved in the planning process, and do all have a voice?

Instructional Task: Ultimate Games

■ PRACTICE TASK

Students play 4 v 4, implementing the plans that they created and using the skills and strategies that they've learned.

Refinement

Let students modify their plans, if needed.

Guiding questions for students:

- How are the plans working?
- Does either of the plans need to be adjusted? If so, how?
- How are you working as teammates and communicating together?

EMBEDDED OUTCOME: S4.M6.7 Remind students of the importance of following rules and etiquette by letting them self-officiate the ultimate game.

Student Choices/Differentiation

- Teams are grouped by ability.
- Adjust game space to increase or decrease difficulty.
- Let students self-officiate the game.

What to Look For

- Students are implementing their written plans.
- Students are using appropriate communication.

Formal and Informal Assessments

Checklist or rubric for catching. The teacher-created assessment can evaluate process (critical elements) and product (how many catches the student makes).

Closure

- Discuss with students how the class performed on its catching assessment.
- Have students describe how their plans and games went, and discuss what you observed.
- Discuss how students will be tested on the rules of ultimate and how you will assess their offensive and defensive strategies during game play.

Reflection

- How are students doing with their plans? What suggestions can you provide next class before the games?
- What guidance can you provide to help struggling teams make their plans more likely to succeed?

Homework

Review the rules of ultimate and the game-play assessment rubric posted on the school's physical education website.

Resources

Baccarini, M., & Booth, T. (2008). *Essential ultimate: Teaching, coaching, and playing.* Champaign, IL: Human Kinetics.

Dougherty, N.J. (Ed.) (2010). *Physical activity & sport for the secondary school student.* 6th ed. Reston, VA: National Association for Sport and Physical Education.

Parinella, J., & Zaslow, E. (2004). *Ultimate: Techniques & tactics.* Champaign, IL: Human Kinetics.

Internet keyword search: "how to catch a disc," "invasion game strategies"

LESSON 8: GAME AND ASSESSMENT DAY

Grade-Level Outcomes

Primary Outcomes

Offensive skills: Executes at least two of the following to create open space during modified game play: pivots, fakes, jab steps, screens. (S1.M6.8)

Reducing space by changing size & shape: Reduces open space on defense by staying on the goal side of the offensive player and reducing the distance to him/her (third-party perspective). (S2.M4.8)

Transitions: Transitions from offense to defense or defense to offense by recovering quickly, communicating with teammates and capitalizing on an advantage. (S2.M6.8)

Creating space using width & length: Creates open space by staying spread on offense, cutting and passing quickly, and using fakes off ball. (S2.M3.8)

Embedded Outcome

Rules & etiquette: Demonstrates knowledge of rules and etiquette by self-officiating modified physical activities and games or following parameters to create or modify a dance. (S4.M6.7)

Lesson Objectives

The learner will:

- demonstrate on a test his or her knowledge of ultimate rules.
- demonstrate the offensive and defensive strategies that he or she has learned while playing ultimate in this module.
- use proper transitions and offensive skills during the 4 v 4 ultimate games.

Equipment and Materials

- 1 disc for each field
- 1 field for every 2 teams
- 1 assessment for every student

Introduction

Today, you will demonstrate your ability to perform offensive and defensive strategies while playing 4 v 4 modified games of ultimate.

Instructional Task: Ultimate

■ PRACTICE TASK

In grids, students play modified games of 4 v 4 ultimate disc or ball.

Assess students during modified game play on their ability to create open space (Outcomes S1.M6.8 and S2.M3.8), reduce open space (Outcome S2.M4.8), and transition from offense to defense (Outcome S2.M6.8).

We'll play a round-robin tournament, with the winners getting a golden disc!

Extension

Using the assessment tool, ask students to explain what they should be doing and why, to help them understand what you are looking for and on what they will be assessed.

Refinement

If needed, stop games to refine skills or explain rules or cognitive concepts taught during the module.

EMBEDDED OUTCOME: S4.M6.7 Discuss with students common etiquette and self-officiating procedures and principles before starting game play.

Student Choices/Differentiation

Use a ball instead of a disc.

What to Look For

- Are students able to create open space?
- When students are on defense, are they able to reduce open space?
- Are students transitioning from offense to defense or defense to offense?
- Are students self-officiating and holding each other accountable to the rules?

Instructional Task: Knowledge Test on Rules

■ PRACTICE TASK

While their teams are not playing, students take a test on the rules or other outcomes that you determine.

Student Choices/Differentiation

Modify for individual student needs.

What to Look For

Are students able to show an understanding of the rules and strategies of ultimate?

Formal and Informal Assessments

- Assessment of rules knowledge and application during game play
- Knowledge assessment of rules

Closure

- With team members, provide examples of the growth that you have observed in skill, teamwork, and strategies. Students can do this with the video recordings in the first lessons and what you and students have observed.
- Have students share their positive experiences from the module.

Reflection

- How did the module go?
- What strategies within the lessons could I tweak to help students learn the skills that they were lacking?
- What worked well? What did not?

Homework

Provide instructions for students to view or read for the next module.

Resource

SHAPE America – Society of Health and Physical Educators. (2014). *National Standards & Grade-Level Outcomes for k-12 physical education.* Champaign, IL; Human Kinetics.

SOCCER MODULE

Lessons in this module were contributed by Brad Rettig, a middle school physical education teacher in Lincoln, NE, Public Schools.

Grade-Level Outcomes Addressed, by Lesson	Lessons							
	1	2	3	4	5	6	7	8
Standard 1. The physically literate individual demonstrates competency in a variety of motor skills and movement patterns.								
Passes and receives with feet in combination with locomotor patterns of running and change of direction & speed with competency in invasion games such as soccer or speedball. (S1.M4.7)	P	P					P	
Performs the following offensive skills without defensive pressure: pivot, give & go, and fakes. (S1.M7.6)					P			
Foot-dribbles or dribbles with an implement with control, changing speed and direction in a variety of practice tasks. (S1.M9.6)	P		P					
Foot-dribbles or dribbles with an implement combined with passing in a variety of practice tasks. (S1.M9.7)		P	P					
Shoots on goal with power in a dynamic environment as appropriate to the activity. (S1.M10.6)			P			E		
Maintains defensive-ready position, with weight on balls of feet, arms extended and eyes on midsection of the offensive player. (S1.M11.6)			P					
Slides in all directions while on defense without crossing feet. (S1.M11.7)			P					
Standard 2. The physically literate individual applies knowledge of concepts, principles, strategies and tactics related to movement and performance.								
Creates open space by using locomotor movements (e.g., walking, running, jumping & landing) in combination with movement (e.g., varying pathways; change of speed, direction or pace). (S2.M1.6)			E		P			
Executes at least one of the following offensive tactics to create open space: moves to open space without the ball; uses a variety of passes, pivots and fakes; give & go. (S2.M2.6)			P	P				
Reduces open space on defense by making the body larger and reducing passing angles. (S2.M4.6)					P	P		
Transitions from offense to defense or defense to offense by recovering quickly. (S2.M6.6)				P				
Standard 3. The physically literate individual demonstrates the knowledge and skills to achieve and maintain a health-enhancing level of physical activity and fitness.								
Standard 4. The physically literate individual exhibits responsible personal and social behavior that respects self and others.								
Exhibits responsible social behaviors by cooperating with classmates, demonstrating inclusive behaviors and supporting classmates. (S4.M1.7)			E					
Demonstrates self-responsibility by implementing specific corrective feedback to improve performance. (S4.M3.6)			E		E			
Accepts differences among classmates in physical development, maturation and varying skill levels by providing encouragement and positive feedback. (S4.M4.6)	E			E				
Responds appropriately to participants' ethical and unethical behavior during physical activity by using rules and guidelines for resolving conflicts. (S4.M4.8)								E
Identifies the rules and etiquette for physical activities/games and dance activities. (S4.M6.6)						P		
Demonstrates knowledge of rules and etiquette by self-officiating modified physical activities and games or following parameters to create or modify a dance. (S4.M6.7)								P
Standard 5. The physically literate individual recognizes the value of physical activity for health, enjoyment, challenge, self-expression and/or social interaction.								
Demonstrates respect for self and others in activities and games by following the rules, encouraging others and playing in the spirit of the game or activity. (S5.M6.6)		E					E	
Demonstrates respect for self by asking for help and helping others in various physical activates. (S5.M6.8)						E		

P = Primary; E = Embedded

LESSON 1: DRIBBLING AND PASSING

Grade-Level Outcomes

Primary Outcomes

Dribbling/ball control: Foot-dribbles or dribbles with an implement with control, changing speed and direction in a variety of practice tasks. (S1.M9.6)

Passing & receiving: Passes and receives with feet in combination with locomotor patterns of running and change of direction & speed with competency in invasion games such as soccer or speedball. (S1.M4.7)

Embedded Outcome

Working with others: Accepts differences among classmates in physical development, maturation and varying skills levels by providing encouragement and positive feedback. (S4.M4.6)

Lesson Objectives

The learner will:

- demonstrate the critical elements of dribbling.
- demonstrate the critical elements of passing and receiving.

Equipment and Materials

- Soccer balls for every student
- 5 cones per grid

Introduction

Today, we will start our soccer module.

Ask students what they know about soccer and who has played. Watch video clips of current soccer games, local or worldwide. Explain and demonstrate to students the critical elements of dribbling, passing, and receiving a pass.

Instructional Task: Dribbling

■ PRACTICE TASK

In grids of 10 × 10 yards or meters, place five cones spread out within the grid. Students will work on dribbling and changing direction.

In each grid, four students play follow the leader to each cone. After they have dribbled to five cones, the leader switches.

Students should dribble to each cone in a line no more than 4 to 6 feet (1.2 to 1.8 m) wide, and the ball should stay within that distance as well.

During this time, conduct a pre-assessment to determine students' dribbling skill levels.

Extensions

- Students can pick up the speed as long as they are keeping control of the ball and staying close together.
- Repeat, using students in place of the cones to simulate ball control with a defender (eyes up).
- Pre-assessment checklist: dribbling using cues.

Guiding questions for students:

- Why is it important to keep the ball 3 to 5 feet (1 to 1.5 m) in front of you while dribbling uncontested?
- Why should you use the instep and not your toes while dribbling?

Discuss with students ways to work together and encourage each other, as each student is going to lead or follow at a different pace due to ability. Every student should be accepting and helpful to their classmates. Give positive examples of what you have seen.

Refinement

Remind students to use the instep while dribbling.

Student Choices/Differentiation

- The first time through with each leader, you might want everyone to walk so that they understand what to do and don't get separated.
- For students or groups that have trouble dribbling, the groups can walk or move at a slower pace.
- Each time through, students can pick up the speed as long as they maintain control of the ball and stay close together.

What to Look For

- Are students applying the critical elements of dribbling?
- Are students keeping the ball in line while dribbling?
- Are students staying within 6 feet (1.8 m) of each other?
- What part of this is difficult or challenging?

Instructional Task: Passing and Receiving

▩ PRACTICE TASK

Within the same grid, each student dribbles to a cone (one cone should be open). Using the critical elements of passing and receiving, each student passes the ball to a person at a cone. Once each student passes the ball, he must run to an open cone.

Extensions

- Repeat, with receiver moving to a cone and the ball passed to the cone that receiver is moving toward.
- Repeat with passer and receiver moving.
- Repeat with a passive defender on the passer.

Guiding questions for students:

- Why is it important to collect and receive the ball before passing it?
- Discuss what you are seeing that is creating good passes, as well as what students are doing that is causing passes to be unsuccessful.
- Ask students how running to a cone after a pass relates to a soccer game.

Student Choices/Differentiation

- Groups can be smaller, with two or three students and three or four cones, to allow for more practice touches and less confusion about whom to pass to.
- Students can increase or decrease speed or playing distance according to skill level.

What to Look For

- Are students using correct form while passing?
- Can students pass the ball to a person who is stationary?
- How many students are ready to pass to a moving person?
- Are students able to collect the ball from a pass while stationary?

Formal and Informal Assessments

Pre-assessment checklist: dribbling using cues

Closure

Discuss and have students demonstrate the critical elements of passing, receiving a pass, and dribbling.

Reflection

- How many students have played soccer before on a team?
- From your informal assessment during the dribbling, at what level are most students?
- Are students making accurate passes?
- Are they able to receive a pass?
- You might need to conduct receiving and passing drills during the next class before starting the next lesson.

Homework

Have students dribble at home or during recess. Have them work on passing and receiving a pass with someone, if they can. If not, passing against a wall will work. Have students review critical-elements handouts and videos posted to the school's physical education website.

Resources

Dougherty, N.J. (Ed.) (2010). *Physical activity & sport for the secondary school student.* 6th ed. Reston, VA: National Association for Sport and Physical Education.

Internet keyword search: "soccer fundamentals," "soccer skills"

LESSON 2: DRIBBLING AND PASSING

Grade-Level Outcomes

Primary Outcomes

Dribbling/ball control: Foot-dribbles or dribbles with an implement combined with passing in a variety of practice tasks. (S1.M9.7)

Passing & receiving: Passes and receives with feet in combination with locomotor patterns of running and change of direction & speed with competency in invasion games such as soccer or speedball. (S1.M4.7)

Embedded Outcome

Social interaction: Demonstrates respect for self and others in activities and games by following the rules, encouraging others and playing in the spirit of the game or activity. (S5.M6.6)

Lesson Objectives

The learner will:

- develop dribbling skills to move in a variety of directions with control of the ball.
- develop passing skills off the dribble with a change of direction and speed.

Equipment and Materials

- Soccer balls for every student
- Cones

Introduction

Review skills learned from Lesson 1. Call on students to demonstrate the critical elements of the passing, receiving a pass, and dribbling skills learned. Review the critical elements for each and explain how students will be building from what they learned previously to more game-like situations.

Instructional Task:
Dribbling While Being Aware of Your Surroundings

■ PRACTICE TASK

In grids of 7 × 7 yards or meters, six students dribble, focusing on the critical elements and spatial awareness.

Each student has a soccer ball, dribbling at a quick pace within the grid, while not running into others or losing control of the ball.

Extension

Repeat, but have students accelerate two steps at the sound of a whistle, still maintaining control.

Guiding questions for students:

- Why is it important to keep the ball close?
- Why is important to look up and not at the ball?

Refinement

Correct students if they are

- using the toes instead of the instep,
- not keeping the ball 3 to 5 feet (1 to 1.5 m) in front, or
- not keeping the eyes up.

Student Choices/Differentiation

For students who are struggling, slow the pace to a walk. They can keep the ball closer to them than 3 feet to maintain control. They may look down at the ball more often to maintain contact and control.

What to Look For

- Are students applying the critical elements?
- Are students' eyes looking forward to see where others are?
- Are students keeping control of the ball and within the grid?

Instructional Task: Dribbling Take-Away

■ PRACTICE TASK

In grids with five students, students play a game of take-away. Each student has his own ball, which he tries to protect while also knocking another player's ball out of the grid. Play for a set time.

Once a ball is stolen or goes out of bounds, that student is out. To get back in, students must recite one of the critical elements.

Refinement

Students must look up while dribbling.

Guiding questions for students:

After each game, discuss the following:

- Why were you successful? Why were you not successful?
- Was it skill level, strategy, or teamwork?

EMBEDDED OUTCOME: S5.M6.6. While dribbling within general space and protecting the ball, discuss with students the spirit of the game and ways to stay within it.

Guiding questions for students:

- What are examples of play that reflects the spirit of the game?
- What are examples of play that does not?

Student Choices/Differentiation

- The size of the grid can be larger or smaller, depending on student needs.
- Students can choose their own groups or be grouped by ability.
- Review the critical elements for dribbling to help students who are struggling and easily losing the ball.

What to Look For

- Which students can control the soccer ball and dribble using the critical elements?
- How are students working together?
- Do students have any prior knowledge of defensive strategies and how to take the ball away?

Instructional Task: Passing Off the Dribble

■ PRACTICE TASK

With two soccer balls, have four students pass continuously to each other.

Students must remain moving within the grid so that the student passing has to work on using the critical elements and passing to a moving target and receiving a pass on the move. Students have five dribbles to set themselves up to pass.

Extensions

- Repeat with a passive defender on the receiver.
- Repeat with a passive defender on the passer.
- Repeat, allowing one defender to be more active.
- Repeat with both defenders active.

Guiding questions for students:

- Why is it important to gain control of the soccer ball before passing it?
- How do you use your feet to collect a pass?
- Why is it important to lead the person you are passing to?

Student Choices/Differentiation

- Students who are still working on the critical elements should trap the ball and kick from a stationary position.
- If the use of two soccer balls is making it difficult, use only one or limit the number of students in the grid.
- If students are not moving around, add a third soccer ball and enforce the rule that everyone must be passed to before repeating a person, and order does not matter.

What to Look For

- Are students using the critical elements for passing?
- Do students seem to want to stop the ball before passing?
- Are students moving continuously?
- How accurate are the passes?

Formal and Informal Assessments

Informal assessment

Closure

- Ask students to describe and show the critical elements of passing, dribbling, and receiving a pass.
- Discuss what was observed today.

Reflection

- Are students able to perform the critical elements of dribbling in a dynamic environment?
- At what level are students with passing both from stationary position and off the dribble?

Homework

At home or during recess, work on passing and dribbling.

If possible with another person, work on passing to a moving target and receiving a pass.

Resources

McManama, J., Hicks, L., & Urtel, M. (2010). *Physical education activity handbook*. 12th ed. San Francisco: Benjamin Cummings.

Internet keyword search: "soccer dribbling," "soccer passing"

LESSON 3: DEFENDING AND SHOOTING

Grade-Level Outcomes

Primary Outcomes

Dribbling/ball control: Foot-dribbles or dribbles with an implement with control, changing speed and direction in a variety of practice tasks. (S1.M9.6)

Dribbling/ball control: Foot-dribbles or dribbles with an implement combined with passing in a variety of practice tasks. (S1.M9.7)

Creating open space with offensive tactics: Executes at least one of the following offensive tactics to create open space: moves to open space without the ball; uses a variety of passes, pivots and fakes; give and go. (S2.M2.6)

Shooting on goal: Shoots on goal with power in a dynamic environment as appropriate to the activity. (S1.M10.6)

Defensive skills: Maintains defensive-ready position, with weight on balls of feet, arms extended and eyes on midsection of the offensive player. (S1.M11.6)

Defensive skills: Slides in all directions while on defense without crossing feet. (S1.M11.7)

Embedded Outcomes

Personal responsibility: Exhibits responsible social behaviors by cooperating with classmates, demonstrating inclusive behaviors and supporting classmates. (S4.M1.7)

Accepting feedback: Demonstrates self-responsibility by implementing specific corrective feedback to improve performance. (S4.M3.6)

Creating space with movement: Creates open space by using locomotor movements (e.g., walking, running, jumping & landing) in combination with movement (e.g., varying pathways; change of speed, direction or pace). (S2.M1.6)

Lesson Objectives

The learner will:

- demonstrate proper technique to control the soccer ball while dribbling.
- demonstrate how to pass the ball correctly while dribbling.
- demonstrate the proper technique for shooting on goal from a variety of angles.
- demonstrate a variety of passes to create open space.
- use the proper ready position when playing defense.
- use the slide technique to defend.

Equipment and Materials

- 3 soccer balls for each grid
- Enough modified goals for every 3 or 4 students
- 3 or 4 soccer balls at each goal
- Video-recording device

Introduction

As a class, bring students up to demonstrate how to pass and receive on the move.

In today's activities, we will move while passing and receive passes on the move. We also will work on dribbling and protecting the ball.

During students' demonstration on how to dribble, discuss how to move in different directions. Spend the last part of class working on shooting. Demonstrate how to shoot and the difference between the critical elements of passing and shooting.

Instructional Task: Defending

■ PRACTICE TASK

In pairs, have students dribble 10 yards or meters at half speed with changes of direction while their partners practice defensive positioning and sliding. Defender (passive) may not take the ball from the dribbler. Switch roles.

Extensions

- Repeat, with dribbler moving at a faster speed.
- Repeat, with defender allowed to take the ball when it's off the dribbler's foot (semi-active defender).

Refinement

Make sure that students are in the proper ready position (weight on balls of feet, arms extended, and eyes on midsection).

Guiding questions for students:

- How did being guarded change the way you were dribbling?
- Did you find yourself keeping the ball closer?
- Where were your eyes focused?

Student Choices/Differentiation

- Do not use ball for initial practice.
- Stay at slower speed if defender cannot maintain position.

What to Look For

- Are defenders staying low and on the balls of their feet?
- Are they sliding when the dribbler tries to go by?
- Are their eyes on the midsection of the dribbler or the ball?

Instructional Task: Dribbling and Possession

■ PRACTICE TASK

In grids, set up a game with six students and three soccer balls. The three students without a ball try to steal one away from the three students who have them (like keep-away). Games are set by time limits (45 seconds to 2 minutes), and the objective is to end up with possession of a soccer ball.

Refinement

Remind dribblers to hold their arms away from the body to make themselves bigger to help protect the ball.

Guiding questions for students:

- Why is it important to keep the ball close to you while dribbling?
- While trying to take the ball away, where should you look so as not be faked out?

EMBEDDED OUTCOME: S4.M1.7 Discuss with students appropriate social behaviors and cooperating with classmates during the dribbling activity.

Student Choices/Differentiation

- Change the size of the grid to meet student needs.
- Change the number of students or balls in each grid, if needed.
- If students have difficulty maintaining possession, reduce the number of defenders to two.

What to Look For

- What part of the feet are students using to dribble?
- Are students keeping the ball close?
- Are students working to steal the ball away?
- Are students being too aggressive when trying to steal the ball?

Instructional Task: Passing and Receiving: 4 v 2 Keep-Away

■ PRACTICE TASK

In a grid with six students, play 4 v 2 keep-away, with four offensive players and two defensive. If the ball is stolen or kicked out of bounds, the defender who stole or caused the ball to go out of bounds will trade places. Students may move anywhere inside the grid.

Extensions

- Repeat task for a set time with the same offensive players. Award points for a give and go or specified type of pass. Rotate roles.
- Repeat, awarding a point for a controlled turn and pass.
- Add a third defender.

EMBEDDED OUTCOME: S2.M1.6 Use this task to point out examples of where students are moving off the ball to get open, and identify how they are doing it.

Guiding questions for students:

- Why is movement important in keeping possession of the ball?
- What part of the foot should you use for passes?
- Why is it important to control the ball before passing?

Student Choices/Differentiation

- Start off with one soccer ball. If people in the middle are not able to steal the ball or the four are not moving around enough, add a second ball.
- If one person is constantly in the center, give her tips based on what she is doing to help her become more successful.

What to Look For

- Are students using proper passing techniques?
- Is every student getting involved?
- Are students moving around to get open or staying in the same spot?

Instructional Task: Shooting on Goal

■ PRACTICE TASK

Without a goalie, have students practice shooting on the modified goal from 15 feet (4.6 m) away. Play with three or four students to a goal.

One student waits for the kicked ball. The passer dribbles to a point, passes the ball to the shooter, and then waits for his turn to shoot. The shooter collects or traps the ball, shoots on goal, and then jogs next to the goal to retrieve the next shot. The student who was waiting for the ball is now the passer.

Extensions

- After students have had success, let them start from the center and then move the spot to the left and right for angle shooting.
- Repeat, adding a passive defender.

- Repeat with a passer. Receiver collects the ball and then shoots.
- Repeat, adding a semi-active defender.

Guiding questions for students:

- What part of the foot should you be kicking with?
- Why is the follow-through important for your shot?

Extensions

- Students can use a teacher-generated checklist on dribbling, passing, and shooting.
- Students may use a flip camera or other video device to record peers' performances.

EMBEDDED OUTCOME: S4.M3.6 During the peer assessment, students should show self-responsibility by implementing corrective feedback from a checklist scored by their peers.

Refinements

Make sure that students are using the correct form in dribbling, passing, and shooting.

Student Choices/Differentiation

- If students are struggling, have them take more time to set up their shots, and go over how to kick the ball.
- Use a passive defender instead of a semi-active one, according to skill level.
- Students may move back to 20 to 25 feet (6 to 7.5 m) if they make the shot continually.
- Students can use non-dominant foot if they are ready for a more advanced skill.

What to Look For

- Are students using the critical elements for shooting?
- How is the accuracy of the students' shots at different angles?
- Which students are able to shoot with both feet?

Formal and Informal Assessments

Exit slip: List two or three critical elements of proper defensive positions or tactics.

Closure

- Discuss with students what they learned from the peer assessment. Demonstrate correct elements and what was not always being performed.
- Have students reflect on their shooting and explain how they think it went. Provide feedback as to what you saw, as well.

Reflection

- How are students developing in their passing and dribbling?
- Does it appear that students are practicing to become better?
- How did the shooting practice task go?
- Are students working on the elements to become more accurate while shooting?

Homework

At home or during recess, practice passing, dribbling, and shooting, using the critical elements.

Students should review the rules on the school's physical education website.

Resources

McManama, J., Hicks, L., & Urtel, M. (2010). *Physical education activity handbook.* 12th ed. San Francisco: Benjamin Cummings.

Internet keyword search: "passing and receiving in soccer," "shooting on goals in soccer"

LESSON 4: THROW-INS AND TRANSITIONS

Grade-Level Outcomes

Primary Outcomes

Creates open space with offensive tactics: Executes at least one of the following offensive tactics to create open space: moves to open space without the ball; uses a variety of passes, pivots and fakes; give and go. (S2.M2.6)

Transitions: Transitions from offense to defense or defense to offense by recovering quickly. (S2.M6.6)

Embedded Outcome

Working with others: Accepts differences among classmates in physical development, maturation and varying skill levels by providing encouragement and positive feedback. (S4.M4.6)

Lesson Objectives

The learner will:
- know how and when to perform a throw-in.
- create open space by applying the skills learned during pin soccer.
- transition from offense to defense and defense to offense quickly.

Equipment and Materials

- 1 soccer ball for every 2 students
- 2 pins and 1 soccer ball for every field

Introduction

Keep studying the rules of soccer. Today, we will learn how to perform throw-ins and when they occur.

Explain and then have students model how to perform throw-ins. Discuss with students how they will apply the skills they have learned thus far in a modified game. Explain how they will play pin soccer, including the rules. Review the skills and answer any questions.

Instructional Task: Throw-Ins

■ PRACTICE TASK

Students learn how to throw the ball into play and how to collect the throw-in. Group students in partners about 5 yards or meters apart:
- One partner throws the ball in and the other uses his body and feet to trap the ball.
- Once the receiver gains possession of the ball, he switches roles and performs a throw-in.

Extension

Collect the throw-in when the ball is not thrown at the feet. (Players use the body, chest, torso, and legs to drop the ball to the ground to collect it.)

Refinement

Remind students to drag the foot and keep it on the ground.

Guiding questions for students:

- Why is it important to step while throwing in?
- When collecting the throw-in, what part of your body can you use?
- When performing throw-ins, where are you aiming and why?

EMBEDDED OUTCOME: S4.M4.6. Discuss with students the differences in skill level that classmates might have in physical development, maturation, and varying skill levels. Provide opportunities in this task for students to offer classmates encouragement and positive feedback.

Student Choices/Differentiation

- If students are struggling with stepping, have them work on throwing the ball with their arms only.
- For lower-skilled students, have them focus on stepping and dragging the foot without the ball.

What to Look For

- Are students using correct technique and making legal throw-ins?
- How are they collecting the throw-ins?

Instructional Task: Creating Open Space

▧ PRACTICE TASK

In grids, four students move throughout the grid, finding open areas to pass and receive passes.

Using the traditional pass with the inside of the foot, students pass to open areas or lead the person they are passing to toward an open area.

Students also practice long passes. Using the laces of the shoe as the contact point, they swing with power to move the ball a greater distance to open up space or get the ball away from close defenders.

Students use the heel or sole of the shoe to pass the ball backward, away from defenders.

Extension

One or two students in the grid become defenders trying to get the ball away, as the other three make passes to create space.

Guiding questions for students:

- How does each pass help create space?
- What changes does adding defenders make?

Student Choices/Differentiation

- Extend the grid size when adding the defensive person.
- Focus on one type of pass if a student is struggling to perform one or more.

What to Look For

- Are students using correct technique for the passes they are intending?
- Are they able to create open space with their passes?
- Is there a pass that needs to be practiced more or retaught?

Instructional Task: Pin Soccer

▧ PRACTICE TASK

Put one pin on each side of the field about a quarter way up the field, with a 15 × 15-foot (4.5 × 4.5 m) area around the pin that no one may enter. In teams of four or five, students try to knock over the other team's pin by kicking the ball. If the ball goes out of bounds, students put it back into play by throw-in.

When a pin is knocked down, the scoring team immediately drops back on defense, and the defensive team goes on attack. Emphasize transitioning from offense to defense and back again.

Games are played for 4 to 5 minutes, and then teams rotate to a new field.

Extension

Limit the number of dribbles players may take after receiving the ball. That forces them to pass, creating a challenge for the ball handler and creating greater need for effective offensive transitioning.

Refinements

- When on offense, continue to move around and into areas where defenders are not.
- While passing, position the pass to an area that helps a teammate find an open area to continue to move the ball down the field, or take an open shot using the passing techniques from the previous practice task.

Guiding questions for students:

- Why is it important to find or create open space?
- How can this be done?
- What are some key points for transitioning from offense to defense and defense to offense?
- How does the defender need to be positioned to cover more than one offensive play?
- Where are you aiming when throwing in and why?

Student Choices/Differentiation

- Reduce or increase the size of the playing zone where the pin is located, based on students' ability to knock the pin over.
- Make team size smaller to increase the number of touches for each student.

What to Look For

- Are students using the correct throw-in techniques? (See following evaluation sheet.)
- Are students using the skills that they have learned to move into or create open space?
- Are students switching from offense to defense and knowing what to do?

Formal and Informal Assessments

- Informal assessment
- Exit slip: List two or three critical elements of transitions from offense to defense or defense to offense.

Closure

- Review with students how to perform the throw-in and when it occurs.
- Discuss with students how they applied the skills and how they worked together as a team.

Reflection

- Do students understand how to throw the ball in and when to do so?
- How did the teams work together on offense and on defense?
- What can you take away from this to discuss with students in the next lessons?

Homework

Review the rules of soccer.

At home or during recess, continue to work on the skills and critical elements that we have learned (especially the different kicks and transitions).

Resources

Internet keyword search: "types of kicks," "transitions in invasion sports"

THROW-IN EVALUATION

Name: _____ Period: _____

Throw-In Technique

Given multiple attempts, the thrower performs the following consistently:

1. Keeps two hands on ball until release. _____ Yes _____ No

2. While preparing to throw, ball is in hands in front of body. Thrower then brings ball over and behind head as he or she steps forward. _____ Yes _____ No

3. As the thrower steps forward, he brings ball over the head with both hands. _____ Yes _____ No

4. Thrower follows through with arms extended forward from behind head toward target, while stepping forward. _____ Yes _____ No

5. Both feet are on the ground at all times; dragging one foot is allowed while stepping forward. _____ Yes _____ No

Score out of 5: _____

Throw-In Attempts

Total _____ of 12

11-12 = A   9-10 = B   7-9=C 6 = D 1-5 =F

	Attempt 1	Attempt 2	Attempt 3
Grip: Two hands placed on ball until release.			
While getting ready to throw, thrower has ball in hands in front of body; thrower then brings ball over and behind head, elbows bent at 90 degrees.			
Follows through with arms extended forward from behind head toward target, while stepping forward.			
Both feet are on the ground at all times. Dragging one foot is allowed while stepping, bringing momentum forward.			

From R.J. Doan, L.C. MacDonald, and S. Chepko, eds., 2017, *Lesson planning for middle school physical education* (Reston, VA: SHAPE America; Champaign, IL: Human Kinetics).

LESSON 5:
RULES AND MODIFIED GAME PLAY

Grade-Level Outcomes

Primary Outcomes

Creating space with movement: Creates open space by using locomotor movements (e.g., walking, running, jumping & landing) in combination with movement (e.g., varying pathways; change of speed, direction or space). (S2.M1.6)

Reducing space by changing size & shape: Reduces open space on defense by making the body larger and reducing passing angles. (S2.M4.6)

Rules & etiquette: Identifies the rules and etiquette for physical activities/games and dance activities. (S4.M6.6)

Offensive skills: Performs the following offensive skills without defensive pressure: pivot, give & go, and fakes. (S1.M7.6)

Embedded Outcome

Working with others: Demonstrates self-responsibility by implementing specific corrective feedback to improve performance. (S4.M3.6)

Lesson Objectives

The learner will:

- demonstrate appropriate offensive and defensive strategies to create or reduce space during modified game.
- demonstrate basic offensive skills without defensive pressure.
- demonstrate basic soccer rules by performing skits.

Equipment and Materials

- Fields with goals for groups of five
- One ball for each group
- Video devices

Introduction

In today's activities, students will work together on offense and defensive strategies, as well as on applying the skills they have learned to games of 3 v 2 soccer. Discuss and demonstrate the importance of creating open space on offense and how to do it.

Instructional Task: Dribbling and Passing

■ PRACTICE TASK

Play in grids, with two soccer balls for five students. All five students work together to apply dribbling and passing skills. They stay spread out, get open, and create open space.

Students with the ball look for someone to pass to. Students who don't have the ball move to receive a pass.

Extensions

- Make the playing space larger and have students add a pivot (turn), give and go, and fakes.
- Add a semi-active defender who can intercept passes but not take the ball off the foot of a player.

Guiding questions for students:
- How are the different types of passes helpful?
- How will they be helpful in 3 v 2 or in game play?
- During the extension, we added offensive tactic skills. What was the most difficult and easiest to perform?

Refinements
- Quick passes: A student should try to pass the ball to a teammate within 5 seconds of receiving it. If possible, use one touch to receive and pass.
- Students should be practicing and applying the three types of passes they worked on during the last class.

Student Choices/Differentiation
- Use only one ball if students are confused or not able to focus on the person passing to them with two balls in play.
- Have students focus on one skill to improve on rather than three types of passes and different ways to create space.

What to Look For
- Are students able to use different types of passes to create space?
- Are students demonstrating proper technique for passing?
- Are students able to add a pivot, give and go, and fakes?

Instructional Task: 3 v 2 Soccer

■ **PRACTICE TASK**

Using one soccer ball and a modified field with one goal, three students work together applying dribbling, passing, trapping, and shooting skills that they have learned to create open space and score.

The two students on defense work together to fill in the passing lanes to steal the ball away or prevent a goal.

After the ball is taken away or a goal is made, have students switch positions.

Extensions
- Repeat the activity but even up the sides.
- Repeat the activity but go to 4 v 3 in a larger grid.
- Add a couple of students to each grid. Their role is to evaluate their peers using a teacher-generated checklist with the critical elements. Students can use a video device or not.

EMBEDDED OUTCOME: S4.M3.6. Discuss with students ways to implement your feedback or feedback from peers to improve performance.

Refinements
- Limit the number of dribbles a student may take to force passing and getting teammates involved to create open space.
- Set a minimum number of passes that students must make before shooting a goal.
- If students are struggling to create space (e.g., bunching together; one person is dribbling everywhere or not working with others), divide the field in thirds so that each person on offense has to stay within her length of the field. Defense can go anywhere.

Guiding questions for students:
- Ask students to explain how they are working together to create open space.
- Ask for examples that lead to open space and examples that did not lead to open space.

Student Choices/Differentiation

Size of the field may be smaller or larger based on ability.

What to Look For

- Are students moving to create open space?
- Are students moving close to one another or away from each other?
- Are students moving into a space to give themselves an advantage?
- What skills are students most comfortable with to create open space? What will need more work?
- Are students able to take the ball away?

Instructional Task: Review the Rules of Soccer

■ PRACTICE TASK

Go over the rules that you've posted on the school's physical education website.

Extension

In groups of three or four, students draw a rule out of a hat. They are to come up with a skit that demonstrates the importance of the rule and how it applies to soccer.

Refinements

Make sure students are under control and performing their skits safely.

Student Choices/Differentiation

Modify as needed on an individual basis using pictures, videos, and demonstrations.

What to Look For

Do students know the rules from the questions asked?

Formal and Informal Assessments

Exit slip: Explain three rules that are important in soccer.

Closure

- Provide examples from modified game and discuss how students did with creating open space and working together on offense.
- Have students explain and provide examples of what they did on defense to be successful.
- What are ways you successfully implemented feedback to improve skills?

Reflection

- What skills are students missing or struggling with on offense and defense?
- How did students rotate through the grids?
- Were students working together to apply offensive and defensive strategies?

Homework

Review the rules of soccer to prepare for the upcoming games and quiz.
Practice passing, dribbling, shooting, and throw-ins.

Resources

Internet keyword search: "soccer rules," "offensive and defensive soccer skills"

LESSON 6: DEFENDING

Grade-Level Outcomes

Primary Outcome

Reducing open space by changing size & shape: Reduces open space on defense by making the body larger and reducing passing angles. (S2.M4.6)

Embedded Outcomes

Social interaction: Demonstrates respect for self by asking for help and helping others in various physical activities. (S5.M6.8)

Shooting on goal: Shoots on goal with power in a dynamic environment as appropriate to the activity. (S1.M10.6)

Lesson Objectives

The learner will:

- demonstrate knowledge of the rules and strategies of playing goalkeeper to prevent goals and keep the goalkeeper safe.
- learn to reduce passing angles on defense.
- demonstrate the knowledge and skills to apply the rules, skills, and strategies during modified soccer games.

Equipment and Materials

- 1 soccer ball for every 5 students
- 1 goal for every 5 students
- Marked fields with 2 goals for every 8 students
- 1 soccer ball per field
- Jerseys for each field

Introduction

Today, we will focus on defensive play in soccer and will begin playing modified games. Before we begin our games, we will review the rules and also practice shooting on goal with a goalie.

Discuss the rules, and explain and demonstrate strategies of the goalkeeper position and ways to keep the goalkeeper safe.

Instructional Task: Closing Space

■ PRACTICE TASK

Demonstrate the defensive position for off-ball players.

In grids, play 2 v 2, with offensive players scoring when they cross the end line. Defender on the ball must try to take it from the offensive player, while the off-ball player reduces the passing angle and anticipates the pass. Defensive players score when they intercept the ball. Set time (45 seconds) and switch.

Extensions

- Demonstrate the position for one pass away and two passes away.
- Repeat with 3 v 3.

Student Choices/Differentiation

- To aid defenders, make the grid smaller.
- To challenge defenders, increase the size of the grid or add an extra offensive player.

What to Look For

- While on offense, are players moving to get open without the ball?
- Can defenders anticipate the passing angle?
- Are defenders playing the ball closely?
- Are the off-ball defenders diagonal to the ball and anticipating the pass?

Instructional Task: Modified Game of 4 v 4

■ PRACTICE TASK

Review the rules of soccer, including any modified rules for the activity.

Play 4-minute games of 4 v 4, applying the rules and strategies learned. Teams score when they pass and receive the ball over the end line.

After the 4 minutes, have teams rotate to another field; have teams who won play each other and those who lost play each other. Keeping like teams together should keep engagement high and skill levels matched.

Extensions

- Repeat, limiting the number of dribbles.
- Repeat, requiring a minimum number of passes to score.
- Repeat, adding a neutral post to increase transition opportunities.

Guiding questions for students:

- Is your team staying spread, working together, passing, and communicating to move the ball down the field?
- On defense, are you communicating and filling in the passing or dribbling lanes, making it difficult for the offense to score?

EMBEDDED OUTCOME: S5.M6.8. Before the games, review the advantages of asking for help and helping others learn the game of soccer (especially with regard to rules). Remind students that it's okay if they do not know the rules, skills, or tactics well *only* if they ask for help.

Student Choices/Differentiation

- Students choose own teams.
- Adjust size of game space.
- Allow choice of ball.

What to Look For

- While on offense, are players moving to get open without the ball?
- Are defenders playing the ball closely?
- Are the off-ball defenders diagonal to the ball and anticipating the pass?

Instructional Task: Goalkeeping

■ PRACTICE TASK

Explain the keeper's role and rules.

Emphasize reduction of passing angles as an extension of defense.

Set up stations with mini-goals for students who want to try this position. Students who don't want to try this position continue in their modified games.

- Stopping balls on the ground: Students dribble softer balls and shoot (half speed) along the ground to allow keeper to practice stopping low shots. Release must be at least 10 yards or meters out (mark with cone). Shooter moves to the side of the practice area. Keeper picks up the ball and throws to shooter. Rotate keeper after five attempts.

- Stopping balls in the air: Students dribble softer balls and shoot (half speed) at waist or shoulder height to allow keeper to practice stopping balls in the air. Release must be at least 10 yards or meters away. Shooter moves to the side of the practice area. Keeper picks up the ball and throws to shooter. Rotate keeper after five attempts.

Extensions

- Add a defender on the shooter.
- Repeat at game speed.
- Add a pass before the shot.

EMBEDDED OUTCOME: S1.M10.6. Use the keeper stations for students to practice their shooting when they are not in goal. Emphasize aiming for open space.

Guiding questions for students:

- As goalie, when and why did you change positions or move?
- As goalie, what do you need to do to protect yourself?
- What advantage does passing before shooting give the offense?

EMBEDDED OUTCOME: S5.M6.8. Before this activity begins, remind students about working together to help one another improve in all of the skills they are working on.

Student Choices/Differentiation

- Throw or roll balls instead of shooting.
- Adjust speed and distance of shots.

What to Look For

- Are the goalies putting themselves in a position to stop the ball?
- Are they coming out to reduce the angle?
- Are they releasing the ball with control to the player on the side?

Instructional Task: Soccer Quiz

■ PRACTICE TASK

Administer a handout cognitive test that covers rules, skills, and strategy taught throughout the module.

Student Choices/Differentiation

- If needed, pull students aside to read questions from the quiz aloud before or after class.
- Modify assessment, as needed, to address student needs.

What to Look For

Students demonstrate that they know the terms, rules, and strategies of soccer.

Formal and Informal Assessments

Knowledge test of the rules, strategy, and scoring

Closure

- Review the role of the goalie and strategies to stop shots and keep the goalie safe.
- Discuss how students worked together during the game and how they applied the skills and strategies learned.
- Inform students that you will assess their skills in the next class and share the assessment with them.

Reflection

What skills are students missing, and what do they need to spend more time on next class?

Homework

Practice passing and collecting to prepare for formal assessment next class.

Resources

Internet keyword search: "soccer fundamentals," "skills and rules of soccer," "basic rules"

LESSON 7:
ASSESSMENT AND 4 V 4 GAME PLAY

Grade-Level Outcomes

Primary Outcome

Passing & receiving: Passes and receives with feet in combination with locomotor patterns of running and change of direction & speed with competency in invasion games such as soccer or speedball. (S1.M4.7)

Embedded Outcome

Social interaction: Demonstrates respect for self and others in activities and games by following the rules, encouraging others and playing in the spirit of the game or activity. (S5.M6.6)

Lesson Objectives

The learner will:

- demonstrate passing with correct form.
- demonstrate a legal throw-in, applying the critical elements.
- demonstrate how to collect the ball in a variety of ways.

Equipment and Materials

- 1 ball for every 3 students
- Marked fields for teams of 4
- 1 set of jerseys for each field

Introduction

Today, you will demonstrate your ability to pass, collect, and throw in using correct form.

Review the critical elements with students and explain the lesson.

When we are finished with this, we will continue playing 4 v 4.

Review with students what they did well and what they can work on to improve.

Instructional Task:
Assessment of Collecting, Passing, and Throw-Ins

■ PRACTICE TASK

Students perform throw-ins, collecting, and passing in groups of three.

The assessments can be scored live or recorded to be scored at a later time.

Extension

To make the assessment more game-like, add a passive or semi-active defender to the passer and receiver.

Refinement

Before they begin, talk with students about helping one another by providing feedback to help other students improve their skills.

First: Partner A performs a correct throw-in to partner B. Partner B uses appropriate technique to collect the ball and once collected, pass the ball quickly to partner C.

Second: Partner C then traps the ball and starts the process over but can now perform a throw-in to either partner as students continue to demonstrate their ability to throw in, trap, and pass.

Student Choices/Differentiation

If a student is continually receiving a bad throw-in or pass, provide one for her so she may have a better opportunity to demonstrate how to collect.

What to Look For

Using the assessment checklist, identify which critical elements students are proficient in and which ones they need to continue to work on.

Instructional Task: 4 v 4

■ PRACTICE TASK

In teams of four, students play 4-minute modified soccer games using the skills and strategies that they have learned during the module. Students self-officiate.

Refinement

Stop the game and discuss any rules that need clarification.

Guiding questions for students:

- How are you working together to try to score?
- How are you working together to defend?

EMBEDDED OUTCOME: S5.M6.6. Talk with students about following the rules while encouraging fellow classmates to help make soccer fun and enjoyable.

Student Choices/Differentiation

- Students can choose to practice any of the practice tasks from previous lessons.
- Students may choose their playing partners.

What to Look For

- How are students implementing the skills that they have been learning?
- On offense, are students creating open space through dribbling and applying different types of passes?
- On defense, are students reducing open space and getting in passing lanes?
- Are students working with and encouraging one another?

Formal and Informal Assessments

Formal skills assessment on trapping, passing, and throw-ins (teacher-created rubric or checklist)

Closure

- Discuss with students in general how the assessment went and what you observed. Model for students what they did well and what they still need to work on.
- Discuss how the 4 v 4 games went and skills or rules that need clarification. Remind students about evaluation of officiating skills in next class.

Reflection

- How did the skills assessment go?
- How are students doing at self-officiating their soccer games?
- What will you need to discuss again before students are evaluated on their ability to officiate their own games?

Homework

Review the rules of soccer, and practice at home or during recess time any individual skills that you need to work on.

Resources

Dougherty, N.J. (Ed.) (2010). *Physical activity & sport for the secondary school student.* 6th ed. Reston, VA: National Association for Sport and Physical Education.

McManama, J., Hicks, L., & Urtel, M. (2010). *Physical education activity handbook.* 12th ed. San Francisco: Benjamin Cummings.

LESSON 8: OFFICIATING AND GAME PLAY

Grade-Level Outcomes

Primary Outcome

Rules & etiquette: Demonstrates knowledge of rules and etiquette by self-officiating modified physical activities and games or following parameters to create or modify a dance. (S4.M6.7)

Embedded Outcome

Working with others: Responds appropriately to participants' ethical and unethical behavior during physical activity by using rules and guidelines for resolving conflicts. (S4.M4.8)

Lesson Objectives

The learner will demonstrate sufficient knowledge of skills and rules to participate in and self-officiate soccer games.

Equipment and Materials

- Marked fields with 2 goals for every 8 students
- 1 soccer ball per field
- Jerseys for each field

Introduction

Today is our last day of soccer. During our games today, you will be assessed on your ability to self-officiate the soccer games while demonstrating your knowledge of the rules by applying them and holding others to them.

Instructional Task: Officiating

■ PRACTICE TASK

Review general soccer rules with students.

Show video clips of soccer officials.

Have students practice basic calls (offside, goal, hand ball, etc.).

Extension

Have groups of students watch video clips of game play and try to make the call. Discuss the call with the groups and the difficulty of making the call.

Student Choices/Differentiation

- Have examples of videos with calls to demonstrate for students who are struggling.
- Use Internet searches for examples.

What to Look For

Students have a basic understanding of officiating soccer.

Instructional Task: 4 vs 4

■ PRACTICE TASK

Students continue with their 4 v 4 games.

Games are 4 to 5 minutes long, with assessment occurring during game play.

After time is up, teams rotate to play teams with the same ability level.

Extension

During game play, assess students on their officiating skills by their ability to hold themselves and others to the rules of soccer.

EMBEDDED OUTCOME: S4.M3.8. While students are officiating, remind them to work with others by responding appropriately and following the rules of the game.

Student Choices/Differentiation

- Adjust teams, as needed, for appropriate skill level.
- Modify assessment on an individual basis for individual circumstances.

What to Look For

- Are students applying the rules of soccer correctly?
- If someone does not follow the rules, are students holding the person accountable or letting it go?

Formal and Informal Assessments

- Formal skills assessment on trapping, passing, and throw-ins (teacher-created rubric or checklist)
- Self-reflection on officiating experiences

Closure

- Discuss with students what you saw today in their ability to self-officiate and demonstrate their knowledge of soccer.
- Describe the growth that you've observed over this unit in both knowledge and skill.
- Talk about how students interacted together and areas in which they can improve moving forward into the next unit.

Reflection

- How did the unit go?
- What did students pick up quickly, and why might that be?
- What might students need more time or practice on the next time this is taught?
- Did you have enough equipment or might you need something else or more next time?

Homework

Have students write a self-reflection on their officiating experience. Prompts:

What did you like about officiating?

What didn't you like?

Was it more difficult or easier than you thought it would be? Why?

Have students review the information from the school's physical education website before the next class about the upcoming module.

Resources

Dougherty, N.J. (Ed.) (2010). *Physical activity & sport for the secondary school student.* 6th ed. Reston, VA: National Association for Sport and Physical Education.

McManama, J., Hicks, L., & Urtel, M. (2010). *Physical education activity handbook.* 12th ed. San Francisco: Benjamin Cummings.

CHAPTER 6

Applying Students' Skills and Knowledge to Net and Wall Games

For most students, striking is the last fundamental motor skill to mature (SHAPE America, 2014, p. 85). Students need multiple opportunities to practice with different-sized implements (hands, short- and long-handled implements) as well as objects to strike (balls, balloons, etc.) to improve. This chapter provides a model for teaching striking that can be applied to net and wall games.

The Volleyball Module focuses on the two most important volleyball skills for students to learn: forearm pass and serve. The practice tasks in this module focus on encouraging students to become proficient at both of these critical striking skills instead of trying to introduce them to all volleyball skills. The Pickleball Module provides opportunity to strike with a short implement. The Badminton Module provides practice tasks with multiple opportunities to improve striking with a long implement. All modules provide practice tasks designed to progress from controlled to game-like environments.

For easy reference, each module begins with a block plan chart of the Grade-Level Outcomes addressed within the module. Each module addresses multiple National Standards, although most of the primary outcomes reside under Standard 1. For the Volleyball Module, the main focus is on Standard 1 outcomes, but the lessons also place a strong emphasis on Standard 4 through the use of embedded outcomes. These outcomes are related to working with others, responsibility, and safety while engaging in physical activity. The Pickleball Module emphasizes executing legal serves (Outcome S1.M12) and using a mature forehand and backhand stroke (Outcome S1.M14). The last module, for badminton, focuses on executing legal serves (Outcome S1.M12); striking with a mature overhand pattern (Outcome S1.M13); and demonstrating the mature forehand and backhand strokes (Outcome S1.M14). The module also has students create and maintain a physical activity log (Outcome S3.M16) for tracking physical activity during lessons and outside of class. In the Pickleball and Badminton Modules, you will find many outcomes embedded from Standards 2, 4, and 5. The most important component for improving striking is the number of opportunities that students have to make contact with a moving object (SHAPE America, 2014, p. 85). All three modules in this chapter maximize practice opportunities to improve striking and playing tactics in net and wall games.

VOLLEYBALL MODULE

Lessons in this module were contributed by Robert J. Doan, assistant professor of physical education in the University of Southern Mississippi's School of Kinesiology.

Grade-Level Outcomes Addressed, by Lesson	1	2	3	4	5	6	7	8
Standard 1. The physically literate individual demonstrates competency in a variety of motor skills and movement patterns.								
Performs a legal underhand serve with control for net/wall games such as badminton, volleyball or pickleball. (S1.M12.6)		P	P					
Executes consistently (at least 70% of the time) a legal underhand serve to a predetermined target for net/wall games such as badminton, volleyball or pickleball. (S1.M12.7)					P			
Executes consistently (at least 70% of the time) a legal underhand serve for distance and accuracy for net/wall games such as badminton, volleyball or pickleball. (S1.M12.8)						P	P	P
Strikes with a mature overhand pattern in a nondynamic environment for net/wall games such as volleyball, handball, badminton or tennis. (S1.M13.6)							P	
Transfers weight with correct timing for the striking pattern. (S1.M15.6)			E					
Two-hand-volleys with control in a variety of practice tasks. (S1.M17.6)	P	P	P					
Two-hand-volleys with control in a dynamic environment. (S1.M17.7)	P	P	P	P	P	P		
Two-hand-volleys with control in a small-sided game. (S1.M17.8)							P	P
Standard 2. The physically literate individual applies knowledge of concepts, principles, strategies and tactics related to movement and performance.								
Creates open space in net/wall games with a short-handled implement by varying force and direction. (S2.M7.6)				P				
Creates open space in net/wall games with either a long- or short-handled implement by varying force or direction, or by moving opponent from side to side and/or forward and back. (S2.M7.8)						P		
Reduces offensive options for opponents by returning to mid-court position. (S2.M8.6)						E		
Selects offensive shot based on opponent's location (hit where opponent is not). (S2.M8.7)					P			
Standard 3. The physically literate individual demonstrates the knowledge and skills to achieve and maintain a health-enhancing level of physical activity and fitness.								
Standard 4. The physically literate individual exhibits responsible personal and social behavior that respects self and others.								
Exhibits personal responsibility by using appropriate etiquette, demonstrating respect for facilities and exhibiting safe behaviors. (S4.M1.6)						E		
Exhibits responsible social behaviors by cooperating with classmates, demonstrating inclusive behaviors and supporting classmates. (S4.M1.7)	E							
Demonstrates self-responsibility by implementing specific corrective feedback to improve performance. (S4.M3.6)		E						
Provides encouragement and feedback to peers without prompting from the teacher. (S4.M3.8)							E	
Cooperates with a small group of classmates during adventure activities, game play or team-building activities. (S4.M5.6)				E				E
Standard 5. The physically literate individual recognizes the value of physical activity for health, enjoyment, challenge, self-expression and/or social interaction.								

P = Primary; E = Embedded

LESSON 1: INTRODUCTION TO THE FOREARM PASS

Grade-Level Outcomes

Primary Outcomes

Two-hand volley: Two-hand-volleys with control in a variety of practice tasks. (S1.M17.6)

Two-hand volley: Two-hand-volleys with control in a dynamic environment. (S1.M17.7)

Embedded Outcome

Personal responsibility: Exhibits responsible social behaviors by cooperating with classmates, demonstrating inclusive behaviors and supporting classmates. (S4.M1.7)

Lesson Objectives

The learner will:

- demonstrate the proper hand, arm, and body positioning for the forearm pass.
- perform a forearm pass from a dropped ball.
- perform a forearm pass from a ball tossed predictably to the performer.
- perform a forearm pass with a ball tossed unpredictably to the performer.

Equipment and Materials

- Volleyballs (mix of regulation and trainer volleyballs), 1 for every 2 or 3 students
- Cones, 4 for each group of students

Introduction

Today, we are going to start our module on volleyball.

Show a video clip of Olympic indoor volleyball.

As you can see, volleyball is a fast and fun sport to play. We will begin our module with one of the basic and most important skills, the forearm pass.

Instructional Task:
Learning Hand Position for Forearm Pass

■ PRACTICE TASK

Teacher demonstrates proper arm, hand, feet, and body placement for the forearm pass.

In performing the forearm pass, what you are really doing is giving the volleyball a platform to rebound.

Extensions

- In pairs, one partner practices the stance while the other partner checks for proper positioning.
- Peer assessment: Use a checklist with the critical elements of the forearm pass position.

Refinement

To increase success, students should make a flat surface with their forearms.

Guiding questions for students:

- Where is your forearm?
- Why are forearms important in volleyball?
- What happens if your forearms are not flat? (Less control over where the ball goes.)

Student Choices/Differentiation

- Students can refer to the poster displayed in the gymnasium.
- Students can review the proper mechanics video.
- If students have success, they can mimic hitting a volleyball from their stance.

What to Look For

- Students make a fist with the left hand, thumb on top, and wrap the right hand around the fist, laying thumbs flat and parallel, with wrists and elbows hyperextended. This creates a platform for contacting the ball.
- Arms are away from body, feet shoulder-width apart, and knees bent (ready position).

Instructional Task:
Forearm Pass With Emphasis on Shoulder Shrug

▓ PRACTICE TASK

Demonstrate the following: Performer kneels on one knee; partner holds the volleyball directly above performer's "platform"; ball is dropped and performer shrugs the ball back to tosser.

Guiding questions for students:

- Did you swing your arms? (No.)
- Why do you think you needed only to shrug your shoulders instead of swinging your arms? (Because of the force of the ball from gravity.)
- When the ball is coming with a lot of force (spiked ball), do you think you need to swing your arms or shrug your shoulders? (Shrug.) Why? (When the ball comes with force, the greater the force, the higher the rebound.)

Extension

In pairs, students take turns with the forearm pass shrug drill.

Refinement

Make sure that students are shrugging their shoulders and not swinging their arms.

Student Choices/Differentiation

- Performers may begin in a chair instead of kneeling; partner dropping ball may need to stand on a chair.
- Performers can choose a volleyball trainer or regulation-sized volleyball.
- Students may challenge themselves to shrug the ball directly to the tosser's hands.

What to Look For

- Proper hand and arm positioning before ball is dropped.
- Little to no arm movement (mostly shoulders).

Instructional Task: Forearm Pass in Grids

▓ PRACTICE TASK

In grids, students work in pairs as you assign tasks in a controlled environment, moving toward an uncontrolled environment.

Call out a command. Students practice the task five times and then switch so that their partners can perform the same command. Call out another command.

Partners must cooperate by making good tosses. Partners also should encourage each other.

First: Toss the volleyball so that your partner can easily bump (shrug) it back to you for five hits.

Second: Toss the volleyball so that your partner has to take a quick step to the right to hit the ball.

Third: Toss the volleyball so that your partner has to take a quick step to the left to hit the ball.

Fourth: Toss the volleyball so that your partner has to take a quick step forward to hit the ball.

Fifth: Toss the volleyball so that your partner has to take a quick step back while still hitting with a forearm pass.

Extension

We now will move into a more game-like, or uncontrolled, setting. The partner tossing now should toss the ball using any of the previous commands, but do not let the hitter know which one you are going to use. Make sure that you still are tossing at the midsection and are using only the forehand or backhand shot. Switch after five tosses.

Repeat this extension until many students have had success.

Refinements

Stop the task and remind students of any of the following common errors:

- Students are shrugging their shoulders.
- Students are bending their knees and getting their bottoms down.
- Students assume the ready position before the toss.
- Tossers are not making appropriate tosses.

EMBEDDED OUTCOME: S4.M1.7 A good forearm pass begins with a good toss. Discuss with students the importance of cooperating with classmates and supporting them while they learn the skill by providing the best opportunities to learn with respectable tosses.

Student Choices/Differentiation

- Encourage students to discuss the distance that the performers feel will best help them learn.
- If the class is struggling with an extension, stay at that particular extension for a couple more rounds before moving to the next.
- Performers can choose a volleyball trainer or regulation-sized volleyball.
- Challenge higher-skilled students to pass ball directly to tosser.

What to Look For

- Toss is appropriate.
- Contact point is the forearm, with arms extended away from body.
- Little to no arm swing.

Formal and Informal Assessments

- Informal assessments
- Peer assessments: critical elements of forearm pass checklist

Closure

- What are the critical elements of the forearm pass?
- Why should we shrug our shoulders instead of swinging our arms to hit?
- In what ways did you help your peers improve their volleyball skills today?

Great job on the first day of volleyball. We will review the forearm pass in our next class and learn the underhand serve.

Reflection

- Did students have enough time to practice the forearm pass today?
- Were most students shrugging their shoulders?
- When students moved to uncontrolled tosses, did they maintain good form?
- Did students give good tosses to their partners?

Homework

If you have a volleyball or a soft ball at home, practice any of the forearm pass tasks that we performed in today's class. You also can view the videos and handouts on the school's physical education website if you need help with the critical elements of the forearm pass.

Resources

McManama, J., Hicks, L., & Urtel, M. (2010). *Physical education activity handbook.* 12th ed. San Francisco: Benjamin Cummings.

Internet keyword search: "Olympic volleyball highlights," "forearm pass volleyball"

LESSON 2: REVIEW OF PASS AND INTRODUCTION TO SERVE

Grade-Level Outcomes

Primary Outcomes

Two-hand volley: Two-hand-volleys with control in a variety of practice tasks. (S1.M17.6)

Two-hand volley: Two-hand-volleys with control in a dynamic environment. (S1.M17.7)

Serving: Performs a legal underhand serve with control for net/wall games such as badminton, volleyball or pickleball. (S1.M12.6)

Embedded Outcome

Accepting feedback: Demonstrates self-responsibility by implementing specific corrective feedback to improve performance. (S4.M3.6)

Lesson Objectives

The learner will:

- perform a forearm pass with a ball tossed predictably and unpredictably, with space adjustment, to a target while varying the force of the pass.
- practice the underhand serve movement pattern.

Equipment and Materials

- Volleyballs: mix of foam, trainer, and regulation volleyballs
- Video recorders
- Cones or poly spots for grid boundaries

Introduction

In our previous class, we learned the most important skill, the forearm pass. We will continue to practice this skill as well as learn the underhand serve today. Make sure that you are not sacrificing skill for performance.

Instructional Task: Review Hand Position, Platform, Body Position, and Contact for a Forearm Pass

■ PRACTICE TASK

Check students' positioning in working pairs, as they toss in sets of 10 to review the forearm pass.

Extension

Using flip videos, students work in groups of three or four to perform a peer evaluation with a checklist.

Refinement

Make sure that students have a flat platform and are not swinging their arms to hit the ball (shoulder shrug).

EMBEDDED OUTCOME: S4.M3.6. Discuss with students the importance of self-responsibility for implementing corrective feedback offered by others to improve their performance. It can be difficult to hear at times, but we all need feedback to improve performance.

Student Choices/Differentiation

Performers may choose foam, trainer, or regulation volleyballs.

What to Look For

- Proper hand, arm, and knee positioning.
- Proper contact with volleyball.

Instructional Task: Forearm Pass in Grids Review

■ PRACTICE TASK

Using the same grids from the last class, students practice the forearm pass in grids. The task should move from a controlled to an uncontrolled environment.

Call out a command. Students practice the task five times and then switch so that their partners can perform the same command.

Partners must cooperate by making good tosses. Partners also should encourage each other.

First: Toss the volleyball so that your partner can easily bump (shrug) it back to you for five hits.

Second: Toss the volleyball so that your partner has to take a quick step to the right to hit the ball.

Third: Toss the volleyball so that your partner has to take a quick step to the left to hit the ball.

Fourth: Toss the volleyball so that your partner has to take a quick step forward to hit the ball.

Fifth: Toss the volleyball so that your partner has to take a quick step back while still hitting with a forearm pass.

Extension

We now will move into a more game-like, or uncontrolled, setting. The partner tossing now should toss the ball using any of the previous commands, but do not let the hitter know which one you are going to use.

Refinement

Make sure that students are bending their knees and shrugging their shoulders so that they hit the ball back to partners with control.

Student Choices/Differentiation

- Performers can choose foam, trainer, or regulation volleyballs.
- Students might need to start with one tosser, increasing distance of toss gradually as performer learns first to impart force. Tosser then may decrease distance gradually as performer adjusts forearm pass accordingly.

What to Look For

- Performer should be using legs (stepping forward) and arm shrug to add force from near toss to project ball to target.
- Performer should be absorbing force with arms and body from distance toss to control forearm pass to target.

Instructional Task: Introduction to Serve

■ PRACTICE TASK

- Demonstrate the underhand serve.
- Students mimic the underhand serve.

Extensions

- Peer-assess a partner's striking movement pattern with a checklist and video recorder.
- Have students start exploring serving with a ball in general space.

Refinement

Refine skill by breaking down the movement pattern and stressing critical elements, if needed.

Student Choices/Differentiation

- Students may view a video of the correct movement form.
- Higher-skilled students may show weight transfer.
- Performers may choose foam, trainer, or regulation volleyballs.

What to Look For

- The correct foot is forward.
- Students are swinging arms in a controlled manner.
- Knees are bent.
- Hitting surface is flat.

Formal and Informal Assessments

- Peer checklist with critical elements for the forearm pass.
- Peer assessment: Using a video recorder and checklist, measure critical elements of the underhand serve.

Closure

- Did you feel more comfortable with the forearm pass today?
- Was anyone successful passing the ball without making your partner move?
- Who can name the critical elements of the forearm pass? What about the underhand serve?

Tomorrow, we will practice serving with the ball and how to receive a serve.

Reflection

- Did most of students have success during the forearm pass drill in the controlled environment?
- Did skill level suffer in the uncontrolled environment?
- Are students using the checklist correctly during the peer evaluations?

Homework

If you have a volleyball at home, practice the forearm pass with a family member or friend. To improve your skill, review the critical elements and videos of the forearm pass and underhand serve on the school's physical education website.

Resources

McManama, J., Hicks, L., & Urtel, M. (2010). *Physical education activity handbook.* 12th ed. San Francisco: Benjamin Cummings.

Internet keyword search: "underhand serve volleyball," "forearm pass volleyball," "volleyball for beginners"

LESSON 3: SERVE AND SERVE RECEIVE

Grade-Level Outcomes

Primary Outcomes

Serving: Performs a legal underhand serve with control for net/wall games such as badminton, volleyball or pickleball. (S1.M12.6)

Two-hand volley: Two-hand-volleys with control in a variety of practice tasks. (S1.M17.6)

Two-hand volley: Two-hand-volleys with control in a dynamic environment. (S1.M17.7)

Embedded Outcome

Weight transfer: Transfers weight with correct timing for the striking pattern. (S1.M15.6)

Lesson Objectives

The learner will:

- explore the underhand serve.
- demonstrate successful digs (serve receive) from a partner toss.
- combine the serve and serve receive, with a partner, in a modified game.

Equipment and Materials

- Volleyballs: mix of foam, trainer, and regulation volleyballs
- Nets
- Cones

Introduction

A regulation game of volleyball cannot be played without the serve. Many coaches believe that the key to winning the game is effective serving and serve receiving. In today's class, we will explore serving and serve receiving.

Instructional Task:
Review Underhand Serve Motor Pattern

■ PRACTICE TASK

Demonstrate and review the underhand serve.

Extension

Have students practice the underhand serve motor pattern without the ball.

Student Choices/Differentiation

Students may view video or critical elements provided.

What to Look For

- The correct foot is forward.
- Students are swinging arms in a controlled manner.
- Knees are bent.
- Hitting surface is flat.

Instructional Task: Explore Underhand Serving

■ PRACTICE TASK

Divide class in half. One half stands on one side of the gym while the other half stands on the other side. Students practice the underhand serve on their own for 5 minutes.

Guiding questions for students:

- Did anyone serve the ball directly where you wanted to?
- What are some possible reasons why the ball did not go where you wanted it to go? (Arm crossing over the body, improper follow-through, not enough strength, etc.)

Extension

Choose one of the reasons that students provided for an improper serve and discuss why it is important. Follow the discussion with practice trials focused on the reason discussed.

Refinement

Whichever critical feature is being worked on, make sure to stress the element during the task. An example: If students are not following through, have them perform the serve and follow through (point) to the target after contact.

EMBEDDED OUTCOME: S1.M15.6. Discuss with students the importance of weight transfer when serving. Transfer weight with correct timing for the striking pattern.

Extension

Have students practice the serve again while using the concept of weight transfer.

Student Choices/Differentiation

- Have different-sized volleyballs available.
- Students may view video or critical elements provided.

What to Look For

- Students are exploring serving by varying speeds, weight transfer, and directions.
- Students are working to improve skills through extensions and refinements.

Instructional Task: Serve Receive

■ PRACTICE TASK

In pairs, students stand 4 to 7 yards or meters away from each other. The tosser throws the ball (respectfully) toward a partner with force so that the partner can dig the ball back to the tosser. After five hits, partners switch roles.

Extension

After tossers throw the ball, have them keep their hands above the head. Challenge students to dig the ball back to their partners so that the tossers can catch the ball above the head.

Refinement

Make sure that students are shrugging shoulders and not swinging arms.

Student Choices/Differentiation

- Students may change the distance between tosser and receiver.
- Students may use different-sized volleyballs.

What to Look For

- Respectful tosses
- Shoulder shrugs
- Ready position

Instructional Task: Combining Serve and Serve Receive

◼ PRACTICE TASK

- Pair students.
- One student serves the ball while the other student controls the serve with a dig.
- Students rotate between server and receiver.

Extension

- Combine two groups to have groups of four.
- One student is the server, one is the receiver of the serve whose goal is to dig the ball to the passer, one is the passer who passes to the hitter, and the last is the hitter.

Student Choices/Differentiation

Students can use a volleyball net, badminton net, or no net during this activity.

What to Look For

Students are using proper technique for the serve and serve receive.

Formal and Informal Assessments

- Informal assessments
- Exit slip: What are the critical elements of the underhand serve?

Closure

- Who can share one of the problems you had while we were exploring serving? What did you do to fix the problem?
- How is weight transfer important in serving?
- Was any group successful in the last activity (serve, dig, pass, hit)?

We will continue to practice these skills and others in the upcoming lessons.

Reflection

- What level of success did students have in serving?
- Were they able to self-correct during the extensions and refinements with the serve?
- Are students shrugging their shoulders or swinging their arms during the serve receive activities?

Homework

At home, practice any of the skills that we have learned. Review the critical elements and skill videos that are posted to the school's physical education website.

Resources

McManama, J., Hicks, L., & Urtel, M. (2010). *Physical education activity handbook*. 12th ed. San Francisco: Benjamin Cummings.

Internet keyword search: "underhand serve volleyball," "volleyball digs," "volleyball serve receive," "volleyball for beginners"

LESSON 4: INTRODUCTION TO TACTICS

Grade-Level Outcomes

Primary Outcomes

Two-hand volley: Two-hand-volleys with control in a dynamic environment. (S1.M17.7)

Creating space through variation: Creates open space in net/wall games with a short-handled implement by varying force and direction. (S2.M7.6)

Embedded Outcome

Working with others: Cooperates with a small group of classmates during adventure activities, game play or team-building activities. (S4.M5.6)

Lesson Objectives

The learner will:

- call for the ball as it approaches the net.
- perform a forearm pass to intended target.
- work with teammates to control the ball before passing it over the net.
- vary force and direction of attacks to create space during modified game.

Equipment and Materials

- Volleyballs: mix of foam, trainer, and regulation volleyballs
- Cones for boundaries
- Nets

Introduction

Today, we will put two players on the court at the same time to play one ball. Communication in volleyball is an important skill, and "calling" for the ball is communicating to teammates that you are going to play the ball. Sounds easy, right? This can be tricky, even for advanced players. Learning this skill will help you when we start game play. We also will work on some offensive strategies in today's lesson.

Instructional Task: Review Forearm Pass

■ PRACTICE TASK

In grids, students practice the forearm pass.

Refinement

Make sure that students are starting in the ready position (low base of support).

Student Choices/Differentiation

Students may practice at the controlled or uncontrolled levels.

What to Look For

Students are using the critical elements of the forearm pass.

Instructional Task:
Calling for the Ball and Passing to a Target

■ PRACTICE TASK

- Demonstrate by calling the ball as it approaches the net. Calls should be short and loud enough for teammates to hear: "Mine," "I got it," "Me."
- Set-up: On half of a volleyball court, two lines of students stand behind the end line. One catcher (target) stands 3 feet (0.9 m) from the net, with two to four tossers across the net.
- First student in each line steps to mid-court, side by side. One tosser from across the net tosses the ball over the net toward a player, who calls for it and passes it to the target. Target rolls ball under net to tosser (or tosser shags errant pass); next two passers step onto court as other passers return to line. Signal groups to rotate frequently.

Refinement

Make sure that students are loud enough when they call for the ball.

Student Choices/Differentiation

Tosses should become less predictable as students' skills progress. Tosses can be put intentionally between the two passers, forcing them to increase communication on the floor.

What to Look For

- Students are using appropriate communication skills.
- Students toss the ball respectfully.

Instructional Task: Triad—Toss, Pass, Hit

■ PRACTICE TASK

- Divide students into groups of three.
- The groups include a tosser, a passer, and a hitter in a triangle position. The passer and hitter should be close to the net, while the tosser should be 5 to 7 yards or meters back. The tosser tosses the ball to the passer. The passer controls the toss by using a forearm pass to the hitter. The hitter then forearm-passes the ball over the net. Students rotate after two or three trials.

Extension

Students can try attacking the ball with an overhead forearm strike, if comfortable.

Refinement

If using a net, make sure that students are far enough away from it so that they don't hit it when they pass or hit.

Student Choices/Differentiation

- Students may modify the task to toss, pass, and catch.
- Students may use a net or not.
- Students may use trainer volleyballs or deflate the regulation-sized ball a little to make it softer.
- Students may attack the ball with an overhead forearm strike but must keep feet on the ground.

What to Look For

- Tosses are accurate.
- Passer is in ready position.
- Passer uses arms and shoulders to shrug the ball to hitter.
- All three students control the ball.
- Hitter attempts to hit the ball over the net.

Instructional Task: 3 v 3 Volleyball Without Hitting

■ PRACTICE TASK

Using a modified court with smaller boundaries, students play the game of volleyball without hitting the ball. They toss the ball respectfully over the net, trying to win a point.

This game works on the tactic of hitting to open space.

Extension

To help students with force and direction, modify the playing surface:

- Make the court long and narrow.
- Make the court short and wide.

Guiding questions for students:

- How did modifying the playing surface change your strategy?
- When the court was long and narrow, how did you use force and direction to be successful?
- When the court was short and wide, how did you use force and direction to be successful?

Refinements

- Make sure that students are tossing the ball (not throwing it).
- Make sure that students are using all of the space.

Extension

Have students practice using three "hits" to send the ball over the net. They still are not hitting, but they can toss the ball to teammates and send the third ball over.

EMBEDDED OUTCOME: S4.M5.6. Discuss ways in which students can cooperate during the modified game so that all are learning during the game.

Student Choices/Differentiation

- Students can use a volleyball net, badminton net, or no net during this activity.
- Students may use different-sized volleyballs.
- Make playing boundaries larger or smaller, according to skill level.

What to Look For

- Students are using the tactic of varying force and direction.
- Students are being respectful to peers during the activity.

Formal and Informal Assessments

Informal assessments

Closure

- Close your eyes and hold up the number of fingers that represent, on a scale of 1 to 10, how comfortable you are using the forearm pass. (If you ask students to do this with peers watching, they'll be more likely to report higher comfort levels than they actually feel, to avoid embarrassment.)
- What are important things to consider during the toss, pass, and hit activity that we did in today's class?
- Why is it important to communicate?

We will continue to work on tactics and our volleyball skills in the next class. Keep practicing!

Reflection

- Were students working together in today's class?
- Did students vary force and direction during the 3 v 3 activity?
- During the triad activity, were students successful in completing the three tasks?

Homework

Continue to improve your skills in volleyball by playing the 3 v 3 modified game that we played in class. Even if you don't have a volleyball, you can practice this task with any type of ball or even rolled-up paper.

Resources

McManama, J., Hicks, L., & Urtel, M. (2010). *Physical education activity handbook.* 12th ed. San Francisco: Benjamin Cummings.

Mitchell, S., Oslin, J., & Griffin, L. (2013). *Teaching sport concepts and skills: A tactical games approach for ages 7 to 18.* Champaign, IL: Human Kinetics.

Internet keyword search: "creating open space in volleyball," "volleyball for beginners"

LESSON 5:
REFINING SKILLS AND SERVING TACTICS

Grade-Level Outcomes

Primary Outcomes

Using tactics & shots: Selects offensive shot based on opponent's location (hit where opponent is not). (S2.M8.7)

Serving: Executes consistently (at least 70% of the time) a legal underhand serve to a predetermined target for net/wall games such as badminton, volleyball or pickleball. (S1.M12.7)

Two-hand volley: Two-hand-volleys with control in a dynamic environment. (S1.M17.7)

Embedded Outcome

Personal responsibility: Exhibits personal responsibility by using appropriate etiquette, demonstrating respect for facilities and exhibiting safe behaviors. (S4.M1.6)

Lesson Objectives

The learner will:

- continue to improve control of the forearm pass.
- serve with at least 70 percent accuracy during the serving review.
- learn and use basic serving strategies.

Equipment and Materials

- Different-sized volleyballs
- Volleyball nets
- Cones or poly spots

Introduction

Today, we will work on controlling our forearm passes. Why do you think it is important to control our passes? We also will practice our serves and learn multiple serving strategies.

Instructional Task: Review Forearm Pass

■ PRACTICE TASK

In grids, students practice the forearm pass in controlled and uncontrolled environments.

Extension

Students may play a game of keep it alive, using only the forearm pass.

Refinement

For safety and to keep students from developing bad habits, when the ball is passed 2 to 3 feet (0.6 to 0.9 m) away from a partner, the game should be stopped and restarted with a toss.

Student Choices/Differentiation

Change distance of tosser, according to skill level.

What to Look For

- Students display critical elements of the forearm pass.
- Students are practicing in a controlled manner (no high-flying passes).

Instructional Task: Forearm Pass to Yourself

▦ PRACTICE TASK

To work on control, students practice forearm-passing to themselves.

In pairs, one student tosses the ball to a partner. The partner forearm-passes the ball just above his own head. When the ball comes down, the partner forearm-passes the ball back to the tosser, who catches the ball. Students rotate after five trials.

Extension

Instead of the tossers catching the ball, they forearm-pass the ball to themselves and then pass it back to their partners. Students can see how many passes they can complete until the ball touches the ground.

Refinement

Students must absorb the ball with a shoulder shrug. If they swing their arms, it is less likely that they will be able to control the ball to forearm-pass it where they want it to go.

Student Choices/Differentiation

- If students are having difficulty with the task, have them go back to initial passing drills in grids.
- Students may use different-sized volleyballs.
- Vary the distance of the partners.

What to Look For

- Students are shrugging the shoulders instead of swinging their arms.
- Ball is controlled after pass (students aren't chasing the ball all over the gym).
- Students are bending their knees and following through with the pass.
- Students are calling for the ball.

Instructional Task: Review Serve

▦ PRACTICE TASK

- Go over the critical elements of the underhand serve, and have students practice serving the ball to a partner.
- Students practice the underhand serve across the net, trying for 70 percent of the serves to fall legally in the opponent's court.

Extension

If students are experiencing a high rate of success, teach them the overhand serve.

Refinement

- Make sure that students are using proper weight-transfer skills.
- Have students work on speed first, then refine skills for accuracy.

Student Choices/Differentiation

- Students may use a net or not.
- Students may use different-sized volleyballs.
- Students may vary distance of the serve.

What to Look For

Students display proper critical elements of the serve.

Instructional Task: Review Serve

■ PRACTICE TASK

- Go over critical elements of the underhand serve, and have students practice serving the ball to a partner.
- Students practice the underhand serve across the net, trying for 70 percent of the serves to fall legally in the opponent's court.

Extension

If students are experiencing a high success rate, teach them the overhand serve.

Refinements

- Make sure that students are using proper weight-transfer skills.
- Have students work on speed first, then refine skills for accuracy.

Student Choices/Differentiation

- Students may use a net or not.
- Students may use different-sized volleyballs.
- Students may vary distance of the serve.

What to Look For

Students display critical elements of the underhand serve.

Instructional Task: Serving Strategy

■ PRACTICE TASK

Discuss with students different serve strategies. Be sure to cover:

- Varying speeds
- Varying distances
- Float serve
- Topspin
- Choosing whom to serve to
- Serving between players
- Serving against different defenses
- Serving toward the lines

Have students play a modified game of volleyball, working on the serve. Students toss the ball over the net, trying to use one of the previous strategies. The opposing team attempts to return the serve. Once the team returns the serve or fails to do so, the point is awarded and the opposing team rotates and has a chance to serve.

EMBEDDED OUTCOME: S4.M1.6. Even though you are working on strategy, students still should act respectfully toward classmates. Make sure that students exhibit personal responsibility by using appropriate etiquette when tossing or serving to teammates (e.g., not always serving to low-skilled players).

Refinement

The higher the angle of the serve, the easier it is for the defense to react and return the serve successfully. Have students try to keep serves low, yet make sure that they go over the net.

Extensions

If students are having a lot of success in the game, have them use a legal serve instead of a toss or throw. The game stops after the team returns or misses the serve because the objective of the game is serving strategy, and you want students to have a high number of practice trials.

Student Choices/Differentiation

- Students may use different-sized volleyballs.
- Students may move up if they're having a hard time getting the ball over the net.
- Some students might not use a net in this activity.

What to Look For

- Students are using a serve strategy that the class has discussed.
- Students are serving to corners of the court or between opposing players.
- Serve has a low angle instead of a high angle over the net.

Formal and Informal Assessments

Exit slip: Name three serve strategies that we can use in volleyball.

Closure

- Why is it important to control your forearm passes?
- What did you do that was critical to succeeding when you worked on passing the ball today?
- What is important to consider when serving a volleyball over the net?

Keep practicing your volleyball passes and serves. We have three more lessons in volleyball.

Reflection

- Were students successful in controlling the forearm pass today?
- Did students use the serving strategies?
- Were students respectful toward their classmates during the task today?
- Do I need to spend extra time on serving, forearm pass, serve receive, or strategies in the next class?

Homework

Share what you learned with a friend or family member. Keep practicing your forearm pass and underhand serves. Feel free to review the volleyball material posted to the physical education website.

Resources

McManama, J., Hicks, L., & Urtel, M. (2010). *Physical education activity handbook.* 12th ed. San Francisco: Benjamin Cummings.

Mitchell, S., Oslin, J., & Griffin, L. (2013). *Teaching sport concepts and skills: A tactical games approach for ages 7 to 18.* Champaign, IL: Human Kinetics.

Internet keyword search: "serve strategies in volleyball," "volleyball for beginners"

LESSON 6:
RULES AND MODIFIED GAME PLAY

Grade-Level Outcomes

Primary Outcomes

Serving: Executes consistently (at least 70% of the time) a legal underhand serve for distance and accuracy for net/wall games such as badminton, volleyball or pickleball. (S1.M12.8)

Creating space through variation: Creates open space in net/wall games with either a long- or short-handled implement by varying force or direction, or by moving opponent from side to side and/or forward and back. (S2.M7.8)

Two-hand volley: Two-hand-volleys with control in a dynamic environment. (S1.M17.7)

Embedded Outcome

Using tactics & shots: Reduces offensive options for opponents by returning to mid-court position. (S2.M8.6)

Lesson Objectives

The learner will:

- learn the basic rules of volleyball.
- practice serving for accuracy.
- use offensive and defensive strategies in a modified game.
- practice the forearm pass for accuracy.

Equipment and Materials

- Volleyballs: mix of foam, trainer, and regulation volleyballs
- Cones for boundaries
- Net
- Hoops

Introduction

We will continue to work on our skills and volleyball strategy in our class today. First, we will learn the basic rules of volleyball so that you can play the game with friends and family. We also will practice our forearm passes and serving, and we will play a modified game. We are getting closer to our skills test, so make sure that you work hard in class today.

Instructional Task: Basic Volleyball Rules

■ PRACTICE TASK

Divide students into groups and give each group a rule category. Students should teach the class the rule, possible purposes of the rule, and infractions of the rule.

Possible rule categories to choose from:

- Serving
- Net and center line
- Ball handling
- Boundaries
- Scoring

Extensions

- Students may come up with skits of what to do or not do related to the rule.
- Review scoring of skits.

Student Choices/Differentiation

Students may use Internet searches and videos to learn rules.

What to Look For

- Students understand the basic rules to play a game of volleyball.
- Measure students against the rubric that you created to analyze the skits. The rubric should include knowledge of the rules, possible purposes of the rules, and infractions of the rules.
- All students participate in the skits.

Instructional Task: Serve for Accuracy

■ PRACTICE TASK

Students practice the underhand serve across the net, trying for 70 percent of the serves to fall legally in the opponents' court.

Extension

Place hoops in the corners of the court. If a student serves the ball and it lands in the opponents' court, he receives a point. If the ball lands in a hoop, he receives 2 points.

Refinement

Make sure that students are serving to different spots on the court.

Student Choices/Differentiation

- Students may use different-sized volleyballs.
- Students may vary distances of serve according to skill level.

What to Look For

- Students are using the critical elements of the underhand serve.
- Students are varying locations of their serves.

Instructional Task: Forearm Pass Challenge

■ PRACTICE TASK

- Challenge students to forearm-pass the ball to hoops along the court.
- Place one hoop near the net (where setter should be). Place other hoops near the net where attackers might be or near the attack line (back row attack).

Extension

Place hoops on opposite side of net to symbolize a free ball. Students each receive 1 point for a free ball landing legally in the opponents' court. The student receives 2 points if the ball hits inside a hoop placed toward the back corners of the court.

Refinement

Make sure that students are guiding the ball and following through with the pass.

Student Choices/Differentiation

- If students are having difficulty placing passes into the hoops, have them ignore the hoops and focus on successful passes.
- Challenge students to score as many points as possible.

What to Look For

- Students are using all the critical elements of the forearm pass.
- Students are guiding the ball with the proper follow-through on their passes.

Instructional Task: 3 v 3 Volleyball—Open Space

■ PRACTICE TASK

- Using a modified court (smaller boundaries), students play a modified game of volleyball, trying to move the opponents.
- This game works on the tactic of hitting to open space.

Extensions

To help students with force and direction, modify the playing surface:

- Make the court long and narrow.
- Make the court short and wide.

Refinement

Make sure that students use all of the space.

Extension

Have students practice using three hits to put the ball over the net.

EMBEDDED OUTCOME: S2.M8.6. To help students on defense, teach them the importance of returning to mid-court to play defense.

Guiding questions for students:

- Why is it important to return to mid-court after you hit?
- What are some reasons why one might not do so?

Student Choices/Differentiation

- Students can use a volleyball net, badminton net, or no net during this activity.
- Students may use different-size equipment.
- Playing boundaries may be larger or smaller according to skill level.
- The game can start with a serve or a toss.

What to Look For

- Students are hitting to open space.
- Students are sending the ball over with a low angle instead of a high, arching attack.

Formal and Informal Assessments

- Informal assessments
- Exit slip: Give students a drawing of a modified court (short and wide or long and narrow). Ask them to mark an X where the offense should hit the ball.

Closure

- Think, pair, share activity: What is the most important rule in volleyball?
- What strategy can you use to succeed while on offense in volleyball?
- What strategy can you use on defense?
- Where is the ideal place to send a free ball over the net in volleyball?

Reflection

- Are students sending their serves over the net consistently?
- Are students controlling their passes?
- Are students using both offensive and defensive strategies?

Homework

Review key volleyball rules posted on the school's physical education website. I also posted the forearm pass and serve skills test. Make sure that you look over the assessments and practice the skills before the next class.

Resources

McManama, J., Hicks, L., & Urtel, M. (2010). *Physical education activity handbook*. 12th ed. San Francisco: Benjamin Cummings.

Mitchell, S., Oslin, J., & Griffin, L. (2013). *Teaching sport concepts and skills: A tactical games approach for ages 7 to 18*. Champaign, IL: Human Kinetics.

Internet keyword search: "creating open space in volleyball," "defensive strategies in volleyball," "returning to mid-court," "volleyball for beginners"

LESSON 7: PRACTICE DAY AND FOREARM STRIKE

Grade-Level Outcomes

Primary Outcomes

Striking: Strikes with a mature overhand pattern in a nondynamic environment for net/wall games such as volleyball, handball, badminton or tennis. (S1.M13.6)

Two-hand volley: Two-hand-volleys with control in a small-sided game. (S1.M17.8)

Serving: Executes consistently (at least 70% of the time) a legal underhand serve for distance and accuracy for net/wall games such as badminton, volleyball or pickleball. (S1.M12.8)

Embedded Outcome

Accepting feedback: Provides encouragement and feedback to peers without prompting from the teacher. (S4.M3.8)

Lesson Objectives

The learner will:

- review basic volleyball rules.
- practice the keep it alive and serve assessments.
- learn the overhead forearm strike.

Equipment and Materials

- Volleyballs: mix of foam, trainer, and regulation volleyballs
- Cones or tape for boundaries for serve test
- Net

Introduction

In our last class, we learned basic rules of volleyball. We will review these rules and practice our end-of-the-module assessments. We also will learn a new skill today called the overhead forearm strike.

Instructional Task: Review Rules

■ PRACTICE TASK

Review basic rules of volleyball with a PowerPoint. Be sure to cover:

- In and out calls
- Number of hits
- Serve rotations
- Scoring
- Improper serves
- Net and center line violations

Extension

Have students review videos of rule violations. Students can think, pair, and share after each video. Think, pair, share informal assessment.

Student Choices/Differentiation

Students may review handouts or pictures from the website.

What to Look For

Students know the basic rules of volleyball.

Instructional Task: Keep It Alive Assessment—Practice

■ PRACTICE TASK

Review the assessment protocol and rubric with students.

Have groups of four to six students practice the keep it alive assessment.

Extension

Have two groups work together. One group performs the assessment, and the second group uses the rubric to assess the first group. After the assessment, the assessing group shares its assessment and offers constructive feedback. The groups then switch roles.

EMBEDDED OUTCOME: S4.M2.8 Discuss with students the importance of offering their peers encouragement and feedback on their performance.

Guiding questions for students:

We all need feedback to improve performance. As a teacher, I can offer only so much feedback because we have so many students in the class. So, it's important that you help one another with feedback, as well.

- What can you do to offer encouragement to your peers?
- What can you do to offer feedback to your peers?

Student Choices/Differentiation

- Students may use different-sized volleyballs.
- Groups may vary space between players, according to skill level.
- Show students a video of students performing the assessment.

What to Look For

- Students are using proper form and controlling their passes.
- Students are calling for the ball.
- Students are using the rubric correctly and offering constructive feedback.

Instructional Task: Overhead Forearm Strike Over Net

■ PRACTICE TASK

Demonstrate the overhead forearm strike in volleyball.

Have students practice the strike without the ball.

Extension

In grids, students practice the overhead forearm strike from a standing position.

Guiding questions for students:

- What are the benefits of using the skill?
- When would you use the overhead forearm strike?

Refinement

Make sure that students are reaching all the way back to strike the ball.

Student Choices/Differentiation

- Students may use different-sized volleyballs.
- Students may vary the distance of the toss.

What to Look For

Students are using the critical elements of the overhead forearm strike (weight transfer, reaching back, open-hand contact, and follow-through).

Instructional Task: Serving Assessment—Practice

■ PRACTICE TASK

Review the assessment protocol and rubric with students.

Students practice their serves, trying to score points according to the assessment.

Extension

Create a rubric that includes the critical elements of the underhand serve to measure the process as well.

Student Choices/Differentiation

- Students may use different-sized volleyballs.
- Students may vary the distance of the serve.
- Show students a video of students performing the assessment.

What to Look For

Students are serving the ball correctly over the net.

Formal and Informal Assessments

- Think, pair, share informal assessment: Rules
- Keep It Alive assessment

Closure

- Why do we use the overhead forearm strike?
- Does everyone feel comfortable with the test protocols for the forearm pass and serve?
- Who has questions about how you will be graded?

Reflection

- Did students have success at both of the assessment practice tasks today?
- Did students use the overhead forearm strike properly?
- Did students display a good grasp of the rules?

Homework

Review the rules and both skills assessments for tomorrow's last day of the module. Practice the skills and be ready to perform the test tomorrow!

Resources

Lacy, A. (2015). *Measurement and evaluation in physical education and exercise science.* 7th ed. San Francisco: Benjamin Cummings.

South Carolina Physical Education Assessment Program. (2010). *Middle School Physical Education Assessment Manual.* South Carolina Alliance for Health, Physical Education, Recreation and Dance. www.scahperd.org/wp-content/uploads/2015/04/MS-Notebook-Final-Sept-23.pdf.

SOUTH CAROLINA PHYSICAL EDUCATION ASSESSMENT PROGRAM
MIDDLE SCHOOL VOLLEYBALL

Assessment Task

Play a game of keep it alive using proper technique on forearm passes and overhead sets, communication with group members, moving to the ball, and returning to ready position.

Specific Protocol: Directions to Students

You will play a 5-minute game of keep it alive in circle formation, using forearm passes and overhead sets, in groups of five. You will start with a toss to someone in the circle, and play will continue until the ball hits the floor or is hit illegally. After 2½ minutes, the group should stop play and switch positions within the circle so that you are standing between different players. After changing positions, continue play. Communicate with the group that you are going to take a hit by calling the volleyball ("Mine," "I've got it") just before taking the hit. You will be assessed on your ability to execute effective forearm passes and overhead sets, communicate with your group that you will take the hit, move to the ball, and return to a ready position.

Criteria for Assessment

- The student demonstrates good form while using overhead sets and forearm passes.
- The student returns a playable ball effectively.
- The student communicates with group members during play. (Calls the ball: "Mine," "I've got it," etc.)
- The student moves to the ball and returns to ready position after the hit.

Equipment and Facilities

One half of a volleyball court or a marked 30- × 30-foot (9 × 9 m) square per group
Two volleyballs (trainer or official) to ensure uninterrupted play

Camera Location and Operation

The camera may be placed at a high level, such as the bleacher area, or on the floor, approximately 12 feet (3.5 m) from the 30- × 30-foot square and centered on the circular group. Keep the camera stationary and recording once play has started. Each group should be recorded for 5 minutes.

Testing Situation

Read the testing protocol to the group of students being tested. Give each group 5 minutes to warm up. Start each group and the camera at the same time. Be sure that player positions in the circle are switched after 2½ minutes so that neither weak nor strong players are placed at a disadvantage.

South Carolina Physical Education Program Assessment

Middle School Volleyball Assessment Task Scoring Rubric

Level 3

Consistently uses overhead sets and forearm passes showing good form*
Consistently returns a playable ball effectively
Consistently communicates with group members during play
Consistently moves to the ball and returns to a ready position

Level 2

Usually uses overhead sets and forearm passes showing good form
Usually returns a playable ball effectively
Usually communicates with group members during play
Usually moves to the ball and returns to a ready position

(continued)

(continued)

Level 1

Sometimes uses overhead sets and forearm passes showing good form

Sometimes returns a playable ball effectively

Sometimes communicates with group members during play

Sometimes moves to the ball and returns to a ready position

Level 0

Rarely uses overhead sets and forearm passes showing good form

Rarely returns a playable ball effectively

Rarely communicates with group members during play

Rarely moves to the ball and returns to a ready position

*Good form is identified using the following performance cues:

Overhead Set	Forearm Pass
Knees bent to straight	Knees bent to straight
Window overhead	Arms extended, hands together
Elbows out (chicken wings)	Forearm hit and shoulder shrug
Extension and follow-through	Follow-through: arms below shoulders

South Carolina Physical Education Assessment Program
Volleyball Summary Score Sheet

School: _____ Date Collected: _____

Teacher: _____ Semester: _____ Class Period: _____

Coder: _____ Date Coded: _____

Students must appear on this sheet in the order in which they appear on the videotape.

Student # *	Student name	Student gender	Forearm pass/ Overhead set form	Effective play	Communi- cation	Moves to ball and returns to ready position	Level (0-3)

LESSON 8: ASSESSMENT AND GAME DAY

Grade-Level Outcomes

Primary Outcomes

Serving: Executes consistently (at least 70% of the time) a legal underhand serve for distance and accuracy for net/wall games such as badminton, volleyball or pickleball. (S1.M12.8)

Two-hand volley: Two-hand-volleys with control in a small-sided game. (S1.M17.8)

Embedded Outcome

Working with others: Cooperates with a small group of classmates during adventure activities, game play or team-building activities. (S4.M5.6)

Lesson Objectives

The learner will:

- practice the forearm pass and underhand serve before taking the skills test.
- demonstrate the forearm pass and underhand serve skills on the skills test.
- demonstrate knowledge of rules and strategies on the cognitive test.
- participate in a modified 3 v 3 volleyball game.

Equipment and Materials

- Volleyballs: mix of foam, trainer, and regulation volleyballs
- Cones or tape for boundaries for serve test
- Net
- Paper and pencils

Introduction

This is the last day of our Volleyball Module. We will work through the assessments in stations. Make sure that you work hard to produce your best work and stay on task.

Instructional Task: Practice Forearm Pass

■ PRACTICE TASK

In grids, students practice the forearm pass in controlled and uncontrolled environments.

Extension

Students may practice controlling the ball by passing the ball to themselves before passing to the partner.

Refinement

Make sure that students are controlling their passes by keeping the passes low.

Student Choices/Differentiation

- Students may pass continuously or from a partner toss.
- Students may vary ball size and distance between pairs.

What to Look For

- Students are using controlled passes.
- Students are using the critical elements of the forearm pass.

Instructional Task: Practice Serving

■ PRACTICE TASK

Students practice the underhand serve across the net, trying for 70 percent of the serves to fall legally in the opponents' court.

Refinement

Make sure that students are serving to different spots on the court.

Student Choices/Differentiation

Students may use different-sized balls and vary distances of the serve according to skill level.

What to Look For

- Students use the critical elements of the underhand serve.
- Students vary locations of the serve.

Instructional Task: Stations

■ PRACTICE TASK

Have students work through the following stations:

- Keep it alive assessment
- Serving assessment
- 3 v 3 game play
- Cognitive test

EMBEDDED OUTCOME: S4.M6.7 Discuss with students the importance of cooperating during the stations in class today.

Guiding questions for students:

- Why is it important to stay on task today?
- In what ways can you work together to stay on task?
- In what ways can you help one another by cooperating during the test today?

Student Choices/Differentiation

- Students may modify assessments according to class skill level or skills taught.
- During the 3 v 3 game, students may choose to work on Standard 2 skills (applying knowledge of concepts, principles, strategies and tactics) by throwing the ball (not hitting; see lesson 4 for practice task).

What to Look For

- Passes and serves are successful.
- Students know the basic rules and strategies.
- Students play a 3 v 3 modified game of volleyball successfully (not formally assessed).

Formal and Informal Assessments

- AAHPERD serve test
- Keep It Alive assessment
- Cognitive test on rules and strategies

Closure

- On a scale from 1 to 10, how well do you think you performed on the skills test today?
- On a scale from 1 to 10, how much do you think you've improved in the game of volleyball?

I hope you will keep improving your volleyball skills. It's a fun game, and I enjoyed watching you improve over the course of the module.

In our next class, we will start our next module. Review the module outline and the critical elements of the first skill by next class.

Reflection

- How did students perform on the skills test?
- Should I have spent more or less time on any of the skills taught in the module?
- Did students improve over the module?

Homework

Review the outline for the next module and the critical elements of the first skill by next class.

Resources

Lacy, A. (2015). *Measurement and evaluation in physical education and exercise science.* 7th ed. San Francisco: Benjamin Cummings.

South Carolina Physical Education Assessment Program. (2010). *Middle School Physical Education Assessment Manual.* South Carolina Alliance for Health, Physical Education, Recreation and Dance. www.//scahperd.org/wp-content/uploads/2015/04/MS-Notebook-Final-Sept-23.pdf.

Modified or adopted cognitive test from Internet or volleyball books.

PICKLEBALL MODULE

Lessons in this module were contributed by Brad Rettig, a middle school physical education teacher in Lincoln, NE, Public Schools.

Grade-Level Outcomes Addressed, by Lesson	1	2	3	4	5	6	7	8
Standard 1. The physically literate individual demonstrates competency in a variety of motor skills and movement patterns.								
Performs a legal underhand serve with control for net/wall games such as badminton, volleyball or pickleball. (S1.M12.6)		P						P
Executes consistently (at least 70% of the time) a legal underhand serve to a predetermined target for net/wall games such as badminton, volleyball or pickleball. (S1.M12.7)		P				P		
Demonstrates the mature form of the forehand and backhand strokes with a short-handled implement in net games such as paddle ball, pickleball or short-handled racket tennis. (S1.M14.6)	P		P		P			P
Transfers weight with correct timing for the striking pattern. (S1.M15.6)	P							
Forehand- and backhand-volleys with a mature form and control using a short-handled implement. (S1.M16.7)						P		
Standard 2. The physically literate individual applies knowledge of concepts, principles, strategies and tactics related to movement and performance.								
Reduces offensive options for opponents by returning to mid-court position. (S2.M8.6)				P	P			
Selects offensive shot based on opponent's location (hit where opponent is not). (S2.M8.7)							P	
Standard 3. The physically literate individual demonstrates the knowledge and skills to achieve and maintain a health-enhancing level of physical activity and fitness.								
Identifies the components of skill-related fitness. (S3.M7. 6)					E			
Standard 4. The physically literate individual exhibits responsible personal and social behavior that respects self and others.								
Demonstrates self-responsibility by implementing specific corrective feedback to improve performance. (S4.M3.6)		E						
Provides corrective feedback to a peer, using teacher-generated guidelines, and incorporating appropriate tone and other communication skills. (S4.M3.7)			E		E			
Accepts differences among classmates in physical development, maturation and varying skill levels by providing encouragement and positive feedback. (S4.M4.6)			E					
Responds appropriately to participants' ethical and unethical behavior during physical activity by using rules and guidelines for resolving conflicts. (S4.M4.8)								E
Demonstrates knowledge of rules and etiquette by self-officiating modified physical activities and games or following parameters to create or modify a dance. (S4.M6.7)								P
Applies rules and etiquette by acting as an official for modified physical activities and games and creating dance routines within a given set of parameters. (S4.M6.8)					E		E	
Standard 5. The physically literate individual recognizes the value of physical activity for health, enjoyment, challenge, self-expression and/or social interaction.								
Recognizes individual challenges and copes in a positive way, such as extending effort, asking for help or feedback or modifying the tasks. (S5.M3.6)						P		
Demonstrates respect for self and others in activities and games by following the rules, encouraging others and playing in the spirit of the game or activity. (S5.M6.6)								E
Demonstrates respect for self by asking for help and helping others in various physical activities. (S5.M6.8)	E							

P = Primary; E = Embedded

LESSON 1:
FOREHAND AND BACKHAND STRIKING

Grade-Level Outcomes

Primary Outcomes

Forehand & backhand: Demonstrates the mature form of the forehand and backhand strokes with a short-handled implement in net games such as paddle ball, pickleball or short-handled racket tennis. (S1.M14.6)

Weight transfer: Transfers weight with correct timing for the striking pattern. (S1.M15.6)

Embedded Outcome

Social interaction: Demonstrates respect for self by asking for help and helping others in various physical activities. (S5.M6.8)

Lesson Objectives

The learner will:

- learn the basic pickleball grips: backhand, continental, and eastern forehand.
- recall the critical elements of the forehand and backhand and implement the elements during the practice tasks.
- demonstrate correct forehand technique with the paddle.
- demonstrate correct backhand technique with the paddle.
- transfer weight to effectively generate force during the striking pattern.

Equipment and Materials

- Enough paddles for every student
- 2 balls per grid
- Enough grid space to perform the practice tasks
- Nets if they are used during the practice task

Introduction

Today, we will begin our module on pickleball, which is played with a short-handled implement. How many of you have played tennis or badminton before? You will find pickleball similar but also different. Be sure to listen, ask questions, and apply the correct rules and techniques while playing pickleball. The skills that you will learn include serving and returning the ball by using the forehand and backhand. Today, you will learn how to serve by watching videos and with peer help, teacher guidance, and self-evaluation.

Show the class a video clip of a game of pickleball.

Instructional Task: Grips and Pre-test

■ PRACTICE TASK

Demonstrate and have students practice (without striking a ball) the continental and eastern forehand grips as well as the backhand grip.

Extensions

- In grids of two, students toss the ball to each other, allowing them to explore the forehand and backhand grips.
- While students are exploring the grips, do a quick pre-test on the forearm and backhand pickleball strike.

Guiding questions for students:

- Which grip is more comfortable to you?
- What are the critical elements of each grip?

Student Choices/Differentiation

- Students may toss the ball from a variety of trajectories.
- Students may use a net or not.
- Students may watch videos or review handouts if they need extra guidance.

What to Look For

- Students are using the correct hand position.
- Students are using the correct critical elements when performing the skills, while mimicking as well as exploring.
- Pre-assessment: Use a product skills test (award scores to students hitting the ball to different sections of the court) or a process skills test (how well they perform the critical elements).

Instructional Task:
Students Practice the Forehand and Backhand

■ PRACTICE TASK

In grids of two, students toss the ball to each other, allowing them to explore the forehand.

Call out a command. Students practice the task five times and then switch so that their partners can perform the same command. Call out another command.

Partners must cooperate by making good tosses. Partners should encourage each other.

First: Toss the ball to the middle section of your partner's forearm side for five hits.
Same task with backhand.
Second: Toss the ball so that your partner has to take a quick step to the forearm side to hit the ball.
Same task with backhand (step toward backhand side).
Third: Toss the ball so that your partner has to take a quick step forward and hit a forehand shot.
Same task with backhand.
Fourth: Toss the ball so that your partner has to take a quick step back while still hitting a forehand stroke.
Same task with backhand.

Extension

We now will move into a more game-like, or uncontrolled, setting. The partner tossing should now toss the ball using any of the previous commands. Make sure that you still are tossing at the midsection and still are using only the forehand or backhand stroke. Switch after five tosses.

Repeat this extension until many have had success.

Refinement

Observe the weight transfer during the stroke. Reinforce that the weight should shift from the back foot to the front foot by the time the paddle contacts the ball.

Guiding questions for students:

- Ask students to review the cues and explain what they are doing well and what they need to adjust.
- Which is more difficult to strike: forehand or backhand? Why?
- Did anyone swing and miss the ball? (Remind students to bend their knees and really watch the ball.)

EMBEDDED OUTCOME: S5.M6.8. Encourage students to have respect and improve themselves by asking for help from others while learning the forearm and backhand strikes in pickleball.

Extension

Students can work on adding topspin and backspin while performing the forehand strike.

Student Choices/Differentiation

- Students may toss the ball from a variety of trajectories.
- Students may use a net or not.
- Students may choose partners.

What to Look For

- From ready position, students turn sideways to the target while bringing the racket back.
- Students step toward the target, striking the ball off the forward foot.
- Students follow through with racket to opposite side.
- Students create topspin by angling the paddle face slightly closed and moving it from low to high.
- Students create backspin by angling the paddle face slightly open and moving it from high to low.

Formal and Informal Assessments

Pre-assessment: process or product skills test

Closure

- With the class, discuss what you observed while students practiced the forehand.
- What are the critical elements of the grips?
- What are the critical elements of the forearm? Backhand?
- What does weight transfer have to do with pickleball?
- Who can tell me how to create backspin and topspin?

Reflection

- How are students performing the forehand and backhand? Which elements are they struggling with?
- Were students using their time wisely today?
- Did students ask for help and respect others today?

Homework

Practice the forehand and backhand strokes at home. Try to focus on transferring weight and swinging the arm without turning the wrist.

Resources

Curtis, J. (1998). *Pickle-ball for player & teacher.* Boston: Brooks/Cole Cengage Learning.

Dougherty, N.J. (Ed.) (2010). *Physical activity & sport for the secondary school student.* 6th ed. Reston, VA: National Association for Sport and Physical Education.

Pickleball Channel: www.pickleballchannel.com

Internet keyword search: "forehand and backhand striking in pickleball"

LESSON 2: SERVES

Grade-Level Outcomes

Primary Outcomes

Serving: Performs a legal underhand serve with control for net/wall games such as badminton, volleyball or pickleball. (S1.M12.6)

Serving: Executes consistently (at least 70% of the time) a legal underhand serve to a predetermined target for net/wall games such as badminton, volleyball or pickleball. (S1.M12.7)

Embedded Outcome

Accepting feedback: Demonstrates self-responsibility by implementing specific corrective feedback to improve performance. (S4.M3.6)

Lesson Objectives

The learner will:

- practice serving in grids.
- practice receiving a serve.
- evaluate her serve to understand what critical elements she is able to perform and which ones she needs to adjust.

Equipment and Materials

- Grids for groups of 4
- Enough paddles for each student
- 2 balls for each group, with extra quickly available as needed
- Recording devices for group

Introduction

I hope that you practiced striking at home because the forearm and backhand are the most important strokes in pickleball. Every day, try to strike using a short-handled implement. This will help you become proficient in pickleball. Today, we will learn how to serve in pickleball.

Show video clip found by using the key terms "serving in pickleball" or "starting a game of pickleball."

Instructional Task: Students Explore Serving

▓ PRACTICE TASK

In grids, four students explore serving from multiple distances and angles to get a feel for the paddle, the ball, and serving.

Extensions

- Same activity, but add a net.
- Challenge students to serve deep, short, low, etc.

Guiding questions for students:

- How does this serve compare to the serve in other sports?
- What differences in this serve need to be implemented for a successful and legal serve?

EMBEDDED OUTCOME: S4.M3.6. Ask students how they are offering feedback to help other students know what they are doing well and what they can work on.

Student Choices/Differentiation
- The size of the ball can be larger or something that floats in the air longer, allowing students a better opportunity to connect with the ball.
- Students may choose their own groups.
- A net does not need to be used, allowing students to focus on the correct technique for serving.

What to Look For
- Students toss the ball slightly in the air, 12 inches (30 cm) or less above waist.
- Students keep their eyes on the ball from toss to hit.
- Students step with opposition as they serve.
- Students keep the wrist locked and use their arm swing to send the ball where they want it to go.
- Contact occurs below the waist.
- Students are using the correct grip.

Instructional Task: Self-Evaluating the Serve

■ **PRACTICE TASK**

In grids with four or five students, use a device to record their serves. Students self-evaluate how they are doing by comparing their serves to the cues and a video on the proper serving technique.

Refinement
Make sure that students are evaluating using the critical elements of the serve.

Guiding questions for students:
- What did you notice about what you were doing correctly?
- What did you notice that needed changing?
- Did your serve become better after you made the change? Why or why not?

Student Choices/Differentiation
- Students may use a different-sized ball or object to serve.
- They may serve over a net.
- If they are using a net, the distance they are serving from may be shortened to continue their focus on serving and not power and distance.

What to Look For
- Are students noticing what they are doing correctly or incorrectly?
- Are students trying to adjust their serve based on what they are seeing?
- How are students working together to help each other? Are they offering feedback appropriately to help their peers learn?

Instructional Task: Serve and Serve Receive

■ **PRACTICE TASK**

In groups of four in grids or a pickleball court, players practice the serve, which is returned by the receiver.

Both players on one side can serve at the same time. Students take five serves and switch to receiving.

Extensions
- Repeat, specifying the location of the serve.
- Repeat, specifying the location of the return (down the line, cross-court).

Refinements

- Stop the activity and practice the serve or serve receive if students are performing incorrectly.
- Make sure that students are starting in a ready position.

Student Choices/Differentiation

- Students focus on performing the critical elements of the serve correctly and then sending the ball over the net.
- On the return, students focus on critical elements and making contact with the ball.

What to Look For

- Which students are applying the critical elements correctly for the serve, forehand, and backhand?
- What critical elements are students struggling with?

Formal and Informal Assessments

Using a checklist of the critical elements for serving, students self-evaluate how they are performing each element of the serve.

Closure

- Ask students who would be willing to share their video of the serve and break down what they were performing correctly and what they needed to adjust.
- Discuss with students what was observed as a group and what was noticed about students working together helping each other.

Reflection

- Are students able to serve with correct form?
- How many students were past using correct form and working on accuracy or serving over the net and having the ball land in play?
- What will need to be reviewed based on what you observed today?

Homework

Have students continue to watch the video of how to serve correctly and watch video of themselves, if technology allows.

Have them practice the serve and general striking with a short implement at home or at school.

Resources

Curtis, J. (1998). *Pickle-ball for player & teacher.* Boston: Brooks/Cole Cengage Learning.

Dougherty, N.J. (Ed.) (2010). *Physical activity & sport for the secondary school student.* 6th ed. Reston, VA: National Association for Sport and Physical Education.

Pickleball Channel: www.pickleballchannel.com

USA Pickleball Assocation: www.usapa.org

Internet keyword search: "pickleball serves"

LESSON 3:
FOREHAND AND BACKHAND PRACTICE

Grade-Level Outcomes

Primary Outcome

Forehand & backhand: Demonstrates the mature form of the forehand and backhand strokes with a short-handled implement in net games such as paddle ball, pickleball or short-handled racket tennis. (S1.M14.6)

Embedded Outcome

Working with others: Accepts differences among classmates in physical development, maturation and varying skill levels by providing encouragement and positive feedback. (S4.M4.6)

Lesson Objectives

The learner will:

- demonstrate critical elements of the forehand and backhand grips.
- apply the critical elements of the forehand and backhand strokes during the practice task.

Equipment and Materials

- Enough paddles for every student
- 2 to 4 balls per grid
- Enough courts for groups of 4

Introduction

We learned the basic skills of pickleball so far. Today, we will practice the skills more. It can take a lot of practice to become an expert at striking. Let's see how much we can improve with working hard in today's lesson. Can anyone tell me the critical elements of the forehand and backhand strokes?

Instructional Task: Review Grip, Forehand, and Backhand From a Partner Toss

■ PRACTICE TASK

Check students' grips as they work in grids.

Have students toss a yarn ball or hit a shuttle to a partner, exploring backhand and forehand striking.

Extension

Move from a controlled environment to an unpredictable environment.

Refinement

Refine skill as needed. Spend as much time as needed so that at least 80 percent of students are successful.

EMBEDDED OUTCOME: S4.M4.6. Encourage students to provide positive feedback and support to classmates.

Student Choices/Differentiation

- Students may toss the ball from a variety of trajectories.
- A net does not need to be used.
- If a student is struggling to contact the ball, have the tosser throw the ball in front of the student and to the backhand side until he becomes proficient and can move to practicing from a variety of angles.

- To increase accuracy for those who have the correct form, place hoops or markings down for the student to aim toward.

What to Look For

Forehand

- Students are using the V-grip.
- From ready position, students turn body while bringing the paddle back.
- Non-dominant shoulder is pointed toward the target.
- Students step forward with non-dominant leg.
- Paddle swings parallel to the ground.
- Contact occurs next to forward leg, and follow-through continues after contact.

Backhand

- From ready position, students turn sideways to the target while bringing the paddle back.
- Dominant shoulder is facing the target.
- Students step toward the target, striking ball in front of the body.
- Students contact the ball as they are stepping forward and follow through after contact.

Instructional Task: Topspin and Backspin

■ PRACTICE TASK

In the same grids, students practice adding topspin and backspin to a ball tossed directly in front of them.

Extensions

- Students can aim for the hoops or markings on the court or grid.
- Challenge students to perform the strokes from a variety of trajectories and angles.

Refinement

Make sure that students are striking the ball high to low (backspin) or low to high (topspin).

Guiding questions for students:

- What causes the ball to have topspin?
- What did you do that created backspin on the ball?
- How does your arm swing affect your spin?
- How does the trajectory of the ball influence the type of spin you choose to use?

Student Choices/Differentiation

- Students not yet ready to focus on the spin may continue to practice the basic forehand and backhand strokes.
- Students may continue to have the ball thrown from a variety of trajectories and speeds.
- Students may review clips about applying spin.

What to Look For

- For backspin, the stroke on the ball comes from a high to low position, causing the ball to spin backward after it is struck.
  - Is the stroke high to low?
  - Is the ball rotating backward?
- For topspin, the stroke on the ball must come from a low to high position, causing the ball to spin forward after it is struck.
  - Is the stroke low to high?
  - Is the ball rotating forward?

Instructional Task: Forehand and Backhand From a Serve

■ PRACTICE TASK

Students continue to work on serving, applying the critical elements.

Students who are ready can use either the forehand or backhand to return the serve.

Extension

Students can play a modified game of pickleball. The server scores a point for serving the ball correctly to a partner. The receiver scores a point for returning the serve correctly. Students play for a set amount of time and switch playing partners.

Student Choices/Differentiation

- Students may choose the swing that they feel will be most successful, based on the serve.
- Students may choose to use topspin or backspin on their returns.

What to Look For

- While serving, are students applying the critical elements?
- Are students in the correct position to return the ball?
- Are students using the correct grip and swing, based on the position they have put themselves in?
- Are students trying to create topspin or backspin?

Formal and Informal Assessments

- Informal
- Exit slip: What are the critical elements of striking for topspin and backspin?

Closure

- Ask students to explain and demonstrate how to perform the forehand and backhand strokes.
- Have students give examples of what helped them be successful and what challenged them.
- Ask students to explain and demonstrate backspin and topspin.
- Use examples from what was observed to help students in learning these skills.

Reflection

- What level have students reached in learning the different strokes?
- How many students were able to practice and show understanding of topspin and backspin?

Homework

Practice the backhand movement even if you do not have the equipment. Use a hairbrush or similar object to practice grips and swings. Review the critical elements of all strokes and serves taught so far, posted on the school's physical education website.

Resources

Curtis, J. (1998). *Pickle-ball for player & teacher.* Boston: Brooks/Cole Cengage Learning.

Dougherty, N.J. (Ed.) (2010). *Physical activity & sport for the secondary school student.* 6th ed. Reston, VA: National Association for Sport and Physical Education.

Pickleball Channel: www.pickleballchannel.com

USA Pickleball Assocation: www.usapa.org

LESSON 4: STRATEGIES

Grade-Level Outcomes

Primary Outcome

Using tactics & shots: Reduces offensive options for opponents by returning to mid-court position. (S2.M8.6)

Embedded Outcome

Accepting feedback: Provides corrective feedback to a peer, using teacher-generated guidelines, and incorporating appropriate tone and other communication skills. (S4.M3.7)

Lesson Objectives

The learner will:

- apply the footwork learned by moving to a mid-court position after returning a serve.
- demonstrate the dink shot correctly.

Equipment and Materials

- 1 paddle for each student
- 1 ball for every 3 students
- Recording device for each group
- Grid space with a net for each group

Introduction

When playing any game, strategies are involved. In pickleball, body position on the court is important to strategy. Today, we will discuss and practice our footwork to keep ourselves in the optimal position after each hit for returning the ball.

Instructional Task: Returning to Home Base—Forehand

■ PRACTICE TASK

In groups of three, two students volley the ball using a forehand shot. After each return, students return to the center location.

The partner not volleying conducts a peer assessment using a video camera.

Refinement

Place a piece of tape to mark the home position to give students a visual of where to be.

Extension

Start the activity with a serve.

Guiding questions for students:

- Why is it important to move back into a central position on the court?
- How does reaching for a shot (not moving back to home position) affect the outcome of shots?

EMBEDDED OUTCOME: S4.M3.7 For the peer assessment, use teacher-generated guidelines. Discuss with students the proper way to offer feedback (when to do so, what tone of voice, etc.) to their peers using these guidelines. The assessment can address the critical elements of the footwork or a tally of times that students move back to home position.

Student Choices/Differentiation

- Students may use a different-sized ball if the speed or size of the ball is keeping them from having success.
- If students are not accurate with their forehand returns, have them toss the ball to their partners' forehand side instead of hitting.
- Students can challenge themselves to move partners to the corners of the court, forcing a longer recovery to home base.

What to Look For

- Students are stepping with the correct foot.
- Students are stepping back to the center after the swing.
- Students are performing the forehand correctly in order to step back to mid-court correctly and efficiently.

Instructional Task: Returning to Home Base—Backhand

■ PRACTICE TASK

Same task as before but now use backhand.

Extension

In groups of four, two players volley and return home for 30 seconds while partners count the number of times they hit the home spot. Switch.

Guiding questions for students:

- How is moving back into position similar and different between the backhand and forehand?
- Is it harder to get back using the backhand?

EMBEDDED OUTCOME: S4.M3.7 For the peer assessment, use teacher-generated guidelines. Discuss with students the proper way to offer feedback (when to do so, what tone of voice, etc.) to their peers using these guidelines. The assessment can address the critical elements of the footwork or a tally of times that students move back to home position.

Student Choices/Differentiation

- Students may use a different-sized ball if the speed or size of the ball is keeping them from having success.
- If students are not accurate with their backhand returns, have them toss the ball to their partners' backhand side instead of hitting.
- Students can challenge themselves to move partners to the corners of the court, forcing a longer recovery to home base.

What to Look For

- Students are stepping with the correct foot.
- Students are stepping back to the center after the swing.
- Students are performing the backhand correctly in order to step back to mid-court correctly and efficiently.

Instructional Task: Dinking

■ **PRACTICE TASK**

In grids, students work on the dink shot (soft shot hit within the no-volley zone to the opponents' no-volley zone), attempting to keep the ball from hitting the ground.

Extensions

- Repeat, but attempt to hit to a specific target. Lay a piece of paper on the court in the shallow (close to the net) part of the no-volley zone.
- Repeat from the back half of the court (drop shot).

Refinement

If the ball is going into the net, focus on lifting with the legs. If it's going too deep, try to use backspin.

Guiding questions for students:

- How does the footwork you learned in the previous practice task help in this activity?
- When would you use this shot?
- What other sports have a similar shot?

Student Choices/Differentiation

- Students may use a lighter ball that stays in the air to help keep it from hitting the ground.
- Students may choose to volley (no bounce) or let the ball bounce once.

What to Look For

- Students are using proper technique to return the ball.
- Students are using correct footwork, placing them in the correct area in order to be successful.

Formal and Informal Assessments

Peer assessment: Moving back to home position

Closure

- Ask students to explain why their footwork is important for defensive and offensive strategy.
- Review the correct form for the backhand and forehand, demonstrating how this relates to proper footwork.

Reflection

- Are students demonstrating an understanding of stepping with the correct foot after hitting shots?
- Which students are not successful with making contact with the forehand or backhand hits consistently enough to focus on proper footwork? What will I do next class to give them more support?

Homework

Using the handouts or website, review the rules of pickleball in order to officiate the games tomorrow.

Resources

Curtis, J. (1998). *Pickle-ball for player & teacher.* Boston: Brooks/Cole Cengage Learning.

Dougherty, N.J. (Ed.) (2010). *Physical activity & sport for the secondary school student.* 6th ed. Reston, VA: National Association for Sport and Physical Education.

Pickleball Channel: www.pickleballchannel.com

USA Pickleball Assocation: www.usapa.org

LESSON 5: RULES, MODIFIED GAME PLAY, AND FITNESS

Grade-Level Outcomes

Primary Outcomes

Using tactics & shots: Reduces offensive options for opponents by returning to mid-court position. (S2.M8.6)

Forehand & backhand: Demonstrates the mature form of the forehand and backhand strokes with a short-handled implement in net games such as paddle ball, pickleball or short-handled racket tennis. (S1.M14.6)

Embedded Outcomes

Rules & etiquette: Applies rules and etiquette by acting as an official for modified physical activities and games and creating dance routines within a given set of parameters. (S4.M6.8)

Fitness knowledge: Identifies the components of skill-related fitness. (S3.M7. 6)

Lesson Objectives

The learner will:

- demonstrate the ability to use the forehand, backhand, and footwork while playing four square.
- apply the rules of pickleball during match play.

Equipment and Materials

- Whiteboard or like item for rules
- Device to project video of pickleball to discuss rules
- Paddles for each student
- 2 balls per court, with extra easily available
- 1 court for 3 teams

Introduction

For homework, you were to review the rules of pickleball. Today, we will review the rules and play a couple of modified games of pickleball. We also will discuss the role that pickleball can play in our overall health. Does anyone have any general questions before we go over the rules?

Instructional Task: Rules Discussion

■ PRACTICE TASK

Students gather around the whiteboard to discuss the rules. Be sure to cover the following:

- Court lines and boundaries
- Serving
- Scoring
- Etiquette

Extension

Show video clips of pickleball games that demonstrate each rule.

Guiding questions for students:

Individual questions:

- Where are the players in the video clip serving?
- Where did the ball go when it was served? Was this a legal serve? Why or why not?
- How is the game scored?
- Who served after the point was scored?

Partner questions:

- With your partner, discuss what happened when the ball landed on the line.
- How does the serve rotate between partners and the other team in doubles?

All-class questions:

- With your fingers, indicate how many times the ball may bounce in the court.
- Thumbs up for yes, down for no: Was the serve in or out?

Refinement

If students need more explanations, gather them around a court and demonstrate different rules of the game, getting students involved, and explain what occurred and how it related to pickleball rules.

Student Choices/Differentiation

Students may refer to handouts or video clips, when needed.

What to Look For

- Students understand the basic rules of pickleball.
- Each student can explain, demonstrate, and recall the rules.
- Students know how to score.
- Students recall and use basic pickleball etiquette.

Instructional Task: Pickleball Four Square

■ PRACTICE TASK

In groups of four using the net and center lines, students play four-square pickleball in the no-volley zone.

First objective: to apply the forehand and backhand strokes using correct technique.

Second objective: to apply proper footwork, aligned to the forehand and backhand so they can return to mid-court, which will reduce the options for the opponents.

Extra students not playing can help officiate.

The rules are the same as for four square, but smashing is not allowed. An underhand serve starts the game.

Refinements

Even though we are playing a modified game, the focus of this activity is on improving skill rather than on winning.

Make sure that students return to mid-court position after hitting the ball.

Guiding questions for students:

- How does this game help develop skills needed for pickleball?
- As you are playing, what is causing you to be successful and what is causing you to struggle?
- What skills do you need to work on?

EMBEDDED OUTCOME: S4.M6.8. Teach students the rules and how to apply them for the game of pickleball four square. Have students self-officiate the game.

Student Choices/Differentiation

- The size of the four-square court may be adjusted.
- The size and type of ball may be changed, as well.
- Teams may rotate to other courts after games to play and officiate new teams.
- Move teams around, allowing them to play teams of like abilities.

What to Look For

- Students are using proper technique for backhand and forehand.
- Their footwork and positioning are correct.
- Students are putting themselves in position to reduce opponents' offensive options.

Instructional Task: Kings of the Court

■ PRACTICE TASK

At each court, position three teams of two. One team will officiate and keep score, and the other two will play.

Set up multiple courts throughout the gym, with numbers marked with a cone. Play a 10- to 12-minute game of pickleball. At the end of time, instruct the high scores to move to the lower-number court (e.g., if they won on court 4, then they move to court 3), and have the team with the fewest points move up a court (e.g., example if they did not win on court 4, then they move to court 5). Keep the rotation for the remainder of class.

Extension

Assign extra points for using a certain shot (e.g., the dink).

EMBEDDED OUTCOME: S4.M6.8. Have students self-officiate the pickleball games, ensuring that all rules, scoring, and etiquette are followed.

EMBEDDED OUTCOME: S3.M7.6. Lead a discussion on how pickleball can contribute to a physical activity or fitness plan.

Guiding questions for students:

- Did your heart rate go up while playing the game?
- What kinds of fitness do you think you need to play pickleball?
- Identify the components of skill-related fitness that you use in this game.

Student Choices/Differentiation

If students are struggling, give them the opportunity to practice any of the practice tasks taught in this module off the court.

What to Look For

- Students are using proper serving techniques.
- Students know the rules.
- Students are working together and listening to their peers.

Formal and Informal Assessments

Exit slip: List three ways in which pickleball can contribute to a physical activity or fitness plan.

Closure

- As a group, discuss what was observed from four square.
- Ask how students were able to apply their skills during the game.
- Discuss and provide examples of how students work together in teams as well as help officiate the games.

Reflection

- How is students' technique for the skills that we have been working on?
- Do students know the rules?
- How well did the teams work together, and how did they interact with students who were officiating the game?

Homework

Review the rules of pickleball, because we will have a test at the end of the module. Next class, we will learn to play doubles, so pay close attention to doubles rules while you study.

Resources

Curtis, J. (1998). *Pickle-ball for player & teacher.* Boston: Brooks/Cole Cengage Learning.

Dougherty, N.J. (Ed.) (2010). *Physical activity & sport for the secondary school student.* 6th ed. Reston, VA: National Association for Sport and Physical Education.

Pickleball Channel: www.pickleballchannel.com

USA Pickleball Association: www.usapa.org

Internet keyword search: "rules for pickleball," "fitness concepts of net games"

LESSON 6: DOUBLES

Grade-Level Outcomes

Primary Outcomes

Volley: Forehand- and backhand-volleys with a mature form and control using a short-handled implement. (S1.M16.7)

Serving: Executes consistently (at least 70% of the time) a legal underhand serve to a predetermined target for net/wall games such as badminton, volleyball or pickleball. (S1.M12.7)

Challenge: Recognizes individual challenges and copes in a positive way, such as extending effort, asking for help or feedback and/or modifying the tasks. (S5.M3.6)

Embedded Outcome

Accepting feedback: Provides corrective feedback to a peer, using teacher-generated guidelines, and incorporating appropriate tone and other communication skills. (S4.M3.7)

Lesson Objectives

The learner will:

- demonstrate the ability to serve for accuracy, hitting a variety of targets.
- volley with a mature form with a partner.
- reflect on his performance in a successful way during the doubles play.

Equipment and Materials

- 1 paddle for each student
- 1 ball per 2 people
- 1 recording device for every 2 to 4 students
- 1 court for each group

Introduction

In the previous class, we played kings of the court. What did you learn from doing this that might help during doubles game play today? How important is it to be able to serve? Today, we will spend the first part of class working on the serve and the remainder of the lesson on doubles. You'll also have an opportunity to video-assess your skills during the doubles play. Between games, you will watch the first 3 minutes and note what you did well with regard to skill and positioning, and what you will need to adjust.

Instructional Task: Serving for Accuracy

■ PRACTICE TASK

In grids, students practice serving using correct technique and focusing on hitting specific marks on the court. Each mark is worth a certain number of points. The larger the marker, the fewer the points.

Extension

After practicing this for a while, students create teams and play against each other by adding up points or individually.

Refinement

Students should be practicing using the proper movement pattern. Make sure that students are not sacrificing form for accuracy.

Student Choices/Differentiation

- Students may choose what target they want to hit.
- Students may move up to serve, if they need to.

What to Look For

- Students are using correct technique and applying the critical elements for serving.
- Students are serving accurately.

Instructional Task: Volleying

■ PRACTICE TASK

In grids, students practice volleying skills.

Starting 4 to 6 feet (1.2 to 1.8 m) apart, students practice hitting the ball back and forth without letting it touch the ground.

Have students begin by volleying to a partner for a set time. If students hit a ball that makes the partner move 2 to 3 feet (0.6 to 0.9 m), stop the drill and start over (for safety reasons).

Students can use forehand, backhand, or both during this task.

Extensions

- If students are having success, they can start 2 feet (0.6 m) closer or farther away.
- Repeat with students attempting to volley to an open space.

Refinement

Make sure that students are in an athletic stance to start and after each hit.

Guiding questions for students:

- When would you use the skill of volleying?
- What strategy (offensive or defensive) would this skill fit into?

Student Choices/Differentiation

- Students may choose distance to start.
- Students may use different-sized equipment (balloon, yarn or tennis ball, etc.).

What to Look For

- Students are using critical elements of the forehand and backhand volley.
- Students are moving back to home positon.

Instructional Task:
Doubles Game Play and Peer Recording

■ PRACTICE TASK

During the doubles game, three teams are at each court. Two teams playing apply the skills and rules, while the other team is recording the game and helping to officiate.

Games are played for 10 minutes. Teams rotate on the court.

Guiding questions for students:

- How are the rules different for singles and doubles?
- Why is communication important in doubles?

Student Choices/Differentiation

- Game rules may be modified on an individual or class basis, if needed.
- Modifications may include letting the ball bounce twice.
- Moving up the server or allowing the serve to be played from anywhere as long as it clears the net are other options.

What to Look For

- The team not playing is recording the teams that are playing.
- Students are working together so all students are able to be recorded.
- Students are holding each other accountable for implementing the rules correctly.
- Students' placement on the court is allowing them to perform the skills that they have learned and practiced.

Instructional Task: Students View Video

■ PRACTICE TASK

Students have a chance to view their videos from doubles play. While watching their videos, students reflect on the following:

- Is their footwork and positioning correct?
- Are they making efficient movements toward the ball?
- Are they putting themselves in a tactical position on defense to be able to cover their area and make an offensive shot?
- Are they recognizing the open spaces and trying to put their shots there?
- Are they taking more steps than needed?
- Are they able to return to their defensive positions in one or two steps?

EMBEDDED OUTCOME: S4.M3.7. Teach students to provide corrective feedback using teacher-generated guidelines to their peers while reviewing their videos. Choose any of the previous questions, and have students offer feedback to a peer.

Student Choices/Differentiation

- Show an example from a previous class on the proper way to reflect.
- Provide critical elements for students to use while evaluating technique, and provide examples of what feedback should sound like in order to be appropriate and meaningful.

What to Look For

- Students are noticing what they are doing incorrectly and are attempting to change what they are doing.
- Students are helping classmates by providing corrective feedback based on the cues and encouraging them by letting them know what they are doing well.

Formal and Informal Assessments

Written reflection of teacher-generated questions for their play during doubles

Closure

Using student recordings, select a couple of groups to show and discuss what they talked about and learned while watching themselves.

Reflection

- How was the skill of students?
- Does it seem like they know how to play and the rules?
- After reviewing students' corrective feedback, does it appear students know if the skills are being performed correctly?
- How did students do with the peer review?

Homework

Review rules for singles and doubles of pickleball. Keep practicing the skills at home.

Resources

Curtis, J. (1998). *Pickle-ball for player & teacher.* Boston: Brooks/Cole Cengage Learning.

Dougherty, N.J. (Ed.) (2010). *Physical activity & sport for the secondary school student.* 6th ed. Reston, VA: National Association for Sport and Physical Education.

Pickleball Channel: www.pickleballchannel.com

USA Pickleball Assocation: www.usapa.org

Internet keyword search: "doubles in pickleball"

LESSON 7: SHOT SELECTION

Grade-Level Outcomes

Primary Outcome

Using tactics & shots: Selects offensive shot based on opponent's location (hit where opponent is not). (S2.M8.7)

Embedded Outcome

Rules & etiquette: Applies rules and etiquette by acting as an official for modified physical activities and games and creating dance routines within a given set of parameters. (S4.M6.8)

Lesson Objectives

The learner will select and implement a shot based on the location of the opponent in order to hit the ball into open space.

Equipment and Materials

- Enough rackets for each player
- 1 ball for every group of 2
- Enough grids and spacing for each group
- 1 court for every 3 teams

Introduction

Today, we will focus on shot selection during singles and doubles. Using the correct shots not only will help win the point but also will help save energy. The goal is to make the opponent move a lot, causing tiredness and incorrect form, while you move minimally, saving energy and giving you a better chance for a full movement pattern when you swing.

Instructional Task: Shot Selection Drill

■ PRACTICE TASK

The purpose of this task is to use the best stroke and spin in order to make the ball difficult to return.

Teach how each type of shot should be used in singles and doubles play to increase the chance of winning the point.

In grids, students work together to practice ball placement from a serve or returned hit.

The student receiving the serve tries to direct her shot away from the server using any of the strokes or spins learned.

On one half of the court, place a marker or tape near the baseline, near the center line, and near the sideline. Form groups of four, with two players on each baseline. The first player on the marked side of the court (defense) hits the ball over the net and moves from home to one of the markers. The first player on the offensive side chooses a shot based on the opponent's location. The player calls out the shot (down the line, cross-court, or dink or drop) and tries to execute it. Players return to the end of their lines. After 3 minutes, switch sides.

Extension

Add a marker in the no-volley zone, and have players try to pass the net player.

Guiding questions for students:

- What's the best location for your shot if your opponent is pulled wide?
- What if the opponent is too deep?
- Too close to the net?

After each return, students should ask themselves if the shot was good and why.

If not, what should be done differently next time? Students can place these answers in a notebook to study at a later date.

Student Choices/Differentiation

- Execute at half speed or walk through the shot selection if students have trouble recognizing the open spaces.
- Provide videos, pictures, and diagrams to help students understand.

What to Look For

- Students recognize the open space.
- Students are looking to see where the opponent is before hitting.
- Students have enough control on their shots to be accurate when they do see the spaces.

Instructional Task: Doducles

■ PRACTICE TASK

At each court, one team officiates and the other two play doubles. Students implement the skills, strategies, and tactics they've learned. These will be assessed during the next class period.

Refinement

Stop all students to demonstrate and discuss any rules, skills, or strategies that are being continually performed incorrectly as a class to help with any skills or written assessments.

EMBEDDED OUTCOME: S4.M6.8. Discuss with students the importance of officiating. As officials, make sure students understand the rules and hold each other to them.

Student Choices/Differentiation

If students are struggling, give them the opportunity to practice any of the practice tasks taught in this module off the court.

What to Look For

- Students are performing the critical elements for the serve, forehand, and backhand correctly.
- Students are demonstrating knowledge and understanding of the rules and holding both teams to them while they play.

Instructional Task: Written Strategy

■ PRACTICE TASK

Show videos and describe the different doubles strategy positions (up and back, side by side, etc.).

Now that students have seen and had time to practice some of the strategies, they work together on a written plan for attacking or defending.

To help students with strategy using shot selection, create a handout of practice problems. Practice problems can include fill-in-the-blank questions with missing shots in the sequence, and diagrams showing where players are on the court, asking what shots they should make.

Extension

Students create their own practice problems and share them with friends (who then write how to defend against the plans).

Guiding questions for students:

- How will this strategy help you attack on offense?
- Why do you believe this will be effective?
- Why do you believe this strategy will help you on defense?

Student Choices/Differentiation

Provide options for offense or defense, and have students choose one and explain verbally why they think they will be effective.

What to Look For

- Students have enough understanding of the game to make strategies.
- Students know offense well enough to make and explain strategies.
- Students know what they can do to help themselves on defense both in positioning and returns.

Formal and Informal Assessments

Create a written plan for attacking or defending in pickleball.

Closure

- Gather students around to discuss what was observed and to review one last time the correct technique for the forehand, backhand, and serve.
- Review the rules, providing examples of what was observed for correct or incorrect officiating.

Reflection

- Are students able to apply the proper technique and appropriate spins to get the ball into open spaces?
- How are students doing officiating and keeping score during the games?

Homework

Practice the forehand, backhand, and serve, which will be assessed during game play during our next class.

Refer students to the school's physical education website to review the assessments.

Encourage students to study for the pickleball cognitive test.

Resources

Curtis, J. (1998). *Pickle-ball for player & teacher.* Boston: Brooks/Cole Cengage Learning.

Dougherty, N.J. (Ed.) (2010). *Physical activity & sport for the secondary school student.* 6th ed. Reston, VA: National Association for Sport and Physical Education.

Pickleball Channel: www.pickleballchannel.com

USA Pickleball Assocation: www.usapa.org

Internet keyword search: "offensive strategies in pickleball," "defensive strategies in pickleball," "proper shot selection in pickleball"

LESSON 8: GAME AND TESTING DAY

Grade-Level Outcomes

Primary Outcomes

Forehand & backhand: Demonstrates the mature form of the forehand and backhand strokes with a short-handled implement in net games such as paddle ball, pickleball or short-handled racket tennis. (S1.M14.6)

Serving: Performs a legal underhand serve with control for net/wall games such as badminton, volleyball or pickleball. (S1.M12.6)

Rules & etiquette: Demonstrates knowledge of rules and etiquette by self-officiating modified physical activities and games or following parameters to create or modify a dance. (S4.M6.7)

Embedded Outcomes

Working with others: Responds appropriately to participants' ethical and unethical behavior during physical activity by using rules and guidelines for resolving conflicts. (S4.M4.8)

Social interaction: Demonstrates respect for self and others in activities and games by following the rules, encouraging others and playing in the spirit of the game or activity. (S5.M6.6)

Lesson Objectives

The learner will:

- demonstrate basic skills during game play.
- demonstrate his knowledge and understanding of the rules, strategies, and tactics on a knowledge test.

Equipment and Materials

- 1 paddle for each student
- 1 ball for each group
- Assessments for the serve, backhand, and forehand, 1 for each student
- Assessments for the knowledge test, 1 for each student

Introduction

Today, we will incorporate all the skills and knowledge we have learned into pickleball games. During these games, you will be assessed on your ability to demonstrate the following skills using correct form: the serve, the forehand, and the backhand, as well as your knowledge and understanding of the rules and strategies. The skills will be assessed as you play, and the rules and strategies will be assessed from a test while you are not playing.

Instructional Task: Doubles Skills Assessment

■ PRACTICE TASK

EMBEDDED OUTCOME: S5.M6.6. Discuss with students what it means to be respectful. Have students give examples of what this should look like while playing doubles.

Students also should give examples of what it sounds and looks like to encourage others, even those you are playing against.

Assess students while they play a game of doubles. Skills to assess:

- serve
- forehand
- backhand

Extensions
- Assess the dink/drop shot and volley
- Assess strategies during game play

EMBEDDED OUTCOME: S4.M4.8. While students are playing, they should follow the rules and demonstrate good sportsmanship before, during, and after the game.

Student Choices/Differentiation
- Modify on an individual basis to meet students' needs.
- Students may chose partners.

What to Look For
During the games, assess students' ability to perform the critical elements of the serve, backhand, and forehand.

Instructional Task: Knowledge Assessment of Pickleball

■ PRACTICE TASK
Students who are not playing take the knowledge assessment on rules and strategies of pickleball.

Student Choices/Differentiation
- If needed, pull students aside to read aloud before or after class.
- Modify assessment as needed to address student needs.

What to Look For
Students demonstrate that they know the terms, rules, and strategies of pickleball.

Formal and Informal Assessments
- Checklist or rubric for skills test of forehand, backhand, and serve during game play
- Knowledge test of the rules, strategy, and scoring

Closure
- Bring students together to discuss the success observed over the module.
- Highlight gains, notable effort, and sportsmanship of individuals.
- Discuss any areas that may need improvement that could also transfer over to upcoming modules.

Reflection
- What skills did students struggle with, and what helped them become proficient?
- What skills did students struggle with and in which they did not become as proficient as desired?
- What areas may need more time, and what areas could take less time to help students become more successful?

Homework
Have students look over the next module, and be ready to talk about the specific questions, objectives, or skills desired.

Resources

Curtis, J. (1998). *Pickle-ball for player & teacher.* Boston: Brooks/Cole Cengage Learning.
Pickleball Channel: www.pickleballchannel.com
USA Pickleball Assocation: www.usapa.org

BADMINTON MODULE

Lessons in this module were contributed by Robert J. Doan, assistant professor of physical education in the University of Southern Mississippi's School of Kinesiology.

Grade-Level Outcomes Addressed, by Lesson	Lessons							
	1	2	3	4	5	6	7	8
Standard 1. The physically literate individual demonstrates competency in a variety of motor skills and movement patterns.								
Performs a legal underhand serve with control for net/wall games such as badminton, volleyball or pickleball. (S1.M12.6)				P	P	P		
Executes consistently (at least 70% of the time) a legal underhand serve to a predetermined target for net/wall games such as badminton, volleyball or pickleball. (S1.M12.7)				P				
Strikes with a mature overhand pattern in a nondynamic environment for net/wall games such as volleyball, handball, badminton or tennis. (S1.M13.6)					P	P	P	
Strikes with a mature overhand pattern in a dynamic environment for net/wall games such as volleyball, handball, badminton or tennis. (S1.M13.7)	P	P	P					
Demonstrates the mature form of forehand and backhand strokes with a long-handled implement in net games such as badminton or tennis. (S1.M14.7)	P	P						
Demonstrates the mature form of forehand and backhand strokes with a short- or long-handled implement with power and accuracy in net games such as pickleball, tennis, badminton or paddle ball. (S1.M14.8)								P
Standard 2. The physically literate individual applies knowledge of concepts, principles, strategies and tactics related to movement and performance.								
Creates open space in net/wall games with a long-handled implement by varying force and direction, and by moving opponent from side to side. (S2.M7.7)			P					
Creates open space in net/wall games with either a long- or short-handled implement by varying force or direction, or by moving opponent from side to side and/or forward and back. (S2.M7.8)						p	P	P
Reduces offensive options for opponents by returning to mid-court position. (S2.M8.6)			P			P		
Selects offensive shot based on opponent's location (hit where opponent is not). (S2.M8.7)					P		P	
Standard 3. The physically literate individual demonstrates the knowledge and skills to achieve and maintain a health-enhancing level of physical activity and fitness.								
Maintains a physical activity log for at least 2 weeks and reflects on activity levels as documented in the log. (S3.M16.6)	E							E
Standard 4. The physically literate individual exhibits responsible personal and social behavior that respects self and others.								
Exhibits responsible social behaviors by cooperating with classmates, demonstrating inclusive behaviors and supporting classmates. (S4.M1.7)			E					
Demonstrates self-responsibility by implementing specific corrective feedback to improve performance. (S4.M3.6)		E						
Provides corrective feedback to a peer, using teacher-generated guidelines, and incorporating appropriate tone and other communication skills. (S4.M3.7)						E		
Accepts differences among classmates in physical development, maturation and varying skill levels by providing encouragement and positive feedback. (S4.M4.6)	E			E				
Demonstrates knowledge of rules and etiquette by self-officiating modified physical activities and games or following parameters to create or modify a dance. (S4.M6.7)								E
Standard 5. The physically literate individual recognizes the value of physical activity for health, enjoyment, challenge, self-expression and/or social interaction.								
Demonstrates respect for self and others in activities and games by following the rules, encouraging others and playing in the spirit of the game or activity. (S5.M6.6)							E	
Demonstrates the importance of social interaction by helping and encouraging others, avoiding trash talk and providing support to classmates. (S5.M6.7)							E	

P = Primary; E = Embedded

LESSON 1:
FOREHAND AND BACKHAND CLEARS

Grade-Level Outcomes

Primary Outcomes

Striking: Strikes with a mature overhand pattern in a dynamic environment for net/wall games such as volleyball, handball, badminton or tennis. (S1.M13.7)

Forehand & backhand: Demonstrates the mature form of forehand and backhand strokes with a long-handled implement in net games such as badminton or tennis. (S1.M14.7)

Embedded Outcomes

Working with others: Accepts differences among classmates in physical development, maturation and varying skill levels by providing encouragement and positive feedback. (S4.M4.6)

Assessment & program planning: Maintains a physical activity log for at least 2 weeks and reflects on activity levels as documented in the log. (S3.M16.6)

Lesson Objectives

The learner will:

- demonstrate the ability to perform both the V-grip and thumb grip.
- demonstrate the ability to perform the forehand clear shot by completing three out of five attempts successfully during the grids practice task.
- demonstrate the ability to perform the backhand clear shot by completing three out of five attempts successfully during the grids practice task.

Equipment and Materials

- Yarn balls and shuttles: at least 5 for every 2 students
- Badminton rackets and long-handled lollipop paddles: 1 per student
- 4 cones for grids: 4 cones for every 2 students
- Tape for targets on wall
- Pedometers

Introduction

Today, we will start our next module on striking with a long implement. We will use the sport of badminton to do so. We will start with grips, forehand clears, and backhand clears. Throughout the unit, we will progress to more advanced motor skills, such as smashes and drop shots, as well as learn the rules and basic tactics to succeed in game play.

Show a badminton video clip to pique students' interest.

EMBEDDED OUTCOME: S3.M16.6 *During this module, we will track our physical activity with step counts. It will be interesting to see how our step-count goals are different in badminton than in some other modules that we have completed. Track your step count for each lesson and track your physical activity outside of class, as well.*

Instructional Task:
Explore Striking With a Long-Handled Implement

■ PRACTICE TASK

Working in grids, students explore striking with a partner as a pre-assessment for the module.

Guiding questions for students:

Discuss with students the similar characteristics of badminton and other sports.

- Did you see a pattern of hitting the shuttle hard and soft?
- What other sports use a long-handled implement?
- On what trajectory does the shuttle move after you hit it?

Extension

Have students explore striking again after the brief discussion about skill transfer.

Student Choices/Differentiation

Students can use a badminton racket or lollipop paddle for striking and a shuttle or yarn balls to hit.

What to Look For

Observe in the pre-assessment:

- Movement patterns
- Types of shots students take
- Court movement
- Common errors in skill and tactics

Instructional Task: Learning Grips

■ PRACTICE TASK

Demonstrate the V-grip and thumb grip.

Students practice the grips.

Extension

Have students place rackets on the ground. When you say "go," students pick up their rackets with the V-grip or thumb grip according to your demand.

Refinement

Refine skill by reviewing pictures of the grips on the school's physical education website. Post an instructional video of the grips to the school's website.

Student Choices/Differentiation

Students can use lollipop paddles or badminton rackets.

What to Look For

- V-grip: Students use a V-grip (thumb and index finger form a V) and not a fist-like grip (they form a U).
- Students do not use a flattened thumb—when students press the thumb flat against the racket handle—a common error for the thumb grip. A flattened thumb causes tension, which hinders power.

Instructional Task: Forehand Strike Movement Pattern

■ PRACTICE TASK

Demonstrate the forehand strike movement pattern.

Students will mimic the striking motion.

Refinement

Refine skill by breaking down the movement pattern and stressing critical elements if needed.

Extension

Peer-assess a partner's striking movement pattern using a checklist.

EMBEDDED OUTCOME: S4.M4.6 Remind students that not all classmates are at the same skill level. Discuss encouraging their peers and offering positive feedback during class so that all students can improve their skills.

Student Choices/Differentiation

Students may use lollipop paddles or badminton rackets.

What to Look For

- The arm action is back to front, rather than sidearm or overhead.
- Students either stand in a forward or backward stance or step forward on the opposite foot.
- Students swing through the shuttlecock, not at it.
- The swing is low to high.

Instructional Task: Forehand Strike Against Wall

■ PRACTICE TASK

One student kneels and soft-tosses the ball to a partner, who forehand-strikes the ball into the wall. Students should stand at least 10 feet (3 m) from the wall. Students switch after every 10 hits.

Extensions

- Try to hit a spot on the wall.
- Try changing the yarn ball to a shuttle.

Student Choices/Differentiation

Staying with the foam ball or moving to a balloon, moving closer to the wall, and taking breaks to practice only the movement pattern without the partner tossing the ball are all ways to modify the activity according to skill level.

What to Look For

- The racket face is flat for the contact.
- Students are beginning to pull the racket way back in preparation for the contact.
- Students are following through in the direction of the target.

Instructional Task: Forehand and Backhand Strike in Grids

■ PRACTICE TASK

Teaching in grids, assign tasks from the controlled environment, moving toward an uncontrolled environment.

Call out a command. The students practice the task five times and then switch so their partners can perform the same command. Call out another command.

Partners must cooperate by making good tosses. Partners also should encourage each other.

First: Toss the yarn ball to the middle section of your partner's forearm side for five hits.

Same task with backhand.

Second: Toss the yarn ball so that your partner has to take a quick step to the forearm side to hit the shuttle.

Same task with backhand (step toward backhand side).

Third: Toss the yarn ball so that your partner has to take a quick step forward and hit a forehand shot.

Same task with backhand.

Fourth: Toss the yarn ball so that your partner has to take a quick step back while still hitting a forehand shot.

Same task with backhand.

Extension

We now will move into a more game-like, or uncontrolled, setting. The partner tossing should choose randomly any of the previous tasks. Make sure that you still are tossing at the midsection and using only the forehand or backhand shot. Switch after five tosses.

Repeat this extension until many have had success.

Refinement

Make sure that students are swinging with a full movement pattern. Tell students to fully strike the ball (instead of tapping it to their partners).

Student Choices/Differentiation

- If the class is struggling with an extension, stay at that particular extension for a couple more rounds before moving to the next one.
- Start with yarn balls, and if students are having a high incidence of success, switch to shuttles.

What to Look For

- The biggest concern in this task is students' not having a full movement pattern. They cut the hit short to hit the shuttle back to their partners instead of using a full motor pattern, hitting the ball as hard as they can. Make sure that they hit the yarn balls as hard as they can and complete the full movement pattern with a follow-through.
- If students are swinging and missing, make sure that they're tracking the shuttle all the way to the target.

Formal and Informal Assessments

- Informal assessments
- Peer assessment: Students use a teacher-created checklist to assess partners' movement patterns.
- Exit slip: What are the critical elements of the two types of clears that we learned today?

Closure

- What types of grips did you learn today?
- Name three critical elements of the forehand clear.
- Name three critical elements of the backhand clear.
- Give some examples of cooperation in today's class.

Keep practicing the skills at home, if you can. In our next lesson, we will learn the overhead and underhand clear shots.

Reflection

- Do students strike the shuttle so that it travels forward instead of mostly upward?
- Are they able to transfer the striking movement pattern with the long implement, making sure that they complete the strike with a follow-through?
- Are students getting enough practice hits throughout the lesson?

Homework

Striking (with hand, short implement, or long implement) will help support what students are learning in physical education class. It doesn't matter what piece of equipment or ball they use, as long as they practice the movement pattern and eye–hand coordination.

Students should take home the worksheet with pictures of the grips and the critical elements of the forehand and backhand clear. They also can review the grips and instruction videos that you can post to the school's physical education website.

EMBEDDED OUTCOME: S3.M16.6. Remind students to record their step counts during physical education class, daily physical activity time, and their reflections in a personal log after each lesson in the module.

Resources

Ballou, R. (1992). *Badminton for beginners*. Englewood, CO: Morton.

Grice, T. (2008). *Badminton: Steps to success*. Champaign, IL: Human Kinetics.

The Badminton Bible: www.badmintonbible.com

Internet keyword search: "V-grip and thumb grip in badminton," "forehand and backhand clear shots in badminton"

LESSON 2: CLEARS DAY 2

Grade-Level Outcomes

Primary Outcomes

Striking: Strikes with a mature overhand pattern in a dynamic environment for net/wall games such as volleyball, handball, badminton or tennis. (S1.M13.7)

Forehand & backhand: Demonstrates the mature form of forehand and backhand strokes with a long-handled implement in net games such as badminton or tennis. (S1.M14.7)

Embedded Outcome

Accepting feedback: Demonstrates self-responsibility by implementing specific corrective feedback to improve performance. (S4.M3.6)

Lesson Objectives

The learner will:

- demonstrate the ability to perform the overhead clear shot by completing three out of five attempts successfully during the grids practice task.
- demonstrate the ability to perform the underhand clear shot by completing three out of five attempts successfully during the grids practice task.

Equipment and Materials

- Yarn balls and shuttles: at least 5 for every 2 students
- Badminton rackets and long-handled lollipop paddles: 1 per student
- 4 cones for grids: 4 cones for every 2 students
- Tape for targets on wall
- Pedometers

Introduction

Today we will learn two more clear shots in badminton. Last class, we learned the forehand and backhand clear shots, and today we will learn the overhead and underhand clears. The clear shots are the most common shots and are the most effective shots for moving your opponent to the back of the court.

Instructional Task: Review Grip and Striking Forehand and Backhand With Long-Handled Implement

■ PRACTICE TASK

In grids, check students' grips and have students explore striking with a partner.

Have students toss yarn balls or hit shuttles to a partner, exploring backhand and forehand striking. Move from a controlled environment to an unpredictable environment.

Refinement

Refine skill as needed. Spend as much time as needed to have at least 80 percent of the class successful.

Student Choices/Differentiation

Students can use a badminton racket or lollipop paddle for striking and a shuttle or yarn balls to hit.

What to Look For

- Make sure that students are striking with the full striking movement pattern.
- This task can be used as an informal assessment to gauge where students are in this skill after one day of striking.

Instructional Task:
Overhead and Underhand Strike Movement Pattern

■ PRACTICE TASK

Demonstrate and have students mimic the striking motion.

Refinement

Refine skill by breaking down the movement pattern and stressing critical elements if needed.

Extension

Students can peer-assess their partners' movement patterns with a video device and critical elements checklist.

Peer assessment: critical elements of the movement pattern

Student Choices/Differentiation

Students may use lollipop paddles or badminton rackets.

What to Look For

- Students position their bodies so that they are under and slightly behind where they are dropping the shuttle, the racket in back-scratching position.
- Students snap the wrist and follow through.
- Students step or lunge and rotate forearm so racket is brought explosively up.

Instructional Task:
Overhead and Underhand Strike in Grids

■ PRACTICE TASK

Teaching in grids, assign tasks from the controlled environment, moving toward an uncontrolled environment.

Call out a command. Students practice the task five times and then switch so that their partners can perform the same command. Call out another command.

Partners must cooperate for good tosses. Partners should provide feedback to each other.

First: Toss or strike the yarn ball high into the area toward your partner and strike for five hits.

Same task with underhand strike.

Second: Toss or strike the yarn ball so that your partner has to take a quick step to the forearm side to hit the shuttle above the head.

Same task with underhand strike.

Third: Toss or strike the yarn ball so that your partner has to take a quick step forward and hit an overhead shot.

Same task with underhand strike.

Fourth: Toss or strike the yarn ball so that your partner has to take a quick step back while still hitting an overhead shot.

Same task with underhand strike.

Extension

We now will move into a more game-like, or uncontrolled, setting. The partner tossing or striking should choose randomly any of the previous tasks. Make sure that the striker is using only the overhead or underhand clear. Switch after five tosses.

Repeat this extension until many have had success.

Student Choices/Differentiation

If the class is struggling with an extension, stay at that particular extension for a couple more rounds before moving to the next one.

Start with yarn balls, and if students are having a high incidence of success, switch to shuttles.

What to Look For

- The biggest concern in this task is students' not having a full movement pattern. They cut the movement pattern short to hit the shuttle back to their partners instead of using a full motor pattern, hitting the ball or shuttle as hard as they can. Make sure that they are hitting the yarn balls or shuttles as hard as they can and completing the full movement pattern with a follow-through.
- If students are swinging and missing, make sure that they are tracking the shuttle all the way to the target.

Instructional Task: Clear-Shot Rally

■ PRACTICE TASK

- Place tape 4 feet (1.2 m) inside the back boundary lines of the court.
- Partners rally clear shots from behind the taped lines, trying to drive each other all the way back to or outside their back boundary lines. Players may use forehand, backhand, overhead, and underhand clear shots.
- Partners may not step across the taped lines to return shots.

Extension

Peers assess a partner's striking movement pattern using a teacher-generated checklist.

EMBEDDED OUTCOME: S4.M3.6 Hand out a list of examples of proper and improper corrective feedback. Discuss with students which feedback statements are helpful and which are not as helpful. Encourage students to use appropriate feedback statements to improve performance.

Student Choices/Differentiation

Staying with the foam ball or moving to a shuttle, moving closer to the net, and taking breaks to practice only the movement pattern without the partner hitting the ball are all ways to modify the activity.

What to Look For

- Students are getting in position to make the clear shots.
- Rackets are in back-scratching position.
- Students are stepping into shots.

Formal and Informal Assessments

- Informal assessment
- Have two students rally and a third watch (or video-record) the movement pattern to give feedback. Rotate after 10 strikes.

Closure

- Name three critical elements of the overhead clear.
- Name three critical elements of the underhand clear.
- Give an example of feedback that you shared with your partner.

Keep practicing the skills at home, and in the next class, we will continue to practice clears as well as add strategy.

Reflection

- Do students strike the shuttle so that it travels forward instead of mostly upward?
- In the uncontrolled environments, does the movement pattern change?
- Are students at all skill levels improving?

Homework

Striking (with hand, short implement, or long implement) will help support what students are learning in physical education class. It does not matter what piece of equipment or ball they use, as long as they are practicing the movement pattern and eye–hand coordination.

Students should review instructional videos for clear shots and strategy that are posted to the school's physical education website.

Students can update their physical activity logs.

Resources

Ballou, R. (1992). *Badminton for beginners*. Englewood, CO: Morton.

Grice, T. (2008). *Badminton: Steps to success*. Champaign, IL: Human Kinetics.

The Badminton Bible: www.badmintonbible.com

Internet keyword search: "overhead and underhand clear shots in badminton"

LESSON 3: INTRODUCTION TO STRATEGY

Grade-Level Outcomes

Primary Outcomes

Striking: Strikes with a mature overhand pattern in a dynamic environment for net/wall games such as volleyball, handball, badminton or tennis. (S1.M13.7)

Creating space through variation: Creates open space in net/wall games with a long-handled implement by varying force and direction, and by moving opponent from side to side. (S2.M7.7)

Using tactics & shots: Reduces offensive options for opponents by returning to mid-court position. (S2.M8.6)

Embedded Outcome

Personal responsibility: Exhibits responsible social behaviors by cooperating with classmates, demonstrating inclusive behaviors and supporting classmates. (S4.M1.7)

Lesson Objectives

The learner will:

- perform clear shots correctly during the uncontrolled environment practice task.
- perform the basic offensive strategy of moving an opponent from side to side during the practice task.
- perform the basic defensive strategy of returning to mid-court or home base after hitting clear shots in the practice task.

Equipment and Materials

- Yarn balls and shuttles: at least 5 for every 2 students
- Badminton rackets and long-handled lollipop paddles: 1 per student
- 4 cones for grids: 4 cones for every 2 students
- Pedometers

Introduction

Today, we will practice the four clear shots that you have learned so far in our Badminton Module. We also will learn basic offensive and defensive strategies that will improve your game play later in the module.

Show a video clip of a badminton game in which players are using multiple strategies.

Instructional Task: Review Striking Forehand, Backhand, Overhead, and Underhand

■ PRACTICE TASK

Working in grids, students toss or strike a yarn ball or shuttle to a partner, exploring the four types of clear shots. Move from a controlled environment to an unpredictable environment.

Spend as much time in skill practice as needed so that at least 80 percent of students are successful.

Student Choices/Differentiation

Students may use a badminton racket or lollipop paddle for striking and a shuttle or yarn balls to hit.

What to Look For

- Students are striking with the full striking movement pattern.
- This task can be used as an informal assessment to gauge where your students are in this skill after two days of striking and learning clear shots.

Instructional Task: Clear-Shot Rally

■ PRACTICE TASK

Similar to the task in Lesson 2, place tape 4 feet (1.2 m) inside the back boundary lines of the court. Partners rally clear shots from behind the taped lines, trying to drive each other all the way back to or outside of the back boundary lines. Partners may not step across the taped line to return shots.

Extension

Use flip cameras or iPads to film rally. Have students review their performance and look for errors in their movement patterns.

Refinement

Students need to follow through with their shots to have a mature movement pattern. Stop the practice task if students are not following through with their hits.

Student Choices/Differentiation

- Students may focus on certain clear shots or challenge themselves to use all four.
- Students may use yarn balls or shuttles.
- Students may move closer, if needed.

What to Look For

Students are driving the shots deep into the court.

Instructional Task: Moving Opponent From Side to Side and Moving Back to Home Base

■ PRACTICE TASK

Introduce the strategy of moving the opponent with clears.

Students work in pairs, one on each side of the court (or in grids) at home base. Student A throws the ball or shuttle to the back court to move her opponent. Student B should catch the ball or shuttle and move back to home base.

Extensions

- Student A throws the ball or shuttle to the back court. Student B returns it with a clear shot and moves back to home base.
- Student A strikes the ball or shuttle to the back court. Student B returns it with a clear shot and moves back to home base.

Refinement

Refine skill or tactics as needed. For example, for each attempt, students can track points: 1 for a successful clear and 1 for a return to home base. This reinforces the importance of positioning as well as the shot.

EMBEDDED OUTCOME: S4.M1.7. Have students support their peers by encouraging them to return to home base after each hit.

Student Choices/Differentiation

- Start in a controlled environment and then move to an uncontrolled environment.
- Stay on progression until students attain a high level of success.
- Students may use a yarn ball or shuttle, depending on skill level.

What to Look For

- The tosser or striker should be placing clear shots deep in opponent's court using correct technique.
- The receiver is assuming an athletic position to return the clear shot, hitting the shot, and then returning to home base.

Formal and Informal Assessments

- Informal and peer assessments for this lesson
- Exit slip: Please describe one offensive and one defensive strategy in badminton.

Closure

- Describe the offensive strategy that we covered today.
- What is the most important defensive strategy that you learned today?
- How did tracking points for returning to home base affect your play?

Keep practicing the skills at home. If you have equipment, practice the motor skills. If you do not have equipment, practice the tactics with a small ball.

Next class, we will add serves.

Reflection

- Are all students performing the clear shots with a mature movement pattern?
- Did students use the strategies (offensive and defensive) in the last activity?
- Are students encouraging one another, or do I need to revisit this in the next lesson?

Homework

Striking (long implement) will help support what students are learning in physical education class. Practice the basic strategies taught with badminton equipment or simply a ball and a court. Also, review the previous instructional videos as well as the serve videos that are posted to the school's physical education website.

Students can update their physical activity logs.

Resources

Ballou, R. (1992). *Badminton for beginners*. Englewood, CO: Morton.

Grice, T. (2008). *Badminton: Steps to success*. Champaign, IL: Human Kinetics.

The Badminton Bible: www.badmintonbible.com

Internet keyword search: "offensive and defensive strategies in badminton"

LESSON 4: SERVING

Grade-Level Outcomes

Primary Outcomes

Serving: Performs a legal underhand serve with control for net/wall games such as badminton, volleyball or pickleball. (S1.M12.6)

Serving: Executes consistently (at least 70% of the time) a legal underhand serve to a predetermined target for net/wall games such as badminton, volleyball or pickleball. (S1.M12.7)

Embedded Outcome

Working with others: Accepts differences among classmates in physical development, maturation and varying skill levels by providing encouragement and positive feedback. (S4.M4.6)

Lesson Objectives

The learner will:

- demonstrate the ability to perform the long serve by completing three out of five attempts during the grids practice task.
- demonstrate the ability to perform the short serve by completing three out of five attempts during the grids practice task.
- perform short and long serves with at least 70 percent accuracy during the hoop practice task.

Equipment and Materials

- Yarn balls and shuttles: at least 5 for every 2 students
- Badminton rackets and long-handled lollipop paddles: 1 per student
- 4 cones for grids: 4 cones for every 2 students
- Tape for targets on wall
- Hoops
- Poly spots
- Pedometers

Introduction

Today, we will learn the important skill of serving. There are two types of serves in badminton, and they are important to learn since we start each point with a serve.

Show a quick video clip of badminton serves.

Instructional Task:
Explore Short and Long Serves in Badminton

■ PRACTICE TASK

Working in grids, students explore serving with a partner.

Guiding questions for students:

Discuss with students the similar characteristics of badminton serves and other sports.

- Did you see a pattern of hitting the shuttle hard and soft?
- What other sports use a serve to start the game?
- Is it difficult to hit the shuttle?

Extension

Have students explore serving again after this brief discussion.

Student Choices/Differentiation

Students may use badminton rackets for striking and a shuttle or yarn balls to hit.

What to Look For

Observe in the pre-assessment:

- Movement patterns
- Whether students are using the short- or long-serve technique
- Whether students are hitting to all areas of the serve box
- Common errors in skill and tactics

Instructional Task:
Short- and Long-Serve Movement Pattern

▓ PRACTICE TASK

Demonstrate and have students mimic the striking motion for short and long serves.

Refinement

Break down the movement pattern and stress critical elements.

Student Choices/Differentiation

Students may use lollipop paddles or badminton rackets.

What to Look For

- Long serve: Students drop shuttle before starting swing, drop shuttle in front and to the side, contact shuttle at knee height, and hit shuttle up and out.
- Short serve: Students drop shuttle before starting swing, drop shuttle in front and to the side, contact shuttle at thigh height, push the shuttle rather than hitting it, and keep shot as low and short as possible.

Instructional Task: Short and Long Serve to Wall

▓ PRACTICE TASK

This task is designed for beginners who are struggling with the timing of the drop and swing. Have students face the wall and practice hitting or pushing the shuttle into the wall, focusing on the timing of the drop and swing.

Extension

When students are having more success, have them back up and try hitting a specified spot on the wall.

Refinement

Many students toss the shuttle or strike the shuttle above the waist. Stop the task and help students master the movement pattern before moving on.

Student Choices/Differentiation

Practice just hitting the shuttle (eye–hand coordination), taking breaks to practice only the movement pattern without the shuttle.

What to Look For

- Students are dropping the shuttle before starting the swing.
- Students are dropping the shuttle in front of and to the side of the body, far enough away to force the hitting arm to reach slightly.
- Contact is at knee height (long serve) or thigh height (short serve).

Instructional Task: Long and Short Serves in Grids

■ PRACTICE TASK

Teaching in grids, assign tasks from the controlled environment, moving toward an uncontrolled environment.

Call out a command. Students practice the task five times and then switch so that their partners can perform the same command. Call out another command.

First: Long serve to back of grid (up and out); partner should stand closer to server to simulate opponent playing up.

Second: Short serve (low and short); partner should stand closer to back of grid to simulate opponent playing back.

Third: Server hits a short or long serve according to partner's stance in the grid (uncontrolled).

Refinement

Stop drill and refine skill if students are not pushing the shuttle deep on long serves or are not hitting with a low trajectory while using the short serve.

Student Choices/Differentiation

If the class is struggling with an extension, stay at that particular extension for a couple more rounds before moving to the next. If a student is struggling, have him switch to yarn balls.

What to Look For

Students are hitting long serves up and out and are hitting short serves low and short.

Instructional Task: Serve Into a Hoop

■ PRACTICE TASK

In grids or on a court, arrange hoops for short and long serves. Have students practice serving to the targets.

Extension

Point-system assessment: Add poly spots and assess serving accuracy. Legal serve = 1 point; into hoop = 2 points; and onto specific spot = 3 points.

EMBEDDED OUTCOME (S4.M4.6): Students have a variety of skill levels on serves, and this would be a great time to teach them to accept differences among classmates and provide encouragement and positive feedback.

Student Choices/Differentiation

To make the task more difficult, include a net. Make the target larger or smaller, according to skill level.

What to Look For

- Students serve long for a long serve and low and short for the short serve.
- Students are serving accurately.

Formal and Informal Assessments

- Informal
- Point-system assessment
- Exit slip: List the critical elements of the serve and what happens when one of the elements is not followed. (Example: When contacted above the knee, the shuttle will go straight up in the air.)

Closure

- Where on the court do you want a short serve to drop?
- Where on the court do you want a long serve to drop?
- Did any classmates encourage you today in class?

Practice the two types of skills at home, if you can. In our next class, we will work on the drop shot.

Reflection

- Are most students using legal serves?
- Did students have enough practice opportunities for the serve?
- Did the high-skilled students have a high amount of success hitting the poly spots?

Homework

If students have access to equipment, practice the short and long serves. If students do not, they can still practice dropping a ball and striking the ball with the hand (focusing on striking below the waist). Review the instructional videos for the serves and clears, and learn the drop shot from the videos posted to the school's physical education website.

Students can update their physical activity logs.

Resources

Ballou, R. (1992). *Badminton for beginners*. Englewood, CO: Morton.

Grice, T. (2008). *Badminton: Steps to success*. Champaign, IL: Human Kinetics.

The Badminton Bible: www.badmintonbible.com

Internet keyword search: "long and short serves in badminton"

LESSON 5:
SERVE STRATEGY AND DROP SHOTS

Grade-Level Outcomes

Primary Outcomes

Serving: Performs a legal underhand serve with control for net/wall games such as badminton, volleyball or pickleball. (S1.M12.6)

Striking: Strikes with a mature overhand pattern in a nondynamic environment for net/wall games such as volleyball, handball, badminton or tennis. (S1.M13.6)

Creating space through variation: Creates open space in net/wall games with either a long- or short-handled implement by varying force or direction, or by moving opponent side to side and/or forward and back. (S2.M7.8)

Using tactics & shots: Selects offensive shot based on opponent's location (hit where opponent is not). (S2.M8.7)

Embedded Outcome

Accepting feedback: Provides corrective feedback to a peer, using teacher-generated guidelines, and incorporating appropriate tone and other communication skills. (S4.M3.7)

Lesson Objectives

The learner will:

- demonstrate the ability to perform the drop shot movement pattern during the mimic-with-teacher task.
- perform basic offensive and defensive strategies during the clear-rally practice task.
- select offensive shots, including serves, based on the opponent's location during a grid extension activity.

Equipment and Materials

- Yarn balls and shuttles: at least 5 for every 2 students
- Badminton rackets and long-handled lollipop paddles: 1 per student
- Cones
- Pedometers

Introduction

Today, we will review the badminton serves, discuss strategy for serves, and learn the drop shot. The strategy that we used in earlier lessons involved moving the opponent from side to side. The drop shot, combined with the clear, will help move the opponent forward and back.

Instructional Task:
Review Short and Long Serves in Badminton

■ PRACTICE TASK

Working in grids, students practice short and long serves with a partner.

As in previous lessons, move from a controlled environment to an unpredictable environment.

Refinement

Refine skill as needed. Spend as much time as needed until at least 80 percent of students are successful.

Student Choices/Differentiation

Students may use badminton rackets for striking and a shuttle or yarn balls to hit.

What to Look For

This task can be used as a pre-assessment to gauge where your students are in this skill starting day two of serves.

Instructional Task: Short- and Long-Serve Strategy

■ PRACTICE TASK

Discuss long- and short-serve strategies.

Guiding questions for students:

- If the long serve does not go deep, what can the opponent do?
- If the short serve is higher than anticipated, how does that put you on the defensive?
- How do you know what type of serve to use?

Extension

- In grids, students hit long or short serves based on partner's location. Partner hits return and moves to home base.
- Repeat five times and change roles.

Refinement

Refine skill by reviewing pictures or videos of the strategies posted on the school's physical education website.

Student Choices/Differentiation

Students may throw a ball instead of striking if their skill level is low. (The task is designed for learning strategy.)

What to Look For

- Students make the right choice for serve location based on the partner's position.
- Students use proper movement pattern.

Instructional Task: Drop Shots

■ PRACTICE TASK

Demonstrate the drop shot, and mimic the shot along with the class.

Extension

In grids, students practice the drop shot. A partner hits a high clear for the striker to hit.

Refinement

Make sure that students are using proper movement pattern and are not merely blocking the opponent's shot from going over the net.

Student Choices/Differentiation

If students struggle with hitting a high shot with a shuttle, they may throw or strike a ball.

What to Look For

- Racket makes contact in front of body.
- Students slow speed of racket head just before contacting shuttle.
- Racket face is angled slightly downward.
- Students guide shuttle over net with wrist action and follow-through.

Instructional Task: Review Clears

▣ PRACTICE TASK

Working in grids, students toss or strike a yarn ball or shuttle to a partner to explore the four types of clear shots. Move from a controlled environment to an unpredictable environment.

Spend as much time in skill practice as needed so that at least 80 percent of students are successful.

Refinements

- Review critical elements if needed.
- Make sure that students are using their entire bodies to hit the clears.

Extensions

- Students must use at least three of the clear shots in a row.
- If students are having success, add the drop shot.

Student Choices/Differentiation

- Students may focus on certain clear shots or challenge themselves to use all four.
- Students may use yarn balls or shuttles.
- Students may move closer, if needed.

What to Look For

- Students' movement patterns are correct.
- The task is to review and refine the clear movement pattern before moving into a modified game.

Instructional Task:
Modified Game With Only Serve and Clear Shots

▣ PRACTICE TASK

Two students per court play a clear rally. Make the court wider by 2 feet (0.6 m) on each side, and place a cone in the middle of the court. The objective is to move the opponent from side to side as students volley back and forth. Every time a player moves an opponent to the other side of the cone, she receives a point. The game should start with a serve and be played for 5 minutes. After 5 minutes switch opponents.

Guiding questions for students:

- Why is it important to move your opponent from side to side?
- What advantage does this tactic give you?
- How can you counter or defend this tactic?

Refinements

Refine skill or strategy as needed. Make sure that students are moving their opponents by using the correct shot sequence.

EMBEDDED OUTCOME: S4.M3.7 This is a great opportunity to teach students to provide corrective feedback to a peer using teacher-generated guidelines (court markings, strategies, etc.).

Student Choices/Differentiation

- If students are struggling with the skills, stop and refine the skills.
- If students are struggling with the tactic, refine the tactic to throwing yarn balls instead of striking shuttles.

What to Look For

- Students are hitting long serves up and out, and they are hitting short serves low and short.
- All four clears have mature movement patterns.
- Students are providing corrective feedback to their partners.

Formal and Informal Assessments

- Informal
- Peer assessments using teacher-generated guidelines
- Exit slip: Please list two serving rules and one serving strategy.

Closure

- Who can describe the short-serve strategy?
- Who can describe the long-serve strategy?
- If your opponent is surprised with a long serve and has to work hard to save the point with the overhead clear, what shot should you follow with?
- How are your physical activity logs coming along?
- Do you see a difference in your step counts in this module compared to other modules?

Keep practicing the skills at home if you can. In our next lesson, we will learn the smash.

Reflection

- Are students having a high incidence of success in making legal serves?
- Did students move the opponent from side to side in modified games?
- Are students using a mature movement pattern during modified games?

Homework

If students have access to equipment, practice the serves and drop shot movement patterns. If students don't, they can practice dropping a ball and striking it with their hands (focus on striking it below the waist) or the movement patterns without equipment. Review the instructional videos for the serves, clears, and drops, and learn the smash from the videos posted to the school's physical education website.

Students can update their physical activity logs.

Resources

Ballou, R. (1992). *Badminton for beginners*. Englewood, CO: Morton.

Grice, T. (2008). *Badminton: Steps to success*. Champaign, IL: Human Kinetics.

The Badminton Bible: www.badmintonbible.com

Internet keyword search: "drop shot in badminton," "serving strategy in badminton," "clear shots in badminton"

LESSON 6: SMASH

Grade-Level Outcomes

Primary Outcomes

Serving: Performs a legal underhand serve with control for net/wall games such as badminton, volleyball or pickleball. (S1.M12.6)

Striking: Strikes with a mature overhand pattern in a nondynamic environment for net/wall games such as volleyball, handball, badminton or tennis. (S1.M13.6)

Creating space through variation: Creates open space in net/wall games with either a long- or short-handled implement by varying force or direction, or by moving opponent side to side and/or forward and back. (S2.M7.8)

Using tactics & shots: Reduces offensive options for opponents by returning to mid-court position. (S2.M8.6)

Embedded Outcome

Social interaction: Demonstrates the importance of social interaction by helping and encouraging others, avoiding trash talk and providing support to classmates. (S5.M6.7)

Lesson Objectives

The learner will:
- demonstrate the ability to perform the smash shot by completing three out of five attempts during the grids practice task.
- perform basic offensive and defensive strategies during the clear-rally practice task.
- reduce offensive options for opponents by returning to mid-court positions during the modified game.

Equipment and Materials
- Yarn balls and shuttles: at least 5 for every 2 students
- Badminton rackets and long-handled lollipop paddles: 1 per student
- Cones
- Pedometers

Introduction

Today, we will learn the smash and practice the drop shots, serves, and basic offensive and defensive strategies. The smash is an advanced skill that, when mastered, can be a very important tool in your offensive strategy.

Show video clip of players using a smash in a game.

Instructional Task: Review Drop Shots and Serve

■ PRACTICE TASK

Working in grids, students practice drop shots and serves with a partner.

One partner serves and the other receives. The receiver practices the overhand drop shot, concentrating on the proper mechanics of the swing and adjusting racket speed just before contact.

Refinement

Choose any of the critical elements for the drop shot or serve.

Student Choices/Differentiation

Students may focus on only one serve (short or long).

What to Look For

Students are using the correct movement pattern for serves as well as the drop shot.

Instructional Task: Drop Into Hoop

■ PRACTICE TASK

Place two hoops per set of partners end to end under a net, extending an equal distance into each court.

Partners take positions opposite each other and one step behind their hoops, facing each other. Students rally back and forth using underhand hits so that the shuttle falls into the hoop area closest to their partner.

Extension

Challenge students to see how many hits they can drop into the hoop with 10 tries.

Student Choices/Differentiation

- Students can move hoops.
- Students can place smaller hoops inside of larger hoops and try to place the shuttle in the smaller hoops.

What to Look For

- The racket face is angled slightly downward.
- Students are guiding the shuttle over the net with wrist action and follow-through.

Instructional Task: Defensive Strategies

■ PRACTICE TASK

Discuss basic defensive strategies.

Guiding questions for students:

- Why is getting back to home base important as a defensive strategy?
- What shot selection should you use if you are having difficulty getting back under control to home base?
- Who can describe how a good offense can also be a good defense?

Student Choices/Differentiation

Show videos if students need extra help.

What to Look For

Students understand basic defensive strategies.

Instructional Task: Modified Game

■ PRACTICE TASK

Students play a game using only the skills of clears (overhead, underhand, forehand, and backhand), serves, and drop shots. After playing for 7 to 10 minutes, students switch partners.

Refinement

If a student is not performing a shot, make it an emphasis by rewarding him with 2 points for using it. Example: Drop shots that score a point earn 2 points instead of 1.

This is a great opportunity to teach students the importance of social interaction. Help students understand how avoiding trash talk and encouraging others can be fun and useful during game play.

Student Choices/Differentiation

Encourage students to play with peers of the same ability.

What to Look For

- Students are using mature movement patterns.
- Students are hitting to move opponents.
- Students are making an attempt to get back to home base.

Instructional Task: Introducing the Smash

■ PRACTICE TASK

Demonstrate the smash shot, and mimic the shot with the class.

Extensions

- Peers assess a partner's striking movement pattern using a checklist.
- In grids, students practice the smash shot. A partner hits a high clear for the striker to hit a smash.
- One partner serves and the other receives. The receiver practices the smash shot, concentrating on the proper mechanics of the swing and adjusting racket speed just before contact.

Refinement

Make sure that students are reaching all the way back in their movement patterns.

Student Choices/Differentiation

- Students may review skills videos, if needed.
- If students struggle with hitting a high shot with a shuttle, they may throw or strike a ball.

What to Look For

- Students contact the shuttle ahead of racket shoulder.
- Racket face is angling downward at contact (a sharp downward angle is as important as shuttle speed).
- The serves are high enough for the students to smash.
- Students move their feet to position themselves under the shuttle.

Formal and Informal Assessments

- Informal assessments
- Peer assessments: critical elements checklist of partners' movement pattern

Closure

- Name three critical elements of the smash.
- Name three critical elements of the drop shot.

Keep practicing the skills at home if you can, and the next lesson we will review the smash and learn how to defend against the smash with the block shot.

Reflection

- Are students maintaining success with the clears and serves, or do I need to revisit them next class?
- Are students reaching all the way back for the smash?
- Are students hitting the shuttle right at their opponents, or are they hitting away to make them move?

Homework

If you have access to equipment, practice the smash and drop shot movement patterns. If you don't, you can practice dropping a ball and striking the ball with your hand (focusing on striking below the waist) or the movement patterns without equipment. Review the instructional videos for the serves, clears, and drops, and learn the block from the videos posted to the school's physical education website.

Students can update their physical activity logs.

Resources

Ballou, R. (1992). *Badminton for beginners*. Englewood, CO: Morton.

Grice, T. (2008). *Badminton: Steps to success*. Champaign, IL: Human Kinetics.

The Badminton Bible: www.badmintonbible.com

Internet keyword search: "badminton smash"

LESSON 7: BLOCKING AND DOUBLES PLAY

Grade-Level Outcomes

Primary Outcomes

Striking: Strikes with a mature overhand pattern in a nondynamic environment for net/wall games such as volleyball, handball, badminton or tennis. (S1.M13.6)

Creating space through variation: Creates open space in net/wall games with either a long- or short-handled implement by varying force or direction, or by moving opponent from side to side and/or forward and back. (S2.M7.8)

Using tactics & shots: Selects offensive shot based on opponent's location (hit where opponent is not). (S2.M8.7)

Embedded Outcome

Social interaction: Demonstrates respect for self and others in activities and games by following the rules, encouraging others and playing in the spirit of the game or activity. (S5.M6.6)

Lesson Objectives

The learner will:

- demonstrate the ability to perform the smash or block by completing three out of five attempts during the grids practice task.
- perform basic offensive and defensive strategies in a modified game.
- apply the rules and strategies of doubles badminton in a modified game.

Equipment and Materials

- Yarn balls and shuttles: at least 5 for every 2 students
- Badminton rackets and long-handled lollipop paddles: 1 per student
- Cones
- Pedometers

Introduction

Today, we will add our last skill—blocking—and learn offensive and defensive strategies in the game of doubles. You will find that doubles can be challenging but a lot of fun.

Instructional Task: Shadow Drill

■ PRACTICE TASK

Have students in scatter formation around the gym, 6 to 8 feet (1.8 to 2.4 m) apart. Have them practice the smash shot without the shuttle, concentrating on a powerful swing, driving sharply downward and rotating the wrist fully. Their swings should generate a strong swishing sound.

Student Choices/Differentiation

Students may review videos if needed.

What to Look For

- The strokes are powerful.
- Students are rotating their wrists fully.
- Students are following through.

Instructional Task: Smash in Grids

■ PRACTICE TASK

Working in grids, students practice smash hits with a partner.

As in previous lessons, move from a controlled environment (hitting the clear or serve high right at the student) to an uncontrolled environment (hitting the serve or clear so that the student must move to hit the smash).

Refinement

Refine skill as needed. Spend as much time as needed so that at least 80 percent of students are successful.

Student Choices/Differentiation

Students may use badminton rackets for striking and a shuttle or yarn balls to hit.

What to Look For

This task can be used as a review or formative assessment to gauge where your students are in this skill.

Instructional Task: Learning to Block

■ PRACTICE TASK

Demonstrate the block, and mimic the shot along with the class.

Extensions

Have students peer-assess one another by video-recording their mimicked block shots. Have students focus on body position.

Refinement

Review pictures and videos of the block shot posted on the school's physical education website.

Student Choices/Differentiation

Students can use lollipop paddles or badminton rackets.

What to Look For

- Stroke does not require backswing.
- Students react as quickly as possible, trying to get racket head in front of body and to the shuttle.
- Students use proper body alignment to maintain balance.

Instructional Task: Smash and Block in Grids

■ PRACTICE TASK

Working in grids, students explore the smash and block shots with a partner.

Extensions

- Have students toss or strike a yarn ball or shuttle to a partner, exploring the smash and block shots. Partner 1 hits a high underhand clear that the partner smashes. The returner attempts to block the smash and send it over the net.
- Spend as much time in skill practice as needed so that at least 80 percent of students are successful.

Refinement

Make sure that students are using a mature movement pattern for both the block and the smash. Review critical elements and practice the pattern, if needed.

Student Choices/Differentiation

- Students may use yarn balls or shuttles.
- Students may vary distances according to comfort levels.

What to Look For

- Students are using correct movement patterns, specifically, reaching all the way back for the smash and the follow-through.
- Students are in an athletic position with racket up to defend, using the block.

Instructional Task:
Learning Doubles Rules and Strategies

■ PRACTICE TASK

Review rules and strategies for playing doubles badminton. Make sure that students know the front-and-back formations as well as the side-by-side formations.

Guiding questions for students:

- What similarities and differences between other sports and badminton have you learned already?
- Why do you think the serving boundaries are different in doubles?
- What advantages and disadvantages do the different formations have?

Refinement

Make sure that students know the differences between singles and doubles badminton.

Student Choices/Differentiation

Students may review videos posted on the school's physical education website.

What to Look For

- Students know the basic rules of doubles.
- Students know both the front-and-back and side-by-side offensive and defensive strategies.

Instructional Task:
Modified Doubles Game Using Strategies

■ PRACTICE TASK

Using a foam ball and no rackets, students play a game of doubles badminton, focusing on the type of shots and shot placement that they should use in badminton.

Students should practice side-by-side defense as well as front-and-back defense.

Extensions

- The scoring of the game can be modified. If a team makes an offensive shot that is one of the strategies, the team receives a point (no matter what happens in the game).
- Students play the same task but this time use rackets and shuttles.

EMBEDDED OUTCOME: S5.M6.6. This is a great opportunity to teach students respect for self and others in activities and games by following the rules of the modified game. Also, the purpose of the activity is to work on offensive and defensive strategies using alignment and shot selection. Encourage students to play in the spirit of the activity so everyone is learning the doubles strategy.

Student Choices/Differentiation

- To speed up the game, use a smaller and faster ball.
- To slow down the game, use a lighter and bigger ball.

What to Look For

- Students focus on attacking the type of defense that the other team is using.
- Students use the correct shots (even though they are throwing the ball) against the defensive team's alignment.

Formal and Informal Assessments

- Peer assessment: informal feedback on the partner's body alignment during the block
- Exit slip: Please list the critical elements of the smash and block.

Closure

- Name three critical elements of the smash.
- Name three critical elements of the block.
- What offensive and defensive strategies did you learn today?

Keep practicing the skills at home if you can, and the next lesson we will review skills and play modified games.

Reflection

- Are students moving their opponents in the games?
- Are students using the offensive and defensive alignments correctly?
- Are students developing shot sequences to improve offensive and defensive strategies?

Homework

If students have access to equipment, they can practice the badminton skills and strategies taught throughout the module. If they don't, they can practice the strategies by using a ball to move their opponents; review the instructional videos for the serve, clear, drop, smash, and block; and review videos posted to the school's physical education website.

Students can update their physical activity logs.

Resources

Ballou, R. (1992). *Badminton for beginners*. Englewood, CO: Morton.

Grice, T. (2008). *Badminton: Steps to success*. Champaign, IL: Human Kinetics.

The Badminton Bible: www.badmintonbible.com

Internet keyword search: "blocking in badminton," "offensive and defensive strategies in doubles badminton"

LESSON 8: TESTING AND GAME DAY

Grade-Level Outcomes

Primary Outcomes

Forehand & backhand: Demonstrates the mature form of forehand and backhand strokes with a short- or long-handled implement with power and accuracy in net games such as pickleball, tennis, badminton or paddle ball. (S1.M14.8)

Embedded Outcomes

Rules & etiquette: Demonstrates knowledge of rules and etiquette by self-officiating modified physical activities and games or following parameters to create or modify a dance. (S4.M6.7)

Assessment & program planning: Maintains a physical activity log for at least 2 weeks and reflects on activity levels as documented in the log. (S3.M16.6)

Lesson Objective

The learner will perform a variety of badminton skills during game play.

Note: Assess student skills and use of strategies during game play.

Equipment and Materials

- Yarn balls and shuttles: at least 5 for every 2 students
- Badminton rackets and long-handled lollipop paddles: 1 per student
- Badminton courts
- Pedometers

Introduction

Today, we will finish our Badminton Module. We will review basic rules and strategies, we'll warm up using the skills that we've learned, and then we'll play singles and doubles badminton.

Instructional Task: Rules of the Game

■ PRACTICE TASK

Review the rules of the game. Be sure to review serving rules, boundaries, points, beginning and ending game, etc.

Extension

Reviewing offensive and defensive strategies can be helpful as well.

Student Choices/Differentiation

Students may review videos or handouts that are posted on the school's physical education website.

What to Look For

The goal of this activity is to review or tie in any loose ends so that students are able to play the game of badminton.

Instructional Task: Review Badminton Shots

■ PRACTICE TASK

In grids, students warm up using a variety of badminton shots.

Have students start with a long or short serve, and have students practice all badminton shots that were taught in the module.

Extension

Challenge students to use all types of shots during this warm-up activity.

Refinement

Stop the activity and correct any movement pattern that needs correcting.

Student Choices/Differentiation

Students may agree to stick with clears and drop shots or choose to include the smash and block.

What to Look For

This can be a great last look at what skills need to be refined before moving into game play.

Instructional Task: Singles or Doubles Game Play

■ PRACTICE TASK

Set up multiple courts throughout the gym, with numbers marked with a cone.

Play a 10- to 12-minute game of badminton, either singles or doubles. At the end of time, instruct the high scores to move to the lower-numbered court (e.g., if they won on court 4, then they move to court 3), and have the player or team with the fewest points move up a court (e.g., if they did not win on court 4, then they move to court 5). Keep the rotation for the remainder of class.

Students are expected to self-officiate.

If the class is playing doubles, switch partners after a couple of rotations.

Refinement

Even though it is game play, feel free to refine skills or strategies, if needed.

Extension

During game play, assess students on their skill.

EMBEDDED OUTCOME: S4.M6.7 This is a great opportunity to teach students important components of self-officiating modified physical activities. Review with them when to enforce rules, how to stop the game properly, the appropriate response to a call made by an official, etc.

Student Choices/Differentiation

If students are struggling, give them the opportunity to practice off the court any of the practice tasks taught in this module.

What to Look For

The goals are to keep students moving and to match students of similar ability levels.

Formal and Informal Assessments

Formal badminton assessment: Use a badminton rubric that evaluates all or selected skills taught during game play.

Closure

- List two major muscle groups that we use in badminton.
- Name three important rules in the game of badminton.
- Name three offensive or defensive strategies in the game of badminton.

Keep practicing the skills and playing the game of badminton when you can.

Reflection

- Do students understand basic offensive and defensive strategies?
- Do students use all shots or focus only on using the overhead clear shots?
- Can students self-officiate the game of badminton?

Homework

Keep practicing your skills by playing the game of badminton with your family and friends.

Review the material on the school's physical education website for the next module.

EMBEDDED OUTCOME: S3.M16.6. Have students reflect on their physical activity logs. Some possible questions:

- Are you surprised by your step counts during the badminton module?
- In which lesson did you see the highest step count? Which had the lowest? Why do you think the step counts were high or low for those lessons?
- Please reflect on your after-school physical activity.
- Are you happy with the log?
- What would you change or would like to improve?
- What are some strategies to improve?

Resources

Ballou, R. (1992). *Badminton for beginners*. Englewood, CO: Morton.

Grice, T. (2008). *Badminton: Steps to success*. Champaign, IL: Human Kinetics.

The Badminton Bible: www.badmintonbible.com

CHAPTER 7

Applying Students' Skills and Knowledge to Fielding and Striking Games and Target Games

National Standards & Grade-Level Outcomes for K-12 Physical Education (SHAPE America, 2014) breaks the games and sports category into target, invasion, fielding and striking, and net and wall games. This chapter includes modules on both fielding and striking games and target games. Fielding and striking games (e.g., softball, baseball, cricket, Wiffle ball) involve a complex set of offensive and defensive strategies. They also require challenging skills, such as catching and throwing under a variety of conditions and batting to open space. Wiffle ball has several advantages as an activity for the physical education setting: (a) It teaches all the common skills and concepts of fielding and striking games in a form that requires little specialized equipment; (b) it can be adapted for indoor and outdoor play; (c) it can be played safely by students of all abilities; and (d) it can be played recreationally at home. The Wiffle Ball Module provides a model for teaching this complex game that you can apply to other fielding and striking activities.

The other two modules in this chapter are for target games. In that category of games, accuracy is paramount: Think of activities such as golf, bowling, and archery. The eight-lesson Disc Golf Module involves a target game with a unique throwing pattern (throwing a disc). Students progress through practice tasks using proper throwing mechanics at varying speeds and trajectories to hit a target. The Recreational Target Games Module includes several games that employ similar skills and concepts. The module concludes with a fun-filled target games carnival that includes games such as bowling, croquet, and bocce.

For easy reference, each module begins with a block plan chart of the Grade-Level Outcomes that are addressed in the lessons. Each module includes multiple National Standards, although most of the primary outcomes reside under Standard 1. For the eight-lesson Wiffle Ball Module, the main focus is on demonstrating a mature movement pattern for catching (Outcome S1.M21), throwing (Outcome S1.M2), and striking (Outcome S1.M20), but it also addresses positioning on defense based on game situations (Outcome S2.M11.7). The module also addresses Outcome S3.M16.6, which involves developing a physical activity log, throughout the lessons, as well as addressing multiple outcomes under Standard 4. In the Disc Golf and eight-lesson Recreational Target Games Modules, the primary outcome addressed is S1.M18.6, which prescribes demonstrating a mature throwing pattern in a modified target game. Both modules address appropriate shot selection and varying speed, force, and trajectory, using outcomes under Standard 2, and multiple embedded outcomes under Standards 4 and 5. These modules provide great examples of implementing multiple fielding, striking, and target game outcomes in your curriculum.

WIFFLE BALL MODULE

Lessons in this module were contributed by JoEllen Bailey, associate professor of physical education at State University of New York College at Cortland and a former junior high health and physical education teacher in Lindstrom, MN.

Grade-Level Outcomes Addressed, by Lesson	1	2	3	4	5	6	7	8
Standard 1. The physically literate individual demonstrates competency in a variety of motor skills and movement patterns.								
Throws with a mature pattern for distance or power appropriate to the practice task (e.g., distance = outfield to home plate; power = 2nd base to 1st base). (S1.M2.6)	P							
Throws with a mature pattern for distance or power appropriate to the activity in a dynamic environment. (S1.M2.7)							P	
Executes at least one of the following designed to create open space during small-sided game play: pivots, fakes, jab steps. (S1.M6.7)		P	P					
Strikes a pitched ball with an implement with force in a variety of practice tasks. (S1.M20.6)							P	
Strikes a pitched ball with an implement to open space in a variety of practice tasks. (S1.M20.7)				P				
Catches, with a mature pattern, from different trajectories using a variety of objects in small-sided game play. (S1.M21.7)	P	P	P	P	P		P	
Standard 2. The physically literate individual applies knowledge of concepts, principles, strategies and tactics related to movement and performance.								
Identifies open spaces and attempts to strike object into that space. (S2.M10.6)								P
Selects the correct defensive play based on the situation (e.g., number of outs). (S2.M11.7)	P	P	P			P		P
Reduces open spaces in the field by working with teammates to maximize coverage. (S2.M11.8)				P				
Standard 3. The physically literate individual demonstrates the knowledge and skills to achieve and maintain a health-enhancing level of physical activity and fitness.								
Describes how muscles pull on bones to create movement in pairs by relaxing and contracting. (S3.M14.7)						E		
Maintains a physical activity log for at least 2 weeks and reflects on activity levels as documented in the log. (S3.M16.6)	E							E
Standard 4. The physically literate individual exhibits responsible personal and social behavior that respects self and others.								
Exhibits responsible social behaviors by cooperating with classmates, demonstrating inclusive behaviors and supporting classmates. (S4.M1.7)							E	
Provides corrective feedback to a peer, using teacher-generated guidelines, and incorporating appropriate tone and other communication skills. (S4.M3.7)					E			
Cooperates with a small group of classmates during adventure activities, game play or team-building activities. (S4.M5.6)		E						
Problem-solves with a small group of classmates during adventure activities, small-group initiatives or game play. (S4.M5.7)	E		E					
Demonstrates knowledge of rules and etiquette by self-officiating modified physical activities and games or following parameters to create or modify a dance. (S4.M6.7)				E				
Applies rules and etiquette by acting as an official for modified physical activities and games and creating dance routines within a given set of parameters. (S4.M6.8)							P	
Standard 5. The physically literate individual recognizes the value of physical activity for health, enjoyment, challenge, self-expression and/or social interaction.								
Demonstrates the importance of social interaction by helping and encouraging others, avoiding trash talk and providing support to classmates. (S5.M6.7)								E

P = Primary; E = Embedded

LESSON 1:
THROWING, CATCHING, AND DEFENSE

Grade-Level Outcomes

Primary Outcomes

Throwing: Throws with a mature pattern for distance or power appropriate to the practice task (e.g., distance = outfield to home plate; power = 2nd base to 1st base). (S1.M2.6)

Catching: Catches, with a mature pattern, from different trajectories using a variety of objects in small-sided game play. (S1.M21.7)

Reducing space: Selects the correct defensive play based on the situation (e.g., number of outs). (S2.M11.7)

Embedded Outcomes

Assessment & program planning: Maintains a physical activity log for at least 2 weeks and reflects on activity levels as documented in the log. (S3.M16.6)

Working with others: Problem-solves with a small group of classmates during adventure activities, small-group initiatives or game play. (S4.M5.7)

Lesson Objectives

The learner will:

- demonstrate proper throwing technique using all critical elements of a mature pattern during the four-corners practice task.
- demonstrate proper catching technique using all critical elements of a mature pattern during the four-corners practice task.
- demonstrate appropriate footwork three out of five times when playing a base for a force out during partner practice.

Equipment and Materials

- Ball options: tennis balls, Wiffle balls, racquetballs, foam balls, etc.
- Four-base grid options: bases spray-painted on grass, rubber bases, poly spots
- Cones
- Pedometers

Introduction

Pique students' interest by commenting or asking questions about a local softball team or a favorite baseball team. Discuss Wiffle ball as a safe activity option for softball or baseball. Explain that today's lesson involves throwing and catching; provide a brief overview of the module. Ask about students' participation in after-school or community softball or baseball programs (embedded outcome: S3.M16.6).

We also will continue tracking our physical activity with this module. I will provide you with an individual step-count goal for each lesson, as well as asking you to track your physical activity outside of class.

Instructional Task: Catching Warm-Up

■ PRACTICE TASK

Catch on the run

Partners with one ball travel within cones while underhand tossing and catching. Partners count all successful catches in the time period (30 seconds to 1 minute). Give safety reminders about avoiding others. Partners need to communicate.

Guiding questions for students:

- What did you do to be successful?
- How did you toss?
- How did you catch?
- How did you catch a ball that was high?
- How did you catch a ball that was low?

Extensions

- Have partners talk to develop strategies for improving the number of successful catches.
- Repeat the same activity one or two more times, using the same time period.

Student Choices/Differentiation

- Partners choose the type of ball they want to use.
- Partners may decide how fast they want to move.
- Partners may decide how far apart they want to be (minimum of two arm lengths).

What to Look For

Critical elements for catching:

1. Watch the ball to anticipate its flight.
2. Get both hands ready: "When it's high, thumbs will meet; pinkies touch when it's at your feet."
3. Absorb the ball into the body.

Instructional Task:
Throwing and Catching Practice and Pre-Assessment

▪ PRACTICE TASK

Four-corners throwing

In a grid formation (four bases), one student is at each base. One student with the ball begins by throwing to the next student, clockwise around the bases. Students continue throwing for a designated time (at least five times around the grid). Students call for the ball.

Be sure to stagger the grids so any overthrows are not in line with the next grid.

The group should take two or three extra balls in case students lose one from the playing area.

Guiding questions for students:

- What do your feet do when you throw?
- Why do you want to turn your body when you throw?
- Why should you reach high when the ball is behind you?
- When you catch, what can you do to make sure the thrower knows where to throw? (Answer: Say the thrower's name and "right here.")

Extension

- Do the same activity but counterclockwise.

Guiding questions for students:

- Which direction of throwing was easier? Why?
- What do you need to do with your feet if you have to catch a ball and then turn to your throwing side to make your throw?
- Does anyone know what that movement with your feet is called? (Answer: crow hop)
- How does the crow hop help your throw?

- Groups go back to their grids and throw three more times around the bases, focusing on the crow hop.
- Each group then creates a different throwing pattern that might include throwing across the grid, along with throwing around the grid.
- Challenge each group to make at least 12 successful throws and catches using the new pattern.

Refinement

Make sure that students are stepping toward the target when they throw.

Student Choices/Differentiation

- Each group of four students chooses the type of ball it would like to use and also chooses the size of grid.
- If a group is having difficulty with successful throws and catches, decrease the size of the grid.

What to Look For

Critical elements for throwing:

1. Step to the target.
2. Reach high with the ball and point at the target (T position).
3. Turn and push off back foot.
4. Release high and follow through down across the body.

Critical elements for the crow hop:

1. Straddle an imaginary (or real) line.
2. Jump in the air, turn to the throwing side, and land with the throwing side foot on the line.
3. Step to the target with non-throwing-side foot.

Focus feedback on throwing in the first activity and then on the crow hop and calling for the ball in the second and third activities.

Pre-assessment

Use a simple checklist or rating scale (see example) on a single recording sheet or portable electronic device for assessing throwing and catching during this task.

Instructional Task: Footwork at a Base for a Force Out

■ PRACTICE TASK

Ask students about the rules for getting runners out, and follow up with "why" questions (e.g., Why should you move to the side of the base that is closest to the thrower? Answer: to catch the ball sooner, giving you a better chance of getting the runner out).

Play the base

In the same groups of four, students make partners. Each set of partners uses one base; one partner underhand tosses the ball to the partner who is practicing the footwork for making a force out at a base. After five throws, partners switch places.

Give safety reminders about making sure that the receiver is ready before throwing.

Extensions

- The tosser should now throw from different angles to the partner playing the base to make that partner move to the side or corner of the base that is closest to the throw.
- Have the student playing the base begin several steps away from the base and then run to the base, turn, and make the catch.

THROWING AND CATCHING RATING SCALE

Critical Elements for Catching

- Watch the ball to anticipate its flight.
- Step toward the target.
- Get both hands ready. "When it's high, thumbs will meet; pinkies touch when it's at your feet."
- Absorb the ball into the body.
- Release high and follow through

Critical Elements for Throwing

Reach high with the ball and point to target.

Turn and push off back foot across the body.

Rating Scale

3 Student performs the skill consistently, using all critical elements properly; skill appears automatic.

2 Student performs the skill using critical elements; repetitions may not be similar; cognitive concentration necessary.

1 Student attempts the skill; performance of critical elements is inconsistent.

Directions: Enter a number that best represents each student's performance of each skill. Use the "Needs Practice" column for notes on follow-up.

Student name	Catching score	Needs practice	Throwing score	Needs practice

From R.J. Doan, L.C. MacDonald, and S. Chepko, eds., 2017, *Lesson planning for middle school physical education* (Reston, VA: SHAPE America; Champaign, IL: Human Kinetics).

Student Choices/Differentiation

- Partners choose the type of ball they want to use.
- Partners determine the distance from the thrower to the partner covering the base.
- Partners determine the variation in the direction from which the throw is made.
- Partners determine the starting position of the student playing the base (right next to the base or several steps from the base).

What to Look For

Critical elements for footwork at a base for a force out:

1. Standing with back to the base, move to the side of the base that is closest to the thrower.
2. Face the direction from which the throw is coming, and put the throwing-side foot on the edge of the base (toes pointing down).
3. Put both hands up to show a target.
4. Call to the thrower.
5. Step forward to catch the ball, keeping the other foot in contact with the base.

Instructional Task:
Game Application of Throwing, Catching, Playing a Base

■ PRACTICE TASK

2 v 2:

Using the same grids and groups of four, two students play first- and second-base defensive positions. The other two are at home base as the offensive team. An offensive player throws the ball toward the right side of the grid and runs through first base. The defensive team fields the ball and works to make a force out at first base. After each of the offensive players have had three "at bats," the teams switch roles.

Have the thrower run to a cone 6 to 8 feet (1.8 to 2.4 m) beyond first base to prevent collisions at the base.

Refinement

Make sure that students are keeping one foot on the edge of the base.

EMBEDDED OUTCOME: S4.M5.7. As a problem-solving challenge, students work in groups to determine which defensive player will field the ball and who will cover the base. Students can discuss and implement strategy.

Student Choices/Differentiation

Each group of four should choose the type of ball it would like to use and also choose the size of the grid.

What to Look For

- Students look before throwing.
- Students make accurate throws.
- Students are able to catch under pressure.
- Students are able to apply their base-playing skills in the modified game.
- Students play the base, keeping one foot just on the edge of the base and not on top of it.

Formal and Informal Assessments

- During the lesson introduction, ask students about their softball or baseball participation in after-school or community programs.
- Use a throwing and catching checklist or rating scale.

Closure

Today, we reviewed the catching and throwing skills that you'd learned previously, and also, you learned some new skills—crow hop and playing a base for a force out.

If students are primarily at the pre-control and control levels in throwing and catching skills, use questions such as:

- What are some things to remember about catching a ball?
- Why are those things important?
- What do you have to do to be an accurate thrower?
- Show me how you do a crow hop. Why do we have to do that when throwing?

If students are primarily competent and proficient in throwing and catching skills, ask questions such as: Who can show me the footwork of how to get a runner out at a base? Can someone else explain the important things to remember about the footwork? When you were playing 2 v 2, how did you know which person was going to cover the base? How did you cooperate? Did you talk to each other? When you were the thrower, where did you throw the ball to give yourself a better chance at being safe? Why did that work? Would you try anything different next time?

Reflection

- At what level are students' throwing and catching abilities?
- Is more teaching and practice time needed on those basic skills?
- Can students begin to combine throwing and catching with other skills?
- Are they grasping the offensive strategy of where to hit a ball and the defensive strategy of how to get a runner out at first?
- Are they remembering to communicate with each other?

Homework

Practice the crow hop at home with or without throwing a ball. Watch yourself in a mirror performing the crow hop with the throwing motion.

EMBEDDED OUTCOME: S3.M16.6 Remind students to record physical education step counts, daily physical activity time, and reflections in a personal log after each lesson in the module.

Resources

Graham, G., Holt/Hale, S.A., & Parker, M. (2012). *Children moving: A reflective approach to teaching physical education*. 9th ed. New York: McGraw-Hill Education.

Mitchell, S.A., Oslin, J.L., & Griffin, L.L. (2013). *Teaching sport concepts and skills: A tactical games approach*. 3rd ed. Champaign, IL: Human Kinetics.

Potter, D.L., & Johnson, L. (2007). *Teaching softball: Steps to success*. 3rd ed. Champaign, IL: Human Kinetics.

LESSON 2:
OFFENSIVE AND DEFENSIVE SKILLS

Grade-Level Outcomes

Primary Outcomes

Catching: Catches, with a mature pattern, from different trajectories using a variety of objects in small-sided game play. (S1.M21.7)

Offensive skills: Executes at least one of the following designed to create open space during small-sided game play: pivots, fakes, jab steps. (S1.M6.7)

Reducing space: Selects the correct defensive play based on the situation (e.g., number of outs). (S2.M11.7)

Embedded Outcome

Working with others: Cooperates with a small group of classmates during adventure activities, game play or team-building activities. (S4.M5.6)

Lesson Objectives

The learner will:

- demonstrate proper catching technique using all critical elements of a mature pattern during the four-corners practice task.
- demonstrate techniques (pivot, fake, jab step) to avoid being tagged when running the bases during the tag 'em out and pickle game practice tasks.

Equipment and Materials

- Ball options: tennis balls, Wiffle balls, racquetballs, foam balls, etc.
- Four-base grid options: bases spray-painted on grass, rubber bases, poly spots
- Cones
- Pedometers

Introduction

Begin with a review of footwork at a base for a force out. Do a recognition check for understanding. Demonstrate the footwork two times, one done correctly and one incorrectly. Ask students which one was correct and why. Follow up with "why" questions about the footwork (e.g., Why is it important to put your foot on the edge of the base? Answer: So you can catch the ball sooner and you don't trip the runner). Provide an individual step-count goal.

Instructional Task: Throwing and Catching Practice

■ PRACTICE TASK

Four-corners throwing:

In a grid formation (four bases), one student is at each base. Based on your whistle, students throw clockwise and then counterclockwise.

Be sure to stagger the grids so that any overthrows are not in line with the next grid.

Each group should take two or three extra balls in case throws go astray. Give safety reminders about looking before throwing.

Refinements

- Crow hop: Use a low and quick step for a short throw. Exaggerate a high step to make a long throw.
- Footwork on base: Wait to put your foot on the base until you know the direction the throw is coming from.

- Calling for the ball: Repeat, calling for the ball multiple times.
- Students self-assess on the critical elements for catching.

Student Choices/Differentiation

- Each group of four should choose the type of ball it would like to use and also choose the size of the grid.
- If a group is having difficulty with throwing and catching successfully, decrease the size of the grid.

What to Look For

Focus feedback on throwing in the first activity and then on the crow hop and calling for the ball in the second and third activities.

Instructional Task: Tagging Runners

■ PRACTICE TASK

Ask students about the rules for tagging unforced runners out, asking primarily "why" questions (e.g., Why should you hold the ball with two hands when tagging a runner? Answer: to ensure that the ball is held securely) to check for understanding.

Tag 'em out: In the same groups of four, one student is the defender of a base, one throws the ball to the defender, and the other two take turns as runners coming from the previous base. The defender tries to tag the runner, while the runner tries to avoid being tagged before she reaches the base. After five throws, students rotate to a new position: thrower, defender, runner 1, runner 2.

Do not allow sliding into a base.

Emphasize that the tagger should stand outside of the baseline to avoid collisions.

Extensions

- Increase the distance of the throw.
- Increase the tagger's distance from the base.

Student Choices/Differentiation

Each group of four should choose the type of ball it would like to use and also choose the size of the grid.

What to Look For

- Runners use pivots, fakes, and/or jab steps to evade being tagged.
- Critical elements for tagging a runner:
    1. Hold the ball with two hands.
    2. Tag the runner on the upper body.
    3. Stand to the side of the baseline to avoid collisions.

Instructional Task: Game Application of Defending a Base With Unforced Runners (Tactical Approach)

■ PRACTICE TASK

Pickle game:

In groups of four (three on defense and one on offense),

- two defenders start at one of the bases and one starts at the other base; one defender from the group of two has a ball;
- the runner starts in the middle;
- play begins when the defender with the ball moves;

- defenders throw the ball back and forth, trying to tag the runner out before she reaches either base;
- when a defender throws the ball, he runs to cover the base of the player to whom he threw;
- runner scores a point when reaching either of the bases without being tagged; and
- after three tries, the runner switches with a defender.

Keep track of points scored individually. Do not allow sliding or diving into a base. Emphasize that the tagger should stand outside of the baseline to avoid collisions.

Guiding questions for students:
- What was the runner's goal? (Answer: to reach either base without being tagged)
- What did you do as the runner to keep from getting tagged? (Answer: watched the player with the ball; changed directions when he threw the ball; used a fake, pivot, or jab step to avoid the defender's tag)
- What was the defenders' goal? (Answer: to tag the runner before she got to a base)
- As defenders, how did the three of you move between the two bases so that you worked together efficiently? (Answer: We followed our throws to rotate to the other base.)
- What did your throws look like, or what kind of throws did you make? (Answer: short throws made with the wrist, just like throwing a dart)
- How did you communicate so that you knew when to throw the ball? (Answer: We told the thrower when to throw the ball to us.)

Extension
Have each group run a shuttle relay, using dart throws on the run, the receivers calling for the ball and throwers following their throws to the next base. Each group keeps a continuous shuttle going until all members have returned to their starting positions without dropping the ball.

Student Choices/Differentiation
Each group of four should choose the type of ball it would like to use and the distance between the two bases.

What to Look For
Critical elements for defenders:
- Run fast to cover the base.
- Keep the ball high (throwing hand).
- Use a dart throw.
- Follow your throw.

Critical elements for runners:
- Watch the ball.
- Change directions when the defenders throw the ball.
- Use a fake, pivot, or jab step to avoid the tag.

Formal and Informal Assessments
Self-assessment of catching

Closure
- Discuss tagging runners (defending a base with unforced runners).
- Groups of four discuss: When playing the pickle game, what can a runner do to reach a base?
- What should a defender do to tag the runner out?

Reflection

- Are students' throwing and catching skills at the competency level so that they can use them in small-sided game play?
- Do students understand the difference between forced and unforced runners?

Homework

Ask students to update their physical activity logs.

Part or whole worksheet (see example): Have students list the critical elements of catching a thrown ball, then identify one element to take away. Have students respond to the following questions: What would happen to the skill if this part was missing? Why do we need to do that part of the skill?

Resources

Bailey, J. (2008). Rundowns in physical education? Try the tactical approach. *Strategies, 22*(2), 10-12.

Graham, G. (2008). *Teaching children physical education: Becoming a master teacher.* 3rd ed. Champaign, IL: Human Kinetics.

Mitchell, S.A., Oslin, J.L., & Griffin, L.L. (2013). *Teaching sport concepts and skills: A tactical games approach.* 3rd ed. Champaign, IL: Human Kinetics.

Potter, D.L., & Johnson, L. (2007). *Teaching softball: Steps to success.* 3rd ed. Champaign, IL: Human Kinetics.

PART OR WHOLE ASSIGNMENT: CATCHING

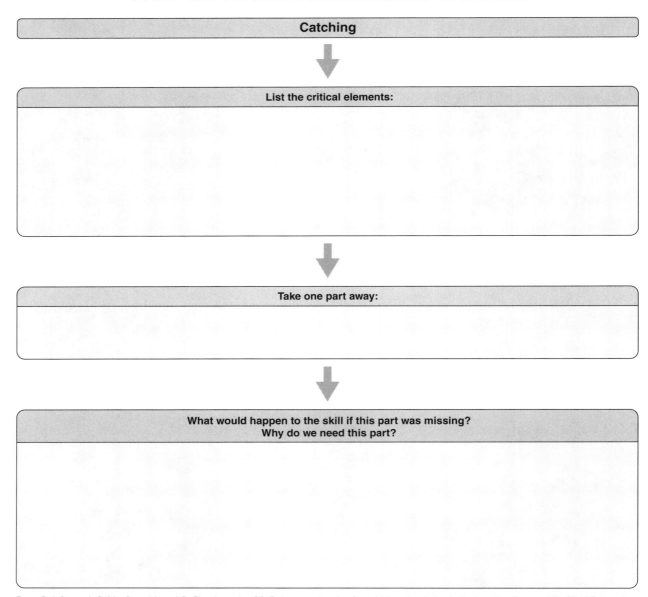

Catching

⬇

List the critical elements:

⬇

Take one part away:

⬇

What would happen to the skill if this part was missing?
Why do we need this part?

From R.J. Doan, L.C. MacDonald, and S. Chepko, eds., 2017, *Lesson planning for middle school physical education* (Reston, VA: SHAPE America; Champaign, IL: Human Kinetics).

LESSON 3: FIELDING GROUND BALLS AND DECISION MAKING ON DEFENSE

Grade-Level Outcomes

Primary Outcomes

Offensive skills: Executes at least one of the following designed to create open space during small-sided game play: pivots, fakes, jab steps. (S1.M6.7)

Catching: Catches, with a mature pattern, from different trajectories using a variety of objects in small-sided game play. (S1.M21.7)

Reducing space: Selects the correct defensive play based on the situation (e.g., number of outs). (S2.M11.7)

Embedded Outcome

Working with others: Problem-solves with a small group of classmates during adventure activities, small-group initiatives or game play. (S4.M5.7)

Lesson Objectives

The learner will:

- demonstrate techniques (pivot, fake, jab step) to avoid being tagged at least two out of three times during the pickle or trickle game.
- demonstrate proper ground-ball fielding technique, using all critical elements of a mature pattern during partner fielding practice tasks.
- make appropriate decisions when playing defense for a tag out during the one player game application.

Equipment and Materials

- Ball options: tennis balls, Wiffle balls, racquetballs, foam balls, etc.
- Four-base grid options: bases spray-painted on grass, rubber bases, poly spots
- Cones
- Pedometers

Introduction

Begin with a review of tagging unforced runners. Invite four skilled students to demonstrate the pickle game. After the runner returns to the base of origin, advances to the next base, or is tagged out, ask questions about the strategy of both the defensive players and the runner. Explain that, later in the lesson, students also will practice fielding ground balls. Ask students, "If you hit a high percentage of ground balls as a batter, do you think you will be very successful? Why or why not?" "If you can field ground balls well, your team will have a better chance of getting batters out." Provide an individual step-count goal.

Instructional Task: Review Tagging Unforced Runners

■ PRACTICE TASK

In ability groups of four, play the pickle game from Lesson 2.

Do not allow sliding or diving into a base. Emphasize that the tagger should stand outside of the baseline to avoid collisions.

Refinements

- Defense: Make the runner commit. Throw the ball with just a wrist snap. As a receiver, call for the ball.
- Runner: Don't commit to a base until the defense makes you go that way. Avoid a tag by ducking and rolling under the non-ball side of the defender.

Student Choices/Differentiation

- The group of four should choose the type of ball they would like to use and also choose the distance between the two bases.
- Groups of students at the utilization or proficiency level of what Graham, Holt/Hale, and Parker refer to as the generic levels of skill development (GLSP) (2012) could be invited to try trickle, in which one more base is added to form a triangle. At least four defenders are needed along with two runners.

What to Look For

Critical elements for defenders:

1. Run fast to cover the base.
2. Keep the ball high (throwing hand).
3. Use a dart throw.
4. Follow your throw.

Critical elements for runners:

1. Watch the ball.
2. Change directions when the defenders throw the ball.
3. Use a fake, pivot, or jab step to avoid the tag.

Instructional Task: Fielding Ground Balls

■ PRACTICE TASK

Demonstrate technique for fielding grounders.

Guiding questions for students:

- Ask questions about specific aspects of fielding ground balls (e.g., How did Mary have her feet when she was waiting for the ball?).
- Follow up the response with a "why" question (e.g., Why should Mary's feet be spaced wide apart?).

Continue by demonstrating the movement needed when a ball is coming at a fielder to one side or the other (shuffle or slide if ball is close; cross over and square up if not close).

Extensions

- Triangles: In partners about 5 feet (1.5 m) apart with a ball of choice, one student rolls a grounder directly at the partner, who is kneeling with knees apart and hands out in front. (The knees form the base of the triangle, and the hands are the point of the triangle.) Partner fields the ball and tosses the ball back. Repeat 10 times and switch.
- Two-ball pick-up: In partners with two balls of choice, one student rolls a grounder just to the side of the partner, making him slide over to field it. Fielder underhand tosses the ball back to the partner. Tosser immediately rolls the second ball to the opposite side, making the fielder slide over to field it between the feet and toss it back. Tosser immediately rolls the other ball back to the other side and continues for 10 pick-ups. Partners switch.
- Two-ball pick-up extended: Same as two-ball pick-up but the ball is rolled farther out to the side, making the fielder use a crossover step to get to the ball. After 10 pick-ups, partners switch.

Refinement

Keep both palms open to the oncoming ball. When moving to the side, keep your shoulders square to the ball. Stay low while moving to the ball.

Student Choices/Differentiation

- Partners should choose the type of ball they want to use in the fielding activities.
- Partners can determine the distance apart they want to be.
- Partners can determine the speed at which the balls are thrown during the pick-up activities.

What to Look For

Critical elements for fielding ground balls:

- Assume a low ready position with feet apart.
- Both hands are out in front forming a triangle, with the feet as the base and the hands as the point.
- "Alligator"(the fielder places one hand under the ball to scoop it and uses the other hand to clamp down on the ball to secure it, like an alligator's jaw) the ball and absorb it into the body.
- Crow-hop and transfer into throwing position.
- Is the force or speed of the throws or tosses appropriate for the skill of the receiver?
- Are students looking to see that the receiver is ready before throwing?

Instructional Task: Game Application—Combining Fielding, Throwing, Catching, and Tagging Runners

■ PRACTICE TASK

Explain and demonstrate the game.

Emphasize correct fielding and tagging technique, along with running strategy.

One Player

- Form teams of six to eight students.
- One player begins in the field, while the remaining players are members of the offensive team.
- One person on the offensive team throws a ground ball into the field (four bases at skill-appropriate distance).
- The whole offensive team then runs the bases behind the batter.
- The base runners can pass one another as they round the bases, but stopping on the bases is not allowed.
- Cones can be used to represent the bases, and the runners just run past them.
- After the ball is thrown, the defensive player retrieves the ball and begins to tag runners with the ball.
- As runners are tagged, they immediately become part of the defensive team and assist in tagging other runners.
- When runners reach home, they are safe.
- When *all* runners reach home, a new "batter" starts the process again, with all of the tagged players helping in the field as part of the defensive team.
- Eventually, there will be a team of fielders with only one batter.
- This batter then becomes the new defensive player for the next game.

Give safety reminders for runners to look where they are going and avoid other runners.

Set up playing areas so they radiate out from a central open space.

Refinement

Defense: Get in a low ready position to field a ground ball. Before the ball is thrown, look to see how you could assist the person who fields the ball or what you will do with the ball if you field it. Make the runners change directions to make a tag on their backs and avoid collisions.

EMBEDDED OUTCOME: S4.M5.7. After a few turns, stop and ask questions about the defensive strategies that were successful or the strategies that could be implemented to be more successful getting runners out. Allow time for students to talk with a partner, and then suggest ideas to the class. Continue play.

Student Choices/Differentiation

- The student who is throwing can choose the type of ball to throw. Available options should include balls that have a limited flight.
- Rather than throwing, the offensive player can hit off a tee, hit a soft toss, or fungo hit.
- Begin the game with a skilled player as the lone defensive player.
- More than one player can begin on defense if it is too difficult to get runners out.
- Make the distance between bases greater if it is too easy to get runners out; make the distance shorter if it is too difficult to get runners out.

What to Look For

Critical elements for defenders:

- Use correct fielding technique for ground balls.
- Make appropriate decisions about which runners to attempt to tag.
- Use proper tagging technique.
- Successful cooperation among defensive players allows for tagging multiple runners.

Critical elements for runners:

- Watch the ball.
- Change directions when the defenders throw the ball.
- Use a fake, pivot, or jab step to avoid the tag.

Formal and Informal Assessments

Student self-assessment of fielding critical elements in the lesson closure

Closure

- Ask students about defensive decisions when playing the one player game (e.g., If the fielder picks up the ball on the left side of the field, what should she do?).
- When the "one player" has tagged one runner and now there are two players on defense, what can they do to get more runners out?
- How many defensive players would be ideal to be very effective at getting runners out?
- Have students complete a written self-assessment of fielding using a rating scale. Rate yourself on each of the critical elements of fielding as follows: (1) This part is easy for me. (2) I have to concentrate to be able to do this part. (3) I need more practice on this part.
  - Assume low ready position with feet apart.
  - Both hands are out in front with palms up.
  - "Alligator" the ball and absorb it into the body.
  - Crow-hop and transfer into throwing position.

Reflection

- After two lessons that include tagging an unforced runner, are students progressing in their understanding and demonstration of defensive strategies?
- What is their level of ability in fielding ground balls?
- Is continued practice with the isolated skill needed, or can students combine the skill with throwing and apply the skills in game-like situations?

Homework

Ask students to update their physical activity logs.

Play one of the games taught in today's lesson with a friend or family member.

Resources

Bailey, J. (2008). Rundowns in physical education? Try the tactical approach. *Strategies, 22*(2), 10-12.

Graham, G. (2008). *Teaching children physical education: Becoming a master teacher.* 3rd ed. Champaign, IL: Human Kinetics. (CFUs)

Potter, D.L., & Johnson, L. (2007). *Teaching softball: Steps to success.* 3rd ed. Champaign, IL: Human Kinetics.

Internet keyword search: "fungo hitting," "soft toss hitting"

LESSON 4: FIELDING FLY BALLS

Grade-Level Outcomes

Primary Outcomes

Catching: Catches, with a mature pattern, from different trajectories using a variety of objects in small-sided game play. (S1.M21.7)

Reducing space: Reduces open spaces in the field by working with teammates to maximize coverage. (S2.M11.8)

Embedded Outcome

Rules & etiquette: Demonstrates knowledge of rules and etiquette by self-officiating modified physical activities and games or following parameters to create or modify a dance. (S4.M6.7)

Lesson Objectives

The learner will:

- demonstrate proper ground-ball fielding technique using all critical elements of a mature pattern during small-group fielding practice tasks and game application.
- demonstrate proper fly-ball fielding technique using all critical elements of a mature pattern during small-group fielding practice tasks and game application.
- work with teammates by calling for fly balls in the game application of over the line.

Equipment and Materials

- Ball options: tennis balls, Wiffle balls, racquetballs, foam balls, etc.; 5 balls for each group of 3 students
- Pails, buckets, or bags for the balls
- Bat options: Wiffle bats of different sizes, tennis rackets, wooden paddles
- Four-base grid options: bases spray-painted on grass, rubber bases, poly spots, cones
- Cones for over the line: 4 cones for each game setup
- Pedometers

Introduction

Begin with a review of fielding ground balls. Check for understanding on fielding a ball that doesn't come right at you. Demonstrate the technique two times, one done correctly and one incorrectly. Ask students which one was correct and why. Follow up with "why" questions about the technique (e.g., Why is it important to get behind the ball? How should your feet move if the ball is within one or two steps? How should your feet move if the ball is farther away?). Provide step-count goal for groups of three.

Instructional Task: Review Fielding Ground Balls

■ **PRACTICE TASK**

Field and throw:

In a grid formation (four bases), with one student at each of three bases in the grid; one student as the thrower, one as the fielder, and one as the receiver. Begin with five balls of choice.

First: The thrower throws a ground ball to the fielder, who fields the ball and throws through the grid to the receiver. The receiver drops the caught ball on the ground beside him. Continue with all five balls. Then, the receiver becomes the thrower, the thrower becomes the fielder, and the fielder moves to the open base and becomes the receiver. Repeat the process with the five balls. After the third rotation, all three students will have fielded at least five ground balls and thrown them to a catcher.

Second: Have the thrower alternate throwing the ball to opposite sides of the fielder. The fielder must move to get behind the ball to field it cleanly and then throw to the catcher. Use the same rotation system so that each player has five opportunities to field a ground ball.

Third: With the same setup, repetitions, and rotation, the thrower throws the ball in the general direction of the fielder, so that the fielder has to move to field the ball.

Use small pails, buckets, or bags to carry the sets of five balls for groups of students.

If class size or lack of equipment dictates larger groups, have students back up the fielder, back up the catcher, or feed balls to the thrower. Students who are backing up another student should be at a safe distance (5 to 10 feet; 1.5 to 3 m). They then rotate into the drill.

Extension

Partners use technology to record peers' fielding technique for ground balls. Provide a teacher-generated checklist with the critical elements.

Student Choices/Differentiation

- Groups should choose the type of balls they want to use in the fielding activities.
- Groups may determine the distance apart they want to be.
- Groups may determine the speed at which the balls are thrown during the practice tasks.
- Groups may determine whether the ball is hit fungo-style rather than thrown.

What to Look For

Critical elements for fielding ground balls:

1. Assume a low ready position, with feet apart.
2. Both hands are out in front, with palms up.
3. "Alligator" the ball and absorb it into the body.
4. Crow-hop and transfer into throwing position.
5. Is the force or speed of the throws or tosses appropriate for the skill of the receiver?
6. Are students looking to see that the receiver is ready before throwing?

Instructional Task: Fielding Fly Balls

■ PRACTICE TASK

Demonstrate technique for fielding fly balls. Remind students that the technique is similar to catching a thrown ball. Review by having two or three students explain and demonstrate a critical element that they chose to "remove" from catching and what would happen with that element missing from the skill. Demonstrate the proper footwork for catching fly balls in all directions:

- Front: jab step
- Sides: crossover step
- Behind: drop step

Shadow Drill

Stand in front of the class with a ball in one hand. Students are scattered in personal space. Hold the ball in the air, moving it either to one side, back overhead, or out in front at an angle. Students respond by moving in that direction, using proper footwork (jab, crossover, or drop step). Continue to move the group up, back, and to the sides.

Make sure that students have enough personal space so that if someone makes an inaccurate movement, she will not run into another student.

Catch and Throw

Use the same organization and implementation as in the earlier field and throw practice task.

First: The thrower throws fly balls directly to the fielder.

Second: The thrower throws fly balls alternately to both sides, making the fielder take two or three steps to the side to catch the ball.

Third: The thrower throws fly balls alternately in front of the fielder and then behind the fielder.

Fourth: The thrower may throw fly balls in any direction near the fielder.

Partner Catching

Using the same grids and groups of three as in the previous fielding tasks, two students are fielders and one student is a thrower. Identify which fielder has priority. The thrower throws a fly ball between the two fielders to practice calling for the ball. The caught ball is tossed back to the thrower. Repeat for five throws and rotate positions.

Student Choices/Differentiation

- Groups should choose the type of balls that they want to use in the fielding activities.
- Groups may determine how far apart they want to be.
- Groups may determine the difficulty of the fly balls that are thrown.

What to Look For

Critical elements for fielding fly balls (similar to catching from Lesson 1):

1. Assume an athletic stance, with non-throwing-side foot slightly ahead.
2. Call for the ball.
3. Both hands are ready for a two-hand catch: "When it's high, thumbs will meet; pinkies touch when it's at your feet."
4. Absorb the ball into the body.
5. Crow-hop and throw: "Thumb to the thigh and up to the sky" (big arm circle).

Critical elements for jab steps (balls hit in front of the player):

1. Take a quick and short step toward the ball to start momentum.
2. Run hard for the ball, pumping both arms.

Critical elements for crossover steps (balls hit to the side):

1. Pivot the foot on the ball side.
2. Cross over with the foot on the non-ball side.
3. Run hard to the ball.
4. Square up to the fly ball, and get in ready position to make the catch.

Critical elements for drop steps (balls hit behind the player):

1. Step backward at an angle, with the foot on the ball side.
2. Turn body and run, pumping both arms.
3. Square up to the fly ball if possible, and get in ready position to make the catch.

Critical elements for fly ball communication:

1. Determine specific words to call for the ball (e.g., "mine" or "I got it")
2. Determine fielding priorities:
   - Outfielders have priority over infielders.
   - Center fielder has priority over all others.
   - Shortstop has priority over all infielders.
   - Force or speed of fielders' throws or tosses are appropriate for the skill of the receiver.

- Students look to see that the receiver is ready before throwing.
- Fielders call for the fly ball in the practice task.

Instructional Task:
Game Application of Fielding Fly Balls and Ground Balls

■ PRACTICE TASK

Over the line:

Set up playing areas so that they radiate out from a central open space. Have three players per team: one thrower acting as a hitter, and two fielders.

Thrower throws from home plate area.

Mark a line with two cones that fielders must stay behind (20 to 30 feet [6 to 9 m] from home).

Mark sidelines with two more cones that make an alley to play within (30 to 50 feet [9 to 15 m] wide).

Hits: ball thrown into the alley past the line on the fly without being caught; any ball dropped by the fielders; fielders cross "the line" when catching the ball

Outs: two foul balls by the thrower (outside the alley); fly balls caught in the air

Runs: three "hits" in an inning scores one run; each additional "hit" in that inning scores another run

Players rotate after three outs.

Refinements

- Defense: Spread out to cover all types and distances of hits. Fielder farthest away from home has priority on fly balls.
- Offense: Use a high crow hop to throw for more distance.

EMBEDDED OUTCOME: S4.M6.7. Students should understand and follow the rules so that they can self-officiate a small-sided game.

Student Choices/Differentiation

- Adjust the scoring, the number of outs, or both.
- Students determine the distance between home and the line, along with size of the alley.
- Groups choose the type of ball used.

What to Look For

Critical elements for defense:

1. Players use correct fielding technique for ground balls.
2. Players use correct fielding technique for fly balls.
3. Fielders call for fly balls.
4. Defensive players cooperate to catch fly balls.
5. Players count outs accurately.

Critical elements for offense:

1. Players place hits strategically into the alley between fielders.
2. Players count runs accurately.

Formal and Informal Assessments

- Checks for understanding: fielding technique for ground balls (formal peer assessment) and fly balls (informal)
- Exit slip: Describe the proper communication and who has priority for fly balls in Wiffle ball.

Closure

If students are primarily at the pre-control and control levels in fielding skills, use questions such as:

- What are some things to remember about fielding a ground ball?
- Why are those things important?
- Show me how you make a triangle when fielding a ground ball.
- How should your feet be positioned when catching a fly ball?
- Why is it important to call for the ball when catching a fly ball?

If students are primarily at the utilization and proficient levels of GLSP (Graham, Holt/Hale, & Parker, 2012) in fielding skills, ask questions such as:

- Can someone show me the difference between the throwing-arm motion when you are close to a target and when you are farther away?
- If you were using a glove, how would you try to field a ball that is on your throwing side?
- When you were playing over the line, how did you position yourselves when on defense?
- Why did you try that strategy? Did it work?

Reflection

- Are students able to use their fielding skills in modified game play?
- Are students working together when playing defense?
- Are students ready to move on to a new skill?

Homework

Ask students to update their physical activity logs.
Collect part or whole homework from Lesson 2.

Resources

Graham, G. (2008). *Teaching children physical education: Becoming a master teacher.* 3rd ed. Champaign, IL: Human Kinetics.

Graham, G., Holt/Hale, S.A., & Parker, M. (2012). *Children moving: A reflective approach to teaching physical education.* 9th ed. New York: McGraw-Hill Education.

Old Mission Beach Athletic Club. (2015). Official over the line rules. Retrieved from www.ombac.org.

Internet keyword search: "fly ball priority"

LESSON 5: HITTING

Grade-Level Outcomes

Primary Outcomes

Catching: Catches, with a mature pattern, from different trajectories using a variety of objects in small-sided game play. (S1.M21.7)

Striking: Strikes a pitched ball with an implement to open space in a variety of practice tasks. (S1.M20.7)

Embedded Outcome

Accepting feedback: Provides corrective feedback to a peer, using teacher-generated guidelines, and incorporating appropriate tone and other communication skills. (S4.M3.7)

Lesson Objectives

The learner will:

- demonstrate the proper footwork for fielding fly balls, using all critical elements of a mature pattern during small-group fielding practice tasks and game application.
- hit a pitched ball into open space using proper striking form during small-sided game play.

Equipment and Materials

- Ball options: tennis balls, Wiffle balls, racquetballs, foam balls, etc.
- Bat options: Wiffle bats of different sizes, tennis rackets, wooden paddles, wooden dowels
- Home plates
- Cones or markers (6 for each group of 4 students)
- Pedometers
- iPads or digital video cameras

Introduction

Begin with a review of catching fly balls. Do a performance check for understanding, by asking all students to show you the position of their bodies when catching a fly ball. Ask questions about the technique, specifically "why" questions (e.g., Why should the non-throwing-side foot be slightly ahead? Why do we need to have two hands ready to catch? Why do we use the crow hop?). Provide an individual step-count goal.

Instructional Task: Review Catching Fly Balls

■ PRACTICE TASK

Partner Fly Balls

One partner is the tosser and the other is the fielder.

- Tosser makes an underhand toss for a short fly ball directly in front of the fielding partner.
- Fielder runs in to catch the short fly ball and returns the ball to the tosser.
- The tosser then throws a fly ball over the head of the fielder, making him drop-step and run back to catch the overhead fly ball.
- The fielder throws the ball back to the tosser.
- The pattern continues with a short fly ball and then an overhead fly ball until 10 throws have been made or the designated time is up.

In the partner activities, each set of partners should take two balls of choice in case one goes out of play.

Extension

X-ball catching: Partners are set up as in the previous fly ball practice task. Four throws and attempted catches are made before partners switch. The tosser makes the following throws so that the fielder is making catches in the four corners of an X:

- Short fly to the right
- Overhead fly to the left
- Short fly straight ahead
- Overhead fly to the right

Refinement

Many students have trouble with footwork. Stop the drill and practice footwork if needed.

Student Choices/Differentiation

- Partners choose the type of ball they want to use in the fielding activities.
- Partners determine the distance apart they want to be.
- Partners determine the speed at which the balls are thrown.

What to Look For

Critical elements for fielding fly balls:

1. Fielders assume an athletic stance, with non-throwing-side foot slightly ahead.
2. Fielders call for the ball.
3. Fielders have both hands ready for a two-hand catch: "When it's high, thumbs will meet; pinkies touch when it's at your feet."
4. Fielders absorb the ball into the body.
5. Fielders crow-hop and throw: "Thumb to the thigh and up to the sky" (big arm circle).

Critical elements for jab steps (balls hit in front of the player):

1. Fielders take a quick and short step toward the ball to start momentum.
2. Fielders run hard for the ball, pumping both arms.

Critical elements for crossover steps (balls hit to the side):

1. Fielders pivot the foot on the ball side.
2. Fielders cross over with the foot on the non-ball side.
3. Fielders run hard to the ball.
4. Fielders square up to the fly ball, and get in ready position to make the catch.

Critical elements for drop steps (balls hit behind the player):

1. Step backward at an angle with the foot on the ball side.
2. Turn body and run, pumping both arms.
3. Square up to the fly ball, if possible, and get in ready position to make the catch.

Instructional Task: Hitting (Striking)

■ PRACTICE TASK

Demonstrate the technique of hitting. Discuss the bat as a lever, along with the relationship between the length of the lever and the speed of the swing. Remind students that they have been previously taught the skill of hitting, but there are more details to learn to be a successful hitter.

Hitting progression:

Each student has her own bat, or partners share one bat and give feedback when watching each other. Students are in self-space, all facing the same direction. Intersperse skilled students who may help others. Emphasize safety.

- Students show the proper grip on the bat. Put the bat out to show it as an extension of the arm.
- Students show proper ready position and jump straight up from that position (possible only if the ready position is balanced).
- Students take dry swings in slow motion. Stop the swing at the contact point to show that the top hand is in a hand-shaking position.
- Students put bat behind back, hooking it in their arms, and a ball beside the back heel. They rotate and push the ball with the back heel if they are "squishing the bug" properly.

Extensions

- Hitting practice: Using a home plate to show pitch location, partners hit off a tee, do a soft toss, or hit a pitched ball. Switch by repetitions or by time.
- Assign a peer assessment of hitting.

EMBEDDED OUTCOME: S4.M3.7 Using appropriate technology (e.g., iPads, digital cameras), students record each other hitting off a tee or hitting a soft toss. Students watch the video together and complete a written peer-assessment checklist.

Refinement

Step toward the pitch. Hit *through* the ball. Chin moves from front shoulder to back shoulder.

Guiding questions for students:
- Why do you line up your "door-knocking" knuckles when gripping the bat?
- How do you make your stance balanced?
- Why do you want to take just a short stride?
- At the contact point, why should your top hand be in a hand-shaking position?
- What is the purpose of the follow-through?

Video analysis: Teacher-created checklist or rubric of critical elements

Student Choices/Differentiation

- Partners choose the type of balls they want to use in the hitting activities.
- Partners choose the type of bat they want to use in the hitting activities.
- Partners choose to use a tee, hit a soft toss, or hit a pitched ball.
- Higher-skilled students practice hitting inside or outside pitches by setting up the tee in those locations, soft-tossing to those locations, or pitching to those locations.

What to Look For

Critical elements for striking:
- Batters use the proper grip (door-knocking knuckles lined up).
- Batters assume a hitting-ready position (balanced athletic stance).
- Batters step and extend (take a short stride toward the pitch, begin to turn, throw hands out).
- Batters rotate (twist trunk so that back leg forms an L and back foot "squishes the bug").
- Batters follow through, continuing the swing to roll wrists over and wrap bat around the back.

Soft toss:

1. One partner with a bat stands in hitting stance.
2. Other partner kneels facing the batter, but off to the side and slightly ahead of the batter.
3. The partner who is kneeling makes a slow toss into the batter's hitting zone.

Instructional Task: Game Application of Hitting

■ PRACTICE TASK

2 v 2 hitting:

Groups of four play 2 v 2. From home plate, two foul lines go out about 60 feet (18 m) to form a triangular-shaped playing area. Place markers about 20 feet (6 m) apart at the 60-foot home run line. Put another set of markers about 40 feet (12 m) from home plate that designate a triple. Add a third set of markers about 20 feet from home plate that designate a double. A ball hit between home plate and 20 feet is considered a single.

Teams: The offensive team includes a hitter and on-deck hitter. No base running is included. The defensive team includes a pitcher and catcher.

Scoring: A ball hit in the single area moves an imaginary runner to first; double area moves all runners two bases; triple area moves all runners three bases; home run area scores all runners.

Outs: The hitter strikes out (swing and miss or foul balls count as strikes). Three outs and the teams switch.

Emphasize safety. Set up playing areas so they radiate out from a central open space.

Refinement

Know your best pitch area to hit. With no strikes, the area is small. With one strike, the area is larger. With two strikes, the area becomes the entire strike zone.

Student Choices/Differentiation

- Groups choose the type of bats and balls they want to use in the game.
- Groups determine the size of their playing area.
- Groups determine the number of strikes per batter and the number of outs per team.

What to Look For

Critical elements for striking:

1. Use the proper grip (door-knocking knuckles lined up).
2. Assume the ready position (balanced athletic stance).
3. Step and extend (take a short stride toward the pitch, begin to turn, throw hands out).
4. Rotate (twist trunk so that back leg forms an L and back foot "squishes the bug").
5. Follow through (continue the swing to roll wrists over and wrap bat around the back).

Critical elements for pitch selection:

1. Strike zone is from knees to shoulders.
2. Students should know the pitch location that is ideal for their swing.
3. Students make decision to swing according to the pitch location and the strike count.
   - With no strikes, perfect pitch area is very small.
   - With one strike, perfect pitch area becomes larger.
   - With two strikes, perfect pitch area is very large within the strike zone.

Organization and Safety

- Ensure that the size of the playing space is appropriate to students' skill level.
- Give safety reminders for students to look that the batter and catcher are ready before pitching.
- Have the catcher stand back at least 5 feet (1.5 m) behind the hitter. Have the on-deck hitter stand on the right side, well away from the hitter and catcher.
- Set up playing areas so they radiate out from a central open space.

Formal and Informal Assessments

- Checks for understanding of catching fly balls and hitting
- Peer assessment of hitting technique (rubric or checklist of critical elements)

Closure

If students are primarily at the pre-control and control levels in hitting skills, use questions such as:

- What are some things to remember about hitting a ball?
- Why are those things important?
- Show me how you get into your hitting stance. Why do you want to "squish the bug" with your back foot?
- What does the follow-through look like?

If students are primarily at the utilization and proficient levels of GLSP (Graham, Holt/Hale, & Parker, 2012) in hitting skills, ask questions such as:

- Can someone show me the difference between hitting an inside pitch and an outside pitch?
- In what game situations would you try to hit to the right side of the field?
- When you were playing the 2 v 2 hitting game, what did you need to do as a hitter to be successful?
- How did you work with your partner?
- Was it easy to score runs? Why or why not?

Reflection

- Are students able to use their hitting skills in modified game play?
- Are students working together in game applications of the skill?
- Are students ready to add base running to the hitting skill?

Homework

Ask students to come back to the next class with the answer to the question: Which class of lever would swinging a bat represent?

Practice the hitting motion at home by getting in the batting stance with hands on hips, putting a ball by the back heel, and "squishing the bug" to make the ball move away from the foot. Do 20 trials.

Ask students to update their physical activity logs.

Resources

Wiffle Ball: www.wiffle.com

Internet keyword search: "proper footwork for outfielders," "catching fly balls," "fielding fly balls," "softball hitting mechanics," "baseball hitting mechanics"

LESSON 6: BASE RUNNING

Grade-Level Outcomes

Primary Outcome

Reducing space: Selects the correct defensive play based on the situation (e.g., number of outs). (S2.M11.7) Note: Use this outcome to address offensive play.

Embedded Outcome

Fitness knowledge: Describes how muscles pull on bones to create movement in pairs by relaxing and contracting. (S3.M14.7)

Lesson Objectives

The learner will:

- demonstrate proper technique in running through first base on a batted ball during practice tasks or small-sided game play.
- demonstrate proper technique in rounding a base during practice tasks or small-sided game play.
- demonstrate proper technique in stopping at a base during base running practice tasks or small-sided game play.

Equipment and Materials

- Ball options: tennis balls, Wiffle balls, racquetballs, foam balls, etc.
- Bat options: Wiffle bats of different sizes, tennis rackets, wooden paddles
- Home plates and bases
- Pedometers

Introduction

With students in partners, have them write down as many base running rules as possible. Possible answers include running in baseline, forced-to-run situations, not-forced-to-run situations, tagging up on a fly ball, and over-running first base. Discuss students' responses and demonstrate, if necessary. Briefly discuss the homework assignment. Give an individual step-count goal.

Instructional Task: Tactical Base Running Game

■ PRACTICE TASK

2 v 2 Wiffle ball:

Create teams of two players. Two teams of players use only home, first, and third bases.

Offense

- Batter has a choice to run to first or third base. The batter can run only to an unoccupied base.
- Runners may not run directly from first base to third base.
- Runners must run on each hit.

Defense

- A ball caught in the air is an out.
- Outs also are made by tagging the base before the runner arrives, or by tagging the runner.

Set up playing areas so that they radiate out from a central open space.

Guiding questions for students:

- What did you do as a batter to help you reach a base? (Possible answers: look at where my partner was, hit to an open area, run to the closer base if it was open)

- Did those strategies work? Why or why not?
- What did you do to reach the base quickly? (Possible answers: sprint out of the batter's box, run hard, run in a straight line, run through the base)
- Why don't you want to stop at the base? (Answer: have to slow down)
- What part of the base did you try to touch to be sure that you were safe? (Answer: the front edge)
- How did you stand on the base when your partner was hitting? (Answer: like a runner in a race)

Student Choices/Differentiation

- Allow students to set up the bases at a distance they choose. One base must be half the distance of the other.
- Allow individual choices for the type of bat and ball used.
- Batter can throw, fungo hit, hit off a tee, hit a soft toss, or have the ball pitched.
- Teams switch after three outs or after each batter hits three times.

What to Look For
Critical elements for base running:
1. Drop the bat after the swing.
2. Sprint out of the box.
3. Run on the outside of the imaginary first-base line.
4. Step on the front edge of the base.
5. Run through first base.

Instructional Task: Base Running Practice Tasks

■ PRACTICE TASK

Make groups of four students, and have them set up two bases about 30 feet (9 m) apart.

Base running progression:

Explain and demonstrate each technique. Have students practice after each demonstration.
- Running through first base
- Rounding first base and returning to the base
- Leadoff position
- Stopping on a base

Refinement

Make sure that students are exploding out of their lead-up stance.

EMBEDDED OUTCOME: S3.M14.7. Through guiding questions, discuss muscle groups and how they work in pairs to produce movement.

Guiding questions for students:
- What muscle groups are you using when you run?
- Which muscles help you straighten out your legs at the knees and at the hips?
- What muscles help you bend your legs at the knees and at the hips?
- What muscle groups are you using in the upper body?

Student Choices/Differentiation
- Students may vary distance.
- Students may chose who they work with.

What to Look For

Critical elements for sprinting out of the batter's box:

1. Drop bat down after follow-through rather than throwing the bat.
2. First step is with the back foot.

Critical elements for running through first base and home plate:

1. Run to the right side of an imaginary baseline (home to first or third to home).
2. Step on the front edge of the base.
3. Run past the base and straight through.

Critical elements for rounding a base:

1. Halfway to the base, angle out and then back in toward the base.
2. Step on the inside corner of the base.
3. Lean to the infield side of the base.

Critical elements for the leadoff position:

1. Use a runner's standing start, with the back foot pushing against the edge of the base.
2. Use a forward lean, with arms in position to sprint.

Critical elements for stopping at a base:

1. Run hard in a straight line to the base.
2. Step on the front edge of the base.
3. Keep the first foot on the base, step over the base with the other foot, and lower the body to stop momentum.

Instructional Task: Game Application of Base Running

■ PRACTICE TASK

4 v 4 Wiffle ball:

Combine teams of two to create teams of four players. Two teams of players use an entire grid of bases. Set up playing areas so they radiate out from a central open space.

Offense

- Runners run bases as in regulation softball or baseball.
- The runners are forced to run only by the batter or a runner behind them.

Defense

- A ball caught in the air is an out.
- Outs can also be made by tagging the base before the runner arrives, or by tagging the runner.
- Teams switch after three outs.

Extensions

- Have students perform a self-assessment on their base-running skills.
- Evaluate students using the Game Performance Assessment Instrument (GPAI) (Oslin et al.).

Refinements

- Runner on first: Run on a ground ball. Go part way on a fly ball.
- Unforced runner on second: Run on a ground ball to the right side. Tag up on a fly ball to the right side.
- Unforced runner on third: Run on a deep ground ball to the right. Tag up on any fly ball.

Student Choices/Differentiation

- Allow students to set up the bases at a distance they choose.
- Allow individual choices for the type of bat and ball used.
- Batter can throw, fungo hit, hit off a tee, hit a soft toss, or have the ball pitched.
- Teams switch after three outs or after each batter hits three times.

What to Look For

Critical elements for base running:

1. Drop the bat after the swing.
2. Sprint out of the box.
3. Run on the outside of the imaginary first-base line.
4. Step on the front edge of the base.
5. Run through first base.
6. Make proper decisions about advancing to the next base.

Are team members cooperating to make the outs?

Formal and Informal Assessments

- Complete the GPAI for base-running decisions.
- Self-assessment: Have students rate themselves on a teacher-created rubric on the following:
  - Using all of the base-running aspects of sprinting out of the batter's box
  - Running through first base
  - Rounding a base
  - Leading off
  - Stopping on a base

Closure

Discuss base running:

- If you were on first base and the ball was hit on the ground (hit in the air), what would you do?
- If you were on second base and there was no runner on first and a ball was hit on the ground (hit in the air), what would you do?
- If you were on third base and not forced to go, where would the ball need to be hit for you to run?
- What would you do if the ball was hit in the air?

Reflection

- Are students using the correct base-running techniques?
- Are students making appropriate decisions about when to run?

Homework

Give students a worksheet that requires them to identify primary muscle groups used when a person runs the bases.

Resources

Docheff, D., & Hunkapiller, J. (1999). Two-on-two softball. *Strategies, 13*(4), 13-15.

Mitchell, S.A., Oslin, J.L., & Griffin, L.L. (2013). *Teaching sport concepts and skills: A tactical games approach.* 3rd ed. Champaign, IL: Human Kinetics.

Internet keyword search: "softball base running," "baseball base running"

LESSON 7: WIFFLE BALL STATIONS

Grade-Level Outcomes

Primary Outcomes

Throwing: Throws with a mature pattern for distance or power appropriate to the activity in a dynamic environment. (S1.M2.7)

Catching: Catches, with a mature pattern, from different trajectories using a variety of objects in small-sided game play. (S1.M21.7)

Striking: Strikes a pitched ball with an implement with force in a variety of practice tasks. (S1.M20.6)

Rules & etiquette: Applies rules and etiquette by acting as an official for modified physical activities and games and creating dance routines within a given set of parameters. (S4.M6.8)

Embedded Outcome

Personal Responsibility: Exhibits responsible social behaviors by cooperating with classmates, demonstrating inclusive behaviors and supporting classmates. (S4.M1.7)

Lesson Objectives

The learner will:

- demonstrate proper throwing technique using all critical elements of a mature pattern during the post-assessment.
- demonstrate proper catching technique using all critical elements of a mature pattern during the post-assessment.
- demonstrate proper technique to field a ground ball using all critical elements of a mature pattern during peer assessment.
- demonstrate proper base-running technique using all critical elements of a mature skill pattern during the team base-running activity.
- provide correct visual and verbal direction to batter-runners during the base-running activity.

Equipment and Materials

- Ball options: tennis balls, Wiffle balls, racquetballs, foam balls, etc.
- Bat options: Wiffle bats of different sizes
- Home plates or bases
- Batting tees
- Pedometers, iPads, and stopwatches

Introduction

Begin with a review of base running. Ask students to find a partner and discuss what is important for a base runner to do when hitting a single, a double, a triple, and a home run. Give partners time to converse and then have groups report on their base-running suggestions. Provide a team of four students a step-count goal for today.

Instructional Task: Review Base Running

■ PRACTICE TASK

Explain and demonstrate visual and verbal signals given by a first base coach.

Fantasy teams:

Groups of four to six use a grid of four bases. One student begins as a first base coach. One student role-plays as the game announcer, reporting on the base runner's pretend hit, defensive play, and base-running result. One student is the batter/base runner, who pretends to hit a ball and then runs to first. The base coach gives the runner direction to run through the base, round the base, or continue to second base. One or more students are on deck to become the batter. Students rotate from announcer to on deck, to batter/runner to base coach.

Extension

With the same setup, batter/runners are timed by another student swinging a bat and then running through first base. Students repeat to improve their time. Students can then predict their time for a double, attempt a double, and use group members' feedback to improve their times.

Refinements

- Pump your arms from "pocket to chin" when running.
- Lean toward the infield when rounding a base.
- To get faster, increase your stride length, increase your stride rate, or do both.

Student Choices/Differentiation

Groups can extend or shorten the size of their grids.

What to Look For

Critical elements for base running:

1. Drop the bat after the swing.
2. Sprint out of the batter's box.
3. Run on the outside of the imaginary first-base line.
4. Step on the front edge of the base.
5. Run through first base.
6. Make proper decisions about advancing to the next base.

Critical elements for first base coaching:

1. Point toward the right field foul line; say, "Run through, run through!"
2. Make small circle with one arm; say, "Round, round, round!"
3. Point toward second base; say, "Go two, go two, go two!"

Instructional Task: Station work

■ PRACTICE TASK

In groups of four, students rotate through all stations. Set up the stations so that you can monitor the written test station while also completing the throwing and catching post-assessment station.

- Throwing and catching post-assessment done by teacher
- Written test on rules
- Peer assessment of fielding grounders (one hitter, one catcher, one fielder, one assessor); use written checklists, iPads, or both
- Stacked Wiffle balls on tee challenge: Stack two Wiffle balls on a tee. Batter attempts to hit the bottom ball and make the top ball drop onto the tee. (A quick swing is needed for this to work!)
- Catching tricks: Toss, clap hands, catch; toss, turn 180 degrees or 360 degrees, catch; toss and catch behind back; juggle three small balls.
- Pitching with a Wiffle ball: Experiment with different grips and wrist snaps when throwing overhand; have an iPad at this station to show video clips of athletes throwing different baseball pitches (fastball, curve, slider).

Refinement

Stop activity and refine any skills taught that need to be corrected.

Students should cooperate with others in their group to successfully complete the station tasks.

Student Choices/Differentiation

- Groups of students choose the type of bat and ball used, along with the distance apart in the station activities.
- In the hitting assessment, allow students to hit a soft toss or off of a tee.

What to Look For

- Grip the ball like a softball or baseball, with two or three fingers on top of the ball (depending on the size of students' hands).
- Different pitches can be thrown overhand like a baseball.
- The direction of the wrist snap is not crucial in making the ball move. Because the holes are on just one half of the ball, the air pressure difference will make the ball move if it is thrown hard enough.
- Straight: The holes of the Wiffle ball are on the top by the two or three fingers and the wrist is snapped over the top of the ball.
- Curve: The holes of the Wiffle ball are on the thumb side of the grip. The wrist is snapped so the palm goes toward the middle of the body. The throwing-arm elbow goes toward the opposite hip on the follow-through.
- Slider: The holes of the Wiffle ball are on the pinkie side of the grip. The wrist is snapped so the palm goes away from the middle of the body. The follow-through stays on the throwing side of the body.

Formal and Informal Assessments

- Peer assessment of fielding grounders as one of the stations
- Written test on the rules of striking games as one of the stations
- Teacher assessment of catching and throwing skills as one of the stations (same as in Lesson 1)

Closure

- Ask questions about performance at stations regarding technique, strategies, and success.
- Collect homework and ask students questions about muscle groups that extend and contract when running.

Reflection

Enter assessment results (knowledge, catching, throwing, hitting) into spreadsheet and analyze the data. Determine what skills and knowledge should be reviewed in the next lesson.

Homework

Research the rule about a base runner being hit by a batted ball.

Ask students to update their physical activity logs.

Resources

Internet keyword search: "baseball pitching grips," "softball hitting tee drills," "three-ball juggling"

LESSON 8: TESTING DAY

Grade-Level Outcomes

Primary Outcomes

Offensive strategies: Identifies open spaces and attempts to strike object into that space. (S2. M10.6)

Reducing space: Selects the correct defensive play based on the situation (e.g., number of outs). (S2.M11.7)

Embedded Outcomes

Social interaction: Demonstrates the importance of social interaction by helping and encouraging others, avoiding trash talk and providing support to classmates. (S5.M6.7)

Assessment & program planning: Maintains a physical activity log for at least 2 weeks and reflects on activity levels as documented in the log. (S3.M16.6)

Lesson Objectives

The learner will:

- use proper hitting technique and strategy during game play to become a base runner.
- make appropriate defensive decisions during game play to get base runners out.

Equipment and Materials

- Ball options: tennis balls, Wiffle balls, racquetballs, foam balls, etc.
- Bat options: Wiffle bats of different sizes, tennis rackets, wooden paddles
- Home plates or bases
- Pedometers

Introduction

Begin with a discussion about the rule for a base runner being hit by a batted ball. Ask students to explain the rule.

EMBEDDED OUTCOME: S5.M6.7 Discuss cooperation and providing support to classmates. Ask students to give examples of cooperation they have seen in sport activities. Explain why it is important to review knowledge and skills. Provide step-count goals.

Instructional Task: Review of Knowledge or Technique According to Assessment Results

■ PRACTICE TASK

Knowledge review: Begin with partners or small groups discussing a topic, strategy, technique, or rule. Either distribute students with strong knowledge and skills among groups, or group students by ability and provide appropriately challenging questions and tasks for those with strong knowledge and skills.

Extension

Technique review: Repeat one or more practice tasks that have previously been used in the module.

Student Choices/Differentiation

Provide knowledge review activities appropriate to each group's cognitive level (Bloom's Revised Taxonomy):

- Understanding: Match up written terms and definitions.
- Applying: Complete a demonstration of a skill.
- Analyzing: Do a mock interview of a coach.
- Evaluating: Debate a defensive strategy (e.g., infield shift).
- Creating: Develop a radio ad for a local team.

What to Look For

- Ask probing questions when doing knowledge checks for understanding to ensure students understand the "why" behind the response.
- Reinforce appropriate skill with specific and corrective feedback.

Instructional Task:
Game Application of All Wiffle Ball Skills and Strategies

■ PRACTICE TASK

6 v 6 Wiffle ball:

Create teams of six players. Two teams use a grid with four bases. Set up playing areas so they radiate out from a central open space.

EMBEDDED OUTCOME: S5.M6.7. Emphasize cooperation and support for teammates.

Make sure to teach and remind students of the following:

Offense

- Runners run bases as in regulation softball or baseball.
- The runners are forced to run only by the batter or a runner behind them.
- Offense scores a point for every runner who reaches first base.

Defense

- A ball caught in the air is an out.
- Outs can also be made by tagging the base before the runner arrives, or by tagging the runner.
- Defense scores a point for every play that gets a runner out.

Defensive positions are rotated each inning, from pitcher to catcher to infielders to outfielders.

After a specific amount of time, switch opponents. This switch can be done multiple times.

Refinements

- Defense: Before each pitch, decide what you will do with the ball if hit to you on the ground or in the air.
- Runner: Before each pitch, decide what you will do if the ball is hit on the ground or in the air.
- Batter: Before your at-bat, look at the location of the defensive players. Try to hit the ball to an open area.

Extension

Lead students in conducting a self-assessment on their cooperation skills throughout the module.

Student Choices/Differentiation

- Allow students to set up the bases at a distance they choose.
- Allow individual choices for the type of bat and ball used.

- Batters can throw, fungo hit, hit off a tee, hit a soft toss, or have the ball pitched.
- Teams switch offense to defense after three outs or when all six players have batted.

What to Look For

Offense:

- Proper hitting technique
- Proper base-running technique
- Appropriate decision making about advancing to the next base or bases

Defense:

- Proper catching and fielding techniques
- Proper tagging technique
- Proper footwork on bases for force outs
- Appropriate decision making in defending the bases and space
- Cooperation among team members in the field

Formal and Informal Assessments

- Self-assessment on cooperation throughout the module
- Physical activity log reflection

Closure

EMBEDDED OUTCOME: S5.M6.7. Have teams of six discuss what cooperation means within the Wiffle Ball Module. Students then complete a self-assessment of their cooperation skills.

Discuss as a class why cooperation is important and how it can transfer to situations outside of physical education.

Reflection

- What worked well and what did not in the module and why?
- What should be modified, added, or eliminated for the next time the module is taught?

Homework

EMBEDDED OUTCOME: S3.M16.6. Have students reflect on their physical activity logs. Some possible questions:

- Are you surprised with your step counts during the Wiffle Ball Module?
- Compare your steps with those in other modules we have completed.
- Please reflect on your after-school physical activity.
- Are you happy with the log?
- What would you change or would like to improve?
- What are some strategies for improving?

Resources

Graham, G. (2008). *Teaching children physical education: Becoming a master teacher.* 3rd ed. Champaign, IL: Human Kinetics.

Graham, G., Holt/Hale, S.A., & Parker, M. (2012). *Children moving: A reflective approach to teaching physical education.* 9th ed. New York: McGraw-Hill Education.

Old Mission Beach Athletic Club. (2015). Official over the line rules. Retrieved from www.ombac.org.

Internet keyword search: "Bloom's Revised Taxonomy"

DISC GOLF MODULE

Lessons in this module were contributed by Aaron Hart, a lecturer in the physical education department at State University of New York College at Cortland and a former physical education teacher in New York City.

Grade-Level Outcomes Addressed, by Lesson	1	2	3	4	5	6	7	8
Standard 1. The physically literate individual demonstrates competency in a variety of motor skills and movement patterns.								
Demonstrates a mature pattern for a modified target game such as bowling, bocce or horseshoes. (S1.M18.6)	P	P	P		P			
Executes consistently (70% of the time) a mature pattern for target games such as bowling, bocce or horseshoes. (S1.M18.7)						P		
Performs consistently (70% of the time) a mature pattern with accuracy and control for one target game such as bowling or bocce. (S1.M18.8)							P	
Demonstrates correct technique for basic skills in 1 self-selected individual-performance activity. (S1.M24.6)	P							
Demonstrates correct technique for a variety of skills in 1 self-selected individual-performance activity. (S1.M24.7)								P
Standard 2. The physically literate individual applies knowledge of concepts, principles, strategies and tactics related to movement and performance.								
Selects appropriate shot and/or club based on location of the object in relation to the target. (S2.M9.6)	P	P						
Varies the speed, force and trajectory of the shot based on location of the object in relation to the target. (S2.M9.8)			P					
Standard 3. The physically literate individual demonstrates the knowledge and skills to achieve and maintain a health-enhancing level of physical activity and fitness.								
Describes the role of warm-ups and cool-downs before and after physical activity. (S3.M12.6)			P		E			
Designs a warm-up/cool-down regimen for a self-selected physical activity. (S3.M12.7)			P					
Designs and implements a warm-up/cool-down regimen for a self-selected physical activity. (S3.M12.8)			P					
Standard 4. The physically literate individual exhibits responsible personal and social behavior that respects self and others.								
Exhibits personal responsibility by using appropriate etiquette, demonstrating respect for facilities and exhibiting safe behaviors. (S4.M1.6)		E						
Exhibits responsible social behaviors by cooperating with classmates, demonstrating inclusive behaviors and supporting classmates. (S4.M1.7)	E	E		P				
Provides corrective feedback to a peer, using teacher-generated guidelines, and incorporating appropriate tone and other communication skills. (S4.M3.7)		E						
Provides encouragement and feedback to peers without prompting from the teacher. (S4.M3.8)		E						
Identifies the rules and etiquette for physical activities/games and dance activities. (S4.M6.6)		P		E				
Demonstrates knowledge of rules and etiquette by self-officiating modified physical activities and games or following parameters to create or modify a dance. (S4.M6.7)		P		P		P		
Standard 5. The physically literate individual recognizes the value of physical activity for health, enjoyment, challenge, self-expression and/or social interaction.								
Identifies components of physical activity that provide opportunities for reducing stress and for social interaction. (S5.M2.6)			E					
Identifies positive mental and emotional aspects of participating in a variety of physical activities. (S5.M2.7)			E					
Analyzes the empowering consequences of being physically active. (S5.M2.8)			E					
Demonstrates respect for self and others in activities and games by following the rules, encouraging others and playing in the spirit of the game or activity. (S5.M6.6)				E	E			
Demonstrates the importance of social interaction by helping and encouraging others, avoiding trash talk and providing support to classmates. (S5.M6.7)				E				

P = Primary; E = Embedded

LESSON 1: THROWING 101

Grade-Level Outcomes

Primary Outcomes

Throwing: Demonstrates a mature pattern for a modified target game such as bowling, bocce or horseshoes. (S1.M18.6)

Individual-performance activities: Demonstrates correct technique for basic skills in 1 self-selected individual-performance activity. (S1.M24.6)

Shot selection: Selects appropriate shot and/or club based on location of the object in relation to the target. (S2.M9.6)

Embedded Outcome

Personal responsibility: Exhibits responsible social behaviors by cooperating with classmates, demonstrating inclusive behaviors and supporting classmates. (S4.M1.7)

Lesson Objectives

The learner will:

- perform the backhand and forehand throws accurately to a partner.
- perform the basic pancake or clap catch successfully.
- learn how to select the correct shot in disc golf.

Equipment and Materials

- Flying discs: at least 2 for every student
- 12-inch (30 cm) cones (or larger): at least 1 for every 3 students
- Hoops: at least 1 for every 3 students

Introduction

Today, we will start a new module on disc golf. How many of you have played traditional golf or mini-golf? Great! Disc golf is very similar with respect to rules and etiquette. The benefit is that it can be played anywhere with just a flying disc! Today, we'll begin to develop the basic backhand and forehand throwing skills that you'll need to play the game successfully. We'll also work on the most basic type of catch—the pancake catch. Mastering a basic catch will allow you to get more practice with your throws and also to safely participate as multiple discs are being thrown around you.

If possible, show video highlights from the Internet of spectacular disc golf shots (keyword search suggestion: "amazing disc golf shots").

Instructional Task: Throw-Around

■ PRACTICE TASK

Working in groups of two or three, students experiment with different throws into open space around a cone, which is used to indicate their home base.

Refinement

Prompt students to control throws so that they stay within 15 feet (4.5 m) of their home base.

Safety note: To ensure the safety of students, make sure they are spread out in a field and are throwing under control.

Guiding questions for students:

- When you throw the disc, how does the angle affect the accuracy and distance of the throw?
- What type of throw is the most comfortable for you? Why do you think that is?

Student Choices/Differentiation

Students can choose to throw to space and let the disc fall to the ground, or they can toss and catch throws from partners.

What to Look For

- This task can be used as a pre-assessment to gauge prior experience and current skills associated with throwing and catching a disc.
- Observing student performance (check of understanding) provides an effective assessment of students' skill levels and background knowledge.

Instructional Task: Throwing to a Target

■ PRACTICE TASK

Partners take turns throwing backhand to the home base cone, starting from a distance of 6 to 10 feet (2 to 3 m). Each pair of partners is given three or four discs. After the first partner throws all three or four discs, he jogs quickly to retrieve his discs and then return them to the partner waiting.

Practice backhand and then repeat with forehand.

Extension

If pairs/partners hit the cone five times, students take a step back and repeat from a greater distance. If they miss on five consecutive throws, the pairs/partners take a step closer to the target.

EMBEDDED OUTCOME: S4.M1.7. Students cooperate with classmates during practice tasks to maximize opportunities for success. They follow throwing and catching cues while remaining focused on practice tasks and using positive language. Student encourage one another regardless of skill levels.

Student Choices/Differentiation

Students can place a hoop around the cone. If the throw lands in or touches the hoop, count it as a successful throw.

What to Look For

- Backhand throw grip: fingers under, thumb on top
- Backhand throw motion: load to shoulder, step and snap
- Common errors: fingers straight under disc; fail to load; do not execute toward target
- Forehand throw grip: V underneath, thumb on top
- Forehand throw motion: open to load, step and snap
- Formative assessment options: teacher observation and feedback; peer assessment; video analysis via mobile device or tablet
- Check for understanding: Students repeat and demonstrate cues.

Instructional Task: Game of Catch

■ PRACTICE TASK

As discs are being thrown, students should learn how to make basic catches for protection and to make the practice tasks more efficient (not wasting time chasing down discs).

Partners or groups throw and catch using backhand throws and pancake catches from a distance of 15 to 20 feet (4.5 to 6 m) apart. Groups of three may form a passing triangle.

Extensions

- If pairs or groups complete five successful catches, students take a step back and resume from a greater distance.

- To teach catching when students lack throwing skills, group two unskilled throwers with one skilled thrower. Students catch and then jog to return the disc to the thrower.

Student Choices/Differentiation

- Allow students to modify throwing distances within safe limitations. Skilled students can experiment with alternative ways to catch the disc (e.g., one- and two-hand rim catches).
- Students having difficulty controlling both accuracy and velocity should be reminded of the cues and prompted to return to the task of throwing to a target (cone).

What to Look For

- Pancake catch: hands apart, move to disc, clap to catch
- Formative assessment options: teacher observation and feedback using critical-elements checklist; peer assessment; video analysis via mobile device or tablet
- Check for understanding: Students repeat and demonstrate cues.

Formal and Informal Assessments

- Pre-assessment throw-around (eyeball test informal or checklist formal)
- Teacher observation with feedback
- Peer assessment with a critical-elements checklist

Closure

- Who can recite the critical cues for each throw and catch that you learned today?
- Consider one of those cues. How does that cue affect the quality of your performance? What would happen to the throw (or catch) if the cue was ignored or executed poorly?
- Why do you think we began the disc golf unit with these three skills? How might you use these skills later in the unit?

Reflection

- Did students use cues while throwing and catching?
- Did they work cooperatively and meet behavior expectations? If not, how can expectations be reinforced in the next class?
- Are there any safety considerations to address that you were not aware of prior to this lesson?

Homework

Send students home with a handout listing the cues for backhand and forehand throwing, as well as the pancake catch. You may also refer them to the school's physical education website to view skill videos. Students use a disc or paper plate to demonstrate the cues for a family member or friend. Students return a signed worksheet as evidence of completion.

Resources

Windsor Ultimate: www.windsorultimate.com

Internet keyword search: "basic disc golf throws (backhand and forehand)," "shot selection in disc golf"

LESSON 2:
FOREHAND AND BACKHAND THROWS

Grade-Level Outcomes

Primary Outcomes

Rules & etiquette: Identifies the rules and etiquette for physical activities/games and dance activities. (S4.M6.6)

Rules & etiquette: Demonstrates knowledge of rules and etiquette by self-officiating modified physical activities and games or following parameters to create or modify a dance. (S4.M6.7)

Throwing: Demonstrates a mature pattern for a modified target game such as bowling, bocce or horseshoes. (S1.M18.6)

Embedded Outcomes

Personal responsibility: Exhibits personal responsibility by using appropriate etiquette, demonstrating respect for facilities and exhibiting safe behaviors. (S4.M1.6)

Personal responsibility: Exhibits responsible social behaviors by cooperating with classmates, demonstrating inclusive behaviors and supporting classmates. (S4.M1.7)

Lesson Objectives

The learner will:

- demonstrate the rules and etiquette for disc golf as outlined in class with fewer than three teacher reminders during a modified game.
- recite and demonstrate the cues for both the backhand and forehand throws.

Equipment and Materials

- Flying discs: 1 per student
- 12-inch (30 cm) cones (or larger): at least 1 for every 3 students
- Hoops: at least 1 for every 3 students
- A variety of fitness equipment (optional)

Introduction

Did you know that there is a professional disc golf association? Pro disc golfers can earn money and honor by winning professional disc golf events! They use specialized discs for various shots, and they also travel around the world to compete against other elite players. What do you think it takes to become a professional disc golfer? Yes, it takes dedication and a clear understanding of the techniques, strategies, and rules of the sport. In today's lesson you'll begin learning the basic rules and etiquette for the sport while practicing your basic throws.

If possible, show the PDGA website and online highlight videos of professional disc golf events.

Instructional Task: Game of Catch

■ PRACTICE TASK

This game can be used as an instant activity or warm-up. Students quickly form pairs or groups of three and begin throwing and catching using both backhand and forehand throws, as well as the pancake catch.

Extension

Repeat with students reciting the cues for each throw to their partners.

Student Choices/Differentiation

- Students can modify throwing distances within safe limitations.
- Skilled students can experiment with alternative ways to catch the disc (e.g., one- and two-hand rim catches).

What to Look For

- Formative assessment options: teacher observation and feedback, peer assessment
- Check for understanding: Students repeat and demonstrate cues for both partners and teacher.

Instructional Task: Perfect Pace

■ PRACTICE TASK

Form groups of two or three students. Set up a cone 10 to 15 yards or meters from each group's hoop, with all groups throwing in the same direction.

The main objective of disc golf is to reach the target (hole) with as few throws as possible. In the game of perfect pace, one player per group throws from behind the group's cone toward the group's hoop. As soon as the disc lands, the throwing player jogs to it and makes another throw to the hoop. This continues until the player throws into or touches the hoop. She then jogs the disc back to the cone. Players waiting perform an exercise to increase heart rate (e.g., jumping jacks, jogging in place).

Extensions

- Students who are successful with the backhand throw can be prompted to switch to a forehand throw or alternate backhand and forehand.
- Formative assessment option: Video analysis would benefit students in this activity. As students jog to each disc and work at an increased pace, performance cues may be forgotten or dismissed. Video analysis can help highlight technique errors.

Guiding questions for students:

- How many throws did it take you to hit the target?
- Are you following all skill cues when you make a throw?
- Does the pace of your movement affect your accuracy? Why/why not?

EMBEDDED OUTCOME: S4.M1.6. Students should manage movement and performance safely and accurately. The goal should be to keep discs inside of their group's activity area.

Student Choices/Differentiation

- Allow students to modify throwing distances within safe limitations.
- Allow students waiting to choose from a variety of exercises. Provide equipment (e.g., jump rope, exercise band) if available and appropriate.

What to Look For

Students are demonstrating
- backhand and forehand throwing cues,
- continuous physical activity, and
- cooperative behavior.

Instructional Task: Par 2

■ PRACTICE TASK

Order of play is the most important element of disc golf etiquette. It allows matches to run smoothly and safely. The terms *honor* and *away* are used to determine the order of play. *Par* is the set number of throws that players should need to hit the target.

The player throwing off the tee area first has the honor. After all tee shots are made, the player farthest away from the target throws first, while other players stand safely behind the thrower. The player who hits the target using the fewest throws has the honor off of the next tee.

The objective of par 2 is to get your disc into the hoop in two backhand throws. The first honor of this game belongs to the youngest player, with the oldest throwing from the tee area last.

Start with the hoop three large paces from the cone. If every player in the group gets par (2 throws), then move the hoop three paces farther. Continue until someone requires three throws to the target. Then, reset the hoop back to three paces and restart using a forehand throw. Continue resetting the game and alternating between backhand and forehand throws.

EMBEDDED OUTCOMES: S4.M1.6; S4.M1.7 Students demonstrate appropriate etiquette using the terms *honor* and *away* to determine the order of play and maintain a cooperative and safe activity environment.

Student Choices/Differentiation

Students may choose from different-sized targets: hoops (basic) to half cones (advanced).

What to Look For

- Students demonstrate the rules and etiquette for disc golf as outlined in class with fewer than three teacher reminders.
- Provide etiquette scorecards to each group. The objective is to make it through the class with fewer than three reminder checks.
- Reminder checks are given to groups that require a teacher reminder to help them follow etiquette and safety procedures.

Formal and Informal Assessments

- Teacher observation with feedback
- Etiquette scorecard
- Video analysis assessment

Closure

- In disc golf, what is the definition of honor? Away? Par?
- What might happen during a disc golf match if players do not follow the etiquette for order of play?
- What are two things you could do at home to improve your disc golf skills?

Reflection

- Did students demonstrate an understanding of the etiquette of order of play?
- Did students demonstrate proper throwing technique throughout each of the lesson's activities?
- What concepts need to be reinforced in the next lesson?

Homework

Students do the two things for improvement identified in the lesson closure.

Resources

Professional Disc Golf Association: www.pdga.com

Internet keyword search: "rules and etiquette for disc golf"

LESSON 3: THROWING FOR ACCURACY

Grade-Level Outcomes

Primary Outcomes

Throwing: Demonstrates a mature pattern for a modified target game such as bowling, bocce or horseshoes. (S1.M18.6)

Shot selection: Selects appropriate shot and/or club based on location of the object in relation to the target. (S2.M9.6)

Embedded Outcomes

Accepting feedback: Provides corrective feedback to a peer, using teacher-generated guidelines, and incorporating appropriate tone and other communication skills. (S4.M3.7)

Accepting feedback: Provides encouragement and feedback to peers without prompting from the teacher. (S4.M3.8)

Lesson Objectives

The learner will:

- perform the forehand throw for accuracy, hitting a target three out of every five attempts.
- adjust the backhand throw (e.g., force, angle) based on location of target (and objective of activity) to throw in front of (or beyond) a target three out of every five attempts.

Equipment and Materials

- Flying discs: 1 per student
- Cones (various sizes): 2 per student
- Hoops: at least 1 for every 4 students

Introduction

You've learned and reviewed both the backhand and forehand throws in previous lessons. You may have discovered that by adjusting the force of a throw or the angle of release, your throws will change considerably. For beginners, it's best to keep the angle of release lower to the ground. This angle generally results in the best and most predictable accuracy. Today, you'll get an opportunity to adjust your throws to complete very different practice tasks.

Instructional Task: In the Trees—Forehand Throwing

■ PRACTICE TASK

Scatter all cones 10 to 15 feet (3 to 4.5 m) apart in the center of the activity area. Students work in pairs.

Forehand throws may be used to throw around or through obstacles. In this activity, one partner uses a forehand throw to hit as many cones as possible within the activity area. Students throw from behind the cone that was just hit. The other partner walks or jogs the perimeter for 1 minute. After 1 minute, they change roles.

Instruct students to move and throw carefully, watching for other players.

Extensions

- Students who were walking or jogging are prompted to stand along the perimeter and observe the throwers. Students observing should be looking for and identifying mature skill patterns. As roles change, students observing provide one or two items of specific feedback to the throwers using positive language.
- Students may walk and observe if they are able to focus their attention while moving.

EMBEDDED OUTCOMES: S4.M3.7: S4.M3.8. Students should offer specific feedback to each other using positive language and highlighting successful performances. It may be helpful to have students focus on the cues.

Student Choices/Differentiation

If there is a wide spectrum of skills and abilities in the class, split the activity area in half. Place larger cones or targets on one half and smaller cones or targets on the other. Students move freely from one side to the other based on their level of comfort and challenge.

What to Look For

- Students are developing and mature forehand throwing technique. Use a skill-cue checklist (see example) to provide the criteria for the forehand throw.
- Students are demonstrating safe behaviors. Reinforce and provide feedback based on safe and unsafe student behaviors.

Instructional Task: Tee Off

■ PRACTICE TASK

Create one throwing lane for every four students, with a cone to mark the tee area and a hoop 15 feet (4.5 m) away from the cone. All groups throw in the same direction.

The objective of this activity is to backhand throw the disc beyond the hoop from behind the cone. Honors start with the oldest thrower. After all discs are thrown, students jog to retrieve their discs and reset the activity, with the farthest thrower receiving the honors.

Refinements

- Level release. After 3 to 5 minutes of play, stop the activity and review the cues for a backhand throw, emphasizing a level release point.
- Understanding honors. If students are not serving in the correct order, stop the lesson and remind all students how to determine order of play in disc golf, and encourage them to use this etiquette concept in the game of tee off.

Guiding questions for students:

- Can you define the term *release point*?
- Why is it important to understand and recognize your release point?
- How does the angle of your release (e.g., low, level, high) affect your throw?

EMBEDDED OUTCOME: S4.M3.8. Prior to the activity, remind students to encourage one another using positive language. Highlight and reinforce this behavior when it's observed.

Student Choices/Differentiation

Students may adjust the distance of the hoop (less or more difficult) within safe limitations.

If multiple discs are available, students may pair up instead of forming groups of four to give them more practice trials.

What to Look For

- Observe throws with a focus on a level release point.
- Common error: Students release the disc too high, causing the disc to bank and fly off target.

DISC GOLF SKILL-CUE CHECKLIST

Use the following checklists for each disc golf skill to guide deliberate practice.

Backhand

Backhand throw grip:
- ❏ Fingers under
- ❏ Thumb on top

Backhand throw motion:
- ❏ Load to shoulder
- ❏ Step to target
- ❏ Snap to release

Forehand

Forehand throw grip:
- ❏ V underneath
- ❏ Thumb on top

Forehand throw motion:
- ❏ Open to load
- ❏ Step to target
- ❏ Snap to release

Catch

Pancake catch:
- ❏ Hands apart (up and down)
- ❏ Move to disc
- ❏ Clap to catch

From R.J. Doan, L.C. MacDonald, and S. Chepko, eds., 2017, *Lesson planning for middle school physical education* (Reston, VA: SHAPE America; Champaign, IL: Human Kinetics).

Instructional Task: Cut the Grass

■ PRACTICE TASK

Use groups and throwing lanes created for tee off.

The objective of this activity is to backhand throw the disc so that it lands just in front of the hoop. Honors start with the oldest thrower. After all discs are thrown, students jog to retrieve their discs and reset the activity, with the thrower closest to the hoop (without going past it) receiving the honors.

Refinement

Backhand throw, re-emphasizing a level release point.

Guiding questions for students:

- Again, how does the angle of your release (e.g., low, level, high) affect your throw?
- Does anything else affect the accuracy of the throw?

Student Choices/Differentiation

- Skilled students may alternate between backhand and forehand throws.
- Students can throw multiple discs if equipment allows.

What to Look For

Common error: Students release the disc too low, causing the disc to crash close to the thrower and roll away from the play area.

Formal and Informal Assessments

- Teacher observation with feedback
- Skill-cue checklist
- Thumbs-up self-check. Students show a thumbs-up if they feel as if skills are improving.

Closure

- How does the angle of release affect the accuracy of a throw?
- When might it be appropriate for you to change the angle of a throw?
- What safety consideration should you think about with respect to angle of a throw?

Please show me with your thumbs if you feel you are improving in your disc golf skills.

Reflection

- Are students' skills maturing?
- What cues need to be reinforced?
- Did the majority of the class self-report skill improvement via a thumbs-up? If not, why?

Homework

Students perform a web search at home for "flying disc trick shots." Prepare a response to the question: How did the angle of release affect or enable these throws?

Resources

Disc Golf Association: www.discgolf.com

Internet keyword search: "throwing for accuracy in disc golf," "common errors in disc golf"

LESSON 4:
FITNESS AND EXERCISE FOR DISC GOLF

Grade-Level Outcomes

Fitness knowledge: Describes the role of warm-ups and cool-downs before and after physical activity. (S3.M12.6)

Fitness knowledge: Designs a warm-up/cool-down regimen for a self-selected physical activity. (S3.M12.7)

Fitness knowledge: Designs and implements a warm-up/cool-down regimen for a self-selected physical activity. (S3.M12.8)

Embedded Outcomes

Health: Identifies components of physical activity that provide opportunities for reducing stress and for social interaction. (S5.M2.6)

Health: Identifies positive mental and emotional aspects of participating in a variety of physical activities. (S5.M2.7)

Health: Analyzes the empowering consequences of being physically active. (S5.M2.8)

Lesson Objectives

The learner will:

- design a warm-up routine with appropriate exercises to maximize disc golf performance.
- identify exercises that are effective for disc golf training.
- identify and document positive health consequences of participation in disc golf.

Equipment and Materials

- Blank journal page: 1 per student
- Pen or pencil: 1 per student
- Flying discs: 1 per 2 students

Introduction

Each and every component of health- and skill-related fitness can help disc golfers maximize each performance. However, two components of health-related fitness and two components of skill-related fitness are essential for peak performance. They are muscular strength and flexibility, as well as power and coordination. Like all components of fitness, these four components can be developed through training and will benefit from a proper warm-up. Let's explore these concepts in our fourth lesson of disc golf!

Instructional Task: Toss and Talk

■ **PRACTICE TASK**

Partners throw and catch using backhand and forehand throws and pancake catches from a distance of 15 to 20 feet (4.5 to 6 m) apart.

Prompt students to think, pair, and share about the following guiding questions while they throw and catch.

Guiding questions for students:

- Define the components of fitness identified in the introduction. Explain why they're important to disc golf.
- What are the components of an effective warm-up?
- How do disc golfers benefit physically, socially, and emotionally from playing the sport?

EMBEDDED OUTCOMES: S5.M2.6; S5.M2.7; S5.M2.8 Use these guiding questions to ensure students understand the potential wellness benefits of disc golf.

Guiding questions for students:

- In what ways can disc golf reduce stress in your life?
- Many people feel that disc golf provides an opportunity for a positive mental and emotional influence on their lives. Can you identify a couple of reasons why?
- Being physically active can give someone a sense of empowerment. How can disc golf make someone feel that way?

Student Choices/Differentiation

Post questions around the activity area for students to reference throughout this task.

What to Look For

- Students describe multiple components of fitness and their importance to disc golf.
- Students are using proper elements of disc golf while performing the warm-up.
- Students describe multiple benefits of playing disc golf.

Instructional Task: Purposeful Interval Planning

■ PRACTICE TASK

Print a series of exercise routines (www.darebee.com is a great reference) and post them on cones in a circuit throughout the activity area.

Pairs rotate around the circuit, demonstrating each routine with proper form and attention to safety.

Guiding questions for students:

- Which exercises could be used to build an effective warm-up?
- Which exercise could be used to develop the fitness components essential for disc golf?
- Which exercises did you enjoy the most?

Extensions

- Students design a warm-up routine to be performed as an instant activity for the remainder of the disc golf module.
- If time allows, students can design an exercise interval workout that can be done at home to develop muscular strength and flexibility, as well as power and coordination.
- Possible assessment: If time and schedule allow, repeat this instructional task with one station within the circuit as an assessment station. At this station, review students' work with them, providing feedback and direction.

Student Choices/Differentiation

- Provide routines from basic to complex, allowing for different skill and fitness levels.
- For classes struggling with independent participation, select or create a routine to complete as a class.

What to Look For

Student writing samples: Take the time to debrief and then use student writing samples to focus student effort and refine their fitness knowledge.

Formal and Informal Assessments

- Student journal pages
- Assessment station

Closure

- What components of fitness are essential for peak disc golf performance?
- How would you summarize the importance of a warm-up with respect to disc golf performance?
- Can you elaborate on the reasons why power and coordination are essential to the sport of disc golf?

Reflection

- Did students demonstrate an understanding of an effective warm-up routine?
- Did students demonstrate an understanding of health- and skill-related fitness?
- Did I provide targeted and relevant feedback to each student?

Homework

Disc golf interval workouts and warm-ups: Have students practice the interval workout or generated warm-up at home.

Resources

Darebee: www.darebee.com

Internet keyword search: "exercises for disc golf"

LESSON 5: DISC GOLF COURSE CREATION

Grade-Level Outcomes

Primary Outcomes

Throwing: Demonstrates a mature pattern for a modified target game such as bowling, bocce or horseshoes. (S1.M18.6)

Shot selection: Varies the speed, force and trajectory of the shot based on location of the object in relation to the target. (S2.M9.8)

Embedded Outcome

Social interaction: Demonstrates respect for self and others in activities and games by following the rules, encouraging others and playing in the spirit of the game or activity. (S5.M6.6)

Lesson Objectives

The learner will:

- demonstrate a mature throwing pattern for the backhand and forehand throws a minimum of four out of every five throws.
- use appropriate force and trajectory on two out of every three throws.

Equipment and Materials

- Dome cones: enough to create a grid with 9 extra-large stations
- Hoops: 18
- Flying discs: 1 for every student
- 12-inch (30 cm) cones (or larger): 9
- Index cards: 9
- Pencils: 9

Introduction

Today, we'll prepare for our first style of disc golf tournament play called a scramble. To play at your full potential, you'll begin today by completing the warm-up routines that you created last week. Then, you'll begin building the course for your first tournament. A scramble is a team competition that allows everyone to participate and contribute while enjoying the social aspect of disc golf. All players on a team take turns throwing from the tee area. After all throws are made, the team will decide which throw gives them the best advantage for the next shot. All players then take turns throwing from the spot—or lie—of the best shot. The better of the second shots is then determined, and so on until the target is hit. Before we start, does anyone want to share his or her response to the homework assignment?

Instructional Task: Student-Designed Warm-Up Routines

■ PRACTICE TASK

Students enter the activity area and begin completing the warm-up routines they designed in the last class.

Refinement

The first time this task is performed, ask a group to demonstrate its routine. Highlight and praise accurate interpretation of the routine. Pause after two to four exercises, and allow other groups to begin the warm-up task.

Extension

As students perform the warm-up task, ask questions to check for understanding with respect to the benefits of performing a warm-up routine.

- How would you describe this warm-up routine (moderate or vigorous)?
- How will this warm-up affect your disc golf performance? Why?
- Can you modify this warm-up to make it more (or less) vigorous? How could you test your ideas?

Student Choices/Differentiation

- Allow students to choose from classmates' routines based on level of comfort according to the routines' difficulty.
- If students have difficulty staying on task, select a routine from those created and perform it as a group.

What to Look For

Assess for proper form and technique in addition to accurate performance of exercise routines.

Instructional Task: Course Creation and Calibration

■ PRACTICE TASK

It's time to create and practice a disc golf hole to be used in our class scramble tournament.

- Break the class into nine equal groups.
- Assign each group a large station area within a grid.
- Groups are equipped with two hoops, a 12-inch cone (or larger), and enough discs for each member of the group. Use one hoop as the tee area, the other as a hazard.
- The cone acts as the target.
- Each hole will be a par 3 (i.e., most players will reach it in three throws).
- Students calibrate a good distance by practicing the hole three times in scramble format.
- They adjust distance and difficulty as needed.
- Holes are ready when each player hits the target in one to three attempts.
- When complete, students record the hole design on an index card and give the card to you as a reference for next class.

Guiding questions for students:

- Why did you choose to set your golf hole up the way that you did?
- What adjustments did you make after playing it for the first time?
- What do you think makes your setup unique when compared to other groups'?

EMBEDDED OUTCOME: S5.M6.6. This cooperative activity provides opportunities for students to demonstrate respect for self and others by following the activity guidelines, encouraging others, and playing in the spirit of the game.

- Video analysis can be helpful to students. Video-record one player per group, and allow all members of that group to analyze the performance.

Student Choices/Differentiation

- By design, this activity encourages students to be self-directed in a cooperative environment.
- Monitor the holes' designs to make sure there is a range of difficulty.

What to Look For

- While students are engaged in cooperatively building a nine-hole disc golf course, there are several assessment opportunities.
- Teacher observation, rubrics, or checklist-based skill assessment can be done to analyze the forehand and backhand throws. (Cues provided in Lesson 1.)

Instructional Task: Swap and Test (Time Permitting)

■ PRACTICE TASK

Groups rotate one station in either direction and perform three practice runs in scramble format.

Extension

After students perform at least one round, teach them the importance of using the correct force when throwing the disc.

Refinements

- Make sure students are using proper shots and skills and applying the correct force.
- Make sure students are using the proper movement pattern when throwing with higher and lower amounts of force.

Guiding questions for students:

- After each trial run, discuss with your teammates ways to modify your approach to improve your score.
- Summarize your team's shot approach. Was this a good or bad approach?
- What facts would you select to support your answer?
- Identify an area of weakness in the previous approach, and design a stronger approach.

Student Choices/Differentiation

- Students may choose between pars 3, 4, and 5 for their first two attempts at the target.
- To let students experience different hole difficulty, if a par 5 is selected for the first attempt, par 4 will then be selected for the second and par 3 for the third.
- In classes with a large percentage of skilled students, challenge students to modify each hole into a par 4 (or 5).

What to Look For

Focus observation and feedback on shot selection, making sure students are using forehand and backhand shots, proper critical elements, and appropriate force when throwing the disc.

Formal and Informal Assessments

- Teacher observation with feedback
- Rubric or checklist-based skill assessment
- Video analysis

Closure

- What steps did your group take when designing your disc golf hole?
- As you practiced your design, why was it important to focus on proper throwing technique and shot selection?
- Can you provide evidence to support your group's claim that your hole design is an authentic par 3?

Reflection

- Were groups actively engaged in all aspects of the lesson's activities? How might I improve engagement?
- Was feedback relevant and specific enough to help students improve their throwing skills and shot selections?
- What safety cues need to be emphasized prior to tournament play?

Homework

Decide which throw needs the most refinement (forehand or backhand). At home, spend 15 minutes improving that throw. Make sure you focus on the skill cues taught in class. Feel free to observe videos on the web if needed.

Resources

Internet keyword search: "creating your own disc golf course," "disc golf course calibration"

LESSON 6:
OFFICIATING AND TOURNAMENT PRACTICE

Grade-Level Outcomes

Primary Outcomes

Throwing: Executes consistently (70% of the time) a mature pattern for target games such as bowling, bocce or horseshoes. (S1.M18.7)

Rules & etiquette: Demonstrates knowledge of rules and etiquette by self-officiating modified physical activities and games or following parameters to create or modify a dance. (S4.M6.7)

Embedded Outcome

Social interaction: Demonstrates the importance of social interaction by helping and encouraging others, avoiding trash talk and providing support to classmates. (S5.M6.7)

Lesson Objectives

The learner will:

- demonstrate a mature throwing pattern for the backhand and forehand throws a minimum of four out of every five throws.
- self-officiate personal and team play during the scramble tournament, requiring no more than one teacher reminder.

Equipment and Materials

- Dome cones: enough to create a grid with 9 extra-large stations
- Hoops: 18
- Flying discs: 1 for every student
- 12-inch (30 cm) cones (or larger): 9
- Team scorecards: 9
- Pencils: 9

Introduction

After you complete your warm-up routines, it will be time to begin our scramble disc golf tournament. Remember, a scramble is a team competition. All players on a team take turns throwing from the tee area. After all throws are made, the team will decide which throw gives them the best advantage for the next shot. All players will then take turns throwing from the spot—or lie—of the best shot. The better of the second shots is then determined, and so on until the target is hit.

Today, we'll focus on two aspects of successful tournament play: accurate throws and self-officiating. To perform at your personal best, continue to concentrate on mature throwing patterns. Self-officiating means that you'll follow the rules and etiquette of the tournament without teacher reminders. Professional golfers rarely need reminders of rules and how to conduct themselves. Let's work hard to play like professionals today.

Instructional Task: Student-Designed Warm-up Routines

■ PRACTICE TASK

As students enter the activity area, they select a warm-up routine designed by another group and begin completing the routines in preparation for tournament play.

Refinement

Make sure students are using the warm-up properly.

Student Choices/Differentiation

- Groups can view and select preferred warm-up routines, or you can assign routines to each group.
- If students have difficulty staying on task, select a single routine from those created and perform it as a group.

What to Look For

Assess for proper form and technique in addition to accurate performance of exercise routines.

Instructional Task: Self-Officiating in Disc Golf

■ PRACTICE TASK

Discuss with students common self-officiating circumstances.

Extension

Watch video clips that show disc golfers doing different golf etiquette or self-officiating practices. This can be done by pausing the video and asking students what the golfer should do next or what the score should be.

Student Choices/Differentiation

- Have examples prepared beforehand to show lower-skilled students.
- Have a range of etiquette and self-officiating video clips.

What to Look For

- Students are engaged in active discussion.
- Students are applying rules and etiquette correctly during group activity.

Instructional Task: Scramble Tournament

■ PRACTICE TASK

Groups set up the holes that they designed in the last class.

Refinements

- Make sure the course has different levels of difficulty (especially to align to objectives). For example, having narrow fairways forces students to throw straight with different challenges of throwing forehand or backhand.
- Begin the scramble tournament. Here are the guidelines for play:
  - After completing a hole, rotate clockwise and wait patiently for the group ahead of you to finish.
  - The member of your team who hit the target on the last hole has honors and tees off first.
  - Record your score for each hole on the scorecard.
  - Scorecards also include skill-cue reminders and etiquette bonus criteria.
- Make sure students are properly applying rules and etiquette in the game.

Extensions

- Provide more repetitions and focused practice by requiring students to use all backhand throws on all even holes, and all forehand throws on all odd holes.
- Increase the focus on throw accuracy by creating long and narrow station areas for each hole.

EMBEDDED OUTCOME: S5.M6.7 Encourage students to maintain positive social interaction by helping and encouraging others, avoiding trash talk and providing support to classmates. One way to do this is to award sportsmanship or spirit points to teams displaying positive behaviors. Teams can then subtract their spirit points from their total team scores.

DISC GOLF ETIQUETTE SCORECARDS

Carry this scorecard with you during the disc golf practice task. Your team's goal is to make it through the activity with few or no etiquette marks. The teacher or referee will record an etiquette mark if a rule is broken or proper etiquette is not followed.

- ❏ Etiquette mark 1
- ❏ Etiquette mark 2
- ❏ Etiquette mark 3
- ❏ Etiquette mark 4
- ❏ Etiquette mark 5

- -

DISC GOLF ETIQUETTE SCORECARDS

Carry this scorecard with you during the disc golf practice task. Your team's goal is to make it through the activity with few or no etiquette marks. The teacher or referee will record an etiquette mark if a rule is broken or proper etiquette is not followed.

- ❏ Etiquette mark 1
- ❏ Etiquette mark 2
- ❏ Etiquette mark 3
- ❏ Etiquette mark 4
- ❏ Etiquette mark 5

- -

DISC GOLF ETIQUETTE SCORECARDS

Carry this scorecard with you during the disc golf practice task. Your team's goal is to make it through the activity with few or no etiquette marks. The teacher or referee will record an etiquette mark if a rule is broken or proper etiquette is not followed.

- ❏ Etiquette mark 1
- ❏ Etiquette mark 2
- ❏ Etiquette mark 3
- ❏ Etiquette mark 4
- ❏ Etiquette mark 5

- -

DISC GOLF ETIQUETTE SCORECARDS

Carry this scorecard with you during the disc golf practice task. Your team's goal is to make it through the activity with few or no etiquette marks. The teacher or referee will record an etiquette mark if a rule is broken or proper etiquette is not followed.

- ❏ Etiquette mark 1
- ❏ Etiquette mark 2
- ❏ Etiquette mark 3
- ❏ Etiquette mark 4
- ❏ Etiquette mark 5

From R.J. Doan, L.C. MacDonald, and S. Chepko, eds., 2017, *Lesson planning for middle school physical education* (Reston, VA: SHAPE America; Champaign, IL: Human Kinetics).

Student Choices/Differentiation

Students may choose to either use scorecards to track the number of throws in addition to etiquette bonus points, or provide a scorecard to record etiquette items only.

What to Look For

- While students are engaged in the scramble tournament format, there are several options for assessment.
- Teacher observation, rubrics, or checklist-based skill assessment can be done to analyze the forehand and backhand throws. (Cues provided in Lesson 1.)

Formal and Informal Assessments

- Teacher observation with feedback
- Rubric or checklist-based skill assessment
- Video analysis
- Exit slip: Write down any officiating or etiquette issues that you came across in today's lesson. If you did not have any, please write down a couple of rules that you made sure to follow today.

Closure

- What was the most memorable thing that happened during tournament play today? What made that event memorable?
- How is etiquette related to enjoyment? Can you elaborate?
- Did you enjoy the scramble tournament format? What are pros and cons to this type of format?

Reflection

- Did students self-officiate their play?
- What were two common challenges to self-officiating?
- What steps could be taken to help students do a better job of self-officiating?
- What safety cues need to be emphasized during the next round of tournament play?

Homework

Create a golf game at home using soft items that you can throw without breaking anything (use clean socks, foam balls, or beanbags). Select non-breakable items as targets (chairs, the bottom step, a closet door). Find someone to play with and then play from room to room, practicing the golf etiquette and scoring that you learned in class. Keep score on an index card or piece of paper, with bonus points for good sportsmanship and etiquette.

Resources

Internet keyword search: "golf etiquette," "spirit of the game," "scramble golf format"

LESSON 7:
COURSE CREATION AND CALIBRATION

Grade-Level Outcomes

Primary Outcomes

Personal responsibility: Exhibits responsible social behaviors by cooperating with classmates, demonstrating inclusive behaviors and supporting classmates. (S4.M1.7)

Throwing: Performs consistently (70% of the time) a mature pattern with accuracy and control for one target game such as bowling or bocce. (S1.M18.8)

Embedded Outcomes

Rules & etiquette: Identifies the rules and etiquette for physical activities/games and dance activities. (S4.M6.6)

Social interaction: Demonstrates respect for self and others in activities and games by following the rules, encouraging others and playing in the spirit of the game or activity. (S5.M6.6)

Lesson Objectives

The learner will:

- work cooperatively with classmates to create challenging disc golf holes that promote enjoyable and successful participation for the entire class.
- accurately perform a mature throwing pattern for the backhand and forehand throws a minimum of three out of every five throws.

Equipment and Materials

- Dome cones: enough to create a grid with 9 extra-large stations
- Hoops: 18
- Large cones, jump ropes, and other equipment to be used to create a variety of course obstacles
- Flying discs: 1 for every student
- 12-inch (30 cm) cones (or larger): 9
- Index cards: 9
- Pencils: 9

Introduction

Today, you'll prepare for our second style of disc golf tournament play called best ball. Best ball—or disc, in this case—allows players to play an entire hole from start to finish with their own throws and lies. At the end of the hole, each team will use the score from the player who performs the best. After your warm-up routines are complete, you'll begin building the course for your best-ball tournament. As you create a challenging hole with your group, consider the skills and abilities of all of your classmates to be sure all players will enjoy playing the entire class course.

Instructional Task: Mash-Up Warm-Up Routines

■ PRACTICE TASK

Prior to class, select three or four of the best student-generated routines. Take exercises from each one to create a new mash-up routine.

Display the mash-up routine for all students to see as they enter the activity. As students enter, they begin completing the routine.

Extension

Give students the opportunity to lead the warm-up routines.

Student Choices/Differentiation

Provide challenge progressions for the exercises used in the routine. Students may select a challenge level.

What to Look For

Assess for proper form and technique in addition to accurate performance of exercise routines.

Instructional Task: Course Creation and Calibration

■ **PRACTICE TASK**

- Break the group into nine equal groups, creating nine course holes.
- Assign each group a large station area within a grid.
- Group are equipped with two hoops, a 12-inch cone (or larger), a variety of equipment to be used as obstacles, and enough discs for each member of the group.
- Use one hoop as the tee area, the other as a hazard.
- Use other equipment pieces as additional hazards.
- The cone acts as the target.
- Place hazards strategically to increase the difficulty of the hole.
- Each hole is a par 3 (i.e., most players will reach it in three throws).
- Students calibrate a good distance by practicing the hole three times in best-ball format.
- They adjust distance and obstacles as needed.
- Holes are ready when more than 50 percent of team members can reach and hit the target on par.
- When complete, students record the hole design on an index card and give the card to you as a reference for next class.

Extension

Have students create courses with two different skill levels. This may require "pro" and "semi-pro" tee areas.

Refinement

Encourage students to create challenging course holes while also trying to be inclusive of all student skill levels.

Guiding questions for students:

- How will the added obstacles change the way this tournament is played?
- Do you think the increased challenge will make the tournament more or less enjoyable? Why?
- What are ways you can encourage classmates who are struggling because of the increased difficulty of this course?

EMBEDDED OUTCOME: S5.M6.6 This cooperative activity provides opportunities for students to demonstrate respect for self and others by following the activity guidelines, encouraging others, and playing in the spirit of the game.

- Students can conduct peer assessment with a checklist and scorecard on which a partner records the accuracy of one or more performances.

Student Choices/Differentiation

- By design, this activity encourages students to be self-directed in a cooperative environment.
- Students who are ready for greater challenge can institute a one-stroke penalty for hitting a course hazard.
- Students playing the course could select the "pro" area for increased challenge and the "semi-pro" area if they need to develop greater throw accuracy.

What to Look For

- Spreading skill-specific assessments out over the course of multiple lessons allows each student to receive quality and specific feedback to improve skill development and performance.
- The use of a holistic rubric with performance criteria specific to disc golf can help guide formative feedback and provide an outcomes-based summative assessment toward the end of the unit.
- Continue using teacher observation, rubrics, or checklist-based skill assessments.

Instructional Task: Swap and Test (Time Permitting)

■ PRACTICE TASK

Groups rotate one station in either direction and perform three practice runs in best-ball format.

Extension

After each trial run, students discuss with their teammates ways to modify their approach to improve their score.

Student Choices/Differentiation

- As students move to a new hole, they may choose between pars 3, 4, and 5 for their first two attempts at the target.
- If a par 5 is selected for the first attempt, par 4 will then be selected for the second and par 3 for the third.
- This strategy can help set more realistic expectations while challenging students to improve.

What to Look For

Focus observation and feedback on shot selection.

Formal and Informal Assessments

- Teacher observation with feedback
- Rubric or checklist-based skill assessment
- Video analysis

Closure

- Was today's throwing accuracy an improvement over previous performances? Can you explain how your practice habits (or lack thereof) affected your improvement?
- What are two characteristics of a challenging disc golf hole?
- How would you compare and contrast the hole that your team created with the hole that you practiced during the swap and test activity?

EMBEDDED OUTCOME: S4.M6.6. Discuss with students the unique aspect and importance of disc golf etiquette. After the discussion, assign the homework assignment.

Reflection

- Did the additional obstacles enhance the activity? Why or why not?
- What other adjustments could be made to increase both the challenge and enjoyment of tournament play?
- What safety cues need to be emphasized in the next lesson, prior to tournament play?

Homework

Perform a web search for disc golf etiquette. Record what you believe to be the top three components of disc golf etiquette, and be ready to share your research with your classmates.

Resources

Internet keyword search: "best-ball golf format"

LESSON 8: BEST-BALL TOURNAMENT

Grade-Level Outcomes

Primary Outcomes

Rules & etiquette: Demonstrates knowledge of rules and etiquette by self-officiating modified physical activities and games or following parameters to create or modify a dance. (S4.M6.7)

Individual-performance activities: Demonstrates correct technique for a variety of skills in 1 self-selected individual-performance activity. (S1.M24.7)

Embedded Outcome

Fitness Knowledge: Describes the role of warm-ups and cool-downs before and after physical activity. (S3.M12.6)

Lesson Objectives

The learner will:

- demonstrate competency in skill, strategy, and etiquette as described in the criteria listed on the disc golf holistic rubric.
- complete 9 or 18 holes of disc golf while using the best-ball format.

Equipment and Materials

- Dome cones: enough to create a grid with 9 extra-large stations
- Hoops: 18
- Large cones, jump ropes, or other equipment to be used to create a variety of course obstacles
- Flying discs: 1 for every student
- 12-inch (30 cm) cones (or larger): 9
- Team scorecards: 9
- Pencils: 9

Introduction

Let's quickly review your top three disc golf etiquette components before we start today's lesson. Discuss your homework research with a partner for 1 minute, focusing on what components you selected and why. Then, we'll briefly discuss your research as a group.

After you complete your warm-up routines, it will be time to begin our final tournament format: best ball. You've learned and applied a variety of skills and strategies within the lessons of this module. Today, you'll put them all together, and I will complete a final assessment rubric to score your overall performance. (Note: Post rubric criteria for students to view). One very important part of your performance will be to make sure that everyone has a positive physical activity experience. To do that, every member of the class will follow proper golf etiquette, as we just discussed, and encourage each other with absolutely no trash talk. Each team that accomplishes these two goals throughout tournament play will be awarded double spirit points, to be subtracted from the team's total score for the day.

Instructional Task: Student-Designed Warm-Up Routines

■ PRACTICE TASK

At this point, students have performed three variations of student-designed warm-up routines. For the final warm-up of the unit, students can choose their favorite warm-up from previous lessons.

DISC GOLF HOLISTIC PERFORMANCE RUBRIC

	Skill Scoring Criteria	Behavioral Scoring Criteria
Proficient (4)	Demonstrates a mature backhand and forehand throwing pattern consistently, with appropriate speed, force, and trajectory in relation to the target. Demonstrates correct technique for the basic pancake catch consistently.	Works cooperatively and safely with consideration for classmates. Contributes consistently to an inclusive and supportive learning environment. Follows rules and etiquette of disc golf with no reminders from the teacher or peers.
Competent (3)	Demonstrates all skills listed above with only occasional errors. Is purposeful and focused during practice tasks, with a desire to improve.	Works cooperatively and safely without disrupting the learning environment. Follows rules and etiquette of disc golf with no more than one reminder per lesson.
Lacks Competence (2)	Demonstrates all skills listed above with frequent errors. Needs reminders to stay focused and purposeful during practice tasks.	Has difficulty cooperating with classmates. Occasionally creates unsafe or disruptive situations. Requires regular reminders with respect to rules and etiquette.
Well Below Competence (1)	Displays unsatisfactory effort with respect to skill performance and practice.	Demonstrates unsafe and inappropriate behavior often. Is disruptive in class.

	Student name	Skill score	Behavior score	Comments
1				
2				
3				
4				
5				
6				
7				
8				
9				
10				
11				
12				
13				
14				
15				
16				
17				
18				
19				
20				

From R.J. Doan, L.C. MacDonald, and S. Chepko, eds., 2017, *Lesson planning for middle school physical education* (Reston, VA: SHAPE America; Champaign, IL: Human Kinetics).

Extension

Ask students the following questions:

- Why did you select this routine?

- How does a warm-up affect your disc golf performance?

- What makes the warm-up routine that you selected a good one? Provide at least three details.

EMBEDDED OUTCOME: S3.M12.6. Use this opportunity to discuss the role of warm-ups and cool-downs before and after physical activity with regard to disc golf.

Student Choices/Differentiation

If students are having difficulty, provide two or three options from previously performed routines.

What to Look For

Continue observation for accurate performance, and add related questions to check for understanding with respect to fitness knowledge and the role of warm-ups before physical activity.

Instructional Task: Best-Ball Tournament

■ PRACTICE TASK

Groups quickly move to grids and set up the holes designed in the last class.
Begin the best-ball tournament. Here are the guidelines for play:

- Rotate play clockwise, waiting patiently for groups ahead of you to finish.

- Players with the lowest score on the last hole have honors.

- Record your score for each hole on the scorecard.

Play 9 to 18 holes depending on time limitations.

Complete a holistic performance rubric as a summative skill and behavioral assessment for this unit.

Set up a camera on one or more holes to capture the performance of all students as they rotate around the course.

Extensions

- As you complete the holistic performance rubric during tournament play, share your assessment with students, with an emphasis on skill and behavioral improvement.

- Guide the discussion with specific examples of how they can move their rating from lacking competence to competent, or competent to proficient, and so on. Sample dialogue could include: *"When you take your time and concentrate on your skill cues, your movement pattern is mature and your accuracy is very good. However, you're making frequent errors because you rush your throws. What one simple thing could you do to improve and become fully competent?"*

Refinements

- Correct officiating and disc golf etiquette when needed.

- Monitor students' behavior and attitude when needed.

Student Choices/Differentiation

- Providing "pro" and "semi-pro" tee areas in a best-ball tournament can help both high- and low-skilled students feel more comfortable and successful with their participation and contribution to their teams.

- Providing this option to students does require some monitoring to prevent highly skilled students from taking advantage of the shorter distance or better angle to the target.

- Use the video footage of the assessment to analyze student performance, either with or without the student.

DISC GOLF BEST-BALL TOURNAMENT SCORECARD

Team Name: _____   Sign-off Signature: _____

Team Members: _____

Class: _____   Date: _____

Hole 1 Score:_____ (# of throws) Honors:_____ (Player with the fewest throws) Etiquette reminders Reminders ☐ ☐ Trash talk violations Violations ☐ ☐	**Hole 2** Score:_____ (# of throws) Honors:_____ (Player with the fewest throws) Etiquette reminders Reminders ☐ ☐ Trash talk violations Violations ☐ ☐	**Hole 3** Score:_____ (# of throws) Honors:_____ (Player with the fewest throws) Etiquette reminders Reminders ☐ ☐ Trash talk violations Violations ☐ ☐
Hole 4 Score:_____ (# of throws) Honors:_____ (Player with the fewest throws) Etiquette reminders Reminders ☐ ☐ Trash talk violations Violations ☐ ☐	**Hole 5** Score:_____ (# of throws) Honors:_____ (Player with the fewest throws) Etiquette reminders Reminders ☐ ☐ Trash talk violations Violations ☐ ☐	**Hole 6** Score:_____ (# of throws) Honors:_____ (Player with the fewest throws) Etiquette reminders Reminders ☐ ☐ Trash talk violations Violations ☐ ☐
Hole 7 Score:_____ (# of throws) Honors:_____ (Player with the fewest throws) Etiquette reminders Reminders ☐ ☐ Trash talk violations Violations ☐ ☐	**Hole 8** Score:_____ (# of throws) Honors:_____ (Player with the fewest throws) Etiquette reminders Reminders ☐ ☐ Trash talk violations Violations ☐ ☐	**Hole 9** Score:_____ (# of throws) Honors:_____ (Player with the fewest throws) Etiquette reminders Reminders ☐ ☐ Trash talk violations Violations ☐ ☐

For 0 reminder or violation, subtract (−) 4 throws from Total Score for Final Score.

For 1 reminder and 0 violations, keep Total Score as Final Score.

For 2 (or more) reminders and violations, add total of all reminders and violations to Total Score for Final Score.

Total Score: _____   +/− Etiquette: _____   Final Score: _____

From R.J. Doan, L.C. MacDonald, and S. Chepko, eds., 2017, *Lesson planning for middle school physical education* (Reston, VA: SHAPE America; Champaign, IL: Human Kinetics).

What to Look For

Provide best-ball scorecards with room for scoring and etiquette spirit points (see example) for students to self-monitor and complete throughout tournament play. At the end of the lesson, require each scorecard to be signed off by a member of a different team as verification of accumulated spirit points.

Formal and Informal Assessments

- Holistic performance rubric
- Best-ball scorecards
- Disc golf crossword puzzle

Closure

- How can you recognize enjoyment in a physical activity setting? How did our emphasis on personal and social behaviors affect enjoyment during today's tournament play?
- What characteristics of disc golf make it a lifetime physical activity option? How do those characteristics compare or contrast with other physical activity options?

Reflection

- When planning for next year's Disc Golf Module, what improvements can I make in the areas of skill development, fitness, personal behaviors, and social behaviors?
- Were the assessments chosen and created for this module effective with respect to providing both formative and summative performance feedback?

Homework

To be sure that you've remembered the key academic language vocabulary words for disc golf, I've copied a disc golf crossword puzzle for you to complete and return next class. See how many words you can get correct without help or online research. Check the box next to any words you had trouble with, and then use your resources to find the correct answers.

Now that this module is complete, find a friend or family member and create a disc golf course where you live. Be sure to create holes that are safe and respect both people and property.

Resources

Internet keyword search: "best-ball golf format," "disc golf scorecards"

RECREATIONAL TARGET GAMES MODULE

Lessons in this module were contributed by Evelyn Gordon, assistant professor of sport coaching education at the University of Southern Mississippi and a former secondary school teacher.

Grade-Level Outcomes Addressed, by Lesson	Lessons							
	1	2	3	4	5	6	7	8
Standard 1. The physically literate individual demonstrates competency in a variety of motor skills and movement patterns.								
Demonstrates a mature pattern for a modified target game such as bowling, bocce or horseshoes. (S1.M18.6)		P	P	P			P	
Executes consistently (70% of the time) a mature pattern for target games such as bowling, bocce or horseshoes. (S1.M18.7)					P			
Strikes, with an implement, a stationary object for accuracy and distance in activities such as croquet, shuffleboard or golf. (S1.M19.7)						P		
Demonstrates correct technique for basic skills in at least 2 self-selected individual-performance activities. (S1.M24.8)								P
Standard 2. The physically literate individual applies knowledge of concepts, principles, strategies and tactics related to movement and performance.								
Selects appropriate shot and/or club based on location of the object in relation to the target. (S2.M9.6)						P		
Varies the speed and/or trajectory of the shot based on location of the object in relation to the target. (S2.M9.7)		P						
Standard 3. The physically literate individual demonstrates the knowledge and skills to achieve and maintain a health-enhancing level of physical activity and fitness.								
Standard 4. The physically literate individual exhibits responsible personal and social behavior that respects self and others.								
Accepts responsibility for improving one's own levels of physical activity and fitness. (S4.M1.8)					E			
Demonstrates self-responsibility by implementing specific corrective feedback to improve performance. (S4.M3.6)		E						
Cooperates with a small group of classmates during adventure activities, game play or team-building activities. (S4.M5.6)				E		E		
Problem-solves with a small group of classmates during adventure activities, small-group initiatives or game play. (S4.M5.7)				P				
Identifies the rules and etiquette for physical activities/games and dance activities. (S4.M6.6)	P	P					P	
Demonstrates knowledge of rules and etiquette by self-officiating modified physical activities and games or following parameters to create or modify a dance. (S4.M6.7)						P	E	
Applies rules and etiquette by acting as an official for modified physical activities and games and creating dance routines within a given set of parameters. (S4.M6.8)								P
Uses physical activity and fitness equipment appropriately and safely, *with the teacher's guidance.* (S4.M7.6)	E							
Standard 5. The physically literate individual recognizes the value of physical activity for health, enjoyment, challenge, self-expression and/or social interaction.								
Recognizes individual challenges and copes in a positive way, such as extending effort, asking for help or feedback and/or modifying the tasks. (S5.M3.6)			E					
Demonstrates respect for self and others in activities and games by following the rules, encouraging others and playing in the spirit of the game or activity. (S5.M6.6)							E	
Demonstrates the importance of social interaction by helping and encouraging others, avoiding trash talk and providing support to classmates. (S5.M6.7)								E

P = Primary; E = Embedded

LESSON 1: INTRODUCTION TO BOWLING

Grade-Level Outcomes

Primary Outcome

Rules & etiquette: Identifies the rules and etiquette for physical activities/games and dance activities. (S4.M6.6)

Embedded Outcome

Safety: Uses physical activity and fitness equipment appropriately and safely, *with the teacher's guidance.* (S4.M7.6)

Lesson Objectives

The learner will:

- perform correct ball-selection techniques.
- identify basic rules of the game of bowling.

Equipment and Materials

- Bowling balls of varying sizes
- List of basic rules of bowling, or iPads or tablets with Internet connection to access www.rule-sofbowling.com
- Pencils
- If no access to a bowling alley, taped area of regulation bowling lanes if space permits or modified area
- Plastic or used bowling pins
- Scales or previous weights of students (for proper ball weight)

Introduction

We're starting a module on target games today. Does anyone know what a target game is? Can you provide any examples? Target games have been around for a long time and are found in many different cultures. We're going to try a few target games in this module, and the first one is bowling. Have any of you been bowling or attended a birthday party at a bowling alley? Today, we will introduce you to the basics of bowling.

To pique interest in bowling, show a bowling trick-shot video from YouTube.

Instructional Task: Rules of the Game

■ PRACTICE TASK

Review and discuss the rules of bowling from the handout (see resources).

Guiding questions for students:

- Where is the approach?
- Where is the foul line?
- Where are the gutters?

Extensions

- Human bowling lane: After students have studied the rules, have them physically run to certain parts of the lane. This works best in the gymnasium with multiple lanes taped on the floor.
- Have students ask each other questions from the rule sheet or website.

Student Choices/Differentiation

- Students can observe a taped bowling lane with the pins to assist students with different learning styles.
- Human bowling lane: Have students decide if they would rather relay with teammates or have the entire team run to the spot.

What to Look For

- Students should have a basic understanding of the rules.
- For human bowling lane, observe students to ensure each one knows the answers to the questions on basic rules of bowling.

Instructional Task: Ball Selection

■ PRACTICE TASK

Students select an appropriate ball, focusing on appropriate ball size and finger holes.

Extension

This is a good time to use interdisciplinary education (math and percentages). Students select a ball based on 8 to 10 percent of their body weight.

Guiding questions for students:

- If you weigh 100 pounds (45 kg), what is 10 percent of your body weight?
- What would be the minimum weight for your ball at 8 percent?

Student Choices/Differentiation

- Have pictures printed off on the racks to help students with proper ball selection.
- Students may review videos from YouTube on how to choose a bowling ball.

What to Look For

- Ball selection is not too light or too heavy.
- Students' fingers fit properly into the finger holes.

Instructional Task: Proper Equipment Care

■ PRACTICE TASK

Demonstrate placing balls back on the rack properly.

Students practice with a partner. The partner uses a checklist to assess if student is performing the skill correctly.

Refinement

Make sure students are lifting with their legs and are using two hands to carry the ball.

Guiding questions for students:

- What is the proper way to carry a ball back to the rack?
- Are your fingers in the holes or out when placing a ball on the rack?

EMBEDDED OUTCOME: S4.M7.6. Discuss with students the importance of using equipment appropriately to maintain a safe environment during the bowling activities.

Extension

Bottle bowling: Fill 10 empty soda bottles (1 or 2 liter) with sand and number them 1 to 10. Students practice bowling from any distance with non-bowling balls.

Student Choices/Differentiation

Show videos of proper safety procedures when carrying a ball and placing it on the rack, or have more experienced students demonstrate.

Use different-sized soda bottles (1, 2, or 3 liters) for varying skill levels

What to Look For

- Safety
- Both hands holding ball
- Keeping ball at waist when carrying it to the rack
- Not having fingers in the holes when placing ball on the rack
- No swinging the ball wildly

Formal and Informal Assessments

- Informal bowling assessment with human bowling activity; bottle bowling (10 empty soda bottles that are numbered)
- Peer assessment: teacher-generated checklist on proper equipment care

Closure

- How many pins are set in the game of bowling?
- What is the area toward the back of the lane where bowlers take their steps and swing to release the ball?
- What is the area of the lane where the pins are set called?
- Who can point to the foul line?

Reflection

- Do students have the correct ball for successful completion of the future tasks?
- Were the rules clear and precise on the handout?
- Did students display knowledge of proper ball size and rules during the informal assessment?

Homework

Study rules that are posted on the school's physical education website. We will take a quiz on bowling rules and procedures next class.

Resources

Grinfelds, V., & Hultstrand, V. (2003). *Right down your alley: The complete book of bowling.* Belmont, CA: Wadsworth.

Physical and Health Education America: www.pheamerica.org

Rules of Bowling: www.rulesofbowling.com

Internet keyword search: "bowling trick shots," "how to choose a bowling ball"

LESSON 2: THE FOUR-STEP APPROACH

Grade-Level Outcomes

Primary Outcomes

Throwing: Demonstrates a mature pattern for a modified target game such as bowling, bocce or horseshoes. (S1.M18.6)

Rules & etiquette: Identifies the rules and etiquette for physical activities/games and dance activities. (S4.M6.6)

Embedded Outcome

Accepting feedback: Demonstrates self-responsibility by implementing specific corrective feedback to improve performance. (S4.M3.6)

Lesson Objectives

The learner will:

- demonstrate the four-step approach properly.
- demonstrate knowledge of rules of bowling by scoring 70 percent or higher on the quiz.

Equipment and Materials

- 3 to 5 bowling pins per group of 2
- 2 bowling balls or foam balls with holes like a bowling ball per group of 2
- Gym court lines or taped lines on a floor if no access to a bowling lane
- Pencils
- Take-home sheet on how to score in bowling: 1 per student

Introduction

Today, you will take a quick quiz and then learn the four-step approach in bowling. You will also use your ball-selection skills from the last lesson.

Show a video on (keyword: "four-step approach") or demonstrate the four-step approach.

Instructional Task: Bowling Quiz

■ PRACTICE TASK

Students take a multiple-choice and short-answer quiz on basic bowling rules and etiquette.

Extension

The human bowling activity can be used for a warm-up and review of rules.

Student Choices/Differentiation

Students can have more time if needed.

What to Look For

Students know basic rules and etiquette for bowling.

Instructional Task: Four-Step Approach

■ PRACTICE TASK

Demonstrate the four-step approach.

Pair students across from each other. Each one takes a turn at practicing the four-step approach.

- Start with your feet together, the ball at belly button height. Step with your left foot if you are right-handed and your right foot if you are left-handed. The ball should be out in front as you take your first step.
- In the second step, making sure you are holding the ball with one hand, bring the ball to your side. Keep your arm with the ball straight.
- In the third step, move your ball arm back as far as you can. Keep your arm straight.
- In the fourth step (slide), push the ball forward. Bend your knees and release the ball gently on the lane.

Have students shadow practice—no ball, just arm swing and steps—for two or three repetitions.

Refinement

Make sure the steps are smooth (not jerky).

Extensions

- Practice with foam balls or bowling balls until students are comfortable with the approach and underhand roll.
- Repeat with students aiming for pins or other targets.

Student Choices/Differentiation

- Students may select a foam ball or bowling ball if equipment allows.
- If students are having issues, tape cut-out feet shapes on the floor for the left- and right-handed approach so students can practice.

What to Look For

- Proper ball selection, etiquette, and safety: Did students politely walk to the racks to get the correct ball? Did students just grab a ball, or did they remember how to properly select the right ball?
- Observe students' four-step approach (back to wall observation). Watch their step pattern and arm swing, and correct accordingly (left-handed students stepping wrong, right-handed students stepping wrong).
- Ball should be released smoothly and gently, not tossed upward.

Instructional Task: Self-Evaluation

■ PRACTICE TASK

Hand out a short questionnaire for students to evaluate their performance of the four-step approach.

Guiding questions for students:

- Describe or draw step 1, step 2, step 3, and step 4.
- How do you think you performed on each step?

After completing the assessment, students repeat the approach, implementing the feedback.

Extension

Repeat with students completing a peer assessment, or use a device to record the four-step approach. Students compare their self-analysis to the peer analysis.

EMBEDDED OUTCOME: S4.M3.6. Use this task to have students practice implementing feedback from self- or peer-evaluations.

Student Choices/Differentiation

Students may write or draw answers to the questions.

What to Look For

Student comprehension. Do students think they have it or need more time to master the skill?

Instructional Task: Buzzer Beater Bowling

■ PRACTICE TASK

Each paired group has three to five pins and a foam bowling ball. Using the four-step approach, students try to knock all the other team's pins down before all their pins get knocked down. Each team must alternate rolls.

Call out which pins students are to aim for and try to knock over.

Guiding questions for students:

- Was your accuracy affected by competing against another team?
- How did rolling for particular pins affect your technique?

Extension

- Bowling accuracy. Call out which pins students are to aim for and try to knock over.
- Change the number of points per pin and have students add scores.

Student Choices/Differentiation

- Students may have two attempts to knock over pins.
- Students may vary the distance or playing area.

What to Look For

Students are accurately using the four-step approach.

Formal and Informal Assessments

- Rules and etiquette quiz
- Self- and peer-assessment: Teacher-created rubric or checklist
- Informal observation from the instructor

Closure

- How many steps do you take in the approach?
- Demonstrate step 1, step 2, step 3, and step 4.
- Are you curious about how to keep score? (Hand out worksheets on how to keep score, or refer students to the Rules of Bowling website for homework.)

Reflection

- What were some of the issues with the four-step approach?
- Do all students appear to be at the same level? If not, how will I address this issue?
- After reading students' self-evaluations, is there a common thread?

Homework

Pass out a "how to score" teacher-created handout. Have students e-mail the completed handout before the next class.

Resources

Physical and Health Education America: www.pheamerica.org

Rules of Bowling: www.rulesofbowling.com

Internet keyword search: "four-step approach," "buzzer beater bowling," "how to keep score in bowling"

LESSON 3: ACCURACY, VARYING SPEED, AND TRAJECTORIES

Grade-Level Outcomes

Primary Outcomes

Shot selection: Varies the speed and/or trajectory of the shot based on location of the object in relation to the target. (S2.M9.7)

Throwing: Demonstrates a mature pattern for a modified target game such as bowling, bocce or horseshoes. (S1.M18.6)

Embedded Outcome

Challenge: Recognizes individual challenges and copes in a positive way, such as extending effort, asking for help or feedback and/or modifying the tasks. (S5.M3.6)

Lesson Objectives

The learner will:

- demonstrate score-keeping knowledge by taking a short practice quiz.
- demonstrate ball-placement skills by setting a goal on which pins to knock over.
- explore varying speed and trajectory during activities in the lesson.

Equipment and Materials

- Practice quizzes for each student on score keeping
- Pencils
- Calculators
- 10 numbered (1-10) bowling pins per each group and lane or a modified version for a gymnasium
- Bowling balls for each student
- Scorecards or score sheets for accuracy goal

Introduction

I received your handouts. (Go over the results of the homework.) Today, you will have the opportunity to practice keeping score. I have pencils and calculators. If you don't understand completely, it's okay. We will keep working on it.

Instructional Task: Practice Quiz—Scoring

■ PRACTICE TASK

Hand students the practice quiz, pencils, and calculators.

Extensions

- Have students watch a few frames of a bowling video and practice scoring.
- This would also be a perfect cross-curricular activity. Get assistance from the math teachers to help with connecting math content to bowling content.

Student Choices/Differentiation

- Make calculators available to students.
- Have multiple questions within a range of difficulty.

What to Look For

Students can correctly score a bowling game.

Instructional Task: Varying Speed and Trajectory

■ PRACTICE TASK

Have students explore bowling with varying speeds, trajectories, or both.

Challenge students to safely explore throwing fast, slow, and with different angles and spins.

Refinement

Students may get excited trying the different types of rolls. Make sure students are practicing safely and are under control during this activity.

Guiding questions for students:

- What is the benefit of rolling the ball fast? Slow?
- What do you think is the ideal speed to roll the ball?
- Did anyone have success changing the angle of their approach or using a spin?
- When would you want to use the different speeds and trajectories approach and why?

Extension

Have students practice again using the information gained from the class discussion.

Student Choices/Differentiation

- Guide students through the activity with prompts if needed.
- Have students practice using different sizes or types of balls.

What to Look For

- Students are exploring different ways to vary speed and trajectory when bowling.
- Students are implementing strategies from the class discussion.

Instructional Task: Accuracy Bowling

■ PRACTICE TASK

In groups of two or three, practice bowling. If not in a bowling alley, pin setters will be needed.

Students take turns aiming for a selected pin you have designated (usually 1, 2, or 3).

Mix it up for students by varying the numbers.

Refinements

Stop the activity and remind students to:

- use the four-step approach.
- take their time and aim! (But do not change the motor pattern.)
- use the arrows on the lane.

Extension

See if students can match the score of your choice by accurately hitting the correct number of pins.

Student Choices/Differentiation

Students may vary distances according to skill level.

What to Look For

- Students know how to properly select a ball.
- Students are following the rules for etiquette.
- Students are accurately using the four-step approach.
- Accuracy: Students are knocking over the correct pins.

Instructional Task: Low Ball

▓ PRACTICE TASK

Students aim for the outside pins (7 and 10).

Extension

Students set goals on which pin they will knock over (7 or 10). Students keep an accuracy record.

Refinement

Students like to modify their approach or movement pattern when rolling for accuracy. Make sure students are using the proper form.

Guiding questions for students:

- How will you change your aim this time?
- How is this different from the last activity?
- Did you change your angle or speed of the roll to accomplish the task?

Student Choices/Differentiation

- Students may choose the ball.
- If students are having difficulty with this task, they may start closer to the target.

What to Look For

- Students are using the four-step approach accurately.
- Accuracy: Students are knocking over the correct pins.

Formal and Informal Assessments

- Practice quizzes on keeping score
- Goal-setting scorecard for students
- Informal observation from the instructor

Closure

- What were the main ideas of our activities today?
- Do you think you were successful?
- What are some important elements of speed and angles in bowling?

Continue to study the rules of bowling and practice keeping score. I have take-home practice scorecards; hand these out to the people in your row/group.

Reflection

- Did students seem to enjoy the activities today?
- What do students seem to be struggling with from today's activities? (e.g., aiming, four-step approach, scoring)

Homework

Continue to have students review rules and scoring for a quiz.

Resources

Grinfelds, V., & Hultstrand, V. (2003). *Right down your alley: The complete book of bowling.* Belmont, CA: Wadsworth.

Physical and Health Education America: www.pheamerica.org

Print Your Brackets: www.printyourbrackets.com/printable-bowling-score-sheet.html

Rules of Bowling: www.rulesofbowling.com

LESSON 4: CREATING BOWLING TARGET GAMES

Grade-Level Outcomes

Primary Outcomes

Throwing: Demonstrates a mature pattern for a modified target game such as bowling, bocce or horseshoes. (S1.M18.6)

Working with others: Problem-solves with a small group of classmates during adventure activities, small-group initiatives or game play. (S4.M5.7)

Embedded Outcome

Working with others: Cooperates with a small group of classmates during adventure activities, game play or team-building activities. (S4.M5.6)

Lesson Objectives

The learner will:

- continue to work on accuracy.
- practice scoring.
- work with others to create a bowling target game.

Equipment and Materials

- Bowling alley or modified lane in a gymnasium
- Pins if not in bowling alley
- Bowling balls for students
- Pin no-tap scorecards
- Pencils
- Bowling shoes or socks

Introduction

How many of you who have bowled before have ever thought you were bowling a strike but one pin was still standing? Today, you will be introduced to pin no-tap bowling. But first we will warm up by playing a game we learned yesterday, accuracy bowling. Remember to work on your four-step approach and accuracy throughout the lesson.

Instructional Task: Accuracy Bowling

■ PRACTICE TASK

Students form pairs or groups after selecting their balls.

Students take turns aiming for a selected pin you have designated (usually 1, 2, or 3). Mix it up for students by varying the numbers.

See whether students can match the score of your choice by hitting the correct number of pins.

Student Choices/Differentiation

Students may pick the distance to practice for accuracy (if the alley allows).

What to Look For

- Students know how to select a ball properly.
- Students are following the rules for etiquette.
- Students are using the four-step approach accurately.
- Accuracy: Students are knocking over the correct pins.

Instructional Task: Pin No-Tap Bowling

■ PRACTICE TASK

Explain the rules of the game, which are essentially the rules of bowling with a relaxed standard for a strike (e.g., modify to seven, eight, or nine pins on the first ball is a strike).

Students begin bowling as soon as the instructions are over. Each student has two chances.

If you knock down nine pins with your first ball, it counts as a strike. Keep score. You only receive a strike if you knock over nine pins with the first ball.

Refinements

- Make sure students are scoring correctly.
- Students are using the critical elements for speed and accuracy that were taught in previous lessons.

Guiding questions for students:

- How many chances to bowl does each player get?
- What symbol represents a strike on your card?
- How will you adjust for accuracy?

EMBEDDED OUTCOME: S4.M5.6. Reinforce cooperation with students as they participate in the bowling game. Students need to work together to set pins and keep score.

Student Choices/Differentiation

- Students can decide which one goes first. They can select a game such as rock, paper, scissors, or who is the oldest, youngest, tallest, shortest, etc.
- Students can decide to use bumper guards as well.
- Students choose the number of pins for a strike.

What to Look For

- Students are using the four-step approach accurately.
- Students are hitting the front pins accurately.
- Students are keeping scorecards. (Scorecards can be found in Lesson 3.)

Note: Pick up scorecards at the end of the class.

Instructional Task: Create Your Own Bowling Game

■ PRACTICE TASK

In small groups of two to four, come up with your own bowling target game. Be prepared to teach the class the rules and scoring of the game.

Refinement

Make sure students are being safe and are using the critical elements for target games (speed, accuracy, angles, proper movement patterns, etc.).

Extension

Have groups teach each other their created bowling game.

Student Choices/Differentiation

- Have examples of simple and difficult student-generated bowling target games.
- Students may use computers to help in creating the game.
- Students choose balls and targets.

What to Look For

- Students are working together.
- Students are establishing proper rules, scoring, and strategies for their games.
- Students are maintaining safety.

EMBEDDED OUTCOME: S5.M4.6. Ask students to reflect on the enjoyment they get from making accurate shots and bowling well.

Formal and Informal Assessments

- Observation of bowling procedures of students
- Scorecards from pin no-tap
- Exit slip: How does bowling create enjoyment in one's life? Try to be specific!

Closure

- Did you feel more confident in your accuracy?
- How did you adjust for accuracy?
- What symbol do you use for a strike on the score sheet? A spare?

You have a bowling quiz next class. Be sure to look over the rules and practice scoring.

Reflection

- Is this progression working for the majority of students?
- What are some observable problems with students' techniques?

Homework

Study rules of the game from the school's physical education website or handouts, and practice scoring. See if you can teach your parents how to score in bowling!

Resources

Physical and Health Education America: www.pheamerica.org
Rules of Bowling: www.rulesofbowling.com

LESSON 5: BOWLING ASSESSMENT DAY

Grade-Level Outcomes

Primary Outcomes

Rules & etiquette: Demonstrates knowledge of rules and etiquette by self-officiating modified physical activities and games or following parameters to create or modify a dance. (S4.M6.7)

Throwing: Executes consistently (70% of the time) a mature pattern for target games such as bowling, bocce or horseshoes. (S1.M18.7)

Embedded Outcome

Personal responsibility: Accepts responsibility for improving one's own levels of physical activity and fitness. (S4.M1.8)

Lesson Objectives

The learner will:

- demonstrate knowledge of rules, scoring, and etiquette during a formal assessment.
- have completed a full game of bowling and evaluate execution of techniques learned.

Equipment and Materials

- Quizzes
- Bowling alley
- Bowling balls for students
- Pencils
- Scorecards
- Bowling shoes or socks

Introduction

Today, you will take the overall bowling quiz and complete a game. After you turn in your quiz to me, you may gather your balls and shoes. You will score and evaluate your bowling performance. Do you have any questions about the bowling quiz? (Address questions from students.)

Instructional Task: Bowling Quizzes

■ **PRACTICE TASK**

Prior to the quiz, you may answer questions or generate questions to students.

Quizzes can be made or printed off from online resources.

Student Choices/Differentiation

Offer to extend time for any student who needs it.

What to Look For

- Students score 70 percent or higher on the quiz.
- Students know basic rules, etiquette, and scoring.
- Re-assess low performers.

Instructional Task:
Bowling With Scorecard and Self-Evaluation

■ PRACTICE TASK

Students are to bowl one complete game (if time allows, two would be better).

Students score the game.

Assessment: While students are bowling, walk around and assess students' four-step approach.

Extension

Students evaluate performance with a self-reflection essay.

EMBEDDED OUTCOME: S4.M1.8. During the self-reflection, students should accept responsibility to improve their scores as well as fitness levels.

Student Choices/Differentiation

Students may take more time to bowl or may keep score during the bowling activity.

What to Look For

- Students are using the four-step approach accurately.
- Students are hitting the front pins accurately.
- Students are keeping scorecards correctly. (Clarify when needed.)
- Self-evaluations cover issues and successes the students experienced.

Formal and Informal Assessments

- Formal assessment: bowling quiz, scorecard, and self-evaluation
- Observation of students' 4-step approach technique

Closure

- I hope that you enjoyed bowling.
- What was the biggest problem you faced with scoring today?
- Did you enjoy the traditional game or the games that you created more?

In our next class, we will start a target game called croquet.

Reflection

- Was there anything during this lesson that I need to focus on for the next time I teach it?
- How can I involve other areas of study in this bowling unit? (e.g., history, math, art)
- After reviewing the quizzes, what areas need to be stressed the next time bowling is taught?
- After reviewing the scorecards and self-evaluations, which areas should be addressed? (e.g., cheating, self-doubt, lack of skill comprehension)

Homework

Research croquet on the Internet or in a book at the library. Write a brief paragraph of five or six sentences describing what it is.

Resources

Grinfelds, V., & Hultstrand, V. (2003). *Right down your alley. The complete book of bowling.* Belmont, CA: Wadsworth.

Physical and Health Education America: www.pheamerica.org

Rules of Bowling: www.rulesofbowling.com

LESSON 6: CROQUET

Grade-Level Outcomes

Primary Outcomes

Striking: Strikes, with an implement, a stationary object for accuracy and distance in activities such as croquet, shuffleboard or golf. (S1.M19.7)

Shot selection: Selects appropriate shot and/or club based on location of the object in relation to the target. (S2.M9.6)

Embedded Outcomes

Rules & etiquette: Demonstrates knowledge of rules and etiquette by self-officiating modified physical activities and games or following parameters to create or modify a dance. (S4.M6.7)

Working with others: Cooperates with a small group of classmates during adventure activities, game play or team-building activities. (S4.M5.6)

Lesson Objectives

The learner will:

- demonstrate the preferred technique for striking an object (croquet ball) during game play.
- identify the target game characteristics of bowling and croquet.

Equipment and Materials

- Croquet basic rule sheet
- 4 balls (black, blue, red, yellow)
- 4 mallets per team
- 12 hoops and 2 pegs per group
- Croquet courts (how many depends on the number of students in your class)
- Scorecards

Introduction

Today, we will play croquet. Have any of you played this game before? If so, what is the objective of the game? If not, do you know anything about croquet? What does it have in common with bowling? It is a target game!

Instructional Task: Video Relay Review

■ PRACTICE TASK

Have students read over the rules.

One student runs a lap or pre-determined distance. Upon returning to the group, he rolls the dice. The number rolled determines the question that students review on the sheet. The student who checks the answer runs next. The third student becomes the checker while the runner rests. Students rotate in the group.

Extension

Students can provide examples of following and violating the rules.

Refinements

- Make sure students are focused on learning the rules. Some students may be more interested in winning the relays.
- Follow up with questions from the croquet question handout.

EMBEDDED OUTCOME: S4.M5.6. Discuss with students the importance of cooperating as a relay team to achieve the goal. (Win but also learn the rules.)

Student Choices/Differentiation

- Students decide who will run first and who will have the review sheet to check for correct answers.
- Roles can be decided by rolling the dice (highest number picks who does what).
- Music can be played for reinforcement.

What to Look For

- During the video viewing, students are attentive.
- Students are cooperating and following instructions.

Instructional Task: Quick Review of Croquet

■ PRACTICE TASK

Ask questions about the court and game.

Each student runs to a spot or is prompted to answer a question.

Guiding questions for students:

- Stand next to a wicket. Why is this important?
- Stand next to a peg. When is it used?
- What happens when your ball goes out of bounds?
- Describe a mallet.

Extension

No-mallet croquet: Students roll or underhand toss the ball to connect the game of croquet to bowling and bocce.

Student Choices/Differentiation

- Play as a class activity or small-group activity.
- Students decide which method to use: four-step approach or underhand toss during no-mallet croquet.

What to Look For

- Check for understanding. Croquet is an advanced game, and the rules are more complicated than those for bowling or bocce.
- Students make the connection to other target games, striking objects using varying techniques.

Instructional Task: Hitting With a Mallet

■ PRACTICE TASK

Ball striking: Have students explore striking with a mallet using varying levels of force.

Refinements

- Make sure students are following class safety procedures.
- Make sure students are not swinging clubs when other students are close.

Guiding questions for students:

- Was the ball difficult to make contact with when you swung with a high amount of force? How about little force?
- Did the ball go where you wanted it to go?
- What are some ways force and accuracy are important in this game?
- With regard to force and accuracy, how are croquet and bowling different? How are they the same?

Extension

Students practice hitting balls with their mallets:

- Try to hit your ball through the wicket. Position your ball wherever you would like.
- Practice striking your opponent's ball with your ball by hitting it with the mallet.
- Practice hitting the stake. Aim your ball at the stake and hit it.

Guiding questions for students:
- Did you use different force on your club according to the type of shot I asked you to perform?
- Did location matter? How?
- How is this similar to or different from bowling?

Student Choices/Differentiation
- Students may use balls of different sizes and weights.
- Students may need to choke up on the mallet (hands closer to the ground for greater control).

What to Look For
- Students are following the critical elements of striking with a mallet.
- Students are striking with different levels of force.
- Students are having success striking with accuracy.

Instructional Task: Play Croquet Game

■ PRACTICE TASK

Students practice the basic rules and skills of the game.

Guiding questions for students:
- What do you do if you play out of bounds?
- Do you lose a turn if the ball goes out of bounds?

Refinements
- Make sure students are using the proper striking movement pattern.
- Make sure students are following the rules of the game.

Extension

Share with students a rubric for striking in croquet. Have students peer-assess each other to offer feedback on their croquet skills.

EMBEDDED OUTCOME: S4.M6.7 During the game, students self-officiate as they play. Students are expected to implement the rules correctly and score the match accurately.

Student Choices/Differentiation
- Students decide on the type of stroke to use during the game or to use all the strokes.
- Students decide on which team plays first (e.g., through a coin toss).
- Students may use different-sized balls as progression in the game occurs.

What to Look For
- Students are following the rules and engaging in fair play.
- Students are actively engaged in the game.

Formal and Informal Assessments

- Croquet rubric for peer assessment: NATECHPA rubric
- Informal observation and questioning of students as they engage in play

Closure

- What are three strokes used during the game of croquet?
- Demonstrate all three, starting with the croquet. Now to the side. Now through the legs.
- What is the main objective of the game?

Reflection

- Are the rules too complicated? If so, can I make them easier?
- In what ways can I modify the game for higher activity levels from students?

Homework

The goal for the class is to generate a list of target games we can play during our target games carnival. I need each of you to research and provide at least two target games. If you want a challenge, try to provide a target game from a different culture. E-mail me the games you found, and we will decide which ones to include in the carnival.

Study for the cognitive test on basic rules, etiquette, scoring, and strategy of target games. Materials will be posted on the school's physical education website. The test will be given the last day of the module.

Resources

Internet keyword search: "basic skills and rules of croquet," "croquet score cards," "scoring in croquet," "croquet rubrics," "NATECHPA rubric," "croquet for beginners"

CROQUET QUESTION SHEET WITH ANSWERS

1. The objective of croquet is to use a mallet to send a ball through a series of hoops. The formal name for these hoops is also used in the sport of cricket. Which of the following is it?

   Bouncers

   Googlies

   Creases

   *Wickets

2. Croquet uses four differently colored balls, with each side having two of the balls. Which of the following is not one of the four colors?

   Black

   *Orange

   Blue

   Red

3. My partner and I are ready to take the next turn. If we are playing to the standard rules of croquet, what will determine who takes that turn?

   Our opponents decide for us

   The player whose ball is nearest an opponent's ball must take the turn

   *Either of us can play at our discretion

   Players alternate their turns

4. We've got our mallets and balls and proceed on to the croquet lawn. Assuming that this is full size, to which of the following areas is it roughly equivalent?

   Three NFL football fields

   Three boxing rings

   *Three tennis courts

   Three soccer pitches

5. How does a game of croquet finish, assuming it is played to the standard rules?

   When the losing team has had enough and decides to call time

   *When both balls on a team have struck a peg in the center of the lawn

   After precisely two hours

   After every hoop has been passed through three times

Question Sheet for Croquet

1. How many balls do you need to play croquet? (Answer: four balls for up to four people, six balls for six people)

2. What is a wicket? (Answer: A wicket is a horseshoe-shaped wire through which you hit the ball.)

3. What is a roquet? (Answer: When you hit your opponent's ball with yours. You might want to have students demonstrate.)

4. What is the main objective of the game? (Answer: First one to get the ball around the course wins.)

5. What is the protocol if the ball goes out of bounds? (Answer: Place the ball one mallet-head-length from the boundary, close to where the ball went out of bounds.)

6. What color of balls are usually used? (Answer: blue, red, black, and yellow)

From R.J. Doan, L.C. MacDonald, and S. Chepko, eds., 2017, *Lesson planning for middle school physical education* (Reston, VA: SHAPE America; Champaign, IL: Human Kinetics).

LESSON 7: BOCCE BALL

Grade-Level Outcomes

Primary Outcomes

Throwing: Demonstrates a mature pattern for a modified target game such as bowling, bocce or horseshoes. (S1.M18.6)

Rules & etiquette: Identifies the rules and etiquette for physical activities/games and dance activities. (S4.M6.6)

Embedded Outcome

Social interactions: Demonstrates respect for self and others in activities and games by following the rules, encouraging others and playing in the spirit of the game or activity. (S5.M6.6)

Lesson Objectives

The learner will:

- learn the rules and techniques to play bocce ball.
- demonstrate the proper movement pattern for bocce.
- identify the shared characteristics between bocce ball and bowling.

Equipment and Materials

- Rule sheet
- Question sheet
- Dice per group of students
- Flour to mark off the playing area (full sized or modified) on a grassy area
- Up to 10 marked areas
- 10 bocce ball kits

Or

- 80 balls varying in size and color
- 10 small white balls or baseballs or softballs

Introduction

Discuss with students their choices for the target games they selected for the carnival.

We are going to play these games during the target games lesson. How many of you enjoyed bowling and croquet? Are you ready to learn another target game similar to the ones you learned so far? We are going to learn bocce ball. How many of you have heard of that before? I have an introductory video to show you. After the video, I will hand out a rule sheet and explain the outside target.

Instructional Task: Video Jumping Jack Flash

■ PRACTICE TASK

Show students a video with bocce ball

Have students read over the rules.

Have students get into small groups. Hand each group a rule and have students create a skit demonstrating the rule given.

Extension

Students can provide examples of following and violating the rules.

Refinements

- Make sure students are focused on learning the rules. Some students will be more interested in the skit than in learning the rules.
- Follow up with questions from the bocce question handout.

Student Choices/Differentiation

Have examples of skits if needed.

Students may choose groups.

What to Look For

- During the video viewing, students are attentive.
- Students are cooperating and following instructions.

Instructional Task: Tossing the Bocce Ball

▦ PRACTICE TASK

Demonstrate the proper toss.

Students mimic the movement pattern without the ball.

Extensions

- In partners, have students peer-assess each other on the proper movement pattern.
- Have students practice the bocce ball toss, 10 times or more until they are comfortable with the motion.
- Repeat, aiming to get as close to the pallino as possible. Count the number within a set number of inches.

Student Choices/Differentiation

- Students select a practice ball that can be regulation or modified.
- Students can use different-sized balls to assist with accuracy.
- Students can toss the ball like an underhand pitch or using the four-step approach learned from the bowling lessons.

What to Look For

- Are students able to roll or toss the ball fluidly?
- Are they able to apply an appropriate level of force to get the right distance?
- Peer assessment: Students use a teacher-generated checklist to evaluate their peers on the underhand toss movement pattern.

Instructional Task: Game Play

▦ PRACTICE TASK

Teach students how to score. Students pair off or play in small groups.

Refinement

Make sure students who are closest to the ball received the points.

Extension

After one round of play, students change partners or groups and play again.

Guiding questions for students:

- How do you score points in the game?
- After all balls have been thrown, who goes next after points have been totaled?
- What is the white ball called?
- What are the similarities between bowling and bocce?

EMBEDDED OUTCOME: S5.M6.6. Teach students the importance of respecting themselves and others by following the rules and encouraging others to perform their best during the game of bocce ball.

Student Choices/Differentiation

Students choose their partners or groups.

What to Look For

- Are students scoring the match correctly?
- If playing in small groups, are they communicating about strategy?
- Are students supporting one another with positive comments?
- Are they rolling or tossing the ball with appropriate accuracy and distance?

Instructional Task: Bocce Ball Strategy and Tactics

■ PRACTICE TASK

Demonstrate the blocking technique.

Have students practice rolling the balls to block the pallino from their opponents.

Extensions

- Demonstrate the spocking technique. Have students set up their court so the pallino has two or three balls around it. Have students practice spocking.
- After practicing both strategies, have students play another round (frame). Students can award a bonus point for a successful block or spock.

Student Choices/Differentiation

- Students choose their groups or partners.
- Students may review video clips of blocking and spocking.
- Students may choose the distance from the pallino to decrease or increase the level of challenge.

What to Look For

- Are students able to set up the block with their rolls?
- Are students able to make the high toss to hit the pallino?
- Are they able to implement the techniques in the game?

Formal and Informal Assessments

- Observing for proper scoring, strategy, and cooperation
- Peer assessment: underhand movement pattern

Closure

- What are two ways you can get your ball in play? Please demonstrate.
- Which team scores or receives points?
- How was this game similar to and different from bowling and croquet?

Reflection

- How well did the creating skits activity work for learning the rules?
- Did students cooperate well?
- Did students understand scoring?
- Were students able to implement the strategies of the game successfully?

Homework

Practice target games for the upcoming carnival.

Study for the cognitive test on basic rules, etiquette, scoring, and strategy of target games. Materials will be posted on the school's physical education website.

Resources

World Bocce League: www.worldbocce.org (rule sheet and much more)

Internet keyword search: "bocce," "pallino," "blocking in bocce," "rules of bocce," "spocking"

QUESTION SHEET FOR BOCCE BALL

1. How many balls do you use playing bocce ball? (Answer: eight players' balls and one target ball)

2. How many playing balls does each team have? (Answer: four)

3. How do you decide which team goes first? (Answer: coin toss, usually)

4. How do you start the game? (Answer: The pallino, the small white target ball, is tossed by the team who won the coin toss.)

5. How do you score points in bocce ball? (Answer: Get your bocce balls closer to the pallino than the other team.)

From R.J. Doan, L.C. MacDonald, and S. Chepko, eds., 2017, *Lesson planning for middle school physical education* (Reston, VA: SHAPE America; Champaign, IL: Human Kinetics).

LESSON 8: TARGET GAMES CARNIVAL DAY

Grade-Level Outcomes

Primary Outcomes

Individual-performance activities: Demonstrates correct technique for basic skills in at least 2 self-selected individual-performance activities. (S1.M24.8)

Rules & etiquette: Applies rules and etiquette by acting as an official for modified physical activities and games and creating dance routines within a given set of parameters. (S4.M6.8)

Embedded Outcome

Social interaction: Demonstrates the importance of social interaction by helping and encouraging others, avoiding trash talk and providing support to classmates. (S5.M6.7)

Lesson Objectives

The learner will:

- demonstrate basic target games techniques and strategies during the target games carnival.
- demonstrate basic knowledge of the rules, etiquette, scoring, and strategy during a cognitive test.

Equipment and Materials

A variety of equipment depending on the target games selected for the carnival:

- Inflatable ring toss
- Bocce ball court
- Croquet court
- Bowling lane
- Beanbag toss
- Bank a shot (standing tilted board, Wiffle ball, and laundry basket)

Introduction

It's target games carnival day! Using the games you selected, we will play multiple carnival target games. You must participate in at least two games. Here is your bingo card. Get a stamp for each game you play, and you will get a prize at the end of class.

This could be a good time to involve parents and teachers who want to volunteer.

Instructional Task: Target Games Carnival Bingo

■ PRACTICE TASK

Students demonstrate proper techniques for game play at each station.

Examples of games: bowling, bocce ball, croquet, washer pitching, putting green, Velcro-ball target toss

Extension

Peer evaluation or teacher skill evaluation can be done with teacher-created checklist or rubrics.

Refinement

Stop activities to refine skill, scoring, and strategy if needed.

EMBEDDED OUTCOME: S5.M6.7 Discuss with students the importance of social interaction by helping and encouraging others, avoiding trash talk, and providing support to classmates during the target games carnival. Make sure to go over examples of these behaviors.

Student Choices/Differentiation

- Students decide which games to play throughout the day or class.
- Equipment sizes, distances, and target sizes can be varied.

What to Look For

- Students are enjoying the activities.
- Students show proper technique and etiquette during game play.
- Students follow the rules during game play.
- Peer- or teacher-created evaluation: Evaluations can be done for skill, scoring, and strategy.

Instructional Task: Cognitive Test

■ PRACTICE TASK

Administer a knowledge test on the concepts and principles taught during the module.

Student Choices/Differentiation

Students may take extra time if needed.

What to Look For

Students know basic rules, etiquette, scoring, and strategy that were covered throughout the module.

Formal and Informal Assessments

- Bingo card to ensure each student visited two booths
- Peer- or teacher-created assessment
- Cognitive test

Closure

- This concludes our target games module. What similarities did you see in the various target games?
- What are the differences?
- What are the benefits of playing target games?
- What kinds of target games does your family play?

You will receive a survey so you can tell us what you liked best and least. Bring it back to class next time.

Reflection

- Reviewing the bingo cards, which games were visited the most? Least?
- How could we incorporate interdisciplinary study in the carnival?

Homework

Complete the survey to rank the games you played during the target games carnival. Do you have any suggestions for other games?

Please review the material on the school's physical education website for the next module.

Resources

Carnival Game Ideas: www.schoolcarnivals.com

CHAPTER 8

Applying Students' Skills and Knowledge to Outdoor Pursuits

There are many reasons to include outdoor pursuits in the middle school curriculum (Gilbertson, Bates, McLaughlin, & Ewert, 2006). For one thing, these types of activities offer a healthy alternative to traditional games and sports, which have limited appeal for less-skilled and disengaged students (Ntoumanis, Pensgaard, Martin, & Pipe, 2004). For another, many forms of outdoor pursuits are lifelong physical activities that lend themselves to adult and family participation in recreation settings. Perhaps best of all for physical educators, outdoor-pursuit activities provide many options for teaching the skills and knowledge prescribed in the Grade-Level Outcomes under multiple National Standards. Not only do outdoor pursuits such as hiking, backpacking, orienteering, geocaching, ice skating, canoeing, mountain biking, and a host of others help students hone their physical skills and subject knowledge under Standards 1 and 2, but the content area also is rich in opportunities for addressing outcomes under Standards 4 and 5, which emphasize social acceptance and growing autonomy by focusing on the ability to cooperate, work with others, accept feedback, and make healthy choices (SHAPE America, 2014, p. 40).

This chapter contains three modules of lessons on outdoor pursuits. The first module, Geocaching and Orienteering, helps students learn to use multiple navigation devices for exploring the outdoors. The second module, Hiking and Backpacking, teaches students how to plan and prepare properly for hikes and backpacking trips. Continuing with the adventure theme, the third module, Adventure Activities, teaches students basic team-building and challenge activities to enhance their overall well-being and collaborative skills. The activities are geared toward increasing personal confidence and mutual support within a group (Miles & Priest, 1999).

As you will read in the modules, many of the adventure activities fall under the following categories: acquaintance activities (getting to know other group members), ice breakers, communication tasks (decision-making and conflict-resolution activities), and problem-solving and trust-building activities (Rohnke & Butler, 1995). While it would be ideal to offer these activities in a beautiful natural setting, many schools are not in a position to do so because of financial or space constraints. Fortunately, all three of the modules offered here can be adapted easily to a gym, school grounds, or local park or recreation areas.

The eight-lesson Geocaching and Orienteering Module focuses mainly on demonstrating correct technique for a variety of skills (Outcome S1.M22.7), while addressing many other outcomes under Standards 2, 4, and 5. Lessons in the Backpacking and Hiking Module concentrate on teaching basic skills (Outcome S1.M22.6) and a variety of skills (Outcome S1.M22.7) in one self-selected outdoor activity. The lessons also require students to analyze and implement safe protocols (Outcomes S2.M13.7 and S2.M13.8) in outdoor activities, while addressing multiple outcomes under Standards 3, 4, and 5. Finally, the Adventure Activities Module focuses on problem solving in small groups (Outcome S4.M5.7), cooperating with multiple classmates on problem-solving activities (Outcome S4.M5.8), and generating positive strategies for possible solutions when faced with group challenges.

Together, the lessons in these three modules provide a great resource for teaching outdoor pursuits, while guiding students along the path to becoming physically literate individuals, as mapped throughout the National Standards and Grade-Level Outcomes.

GEOCACHING AND ORIENTEERING MODULE

Lessons in this module were contributed by Erin Curran, assistant principal at Swofford Career Center in Inman, SC, and a certified physical education teacher.

Grade-Level Outcomes Addressed, by Lesson	Lessons							
	1	2	3	4	5	6	7	8
Standard 1. The physically literate individual demonstrates competency in a variety of motor skills and movement patterns.								
Demonstrates correct technique for basic skills in 1 self-selected outdoor activity. (S1.M22.6)	P	P			P			
Demonstrates correct technique for a variety of skills in 1 self-selected outdoor activity. (S1.M22.7)			P	P		P	P	P
Standard 2. The physically literate individual applies knowledge of concepts, principles, strategies and tactics related to movement and performance.								
Analyzes the situation and makes adjustments to ensure the safety of self and others. (S2.M13.7)							E	
Implements safe protocols in self-selected outdoor activities. (S2.M13.8)								E
Standard 3. The physically literate individual demonstrates the knowledge and skills to achieve and maintain a health-enhancing level of physical activity and fitness.								
Standard 4. The physically literate individual exhibits responsible personal and social behavior that respects self and others.								
Exhibits responsible social behaviors by cooperating with classmates, demonstrating inclusive behaviors and supporting classmates. (S4.M1.7)		E		E	E			
Independently uses physical activity and exercise equipment properly and safely. (S1.M7.7)						E		
Standard 5. The physically literate individual recognizes the value of physical activity for health, enjoyment, challenge, self-expression and/or social interaction.								
Identifies positive mental and emotional aspects of participating in a variety of physical activities. (S5.M2.7)							E	
Recognizes individual challenges and copes in a positive way, such as extending effort, asking for help or feedback and/or modifying the tasks. (S5.M3.6)	E		E					
Generates positive strategies such as offering suggestions or assistance, leading or following others and providing possible solutions when faced with a group challenge. (S5.M3.7)				E				
Develops a plan of action and makes appropriate decisions based on that plan when faced with an individual challenge. (S5.M3.8)						E		
Demonstrates the importance of social interaction by helping and encouraging others, avoiding trash talk and providing support to classmates. (S5.M6.7)				E				

P = Primary; E = Embedded

LESSON 1: COMPASS BASICS

Grade-Level Outcomes

Primary Outcome

Outdoor pursuits: Demonstrates correct technique for basic skills in 1 self-selected outdoor activity. (S1.M22.6)

Embedded Outcome

Challenge: Recognizes individual challenges and copes in a positive way, such as extending effort, asking for help or feedback and/or modifying the tasks. (S5.M3.6)

Lesson Objectives

The learner will:

- recognize and understand the parts of a compass.
- exhibit knowledge of a compass by translating it to a map.

Equipment and Materials

- Compasses
- Computer to watch video clips
- Paper and pencils

Introduction

To start our module on geocaching and orienteering, today we will learn to read and use a compass effectively. Orienteering is an adventure activity that works not only your body, but your mind, as well. The goal of orienteering is to navigate in sequence between points marked on a map and decide the best route for completing the course in the quickest time. Geocaching is hiding objects for other people to find, using a global positioning device, or GPS. It's sort of like high-tech scavenger hunting.

Show students a video (do a keyword search for "geocaching," "compass," "orienteering," etc.).

Instructional Task: The Basics of the Compass

■ PRACTICE TASK

Conduct an informal pre-assessment.

Guiding questions for students:

- Who has used a compass while on an adventure?
- Who can tell me why someone would use a compass, especially since we have computers, phones, and GPS?

Who can name the parts of a compass?

Teach the components of the compass and the rules of thumb for using one, including:

- the four compass directions and degrees
- the dial
- the needle
- direction of travel
- holding it flat
- moving your body, not the compass
- "red Fred in the shed" to face north

Have students start to explore using the compass with maps after giving them the attached worksheet.

Extension

Have students use the compass to find north, south, east, and west.

Student Choices/Differentiation

- Students may start to use degrees or challenge each other to find secondary directions such as southwest or northeast.
- Show how-to videos (keywords: "compass 101," "how to use a baseplate compass," etc.)

What to Look For

- Students are using the correct vocabulary.
- Do students understand all the parts of the compass?
- Are they using the compass effectively?
- Are they demonstrating the four major directions correctly?

Instructional Task:
Map Drawing and Compass Reading

■ PRACTICE TASK

Students draw maps of the local community, labeling the school, major roads, their homes, and landmarks in the community. Each map should include a compass rose, which helps users orient themselves when using the map by indicating the four major directions: North, South, East, and West. Make sure that the compass directions are correct in the rose.

Extension

Have students check one another's maps for correct orientation. To do that, students hold a compass at waist level and allow it to find its bearings. Students then use these bearings to line up the map's North alignment with the compass's North alignment to determine whether the map is oriented correctly.

EMBEDDED OUTCOME: S5.M3.M6. This is a good opportunity to discuss constructive ways of supporting peers and providing appropriate feedback on their maps.

Student Choices/Differentiation

Students could use technology to make their map or work in groups to enhance understanding.

What to Look For

- Can students use the compass effectively to navigate to a desired location or direction?
- Can students identify the various parts of the compass?
- Are students using teamwork and giving corrective feedback?

Instructional Task: Compass Game

■ PRACTICE TASK

One person is the compass needle in the center of the group. That student's

- front will be north.
- back will be south.
- left will be west.
- right will be east.

"The needle" calls out a direction and other students align themselves with that direction, based on the needle (e.g., they would move to behind the needle for south).

Extension

The needle can change her position by moving around the area and spinning, making classmates have to respond to the movement to find their next placement.

Student Choices/Differentiation

Students may wear a pinny labeled with compass directions to help at the beginning of the activity.

What to Look For

- Are students able to orient themselves to the center person?
- Are they navigating on their own or watching others for direction?

Formal and Informal Assessments

- Informal pre-assessment
- Informal teacher observation

Closure

- Why is it important to learn how to use a compass?
- Why is learning the directions on a compass important, and how can you use them if you are lost?

As you gain more knowledge of the compass and how to use it, you will undertake fun challenges and adventures. We will start with compass work and then go on to geocaching using GPS tracking devices.

Reflection

- Were students able to identify the components of the compass?
- Were students able to use the compass rose to check one another's maps?
- Did students provide constructive ways to support one another during the lesson today?

Homework

Share the video that we watched in class with a friend or family member, and teach him or her how to read and use a compass.

Resources

Internet keyword search: "geocaching," "compass," "orienteering"

Compass illustrations on handout

FIND YOUR WAY WITH A MAP

STEP 1. Place your compass on the area map with the base plate edge connecting where you are with where you want to go.

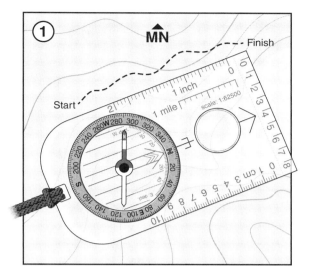

STEP 2. Set the compass heading by turning the compass dial until the N on your compass aligns with magnetic north on the map.

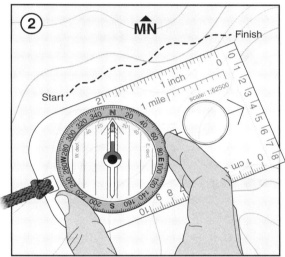

STEP 3. Remove the compass from the map and hold it level in front of you, with the direction-of-travel arrow pointing straight ahead. Turn your body until the red end of the needle is directly over the orienting arrow, pointing to the N on the dial.

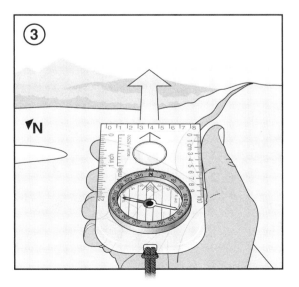

LESSON 2: COMPASS SCAVENGER HUNT

Grade-Level Outcomes

Primary Outcome

Outdoor pursuits: Demonstrates correct technique for basic skills in 1 self-selected outdoor activity. (S1.M22.6)

Embedded Outcome

Personal responsibility: Exhibits responsible social behaviors by cooperating with classmates, demonstrating inclusive behaviors and supporting classmates. (S4.M1.7)

Lesson Objectives

The learner will:

- complete the scavenger hunt by employing compass skills.
- in small groups, create a scavenger hunt with three or four clues.

Equipment and Materials

- Compasses
- Paper and pencils
- Scavenger hunt instructions and clues

Introduction

Today, we will review the parts of the compass and participate in a fun scavenger hunt.

Instructional Task:
Review of Compass and Compass Scavenger Hunt

■ PRACTICE TASK

Before class, set out items for students to find using their compasses.

Review the parts of the compass with students to check for understanding.

Have students complete this task in groups, with partners, or individually. Make stations so that they cannot observe others.

The activity has students using the clues and directions that you provide to progress through the scavenger hunt.

Example: You will start in the doorway that faces the lockers. From that spot, you will go north until you cross the yellow line on the floor. After you cross the yellow line, you will turn east and go to the cone. (Put a few cones out so that students must choose the correct one.) There, you will receive your next clue.

Extensions

- Students draw a map as they progress through the scavenger hunt. It must be readable to others and include the direction, how many paces were traveled, and any landmarks to look for.
- Add activities to the scavenger hunt. Require lunges, wall sits for 30 seconds, or even 10 push-ups or burpees before moving on to find the next clue.
- Students follow other students' maps to see whether they align.

Student Choices/Differentiation

- Have different scavenger hunt routes for the different skill levels (easy, medium, difficult, and extreme).
- Place clues within sight of the last clue to help less-skilled students.

What to Look For

- Are students using the compass effectively?
- Do they understand the basics of the compass and how it works?
- Students are reading their compasses and not guessing throughout the scavenger hunt.

Instructional Task:
Students Create Their Own Scavenger Hunt

■ PRACTICE TASK

Now that they have seen your version of the scavenger hunt, students in small groups create their own scavenger hunts with three or four clues.

All groups start in the same place and end at the same place but take different routes to get there.

EMBEDDED OUTCOME: S4.M1.7 Teach students appropriate social behaviors such as including all group members, supporting all group members' ideas, and working as a team.

Extension

After the groups create their own, have students complete other groups' scavenger hunts.

Guiding questions for students:

- Which scavenger hunt was the easiest? Why?
- Which scavenger hunt was the most difficult? Why?

Student Choices/Differentiation

Partner students evenly so that knowledge can be shared between partners and groups.

What to Look For

- Students are able to write detailed clues.
- Students are writing a scavenger hunt that uses compass directions.
- Students understand why a scavenger hunt is easy or hard.

Note: Use a simple checklist to assess students' scavenger hunts:

- Three or Four clues
- Level of difficulty
- Creativity

Formal and Informal Assessments

Checklist: student-created scavenger hunt

Closure

- Compass reading is an important survival skill, but in today's lesson, it was a matter of surviving the scavenger hunt. How were you able to succeed?
- From time to time, we will fail or get our directions wrong, and it is important to learn from these mistakes. How many of you made a mistake reading your compass today? Can you describe where you went wrong? Learn to correct it and move on, and don't let it frustrate you.

It seems that we are getting better at using the compasses, which is good, because next class we will play a game in which it's important to use the compass quickly to win. We also will use a compass to create directions to a time capsule that we will set so that others can find it.

Reflection

- Did all students have a say in creating the scavenger hunt?
- Did students work together?
- Were the clues too difficult or easy for the teacher-led scavenger hunt?

Homework

Because we will set a time capsule next class, bring something small and non-perishable to add to it. We will vote to determine whether it should be added to our collection of items.

Hand out rubric on time capsule assignment for students to review.

Resources

Internet keyword search: "scavenger hunt with compass," "compass activities"

TIME CAPSULE RUBRIC

Fill out rubric using scale points, with 5 being the highest score and 1 being the lowest, or does not meet standard.

Student name	Correctness	Neatness	Aesthetic-ally pleasing	Compass knowledge	Effort	Ease of interpretation	Completeness	Collaboration with team

From R.J. Doan, L.C. MacDonald, and S. Chepko, eds., 2017, *Lesson planning for middle school physical education* (Reston, VA: SHAPE America; Champaign, IL: Human Kinetics).

LESSON 3: DISC COMPASS GAME

Grade-Level Outcomes

Primary Outcome

Outdoor pursuits: Demonstrates correct technique for a variety of skills in 1 self-selected outdoor activity. (S1.M22.7)

Embedded Outcomes

Challenge: Recognizes individual challenges and copes in a positive way, such as extending effort, asking for help or feedback and/or modifying the tasks. (S5.M3.6)

Social interaction: Demonstrates the importance of social interaction by helping and encouraging others, avoiding trash talk and providing support to classmates. (S5.M6.7)

Lesson Objectives

The learner will:

- draw a detailed map for locating a time capsule.
- work with a partner to navigate through the disc compass game.

Equipment and Materials

- Discs
- 12 labeled cones
- GPS trackers
- Time capsule (e.g., glass jar, sealable plastic container, metal box)

Introduction

Today, you will use your compass skills to create a map to a time capsule. It's important that your map and compass skills be spot-on because someone else will be using your map to find the time capsule. Remember what you have learned about the compass so far, and be sure to involve all of your teammates.

Instructional Task: Time Capsule Burial

■ PRACTICE TASK

Work with students to find a perfect location for a time capsule to be buried and then opened 100 to 150 years from now. Explain to students that those who eventually will open the time capsule will be using the students' compass navigations to locate it.

Draw students a detailed map and the exact steps and key points so that they will be able to locate the time capsule. Have each student create a map and key.

Future generations might not understand English, so students' maps and keys will have to be compass based, not language based.

Extension

Challenge students to use landmarks for their maps that they think will remain for a long time.

Student Choices/Differentiation

- Modify the activity with guidelines on how many steps or key points must be included in the directions.
- Allow students to choose how many steps they want to include. This will encourage them to choose a level of activity that's comfortable for them and allow struggling students to use fewer steps, if they want to.

What to Look For

- Students' maps are easy to understand.
- Strangers could use the maps.
- Students understand how to use a compass to draw a map.
- The maps contain keys and a compass rose.

Instructional Task: Disc Mapping Game

■ PRACTICE TASK

Number the inside of cones from 1 to 12. Use a compass to place the cones in an open field (see diagram). Cone-placement order should start off easy and increase in difficulty as students practice.

Students work in pairs for this game. Hand each pair of students a map showing 12 cones' locations, but without indicating how the cones are numbered. Pairs then set out toward the cone that they think might be number 1. One student in each pair navigates toward the selected cone using a compass. The navigator tells the partner in which direction (north, south, east or west) to throw a disc, toward the selected cone. The navigator must track the number of throws and write the number of cones reached in the correct order. Working together, students should find cones 1-12. Cones should be spread out far enough to challenge the thrower and the navigator.

If partners reach a cone out of order, they must start over.

The partners who navigate the course in the fastest time and with the fewest throws wins.

Rules

- Team members must switch roles at cone 6.
- Teams must hit a cone with the disc before they can lift the cone to find its number.
- Throwers may take no steps while holding the disc (as in ultimate).
- Reaching and lifting cones in the wrong order results in a restart, but partners should use each error to refine their search.

Extensions

- Instruct students to use GPS coordinates to move from cone to cone. Give each pair of students the coordinates to the first cone, where they will find the coordinates to the second cone, and so on. If GPS devices are not available, use simple north, south, east, and west coordinates and number of steps for distances. (Example: Walk east 12 steps, then walk north 24 steps to the cone.)

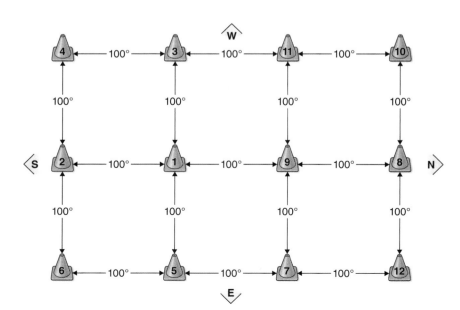

- Students can use different throwing implements, and you can increase or decrease the spacing between cones.
- Add activities by requiring lunges, wall sits for 30 seconds, or even 10 push-ups or burpees before students can move on to the next cone.

Guiding questions for students:
- How did your team remember which cone was which?
- What strategies did you use as you navigated through the course?

EMBEDDED OUTCOME: S5.M6.7 Demonstrate the importance of social interaction by helping and encouraging others, avoiding trash talk and providing support to classmates.

EMBEDDED OUTCOME: S5.M3.6 Discuss the importance of recognizing individual challenges in this activity and how to cope in a positive way, such as extending effort, asking for help or feedback, or modifying tasks.

Student Choices/Differentiation

You can increase or decrease the number of cones in the field to allow students to choose the level of challenge.

What to Look For
- Partners are cooperating with each other.
- Students are safe from errant discs as they navigate the maze.
- Students take responsibility for their team's success and keep score accurately.
- Are they cheating or allowing other classmates to cheat?
- Extension activity: Are students using what they learn from each cone and inferring what their next step should be?

Formal and Informal Assessments

Use the student's map rubric to grade students' maps based on neatness, correctness, aesthetics, effort, and compass-reading knowledge.

Closure
- Do you think you have learned enough about compasses to find your way if you were lost with a map and compass?
- What other skills do you think would help you be able to read a map?

In our next class, we will take the ideas we learned with compasses and move on to geocaching.

Reflection
- Did the teams work together and support everyone?
- Do students understand teamwork and positive social interaction?
- Did students practice game skills and strategy in the compass game?

Homework

Have students complete a compass map of their street or neighborhood, school, community park, church, or building of their choice.

Resources

Internet keyword search: "compass games"

STUDENT'S MAP RUBRIC

Fill out rubric using scale points, with 5 being the highest score and 1 being the lowest, or does not meet standard.

Student name	Correctness	Neatness	Aesthetics	Compass knowledge	Effort	Ease of interpretation	Completeness	Collaboration with team

From R.J. Doan, L.C. MacDonald, and S. Chepko, eds., 2017, *Lesson planning for middle school physical education* (Reston, VA: SHAPE America; Champaign, IL: Human Kinetics).

LESSON 4: INTRODUCTION TO GEOCACHING

Grade-Level Outcomes

Primary Outcome

Outdoor pursuits: Demonstrates correct technique for basic skills in 1 self-selected outdoor activity. (S1.M22.6)

Embedded Outcomes

Challenge: Generates positive strategies such as offering suggestions or assistance, leading or following others and providing possible solutions when faced with a group challenge. (S5.M3.7)

Personal responsibility: Exhibits responsible social behaviors by coopering with classmates, demonstrating inclusive behaviors and supporting classmates. (S4.M1.7)

Lesson Objectives

The learner will:

- describe the components of a GPS used in geocaching.
- use the GPS to find caches.

Equipment and Materials

- GPS trackers or handheld devices with GPS apps
- Worksheets and pencils
- Caches to hide

Introduction

Ask students to share their homework activity.

In the previous three lessons, we have used the compass to find our way. Today, we will add the handheld GPS tracker to our lesson. You will learn about geocaching and the adventures that exist in the sport of caching.

Instructional Task: Rules of Geocaching

■ PRACTICE TASK

What is a cache?

- A cache is a group of items that have been hidden for others to find. It usually is placed in a waterproof container.
- It contains a logbook, a trinket, or both.
- It usually is camouflaged to prevent it from being discovered by someone before the geocacher finds it.

Rules

1. Keep safe!
   - Stay away from traffic.
   - Use the buddy system.
   - Stay away from strangers.
2. Respect the environment.
   - Never bury a cache.
   - Don't deface any object.
   - Don't litter (trash in, trash out).
   - Tread carefully, and avoid things such as sprinkler heads, landscaping lights, and signs.

3. Respect boundaries.
   - Stay off private property.
   - It is unlawful to cache in a national park or wildlife refuge.
4. Respect the game.
   - If you find a cache, keep quiet so that others playing the game can enjoy finding it.
   - If you take something from a cache, you must leave something of equal value.
   - Record in your logbook where you found the cache.
   - Sign the log inside of the cache.
   - Hide the cache in the same way you found it.

Hide a cache for students to find using their GPS skills, and ask them to help others struggling with the task.

Extension

Have students conduct research to find local caches.

Guiding questions for students:
- Why is it important to leave caches as you found them?
- Name three things that you should avoid while geocaching.
- Which type of orienteering do you like better, compass or GPS? Why?
- Do you think geocaching could be a sport?

Student Choices/Differentiation
- Students may use a variety of devices to find geocaches, including a handheld GPS unit or a cell phone or tablet app.
- Have caches hidden as well as placed in open space, to accommodate a range of skill levels.

What to Look For

Students understand the principles and ethical rules of the geocaching activity.

Instructional Task: Students Create Caches With Groups

■ PRACTICE TASK

Play cache hide and seek in small groups.

Provide each group with a treasure to stash and a GPS device. Each group must find a hiding spot for its treasure.

Once its cache is hidden, each group enters the cache's waypoint (its latitude and longitude) into its GPS.

Students return to the class and swap GPS devices to see whether other groups can find their objects. If enough GPS devices are not available, have groups fill out and exchange the Treasure Hide and Seek handout, instead.

EMBEDDED OUTCOME: S4.M1.7 Discuss with students the importance of exhibiting responsible social behaviors by coopering with classmates, demonstrating inclusive behaviors and supporting classmates during this activity.

Extension

Have students start in the gym, where they can see the caches. Students must figure out how to follow the coordinates in another group's GPS to find the correct cache.

Student Choices/Differentiation

Students can create their own caches or use teacher-created ones.

What to Look For

- Students understand the concept of geocaching.
- Students are supporting one another and are providing feedback.
- Students can use the GPS tracking devices effectively.

Instructional Task: Captain on Deck

■ PRACTICE TASK

Students practice their compass points by playing a nautical game.
Learn the movements:

- Captain on deck: Each student must salute the captain (you) and stand still until you say, "At ease" (much like Simon says).
- Captain's ball: Two students join together and dance.
- Row your boat: Three students line up single file and row their boat (canoe style).
- Octopus four: Teammates put their rear ends together and wiggle their arms to create an eight-legged octopus.
- Starfish five: Teammates put their hands together in the air to create a starfish with five arms.
- Beached whale: Students lie down and make whale noises until you call the next action.

Show students the north, south, east, and west points of a compass. Then, repeat the game but change your commands to include the compass points. For example: "octopus to the north" (groups of four must gather in the north) or "starfish to the west" (groups of five must gather in the west). This prompts students to multitask by moving in the compass directions and finding teammates.

Each game action requires a specified number of people, so a few students will be eliminated in each round. Any student who does not make it into a group will have to walk the plank. Eliminated players may re-enter the game after stating compass or geocaching terminology.

Refinement

After the first round, discuss strategies with students.

EMBEDDED OUTCOME: S5.M3.7 Have students discuss positive strategies such as offering suggestions or assistance, leading or following others, and providing possible solutions to help generate success during this activity.

Extension

Teach and use nautical directions: bow (front), stern (rear), port (left), starboard (right). Let students know that using nautical directions can be a little more challenging.

Student Choices/Differentiation

Students can sit down and connect feet for starfish or sit to be in a boat.

What to Look For

- Students are working together.
- Students are following directions.
- Students who are eliminated are listing a wide range of terminology to get back into the game.

Formal and Informal Assessments

Exit slip: Draw and label the GPS device that you used today. Describe what each button does and when you would use it.

Closure

- Had anyone heard of geocaching before today?
- Today, you learned how to use a handheld GPS device instead of relying on the compass. Which do you like better so far?

In our next class, we will set up caches around the school for others to find, so start thinking about a spot. What are some of the basic rules you must follow when you place your caches?

Reflection

- Did students use the rules for geocaching during the activities today?
- Were students comfortable using the GPS devices?
- Were students using correct terms (directions) in the captain on deck activity?
- Where they able to come up with successful strategies during the activity?

Homework

Try to find a neat free application online that could help you geocache outside of school. There are several free apps, so find one that works best for you.

Resources

Geocaching: www.geocaching.com

Internet keyword search: "science spot GPS hide and seek"

TREASURE HIDE AND SEEK

Team members: _____

_____

_____

Steps

1. Find a good place to hide your treasure within the area that your teacher has identified. Place your item in a safe spot, but where it can be seen without having to dig or move objects.

2. Use your GPS receiver to mark the location (waypoint) of your item. Record the waypoint, and the other information called for on this worksheet.

3. Complete the "Find Our Secret Treasure!" slip below and tear it off.

4. Return to home base. Give the teacher your completed slip, as well as your GPS receiver.

Our Hiding Spot

Receiver # _____

Waypoint # _____

Latitude _____

Longitude _____

Location description _____

- -

Tear off this slip and hand it to the teacher after you've filled it out. It will be given to another team, who will try to find your treasure.

Find Our Secret Treasure!

Team members: _____

_____

_____

Receiver # _____

Find waypoint # _____

From R.J. Doan, L.C. MacDonald, and S. Chepko, eds., 2017, *Lesson planning for middle school physical education* (Reston, VA: SHAPE America; Champaign, IL: Human Kinetics).

LESSON 5: SEEKING GEOCACHES

Grade-Level Outcomes

Primary Outcome

Outdoor pursuits: Demonstrates correct technique for a variety of skills in 1 self-selected outdoor activity. (S1.M22.7)

Embedded Outcome

Personal responsibility: Exhibits responsible social behaviors by cooperating with classmates, demonstrating inclusive behaviors and supporting classmates. (S4.M1.7)

Equipment and Materials

- GPS trackers or devices with apps
- Artist handouts
- Pencil

Lesson Objectives

The learner will demonstrate the following parameters for pursuing and finding a cache using a GPS unit:

- draw his or her own initials by setting out waypoints or GPS location points.
- show command of geocaching and using a handheld GPS.

Introduction

In our previous class, we started to use the GPS devices and learned about geocaching. Your homework activity was to find an app. Who found it and will share it? Today, we will build on what we learned, with the chance to be creative and seek geocaches.

Instructional Task: GPS Artist

■ PRACTICE TASK

Students start by drawing a sketch of their initials and writing down directions for following the initials as if they were a course. The letter E, for example, has one line north to south and three lines east to west. Students plotting the letter E would enter those directions into the GPS units to plot out the turns in the letters in their initials. Students then log the waypoints of the letters in their initials on the GPS artist worksheet. Students whose initials create diagonal lines (e.g., X, Z) use ordinal or intermediate directions (e.g., northwest, northeast, southeast, southwest) to describe the locations of different points along their initials.

Extension

Students may choose to spell something other than their initials or may look up GPS art.

Guiding questions for students:

- Were your initials easy to read in the GPS device?
- What problems did you come across?
- How would you do this differently if you had the chance to do it again?
- What else could you draw?

Student Choices/Differentiation

Students may work in pairs to make the task easier or draw out something else that interests them.

What to Look For

- Students have enough GPS skills to be effective.

- Have students chosen something too difficult to map?
- Students are staying on task.
- Students have mastered the concept of direction by being able to label their papers with north, south, east, and west.

Instructional Task: Geocache Around the School Campus

■ PRACTICE TASK

Set out caches around the school campus, with each cache containing stamps for student teams to collect. Load the waypoints for finding the caches into the GPS devices, or give teams the waypoints to load themselves.

Groups find as many caches as they can, using the stamps from the caches as proof.

Extension

Hold a group discussion on responsible social behaviors.

EMBEDDED OUTCOME: S4.M1.7. Teach each group of students how to exhibit responsible social behaviors by sharing its GPS device with all group members, being supportive of group members' suggestions, and cooperating with one another in all aspects of the assignment.

Student Choices/Differentiation

Students may work in larger groups if they find navigating with the GPS devices difficult.

What to Look For

- Students are communicating in an effective manner.
- They are following the guidelines and social etiquette of the geocaching activity.
- Is one group falling behind or largely ahead of the others?

Formal and Informal Assessments

Have students turn in their GPS artwork and points for formal assessment.

Closure

- How do you feel about using the GPS trackers? Are you more confident?
- Now that you have learned to use the GPS and the compass, which is easier?
- Did starting with the compass help you understand the GPS better?

Today, you took the GPS and geocaching to the next level, looking for caches and plotting out points in your own initials. In our next class, you will set out your own caches, so gather into small groups and discuss what you would like to bring in for your cache or where you would like to place it on campus.

Reflection

- Are the groups understanding the assignments, or is one student leading the rest of the group?
- Do students understand the GPS device better than the compass or not as well?
- Are the activities challenging for students?
- Are students engaged in learning as they navigate with the GPS?

Homework

Bring in anything you need in order to make your own cache for the next class.

Resources

The Science Spot: www.sciencespot.net

GPS ARTIST

Name: _____ Date: _____

Design It

Use the space below to plan and sketch. Draw a sketch of your initials, and then write the directions that you would need to follow if you were to follow the letters as a route.

Draw It

Use the GPS unit to create your art. Set waypoints on the GPS that link together in the order in which you place them, creating a pattern or drawing.

Log Your Waypoints

Analyze It

How did you do? Were your initials easy to read? Explain.

What would you do differently if you repeated this activity?

What else could you draw using the skills that you just perfected?

From R.J. Doan, L.C. MacDonald, and S. Chepko, eds., 2017, *Lesson planning for middle school physical education* (Reston, VA: SHAPE America; Champaign, IL: Human Kinetics).

LESSON 6: GEOCACHING AROUND CAMPUS

Grade-Level Outcomes

Primary Outcome

Outdoor pursuits: Demonstrates correct technique for a variety of skills in 1 self-selected outdoor activity. (S1.M22.7)

Embedded Outcomes

Challenge: Develops a plan of action and makes appropriate decisions based on that plan when faced with an individual challenge. (S5.M3.7)

Safety: Independently uses physical activity and exercise equipment properly and safely. (S4.M7.7)

Equipment and Materials

- GPS trackers or devices with apps
- Cache supplies, which could include stamps, stickers, pompon balls, coins, plastic animals, army men, you name it! Don't use anything that's perishable or that would melt or attract animal attention.

Lesson Objective

The learner will:

- demonstrate understanding and ability to use the functions of a GPS unit effectively.
- demonstrate the ability to geocache correctly.

Introduction

In the previous class, you honed your geocaching skills by creating artwork with GPS points and searching for caches. Today, you will continue to build your knowledge of geocaching and challenge classmates to find caches that you have set out.

Instructional Task:
Organize Team Caches and Let Students Explore

■ PRACTICE TASK

Students organize in teams and set out caches for other teams to find. Teams create their caches in the classroom, then place them on the school campus in areas that you have designated. Each team then sets a waypoint for the cache on its GPS.

Have teams set waypoints within 50 feet (15 m) of their caches so that the team seeking cache must use strategy and search to find the cache.

Refinement

Students draw a picture of their team's cache and what the surrounding area looks like to help the seeking team locate it.

Extension

EMBEDDED OUTCOME: S5.M3.7 Help students develop a plan of action and make appropriate decisions based on the plan for this activity.

Once the GPS brings a team close to the cache it is seeking, team members must use inference, reason, and strategy to complete the task.

Student Choices/Differentiation

Change the size of the area in play to make the task easier or more difficult, depending on students' skill levels.

What to Look For

- Students are working together and communicating effectively.
- Groups are organized and efficient in their efforts to hide their caches.
- Students understand the idea of geocaching.
- Students are setting waypoints correctly.

Instructional Task: Locate Caches Set by Other Teams

■ PRACTICE TASK

Students work in small teams or pairs to locate the caches set out by other teams. Each team is expected to locate every other team's cache.

Hand students the rubric and discuss how you will assess them on this activity.

Extensions

- Teams must complete the task before moving on to look for the next hidden cache. The objective is to find each team's cache during the activity, but you can choose to format it as a team competition by timing each group.
- Have students draw or take pictures of each cache to prove that their team located each cache.

Guiding questions for students:

- How will you keep from tipping other students off to where the caches are?
- Once you find a cache, where must you place it and why?

EMBEDDED OUTCOME: S4.M7.7. Teach students how to independently use the GPS device properly and safely while locating caches.

Student Choices/Differentiation

- Most caches are small (about the size of an old film canister or D battery) and are difficult to find, but for this task, students should create larger cache and set waypoints closer than 50 feet (15 m) apart to make it easier for students who are struggling to find caches.
- Allow students who are excelling to be given waypoints set at 100 feet (30 m) apart to increase the challenge.

What to Look For

- Are students practicing safety as they navigate around the area?
- Are they compassionate toward one another, using good sportsmanship?

Note: Use the assessment rubric that follows.

Formal and Informal Assessments

- Assessment rubric
- Exit slips:
  - Test your knowledge of caching.
  - Which team's cache was the hardest to find today and why?
  - Which team's was the easiest?
  - How well did your group work together today?

Closure

- Can you see yourself geocaching in the future?
- What did you like about this activity? What did you not? Explain.
- What are some characteristics of good teammates while you participate and find caches?

Geocaching is gaining popularity, with caches being found all over the country and in parks. In our next class, we will explore some of the worldwide geocaching phenomena.

Reflection

- Do students understand geocaching?
- Can they set waypoints effectively?
- Is anyone falling behind or needing to be challenged?
- Are students enjoying the geocaching unit?
- Have teamwork skills improved during the unit?

Homework

Search the web to find an example of a cache in a park or another state.

Resources

Internet keyword search: "geocaching activities," "geocaching caches"

ASSESSMENT RUBRIC

Name: _____

	Yes	No
Understands how the GPS device works		
Understands how to use and implement the GPS		
Can create coordinates/waypoints using the GPS		
Can find an object using the GPS		
Collaborates and supports others during the lesson		

Using a GPS

Skill				
	Not present (1)	Emerging (2)	Maturing (3)	Applying (4)
Understands how the GPS device works				
Understands how to use and implement the GPS				
Can create coordinates/waypoints using the GPS				
Can find an object using the GPS				
Collaborates and supports others during the lesson				

Total student score: _____

From R.J. Doan, L.C. MacDonald, and S. Chepko, eds., 2017, *Lesson planning for middle school physical education* (Reston, VA: SHAPE America; Champaign, IL: Human Kinetics).

LESSON 7: TEAM TREASURE HUNT

Grade-Level Outcomes

Primary Outcome

Outdoor pursuits: Demonstrates correct technique for a variety of skills in 1 self-selected outdoor activity. (S1.M22.7)

Embedded Outcomes

Outdoor pursuits: Analyzes the situation and makes adjustments to ensure the safety of self and others. (S2.M13.7)

Health: Identifies positive mental and emotional aspects of participating in a variety of physical activities. (S5.M2.7)

Lesson Objectives

The learner will:

- work on developing an appreciation for geocaching through exploring geocaching websites and participating in geocaching activities.
- describe and apply the components of geocaching while participating in a team treasure hunt.

Equipment and Materials

- GPS trackers or devices with apps
- Computer or other device with web search capability
- Cache containers such as old film canisters or small plastic containers
- Cache items, such as coins, stickers, stamps, toy army men, brain teasers, jokes, or anything you can create

Introduction

Today, our goal is to gain a better understanding of geocaching and why so many people choose to participate in it. Geocaching is an international activity that uses GPS devices to help locate caches set out by others that often contain either a log to write who found it or an item to take with you. This is a great lifelong activity that encourages the use of both your mind and body.

Instructional Task: Geocaching Online

■ PRACTICE TASK

Students sign up for a free membership at geocaching.com and explore the world of geocaching. Have students complete the geocaching web search worksheet.

EMBEDDED OUTCOME: S5.M2.7 During the web search, ask students to identify positive mental and emotional aspects of geocaching.

Extension

Have students locate a cache within a 50-mile (80 km) radius of the school (if any exists) and show on Google maps where they think it's located.

Guiding questions for students:

- When involving others in your geocaching, it is important to be accurate. Why do you think that's so?
- If geocaching is not done correctly, what could happen?
- Why is geocaching difficult?
- What do caches usually look like?

Student Choices/Differentiation

Students can conduct an Internet search or scavenger hunt to answer questions that you have set out for them (as long as they follow school Internet rules).

What to Look For

- Are students engaged?
- Are students asking questions?
- Are students on task?

Instructional Task: Team Treasure Hunt

■ PRACTICE TASK

Set out caches around campus, and record their waypoints so that students will be able to enter them into the GPS devices.

Give students clues as to what type of caches they are looking for and what they might be found near. Other helpful hints can be placed in the caches to lead students to the next caches in a scavenger hunt type of activity.

Student groups must follow the clues to find each cache in the correct order.

Refinement

The caches may contain clues to locate something that is around campus but that is not in the GPS. Example: *If you look in the tree to your left, you will find the location of your next cache.* That way, students must find each cache and follow directions to find the next cache location.

EMBEDDED OUTCOME: S2.M13.7. Before students head out on their adventure, discuss with them how to analyze situations and make adjustments while on the hunt to ensure safety of self and others. For example, be sure that students keep their eyes and ears open for cars and other people, look out for animals as they travel through nature to avoid any negative interactions, and heed signs so that they don't trespass.

Student Choices/Differentiation

You could set out differently colored caches to vary the challenge level. Each color could signify a level of difficulty, and students can challenge themselves to find the higher-challenge caches as they go.

What to Look For

- Teams are working together.
- Are teams finding the caches on their own or are they following other teams?
- Is one team struggling with the GPS, teamwork, or sportsmanship?

Formal and Informal Assessments

Geocaching web search

Closure

Today you conducted research on geocaching to help you understand this growing sport. We will finish the module in our next class with an off-campus geocaching field trip. We will go to a local park, where you can locate several caches that were set out by geocachers other than us. Let's quickly review the rules and guidelines of taking an off-campus trip and geocaching.

- What are the benefits of geocaching, and how can this become a lifelong activity?
- Could you use geocaching as exercise? Do you feel it is good for your health?

Reflection

- Are students ready for the off-campus trip?
- Do they understand geocaching and are they starting to enjoy it?
- Are they safe both physically and emotionally while participating in class activities?
- Did they find the computer web search engaging?
- Do students understand the global aspect of geocaching and the large community that participates in the activity?
- Are the GPS units still in good working order for the next use?

Homework

Have students find a cache somewhere other than in their community. It can be near their out-of-town relatives, in the state capital, or even at an amusement park. Have students bring in the location coordinates of the caches that they've found.

Have students study the material on the school's physical education website for a quiz tomorrow.

Resources

Geocaching: www.geocaching.com

GEOCACHING WEB SEARCH

Name: _____ Date: _____

Go to geocaching.com and complete the following web search.

My username:

My password:

1. Define geocaching.

2. List the location of two caches that can be found near the school.

3. List two health benefits of geocaching.

4. Watch the video on tips and tricks of geocaching and list two of those tips and tricks.

5. How can someone have new geocaches published on the website?

6. What type of scale is used to note the difficulty of finding a cache?

7. What do caches usually look like?

8. List three different items that people may place in a cache.

9. List three rules of geocaching.

10. List two reasons why people geocache.

From R.J. Doan, L.C. MacDonald, and S. Chepko, eds., 2017, *Lesson planning for middle school physical education* (Reston, VA: SHAPE America; Champaign, IL: Human Kinetics).

LESSON 8: GEOCACHING FIELD TRIP

Grade-Level Outcomes

Primary Outcome

Outdoor pursuits: Demonstrates correct technique for a variety of skills in 1 self-selected outdoor activity. (S1.M22.7)

Embedded Outcome

Outdoor pursuits: Implements safe protocols in self-selected outdoor activities. (S2.M13.8)

Lesson Objectives

The learner will:

- apply general knowledge and critical-thinking skills to come up with plans for finding geocaches.
- explore ways in which geocaching can become a part of an active lifestyle.
- encourage others to participate in geocaching while on a field trip.

Equipment and Materials

- GPS trackers or devices with apps
- Camera

Introduction

Today, we will bring everything you've learned in our compass and geocaching module together in one final trip to track and find caches located in our community. It is important that you remember to be on your best behavior and represent both yourself and our school in a positive manner. Remember the rules of geocaching, and always stay with a buddy.

Instructional Task: Off-Site Geocaching

■ PRACTICE TASK

Students must find geocaches by using their geocaching.com login info, or you can set caches for them to find. Students must log the caches that they find and report to you about any they cannot find or any that were damaged or misplaced.

EMBEDDED OUTCOME: S2.M13.8 Remind students of the rules and guidelines that you discussed in previous lessons. Have students practice safe protocols while participating in the off-site geocaching activity.

Extensions

- Have the class place a geocache that will stay at the off-campus site so that they can share the location online and with friends and family.
- Have students take pictures with the caches to display.

Guiding questions for students:

- Do you feel as if you have made an impact by leaving your own class cache on site?
- Can geocaching be a healthy, positive activity?

Student Choices/Differentiation

Teams may work with other teams if they are still struggling with the GPS or with finding caches.

What to Look For

- Students are working together in a safe and positive way.
- They understand and respect the guidelines of geocaching.
- They are using their compasses and GPS correctly.

Instructional Task: Quiz and Reflection Assignment

■ PRACTICE TASK

Have students take the geocaching quiz.

Extension

Have students reflect on the module in writing. Students should address the following:

- Do you think you could teach someone else how to geocache?
- What would be the most difficult part and why?
- Do you think you might geocache in the future with either your family or friends? Why or why not?

Be sure to discuss with students how you will assess them on this assignment.

Student Choices/Differentiation

Have pictures or videos available to reinforce questions and answers.

What to Look For

See quiz and reflection rubric.

Formal and Informal Assessments

- Geocaching true or false quiz
- Reflection assignment

Closure

- Do you think geocaching could be a lifelong activity?
- Who thinks that he or she might geocache in the future?

Remember all the great benefits of geocaching, such as being physically active. I encourage you to try to use either geocaching or compass reading with your family.

Reflection

- Are students prepared and educated enough on geocaching to share it with others?
- What could you do differently the next time you teach this module? Anything to delete or add?
- Is there enough community participation in geocaching to support students' new hobby?
- How can geocaching be publicized in the community to further engage students?

Homework

Share what geocaching is with a parent or friend. Keep practicing geocaching in your free time!

Resources

Geocaching: www.geocaching.com

GEOCACHING QUIZ

Select true or false.

1.	Geocaching should always be done alone.	True	False
2.	When you find a cache, it is important to hide it in a new spot.	True	False
3.	You can hide caches on nature preserves and in national parks.	True	False
4.	If you take something out of a cache, you must replace it with something of equal value.	True	False
5.	If you can't find a cache, there is nothing you can do.	True	False
6.	Geocaching can be done with a free app on your phone.	True	False
7.	Caches range in size from very small to very large.	True	False
8.	Anyone can geocache.	True	False
9.	Waypoint is another name for a set location.	True	False
10.	Geocaches should be buried deep in the ground.	True	False
11.	GPS locations are always accurate.	True	False
12.	You should sign the log of any cache you find.	True	False

Geocaching Reflection

Do you think you could teach someone else how to geocache? What would be the most difficult part and why? Do you think you might geocache in the future with either your family or friends? Why or why not?

From R.J. Doan, L.C. MacDonald, and S. Chepko, eds., 2017, *Lesson planning for middle school physical education* (Reston, VA: SHAPE America; Champaign, IL: Human Kinetics).

GEOCACHING RUBRIC

	Not present (1)	Emerging (2)	Maturing (3)	Applying (4)
Follows directions and safety rules effectively throughout the lesson				
Understands how to use and implement the GPS				
Can create coordinates/ waypoints using the GPS				
Can find an object using the GPS				
Collaborates and supports others during the lesson				

Total student score: _____

From R.J. Doan, L.C. MacDonald, and S. Chepko, eds., 2017, *Lesson planning for middle school physical education* (Reston, VA: SHAPE America; Champaign, IL: Human Kinetics).

HIKING AND BACKPACKING MODULE

Lessons in this module were contributed by Erin Curran, assistant principal at Swofford Career Center in Inman, SC, and a certified physical education teacher.

Grade-Level Outcomes Addressed, by Lesson	Lessons							
	1	2	3	4	5	6	7	8
Standard 1. The physically literate individual demonstrates competency in a variety of motor skills and movement patterns.								
Demonstrates correct technique for basic skills in 1 self-selected outdoor activity. (S1.M22.6)	P	P				P		
Demonstrates correct technique for a variety of skills in 1 self-selected outdoor activity. (S1.M22.7)				P				P
Standard 2. The physically literate individual applies knowledge of concepts, principles, strategies and tactics related to movement and performance.								
Analyzes the situation and makes adjustments to ensure the safety of self and others. (S2.M13.7)				P		E	P	
Implements safe protocols in self-selected outdoor activities. (S2.M13.8)	P							
Standard 3. The physically literate individual demonstrates the knowledge and skills to achieve and maintain a health-enhancing level of physical activity and fitness.								
Sets and monitors a self-selected physical activity goal for aerobic and/or muscle- and bone-strengthening activity based on current fitness level. (S3.M8.6)						P		P
Uses available technology to self-monitor quantity of exercise needed for a minimal health standard and/or optimal functioning based on current fitness level. (S3.M8.8)						E		
Maintains a physical activity log for at least 2 weeks and reflects on activity levels as documented in the log. (S3.M16.6)	E							E
Develops strategies for balancing healthy food, snacks and water intake, along with physical activity. (S3.M17.7)	E							
Standard 4. The physically literate individual exhibits responsible personal and social behavior that respects self and others.								
Uses effective self-monitoring skills to incorporate opportunities for physical activity in and outside of school. (S4.M2.8)						P		
Demonstrates cooperation skills by establishing rules and guidelines for resolving conflicts. (S4.M4.7)			E				E	
Uses physical activity and fitness equipment appropriately and safely, *with the teacher's guidance.* (S4.M7.6)	E							
Standard 5. The physically literate individual recognizes the value of physical activity for health, enjoyment, challenge, self-expression and/or social interaction.								
Describes how being physically active leads to a healthy body. (S5.M1.6)					E			
Generates positive strategies such as offering suggestions or assistance, leading or following others and providing possible solutions when faced with a group challenge. (S5.M3.7)			E					
Identifies why self-selected physical activities create enjoyment. (S5.M4.7)				E				

P = Primary; E = Embedded

LESSON 1: INTRODUCTION TO HIKING

Grade-Level Outcomes

Primary Outcome

Outdoor pursuits: Implements safe protocols in self-selected outdoor activities. (S2.M13.8)

Embedded Outcomes

Nutrition: Develops strategies for balancing healthy food, snacks and water intake, along with physical activity. (S3.M17.7)

Safety: Uses physical activity and fitness equipment appropriately and safely, *with the teacher's guidance.* (S4.M7.6)

Assessment & program planning: Maintains a physical activity log for at least 2 weeks and reflects on activity levels as documented in the log. (S3.M16.6)

Lesson Objectives

The learner will:
- identify the baic rules of hiking safety.
- work toward building endurance in hiking.
- convert steps taken into distance covered and calories burned.

Equipment and Materials

- Handouts for each lap around track or trail
- Pedometers

Introduction

In this module, we will focus on the lifelong skills of hiking and backpacking. These are skills that you can use for day trips, overnight trips, and extended trips. Hiking and backpacking are also terrific family activities that you can pursue in almost any environment. Today, we're going to focus on hiking safety and the difference between hiking and backpacking, and we'll start to build up some endurance.

Instructional Task: Introduction to Hiking Safety

■ **PRACTICE TASK**

Pre-assessment

The difference between hiking and backpacking is merely the presence of a pack in backpacking. Divide yourselves into groups, and come up with rules that you think we might need to start our adventure.

Have groups share the rules that they come up with after some discussion time.

Make sure the following is covered:

- Have a buddy wherever you travel.
- Never listen to headphones so that you can hear your surroundings.
- Ensure that someone knows where you are going.
- Keep hands out of pockets so that you can use them if you fall.
- Drink plenty of water.

We will work to learn more as we go, but the skills of hiking and backpacking are as easy as walking. To hike and backpack to new and remote locations, however, we will need to work on endurance.

Extension

Use a PowerPoint presentation to show correct form and posture, or any other pointers that you would like to teach.

Student Choices/Differentiation

- Inexperienced students can watch video clips to learn what hiking and backpacking look like.
- Higher-skilled students may come up with some more advanced rules if they have backpacked or hiked before.

What to Look For

- Students are participating.
- Students know the basic rules to follow during the module.

Instructional Task:
Building Endurance by Gathering Something

■ PRACTICE TASK

Use a track or a nature trail, if available. Scout out a path that you would like students to follow. As they complete each trip around (a lap), students retrieve something to prove the amount of work they have done during the lesson. Be creative! For example, near Thanksgiving, they could earn feathers from a turkey.

Have students record the number of laps that they complete. This will help them set goals as they move through the module.

Extension

Have students determine how many calories they've burned, after calculating how much distance they've covered.

Guiding questions for students:

- How was your personal performance during this activity?
- What can you do to improve your performance the next time we hike?

EMBEDDED OUTCOME: S4. M7.6. Teach students how to use pedometers and why they should use them.

Student Choices/Differentiation

- Students choose their partners so that they move at an effective pace.
- Students may walk at a comfortable pace according to their skill level.

What to Look For

- Have any students chosen the wrong partners and are moving slower than they should?
- Are students moving and enjoying their hike?

Instructional Task: Distance Calculations

■ PRACTICE TASK

Measure the distance of the average student step. Calculate how many steps that students took, based on the distance they documented. Compare students' calculations with yours using a pedometer.

Extensions

- Calculate the number of calories burned over the distance covered to show students that even walking can be effective for burning calories.
- Have students document what they eat or how much water they consume for a week, then discuss the decisions they are making and how they could make healthier choices.

EMBEDDED OUTCOME: S3.M17.7 Use this task to generate discussion about strategies to balance food intake with physical activity.

Student Choices/Differentiation

- Have examples that students can view if they need help.
- Students can work with partners or in small groups.

What to Look For

- Students take personal responsibility for their movements and food and water intake by meeting the daily recommended guidelines.
- Students are making accurate calculations.

Instructional Task: Activity Logs

■ PRACTICE TASK

EMBEDDED OUTCOME: S3.M16.6 Throughout the module, have students keep a log of their physical activity outside of class.

Students can use pedometers, heart rate monitors, other technology, or physical activity estimates.

Student Choices/Differentiation

Students can use instruments that record physical activity.

What to Look For

Students are maintaining physical activity throughout the module.

Formal and Informal Assessments

- Rubric or score system for the items that students collected on their walk
- Pre-assessment on rules

Closure

- Why is it important to learn the techniques and rules for hiking and backpacking?
- What did you learn today?
- What are some of the safety rules we covered?

I hope that you learn to respect nature as well as love to walk for both exercise and health. Usually, people who backpack and hike are in great shape. Walking puts very little strain and stress on joints, and you can walk with anyone almost anywhere.

Reflection

- How well did students do on the pre-assessment?
- Were students excited or lethargic during the endurance activity?
- Did students use pedometers correctly?

Homework

Have students look up hiking opportunities in the local area and tell them to be prepared to discuss them in the next class. Students should log any physical activity outside of class.

Resources

Internet keyword search: "backpacking for beginners," "hiking for beginners"

LESSON 2: RECOGNIZING AND AVOIDING SAFETY THREATS WHILE HIKING

Grade-Level Outcomes

Primary Outcome

Outdoor pursuits: Demonstrates correct technique for basic skills in 1 self-selected outdoor activity. (S1.M22.6)

Embedded Outcome

Working with others: Demonstrate cooperation skills by establishing rules and guidelines for resolving conflicts. (S4.M4.7)

Lesson Objectives

The learner will:

- investigate safety threats while hiking and working respectfully with classmates.
- demonstrate appropriate pacing for different activities.
- maintain or increase endurance.

Equipment and Materials

- Cameras, tablets, smart phones, computers
- Heart rate or physical activity monitors

Introduction

Please share information about any of the hiking trails or places that you found during your homework. I will add these to the school's website to share with all students. Today, we will continue to work on our endurance, but we will start with some of the safety threats you might encounter while hiking in nature.

Instructional Task: Identify Safety Threats

■ PRACTICE TASK

Safety threats students might encounter while hiking and backpacking include but are not limited to the following:

- Poisonous plants
- Disease-carrying insects
- Poisonous snakes
- Predators
- Water parasites
- Extreme temperatures

Have each student create a PowerPoint slide on a hazard that can be found in your area while hiking or backpacking.

Students can use computers or the school's library to complete the task.

Extensions

- Students present their slides or combine them and have the teacher present them.
- Share the scoring rubric with students.

Refinement

Make sure that PowerPoint slides are appropriate (e.g., content relates to activity, students are not using material that is inappropriate for school).

Student Choices/Differentiation

Have notecards with topics ready in case students are not creative or can't think of appropriate topics.

What to Look For

- Pictures
- Three to five bulleted points about each safety threat
- Length of 3 to 5 minutes
- Any other facts or information students deem necessary

Instructional Task: Follow the Leader

■ PRACTICE TASK

The class walks in single file at the pace of the person in the front. The person from the rear has to pick up the pace and walk to the front and then lead the team until the next person comes from the rear and takes over the first position.

Students can walk around the track, through hallways, or around the campus while doing this.

Extension

Students use heart rate or physical activity monitors to track changes in intensity while walking to the front of the team.

Guiding questions for students:

- Who had the quickest pace?
- When you were leading the line, did you want to challenge the team or go easy on your classmates?
- What emotions did you experience?

EMBEDDED OUTCOME: S4.M4.7 Students might need a little help to complete the task as a team. Have students establish rules and guidelines to make sure they cooperate during the activity.

Student Choices/Differentiation

- Students get to choose what path the group walks and the pace if they are in the front, but they must follow the leader at other times.
- You may group students by ability (e.g., split them up into faster- and slower-paced groups) to ensure that everyone is challenged.

What to Look For

- Are all students practicing safe walking methods?
- Are they looking out for each other?
- Is the overall pace quick or slow?

Instructional Task: Slo-Mo Cool-Down

■ PRACTICE TASK

Have students walk in slow motion on the final lap, focusing on the correct walking form: heels hitting the ground first and rolling forward to the toes instead of hitting flat-footed.

Extension

Give students a slow time to shoot for so that they are forced not to rush. Example: "You must take the full 3 minutes to complete this task."

Refinement

Make sure that students are working on the critical elements of walking.

Guiding questions for students:
- Was it difficult to walk this slowly?
- Did you use your muscles more or less as you slowed your pace?

Student Choices/Differentiation

If using music, choose something with a slow tempo.

What to Look For
- Did students pace themselves?
- Are students using opposite arms and opposite legs?
- Are their core muscles tight to ensure correct body alignment?
- Are they using heel-to-toe steps and a proper walking gait?

Formal and Informal Assessments

Assess their PowerPoint slides using a rubric or checkpoints you asked students to cover.

Closure

As we continue our lessons in hiking and backpacking, we will continue to push ourselves in new and unique ways. Be sure to wear appropriate shoes and clothing so that you can enjoy the next day of the module.

Reflection
- Do you think the class is doing a good job of participating?
- Are students working harder than usual in this module? Or less?
- Is teamwork evident even when students walk in groups?

Homework

Teach a friend or neighbor at least one safe practice of hiking.

Resources

Backpacker: www.backpacker.com

REI Co-op: www.rei.com

Washington Trails Association: www.wta.org

PRESENTATION RUBRIC

Name: _____ Topic: _____ Date: _____

Excellent (4 pts)   Good (3 pts)   Average (2 pts)   Poor (1 pt)

1. Visual presentation
2. Length (3 to 5 minutes)
3. Presentation and public speaking
4. Topic covered effectively (three to five bulleted points)
5. Presenter well informed on the facts

From R.J. Doan, L.C. MacDonald, and S. Chepko, eds., 2017, *Lesson planning for middle school physical education* (Reston, VA: SHAPE America; Champaign, IL: Human Kinetics).

LESSON 3: NATURE HIKE

Grade-Level Outcomes

Primary Outcome

Outdoor pursuits: Demonstrates correct technique for basic skills in 1 self-selected outdoor activity. (S1.M22.6)

Embedded Outcome

Challenge: Generates positive strategies such as offering suggestions or assistance, leading or following others and providing possible solutions when faced with a group challenge. (S5.M3.7)

Lesson Objectives

The learner will:

- interpret scavenger hunt clues and develop a plan.
- cooperate with classmates to identify scavenger hunt items and document their location.
- learn how to pick out the correct hiking and backpacking equipment.

Equipment and Materials

- Scavenger hunt handouts
- Cameras or digital devices
- Computers

Introduction

Today, we will apply what we learned about the risks of hiking to complete a scavenger hunt safely. Please use your creativity and show me how exciting your adventure was through your photos.

Instructional Task: Nature Hike and Scavenger Hunt

■ PRACTICE TASK

Students pair up and search the school campus to find and photograph things to use in the scavenger hunt. Each pair's score depends on the number of useful items the partners find.

Let students choose odd things to look for on the scavenger hunt, using the handout as a guide.

At the end of the lesson, students load their pictures onto the computer and share them on the school's website.

Extension

Have students select their favorites (e.g., best picture, most creative picture, best critical-thinking solution to a scavenger hunt item).

Refinement

Make sure students are taking pictures of relevant clues by observing their actions or having them check in every 10 to 15 minutes to report what they have found.

EMBEDDED OUTCOME: S5.M3.7. Review with students what kind of strategies they used to find solutions for the scavenger hunt and how they decided on which to use.

Student Choices/Differentiation

Have pictures that show examples of potential items students could use.

What to Look For

- Are the groups staying together?
- Are students engaged?

Instructional Task:
Select Basic Equipment for Hiking and Backpacking

■ PRACTICE TASK

Hiking and backpacking equipment includes but is not limited to the following:

- Footwear
- Packs
- Clothing
- Sleeping bags and tents
- Food
- Other

Have each student research some or all of this equipment online. Internet-based videos are extremely helpful. Students should be finding different types of equipment and how to use them correctly. Students should create a PowerPoint of their findings.

Students can use computers or the school's library to complete the task.

Extensions

- Students present their research to the class.
- Share the scoring rubric with students.

Student Choices/Differentiation

- Have notecards with topics ready in case students are not creative or can't think of appropriate ways to use the equipment.
- Students can do an Internet search for hiking equipment, backpacking equipment, safe equipment on the trails, etc.

What to Look For

- Pictures
- Three to five bulleted points about each topic
- Length of 3 to 5 minutes
- Any other facts or information students deem necessary

Formal and Informal Assessments

- Grade based on number of items found in scavenger hunt
- Informal teacher observation or checklist to assess students' ability to follow directions and work with a partner
- Rating scale or rubric for equipment activity

Closure

- If you could work by yourself, do you think you would have done better or worse?
- What was your role in the partnership: to take pictures, to look for items, to be creative?
- Did you enjoy this lesson? What would you add to a future scavenger hunt?

Today we searched our surrounding area with scavenger hunt items in mind. These items distracted us at times from the amount of hiking we were doing. Were there any objects that were impossible to find? Did anyone find this object [hold one up]?

Reflection

- Were students working together in the lesson today?
- Did students enjoy searching for different types of equipment?
- Did students discuss meaningful strategies to use during the scavenger hunt?

Homework

Create a walking scavenger hunt around your home, and ask friends or family to try it out. Do not forget to log any physical activity outside of class.

Resources

Internet keyword search: "hiking equipment," "backpacking equipment," "safe equipment on the trails"

EQUIPMENT ACTIVITY RUBRIC

Name: _____ Topic: _____ Date: _____

Excellent (4 pts)   Good (3 pts)   Average (2 pts)   Poor (1 pt)

1. Visual presentation
2. Length (3 to 5 minutes)
3. Presentation and public speaking
4. Topic covered effectively (three to five bulleted points)
5. Presenter well informed on the facts

Photo Scavenger Hunt/Nature Hike

1. Something smooth
2. Something soft
3. A feather
4. Something blue
5. Something alive
6. Three-leaf clover
7. Something with more than four legs
8. Something that pollutes the trail
9. An animal print
10. A trash can
11. Something that makes a circle
12. A three-leaf plant
13. Something brittle
14. A tree bigger around than you
15. A leaf bigger than your face

16. Water
17. Dead tree
18. Moss
19. Something purple
20. A cloud that looks like something
21. A flower
22. Bark
23. Oddly colored leaf
24. Something that can be tied
25. A student who blends into the surroundings
26. Something white
27. A spider web
28. Something that looks like a Y
29. Something hairy
30. Something dangerous to hikers

From R.J. Doan, L.C. MacDonald, and S. Chepko, eds., 2017, *Lesson planning for middle school physical education* (Reston, VA: SHAPE America; Champaign, IL: Human Kinetics).

LESSON 4: FOLLOWING PROCEDURES TO HAVE FUN AND STAY SAFE

Grade-Level Outcomes

Primary Outcome

Outdoor pursuits: Analyzes the situation and makes adjustments to ensure the safety of self and others. (S2.M13.7)

Embedded Outcome

Self-expression & enjoyment: Identifies why self-selected physical activities create enjoyment. (S5.M4.7)

Lesson Objectives

The learner will:

- demonstrate understanding and recognition of signs and symptoms of dehydration.
- demonstrate recognition of the need for leave-no-trace practices and the impact it has on the environment.
- reflect on the enjoyment experienced during a nature walk.

Equipment and Materials

- Paper and pencils
- Cameras, phones, tablets, computers
- Pedometers or heart rate monitors

Introduction

So far, we have learned some of the dangers of hiking, learned what equipment we need for hiking and backpacking, completed a nature scavenger hunt, and built up our endurance for long hikes. Today, we will learn more about the proper procedures for hiking and exploring the woods.

Instructional Task: Leave No Trace

■ PRACTICE TASK

Teach a lesson on leave-no-trace (LNT) trail etiquette and its importance.
Have students explore the website Leave No Trace (www.lnt.org).
Students should research

- what LNT is,
- how they can get involved, and
- quick concepts and plans for learning the LNT principles.

Extension

Have students draw a trailhead sign explaining the LNT trail motto to other hikers.

Guiding questions for students:

- Why do you think it's important to be self-officiating when outdoors?
- Why are there common rules for hiking?
- Do you feel they are important?

Student Choices/Differentiation

Students may work individually, with partners, or in small groups.

What to Look For

- Students are appropriately researching the topic.
- Student understand the basic LNT principles.

Instructional Task: Importance of Hydration

■ PRACTICE TASK

Teach a lesson on water intake and the lifesaving facts students should know.

Assign students a hydration fact that they must further research:

- What are the signs and symptoms of dehydration?
- What should you drink to best re-hydrate?
- How does age affect hydration?
- How much water does your body contain? How much does it lose during a day?
- How quickly can dehydration take effect?
- What are the effects of overhydration?

Have students present their findings to the class while you ensure factual correctness.

Extension

- Have students write down a time when they felt dehydrated and what symptoms they experienced.
- Students can draw a picture that demonstrates the importance of water.

Guiding questions for students:

- Can dehydration happen to anyone?
- Are some people more at risk than others?
- What can we do to avoid this risk?

Student Choices/Differentiation

Have examples of the content that you can share with students in case they are having a difficult time with the research.

What to Look For

Students are able to describe three or four facts on their assigned topics.

Instructional Task: Nature Hike Around Campus

■ PRACTICE TASK

Lead the students in a hike around the school grounds, demonstrating a good pace and how exploring their school surroundings can be fun. If this is not an option, pick a local park or even the hallways of the school for this activity.

Extensions

- Have students take pictures of plants and animals they encounter and then research more details about these species. This may be a good opportunity to work with the biology or science teacher to integrate content.
- Students could break off into groups and have self-led exploration hikes. Larger groups would be best for teacher observation.

Guiding questions for students:

- Why is it important to learn to hike safely and effectively?
- How many people did we pass?
- Draw a picture of the path you took.

EMBEDDED OUTCOME: S5.M4.7 This is an opportunity to have a discussion with students about the role of nature in creating enjoyable physical activity experiences. Students can also write a reflection about how nature impacts their hiking experience.

Student Choices/Differentiation

Parent volunteers may allow for smaller groups and different walking paces.

What to Look For

Ask questions about the hike to check understanding and involvement.

Formal and Informal Assessments

- Rubric or checklist for research tasks
- Exit slip: Explain in your own words what "leave no trace" means. How will you practice this over the next few lessons?

Closure

Tomorrow's challenge is distance, so we will be preparing for a long hike.

You learned the importance of hydration today, so I urge you to come well hydrated and bring a water bottle with you.

Reflection

- Do students understand the importance of hydration?
- Do they understand the concept of leave no trace?
- Are they holding each other accountable while hiking and looking out for group members?

Homework

Write a reflection about how you stay hydrated; include how much water you drink in an average day. Also include what you could do to better hydrate yourself or perhaps signs of dehydration you can observe within yourself.

Resources

Louv, R. (2008). *Last child in the woods: Saving our children from nature-deficit disorder*. Chapel Hill, NC: Algonquin Books.

Leave No Trace: www.lnt.org

Internet keyword search: "dehydration," "drinking water safely while outdoors"

LESSON 5: DISTANCE CHALLENGE

Grade-Level Outcomes

Primary Outcomes

Outdoor pursuits: Demonstrates correct technique for a variety of skills in 1 self-selected outdoor activity. (S1.M22.7)

Fitness knowledge: Sets and monitors a self-selected physical activity goal for aerobic and/or muscle- and bone-strengthening activity based on current fitness level. (S3.M8.6)

Embedded Outcome

Health: Describes how being physically active leads to a healthy body. (S5.M1.6)

Lesson Objectives

The learner will:

- demonstrate recognition of the need for healthy activity and choose to complete the distance challenge.
- formulate a plan for accumulating the most steps or greatest distance during the distance challenge.
- set two or three fitness goals for increasing endurance while backpacking and hiking.

Equipment and Materials

Pedometers or tool/app to track distances

Introduction

Have students turn in their reflections from their homework. Invite students to share thoughts from their reflections.

Today is distance day! Each of you will compete for the greatest distance traveled today!

Instructional Task: Distance Challenge

■ PRACTICE TASK

Use pedometers or counting of laps around the school campus, local park, or track to calculate distance traveled in one class period. Students total their lap counts and reflect on how far they walked.

Classes can compete for the total number of laps completed. Ensure that students are being honest in counting laps through either tallies or collecting an item on each lap to prevent cheating.

Extensions

- Students use baseline scores to set a goal for the end of the module.
- Students discuss and implement a plan to improve their steps or distance traveled.

Guiding questions for students:

Where do you think we could have traveled to if we added all of the class's distance together? Next town, rival school, state capital?

EMBEDDED OUTCOME: S5.M1.6. Discuss with students how being physically active (hiking and backpacking) leads to a healthy body.

Guiding questions for students:

- What type of fitness does this activity build?
- What are the major muscles you used during this lesson?
- If we were backpacking on a trail in the mountains, how would it change the muscles you use?

Student Choices/Differentiation

Students can choose the pace in which they wish to travel, but pacing will be important to maintain their speed.

What to Look For

- How far did students travel?
- Did students show strong work ethic and effort throughout the class period?
- Have students complete the rubric.

Instructional Task: Setting Fitness Goals

■ PRACTICE TASK

Discuss with students proper goal setting for fitness goals related to hiking and backpacking.

Guiding questions for students:

- Why is it important to set realistic fitness goals for hiking and backpacking?
- What can you do to set more realistic goals?
- What are ways to improve your fitness to achieve your goals and make new goals?
- How will you monitor these goals?

Extension

Have students write two or three fitness goals related to hiking and backpacking.

Refinement

Make sure goals are realistic and measureable.

Student Choices/Differentiation

Have examples of realistic and measureable goals.

What to Look For

Make sure goals

- can be reached in a reasonable amount of time,
- are measurable, and
- are related to hiking and backpacking.

Formal and Informal Assessments

Student participation rubric

Closure

- Do you feel more prepared for hiking?
- Did the distance challenge encourage you to test yourself and put more effort into your workout?

Tomorrow, we will discuss what you should take on a backpacking trip. Be prepared, and think about the things you can't live without.

Reflection

- Are students motivated by class competition?
- Are all students writing measurable goals?
- Do students understand the role of backpacking and hiking with regard to physical activity and being healthy?

Homework

Make a list of the items you think are critical for a weekend backpacking trip and bring it to the next class. Do not forget to log any physical activity outside of class.

Resources

The Walking Site: www.thewalkingsite.com

STUDENT PARTICIPATION RUBRIC

Student name: _____

Numbe of laps/distance traveled: _____

Effort: _____

      1: Student put forth little effort.

      2: Student exerted some effort.

      3: Student exerted considerable effort.

Cooperation and attitude: _____

      1: Student exhibited poor cooperation and attitude during activity.

      2: Student exhibited good cooperation and attitude during the activity.

      3. Student exhibited excellent cooperation and attitude during the activity.

From R.J. Doan, L.C. MacDonald, and S. Chepko, eds., 2017, *Lesson planning for middle school physical education* (Reston, VA: SHAPE America; Champaign, IL: Human Kinetics).

LESSON 6: BACKPACKING 101

Grade-Level Outcomes

Primary Outcome

Personal responsibility: Uses effective self-monitoring skills to incorporate opportunities for physical activity in and outside of school. (S4.M2.8)

Embedded Outcomes

Outdoor pursuits: Analyzes the situation and makes adjustments to ensure the safety of self and others. (S2.M13.7)

Fitness knowledge: Uses available technology to self-monitor quantity of exercise needed for a minimal health standard and/or optimal functioning based on current fitness level. (S3.M8.8)

Lesson Objectives

The learner will:

- identify four items a knowledgeable and prepared hiker should pack before leaving for a trip.
- demonstrate the ability to perform parkour activities and challenges alongside classmates.

Equipment and Materials

Flash cards or PowerPoint slides

Introduction

Yesterday's challenge was distance, but today we'll focus on learning about what and how to pack for a trip and the obstacles you may face during a hike.

For homework, you were to find critical items for a weekend backpacking trip. Let's use those items in the first activity.

Instructional Task: Packing for the Trip

■ PRACTICE TASK

Help students understand what they should take with them on both a hiking trip and a backpacking trip.

Have students come up with two things they need to take and one they should not to present to the class (e.g., tent, backpack, fire starter, shovel, knife, sleeping bag, sleeping pad, good shoes, clothing, soap and toiletry items, flashlight, food, and anything else they come up with).

Extension

Let students choose to present something they either should or should not bring on a hiking trip or one of each to the group.

Guiding questions for students:

- Did any groups present an item you hadn't thought about taking?
- Can anyone think of other items that we would need?
- What are a few items that you think people pack that they don't need?

Student Choices/Differentiation

- Make flash cards or PowerPoint slides to help students with items they both should and shouldn't take on the trip.
- Challenge more knowledgeable students to plan for hypothetical extreme conditions (e.g., weather, more difficult trails).

What to Look For

- Use a rubric to look at research done, whether the topic was covered effectively, and if the presenter was well informed.
- Do students understand the equipment needs? Are they bringing enough to be successful? Are they bringing things they don't need?

Instructional Task: Parkour Walking With Teacher

■ PRACTICE TASK

Students follow you around and over obstacles as you perform exercises around the campus or school. Try some of the following, but feel free to create your own:

- Lunges up the stairs
- Wall sits
- Box jumps on curbs
- Maneuver over or under railings
- Vaults over benches
- Push-ups on a bench
- Pretend rope jumping

EMBEDDED OUTCOME: S3.M8.8. Use this activity to review the physical activity standards and how parkour can help meet them.

Extensions

- Let students create new obstacles or split into small groups to create a route for the rest of the class to enjoy.
- Have students take their heart rates or use heart rate monitors to gauge the intensity of the activities.

Refinements

- Ensure students' knees do not go over their toes when they are lunging.
- Ensure students are using the proper technique when they do squats, push-ups, jumps and landings, or any other skill in their course.

EMBEDDED OUTCOME: S2.M13.7. Have students analyze the challenges and tricks that they came up with and find safety concerns or modifications to ensure safety for all participants.

Student Choices/Differentiation

- Students can watch a video clip (search "parkour for kids") to help them understand the activity.
- Challenge students to try new challenges and tricks (within limits of safety).

What to Look For

- Are students participating and committed to their task?
- Are students trying each obstacle?
- Are they staying together as a group?
- Did students create two or three obstacles during their adventure?

Formal and Informal Assessments

Exit slip: Have students draw a parkour route they would lead the rest of the class on. The route should include at least four obstacles or exercises.

Closure

- Explain what parkour is.
- Why do you think so many people are joining the parkour movement?

Reflection

- Did students enjoy parkour?
- Did any students need extensions or refinements to ensure their full participation?

Homework

Find a parkour clip online and describe why you like it. Be sure to give me both the website and your brief write-up. We will watch some of the best videos at the beginning of our next class.

Resources

American Parkour: www.americanparkour.com

LESSON 7: PLANNING YOUR TRIP

Grade-Level Outcomes

Primary Outcomes

Outdoor pursuits: Analyzes the situation and makes adjustments to ensure the safety of self and others. (S2.M13.7)

Outdoor pursuits: Demonstrates correct technique for basic skills in 1 self-selected outdoor activity. (S1.M22.6)

Embedded Outcome

Working with others: Demonstrates cooperation skills by establishing rules and guidelines for resolving conflicts. (S4.M4.7)

Lesson Objectives

The learner will:

- create a backpacking trip plan.
- discuss and create a severe-weather backpacking story.

Equipment and Materials

Computers

Introduction

Who would like to share the parkour video that you found for homework? Today you are going to learn how to plan a hiking trip. Planning a trip is very important because there usually is not a convenience store for miles. So don't forget your toothbrush!

Instructional Task: Exploration Hiking

■ PRACTICE TASK

Your task today is to plan a backpacking trip. In groups and using the Internet, please research the following:

- *Where will you go?*
- *How long will the trip be?*
- *How many miles will you hike?*
- *What will you eat?*

Students form groups of four and plan a trip together, discussing the research topics as well as job duties of each member on the trip.

You will present your findings to the class in a 5-minute presentation that must include all of your group members.

Extension

Share with students the rubric for the assignment.

Guiding questions for students:

- How did you choose where you would go?
- What types of food did you decide to take? Why?
- Who will carry what equipment in the group? Did you share the load, or does each person have his own?

EMBEDDED OUTCOME: S4.M4.7. Before the activity, discuss ways to establish rules or guidelines for resolving any conflicts that might come up as the group works.

Student Choices/Differentiation

- Students may work by themselves or with a partner.
- Have examples of each research area for students having a difficult time explaining their topics or planning their trip.
- Challenge students to plan a trip according to the comfort level of their own hiking and backpacking skills.

What to Look For

- Are students taking this task seriously?
- Are they discussing food and other prep areas for their trip?
- Are they working well as a group?

Instructional Task: Severe Weather

■ PRACTICE TASK

Share with students a story of when you were caught in a weather-related situation.

Guiding questions for students:

- What problems did the weather cause for the backpackers or hikers?
- What would you do in this situation?
- Was there a way to prevent this from happening?

In partners, students create a severe-weather backpacking story, making sure to discuss things the campers should focus on with regard to weather.

Extension

Have students share their stories with the class.

Student Choices/Differentiation

- Students may work by themselves or with a partner.
- Have examples within each research area for students having a difficult time coming up with ideas to explore.

What to Look For

- Are students taking this task seriously?
- Are they discussing food and other prep areas for their trip that can be affected by weather conditions?
- Are they working well as a group?

Formal and Informal Assessments

- Students' backpacking plans
- Teacher-designed rubric or checklist

Closure

- If we left for your planned trips tomorrow, would you be prepared?
- Do you think you would be successful on the trip you planned?
- What if something came up and you had to stay an extra two days. Are you still prepared?

Always be sure to prepare for anything, and use proper backpacking techniques and safety procedures.

Reflection

- Did students go into as much detail as expected?
- Could you take their plans and survive a trip? What's missing that doesn't allow you to do so?

Homework

Discuss your backpacking plan with a friend or relative. Share the things that you would bring and things you would not want to bring on the trip. Do not forget to log any physical activity outside of class. Turn them in next class.

Study for the end-of-module assessment.

Resources

Back Country: www.backcountry.com

Internet keyword search: "packing for a backpacking trip," "how weather conditions affect what to pack for backpacking trips"

LESSON 8:
DISTANCE CHALLENGE WRAP-UP

Grade-Level Outcomes

Primary Outcomes

Outdoor pursuits: Demonstrates correct technique for a variety of skills in 1 self-selected outdoor activity. (S1.M22.7)

Fitness knowledge: Sets and monitors a self-selected physical activity goal for aerobic and/or muscle- and bone-strengthening activity based on current fitness level. (S3.M8.6)

Embedded Outcome

Assessment & program planning: Maintains a physical activity log for at least 2 weeks and reflects on activity levels as documented in the log. (S3.M16.6)

Lesson Objectives

The learner will:
- revisit the distance challenge from previous classes.
- demonstrate knowledge of backpacking and hiking with an end-of-module assessment.

Equipment and Materials
- Pencils and paper
- Physical activity tracking devices

Introduction

For homework, you were supposed to share what you included and what you did not include in your backpacking plan. Did anyone have something they wanted to share from their talks with a relative? Today we are going to finish the module by revisiting the distance challenge we previously completed. Let's see if the fitness activities and goals that we created helped!

Instructional Task: Revisiting the Distance Challenge

■ PRACTICE TASK

In previous lessons students completed a distance challenge and developed realistic fitness goals. Review the scores and goals.

Guiding questions for students:
- Do you think your scores will improve? Why or why not?
- Do you think the goals helped? Why or why not?

Have the class set a class goal for their distance based on their previous data.

Use pedometers or counting of laps around the school campus, a local park, or a track to calculate ultimate distance traveled in one class period. Students total their lap counts and reflect on how far they walked.

Classes can compete for the total number of laps done. Ensure students are being honest in counting laps through either tallies or collecting an item on each lap to prevent cheating.

Extension

Discuss the results with students.

Guiding questions for students:
- Are you happy with the results?
- What are ways to improve your scores?

- How would you modify your goals?
- Do you think you can endure the backpacking trip that you planned in the previous class with your current fitness levels?

Student Choices/Differentiation

Have class totals (not individual) scores posted on schools website.

What to Look For

- Do students understand the importance of attainable goals?
- Are students working to their full potentials?

Instructional Task:
Module Test and Reflection Assignment

■ PRACTICE TASK

Have students take the module test.

Extension

Students turn in their activity logs.

EMBEDDED OUTCOME: S3.M16.6. Have students reflect on the activity logs that they have kept throughout the module.

Guiding questions for students:

- Are you surprised by your activity over the module?
- What were barriers to participating in physical activity?
- What are strategies to overcome the barriers?

Student Choices/Differentiation

Have a list of strategies to provide if needed.

What to Look For

- Students participated in the assessments.
- Students included aerobic activities that will improve endurance.

Formal and Informal Assessments

- Module test
- Reflection assignment

Closure

Throughout this module you learned about hiking and backpacking. I encourage you to continue your activity logs and strive to achieve your goals to improve endurance and stamina. Remember, backpacking and hiking are great family activities. Hopefully you and your family can participate in them soon!

Reflection

- What was your favorite part of this module?
- Do you believe students are prepared for a hiking trip?

Homework

Review material for the next module.

Resources

Internet keyword search: "goal setting," "activity logs," "backpacking," "hiking"

MODULE TEST

Be sure to read all questions carefully and answer to the best of your ability.

1. Walking helps to improve the physiological function of the
   a. heart
   b. lungs
   c. nervous system
   d. all of the above

2. If you are exercising less than 60 minutes, then the best option for hydration is
   a. water
   b. Kool-Aid
   c. Gatorade
   d. juice

3. When walking you should
   a. walk alone
   b. wear headphones
   c. wear dark colors
   d. walk with traffic flow
   e. none of the above

4. On an average day, your body loses approximately how many liters of water?
   a. 2
   b. 2.5
   c. 4
   d. 3

5. Your brain is made up of what percentage of water?
   a. 50%
   b. 60%
   c. 75%
   d. 85%

6. The Surgeon General says you should exercise
   a. once a week for 90 minutes
   b. three times a week for 20 minutes
   c. seven times a week for 10 minutes
   d. all day every day

7. Dehydration can occur in
   a. extreme heat
   b. extreme cold
   c. on any average day
   d. all of the above

8. Can you overhydrate yourself?
   a. yes
   b. no

9. Which is not a good walking surface?
   a. grass
   b. pavement
   c. gravel
   d. extremely uneven rocky surface

10. Who is at the greatest risk of dehydration?
    a. young children
    b. older adults
    c. average people
    d. everyone

11. List two of the walking safety steps we covered in class.
    a. _____
    b. _____

12. Do you think you lead a more active lifestyle now than you did at the beginning of the unit? Have you seen any benefits of the walking program?

    _____
    _____
    _____
    _____
    _____
    _____
    _____
    _____

ADVENTURE ACTIVITIES MODULE

Lessons in this module were contributed by Erin Curran, assistant principal at Swofford Career Center in Inman, SC, and a certified physical education teacher.

Grade-Level Outcomes Addressed, by Lesson	Lessons							
	1	2	3	4	5	6	7	8
Standard 1. The physically literate individual demonstrates competency in a variety of motor skills and movement patterns.								
Demonstrates correct technique for a variety of skills in 1 self-selected outdoor activity. (S1.M22.7)								P
Standard 2. The physically literate individual applies knowledge of concepts, principles, strategies and tactics related to movement and performance.								
Analyzes the situation and makes adjustments to ensure the safety of self and others. (S2.M13.7)							E	P
Standard 3. The physically literate individual demonstrates the knowledge and skills to achieve and maintain a health-enhancing level of physical activity and fitness.								
Uses available technology to self-monitor quantity of exercise needed for a minimal health standard and/or optimal functioning based on current fitness level. (S3.M8.8)							E	
Standard 4. The physically literate individual exhibits responsible personal and social behavior that respects self and others.								
Exhibits responsible social behaviors by cooperating with classmates, demonstrating inclusive behaviors and supporting classmates. (S4.M1.7)						E		
Provides corrective feedback to a peer, using teacher-generated guidelines, and incorporating appropriate tone and other communication skills. (S4.M3.7)				E				
Accepts differences among classmates in physical development, maturation and varying skill levels by providing encouragement and positive feedback. (S4.M4.6)	E							
Demonstrates cooperation skills by establishing rules and guidelines for resolving conflicts. (S4.M4.7)		E						
Responds appropriately to participants' ethical and unethical behavior during physical activity by using rules and guidelines for resolving conflicts. (S4.M4.8)			E					
Problem-solves with a small group of classmates during adventure activities, small-group initiatives or game play. (S4.M5.7)		E	P	P	P		P	
Cooperates with multiple classmates on problem-solving initiatives including adventure activities, large-group initiatives and game play. (S4.M5.8)	P	P	P					
Standard 5. The physically literate individual recognizes the value of physical activity for health, enjoyment, challenge, self-expression and/or social interaction.								
Identifies positive mental and emotional aspects of participating in a variety of physical activities. (S5.M2.7)					E			
Generates positive strategies such as offering suggestions or assistance, leading or following others and providing possible solutions when faced with a group challenge. (S5.M3.7)						P	P	
Demonstrates the importance of social interaction by helping and encouraging others, avoiding trash talk and providing support to classmates. (S5.M6.7)							E	
Demonstrates respect for self by asking for help and helping others in various physical activities. (S5.M6.8)								E

P = Primary; E = Embedded

LESSON 1:
SAFETY AND WORKING TOGETHER 101

Grade-Level Outcomes

Primary Outcome

Working with others: Cooperates with multiple classmates on problem-solving initiatives including adventure activities, large-group initiatives and game play. (S4.M5.8)

Embedded Outcome

Working with others: Accepts differences among classmates in physical development, maturation and varying skill levels by providing encouragement and positive feedback. (S4.M4.6)

Lesson Objective

The learner will cooperate with peers during the different adventure activities in the lesson.

Equipment and Materials

Poly spots or dots

Introduction

Today, we start our adventure activities module. We will start with small challenges and work our way up to larger, more difficult challenges. Throughout this module, you will be expected to work with classmates, to communicate effectively, and to always focus on safety.

Instructional Task:
Explain Expectations and Safety Guidelines

■ PRACTICE TASK

Safety is our top priority during this module.

We will follow the hand contract.

- *Pinky = safety (because it's the weakest finger)*
- *Ring = commitment to ourselves and our task*
- *Middle = anger; we should not bring each other down*
- *Pointer = direction for both you and the group*
- *Thumb = thumb's up or positive interaction*

For more information, perform an Internet search for "team building activity hand contract."

Student Choices/Differentiation

Visual aid if needed

What to Look For

Students are taking the task seriously and understand the importance of respecting the hand contract.

Instructional Task: Scar Story

■ PRACTICE TASK

Students form a circle and share stories about injuries they've sustained or a scar they have from an injury. Every student will have the opportunity to share.

Discuss with students that we all have scars, and it is important to remember as we go throughout this module and the rest of the school year that no one is perfect. We all make mistakes, and we all have scars to remind us of this. We need to accept differences and provide encouragement.

Student Choices/Differentiation

Have a couple of scar stories to share if students are not willing to share theirs.

Students may tell a scar story about someone else if they don't feel comfortable talking about themselves.

What to Look For

Students are participating and willing to engage and share with the group.

Instructional Task: People to People

■ PRACTICE TASK

Students pair up in a small area. Any student without a partner will lead. (If there is an even number of students, you will need to play.)

The leader announces appropriate body parts that the partners will "glue" together (e.g., hand to hand, elbow to shoulder). Partners work together. After a few pairings, the leader announces "people to people," whereupon everyone finds a new partner, including the leader. The next person left without a partner then takes over as leader.

Refinement

Point out and discuss with the class when you see groups who are making tasks look easy by problem solving.

Guiding questions for students:

- What do you think this activity was supposed to teach you?
- Did it matter who your partner was?
- Did you find yourself working with others to scout out your next spot?

Verbal, non-verbal, and physical communication plays an important role in every task we do.

Student Choices/Differentiation

- Challenge students to find a partner who is farthest away.
- Challenge students to find someone who is least or more like themselves.
- Students perform the commands with eyes closed (making sure to open them when the leader calls people to people).

What to Look For

- Student participation
- Cliques that may form
- How students communicate
- Student behavior and attitudes

Ensure that pairs are participating, switching, and not repeating the same partners.

Instructional Task: Group Machine

■ PRACTICE TASK

Students work in assigned teams to create a moving machine.

Each student has to play an active role, and the machine must have sound.

The teacher assigns the type of machine to each group.

Example: Students work together to become a ceiling fan, with someone being the pull string and four people the fan blades, who move around while making a whirring noise.

Extension

Students choose the type of machine they create.

Refinement

Make sure students are participating safely.

Guiding questions for students:

- How did you decide who would play each part of the machine?
- Was anyone in your group taking charge?
- What examples can you give of your group cooperating?

Student Choices/Differentiation

- Students get to choose the objects they become (easy or more difficult).
- The size of the class or groups could be changed to make the challenge harder or easier.
- Provide picture examples if needed.

What to Look For

Are students

- working together?
- playing equal roles?
- stepping into a leadership role?
- falling behind?

Instructional Task: I'll Bet You've Never . . .

■ PRACTICE TASK

Students stand on poly spots in a large circle with ample room between them. One student (or you) is in the middle and says the leading phrase, "I'll bet you've never . . ." Those who have done the activity (including the person in the middle) must find a new dot. Students who have not done the activity must stand where they are.

Someone new is left in the middle to ask the next question.

Rules

1. Students may not move to the dot next to them.
2. Students may not move to the same-color dot they are currently standing on if different colors are available.
3. The content should be school-appropriate.

Refinement

It is important that students ask creative questions and not boring questions such as "I'll bet you've never worn shoes." Re-direct students if the questions are too simplistic.

Student Choices/Differentiation

Lead students into fun, informative questions by giving examples such as "I'll bet you've never eaten alligator, had a pet duck, ridden in a helicopter, tripped and fallen while trying to look cool, or dropped your cell phone in the toilet." The more creative the leadingstatement, the more fun the game is. (Remember that the person in the middle must have completed the activity, though.)

What to Look For
- Ensure that the game doesn't get rough and that students are respectful of one another's space.
- Listen and learn new things about students that you can respond to and may be able to use later.

Formal and Informal Assessments
- Informal assessment during scar activity
- Exit slips:
  - Have students define the hand contract in their own words and what it means for them and their classmates.
  - Have students write one thing they learned about someone else in the class.

Closure
- What are three things we worked on today?
- What could the group do better next time?

Next class, we will continue our adventure activities, so be prepared to work together, problem-solve, and communicate.

Reflection
- How did students work together?
- What are their strengths and weaknesses?
- Do any students need assistance or need activities modified to ensure success?
- Do any students need to be redirected or watched for bullying or negative behaviors?

Homework
Come up with the top five characteristics of a good team member, and be ready to discuss them with the class.

Resources
Curran, E. (2011). Activities and initiatives. *Swofford challenge course manual.* 2nd ed., vol. 1, 19-64. Inman, SC.

Internet keyword search: "team-building hand team contract"

LESSON 2:
COOPERATION AND TEAM BUILDING

Grade-Level Outcomes

Primary Outcome

Working with others: Cooperates with multiple classmates on problem-solving initiatives including adventure activities, large-group initiatives and game play. (S4.M5.8)

Embedded Outcomes

Working with others: Demonstrates cooperation skills by establishing rules and guidelines for resolving conflicts. (S4.M4.7)

Working with others: Problem-solves with a small group of classmates during adventure activities, small-group initiatives or game play. (S4.M5.7)

Lesson Objectives

The learner will:

- work on communication and focused listening skills through basic icebreaker activities.
- cooperate and collaborate to solve problems in the initiatives.

Equipment and Materials

- Poly spots or place markers: 1 per person
- Index cards numbered 1 to the number of students in class (or more)
- Coffee can
- Tennis ball

Introduction

Today, we will continue our adventure activities module. Who can tell me what we did last class? Who is willing to share some of the characteristics of being a good team member from your homework? Why do you think it is important for you to focus on something like team building? Today we will continue to work on cooperation and team-building skills. The challenges will get a little harder. Be ready, use critical thinking, and work together.

Instructional Task: I-So-Ko

■ PRACTICE TASK

Students form a circle, elbow-width apart. Students must conquer three motions and words to understand the game.

1. I: Student brings either arm horizontally across the chest, pointing to the person next to him.
2. So: Student brings either arm above the head and points to the student next to her.
3. Ko: Student places palms together in a spear-like manner and points to anyone in the circle.

The motions must always go in the I-So-Ko order, so "I" points to someone, who must respond with "So" and point to someone, and that person must respond with "Ko" and point to someone else. That person responds with "I" again, and the pattern continues. The students must say the words aloud.

As the game begins, students can get eliminated for the following:

- Going in the wrong order or doing the wrong motion
- Not knowing it's their turn
- Making up their own motion
- Taking too long to respond

Students eliminated become respectful distractors for those still playing.

Guiding questions for students:
- What do you think this activity was supposed to teach you? (Answer: focus)
- Was the game harder or easier when the distractors showed up?
- Did anyone know what was next but couldn't get it out?
- As humans, we rarely get to focus on just one thing. We have a lot of distractions in our lives that can lead to mistakes. Can anyone share a life distractor?

Extension

The students can stop saying the actions and just perform the hand motions.

EMBEDDED OUTCOME: S4.M4.7 As a class, come up with a couple of rules to make sure students are being "respectful distractors" when they are eliminated from the game. For example, students must follow all school rules, and distractors cannot enter the circle, touch the players, or yell in their ears.

Student Choices/Differentiation
- Students first practice the hand motions and words.
- Students can step out of the game setting to practice if needed.

What to Look For
- Are the distractors communicating and cooperating with one another to be more effective?
- Are students focused on the task or trying to get eliminated to become a distractor?

Instructional Task: Silent Lineup

■ PRACTICE TASK

Students must line up according to the number they have drawn. Each student must navigate into the correct order without any type of verbal communication.

Don't assign all sequential numbers (e.g., use 1, 2, 5, 6, 8, 10). That will ensure that students are solving the problem and not just trying to slide into an order.

Extension

Play the game with birthdays, favorite colors, and so on.

Student Choices/Differentiation

Students may take 5 to 10 seconds to talk, if needed.

What to Look For
- What other types of communication surface?
- Are students better or worse at this activity because they can't speak?

Instructional Task: Warp Speed

■ PRACTICE TASK

We are trying to shoot this tennis ball into warp speed. To do that, each of you must touch the ball to transfer your energy as fast as you can. The goal is to pass the ball to each group member faster than other groups. The clock starts when the first person touches the tennis ball and ends when the last person touches it. For your powers to rub off, you must have full contact with the tennis ball and not just place a finger on it.

Extension

Have groups set a time goal for how fast they can complete the task.

Guiding questions for students:

Each of you were important in sending the tennis ball into warp speed.

- What were some events that caused precious time to be lost?
- What are a few ways you can work together to ensure your success as a group?

EMBEDDED OUTCOME: S4.M5.7. Work with students to solve any problems they might have experienced during the activity.

Student Choices/Differentiation

- Different objects besides a tennis ball may be used.
- To make the task more challenging, it can be modified to use students' feet.

What to Look For

- Did the group set a reasonable but challenging goal?
- Are students being creative in the ways they interact with the tennis ball, or are they simply passing it?

Instructional Task: Can-'n-Ball

■ PRACTICE TASK

Students stand in a circle and must pass a can (an old coffee can works well) with a tennis ball in it around the circle using nothing from the shoulders down on their arms. They must stay in their original circle as they get creative to complete their task of looping the group. If either the can or the ball touch the ground at any time, students have to start the task over.

Extension

If the team gets this quickly, you can add a beach ball circulating the opposite way of the can and ball so that the two items must pass each other.

Guiding questions for students:

Talk with students about multiple strategies and how they chose the one they executed.

- Why did you pick the strategy you used?
- Do you think there is an easier way to solve the challenge?
- Do you think you could improve your time or teamwork if you did this challenge again?

Student Choices/Differentiation

- To make the challenge more difficult, students can touch the ground with their feet and nothing else to keep them from sitting.
- To make the challenge easier, students can pass a different item, such as a beach ball.

What to Look For

- When the class reached success, was it because of one person?
- Did the class come together to help others, or was this an individual task?

Formal and Informal Assessments

Exit slip: Name one thing you learned about someone else in today's class (not the same person from last class). Make sure to include the student's name and what you learned.

Closure

- As the activities progressed and became more challenging today, do you think the class rose to the occasion or buckled under pressure? Why or why not?
- If you got to choose an all-star team to complete more challenges tomorrow, who would be your first choice and why?
- Why do you think our physical education class is focusing on these skills?

Come to class tomorrow ready to work together and be successful. The activities gradually progress into more difficult challenges that I know you can succeed in completing.

Reflection

- How well did students work together?
- Was there an activity that was difficult or easy for the class?
- Did students include everyone during these activities?
- Was enough specific feedback given during the activities?

Homework

Teach any of the activities you learned so far to a group of friends or family.

Resources

Curran, E. (2011). Activities and initiatives. *Swofford challenge course manual.* 2nd ed., vol. 1, 19-64. Inman, SC.

Dale, G., & Conant, S. (2004). *101 teambuilding activities: Ideas every coach can use to enhance teamwork, communication, and trust.* Durham, NC: Excellence in Performance.

Internet keyword search: "ice breakers," "team-building games"

LESSON 3: TRUST AND PROBLEM SOLVING

Grade-Level Outcomes

Primary Outcomes

Working with others: Cooperates with multiple classmates on problem-solving initiatives including adventure activities, large-group initiatives and game play. (S4.M5.8)

Working with others: Problem-solves with a small group of classmates during adventure activities, small-group initiatives or game play. (S4.M5.7)

Embedded Outcome

Working with others: Responds appropriately to participants' ethical and unethical behavior during physical activity by using rules and guidelines for resolving conflicts. (S4.M4.8)

Lesson Objectives

The learner will:

- maintain positive communication and interactions during the activities.
- use problem-solving skills to complete group challenges.
- identify how trust in teammates affected solving a challenge.

Equipment and Materials

- Stopwatch
- Tarp large enough for all students to stand on at one time
- 2 by 4s
- Material to make "islands"

Introduction

Today's lesson focuses on team building, trust, and problem solving. During the activities today, you'll need to use effective communication with classmates.

Show a funny video clip of poor communication between people.

Instructional Task: Gator Swamp

▨ PRACTICE TASK

The class must navigate through an alligator-infested swamp. The only way to cross such a dangerous swamp is to use the bridges provided (2 by 4s nailed together or a 4 by 4 post).

You must lay a pathway from one side of the swamp to the other, ensuring every classmate a safe journey.

Alligators live to snack on people, but they also love to nibble on bridges. Throughout this challenge you may not let your bridges touch the swamp. You must use your islands as a safe resting place for the bridges.

Islands can be concrete blocks, paper taped to the floor, or anything else creative.

Safety

In order to keep everyone safe you must avoid doing the following things:

- Jumping from island to island
- Accidentally hitting other classmates with the bridges
- Jumping in or out of the swamp (a bridge must be used to enter and exit the swamp)

Extension

Bridges can float away and be out of use if students let them go.

Guiding questions for students:

- What are some challenges you experienced in this activity?
- Was there a time you thought of giving up?
- What are some strategies that you used from previous lessons?
- How did you perform as a team?
- Where can you improve?
- Can you give some examples of how you demonstrated trust in your teammates?

Student Choices/Differentiation

Bridge length can be the same or varied to get students to think about which bridge should be placed where.

What to Look For

- Are students planning or just doing?
- Do students help one another though the swamp, or are some students left to fend for themselves?

Instructional Task: Magic Carpet

■ PRACTICE TASK

All students stand on a tarp located in an open space. Explain that the tarp is a magic carpet, but unfortunately, it is upside down and cannot be used the way it is. Students must flip the magic carpet into the upright position, but no one is allowed to step off the tarp. Students must navigate around each other to flip the tarp while standing on it. If anyone comes off the tarp, students restart the task.

Refinement

Students must choose how they plan to solve the problem. Refine group work and cooperation, if needed. Possible solutions: Scrunch up the group and start from a corner.

Guiding questions for students:

- How does it feel to succeed?
- Sometimes, we don't like people in our personal space, but in this challenge, they have to be. How did you deal with this?
- Did anyone step up as a leader? If so, why did you follow this student?
- How did you exhibit (or not) trust during this challenge?
- Did anyone experience any conflicts? How were they resolved?
- How did you have to trust your classmates during this activity?

EMBEDDED OUTCOME: S4.M4.8. This activity can be difficult with regard to maintaining integrity. Discuss with students ethical and unethical behaviors during these types of activities. Ask each team to propose guidelines for dealing with unethical behaviors and resolving conflicts. Write these down to use in future lessons.

Student Choices/Differentiation

The tarp can be made bigger or smaller depending on the groups' problem-solving abilities.

What to Look For

- Are student leaders stepping up and taking control?
- Are the leaders the students that the group should follow or simply the loudest people in the class?
- Are students struggling to communicate in such a small space? If so, you may need to call a time-out to let the team talk strategy.

Instructional Task: Report Card

■ PRACTICE TASK

Reflection activity: Have students fill out a report card on how they feel both individually and as a class so far in this module. The report card should include comments and a number or letter grade. Some suggestions for topics on the report card are working together, creativity, maximal effort, behavior, and listening skills.

Extension

Students should complete a reflection sheet.

Student Choices/Differentiation

Show an example of previous classes' Lesson 3 report cards.

What to Look For

Assess S4.M4, S4.M5, and S5.M3, depending on the report card categories.

Formal and Informal Assessments

- Report cards
- Reflection sheets

Closure

- Did you ever feel like giving up today? Why did you choose not to?
- What was the focus of today's activities?
- Why do you think our physical education class is focusing on these skills?

Reflection

- Were all students contributing to the activity?
- Are students' problem-solving or only trying to get through the task?
- Are students ready for higher-risk activities?

Homework

Trust is one of the things we are working on during this module. For the next class, think about a job that uses trust on a daily basis, and be ready to share how that job uses trust and why you selected it.

Resources

Rohnke, K. (2004). *Funn 'n games*. Dubuque, IO: Kendall/Hunt.

STUDENT REFLECTION

1. What did you learn about either yourself or your class today?

2. What do you think the purpose of adventure activities is?

3. Why do you feel that it is or isn't important to take part in adventure activities?

4. What was your favorite activity and why?

5. What was your least favorite activity and why?

6. Can you define what each finger stands for in the hand contract?

7. If you could give yourself a 1 to 10 ranking for your performance, 1 being the lowest and 10 being the highest, what would you give yourself and why?

8. If you could give your team a 1 to 10 ranking for its performance, 1 being the lowest and 10 being the highest, what would you give it and why?

From R.J. Doan, L.C. MacDonald, and S. Chepko, eds., 2017, *Lesson planning for middle school physical education* (Reston, VA: SHAPE America; Champaign, IL: Human Kinetics).

LESSON 4:
PROBLEM-SOLVING CHALLENGES

Grade-Level Outcomes

Primary Outcome

Working with others: Problem-solves with a small group of classmates during adventure activities, small group initiatives or game play. (S4.M5.7)

Embedded Outcomes

Health: Identifies positive mental and emotional aspects of participating in a variety of physical activities. (S5.M2.7)

Accepting feedback: Provides corrective feedback to a peer, using teacher-generated guidelines, and incorporating appropriate tone and other communication skills. (S4.M3.7)

Lesson Objectives

The learner will:

- demonstrate safe working practices while completing activities and initiatives.
- practice problem-solving skills and collaboration in small groups.

Equipment and Materials

- Golden Gate Activity Guidelines
- Building supplies such as sheets of paper, paper clips, straws, toothpicks, tape, rubber bands, string, Popsicle sticks, balloons, or anything else you can get cheaply
- Marbles
- PVC pipes cut in half

Introduction

For homework, you were asked to find jobs that involved a high amount of trust. Does anyone want to share the jobs they found? What do you think it takes for a person to have that kind of trust in a job they go to every day? Today we will work on problem-solving skills and working safely in groups. Take what you have learned in previous lessons and apply them to the challenges you face today.

Instructional Task: Golden Gates

■ PRACTICE TASK

Yesterday, I asked you to think about a job that relies on trust, and you came up with some great ones. Trust is important in almost every profession. Today, you are contractors in charge of a building project. You will have only 30 minutes to build a masterpiece, so trusting your teammates to do their part is very important.

Your goal for the day is to build something that stands by itself and reaches 5 feet in height.

You will start with the following building materials: five sheets of paper, a pencil, three balloons, five feet of string, and a paper bag. You must work as a team to figure out a building strategy and how you will procure more building supplies. You can earn additional supplies through group or individual challenges as listed on the rules sheet also included in your starting materials.

Extensions

- Perhaps a natural disaster comes through and takes out the factory that makes one of the items students are using, making it no longer available.
- Perhaps an item goes on sale and students can buy two for the price of one, doubling the number of goods that the team receives.
- You also can extend the task using an amazing race format, which incorporates challenges along the way that teams must overcome.

Guiding questions for students:

- Who took charge of your building team? Was this student selected? If so, why?
- What materials do you wish you had and why?
- Which materials were unhelpful?
- Did you see any construction techniques in other groups you wished you had used?
- As students build, ask them why they have chosen to implement this strategy. Get them to explain their methods to you.
- Ask how they feel and what their emotions are in the height of the activity and afterward to see if they changed as time ran down and pressure built.

EMBEDDED OUTCOME: S5.M2.7 During the activity, take a break and discuss with students positive mental and emotional aspects of participating in a variety of physical activities, particularly cooperative activities. Teach students how this task is more mental than physical in nature but is still important in order to be a physically literate student.

Student Choices/Differentiation

Students choose their groups.

What to Look For

- What kinds of problem solving can be observed?
- Are students mentally and emotionally supporting each other during both their successes and failures?

Instructional Task: Marble Roll

■ PRACTICE TASK

In small groups, students must use only the PVC pipes to transport the marble into the assigned container. Each group will build a course out of PVC pipes. You can assign the following criteria or create your own:

- Each group will design a course.
- Once the marble is in the PVC pipe, the person holding it may not move his feet.
- Each person must be involved before the marble can be deposited.

Extension

The end location can be made more difficult or obstacles can be put in the way.

EMBEDDED OUTCOME: S4.M3.7 Generate a positive communication feedback sheet. Have students use the handout to provide feedback to their classmates on how well they communicate with each other during this group-challenge activity.

Student Choices/Differentiation

Students get to choose which piece of PVC they would like to use. Offer larger and smaller sizes, longer and shorter pieces, and they can even be painted.

What to Look For

- What is the frustration level of students?
- Are they giving each other feedback on either the strategy or how it is being implemented?
- Are they supporting one another's ideas?

Formal and Informal Assessments

- Informal assessments of students' ability to work together on various task.
- Exit slips:
  - What strategies did your group use to complete the building challenge?
  - If your team failed to meet the challenge or did not perform as well as others, do you think more successful teams got more out of the building challenge than your team? How did you feel if your team either made the height or failed to meet the height and why?

Closure

- As you built your structures and used your teammates to successfully complete the marble roll, what do you think went well? What could the group improve on?
- Some of you took on the responsibility for leading the group while others followed. Why are both roles important?
- Do you think that contractors struggle with some of the same predicaments you struggled with today?
- Each of you has your own thoughts, ideas, and strategies. Did this help or hurt your group today, and why do you think that?

Reflection

- Were all students mentally active in today's lesson?
- Did anyone look frustrated or mentally worn out?
- Do the embedded outcomes need to be developed or practiced more?

Homework

Can you find materials at home similar to the ones provided in today's lesson? Practice building structures at home to exercise your mental skills.

Resources

Curran, E. (2011). Activities and initiatives. *Swofford challenge course manual.* 2nd ed., vol. 1, 19-64. Inman, SC.

Dale, G., & Conant, S. (2004). *101 teambuilding activities: Ideas every coach can use to enhance teamwork, communication, and trust.* Durham, NC: Excellence in Performance.

GOLDEN GATE ACTIVITY GUIDELINES

Structure Build

The objective is to build a stand-alone structure that stands 5 feet (1.5 m) in the air using only the building materials that were issued to your group, or by earning additional materials after completing small challenges. You can complete each task only once to earn objects for your team's creation, so take on as many of the challenges as you can. Each task can earn you up to 5 building supplies (assigned by the teacher). Different team members must participate in each activity (if there are enough). You may alter the items that you earn in any way, but your structure must stand on its own and not be attached to the wall.

Remember: Your goal is to build a solid structure that reaches the 5-foot line marked on the wall.

Challenges to Earn Items

- **50/50 carry:** Four students participate. You must carry a teammate to the yellow line and then have her carry you back. Then, two different teammates will have to complete this same task.

- **Human pyramid:** Six students make a human pyramid.

- **Human knot:** Six students put their right and left hands in and link hands. They then have to untangle themselves without letting go of the hands they are linked to.

- **Human ABC:** At least three students use their bodies to spell out each of the 26 letters in the alphabet, one at a time. Be sure that your team leader checks off each letter.

- **Push-ups:** Team members work together to complete 100 push-ups. Everyone in the group can complete a few, or a few individuals can complete a bunch, as long as you complete 100 as a team.

- **Sing-along:** All team members participate in a sing-along. You choose the song, and all team members must sing the entire song.

- **Team dance moves:** All team members do the same dance at the same time. It can be a dance that you already know, but make sure everyone is participating.

- **Team names:** Someone from your team must learn every other team member's name and give them to the facilitator without using nametags or other team members.

- **Trivia questions:** You must answer six trivia questions correctly to earn your next supply.

- **Moon ball:** Your team must work together to keep a beach ball off the ground for a total of 50 bumps or sets. Each team member must touch the beach ball at least once during the challenge. If the ball touches the ground at any point, the count starts over.

- **Hula-Hoop:** Two team members must Hula-Hoop continuously for 1 minute. (There is only one Hula-Hoop, so you will have to take turns.) The Hula-Hoop must be around your waist.

Trivia Questions

1. **Who is our state's governor?** _____

2. **The first battle of the Civil War took place in which state?** South Carolina

3. **Name seven *Sesame Street* characters.** Elmo, Big Bird, Cookie Monster, Ernie, Bert, Grover, Oscar, Zoe, Abby Cadabby, Gordon, Mr. Snuffleupagus, Baby Alice, Slimey, and any more you can think of

4. **How many justices are on the U.S. Supreme Court?** Nine

5. **What does SPF stand for on sunscreen containers?** Sun protection factor

6. **What was Mickey Mouse's original name? (Hint: It's not Mickey.)** Mortimer Mouse

7. **In basketball, it's called a tip-off; in football, it's a kickoff. What is it called in hockey?** Face-off

8. **What are the three primary colors in art?** Red, blue, yellow

9. **What is the correct musical term that means to play louder, gradually?** Crescendo

10. **What is the (local NFL team) mascot's name?**

11. **What is the person who shoes horses called?** Ferrier

12. **In what year did the United States declare independence from England?** 1776

13. **What is the name of an angle that measures greater than 90 degrees but less than 180 degrees?** Obtuse

14. **In what country are the next Olympics going to be held?** _____

15. **On a standard computer keyboard, which key is the largest?** Spacebar

16. **Mount Rushmore features the faces of four American presidents. Name two of the four:** George Washington, Abraham Lincoln, Thomas Jefferson, Theodore Roosevelt

17. **Who won the Heisman Trophy this year?** _____

18. **What is the word used in tennis for a score of zero?** Love

19. **What is Barbie's kid sister's name?** Skipper (1964)

20. **Which Olympian earned the most individual medals over the course of his or her lifetime?** Michael Phelps

Items You May Earn

4 paper plates

1 roll of tape

Approximately 50 cotton swabs

50 Popsicle sticks

40 drinking straws

250 toothpicks

5 medium balloons (not blown up)

2 foot-long rulers

1 pair of scissors

10 wooden golf tees

10 paper clips

Approximately 30 feet of ribbon

4 plastic forks

Be creative and use whatever you can find or have money for.

From R.J. Doan, L.C. MacDonald, and S. Chepko, eds., 2017, *Lesson planning for middle school physical education* (Reston, VA: SHAPE America; Champaign, IL: Human Kinetics).

LESSON 5: TRUST TO SURVIVE

Grade-Level Outcomes

Primary Outcomes

Working with others: Problem-solves with a small group of classmates during adventure activities, small group initiatives or game play. (S4.M5.7)

Challenge: Generates positive strategies, such as offering suggestions or assistance, leading or following others and providing possible solutions when faced with a group challenge. (S5.M3.7)

Embedded Outcome

Personal responsibility: Exhibits responsible social behaviors by cooperating with classmates, demonstrating inclusive behaviors and supporting classmates. (S4.M1.7)

Lesson Objectives

The learner will:

- express ideas, needs, or solutions to others in the group.
- infer deeper meanings from each activity and how it relates to school or life.
- apply communication and reasoning skills.

Equipment and Materials

- Poly spots
- Hoop or a rope tied into a circle approximately the size of a large hoop
- Objects students wouldn't slip or get injured on
- Rope boundary lines
- Playground balls or something to be used for an egg

Introduction

Last class, we focused on problem solving and teamwork, and we talked a little about leading during the building challenge. Most groups need leaders and followers to succeed, but that relationship doesn't work without trust. Today, I want you to work together and trust your teammates. Remember the hand contract and understand that today, you will need a supportive environment to succeed, because the challenges you face will be more difficult.

Instructional Task: The Nest

■ PRACTICE TASK

Find or make a large egg. Playground balls and beach balls make great large eggs. Students in small groups should create a nest and place it somewhere in the gym or outdoor space. Groups need to move their egg to another small group's nest. The egg must make it back into its mom's nest (be creative with this one) in one piece, but there are a few rules that must be followed:

1. *Don't place a student in the nest.*
2. *Each team member must participate for the success to count.*
3. *If the egg breaks or drops the team must start over.*
4. *Since birds will not recognize eggs as their own with your scent on them, you must complete this challenge without using your arms. You may use your arms only to help a teammate.*

Extension

Place the nest in a high place to force even more strategy into use.

EMBEDDED OUTCOME: S4.M1.7. The rules for this task require inclusion and support. Debrief students on how they accomplished it.

Guiding questions for students:

- Following the four rules can be difficult. How have you chosen to be successful?
- Was it efficient?
- Did you make the challenge harder than it needed to be?
- Who were the leaders in this challenge? Were they different from the last class?

Student Choices/Differentiation

You can either have the egg never touch the ground, or it can be allowed to roll.

What to Look For

- Who is critically thinking to ensure the team is effective in finding a solution?
- How did they get the egg in the nest? Are there other ways? Did the students make the activity harder than it needed to be?
- Has the group's mentality changed at all from "How can *I* complete this task?" to "How will *we* complete this task?"

Instructional Task: Minefield

▪ PRACTICE TASK

Students partner up and choose who will lead whom through the minefield first. The leader of the pair may not touch the person traveling and may communicate vocally with the traveler only from outside the boundary lines. The traveler is blindfolded and is led through a minefield of loose objects. If the traveler hits a mine, he must go back to the beginning.

Extension

The objects can move around to throw off the communicator; partners should switch roles after success.

Student Choices/Differentiation

- Students may go one pair at a time or have all pairs go at the same time for additional distractions.
- Pairs could huddle before they begin to plan strategy.

Guiding questions for students:

- How hard was it to trust a partner to get you through the minefield?
- Were you tempted to cheat and peak? Did you?
- Was it overwhelming to hear other voices besides just your partner's? How did you deal with this?
- What examples of trusting each other can you give for this activity?
- What did this activity teach you?
- How can you apply it to your life?

What to Look For

- Students use strategy and communication effectively.
- Students show integrity.

Instructional Task: Wormhole

▪ PRACTICE TASK

Tell students that a wormhole has opened up to a mythical location. They must help their teammates, one by one, through the wormhole without touching the edge of the hole, because that will shut it down.

Each team member must get through the hole cleanly to bridge to the next location.

The wormhole can be a hoop and the teacher may provide challenges to the class (e.g. selected students might have lost body parts such as their arms or legs, there is minimal light, students need to go through the wormhole backwards).

Discuss safety and ensure that students follow safety measures as they complete the challenge.

Guiding questions for students:

- This activity takes planning and strategy. Who do you think helped your group the most in this area?
- What sacrifices had to be made for the team to succeed?
- How did you gain your teammates' trust so that you could solve the problem?

Student Choices/Differentiation

The hoop can be raised or lowered or made smaller or larger in diameter to change the level of difficulty.

What to Look For

- Students are communicating and working together as a team, with a focus on safety.
- Student leaders are emerging.

Instructional Task: Space Pods

■ PRACTICE TASK

Each team member is issued one space pod from NASA (poly spot). The team must work together to travel through space to the next planet. Students may not touch space (the ground) with any body part without facing death.

They may stand on the space pods to stay safe, but if someone falls off, everyone must start over because the team is lost in space. If someone loses contact with the space pod, even for only a second, the team loses use of it. Some part of one teammate must be touching the pod at all times to keep it from floating away.

Space pods may be shared with others and can support numerous lives at one time.

It's best for students to join together in a line, but explore other ways of completing the task.

Guiding questions for students:

- Does the distance between teammates affect how you communicate?
- Who have you chosen as your leader and why?
- What are the characteristics of a good follower?

Student Choices/Differentiation

Encourage creativity and problem solving as students think the rules through.

What to Look For

- Is the group following the rules? Do they understand their task?
- Are students doing unproductive things or distracting others?

Use information gathered throughout the module on the Adventure Activities Feedback Rubric.

Formal and Informal Assessments

Adventure activities feedback rubric

Closure

- You have completed several adventure challenges in the past few days and have only one more day of challenges before changing pace. Thinking back on what you have done so far, what has your team done well? Where has your team struggled?

- How can you correct some of your struggles for tomorrow's challenges? Has your group grown to trust each other? Do you trust your classmates more than before after completing these challenges?
- Do you think your group would have done well on some of the tough challenges like the wormhole if we had done them the first day of school? Why or why not?

Reflection

- Have your students progressed as the activities have progressed?
- Are students indicating that they need to be challenged more, less, or about the same?
- Have any of the students stepped into a leadership role? Does anyone have too much of a role as a leader and is not giving others in the group an opportunity?

Homework

Find a team-building activity that you would like to try and bring it in to share with the group in the next class. It can be a game, low ropes course element, or critical-thinking challenge like our building challenge.

Resources

Dale, G., & Conant, S. (2004). *101 teambuilding activities: Ideas every coach can use to enhance teamwork, communication, and trust.* Durham, NC: Excellence in Performance.

ADVENTURE ACTIVITIES FEEDBACK RUBRIC

Teacher: _____ Date: _____

School: _____ Weather conditions: _____

Category	Unsatisfactory	Improvable	Satisfactory	Good	Excellent
Safety					
Notes:					
Communication					
Notes:					
Critical thinking					
Notes:					
Leadership					
Notes:					
Goals/Achievement					
Notes:					
Listening skills					
Notes:					
Teamwork					
Notes:					
Active participation					
Notes:					
Overall Class Rating:					

From R.J. Doan, L.C. MacDonald, and S. Chepko, eds., 2017, *Lesson planning for middle school physical education* (Reston, VA: SHAPE America; Champaign, IL: Human Kinetics).

LESSON 6:
STRATEGIC AND CRITICAL THINKING

Grade-Level Outcomes

Primary Outcome

Challenge: Generates positive strategies such as offering suggestions or assistance, leading or following others and providing possible solutions when faced with a group challenge. (S5.M3.7)

Embedded Outcome

Social interaction: Demonstrates the importance of social interaction by helping and encouraging others, avoiding trash talk and providing support to classmates. (S5.M6.7)

Lesson Objectives

The learner will:

- manipulate materials and group ideas to complete the given task.
- apply general knowledge and critical-thinking skills to come up with solutions to each activity.

Equipment and Materials

- Large shoes
- Scooters with ropes attached
- Laundry baskets

Introduction

Today, we will continue our adventure activities module with a strategic and critical-thinking task. Work hard today at being a great team member. We will play one of my favorite games, human hungry, hungry hippos!

Instructional Task: Group Share

■ PRACTICE TASK

Students share their activities from the homework assignment.

Guiding questions for students:

- Why did you choose the activity you did?
- What important concepts (team building, leadership, critical thinking) that we have learned so far apply to the activities you found?
- What are some safety concerns with the activities you found?

Extension

Play one of the activities students provided.

Student Choices/Differentiation

Students can volunteer to explain the activity to the whole group.

What to Look For

Is everyone actively listening?

Instructional Task: Magic Shoes

■ PRACTICE TASK

All students start on one side of a divide. The team is issued one pair of magic shoes that help transport them safely through the mystic area in the middle and to the other side. The goal is to get all students to the other side of the divide. The only way to get to the other side is by using the shoes.

However, there are a few rules:

1. Everyone may wear the shoes only one time and in one direction.
2. The shoes may not be tossed back to the other side.
3. Both shoes must be worn at the same time, and the pair cannot be split up.

The team will have to work together to be successful and get all members to the other side by following the rules.

Get an actual pair of large shoes and paint them a bright color. Allow students to carry one another to get themselves out of trouble. Other props can be added if needed.

Set up a video camera for each team to record their problem solving and solutions. The video will be used later for evaluation.

Guiding questions for students:

- Who had to pull the most weight during the activity?
- Where did your strategy come from?
- Did anyone emerge as a leader?

EMBEDDED OUTCOME: S5.M6.7 Remind students about the importance of supporting one another in these activities. Ask for examples of encouragement and support.

Student Choices/Differentiation

Students may choose a variety of possible solutions for success, but all will require them to work together, support each other, and make sacrifices for group success. Examples:

- Students may have to carry one another.
- They may be allowed to give away their one use of the shoes to someone else if need be.

What to Look For

- Are students safe?
- Are they keeping everyone's strengths and weaknesses in mind?
- Do they understand sacrifices must be made to be successful?
- Are they team players?

Instructional Task: Human Hungry, Hungry Hippos

■ PRACTICE TASK

Have each group choose a "hippo," who will lie belly down on the scooter and collect food. Teammates push the hippo toward the food, and he must collect as many objects as possible using only the laundry hamper. This can be done in heats, using time, or head to head to see which team collects the most.

Teams must push their hippos out and pull them back in with the string.

Allow hippos to use only their hands and arms to gather food.

Extensions

- Rotate the group around and keep a running total to allow each player a chance at being the hungry, hungry hippo.
- Add more hippos to increase competition.

Guiding questions for students:

- How does this game relate to success? You had fun scooting around collecting items, but what can you relate this to?
- Could the hippo have succeeded without the help of his team?

Student Choices/Differentiation

The size of the items collected can change to differentiate the challenge.

What to Look For

- Are students learning from mistakes and correcting them?
- Did they choose the right person to be the hippo?
- Are they using effective strategies?

Instructional Task: Self-Assessment

■ PRACTICE TASK

Using the video from magic shoes, have students self-assess their performance on problem solving and teamwork while coming up with strategies for the activity. Provide prompts to guide their self-evaluation.

Refinement

Make sure students are not just telling you what you can see in the video but are also critically analyzing their performance.

Student Choices/Differentiation

Share a short example of a self-assessment with students.

What to Look For

- Students are objectively viewing the video and critically analyzing their teamwork and problem-solving strategies.
- Students are including things they did well and things they would do differently next time.

Formal and Informal Assessments

Student self-assessment

Closure

- What have you learned about being a teammate during this lesson?
- What are the qualities of a good leader?
- Was problem solving easy or difficult for you?
- Which activity was the most difficult for you today? Why?

Reflection

- Have students gained any team camaraderie?
- Have their communication skills gotten any better?
- Are there students who have drawn away from the adventure activities? How can you reach out to them?
- Are the debrief questions getting good, deep answers or just quick responses?

Homework

Individuals stand out for many different things. For homework I want you to choose an animal that represents how you feel you did during the lesson today. Were you a tiger that took charge and aggressively hunted out an answer, or a sheep that followed the herd and never picked your head up? Were you a turtle that went nice and slow but had the right idea the whole way, or a rabbit that rushed through tasks to find there were better ways to come to the solution? Define your animal and explain why you chose that animal.

Resources

Curran, E. (2011). Activities and initiatives. *Swofford challenge course manual.* 2nd ed., vol. 1, 19-64. Inman, SC.

Rohnke, K. (2004). *Funn 'n Games.* Dubuque, IO: Kendall/Hunt.

LESSON 7: OBSTACLE RACE

Grade-Level Outcomes

Primary Outcome

Working with others: Problem-solves with a small group of classmates during adventure activities, small-group initiatives or game play. (S4.M5.7)

Embedded Outcomes

Outdoor pursuits: Analyzes the situation and makes adjustments to ensure the safety of self and others. (S2.M13.7)

Fitness knowledge: Uses available technology to self-monitor quantity of exercise needed for a minimal health standard and/or optimal functioning based on current fitness level. (S3.M8.8)

Lesson Objectives

The learner will:

- perform obstacle challenges alongside classmates.
- strategize about the best way to get all team members through the obstacles.

Equipment and Materials

- Paper and pencils
- Items for obstacle course

Introduction

Today, we will change things up a bit but still focus on adventure. Instead of focusing so much on trust and team building, we will focus on endurance and toughness. Has anyone ever seen a mud run?

Show a video clip of a mud run.

In class today, we will have a mud run, but without the mud.

Instructional Task: Practice Obstacle Race

■ PRACTICE TASK

In teams, create an obstacle course for students to navigate. The course can review material previously learned or contain silly challenges such as taking a group selfie and getting everyone in before getting the next clue. Be creative and design a fun warm-up activity for your students. Remind students that their whole team must complete each obstacle before moving on to the next one.

Students follow you through obstacles and exercises around the campus or school.

Each obstacle should be broken down and the correct procedure for completion taught. Speed is not the objective; proper technique is.

Place focus on the following:

- Endurance
- Sprinting
- Jumping
- Climbing
- Hanging
- Carrying
- Crawling under obstacles
- Hauling weight
- Swimming (if applicable)

Students should master the proper technique to succeed in any obstacle run. They must determine the best way to ensure that all team members complete the course. All team members should practice each obstacle and, once comfortable, take a complete run-through at half or three-quarter speed.

Students may not move to the next obstacle until all members on the team complete the obstacle.

Have students take their heart rates or use heart rate monitors to gauge intensity of the activities.

Extensions

Let students create new obstacles or split into small groups to create a route for the rest of the class to enjoy.

EMBEDDED OUTCOME: S2.M13.7. Have students analyze the challenges that they came up with and find safety concerns or modifications to ensure safety for all participants.

EMBEDDED OUTCOME: S3.M8.8. Use this activity to review the physical activity standards and how obstacle running can help meet them.

Refinement

Ensure that students' knees do not go over their toes when they are lunging and that they are using proper technique when they do squats, push-ups, jumping and landing, and any other skill embedded in the course.

Student Choices/Differentiation

- This activity could be large scale around the entire school campus or small scale in a gym.
- The possibilities for clues and stations are as endless as your creativity.
- Encourage students to try and create new challenges.

What to Look For

- Are students completing each task as assigned?
- Are students taking lessons learned during the previous six adventure lessons and using them here?
- Are students participating and committed to the task?
- Are students trying each obstacle? Are they staying together as a group?

Formal and Informal Assessments

- Intensity assessment sheet: Create an obstacle course check sheet where students can fill in their heart rates or use heart rate monitors to monitor intensity of each obstacle course element.
- Exit slip: Have students draw an obstacle course of their own and explain why they created the course to look like it does.

Closure

- Obstacle racing is becoming very popular. Color runs, warrior dashes, Spartan races, and tough mudder are lifelong ways to stay in shape. If you had to do some sort of race, which would you choose and why?
- Which obstacle course event was the most intense according to the intensity assessment sheet? Could you have predicted this before participating in the actual course?

Tomorrow, we will continue the module with a unique type of obstacle course.

Reflection

- Do any students need extensions or refinements to ensure their full participation?
- Were students able to understand the connection between physical activity and the use of obstacle courses?
- Did lower-skilled students succeed in the obstacle course? How could the course be modified to ensure that everyone succeeds?

Homework

Find an obstacle run in which you would like to participate one day. Be prepared to discuss what you found during the next class.

Resources

Internet keyword search: "mud run," "homemade obstacle courses"

LESSON 8: AMAZING RACE

Grade-Level Outcomes

Primary Outcomes

Outdoor pursuits: Analyzes the situation and makes adjustments to ensure the safety of self and others. (S2.M13.7)

Outdoor pursuits: Demonstrates correct technique for a variety of skills in 1 self-selected outdoor activity. (S1.M22.7)

Embedded Outcome

Social interaction: Demonstrates respect for self by asking for help and helping others in various physical activities. (S5.M6.8)

Lesson Objectives

The learner will:

- manipulate tasks to complete the obstacles given.
- gain self-respect and develop an increased sense of personal confidence.

Equipment and Materials

- Items for Amazing Race course
- Permission forms (if needed)

Introduction

Please share with us some of the obstacles that you found in your homework. We might not be able to re-create such intense obstacles, but I encourage you to give it your best today and stick with a buddy runner for safety at all times. Has anyone ever seen the television show The Amazing Race? Today, we will put on our own version of the show!

Show a video clip from the show *The Amazing Race.*

Instructional Task: Amazing Race

■ PRACTICE TASK

Break the class into groups. Give each group its first clue. (Beforehand, set out clues that lead to one another.)

Create an obstacle course for students to navigate that resembles the television show *The Amazing Race.*

Amazing Race tasks could include any of the following: Complete a small challenge or puzzle, or complete a challenge of a unit already taught, such as juggling a soccer ball for 10 touches, hitting five 3-point shots, or throwing into a target of some kind. You could set up a mental quiz on items already learned or a physical challenge such as 100 push-ups to be split up among the group.

Find more activities by doing a search with the keywords "Amazing Race challenge."

Students must use solid reasoning to analyze the situations they encounter as they come to each obstacle.

The goal of the activity should be to complete the task while working in groups, not finishing first.

EMBEDDED OUTCOME: S5.M6.8. Discuss with students the importance of asking for help and helping others on some of these challenges so that the team can succeed.

Student Choices/Differentiation

- This activity could be large scale around the entire school campus or small scale in a gym.
- The possibilities for clues and stations are as endless as your creativity.

What to Look For
- Are students completing each task as assigned?
- Are students taking lessons learned during the previous six adventure lessons and using them here?

Instructional Task: Reflections

■ PRACTICE TASK
Have students work in small groups.

Guiding questions for students:
- Which obstacle was the hardest?
- What would you change about the course before another group went through?
- Did anyone encourage you as you completed your run?
- Did you ever feel like giving up? Why didn't you?

Extensions
- Assessment of team members
- Module student reflection

Student Choices/Differentiation
For larger obstacles, a second challenge could be issued for those scared or unable to complete the challenge.

What to Look For
Are students safe at all times?

Formal and Informal Assessments
- Team members' assessment: teacher-created assessment focusing on evaluations of team members (possible elements include being a good team member and problem-solving skills)
- Module reflection

Closure
- If we hosted an obstacle run as a community fund-raising project, which elements would you use?
- What would you change about our run route, and would you prefer for it to be harder or easier?
- If you had to work at our school's obstacle run, which obstacle would you want to work at and why? What would you do to help others be successful there?

Reflection
- Did students seem to have a healthy amount of struggle in the task—that is, it is challenging but can be completed?
- Did students support one another at times of need or struggle?

Homework
Make sure you check the school's physical education website to see what we are covering next!

Resources
Internet keyword search: "Amazing Race challenges," "obstacle courses"

STUDENT REFLECTION

Student's name: _____ Teacher's name: _____

Date: _____

Answer the following questions using a rating scale from 1 to 4. Circle the number that applies.

1	2	3	4
Poor	**Average**	**Good**	**Excellent**

1. How would you rate your experience in adventure education?

    1   2   3   4

2. How would you rate *your* communication efforts?

    1   2   3   4

3. How would you rate the adventure education unit on improving *your* ability to communicate?

    1   2   3   4

4. How would you rate your team's effort?

    1   2   3   4

5. How would you rate your team's communication?

    1   2   3   4

6. How would you rate your team's ability to solve problems?

    1   2   3   4

7. How would you rate *your* role as part of the team?

    1   2   3   4

8. What did you learn from adventure education about either yourself or your class today?

9. How would you rate your team's improvement after completing the adventure education unit from beginning to end?

    1   2   3   4

10. How would you rate the adventure education course on improving your ability to solve problems, work as part of a team, and communicate more effectively?

    1   2   3   4

11. What was your favorite activity in the unit and why?

12. What was your least favorite activity in the unit and why?

13. What could your team have done better to make your group more successful? Be specific and give examples.

14. How will you apply what you learned in adventure education to your daily life and relationships? Be specific and give examples.

15. Did you enjoy your experience with adventure education? Why or why not?

16. If you were allowed to give yourself a letter grade (A to F) for your participation in the sessions, what would it be and why?

17. Do you think your team could have accomplished more overall? **Circle one**:   Yes   No

Additional comments or suggestions:

_____

_____

_____

_____

_____

From R.J. Doan, L.C. MacDonald, and S. Chepko, eds., 2017, *Lesson planning for middle school physical education* (Reston, VA: SHAPE America; Champaign, IL: Human Kinetics).

CHAPTER 9

Applying Students' Skills and Knowledge to Individual-Performance Activities

It's important to expose students to different types of physical activities so that they can find one or more that will interest them—ideally, for a lifetime. Because large-group competitive activities (in which higher-skilled students often dominate) actually can lower some students' interest in physical activity, it's essential that you balance competitive activities with less competitive and individual-performance activities (Hill & Hannon, 2008; Treasure & Roberts, 2001). This chapter focuses on individual-performance activities, featuring modules on in-line skating, mountain biking, and track and field. Those and other individual-performance activities, such as gymnastics, figure skating, wrestling, self-defense, and skateboarding (SHAPE America, 2014), offer many benefits to students in middle school and beyond. Each module in this chapter provides opportunities for students to enhance their skills, their fitness, and their self-confidence. The lessons within each module also offer the possibility of exciting new activities, some by exploring one's environment, be it urban, suburban, or rural.

The eight-lesson Mountain Biking Module, for example, provides a sequence in which students learn basic riding skills that they can apply in their neighborhoods or outdoor wooded environments. The In-Line Skating Module helps students progress safely in their skating skills. The Track and Field Module provides progressions and learning activities for common track and field events, an ancient sport that offers participation opportunities for all who are willing to put forth the effort.

With all individual-performance activities, it's important to consider safety. The In-Line Skating and Mountain Biking Modules provide progressions and notes regarding decisions that you will need to make regarding safety (e.g., when to progress to the next skill, wearing helmets correctly, cleaning equipment). It's also worth noting that these types of activities might require an investment in equipment, such as in-line skates, bikes, and helmets. You can think big and try to access or build a skate park or mountain biking obstacle course or dirt track. Fortunately, one can find many sources for grants (www.skateinschools.com), and working with local community groups and businesses can augment one's basic physical education budget. When the activity is important to students and the community, it's not terribly difficult to marshal their support.

Remember to consider the following, which are important when planning *any* type of activity but are particularly important when planning individual-performance activities:

- the setting,
- previous student learning,
- preparation needed,
- teachable-moment opportunities, and
- opportunities for student reflection.

You will enjoy guiding students to reflect on their learning experiences with questions and prompts throughout the lessons provided here. Although it would be ideal to teach many of these activities outdoors, you can adapt them easily for a gym, school grounds, or local recreation facilities.

For easy reference, each module begins with a block plan chart of the Grade-Level Outcomes that are addressed within the module. Each module incorporates multiple National Standards for K-12 Physical Education, although most of the primary outcomes reside under Standards 4 and 5. Every module in the chapter includes a primary outcome for demonstrating correct technique in a basic self-selected individual-performance activity. The in-line skating lessons include identifying and applying Newton's laws of motion (Outcome S2.M12.7) and using physical activity and fitness equipment appropriately and safely (Outcome S1.M7.6).

In the Mountain Biking Module, students track their physical activity throughout the module while participating in lifetime activities (Outcome S3.M5.6) and use many health concepts to reinforce the lifetime benefits of mountain biking (Outcomes S3.M17.7, S3.M18.7, S5.M1.6, and S5.M1.8). The Track and Field Module includes the role of flexibility in injury prevention (Outcome S3.M10.8) and appropriate warm-ups and cool-downs (Outcome S3.M12.6), as well as multiple embedded outcomes under Standards 4 and 5.

IN-LINE SKATING MODULE

Lessons in this module were contributed by Lori Secrist, assistant principal at the Center for Innovative Learning at Pinecrest in Aiken, SC, and a physical education teacher for 17 years.

Grade-Level Outcomes Addressed, by Lesson	Lessons							
	1	2	3	4	5	6	7	8
Standard 1. The physically literate individual demonstrates competency in a variety of motor skills and movement patterns.								
Shoots on goal with power and accuracy in small-sided game play. (S1.M10.7)						E		
Shoots on goal with a long-handled implement for power and accuracy in modified invasion games such as hockey (floor, field, ice) or lacrosse. (S1.M10.8)						E		
Demonstrates correct technique for basic skills in 1 self-selected individual-performance activity. (S1.M24.6)	P	P	P	P	P	P	P	P
Standard 2. The physically literate individual applies knowledge of concepts, principles, strategies and tactics related to movement and performance.								
Transitions from offense to defense or defense to offense by recovering quickly and communicating with teammates. (S2.M6.7)						E		
Identifies and applies Newton's laws of motion to various dance or movement activities. (S2.M12.7)					P	P		
Standard 3. The physically literate individual demonstrates the knowledge and skills to achieve and maintain a health-enhancing level of physical activity and fitness.								
Identifies major muscles used in selected physical activities. (S3.M14.6)							E	
Standard 4. The physically literate individual exhibits responsible personal and social behavior that respects self and others.								
Exhibits responsible social behaviors by cooperating with classmates, demonstrating inclusive behaviors and supporting classmates. (S4.M1.7)		E						
Provides corrective feedback to a peer, using teacher-generated guidelines, and incorporating appropriate tone and other communication skills. (S4.M3.7)						E		
Accepts differences among classmates in physical development, maturation and varying skill levels by providing encouragement and positive feedback. (S4.M4.6)	E			E				
Problem-solves with a small group of classmates during adventure activities, small-group initiatives or game play. (S4.M5.7)								E
Uses physical activity and fitness equipment appropriately and safely, *with the teacher's guidance*. (S4.M7.6)	P	P			P			
Independently uses physical activity and exercise equipment appropriately and safely. (S4.M7.7)			E					
Standard 5. The physically literate individual recognizes the value of physical activity for health, enjoyment, challenge, self-expression and/or social interaction.								
Demonstrates the importance of social interaction by helping and encouraging others, avoiding trash talk and providing support to classmates. (S5.M6.7)						E		

P = Primary; E = Embedded

LESSON 1: SAFETY

Grade-Level Outcomes

Primary Outcome

Safety: Uses physical activity and fitness equipment appropriately and safely, *with the teacher's guidance.* (S4.M7.6)

Embedded Outcome

Working with others: Accepts differences among classmates in physical development, maturation and varying skill levels by providing encouragement and positive feedback. (S4.M4.6)

Lesson Objectives

The learner will:

- demonstrate proper placement of protective gear.
- inspect gear for damage.
- learn how to fall properly wearing in-line skating protective equipment.

Equipment and Materials

Per student or every two students of similar size:

- Helmet (sanitized between interpersonal use)
- Pair of knee pads
- Pair of elbow pads
- Pair of wrist pads

Introduction

Have you ever seen or heard of the X Games? Do you know of any sports in the X Games?

Show a quick video clip of athletes competing in in-line skating during the X Games.

Today, we will start a module on in-line skating, which is a great activity for exercising, being with friends, and challenging yourself. The focus for our first lesson is going to be learning about the safety gear and how to fall safely.

Instructional Task: Introduction to Safety Gear

■ PRACTICE TASK

Demonstrate how to wear the safety gear properly, including placement on the body and adjustments for proper fit. Be sure to inspect all equipment for damage before student use.

Students practice putting on protective equipment five times and then help their partners do the same.

Once gear is being worn appropriately, instruct students on proper stance while skating. In general terms, students need an athletic stance: head up, elbows bent to approximately 90 degrees, and knees flexed to allow quick position changes required when skating.

Students practice falling forward from the athletic stance—in order—from knees to elbows to hands, five times.

Extensions

- Peer assessment: Students complete a checklist for proper positioning and falling technique.
- Display damaged equipment to help students recognize what it looks like.
- Students time one another for correct gear placement in the least amount of time.
- Plant damaged pieces of equipment (before being worn and used) and intervene if students don't identify them as being unsafe.

Guiding questions for students:

- What does it look like when you fall? (Answer: varies depending on activity, speed, skill)
- How do people usually look when they fall? (Answer: as if they don't know what they are doing)
- What is the proper way to fall? (Answer: from crouched position to knees, then elbows, then hands)

Refinements

- Remind students to have equipment tight, but not to the point that it restricts movement.
- Shake the head to be sure the helmet is snug.

Student Choices/Differentiation

- Students may describe placement of gear to a partner verbally or while fastening it in position physically.
- Students may fall more than five times.
- Students may practice the fall onto a mat to gain trust in the safety equipment placement and the feeling.
- Students may jog or run before falling.
- Students may "sock skate" before falling.

What to Look For

- All protective equipment should fit securely in such a position as to protect the body as intended.
- When students have gear in position, it will look appropriate.
- When students practice falling, gear will not move out of proper position (make adjustments as needed).
- Students fall from crouched position and land initially on knees, then on elbows and hands (as applicable with associated forces).

Safety Notes

- Helmet must fit securely to the head and sit on top (no cowboy hat tilting), with the chin strap buckled under the chin to prevent the helmet from sliding forward or backward.
- Knee and elbow pads must be worn as described by the manufacturer and fit with the protective plastic at the bend of those two joints. Pads must be fastened tightly enough to prevent sliding out of position, but not to constrict movement.
- Wrist pads must be worn as described by the manufacturer. Fit should be snug and supportive to cover the entire wrist and thumb joints.

Instructional Task:
Demonstrate Common Damage to Check

■ PRACTICE TASK

Inspect all equipment for cracks or missing and loose buckles and other fittings.

Guiding questions for students:

- How could the damage occur to equipment? (Answer: speed, improper equipment placement)
- How do you think proper stance helps when skating? (Answer: encourages good skating technique, falling properly and safety)
- Why do you want to try to fall forward? (Answer: safety)

Extensions

- Describe common equipment damage to a partner.
  - Equipment damage to the back of the helmet suggests the skater was standing higher than a crouch and therefore fell backward.

- Wrist pads that are cracked at the wrist joint suggest the skater fell directly on the hands instead of knees first, then elbows, then hands to break the fall. This skater was probably higher than a crouch position.
- Damaged knee pads suggest proper skating and falling techniques.
- Manipulate equipment and have partners make adjustments and repairs to ensure safety.

EMBEDDED OUTCOME: S.4.M4.6. Encourage partners to accept differences among peers and provide positive feedback while inspecting partners' work.

Student Choices/Differentiation

Have a list of equipment issues that students can check off if they are having a hard time finding damage.

What to Look For

- Students can recognize unsafe equipment.
- Students can recognize unsafely placed equipment and manipulate it to a safe state.
- Students attempt to fall forward to utilize padding for protection.

Safety Notes

- Helmets should be free of cracks and have appropriate padding intact.
- Discrepancies should be reported to the teacher and equipment not be used until deemed safe by inspection, repair, or replacement.
- All helmet, knee, elbow, and wrist pad buckles fasten securely and adjust freely. Velcro should be intact and free from debris that weakens the fabric.
- Skates should buckle, brakes should have ample padding, and wheels should be free of debris that prevents smooth rolling.

Formal and Informal Assessments

- Peer assessment using a checklist of equipment positioning and falling technique.
- Exit slip: List five important safety considerations when using in-line skates.

Closure

- Where should pads be worn? (Answer: covering joints, secure fit for movement without sliding out of position)
- Where should the helmet sit? (Answer: top of head, no tilting forward or backward, chin strap secure so no more than three fingers can slide in between your chin and the strap when buckled)
- How should you try to fall? (Answer: from crouched position to knees, then elbows, then hands)
- How will you know if the equipment is being worn properly? (Answer: pads stay in position when you fall)

Reflection

- Did I have enough equipment?
- How can I adjust the time for equipment to avoid loss of skating time?
- Did the equipment fit all students?
- Were students providing positive feedback to each other in today's lesson?

Homework

Seek out videos on in-line skating techniques and share with a friend. Please e-mail me the links of any cool videos I can post to the school's website.

Resources

Keep original manufacturer information and websites handy.

Internet keyword search: "how do I put on knee and elbow pads"

LESSON 2: BRAKING

Grade-Level Outcomes

Primary Outcomes

Safety: Uses physical activity and fitness equipment appropriately and safely, *with the teacher's guidance.* (S4.M7.6)

Individual-performance activities: Demonstrates correct technique for basic skills in 1 self-selected individual-performance activity. (S1.M24.6)

Embedded Outcome

Personal responsibility: Exhibits responsible social behaviors by cooperating with classmates, demonstrating inclusive behaviors and supporting classmates. (S4.M1.7)

Lesson Objectives

The learner will:

- wear equipment properly.
- select appropriate skates for size.
- demonstrate weight transfer to brake position.

Equipment and Materials

Per student or every two students of similar size:

- Helmet (sanitized between interpersonal use)
- Pair of knee pads
- Pair of elbow pads
- Pair of wrist pads
- Pair of in-line skates

Introduction

What did you see in the videos you watched from the previous lesson's homework? (Several students share.) If you saw a fall, how did the skater handle it? Today, we are going to put on our skates, keep working on our falls, and practice the braking position.

Instructional Task:
Continue Safety Gear and Skate Introduction

▦ PRACTICE TASK

Inspect equipment for damage.

Select and adjust skates. Students will need to know their shoe size (round up for half sizes). Explain the importance of a snug (but not too tight) fit using the buckle adjustments.

Students review falling techniques five times.

Students practice lowering center of gravity to promote balance five times.

Extensions

- Practice fastening skates five times.
- Practice putting on skates and fastening them five times.
- Stand in crouched position (wear one or two skates, hold a partner's shoulder who is not wearing skates) five or more times.

Refinements

- Make sure all buckles are secure when fastened.
- Check for athletic stance with knees slightly bent.

EMBEDDED OUTCOME: S4.M1.7 While students are putting on equipment and practicing falls, they should exhibit responsible social behaviors by cooperating with classmates, demonstrating inclusive behaviors, and supporting classmates with encouraging comments. Provide feedback to students about the way they support one another.

Student Choices/Differentiation

- Students inspect equipment for self or partner.
- Students wearing shoes may lend a shoulder to those wearing skates.

What to Look For

- Students report damaged equipment.
- Students fall from knees to elbows to hands.
- Students find skates that match shoe size and select another pair as needed.
- All buckles are secure when fastened.
- Skates are tightened to allow for little or no gaps (long socks are recommended to reduce friction).
- Knees are slightly bent as if sitting in a chair to distribute weight downward instead of forward, fingers point upward, head is up (similar to the athletic stance).

Instructional Task: Brake Position and Promoting Balance

■ PRACTICE TASK

1. *Locate the brake on the right foot by raising the toes while pressing the heel down five times.*

If applicable, students repeat with the left skate five times.

1. *Stand on one foot five times. Repeat with the other foot to feel your weight distribution shift and to become aware of wearing all equipment.*
2. *Squat to a tuck position five times.*
3. *Stand with your feet in the shape of a T five times. Repeat, with your feet in opposite positions.*

Guiding questions for students:

- What happens to your center of gravity when you shift your weight from one skate to the other?
- When would you want to be less balanced? More balanced?
- How would you get into a more balanced position?

Extensions

- Repeat any activity more than five times.
- Vary the speed of the activities.

Refinement

Make sure students are maintaining an appropriate body position, keeping the head up and keeping a balanced center of gravity.

Student Choices/Differentiation

- Students may remain on grass instead of skating on pavement.
- Students take breaks as needed.
- Students may hold a partner's shoulder with dominant hand (partner should wear shoes to assist).

What to Look For

- Students' heads are up, center of gravity is lowered, knees and elbows are bent for balance and control, palms are open.
- Students maintain body position. Their speed is dependent on the comfort level of the skater rather than the assisting partner.
- Students are beginning to establish rhythm of movement, shifting body weight with control.

Note: All skates for the beginning learner have a right-foot brake; some have a break for each foot.

Formal and Informal Assessments

Exit slip: Self-assessment: How do you feel when performing balance activities?

Closure

- What was challenging about the equipment sizing, placement, or adjustment? (varied answers)
- How does crouching help when skating? (Answer: lowers center of gravity)

Reflection

- Did I provide ample choice for differentiation?
- Did I explain the various ways that skates can be adjusted by showing a sample of those with buckles, hook-and-loop fasteners, and laces?
- How can I help those who are missing skill practice time by spending more time with some than others to put on the gear?

Homework

Review all balances wearing shoes, and repeat with socks. Review all balances while standing on a low-level piece of equipment such as a wooden block.

Resources

Miller, L. (2003). *Get rolling: The beginner's guide to in-line skating.* 3rd ed. Danville, CA: Get Rolling Books.

Internet keyword search: "how to learn in-line skating"

LESSON 3: EXPLORING SKATING— JUMPING AND LANDING

Grade-Level Outcomes

Primary Outcome

Individual-performance activities: Demonstrates correct technique for basic skills in 1 self-selected individual-performance activity. (S1.M24.6)

Embedded Outcome

Safety: Independently uses physical activity and exercise equipment appropriately and safely. (S4.M7.7)

Lesson Objectives

The learner will:

- explore skating and stopping with a lowered center of gravity.
- learn basic skills for jumping and landing.

Equipment and Materials

Per student or every two students of similar size:

- Helmet (sanitized between interpersonal use)
- Pair of knee pads
- Pair of elbow pads
- Pair of wrist pads
- Pair of in-line skates
- 5 to 10 12- × 2- × 2-inch (30 × 5 × 5 cm) blocks, carpet squares, or similar pieces of equipment
- Paved and grassed area

Introduction

How does our center of gravity shift when we wear skates? How do we compensate for this? How do our arms and legs help us balance? Today, we're going to work on basic skating technique and different ways of stopping.

Review safety gear placement and inspect equipment before use.

Instructional Task: Control the Body and Skates

■ PRACTICE TASK

In personal space, with a lowered center of gravity, students practice the following five times each:

1. Use the T position for the feet to push off (dominant foot in back).
2. Push off with the dominant foot in back.
3. Position feet like a V and push using an outward stroke.
4. Weight shifts over weight-bearing skate.
5. Take three strides and stop using the brake (raise toes, lower heel and center of gravity, drag the brake).
6. Repeat until comfortable using the brake.

Extensions

- Repeat, using the T stop (place dominant skate behind non-dominant and drag wheels to stop).
- Repeat, using non-dominant foot to drag behind (reverse from above).

EMBEDDED OUTCOME: S4.M7.7. Instead of helping students put on skates and safety equipment, have students independently use equipment appropriately and safely.

Student Choices/Differentiation

Partners may assist with any of the practice tasks, but they must wear shoes.

What to Look For

- Students maintain balance and control of skates.
- Arms extend for balance.
- Weight shifts to appropriate foot for T positioning.

Instructional Task: Jump and Land

■ PRACTICE TASK

Have students work through the following progressions:

- Walk on grass with skates.
- Walk on pavement.
- Do low jumps on grass or pavement.

Extensions

- Do high jumps on grass or pavement.
- Jump and tuck on grass or pavement.
- Step over a small piece of equipment.
- Jump over a small piece of equipment.
- While skating, step or jump over a small piece of equipment.
- Turn blocks or similar items to the elongated position and step or jump over them.

Peer assessment: Describe body positioning to a peer before attempting skills and after landing. Write and share.

Refinements

Remind students to bend their knees and use their arms to maintain a balanced position.

Student Choices/Differentiation

- Students choose whether to attempt more difficult movements.
- Students proceed through tasks at their own pace.

What to Look For

- Students maintain a slightly crouched position before and after movement.
- Feet begin in a V or T position.
- Students use arms for balance.
- Students bend knees to land softly and regain balance immediately using the V position with feet.
- Students use brake to regain balance.
- Students use T position to regain balance.
- Students are able to describe proper body placement to a peer for jumping and landing.

Formal and Informal Assessments

- Peer assessment
- Exit slip: Write the steps for regaining body control. (Answer: 1. Check body position for athletic stance. 2. Check foot position [return to V shape]. 3. Head up.)

Closure

- How does lowering the center of gravity assist you with these tasks? (Answer: promotes stability, engages leg muscles to assist with balance)
- What role do arms play? (Answer: extend to assist with balance, as when Nik Wallenda uses the pole while walking the tight rope)

Reflection

- How many students chose to help others versus practice for their own improvement?
- Are most students able to brake successfully?
- Are they pushing off to skate with confidence?
- Which students need more practice on their jumping and landing?

Homework

Practice foot positioning (T and V using walking speed) from the lesson today, five times for each foot.

Resources

Miller, L. (2003). *Get rolling: The beginner's guide to in-line skating.* 3rd ed. Danforth, CA: Get Rolling Books.

Internet keyword search: "how do I in-line skate," "center of gravity in-line skating," "Nik Wallenda tightrope walking"

LESSON 4: STARTING AND STOPPING

Grade-Level Outcomes

Primary Outcome

Individual-performance activities: Demonstrates correct technique for basic skills in 1 self-selected individual-performance activity. (S1.M24.6)

Embedded Outcome

Working with others: Accepts differences among classmates in physical development, maturation and varying skill levels by providing encouragement and positive feedback. (S4.M4.6)

Lesson Objectives

The learner will:

- explore in-line skate manipulation.
- demonstrate turns while in-line skating.
- combine skills of skating forward, turning, and stopping while navigating an obstacle course.

Equipment and Materials

Per student or every two students of similar size:

- Helmet (sanitized between interpersonal use)
- Pair of knee pads
- Pair of elbow pads
- Pair of wrist pads
- Pair of in-line skates
- 5 to 10 12- × 2- × 2-inch (30 × 5 × 5 cm) blocks, carpet squares, or similar pieces of equipment
- Paved and grassed area
- 4 to 20 cones (any size)

Introduction

Remind students to inspect safety equipment for damage and how to make adjustments.

Is anyone sore from the last lesson? Why do you think you are sore? The low position and push-off of in-line skating can make you sore if you're not used to using your glutes, hamstrings, and quads that way. Today, we're going to review some of the skills that we practiced last time and then learn how to turn on our skates. Before we finish, we'll combine all the skills we've learned so far to skate through an obstacle course.

Instructional Task: Starting and Stopping

■ PRACTICE TASK

Have students review starting and stopping five times each (skating in between so the skills are no longer in isolation).

Extension

Use speed to navigate up or down hills.

EMBEDDED OUTCOME: S4.M4.6. Discuss with students that not all students have the same skill level, and we should accept differences and provide encouragement and positive feedback while practicing skating.

Student Choices/Differentiation

- Students select the speed at which they wish to travel (faster skaters must pass on the right side, allowing ample space).
- Only students wearing shoes may assist skaters.

What to Look For

- From the T or V position, students push outward diagonally and away from the body while shifting weight to the opposite leg.
- Students are repeating the pattern with the opposite leg to develop a comfortable rhythm.
- The upper body shifts weight in the opposite direction of the push to maintain balance.
- Students stop to gain control.

Instructional Task: Turns

■ PRACTICE TASK

Demonstrate the scissor turn. Have students practice the turn five times in each direction at a comfortable pace.

Students can practice the turn around any obstacle or a partner who is wearing shoes to assist.

Extensions

- Demonstrate the crossover turn. Have students practice the turn around any obstacle or partner wearing shoes.
- Students practice both types of turns five times each in both directions.
- Students practice turns with varying speeds (five times per speed).
- Continue station work of all previous skills and have students combine jumping and landing, stopping and turning.

Repeat for a longer turn or step with the non-dominant foot to turn in the opposite direction.

Refinement

For the crossover, reinforce the dominant foot crossing over the weight-bearing foot.

Student Choices/Differentiation

- Students may walk or skate the turns.
- Students may choose the surface (grass or pavement).

What to Look For

- Scissor turns: One foot is slightly in front of the other, but knees are close together. Knees are bent slightly during the turn. Students shift body weight to force momentum left or right.
- Crossover turns: Students step across non-dominant foot and push out with dominant foot. Students shift body weight to non-dominant foot.

Instructional Task: Skating Course

■ PRACTICE TASK

Using stations, students review previously learned skills to navigate an obstacle course: (1) jumping and landing, (2) starting and stopping, (3) turning, and (4) skill combinations.

Set up skating courses with cones and varying degrees of difficulty for learners to practice turns and previously learned skills. Make the turns of varying tightness.

Students navigate the course on skates using scissor-style turns.

Use a checklist or rubric to assess whether students are shifting their weight and center of gravity properly.

Extensions

- Repeat, using crossover-style turns.
- Repeat, navigating at a faster speed but still in control.
- Create obstacle courses for self or others.
- Time partners for obstacle course completion.
- Self-assessment: Students rate their balance and control on a scale of 1 to 10, explaining why they ranked themselves as they did and why they are or are not falling. They also should identify whether they are falling correctly.

You should evaluate whether students are timing the weight shift appropriately and whether they are accounting for how the center of gravity shifts during movement.

Student Choices/Differentiation

- Set up courses of varying difficulty; students choose which course to practice on.
- Students choose the surface (grass or pavement).

What to Look For

- Are students skating with control?
- Are they able to combine skills of turning and stopping?
- Are students shifting their weight correctly and at the appropriate time?
- Are students keeping their center of gravity low and accounting for how the center of gravity shifts during movement?

Formal and Informal Assessments

- Self-assessment of balance and control
- Teacher assessment of weight shifting and center of gravity maintenance

Closure

- List two ways to complete a turn. (Answer: scissors, crossover)
- Share any tips you have found particularly helpful when stopping and starting; when turning; when navigating a hill; when making a speed change. (Answer: ample amount of personal space, use the technique that's most successful when there is no partner to help, crouch lower for turns than when skating in a straight line)

Reflection

- What is the confidence level of the students?
- How should I adjust my instruction accordingly?

Homework

Read Newton's laws of motion. Describe how these laws work when you are skating.

Resources

Miller, L. (2003). *Get rolling: The beginner's guide to in-line skating.* 3rd ed. Danforth, CA: Get Rolling Books.

Internet keyword search: "in-line skating," "how to turn"

LESSON 5:
APPLYING NEWTON'S LAWS TO SKATING

Grade-Level Outcomes

Primary Outcomes

Safety: Uses physical activity and fitness equipment appropriately and safely, *with the teacher's guidance.* (S4.M7.6)

Movement concepts: Identifies and applies Newton's laws of motion to various dance or movement activities. (S2.M12.7)

Individual-performance activities: Demonstrates correct technique for basic skills in 1 self-selected individual-performance activity. (S1.M24.6)

Embedded Outcome

Social interaction: Demonstrates the importance of social interaction by helping and encouraging others, avoiding trash talk and providing support to classmates. (S5.M6.7)

Lesson Objectives

The learner will:
- demonstrate backward skating.
- demonstrate jumping over an obstacle.
- apply Newton's laws to in-line skating.

Equipment and Materials

Per student or every two students of similar size:
- Helmet (sanitized between interpersonal use)
- Pair of knee pads
- Pair of elbow pads
- Pair of wrist pads
- Pair of in-line skates
- 5 to 10 12- × 2- × 2-inch (30 × 5 × 5 cm) blocks, carpet squares, or similar pieces of equipment
- Paved and grassed area
- 4 to 20 cones (any size)
- 5 to 20 small blocks
- Low-level step or ramp with ample space for landings

Introduction

What are Newton's laws of motion? (law of inertia: tendency of objects to continue what they are doing; law of acceleration: the greater the mass, the greater the force needed to move that mass; law of action–reaction: for every action there is an equal and opposite reaction) *How do they apply to in-line skating? If the wheels stop rolling fluidly, you will fall; the relationship among force, mass, and acceleration can make you fall if you skate too fast when your mass isn't distributed correctly by staying low; when you skate, the ground pushes back against you to propel you. We're going to apply these principles while learning to skate backward today.*

Instructional Task:
Skate Backward by Shifting Body Weight Left and Right

■ PRACTICE TASK

Using Newton's laws, we are going to learn how to skate backward.

Instruct students using the following progressions:

- Step side to side: Students gain confidence stepping side to side and maintaining balance; as the heel drives outward, the wheels will begin to roll. Remind students to maintain the crouched position, with head up.
- Carve the letter C: Students begin to make the letter C as the outward leg steps; the hips begin to rotate to assist. Weight shifts from the back wheel to the front wheel as the C is formed.
- Students may opt to carve the letter C with each skate independently at first.
- Skate backward: Momentum created by carving the letter C will propel the skaters backward. Cue students to maintain the crouched position, with head up, glancing backward to ensure safety.

Split the group in two and have half the students practice skating backward at a comfortable speed, trying to maintain a straight line. When they reach their designated area, the other half will go.

Repeat until students are moving more fluidly.

Extensions

- Students may skate backward or forward around obstacles.
- Record students for video analysis.

Refinements

- Emphasize looking over the shoulder to make sure no one collides with another skater.
- Students watch video of themselves performing the skill and discuss body positioning during backward skating.

EMBEDDED OUTCOME: S5.M6.7. Discuss with students that backward skating is a difficult skill and they should encourage one another and be supportive while practicing. Provide feedback to students about how well they support classmates during the practice task.

Guiding questions for students:

- Is the law of inertia greater on surfaces that are paved or grass?
- How does the law of acceleration affect skating on grass?

Student Choices/Differentiation

- Students may practice side-to-side movements on grass or paved surfaces but will likely not feel the wheels begin to roll to encourage movement backward until on paved surfaces.
- Students may skate backward or forward along designated pathways using cones.

What to Look For

- Students begin with feet in the A position.
- Students press the heels outward in or out of sync for speed changes and then back inward like a C to propel.
- Making the C shape is heel driven initially, and then students' weight shifts to the toes for a flick motion to finish the C.
- Students look over the shoulder to navigate.

Instructional Task: Jump and Land

■ PRACTICE TASK

Using Newton's laws, review the previous jumping skills.

- Review jumping: Center weight over skates, set feet shoulder-width apart or slightly wider, bend knees, push upward with legs, keep head up, swing arms with elbows bent.
- Students practice jumping over a variety of obstacles.

Extensions

- Jump with a partner to explore height versus length of jumping.
- Students watch video of themselves performing the skill and discuss body positioning during backward skating.

Guiding questions for students:

- How did Newton's laws help with your jumping practice?
- How does the law of action–reaction explain jumping and landing successfully?
- How did bending the knees and pushing upward help you to jump vertically?
- How does your body absorb the force of landing? How does this action relate to Newton's laws?

Student Choices/Differentiation

- Students can jump up steps if they are spaced well apart to allow time for landing, and then down steps if students can maintain balance jumping upward.
- Students can jump over low-level ramps.
- Students can skate linearly, with small obstacles along the pathway to jump.

What to Look For

- Weight is over skates at all times.
- Arms are used for balance (generally in front or to the side, as needed).
- Knees are bent to begin jump and softened to land.

Formal and Informal Assessments

- Video analysis: backward skating, jumping, and landing
- Exit slip: In your own words, describe how Newton's laws apply to in-line skating.

Closure

Body positioning lends itself to success.

- What are key positioning points for backward skating? (Answer: knees bent, heels in a C)
- What are key positioning points for jumping? (Answer: knees bent, arms for balance, weight on skates)

Reflection

- Do I have enough practice opportunities for all levels of learners regardless of the skill they are mastering?
- Are most of the students getting the feel for skating backward?
- Could we partner students who struggle with balance when looking backward while skating with face-to-face partners who are skating forward to look out behind?

Homework

Think of other uses of Newton's laws of motion in other activities. Discuss your ideas with a friend or family member.

Resources

Miller, L. (2003). *Get rolling: The beginner's guide to in-line skating.* 3rd ed. Danforth, CA: Get Rolling Books.

Internet keyword search: "how to in-line skate backward," "how to in-line skate jump," "Newton's laws and in-line skating"

LESSON 6: FLOOR HOCKEY

Grade-Level Outcomes

Primary Outcomes

Individual-performance activities: Demonstrates correct technique for basic skills in 1 self-selected individual-performance activity. (S1.M24.6)

Movement concepts: Identifies and applies Newton's laws of motion to various dance or movement activities. (S2.M12.7)

Embedded Outcomes

Accepting feedback: Provides corrective feedback to a peer, using teacher-generated guidelines, and incorporating appropriate tone and other communication skills. (S4.M3.7)

Shooting on goal: Shoots on goal with power and accuracy in small-sided game play. (S1.M10.7)

Shooting on goal: Shoots on goal with a long-handled implement for power and accuracy in modified invasion games such as hockey (floor, field, ice) or lacrosse. (S1.M10.8)

Transitions: Transitions from offense to defense or defense to offense by recovering quickly and communicating with teammates. (S2.M6.7)

Lesson Objectives

The learner will:

- demonstrate skating skills while handling a hockey stick and ball.
- apply Newton's laws to striking and collecting a ball with a hockey stick.

Equipment and Materials

Per student or every two students of similar size:

- Helmet (sanitized between interpersonal use)
- Pair of knee pads
- Pair of elbow pads
- Pair of wrist pads
- Pair of in-line skates
- 4 to 20 cones (any size)
- 5 to 20 small blocks
- 1 hockey stick per student
- 2 or 3 street hockey pucks (balls)
- Goals, or 2 cones to use as each goal

Introduction

What are some factors to consider relative to Newton's laws when adding hockey skills? (keeping balance when changing directions, the force of the stick to the puck and the puck pushing back, collisions with other learners, speed changes to chase the puck.) *Today, we will explore some of these, with hockey.*

Instructional Task: Hockey Skill Stations

■ **PRACTICE TASK**

Students practice the following hockey skills without skates:

- Shooting on goal with power and accuracy
- Transitioning from offense to defense or defense to offense by recovering quickly and communicating with teammates

- Dribbling the puck
- Passing the puck with a partner

EMBEDDED OUTCOME: S4.M3.7 Students provide corrective feedback to a peer, using teacher-generated guidelines and incorporating appropriate tone and other communication skills.

Guiding questions for students:
- Consider how the strength of your passes affects your balance when you're wearing shoes instead of skates. How is your balance affected by Newton's laws of motion with respect to the law of action–reaction?
- How are the laws of inertia and acceleration intertwined when you make a poor pass to a partner?

Extensions
- Play a small-sided game of hockey.
- Repeat the stations with skates.

Guiding questions for students:
- How did wearing skates affect your skills?
- Can you justify these changes using Newton's laws of motion?

Refinements
- Stop drills to correct any hockey skills that students are performing improperly (especially if it relates to safety).
- Students should self-identify their skating skills and apply them appropriately to the hockey drills (even though they may be good floor hockey players, they might struggle on skates).

Student Choices/Differentiation
- Students select the varying distances for shots on goal.
- Students may opt out of using a goalie to defend shots on goal.
- Students may dribble around obstacles with stationary or mobile defenders.
- Students may participate in small-sided games ranging from 1 v 1 up to 3 v 3.

What to Look For
- Students use correct body positioning for each skill.
- Students' knees are bent.
- Students maintain body control when using a hockey stick.

Instructional Task: Peer Assessment

■ PRACTICE TASK

Using the skill analysis from previous lessons, students (under your direction) develop checklists to evaluate their skills.

Extension

Have students write a reflection on the process of developing the checklist, or the evaluation of their skills, or both.

Refinement

Help students identify critical elements in their skills. Make sure that students focus on the process instead of only on the product.

Student Choices/Differentiation

Provide an example of an evaluation checklist.

What to Look For

- Students are able to identify critical elements of their skills.
- Students are able to reflect on the assignments.

Formal and Informal Assessments

- Peer assessment
- Reflection activity

Closure

- What issues did you encounter when adding a hockey stick and puck while skating? (Answers: force created while dribbling or passing the puck makes it more difficult to maintain balance, must keep head up to avoid other skaters, must make quick changes in direction with possession changes)
- How did you adjust to avoid falling? (Answer: student feedback, must keep knees bent)

Reflection

- Do students have ample space for skill practice?
- Did I review hockey rules to prevent injuries on plays that would be penalized? (For example: high sticks)

Homework

- Find a video of people skating on ice (figure skaters, speed skaters, hockey players), and note the similarities and differences when compared with in-line skating. For a real challenge, apply Newton's laws!
- We will also take our in-line skating quiz tomorrow. Review the critical elements, safety components, and principles of Newton's laws on the school's physical education website.

Resources

Miller, L. (2003). *Get rolling: The beginner's guide to in-line skating.* 3rd ed. Danforth, CA: Get Rolling Books.

Internet keyword search: "in-line hockey drills," "hockey drills for beginners"

LESSON 7: SKATING STATIONS

Grade-Level Outcomes

Primary Outcome

Individual-performance activities: Demonstrates correct technique for basic skills in 1 self-selected individual-performance activity. (S1.M24.6)

Embedded Outcome

Fitness knowledge: Identifies major muscles used in selected physical activities. (S3.M14.6)

Lesson Objectives

The learner will:
- explore in-line skating with direction changes.
- explore body position in space.
- demonstrate in an assessment a knowledge of skating.

Equipment and Materials

Per student or every two students of similar size:
- Helmet (sanitized between interpersonal use)
- Pair of knee pads
- Pair of elbow pads
- Pair of wrist pads
- Pair of in-line skates
- 5 to 10 12- × 2- × 2-inch (30 × 5 × 5 cm) blocks, carpet squares, or similar pieces of equipment
- 4 to 20 cones (any size)
- 5 to 20 small blocks
- Low-level step or ramp with ample space to land
- 4 to 6 hockey sticks
- 2 or 3 street hockey pucks (balls)
- Goals or 2 cones for each necessary goal

Introduction

What similarities did you notice from doing the homework between using ice skates and in-line skates? Is it possible to practice for tough balancing situations on purpose? What skills should you practice to improve at in-line skating? Today, we will refine our in-line skating skills so we can skate more confidently.

Instructional Task: Skating Stations

■ PRACTICE TASK

Set up stations to improve footwork in four categories. Use cones to designate zones. Students may select one or more activity per station.

Station 1: Speed and Direction Changes
- Skate through speed zones for alternating speeds.
- Practice navigating up and down hills.
- Skate through starting and stopping zones to improve control over speed.

- Navigate around cones to practice left and right direction changes in zigzag lines.
- Skate through direction zones for forward and backward.

Station 2: Turns and Balance

- Cross over while going through a curve.
- Keep both skates in line and shift weight to turn.
- Skate on one leg.
- Navigate through student-created figure eights of various sizes.
- Skate on only two wheels (any combination such as front and back or both back or front wheels).

Station 3: Obstacles

- Jump over low blocks or carpet squares.
- Skate over obstacles such as uneven pavement.
- Jump and turn 180 degrees.
- Jump over low objects and turn.
- Navigate a student-created obstacle course (e.g., hoops, boxes, cones, other objects).

Station 4: Hockey Skills

- Work on passing skills.
- Play a small-sided game (e.g., 2 v 2).
- Work on dribbling skills.
- Do lead-pass drills (pass the puck or ball to where the receiver will be, not where she is at the time it leaves your stick).

Extension

Combine any of the skills.

EMBEDDED OUTCOME: S3.M14.6. At each station, have students discuss the major muscles that they're using.

Refinements

- Suggest that students work on familiar and unfamiliar skills.
- Make sure that students use feedback from video analysis from previous lessons.

Guiding questions for students:

- Describe how to change directions from left to right while skating.
- Name one way to complete a turn while skating.

Student Choices/Differentiation

- Use a timer at stations.
- Challenge higher-skilled students to complete each activity at each station.
- Students complete stations alone or with a partner's assistance or competition.

What to Look For

- Are students centered over their skates?
- Are students persistent and responsible in their learning? (That is, they don't give up but also don't take too much risk for their skill level.)
- Are students using feedback from the video analyses in lesson 5?

Instructional Task: Skating Module Quiz

■ **PRACTICE TASK**

Students should take the end-of-module quiz.

Student Choices/Differentiation

Apply any testing modifications needed.

What to Look For

- Students know the critical elements of the skills taught in the module.
- Students know and are able to apply Newton's laws.
- Students know safety procedures and concepts related to skating.

Formal and Informal Assessments

- Skating module quiz
- Self-reflection homework activity

Closure

- What stations were the most challenging for you?
- What skills did you like best and why?
- Practicing these situations helps us be more prepared when the situation arises unexpectedly.

Reflection

- What were the most popular skills?
- Did I provide ample practice space and equipment?
- Are students improving in more than one area of skating?

Homework

- Complete a self-reflection homework activity.
  - Did I practice familiar and unfamiliar tasks at each station?
  - What are my areas of strength and weakness?
  - What changes in muscle soreness have I noticed after seven lessons of skating as compared to after one lesson?
- Look up some Olympic events on ice skates, and be prepared to share at the beginning of next class.

Resources

Internet keyword search: "how to improve in-line skating," "things to practice for in-line skating," "Rollerblade freestyle slalom (nine-year-old girl)"

LESSON 8: OBSTACLE COURSE AND SKATING ROUTINES

Grade-Level Outcomes

Primary Outcome

Individual-performance activities: Demonstrates correct technique for basic skills in 1 self-selected individual-performance activity. (S1.M24.6)

Embedded Outcome

Working with others: Problem-solves with a small group of classmates during adventure activities, small-group initiatives or game play. (S4.M5.7)

Lesson Objectives

The learner will:

- create and navigate obstacle courses.
- create a skating routine.

Equipment and Materials

Per student or every two students of similar size:

- Helmet (sanitized between interpersonal use)
- Pair of knee pads
- Pair of elbow pads
- Pair of wrist pads
- Pair of in-line skates
- 5 to 10 12- × 2- × 2-inch (30 × 5 × 5 cm) blocks, carpet squares, or similar pieces of equipment
- Paved area
- 4 to 20 cones (any size)
- 5 to 20 small blocks
- Low-level step or ramp with ample space to land
- 20 to 30 ribbon wands

Introduction

Name Olympic sports that involve skating (examples include ice hockey, speed skating, figure skating, and short-track speed skating). *We will explore some of those sports in today's lesson.*

Instructional Task: Create an Obstacle Course

■ **PRACTICE TASK**

Divide the equipment among four to six groups.

Form small groups and create an obstacle course that must include at least four of the following elements of skating at least one time:

- *Speed change*
- *Direction change*
- *Turn*
- *A balancing skill*

- *Jumping*
- *Obstacles*

Recall the stations that you completed last week for ideas.

Students must subdivide their groups to create one aspect of the course.

Students must select one chairperson who may offer a trade in equipment with another group as long as at least four elements are included at least once in her group's obstacle course.

Extension

Each group may test out the other obstacle courses.

Refinement

Pre-determine a student-designated level of difficulty for each course. For example, include at least one course that students feel would be easy to complete.

EMBEDDED OUTCOME: S4.M5.7 Students should practice effective problem-solving skills with a small group of classmates during this activity.

Student Choices/Differentiation

- Allow partners to time each other.
- Group learners of similar abilities.
- Build identical courses for racing as in speed skating.
- Complete less complex courses skating backward only.

What to Look For

- Students begin with feet in the T position.
- Students successfully complete the obstacle courses.
- Students stop with control.
- Each group cooperates to include at least four skating elements in the obstacle course.

Instructional Task: Figure Skating Routine

■ PRACTICE TASK

Have students create a simple or complex figure skating routine.

Routines can include any number of the elements such as jumping, starting and stopping, turning, and changing speed to make the routine 1 to 2 minutes in length.

Extensions

- Teach the routine to a partner.
- Students create judging criteria.
- Perform the routine for faculty and other students.

Student Choices/Differentiation

- Students may work as individuals or with two or three partners in the creation of the routine.
- Students may use props such as ribbons.

What to Look For

- Students' body weight is over skates.
- Students lower center of gravity for speed and stability.
- Students skate with control.

Formal and Informal Assessments

End-of-module homework reflection

Closure

- What opportunities are there in our community for skating?
- In what areas can skating help the body improve? (Answer: cardiorespiratory fitness, muscular strength and endurance, balance)

Reflection

Have all students shown growth in at least one area? How can I improve this unit in the future?

Homework

- End-of-module reflection: How does science affect skating? What elements did you consider when you designed your obstacle course? What are the benefits of skating for a lifetime?
- Tell someone at home your best skating skill, and describe how to complete it.
- Review material on the school's physical education website for the next module.

Resources

Internet keyword search: "Evgenia Medvedeva free skate," "Javier Fernandez free skate," "Duhamel and Radford free skate"

MOUNTAIN BIKING MODULE

Lessons in this module were contributed by Matt Bristol, a PreK-8 physical education teacher at Putney Central School, in Putney, VT.

Grade-Level Outcomes Addressed, by Lesson	Lessons							
	1	2	3	4	5	6	7	8
Standard 1. The physically literate individual demonstrates competency in a variety of motor skills and movement patterns.								
Demonstrates correct technique for basic skills in 1 self-selected outdoor activity. (S1.M22.6)	P	P	P	P	P	P	P	P
Demonstrates correct technique for basic skills in 1 self-selected individual-performance activity. (S1.M24.6)	P	P	P	P	P	P	P	P
Standard 2. The physically literate individual applies knowledge of concepts, principles, strategies and tactics related to movement and performance.								
Standard 3. The physically literate individual demonstrates the knowledge and skills to achieve and maintain a health-enhancing level of physical activity and fitness.								
Participates in a variety of lifetime recreational team sports, outdoor pursuits or dance activities. (S3.M5.6)	E							E
Uses available technology to self-monitor quantity of exercise needed for a minimal health standard and/or optimal functioning based on current fitness level. (S3.M8.8)						P		
Develops strategies for balancing healthy food, snacks and water intake, along with daily physical activity. (S3.M17.7)							P	
Practices strategies for dealing with stress, such as deep breathing, guided visualization and aerobic exercise. (S3.M18.7)					P			
Standard 4. The physically literate individual exhibits responsible personal and social behavior that respects self and others.								
Exhibits responsible social behaviors by cooperating with classmates, demonstrating inclusive behaviors and supporting classmates. (S4.M1.7)							E	
Demonstrates both intrinsic and extrinsic motivation by selecting opportunities to participate in physical activity outside of class. (S4.M2.7)						E		
Demonstrates self-responsibility by implementing specific corrective feedback to improve performance. (S4.M3.6)				P				
Provides corrective feedback to a peer, using teacher-generated guidelines, and incorporating appropriate tone and other communication skills. (S4.M3.7)					E			
Demonstrates cooperation skills by establishing rules and guidelines for resolving conflict. (S4.M4.7)	E							
Problem-solves with a small group of classmates during adventure activities, small-group initiatives or game play. (S4.M5.7)								E
Identifies the rules and etiquette for physical activities/games and dance activities. (S4.M6.6)						E		
Uses physical activity and fitness equipment appropriately and safely, *with the teacher's guidance*. (S4.M7.6)		P						
Standard 5. The physically literate individual recognizes the value of physical activity for health, enjoyment, challenge, self-expression and/or social interaction.								
Describes how being physically active leads to a healthy body. (S5.M1.6)		E						
Identifies different types of physical activities and describes how each exerts a positive effect on health. (S5.M1.7)						E		
Identifies the 5 components of health-related fitness (muscular strength, muscular endurance, flexibility, cardiovascular endurance and body composition) and explains the connections between fitness and overall physical and mental health. (S5.M1.8)								P
Identifies components of physical activity that provide opportunities for reducing stress and for social interaction. (S5.M2.6)					E			
Demonstrates the importance of social interaction by helping and encouraging others, avoiding trash talk and providing support to classmates. (S5.M6.7)			E					

P = Primary; E = Embedded

LESSON 1: EXPLORING THE BIKE

Grade-Level Outcomes

Primary Outcomes

Outdoor pursuits: Demonstrates correct technique for basic skills in 1 self-selected outdoor activity. (S1.M22.6)

Individual-performance activities: Demonstrates correct technique for basic skills in 1 self-selected individual-performance activity. (S1.M24.6)

Embedded Outcomes

Working with others: Demonstrates cooperation skills by establishing rules and guidelines for resolving conflict. (S4.M4.7)

Engages in physical activity: Participates in a variety of lifetime recreational team sports, outdoor pursuits or dance activities. (S3.M5.6)

Lesson Objectives

The learner will:

- identify different parts of a mountain bike.
- demonstrate the ability to fit a helmet and bike properly.
- demonstrate an even pedal stroke on a mountain bike.
- demonstrate the ability to use the brakes to stop.

Equipment and Materials

- Mountain bikes
- Helmets
- Variety of other bicycles (optional)
- Variety of cones
- First aid kit
- Air pump
- Mini tool kit for adjusting and repairing bikes on the go

Introduction

Today, we will explore the world of mountain biking. We first will view a short video (Internet keyword search: mountain biking) *that will give you a better idea of what mountain biking really is. You will have an opportunity to get on the bikes and ride today. But first, you must learn about the bike and bike safety.*

Instructional Task: Exploring the Bike and Bike Safety

■ **PRACTICE TASK**

Working in small groups, take some time to explore a bike:

1. *Examine the bike before getting on.*
2. *Adjust the seat and handlebar height.*
3. *Get on the bike and use your feet to push off the ground. Try putting your feet on the wheels.*

Share and discuss everything you know about mountain biking.

Demonstrate how to fit a helmet.

Have students work in groups while practicing fitting a helmet.

Extensions

- Have students explore a different style of bicycle, such as road or unicycle.
- Have students compare and contrast the bicycles in the room.

EMBEDDED OUTCOME: S4.M4.7 Help students establish rules and guidelines for resolving conflict while working in small groups.

Refinements

- Make sure the helmet fits snugly around the head before adjusting any straps. Some helmets may be too big regardless of how tight the straps are.
- Adjust the ear straps for a tighter, more comfortable fit.

Student Choices/Differentiation

- Students may choose their own small groups.
- Groups may choose the bike that they explore. If there is conflict, they will decide on how to handle it.
- Students may bring in their own bikes and helmets from home.

What to Look For

- Students demonstrate initiative skills by creating their own groups and selecting a bicycle to explore.
- While in groups, students demonstrate active participation in the task.
- Monitor the small-group discussion in order to assess participation levels of all students.

Instructional Task: Selecting and Mounting a Bike and Adjusting the Seat Height

■ PRACTICE TASK

Demonstrate how to find the appropriately sized bike and how to make adjustments to fit individual riders.

Students return to their small groups and practice fitting and mounting a bike.

Peers can assess these skills using a checklist for appropriately sized bicycles and helmets.

Extensions

- Do a running mount.
- Do a rolling dismount.

Refinement

Make sure students are choosing appropriately sized bicycles and that their helmets are fitted properly.

Guiding questions for students:

- What happens when a classmate wants or needs the same bike as you?
- How can you resolve this issue?

Student Choices/Differentiation

- Students may choose to change groups if needed.
- Students will choose their bicycles.
- Guide students toward an appropriate bike if needed.
- Have experienced students help less experienced students.

What to Look For

- Students demonstrate their ability to resolve conflicts when two students want or need the same bike.
- When selecting a bike, students adjust the seat height as needed so that when the student stands next to the bike, the seat rests at hip level.

Instructional Task: Pedal Stroke, Turning, and Braking

■ PRACTICE TASK

Students practice pedaling, turning, and braking on your command.

Individually, students ride through an obstacle course that challenges them to use pedaling, turning, and braking all together.

Refinements

- Students should refrain from using the left brake alone.
- The brake finger should be placed toward the end of the lever for maximum leverage.
- When turning, students should have the outside pedal lower than the inside pedal, and shift their weight to the outside.

Extensions

- Students complete the commands while standing out of the saddle.
- Students practice weaving in and out of cones.
- Students practice breaking out of the saddle and balancing as long as possible before dismounting.
- Students practice 90-degree, 180-degree, and 270-degree turns.
- Formative checklist: mounting/dismounting, pedal stroke, turning, and braking

Student Choices/Differentiation

- Students can work in pairs and share a bike.
- Students are allowed to observe before participating.

What to Look For

- Students demonstrate an even pedal stroke while keeping one finger, lightly, over each brake lever.
- Students release from the saddle when needed in order to maintain balance and dismount properly.
- Students are able to pedal, turn, and brake on command without falling off the bike.

Formal and Informal Assessments

- Peer assessment: bike- and helmet-fitting checklist (see *Bikeology* curriculum)
- Formative checklist: students demonstrate the following skills with safety: mounting and unmounting, pedal stroke, turning, and braking

Closure

- What is something you learned about mountain bikes today?
- How do you appropriately size a bike for yourself?
- How do you resolve conflicts, such as needing the same bike as a classmate?
- What should your helmet look like if you are wearing it properly?
- What bike skills did you practice today?

Reflection

- Were students engaged? Was there too much downtime?
- Is there an equipment issue? Is it okay for students to share bikes, or do they each need their own?
- Can students fit a helmet on their own or with help from a classmate?
- Can students size a bike for themselves or with help from a classmate?

Homework

If you have a bike at home, bike for 20-plus minutes. Make sure to follow the safety guidelines that you learned today and practice mounting and unmounting the bike. If you don't have a bike at home, you can use a school bike to ride at recess. If you elect to use a school bike, you will need to accumulate 20-plus minutes of riding over the course of the week.

Resources

American Alliance for Health, Physical Education, Recreation and Dance. (2014). *Bikeology: A middle and high school bicycle safety curriculum for physical education teachers and recreation specialists*. Reston, VA: Author. Available at www.shapeamerica.org.Bicycle Helmet Safety Institute. (2015). How to fit a helmet. Available at www.bhsi.org.

Lopes, B., & McCormack, L. (2010). *Mastering mountain bike skills*. 2nd ed. Champaign, IL: Human Kinetics.

Internet keyword search: "how to fit and adjust a cycle helmet," "mountain bike skills + tips—10 essential things to know"

LESSON 2: SHIFTING AND ATTACKING

Grade-Level Outcomes

Primary Outcomes

Outdoor pursuits: Demonstrates correct technique for basic skills in 1 self-selected outdoor activity. (S1.M22.6)

Individual-performance activities: Demonstrates correct technique for basic skills in 1 self-selected individual-performance activity. (S1.M24.6)

Safety: Uses physical activity and fitness equipment appropriately and safely, *with the teacher's guidance.* (S4.M7.6)

Embedded Outcome

Health: Describes how being physically active leads to a healthy body. (S5.M1.6)

Lesson Objectives

The learner will:

- demonstrate the skills and knowledge to fit a helmet and bike properly.
- demonstrate the ability to use the brakes to stop.
- learn the skills and knowledge in order to shift gears.
- demonstrate the ability to shift gears.
- demonstrate the attack position.

Equipment and Materials

- Mountain bikes
- Helmets
- Cones
- First aid kit
- Air pump
- Mini tool kit for adjusting and repairing bikes on the go

Introduction

Today, we will continue to explore the mountain bike and will practice a variety of important mountain biking skills. We will start by reviewing bike safety. You will have an opportunity to practice an even pedal stroke, turning, and braking. The new skills that you will learn and practice today include shifting gears, shifting your weight, and the attack position.

Instructional Task: Review Equipment

■ **PRACTICE TASK**

Working in small groups, students fit helmets to their heads and bikes to their bodies. Students check each other for proper fitting.

Extension

Review the following:

- Rolling mount
- Running dismount

Refinement

Make sure students are selecting appropriately sized bikes. Remind them that they should adjust the seat so their toes can touch the ground.

Student Choices/Differentiation

- Students may choose their groups and bikes.
- Provide students with the checklist from the last class if they need a reference.

What to Look For

- Are students checking each other for proper fitting?
- Students find a helmet that fits snugly before adjusting any straps.
- Students adjust straps to keep the helmet in place.
- Students find a bike that fits and adjust the seat so that it comes up to their hips.
- Students are able to reach their toes to the ground while sitting on the bike.

Checklist: Bike and Helmet Fitting

Instructional Task:
Review Pedal Stroke, Braking, and Turning

■ PRACTICE TASK

In pairs, students brainstorm everything they remember about riding with an even pedal stroke and with proper braking and turning techniques. Students should document their brainstorming session with pencil and paper.

In pairs, students practice these skills. One student rides as another student observes.

Refinements

- Students should limit their use of the brakes and keep a consistent pedal stroke.
- When taking sharper turns, students should keep the outside foot down and inside foot up, making sure to find balance on the bike as they lean into the turn.

Extensions

- Students practice keeping an even pedal stroke in a heavier gear.
- Students practice track stands.

Guiding questions for students:

- Are you following the safety guidelines while riding?
- Can you brake and stop safely?
- How do you manipulate the bike and your body in order to turn?

Student Choices/Differentiation

- Student will have access to the field for riding. They may choose their own pathways of travel.
- Students choose their own partners.

What to Look For

- Students hand in documentation of their brainstorming session.
- Students are maintaining consistent pedal stroke.
- Students keep inside pedal up (outside pedal down) while turning.
- Students are accepting of partners' ideas during the brainstorming session.

Instructional Task: Shifting Gears

■ PRACTICE TASK

In groups of four, students practice shifting gears. Each student within the group will have a job. A student will

1. hold the back tire up,
2. use the hand to pedal,
3. shift gears, and
4. observe the gears shifting.

Students should rotate jobs until everyone has had a turn at each job.

Extensions

- Students explore shifting gears independently.
- Teach how to replace a broken chain.

Refinements

- Make sure that students can differentiate between shifting up and shifting down.
- Make sure that they know how to shift on the bike they are using.

Student Choices/Differentiation

- Students choose their own groups and the order of job rotation.
- Students choose what gear they start in and what gears they shift to.

What to Look For

- Students understand that the pedals must be in motion when shifting.
- Students stay mindful of the pedal stroke. They should be shifting gears to keep that stroke consistent.
- Students use their conflict-resolution skills if there is conflict with job rotation.
- Students do not cross their chains.

Instructional Task: Riding in the Cockpit

■ PRACTICE TASK

Read commands out for students to follow.

1. *Push your hips toward the handlebars.*
2. *Get your hips behind the seat.*
3. *Pull your torso toward the pedals.*
4. *Get your shoulders as far away from your feet as possible.*

Give students time to discover the cockpit on their own.

Extension

Students partner up and give each other commands.

Refinement

Students explore the cockpit by moving their bodies into different positions on their bikes. Specifically, look for students to move their knees, hips, and torsos in order to experiment how it affects their riding.

Guiding questions for students:

- What happens when you move and shift your body while riding a bike?
- How does moving your hips affect your balance and overall ride? How about bending your knees?
- What happens when you shift all your weight toward the back of the bike?

Student Choices/Differentiation

- Students choose to skip past a command if they don't feel comfortable or safe attempting the skill.
- Students choose the positions in which they ride.
- If needed, repeat the verbal cues.

What to Look For

Students are discovering techniques for maintaining balance and shifting body weight while riding.

Instructional Task: Attack (Ready) Position

■ PRACTICE TASK

Demonstrate the attack position:

- Heavy feet
- Light hands
- Knees bent
- Hips and weight back
- Head up and eyes out

Allow several students to demonstrate for the class.

All students practice riding in a ready position. Allow students to explore and find their own ready positions.

Guiding questions for students:

- When might you use the attack position?
- Do you think the attack position is useful? Why?
- Why is it called the attack position?

Extensions

- Students use the attack position while traveling through an obstacle course.
- Students use iPads to film each other in the attack position.
- Students use the attack position to do a track stand.
- Students use the attack position on a downhill slope.

Refinements

- Check to make sure that students have their heads up and eyes outs, scanning the area in front of them.
- Make sure students' knees are bent.

EMBEDDED OUTCOME: S5.M1.6. Help students make the connection between mountain biking and improving health.

Ask students the following questions:

- How can being physically active lead to a healthy body?
- Can you use mountain biking to improve your body's health? If yes, how?

Student Choices/Differentiation

- Students choose their pathways as they ride around the field.
- Students may choose to work in pairs and observe each other.
- Students may choose to enter the obstacle course.

What to Look For

- Students explore different body positions until they find a comfortable position on the bike that allows them to maintain maximum balance.
- Students try their best to follow the cues.

Formal and Informal Assessments

- Peer assessments:
  - Checklist for components of attack position
  - Bike- and helmet-fitting checklist
- Exit slips:
  - Describe the attack position.
  - Brainstorming lists

Resources

American Alliance for Health, Physical Education, Recreation and Dance. (2014). *Bikeology: A middle and high school bicycle safety curriculum for physical education teachers and recreation specialists*. Reston, VA: Author. Available at www.shapeamerica.org.

Closure

- What is something you learned about mountain bikes today?
- What bike skills did you practice today?
- What does crossing your gears (chain) mean? What should your gears look like while riding?
- Why do you shift gears?
- Can someone explain what they discovered while they explored the cockpit today?
- What does the attack position look like, and why do you use it?

Reflection

- Can students fit a bike and helmet by themselves?
- Are students improving toward proficiency in skills such as turning and braking?
- Do students understand the concept of gears and shifting gears?
- Can students perform the attack position?
- What skills are students starting to combine? Can they shift in the attack position? Can they safely break out of the attack position?
- Can they turn and shift at the same time?

Homework

In your journal, please write a response to the following prompt: How does mountain biking make you feel? Think about how it makes you feel physically, emotionally, socially. The response has no page minimum or maximum, but it should be thoughtful. Consider the following:

- Does your body and brain feel refreshed after biking? Is your body tired and sore after biking?
- Are you nervous about mountain biking? If so, what makes you nervous?

- Do you get excited for biking? If so, how do you think that affects your experience?
- Is mountain biking something you like to do alone? Would you rather ride with friends? What is the best part about riding with other people?
- Is mountain biking an activity you can see yourself doing for a lifetime? Why or why not?

Resources

American Alliance for Health, Physical Education, Recreation and Dance. (2014). *Bikeology: A middle and high school bicycle safety curriculum for physical education teachers and recreation specialists*. Reston, VA: Author. Available at www.shapeamerica.org.

Lopes, B., & McCormack, L. (2010). *Mastering mountain bike skills*. 2nd ed. Champaign, IL: Human Kinetics.

Internet keyword search: "mountain bike skills + tips—10 essential things to know"

LESSON 3:
CLIMBING AND DESCENDING A HILL

Grade-Level Outcomes

Primary Outcomes

Outdoor pursuits: Demonstrates correct technique for basic skills in 1 self-selected outdoor activity. (S1.M22.6)

Individual-performance activities: Demonstrates correct technique for basic skills in 1 self-selected individual-performance activity. (S1.M24.6)

Embedded Outcome

Social interaction: Demonstrates the importance of social interaction by helping and encouraging others, avoiding trash talk and providing support to classmates. (S5.M6.7)

Lesson Objectives

The learner will:

- demonstrate the ability to shift gears and ride in the attack position.
- acquire the skills and knowledge to be able to climb a hill.
- acquire the skills and knowledge to be able to descend a hill.
- acquire the skills and knowledge to be able to complete a sprint.

Equipment and Materials

- Mountain bikes
- Helmets
- Access to a hill or slope
- First aid kit
- Air pump
- Mini tool kit for adjusting and repairing bikes on the go

Introduction

Today, we will review the skills we learned in the previous classes, including shifting gears and turning. You will learn the skills for climbing and descending a hill safely. Once you feel comfortable with climbing and descending hills, you will learn the skills needed for sprinting. Sprinting is the act of passing other riders and typically includes hard, fast strokes of the pedal. You also will learn the importance of social interaction and supporting your peers while biking, which is more important than any bike skill.

Instructional Task:
Review Shifting Gears and Attack Position

■ PRACTICE TASK

Review discussion of how to shift and why shifting is needed.

Review discussion about the attack position and why it is important.

Guiding questions for students:

- What does the attack position look like? What are the critical elements?
- When would you use the attack position?

Give students verbal commands related to shifting gears and shifting body weight.

- *Shift up.*
- *Shift down.*
- *Push your hips toward the handlebars.*
- *Get your hips behind the seat.*
- *Pull your torso toward the pedals*
- *Get your shoulders as far away from your feet as possible.*

EMBEDDED OUTCOME: S5.M6.7 Discuss with students the importance of social interaction in mountain biking. It is helpful to discuss helping and encouraging others, avoiding trash talk, and providing support to classmates.

Give students time to ride and observe each other in pairs. While riding, students practice

- shifting from an easy gear to a more difficult gear and the attack position.

Extensions

- Students give each other commands.
- Students combine skills, such as shifting gears while riding in the attack position.

Refinements

- Make sure students understand how to shift their bikes.
- Make sure that students get their bottoms out of the saddle.

Guiding questions for students:

- Can you combine the attack position with shifting? Braking? Turning? Why is the combination of these skills so important for biking?
- How can you encourage and support your peers in mountain biking? How can you translate that to the real world?

Student Choices/Differentiation

- Students who need more instruction can work with you during the individual ride time.
- Students choose the rate at which they work through the tasks.

What to Look For

- Students listen respectfully and raise their hands before speaking.
- Students are focused and trying their best to complete the commands.
- Students are on task in small groups and are respectful of their peers. Students encourage their peers to keep trying and congratulate them when a skill is completed.

A peer checklist will be used to document completion of tasks.

Instructional Task: Climbing a Hill

■ PRACTICE TASK

Discuss skills needed for climbing a hill.

Guiding questions for students:

- How should you position your body when climbing a hill?
- What gear should you be in?
- Should you be out of the saddle?

Demonstrate climbing a hill.

In pairs, students practice climbing a hill. Students take turns observing each other.

Refinements

- Shift into a light gear before climbing.
- Shift as needed to keep a consistent pedal stroke.

Extension

Do a rolling dismount after climbing the hill.

Student Choices/Differentiation

- Experienced bikers may demonstrate for other students.
- Inexperienced students may choose an experienced student to practice with.

What to Look For

- Students are respectful listeners during the discussion and demonstrations. Students feel comfortable adding their input during the discussion.
- While practicing, students shift as needed, making sure not to shift down too early. On the incline, students stand out of the saddle, push their weight forward, have slightly bent knees, and drive their pedals in a downward motion.
- Students encourage and support their peers.

Instructional Task: Descending a Hill

■ PRACTICE TASK

Demonstrate how to safely descend a hill.

Students divide into four lines and practice descending.

Refinements

- Make sure students keep their eyes forward while descending.
- Encourage students to descend the hill in the attack position.

Extensions

- Do a running mount before descending.
- Do a rolling dismount.

Student Choices/Differentiation

Students make the choice to attempt the extensions if they feel it's safe.

What to Look For

Students are making smart, safe decisions by analyzing their own skill levels and determining what is safe to practice and what is not.

Instructional Task: Sprinting

■ PRACTICE TASK

Demonstrate and discuss sprinting.

Guiding questions for students:

- What is a sprint?
- Why is a sprint needed?
- When do you sprint?

In pairs, students practice their sprinting in a controlled environment. One student performs while the other observes.

In groups of three, students compete in races of 40 yards or meters. Students practice using the sprint technique to get a good jump off the start line.

Refinements

- Use a higher gear for a stronger, faster sprint.
- Make sure students push down hard on the pedal to gain momentum.

Extension

In groups of two, students practice using the sprint technique to pass each other on a hill.

Student Choices/Differentiation

- Students choose their partners.
- Have stronger riders challenge themselves by starting a bike length behind their opponents.
- Allow students to add people to their group to increase the difficulty of the sprint.
- If students cannot climb hills, they can continue to practice the sprint on flat land.

What to Look For

- Students are using their maximum power to pedal. The pedal stroke should be a pushing down motion as opposed to a perfect circle. Hips should be driven forward toward the handlebars, and the spine should be straight up.
- Students are keeping safety in mind at all times, but especially while riding near or past other bikers.
- When racing, students are cheering each other on, avoiding put-downs, and congratulating each other when the race is over, regardless of the result.

Formal and Informal Assessments

- Peer assessment: peer checklist for previously learned skills and combining skills
- Exit slip: What skills can you, personally, combine in mountain biking?

Closure

- What skills did you practice during your skill session?
- What should your body position look like while descending a hill? While climbing a hill?
- What does it mean to sprint on a bike?
- What skills are easy to combine?

Reflection

- Are students improving toward proficiency in skills such as turning, braking, shifting gears, and attack position?
- Can all students climb and descend hills? Identify students who need modifications.
- Do students understand the concept of sprinting?
- Can students safely combine skills?

Homework

- You must accumulate 40-plus minutes of riding before the week is out. This can be done at home or at recess. You are encouraged to do more than 40 minutes. Please select one skill (e.g., descending a hill, shifting gears) that you have learned in class; practice that one skill during your riding sessions.
- Be ready to report about your training sessions. What skill did you focus on? What went well? What didn't?

Resources

Lopes, B., & McCormack, L. (2010). *Mastering mountain bike skills*. 2nd ed. Champaign, IL: Human Kinetics.

LESSON 4:
LOADING AND UNLOADING: ASSESSMENT

Grade-Level Outcomes

Primary Outcomes

Outdoor pursuits: Demonstrates correct technique for basic skills in 1 self-selected outdoor activity. (S1.M22.6)

Individual-performance activities: Demonstrates correct technique for basic skills in 1 self-selected individual-performance activity. (S1.M24.6)

Accepting feedback: Demonstrates self-responsibility by implementing specific corrective feedback to improve performance. (S4.M3.6)

Embedded Outcome

Accepting feedback: Provides corrective feedback to a peer, using teacher-generated guidelines, and incorporating appropriate tone and other communication skills. (S4.M3.7)

Lesson Objectives

The learner will:

- demonstrate improvement of skills learned previously.
- acquire the skills and knowledge needed to load and unload body weight on a bike.
- acquire the skills and knowledge needed to lift the wheels of the bike off of the ground.
- assess own mountain-biking skills.

Equipment and Materials

- Mountain bikes
- Helmets
- Access to a hill or slope
- Small objects (sticks, rocks, cones)
- Weighted scale
- iPad or voice recorder
- First aid kit
- Air pump
- Mini tool kit for adjusting and repairing bikes on the go

Introduction

Today, you will continue to progress toward proficiency in the skills that you have learned. As a group, you will discuss and create guidelines for providing peer feedback and have opportunities to practice using the guidelines. You will spend the latter part of class learning how to load, unload, and lift your wheels.

Instructional Task: Climbing and Descending Hills

■ PRACTICE TASK

Students practice climbing and descending hills using the skills they learned in the previous class. Students will work in groups of three and rotate jobs:

- Ride.
- Provide feedback.
- Observe the student providing feedback by using a checklist.

MOUNTAIN BIKING

Refinements
- Make sure students don't shift too early.
- Make sure students keep their eyes forward.

Extensions
- Students practice a running mount before descending a hill.
- Students practice a rolling dismount after climbing a hill.

EMBEDDED OUTCOME: S4.M3.7. Hold a group discussion with students about why feedback is important. Together the class will generate guidelines for providing peer feedback.

Guiding questions for students:
- How do you feel when a teacher gives you feedback? When a peer gives you feedback?
- Would you be receptive to feedback?
- How would you want someone to provide feedback to you?

Student Choices/Differentiation
- Students choose their partners.
- Students can choose to focus on just climbing or descending a hill.
- Student can choose to combine the two skills during practice.

What to Look For
- Students are completing the activity with safety and providing encouragement to their classmates.
- Students are giving positive corrective feedback using the peer guidelines.

Checklist
- Student uses a positive tone of voice.
- Student provides helpful advice.
- Student focuses on one aspect of a skill when providing feedback.
- Student is receptive to feedback.

Instructional Task: Loading and Unloading

■ PRACTICE TASK

Demonstrate and discuss loading and unloading on a bicycle. This is also known as weighting and unweighting.

Demonstrate an example of loading and unloading by using a weighted scale. Discuss the effects of one's weight when you crouch down on the scale and quickly stand back up.

Guiding questions for students:
- What is loading and unloading?
- Why do you load?
- Why do you unload?
- When do you load and unload?

Students practice loading and unloading, individually, following your commands.

- Load.
- Unload.

Refinements

- While standing on the ground, pump your body up and down.
- The pump motion should include movement in your legs and arms.

Extensions

- Students practice loading and unloading while riding over small bumps and mounds.
- Students practice loading and unloading in order to ride over small objects (e.g., small sticks, rocks).

Student Choices/Differentiation

- Students choose to stand or sit during discussion.
- Give students an opportunity to load and unload their weight on the scale.
- Students can choose to continue to practice loading and unloading without riding over bumps or objects. When they feel comfortable, they should move onto trying the skill with objects.

What to Look For

- Students demonstrate respectful listening skills and participation by raising their hands and providing input to the conversation.
- Students load their bikes before the bump or mound, unload on the incline, and return to the attack position.
- Students load their bikes by applying weight or force downward on the bike. Unloading is the opposite: Students release their weight from the bike in a controlled upward motion.
- Students load before the object and then unload as they travel over the object.

Instructional Task: Lifting Wheels

■ PRACTICE TASK

Demonstrate and discuss how to lift the front wheel and why it is important.

Guiding questions for students:

- Why is it important to be able to lift your wheel?
- What can you do if you can lift your front wheel?
- How do you lift your front wheel?

In small groups, students practice lifting the front wheel. Group members observe and give feedback using the peer feedback guidelines.

Demonstrate and discuss lifting the back wheel and why it is important.

Guiding questions for students:

- How would you lift your back wheel?
- Why is it important?

After peer reviews, students ride individually.

Guiding questions for students:

- Is it safe for you to attempt wheel lifts?
- Did you appreciate your peers' feedback?
- Did you give helpful feedback to your peers? How did it make you feel?

Refinements

- Make sure students are practicing at slower speeds.
- Make sure students use a strong snapping movement in a downward direction.

Extensions

- Lift the front wheel up and over objects varying in size.
- Lift the back wheel up and over objects varying in size.
- Lift both wheels up and over objects varying in size.
- Do a wheel kick-out.
- Do a wheelie.
- Do a bunny hop.

Student Choices/Differentiation

Students can choose to continue peer observations, using the peer feedback guidelines.

What to Look For

- Students have the bike in a middle gear while practicing the wheel lift. Students should be attempting this skill at a slow speed—high speed is not the key!
- Students start this skill by having the dominant foot in the top of their pedal stroke (11 o'clock). Students should have the torso pushed toward the handlebars. When they want to take off they will snap the dominant foot down aggressively, simultaneously shifting their weight. While they are shifting their weight, they will pull on the handlebars.
- Can students lift their front wheel?
- Regardless of ability, students should strive to challenge themselves within the safety guidelines.

Instructional Task: Assessment

■ PRACTICE TASK

Self-Assessment

Students self-assess by answering a series of yes or no questions. Each question has a place for comments where students can put their thoughts.

- Can you brake and turn?
- Can you shift gears consistently?
- Can you climb and descend hills?
- Do you understand what it means to load and unload your bike?
- Can you load and unload?
- Can you lift your wheels?
- Do you know why this skill is important?
- Do you feel supported by your peers?
- Do you support all of your peers?
- Did you accept peer feedback?
- Did you give peer feedback?

Peer Assessment

- Interview: Students conduct 3-minute interviews with classmates. The interview will address the peer feedback process.
- Students use the self-assessment questionnaire as guiding questions for their interviews.
- Interviews can be voice- or video-recorded.

Student Choices/Differentiation

Provide samples of assessments for students to view.

What to Look For

- Self-assessment questionnaire
- Students are taking the interview process seriously.
- Students are reflecting on their skills accurately.

Formal and Informal Assessments

- Peer assessment: checklist for lifting front wheel
- Exit slips:
  - Self-assessment questionnaire
  - Peer interviews
  - What are the guidelines for providing peer feedback? (Option 1)
  - Why do you need to lift your wheels and how do you do it? (Option 2)

Closure

- Review peer feedback guidelines. Can someone give an example of how to provide feedback respectfully to a peer?
- Why is feedback important? Did you provide feedback to anyone? Did you receive feedback from a peer? How did the feedback interaction go? Positive? Negative?
- Did you learn anything from observing your peers?
- How do you load and unload your bike? Can anyone demonstrate?
- Why is it important to be able to lift your tires off the ground? How do you lift your front wheel off the ground? Your back wheel? Can anyone demonstrate?

Reflection

- Are students mature enough to use the peer feedback guidelines? Did the guidelines prove to be successful? Are there any changes that need to be made to the guidelines?
- Are students attempting to lift their wheels with proper technique? Are there any students who demonstrate unsafe behavior?
- What modifications need to be made and for whom?

Homework

- You must accumulate 20-plus minutes of riding before the week is out. This can be done at home or at recess. You are encouraged to do more than 20 minutes. Please select one skill (e.g., descending a hill, shifting gears, lifting wheels) that you have learned in class; practice that one skill during your riding sessions.
- Be ready to report about your training sessions. What skills did you focus on? What went well? What didn't?
- Journal entry: What skills did you focus on during this week's riding sessions? How have you improved in those skills? How have you improved in mountain biking since the beginning of the unit? Has your attitude toward mountain biking changed? If so, is it a positive or negative change? Why?

Resources

Lopes, B., & McCormack, L. (2010). *Mastering mountain bike skills*. 2nd ed. Champaign, IL: Human Kinetics.

Internet keyword search: "how to bunny hop—MTB skills"

LESSON 5:
FIXING A FLAT TIRE; COPING SKILLS

Grade-Level Outcomes

Primary Outcomes

Outdoor pursuits: Demonstrates correct technique for basic skills in 1 self-selected outdoor activity. (S1.M22.6)

Individual-performance activities: Demonstrates correct technique for basic skills in 1 self-selected individual-performance activity. (S1.M24.6)

Stress management: Practices strategies for dealing with stress, such as deep breathing, guided visualization and aerobic exercise. (S3.M18.7)

Embedded Outcome

Health: Identifies components of physical activity that provide opportunities for reducing stress and for social interaction. (S5.M2.6)

Lesson Objectives

The learner will:

- practice a variety of mountain biking skills.
- acquire skills and knowledge for maintaining stress.
- acquire skills and knowledge to practice guiding visualization.
- acquire skills and knowledge to fix a flat tire.

Equipment and Materials

- Mountain bikes
- Helmets
- Cones
- Obstacle course: sticks, large rocks, logs
- Access to hill or slope
- Extra tubes and tires
- First aid kit
- Air pump
- Mini tool kit for adjusting and repairing bikes on the go
- Electronic tablets

Introduction

Today, you will have a chance to practice the skills that you have learned to this point. These skills include climbing and descending hills, loading and unloading, and lifting tires off the ground. After your practice session, we will discuss and practice strategies for managing stress. Overcoming challenges in mountain biking can take many attempts and lead to frustration. It's important to have some tools to stay calm. Finally, you will learn how to fix a flat tire.

Instructional Task: Review Previously Learned Skills

■ PRACTICE TASK

Discuss previously learned skills and their importance:

- Shifting gears
- Riding in attack position

- Climbing, descending, sprinting
- Loading, unloading
- Lifting wheels

Guiding questions for students:
- How would you climb a hill? How about descend a hill?
- Does loading and unloading help you lift your wheels?

Give spoken commands and cues for students to follow.

- Shift into a lower gear.
- Load and unload your weight.
- Demonstrate the attack position.

Place students in groups for stations. Students should spend approximately 5 minutes at each station.

Stations
1. Attack position and shifting
2. Climbing, descending, and sprinting
3. Loading, unloading, and lifting wheels

Student Choices/Differentiation
- Students select the skills they wish to practice.
- If there are students who excel in certain skills, they can be selected as a station coach.
- Inexperienced students may choose a coach they enjoy working with.

What to Look For
- Students are on task, attempting skills that have been previously taught.
- Students are following the safety guidelines and providing support and encouragement toward each other.
- This a time where students should make connections between skills and have breakthroughs in skill development.
- If students are selected as a station coach, they should be using the peer feedback guidelines that were generated in the previous class.

Instructional Task: Stress Management

■ PRACTICE TASK

Guide students through a discussion about stress and why it is important to manage stress.

Guiding questions for students:
- What is stress?
- What makes you stressed?
- How do you handle your stress?
- How can mountain biking release stress?
- How can mountain biking be stressful?

Share how mountain biking (or other physical activities) and stress are connected in your personal life. To help with this connection, show a YouTube clip to students (keyword search: "guiding imagery," "performance meditation").

With the class, brainstorm connections among mountain biking, stress, and stress management.

EMBEDDED OUTCOME: S5.M2.6. Use the discussion to help students identify the components of mountain biking that can be stress reducing.

Guiding questions for students:

- How can mountain biking be stressful?
- Based on what you have learned this class, how would you dissolve mountain biking stress?

Guide students through a breathing exercise.

Guide students through a visualization exercise.

Give students time to practice a skill with guiding visualization.

Refinements

- Focus on breathing.
- Make sure students "see" themselves doing a skill before attempting the skill.

Extensions

- Students guide themselves in a visualization activity.
- Students guide each other through visualization activities.

Guiding questions for students:

- Why do you need to manage stress?
- How do you talk to yourself? Is it positive? Or negative?
- Do you see yourself using guided visualization? How might it help you attain your goals?

Student Choices/Differentiation

Students select the skill that they wish to envision.

What to Look For

- Students are mimicking your breathing pattern.
- Students are showing respect for their peers by sitting or standing quietly.
- Students are using some quiet time to envision their skills before practicing. Before every attempt, students use the visualization skills that they have learned.

Instructional Task: Fix a Flat Tire and Change a Tube

■ **PRACTICE TASK**

Discuss flat tires; explain how and why flats happen.

Differentiate between fixing a flat and changing a tube.

Show an instructional video on how to fix a flat and change a tube.

Guiding questions for students:

- How can a flat occur?
- What is the difference between fixing a flat and changing a tube?

Demonstrate how to fix a flat and change a tube, and then let students practice fixing the front tire.

Refinement

Make sure students understand how to remove both wheels properly.

Extensions

- Students use electronic tablets to film each other fixing a flat.
- Repeat with students changing a rear flat.

Student Choices/Differentiation

Students review a flat-fixing video or use a checklist to guide them through the steps.

What to Look For

- Students are working in small groups attempting to change a flat tire, following the instructions from the instructional video.
- Are students attempting to change the tube? Are they getting frustrated? If so, are they using their stress management skills?

Students complete a teacher-created activity worksheet: Fixing a Flat.

Instructional Task: Combining Skills

■ PRACTICE TASK

Students challenge their skills by attacking an obstacle course. The course will require them to combine a variety of skills they have learned thus far.

Extension

Students use electronic tablets to film each other and provide feedback.

Guiding questions for students:

- Do you think watching video evidence of yourself riding will prove useful in your learning process?
- Which skills can you combine? Which skills are easy to combine? Which skills are hard to combine?

Student Choices/Differentiation

Modify the course for less and more skilled students.

What to Look For

- Students are on task practicing their mountain biking skills.
- Students take turns going through the obstacle course, demonstrating patience and providing encouragement to peers.

Formal and Informal Assessments

- Teacher-created activity worksheet on fixing a flat tire. Students use video evidence to double-check their peers' work.
- Exit slip: Demonstrate one stress-management tactic.

Closure

- What skills did you practice today?
- What are some examples of stress management skills? When and why do you use these skills?
- Do you think the stress management skills you learned today are going to be useful for you?
- Do you think you could fix a flat tire on your own? In your mind, what is the toughest part of fixing a flat?

Reflection

- Are students improving toward proficiency in a variety of mountain bike skills?
- Do students understand the purpose of obtaining stress management skills?
- Can they manage their stress when it rises?
- Can students change a flat tire? What modifications are needed?

Homework

- You must accumulate 30-plus minutes of riding before the week is out. This can be done at home or at recess. You are encouraged to do more than 30 minutes. Please select one skill (e.g., descending a hill, shifting gears, lifting wheels) that you have learned in classes so far in the module; practice that one skill during your riding sessions.

- Please be ready to report about your training session. What skills did you focus on? What went well? What didn't?

- Journal entry: What has been your favorite part of this mountain biking module and why? Do you have any suggestions for how to make the mountain biking class better?

Resources

American Alliance for Health, Physical Education, Recreation and Dance. (2014). *Bikeology: A middle and high school bicycle safety curriculum for physical education teachers and recreation specialists*. Reston, VA: Author. Available at www.shapeamerica.org.

Internet keyword search: "how to change a mountain bike tire," "how to remove the front wheel of a bicycle," "how to remove the back wheel of a bicycle," "guiding imagery," "performance meditation," "visualization," "relaxation techniques"

LESSON 6: GROUP RIDES IN LINES

Grade-Level Outcomes

Primary Outcomes

Outdoor pursuits: Demonstrates correct technique for basic skills in 1 self-selected outdoor activity. (S1.M22.6)

Individual-performance activities: Demonstrates correct technique for basic skills in 1 self-selected individual-performance activity. (S1.M24.6)

Rules & etiquette: Identifies the rules and etiquette for physical activities/games and dance activities. (S4.M6.6)

Fitness knowledge: Uses available technology to self-monitor quantity of exercise needed for a minimal health standard and/or optimal functioning based on current fitness level. (S3.M8.8)

Embedded Outcomes

Personal responsibility: Demonstrates both intrinsic and extrinsic motivation by selecting opportunities to participate in physical activity outside of class. (S4.M2.7)

Health: Identifies different types of physical activities and describes how each exerts a positive effect on health. (S5.M1.7)

Lesson Objectives

The learner will:
- practice a variety of mountain biking skills.
- use a heart rate monitor to track fitness during a group ride.
- acquire the skills and knowledge to be able to choose a line.
- acquire the skills and knowledge to attack switchbacks.
- demonstrate knowledge of mountain biking via written assessments.

Equipment and Materials

- Mountain bikes
- Helmets
- First aid kit
- Air pump
- Mini tool kit for adjusting and repairing bikes on the go
- Heart rate monitors

Introduction

You will practice a variety of mountain bike skills today. Some will be review and others will be new. You will use heart rate monitors to track your heart rate while biking. You will finish class by taking a summative written assessment.

Instructional Task: On-Campus Group Ride

■ PRACTICE TASK

Review heart rate monitors, and have students fasten them onto their bodies.

Guiding questions for students:
- Why do we use heart rate monitors?
- Why is it important to track your heart rate throughout physical activity?
- Is biking an activity that will keep your heart rate in the moderate to vigorous zone?

Students pair up and ride side by side as you guide them through an on-campus bike ride. Throughout the ride, call out commands for students to follow.

- Brake.
- Shift to a higher gear.
- Shift down.
- Turn left.
- Descend the hill.

Refinement

Make sure students understand how to read the heart rate monitor. They should be checking the monitor periodically.

Extensions

- Have students compare their heart rate scores with the minimal health standard for their age group.
- Challenge students to complete a task within a time frame. For example:
  - Who can ride to the playground and back in under 1 minute?
  - Who can descend a hill followed by climbing a hill? Can you do it in under 1 minute?

EMBEDDED OUTCOME: S5.M1.7. To help students make the connection between mountain biking and positive effects on health, ask the following questions:

- What are different types of physical activities that improve health?
- Does mountain biking fit in with those activities?
- How do any of the activities listed have a positive effect on health?

Student Choices/Differentiation

- Inexperienced riders can choose to ride with a more experienced rider.
- Students can accept or decline the challenges.

What to Look For

- Students are able to apply their own heart rate monitors with little to no help.
- Students are attempting the skills and staying with the group.
- Students are checking their heart rates periodically.
- Students are attempting the challenges. If not, they stay moving to keep their heart rates in the moderate to vigorous zone.

Instructional Task: Choosing a Line

■ PRACTICE TASK

Demonstrate and discuss choosing a line.

Guiding questions for students:

- Why is it important to choose a line?
- What obstacles may appear, and how would you avoid them?
- What proactive steps can you take to ensure your line is safe?

Students practice choosing a line in a controlled setting.

Demonstrate and discuss switchbacks:

- What is a switchback?
- Why is it an important skill to ride a switchback?

In pairs, students practice riding switchbacks in a controlled setting.

Refinements

- Make sure students are looking 10 to 20 feet (3 to 6 m) ahead while choosing their lines.
- Make sure students understand they need to look out for obstacles and make quick decisions on how to get by them.
- Make sure students understand that riding switchbacks requires them to travel in a zigzag or curved pathway.

Extensions

- Students create their own switchbacks using cones.
- Students practice riding switchbacks uphill.

Student Choices/Differentiation

Students choose their lines and the degree of difficulty.

What to Look For

- Observe students' eyes. Students' eyes should be focused out in front of their riding trails, scanning for hazards and turns.
- Students are traveling in zigzag or curved pathways.
- Students are able to explain the line that they took.
- More advanced students lift the back wheel up and kick it out in order to make the switchback turns.

Instructional Task: Riding in Groups

■ PRACTICE TASK

Discuss and demonstrate etiquette for riding in a large group and riding in public.

Guiding questions for students:

- What do think riding etiquette means? What does it look like?
- What kinds of things may you encounter on your bike ride? Should you respect them? How?

In small groups, students practice riding together using the riding etiquette.

Split the class into two larger groups, and have students practice using the riding etiquette.

Gather the class to ride as one group, and practice using the riding etiquette.

Refinement

- Students should understand they might not be the only people on the path or trail.
- Make sure students understand proper riding distance while riding with others.

Extension

Give students prompts to follow. Example: "You are riding on a trail and see a woman with three dogs walking toward you. What do you do?"

Student Choices/Differentiation

Students choose their groups.

What to Look For

- Students are on task riding in their groups, using the riding etiquette to the best of their ability.
- Students are communicating effectively with each other.
- Students are demonstrating previously learned skills.

- Students are providing encouragement and support to their peers.
- Students are providing peer feedback using the peer feedback guidelines.

Administer a teacher-created questionnaire on group riding.

Instructional Task: Written Test

■ PRACTICE TASK

Administer a teacher-created mountain bike knowledge test.

Student Choices/Differentiation

Check IEPs and 504s for students who need test accommodations.

What to Look For

Students are on task, quiet, and focused on their own tests.

Formal and Informal Assessments

- Questionnaire: group riding
- Written test: mountain biking knowledge

Closure

You have made a lot of progress thus far in our mountain biking, and I am really proud of the energy every student has put into this unit. Next class we will learn how to plan out a bike trip and complete the summative skills assessment.

I have planned an organized group ride for later this week. It will occur after school and last one hour. If you come, not only will you benefit from the extra practice but you will also receive extra credit.

- What skills have you learned thus far?
- What skills can you combine?
- What are some embedded outcomes we have discussed in this unit?

Reflection

- Are students progressing toward proficiency in a variety of mountain bike skills?
- Do students understand the importance of choosing a line?
- Can they ride a switchback in a controlled setting?
- Do students understand the importance of bike riding etiquette?

Homework

- You must accumulate 30-plus minutes of riding before the week is out. This can be done at home or at recess. You are encouraged to do more than 30 minutes. Please select one skill (e.g., descending a hill, shifting gears, lifting wheels) that you have learned in classes so far; practice that one skill during your riding sessions.
- Please be ready to report about your training sessions. What skill did you focus on? What went well? What didn't?
- Journal entry: What skills did you focus on during this week's riding sessions? How have you improved in those skills? How have you improved in mountain biking since the beginning of the unit? Has your attitude toward mountain biking changed? If so, is it a positive or negative change? Why?
- Extra credit: An optional off-campus bike ride will take place after school this week. You will receive extra credit for showing up and participating. We will meet in the gym right after school. The bike ride will last one hour.

EMBEDDED OUTCOME: S4.M2.7 The bike ride for extra credit allows students to demonstrate both intrinsic and extrinsic motivation by participating in physical activity outside of class.

Resources

American Alliance for Health, Physical Education, Recreation and Dance. (2014). *Bikeology: A middle and high school bicycle safety curriculum for physical education teachers and recreation specialists*. Reston, VA: Author. Available at www.shapeamerica.org.

Boulder Mountainbike Alliance. (2016). Trail etiquette. Available at www.bouldermountainbike. org under Trails.

Internet keyword search: "how to ride switchbacks on a mountain bike better in 4 minutes"

LESSON 7: PLANNING A RIDE

Grade-Level Outcomes

Primary Outcomes

Outdoor pursuits: Demonstrates correct technique for basic skills in 1 self-selected outdoor activity. (S1.M22.6)

Individual-performance activities: Demonstrates correct technique for basic skills in 1 self-selected individual-performance activity. (S1.M24.6)

Nutrition: Develops strategies for balancing healthy food, snacks and water intake, along with daily physical activity. (S3.M17.7)

Embedded Outcome

Personal responsibility: Exhibits responsible social behaviors by cooperating with classmates, demonstrating inclusive behaviors and supporting classmates. (S4.M1.7)

Lesson Objectives

The learner will:

- learn skills and knowledge for balancing healthy food, snacks, and water intake along with physical activity.
- learn skills and knowledge for planning a bike trip.
- demonstrate the ability to perform a variety of mountain bike skills.
- demonstrate the ability to exhibit responsible social behaviors.

Equipment and Materials

- Mountain bikes
- Helmets
- First aid kit
- Air pump
- Mini tool kit for adjusting and repairing bikes on the go

Introduction

Today, we will prepare for our final class, in which we will take an off-campus ride. We will start today with a short on-campus ride to warm up our bodies. You then will learn how to plan a bike trip and how important proper nutrition is to riding. In groups, you will be asked to plan and map a bike trip. As you work on that project, one group at a time will complete the skills assessment.

Instructional Task: On-Campus Group Ride

■ PRACTICE TASK

Students pair up and ride side by side as you guide them through an on-campus bike ride.

Throughout the ride, give commands for students to complete specific skills.

- Brake to a stop.
- Shift down.
- Shift up.
- Make a 270-degree turn.
- Assume the attack position.

Extensions

- Who can ride to the playground and back in under 1 minute?
- Who can descend this hill and start with a running mount?
- Who can get their front wheel over the small log?

Refinement

Remind students to be respectful of others on the ride. If they can't be respectful, they will ride next to the teacher.

Guiding questions for students:

- What skills did you practice throughout our short ride?
- Did you combine any skills? Which ones?

EMBEDDED OUTCOME: S4.M1.7. Discuss with students why demonstrating responsible social behaviors and cooperating with each other are vital to an enjoyable group ride.

Student Choices/Differentiation

- Students can choose if they want to lead the group.
- Students can choose where in the group they ride.

What to Look For

- Students are attempting the skills and staying with the group.
- Students are demonstrating inclusive behavior and supporting their classmates.

Instructional Task: Planning a Ride

■ PRACTICE TASK

Discuss the importance of planning a ride.

Guiding questions for students:

- Why do you need to plan a ride?
- What emergencies might happen that you should be prepared for?

Discuss the importance of balancing nutrition with physical activity.

Guiding questions for students:

- How can you balance your water and food intake along with physical activity?
- What types of snacks should you bring? How much water?
- Does your route have a stopping point that has access to fresh water?
- What else may you need to bring on your ride besides water and food?
- Do you think what you ate for breakfast will affect your performance? What about what you ate yesterday or last week?

Extension

In groups of three or four, students use local maps to plan a group ride. The ride may be the length of their choice, but the plan must include the following:

- Total miles
- Detailed map of the route
- Planned stopping points
- Planned water and snack breaks
- Estimated time to complete the trip

Skills Test

While students are working on their plans, take one group at a time to complete the skills test.

Student Choices/Differentiation

- Students choose their groups or partners.
- Students decide who will record the trip details.

What to Look For

- Students are respectful listeners and participate in the discussion.
- Students work cooperatively in small groups. They solve conflicts on their own and come to you only in an emergency.
- Students complete the skills assessment. Students show proficiency in a variety of mountain bike skills.

Formal and Informal Assessments

Summative assessment: skills test on mounting, unmounting, even pedal stroke, braking, turning, shifting gears, climbing a hill, and descending a hill

Closure

- Why is it important to balance your diet with physical activity?
- Why is it important to spend time planning before a bike trip?
- Next class will be our last class; we will be taking an off-campus bike trip to celebrate!

Reflection

- Are all students prepared and ready to take an off-campus bike ride? Will it be safe to have everyone come along?
- Do students understand the importance of nutrition and finding a balance between food and physical activity?
- Can students plan a safe bike route?

Homework

- If you have not finished planning your bike route, divide the work you have left with your group members, and finish it for homework.
- Extra credit: Journal entry: How does nutrition affect your performance? What would be your ideal snack for a long ride?

Resources

Nevins, S. (director). (2013). *The weight of the nation for kids* [motion picture]. HBO Home Entertainment.

Nutrition: www.nutrition.gov

USDA Choose My Plate: www.choosemyplate.gov

LESSON 8: OFF-CAMPUS RIDE

Grade-Level Outcomes

Primary Outcomes

Outdoor pursuits: Demonstrates correct technique for basic skills in 1 self-selected outdoor activity. (S1.M22.6)

Individual-performance activities: Demonstrates correct technique for basic skills in 1 self-selected individual-performance activity. (S1.M24.6)

Health: Identifies the 5 components of health-related fitness (muscular strength, muscular endurance, flexibility, cardiovascular endurance and body composition) and explains the connections between fitness and overall physical and mental health. (S5.M1.8)

Embedded Outcomes

Working with others: Problem-solves with a small group of classmates during adventure activities, small-group initiatives or game play. (S4.M5.7)

Engages in physical activity: Participates in a variety of lifetime recreational team sports, outdoor pursuits or dance activities. (S3.M5.6)

Lesson Objectives

The learner will:

- demonstrate a variety of mountain biking skills.
- demonstrate group riding etiquette and positive behavior in public.
- complete an off-campus group ride.
- discuss health-related fitness and connect it to mountain biking.

Equipment and Materials

- Mountain bikes
- Helmets
- First aid kit
- Air pump
- Mini tool kit for adjusting and repairing bikes on the go

Introduction

Today is the last day of our Mountain Biking Module. We will start with review and warm-ups and end with a discussion on health-related fitness. We will spend most of our time on the off-campus bike route, but first we must discuss the route, review safety, and warm up.

Instructional Task: Warm Up

■ **PRACTICE TASK**

Students fit a bike and helmet and ride for 5 minutes.

Extensions

- Who can lift their front wheel over the log?
- Who can do a bunny hop?
- Who can shift gears while in the attack position?

Refinements

- Make sure students are keeping their heart rate in the moderate to vigorous zone.
- Review safety guidelines with students in small groups during the free ride.

Student Choices/Differentiation

Students choose the skills and routes they take during the free ride.

What to Look For

This is free time. Students should be practicing skills of their choice and moving their heart rates into the moderate to vigorous zone.

Instructional Task: Off-Campus Group Ride

■ PRACTICE TASK

Review the safety guidelines and etiquette for group riding.

Explain the planned route.

Go on the group ride, pausing for snacks and water.

EMBEDDED OUTCOME: S4.M5.7 During the break, split students into small groups. Provide each group with a problem that they must solve together.

Examples

- One member of your group ride just realized that he has a flat tire. You have a spare tube but no pump. What do you do?
- You are riding on a trail in the woods. Your group comes across an old bridge that looks unsafe. Do you cross it? Do you backtrack and go the long way around? Is there another solution?

Extensions

- Who can climb the hill in under 30 seconds?
- Who can lead the group to the next pit stop using effective communication?

Refinement

Make sure students can demonstrate the safety guidelines.

Student Choices/Differentiation

- Students choose where in the group they ride.
- Students choose the skills they want to focus on throughout the ride.

What to Look For

- Students are following safety guidelines and biking etiquette.
- Students stay with the group without wandering off.
- Students are practicing a variety of mountain bike skills.

Instructional Task: Health-Related Fitness Discussion

■ PRACTICE TASK

Show students a short video on health-related fitness.

Divide students into small groups, and give each group one component of health-related fitness. Students must brainstorm activities that fit their component.

Students share their ideas with the class.

Guiding questions for students:

- What are the five components of health-related fitness?
- Which health-related fitness component do you feel most comfortable with?

- How is that component related to overall fitness and mental health?
- Can you draw a connection between the five components and what you have previously learned about stress relief and mountain biking?

Refinement

Remind students of the discussion regarding connections between mountain biking and stress management.

Extension

Who can draw connections between all five components and mountain biking?

Student Choices/Differentiation

PowerPoint presentations, handouts, and videos can all help students learn the content.

What to Look For

- Students know basic health-related fitness.
- Students can apply health-related fitness components to mountain biking.

Formal and Informal Assessments

- Turn in journal entries for the module.
- Turn in your physical activity logs.

Closure

What a fun day of mountain biking! That concludes our mountain biking unit. I really hope you enjoyed it and learned not only about mountain biking but about yourself, too.

- What are the biggest take-home messages for you in this unit?
- What was your favorite part of mountain biking?

Reflection

- Was the off-campus ride too challenging? How might I change the route next time?
- What were students' overall attitudes toward mountain biking?
- How would I conduct the overall unit differently next time?

Homework

EMBEDDED OUTCOME: S3.M5.6. Throughout the module, you tracked your mountain biking activity outside of class. Please reflect on your activity logs and then turn them in.

Journal entry: Please write what you consider to be the biggest take-home messages of the Mountain Biking Module.

Resources

Internet keyword search: "health-related fitness," "fitness and mountain biking"

TRACK AND FIELD MODULE

Lessons in this module were contributed by Brad Rettig, a middle school physical education teacher in Lincoln, NE, Public Schools.

Grade-Level Outcomes Addressed, by Lesson	Lessons							
	1	2	3	4	5	6	7	8
Standard 1. The physically literate individual demonstrates competency in a variety of motor skills and movement patterns.								
Demonstrates correct technique for basic skills in 1 self-selected individual-performance activity. (S1.M24.6)	P	P	P		P	P	P	P
Standard 2. The physically literate individual applies knowledge of concepts, principles, strategies and tactics related to movement and performance.								
Describes and applies mechanical advantage(s) for a variety of movement patterns. (S2.M12.8)			P			E		
Standard 3. The physically literate individual demonstrates the knowledge and skills to achieve and maintain a health-enhancing level of physical activity and fitness.								
Describes the role of flexibility in injury prevention. (S3.M10.8)				P				
Describes the role of warm-ups and cool-downs before and after physical activity. (S3.M12.6)				P	P			
Standard 4. The physically literate individual exhibits responsible personal and social behavior that respects self and others.								
Exhibits responsible social behaviors by cooperating with classmates, demonstrating inclusive behaviors and supporting classmates. (S4.M1.7)					E		E	
Demonstrates self-responsibility by implementing specific corrective feedback to improve performance. (S4.M3.6)	E					P		
Accepts differences among classmates in physical development, maturation and varying skill levels by providing encouragement and positive feedback. (S4.M4.6)			E				E	
Identifies the rules and etiquette for physical activities/games and dance activities. (S4.M6.6)		E						
Standard 5. The physically literate individual recognizes the value of physical activity for health, enjoyment, challenge, self-expression and/or social interaction.								
Identifies why self-selected physical activities create enjoyment. (S5.M4.7)				E		E		
Demonstrates the importance of social interaction by helping and encouraging others, avoiding trash talk and providing support to classmates. (S5.M6.7)								E
Demonstrates respect for self by asking for help and helping others in various physical activities. (S5.M6.8)						P		

P = Primary; E = Embedded

LESSON 1: SHOT PUT

Grade-Level Outcomes

Primary Outcome

Individual-performance activities: Demonstrates correct technique for basic skills in 1 self-selected individual-performance activity. (S1.M24.6)

Embedded Outcome

Accepting feedback: Demonstrates self-responsibility by implementing specific corrective feedback to improve performance. (S4.M3.6)

Lesson Objectives

The learner will:

- learn how to use correct form to throw the shot effectively and safely.
- know the rules for throwing the shot.

Equipment and Materials

- Enough softballs for each set of partners or groups
- Open area large enough for multiple students to throw
- 1 or 2 shots, 6 to 8.8 pounds (2.7 to 4 kg), based on age

Introduction

During our Track and Field Module, we will learn a variety of events. The shot put is a field event in which throwers attempt to throw, or put, the shot as far as they can in one throw. There are a couple ways to do that, but we will work on the glide approach. Even though the shot is about the size of a softball, it's much heavier. You will learn the correct way to perform this throw to get the most distance and, most important, keep yourself safe. When performing this event, it's very important that the area around you is clear and that you perform the throwing motion correctly. Make sure to ask questions when you have them.

To increase interest, show students a video clip of students performing the shot put.

Instructional Task: Throw the Shot With Correct Form

■ PRACTICE TASK

Students throw a softball using correct shot put form, rotating a half turn (spin), or 180 degrees.

In pairs, have students throw the softball to general space while you offer corrective feedback on the cues as needed. After all have thrown, have each student collect a softball and give it to the next person. This group goes when all are ready.

Repeat as long as needed.

Remind students of the importance of throwing with correct form and keeping the elbow up, with the shot next to the jaw and neck to prevent injury. They should not throw the shot like a softball.

Refinement

Each time a student throws, give out one or two cues for correcting form. Challenge students to focus on addressing at least one of the cues to improve performance.

EMBEDDED OUTCOME: S4.M3.6. This is a good opportunity to emphasize the importance of taking responsibility for improving performance by using feedback.

Have students record their partners' performance on video and critique it together using a cue sheet.

Student Choices/Differentiation

- If students struggle to complete all the steps, have them try rotating 90 degrees, focusing on last cues.
- If you notice that many students are struggling and their partners are not able to give helpful feedback, limit the number of students throwing to provide feedback to each student.
- Students choose partners.

What to Look For

- Do students face the opposite direction of the throwing area?
- Do students hold the shot with finger pads and fingers (not the palm) next to neck and jaw?
- Do students keep the preferred-arm elbow out away from the body?
- Do students keep the preferred-leg knee in front and bent, with the other leg out and extended?

The Put

- As students turn, do they extend the legs and rotate the hips, keeping the elbow up and away from the body?
- As the hips rotate square, do students extend the throwing arm forward and up so the hand finishes slightly above head level?

Instructional Task:
Using the Glide Approach to Throw the Shot

■ PRACTICE TASK

As students are successful, have them move to practicing the glide approach.

Refinement

Each time a student throws, a partner will provide feedback on one or two cues. Challenge students to focus on correcting one of the cues to improve performance if needed.

Student Choices/Differentiation

Students can continue to practice the previous task if they aren't ready to move on to the glide.

What to Look For

- Is the dominant leg forward while the non-dominant leg remains extended back in the air until the glide is complete?
- Do students skim across to the center of the circle?
- Does the dominant leg pull back to a flexed position under the body at the center of the circle to complete the rest of the throw?

Instructional Task:
Using a 180-Degree Turn With a Weighted Shot

■ PRACTICE TASK

Using the shot, have students use the first practice task technique, with no gliding, to throw the shot.

Extensions

- Add the glide if students are ready.
- Have students video-record themselves and assess their technique based on how they performed the critical elements.

Student Choices/Differentiation

Allow students a choice of shot or softball.

What to Look For

- Refer to first practice task cues.
- It's very important that the thrower does not drop the elbow and keeps the shot next to the jaw and neck until the upward push occurs.

Note: Make sure all critical elements of the throw are achieved before moving to the weighted shot.

Formal and Informal Assessments

- Peer observation of the throw based on critical elements
- Self-reflection and evaluation based on video

Closure

- Ask students if they enjoyed throwing today and why it is important to use correct form when throwing the shot.
- Review the cues and let students know what you observed that went well and some overall tips for what to remember if you work on this later.

Reflection

- Were students using correct form with their arm motion to keep themselves safe?
- How many students were successful at rotating 180 degrees?
- Of students who moved on to the glide, what parts were they struggling with?
- Was the number of students throwing at one time manageable, and was there adequate space to do this?

Homework

Watch a video of a shot put competition. Pay attention to the types of throws competitors use and how they use their bodies throughout the throw.

Resources

American Sport Education Program. (2008). *Coaching youth track and field*. Champaign, IL: Human Kinetics.

Dougherty, N.J. (Ed.) (2010). Physical activity & sport for the secondary school student. 6th ed. Reston, VA: National Association for Sport and Physical Education.

Internet keyword search: "shot put," "glide technique shot put"

LESSON 2: LONG JUMP

Grade-Level Outcomes

Primary Outcome

Individual-performance activities: Demonstrates correct technique for basic skills in 1 self-selected individual-performance activity. (S1.M24.6)

Embedded Outcome

Rules & etiquette: Identifies the rules and etiquette for physical activities/games and dance activities. (S4.M6.6)

Lesson Objectives

The learner will:

- demonstrate the long jump approach to jump from the board.
- perform the long jump correctly.

Equipment and Materials

- Measuring tapes
- Cards to record starting measurements
- Sheet on how to perform the long jump and the rules for the event

Introduction

What did you find in the video clips you saw for homework? Does anyone use the glide technique? I hope you noticed the critical elements that we stressed in the previous class.

Today, you will learn another field event: the long jump. The long jump entails sprinting down a runway and, in one jump, jumping as far as you can into a sand pit. Today, we will work on the sprint up to the board (the place you will jump from) and what to do in the air to help you jump as far as possible.

Show a video clip of the long jump to motivate students.

Instructional Task: Finding the Start Mark

■ PRACTICE TASK

Explain the rules of the long jump, including fouls, and demonstrate the technique.

- From the take-off board, have students sprint away from the sand pit.
- Place a tape measure along the runway to help measure distance from the board.
- Each student's first step is with the preferred foot, and you or a partner counts each preferred-foot step until the student hits eight.
- You or the partner marks the spot, and the student records the distance she should start from. After two or three run-throughs, each student should have a fairly consistent measurement from which to start the long jump.
- Practice with multiple tape measures. Students can do this in groups, marking and counting for one another to save time. Use lines to simulate the take-off board.

Guiding questions for students:

- Why is it important to keep your runway speed consistent?
- How will speed affect your jump?

TRACK AND FIELD

Student Choices/Differentiation

- If needed, students may adjust the number of dominant steps to range from 6 to 10. The goal is to reach top speed but not hold the speed for longer than needed.
- If you can monitor both, have students, when finished, move to the next practice task.

What to Look For

- Are students starting with the dominant leg?
- Are students hitting the board with the dominant foot?
- Do students reach top speed within a given number of steps, while not holding it too long?

Instructional Task: Air Time and Landing

■ PRACTICE TASK

Along the length of the pit, line up students a couple of feet away from the pit. From a standing long jump, students (as many as safety permits) practice circling their arms while in the air and landing with weight going forward. Students practice the task and then move to the end of the line.

Refinement

Focus on keeping momentum going forward and extending legs in front (rather than dropping feet down) to add distance to the jump.

Guiding questions for students:

- Why is it important to keep your head up and not look at the sand?
- How does circling your arms forward help with the distance of the jump?

Student Choices/Differentiation

- This can be done inside on a floor mat if you can't get outside.
- Students having difficulty may work on the flight and landing, focusing on just one critical element at a time.

What to Look For

- While in the air, students circle the arms forward, helping to bring their momentum forward.
- While in the air, students put both feet out in front.
- As students land on their feet, they bring their butts toward their heels.
- Students are looking up as they jump and not at the sand.

Instructional Task: Performing the Long Jump

■ PRACTICE TASK

In small groups, students start at their pre-determined spots and complete the long jump using the correct cues and applying what they have learned.

While students are performing the long jump, others in the jumping group can rotate through officiating tasks, such as measuring the jump, raking the sand, and recording the jump distances.

Extension

Discuss the rules for measuring the long jump, noting the closest part of the body to the take-off board, including falling back or walking out of the sand pit.

EMBEDDED OUTCOME: S4.M6.6. Other groups can answer a few questions on the rules of the long jump and then read about the high jump or view a video clip of this event to give them a better understanding of what they will be learning the next class.

Student Choices/Differentiation

Students having difficulty putting it all together may shorten the number of steps for the run.

What to Look For

- Are students starting with the correct foot?
- Are students sprinting and jumping off the board?
- Are students circling their arms forward while in the air?
- Are jumpers keeping their heads up and not looking down at the board or sand? Looking down leads to stutter steps and results in jumping toward the ground, not up.
- Are jumpers extending their legs out, landing on their feet, and bringing their butts to their heels for maximum distance?

Formal and Informal Assessments

Quiz on rules of the long jump

Closure

- Talk with students about the positive things you saw today.
- Ask students about areas that can be improved, and then ask them why these areas are important and how it will help their jumps.

Reflection

- What went well and why?
- What areas are students struggling with?
- Are they hitting the board because their marks are off or they are looking at the board and stutter-stepping?
- Are they getting their momentum going forward in the air?
- Are they extending their legs out or dropping them down quickly, shortening the length of the jump?

Homework

Watch video clips on the long jump from a recent Olympics or other large meet. Have students come to class prepared to talk about what they think the jumpers were doing to help them be successful.

Resources

American Sport Education Program. (2008). *Coaching youth track and field*. Champaign, IL: Human Kinetics.

Dougherty, N.J. (Ed.) (2010). Physical activity & sport for the secondary school student. 6th ed. Reston, VA: National Association for Sport and Physical Education.

Internet keyword search: "long jump technique"

LESSON 3: HIGH JUMP

Grade-Level Outcomes

Primary Outcomes

Movement concepts: Describes and applies mechanical advantage(s) for a variety of movement patterns. (S2.M12.8)

Individual-performance activities: Demonstrates correct technique for basic skills in 1 self-selected individual-performance activity. (S1.M24.6)

Embedded Outcome

Working with others: Accepts differences among classmates in physical development, maturation and varying skill levels by providing encouragement and positive feedback. (S4.M4.6)

Lesson Objectives

The learner will:

- use the *J* approach correctly when high jumping.
- demonstrate how to put his back to the bar and land on his back.
- describe basic mechanical advantages for attempting the high jump.

Equipment and Materials

- High jump mats
- High jump standards
- 10 cones
- Bungee

Introduction

Does anyone want to share what he observed in the long jump videos? How did the athletes use their bodies and momentum to help their performance? We will explore some of these ideas in today's lesson.

Today, we will learn how to high jump. The high jump is a field event in which athletes try to put their entire bodies over a bar by jumping off of one foot. To succeed in the high jump, you will need to know which of your legs is your preferred leg so that you can run the J approach. That will allow you to jump from the correct side and allow you to use correct form when jumping.

Show students a video of athletes performing the high jump.

Instructional Task: Students Learn the J Approach

■ PRACTICE TASK

Students start on the left or right side of the mat. This starting spot can be pre-determined, chosen by you.

Place cones on both sides as a guide to help students run the *J*.

Each student will run the *J* and jump up, with the dominant leg driving the inside knee up as if doing a layup for maximum height. Students use the mat as a marker or target and do not land on it.

Have students go. This should go quickly.

Extension

After you discuss the mechanical advantages, have students perform the *J* approach again, focusing on their answers to the guiding questions.

EMBEDDED OUTCOME: S4.M4.6. Discuss with students the importance of accepting differences among classmates. Even though we have these differences, it is important to focus on providing encouragement and positive feedback to all classmates.

Refinement

Make sure students are driving the inside knee.

Guiding questions for students:

- Mechanical advantage: Ask students why it is important to jump off the outside leg and drive the inside knee up. (Answer: If the inside leg is the one used to jump, the leg will hit the bar. If the outside leg is used to drive up, the jumper will not be able to use this momentum to turn the body correctly. Driving the inside knee across the body allows the jumper to get the back to the bar.)
- Can you name any mechanical advantages in the shot put and long jump?

Student Choices/Differentiation

- Students who are struggling to jump off the correct leg may switch sides to see if they have picked the wrong side.
- Students who are struggling to do the *J* may run through without jumping.
- If students continue to struggle with the jump, have them take a three-step approach and focus on jumping off the correct leg, driving the opposite knee upward as for a layup.

What to Look For

- Are students running in a *J* shape or diagonal to the mat?
- Are students jumping with the outside leg? (leg away from the mat)
- Are students driving the inside knee up? (leg closest to the mat)

Instructional Task:
Landing on the Back and Kicking Feet Up

■ PRACTICE TASK

Using three sides of the mats, students practice landing on their backs and kicking their feet up.

Place a marker on the floor from where you would like students to jump.

Two students from each of the three sides stand a foot away from the mat with their backs to the mat. Have students jump up and backward so they are landing on their backs on the mat. While in the air, have them kick their feet up, as they will have to do this to get their legs and feet over the bar.

Refinements

- Remind students to land on their backs.
- It is important to kick the legs up so they do not hit or land on the bar.
- While students are jumping, have them emphasize thrusting their arms up to help them explode upward for maximum height.

Student Choices/Differentiation

Students can move closer to the mat for the first attempts and just practice landing without kicking up.

What to Look For

- Do students jump and land on their upper backs?
- Do students kick their feet up so their legs and feet do not touch or hang over the mat when landing?
- Are students swinging their arms up to help drive the body upward?

Instructional Task:
High Jump Using a Modified High Jump Bar

▪ PRACTICE TASK

Students use the *J* approach from their selected side and jump over the bungee between the two standards, using the cues they have practiced from the previous practice tasks.

Extension

Have students record a partner using a video device. Students should discuss how they are performing the critical elements as they wait for their turn to jump.

Refinement

As students jump, ask them what they think they did well and what they could do differently. Provide feedback based on their responses.

Student Choices/Differentiation

- For students who are still not jumping off the correct leg, have them run through again, driving the inside leg up and not landing on the mat.
- For students worried about jumping over the bar, have them do the backward jump over the bungee.

What to Look For

- Students are running the *J* correctly.
- Students are jumping off the correct foot.
- Students are driving the inside knee up and getting their backs to the bar.
- Students are kicking their legs up to send them over the bar.
- Students are landing on their backs.

Formal and Informal Assessments

Video analysis: peer- and self-assessment of jumps as compared with the cues

Closure

- Provide recognition to the class where deserved as well as to those who encouraged others.
- Ask students if they enjoyed the high jump.
- Why is it called the J approach?
- Why is it important to jump off the outside leg and drive the inside knee up?
- Why is it important to kick the legs up? What part of the body should land on the mat?

Reflection

- Which cue did students seem to pick up easily?
- Which cue did students struggle with the most?
- How effectively did students handle the downtime along with the informal peer- and self-assessment when not jumping?

Homework

Have students watch a high jump competition. Students should be able to discuss the mechanical advantages for the high jump.

Resources

American Sport Education Program. (2008). *Coaching youth track and field*. Champaign, IL: Human Kinetics.

Internet keyword search: "high jump techniques"

LESSON 4: WARM-UP AND COOL-DOWN

Grade-Level Outcomes

Primary Outcomes

Fitness knowledge: Describes the role of warm-ups and cool-downs before and after physical activity. (S3.M12.6)

Fitness knowledge: Describes the role of flexibility in injury prevention. (S3.M10.8)

Embedded Outcome

Self-expression & enjoyment: Identifies why self-selected physical activities create enjoyment. (S5.M4.7)

Lesson Objectives

The learner will:

- list the distances run during a track meet and select races to run.
- demonstrate proper warm-up and cool-down techniques before and after running.
- describe why dynamic warm-ups (before activity) and static stretches (after activity) are helpful and important.
- identify the role of flexibility in preventing injury.

Equipment and Materials

- A space to run the selected distances and warm up
- Stopwatch

Introduction

Does anyone want to share what mechanical advantages for the high jump he or she observed for homework? Can anyone apply these advantages to other sports?

Today, we will learn the importance of warming up and cooling down before and after competition.

Discuss with students the distances in a track meet and the races that they will be able to compete in during class. Discuss why it is important to warm up and how performing dymnamic stretching will help your muscles compete at their best level and prevent injury. Show and explain the warm-ups and dynamic stretches that students should perform before they compete.

Instructional Task: Warming Up

■ PRACTICE TASK

Have students warm up and complete dynamic stretches of the muscle groups that they will be using, explaining how that will help prevent injuries.

The warm-up and dynamic stretching should prepare the muscle groups that students will use while running and jumping.

Extensions

- Explain what each warm-up drill or dynamic stretch is doing for each muscle group.
- Discuss why warm-ups and dynamic stretching play an important role in preparing to be active.
- For students who know the muscle grouping names, challenge them to learn the muscles of each group (e.g., hamstring muscles include the semimembranosus, semitendinosus, and biceps femoris).
- Repeat for each muscle group.

Guiding questions for students:

- Why are the following stretches important?
- What is the difference between a dynamic stretch and a static stretch?
- What are two ways to stretch your hamstrings, quads, and calves?

Student Choices/Differentiation

- The warm-up should be based on each student's endurance and ability.
- Provide more than one way to stretch each muscle group.

What to Look For

- Are students completing the dynamic warm-up and doing the warm-up with correct form?
- Do students know the muscle groups and what muscle groups are being stretched?

Instructional Task: Race Selections

▧ PRACTICE TASK

Discuss how to race each distance, focusing on pacing, form, and breathing to help students finish.

Guiding questions for students:

- Why is it important to pace yourself?
- In what ways will proper form help?

Extension

Set predetermined distances at 100, 200, 400, and 800 meters, and students select races they would like to compete in.

Guiding questions for students:

- Why did you select the running events you did?
- Did you enjoy the events or do you wish that you would have picked a different one? Why or why not?

Student Choices/Differentiation

- While practice races are occurring, students are continuing to warm up and perform dynamic stretches.
- Students moderate their speed to get a feel for the length and pacing of the events.

What to Look For

- Are students selecting race distances they are successful at in order to connect it to the embedded objective?
- Are students standing around and talking or continuing to warm up and perform dynamic stretches?

Instructional Task: Cooling Down

▧ PRACTICE TASK

After the races, students jog and walk a determined distance or time and then perform static stretches, discussing what muscle groups each stretch is working on.

Guiding questions for students:

- What muscle groups are being stretched?
- What stretches stretch each muscle group?
- How does static stretching help prevent injury?
- How does static stretching help the muscles after competing or working out?

Extension

Peer assessment: Ask students to demonstrate a static stretch for a specific muscle group and explain what muscles are being stretched.

EMBEDDED OUTCOME: S5.M4.7. During the cool-down period, have students discuss why self-selected physical activities create enjoyment in one's life.

Student Choices/Differentiation

- Ask students if there is an area they would like to stretch more, or show specific stretches for individual students if they feel tight in an area.
- Provide modifications to stretches, if needed.

What to Look For

- Do students know what stretches stretch the different parts of the body and muscle groups?
- Do students know the names of the muscle groups?
- Are students tight and need more time stretching those muscle groups?

Formal and Informal Assessments

- Peer assessment: Using a checklist, students peer-assess classmates' cool-down stretches, looking for correct form and technique.
- Exit slips:
  - Rules for relay races
  - What role does flexibility have in injury prevention?

Closure

- Why is it important to warm up and perform dynamic stretching before being active and static stretching afterward?
- What is the difference between static and dynamic stretches?
- Why are they both important?
- Why is it important to participate in activities that you like?

Reflection

- How did the races go?
- Did students pace themselves?
- Do students know different types of stretches and the muscle groups that they are stretching?

Homework

Using a handout on stretches and dynamic warm-up activities, have students stretch specific muscle groups and complete the dynamic warm-up on their own before the next class.

Resources

American Sport Education Program. (2008). *Coaching youth track and field.* Champaign, IL: Human Kinetics.

Dougherty, N.J. (Ed.) (2010). Physical activity & sport for the secondary school student. 6th ed. Reston, VA: National Association for Sport and Physical Education.

Internet keyword search: "dynamic stretching," "static stretching," "dynamic warm-ups"

LESSON 5: RELAY RACES

Grade-Level Outcomes

Primary Outcomes

Individual-performance activities: Demonstrates correct technique for basic skills in 1 self-selected individual-performance activity. (S1.M24.6)

Fitness knowledge: Describes the role of warm-ups and cool-downs before and after physical activity. (S3.M12.6)

Embedded Outcome

Personal responsibility: Exhibits responsible social behaviors by cooperating with classmates, demonstrating inclusive behaviors and supporting classmates. (S4. M1.7)

Lesson Objectives

The learner will:

- know the different types of relay races.
- know the rules for the 4 × 100 and 4 × 400.
- pass the baton to a moving teammate.
- demonstrate how to warm up and cool down properly.

Equipment and Materials

- Marked-out distances for each relay race
- 1 baton for each team
- Cues for field events

Introduction

Today, we will learn what relay races are and practice two different types. The first relay race will be the 4 × 100 meters and the second will be the 4 × 400 meters. In a relay race, four people on the same team run one at a time with a baton as fast as they can.

Show a video clip of each type of relay race.

When we are done with the relay races, we will review the field events, and then you will spend one day practicing (Lesson 6) your self-selected event before our class track meet. During the practice day, you will be helping each other and providing feedback based on the cues for the events that you choose.

Instructional Task: Warm-Up and Hand-Offs

■ **PRACTICE TASK**

Perform a dynamic warm-up with the class.

Demonstrate the 4 × 100 and the hand-off for a 4 × 100.

Explain relay rules and passing zones.

Demonstrate the 4 × 400 and the hand-offs.

In groups of four, students practice hand-offs.

Extensions

- Teach students the blind hand-off.
- Demonstrate and discuss the differences between the hand-offs used in sprint relays and those used in relays of 400 meters and longer.
- Students evaluate one another using a checklist on critical features of hand-offs.

Guiding questions for students:

- Why is it helpful for the person receiving the baton to be moving forward?
- What is an exchange zone, and what is its purpose?
- What does the hand-off look like for a 4 × 100 and a 4 × 400?

Refinements

- The person receiving the hand-off must be moving forward, not standing still, so that teammates don't run into or over her.

Student Choices/Differentiation

- If you do not have batons, students can use any handheld object or even give high fives.
- Students may run at half speed, three-quarter speed, or full speed during hand-offs.

What to Look For

- Students are performing the proper warm-up that we practiced in previous lessons.
- Students are moving when receiving the hand-off and are not starting off too soon so that their teammate can get to them.
- Students' hands are in the correct position to take the baton.

Instructional Task:
Participate in the 4 × 100 and 4 × 400

■ PRACTICE TASK

Remind students to apply what they learned from the last class when running these distances. Discuss the importance of the following:

- Pacing themselves during the 400 so they don't take off too fast or don't run hard enough and have a lot of energy left
- Running as fast as they can for the entire race during the 4 × 100
- When receiving the baton, starting to run or move forward so their teammate does not have to slow down or stop

Extensions

- Divide the students into two groups for both the 4 × 100 and 4 × 400.
- The first group races while the second group evaluates their peers, using a checklist of the critical features of the handoff. They switch after the race.

Guiding questions for students:

After each race:

- If you ran in this race, how did you pace yourself?
- How did the hand-offs go? What did you learn? What would you do differently?

EMBEDDED OUTCOME: S4.M1.7. Discuss with students proper social behaviors (cooperating with classmates, demonstrating inclusive behaviors, and supporting classmates).

Student Choices/Differentiation

- Students can change the running order.
- Modify the distance for students and space.
- Use different styles of hand-offs.

What to Look For

- Are students pacing themselves well?
- Are students running or moving forward during the hand-offs?

- Are teams able to complete the hand-offs within the correct area?
- Are students encouraging each other?

Instructional Task: Cool Down and Review Procedures for the Field Event Practice

■ PRACTICE TASK

To cool down, each student will jog for 5 minutes and then stretch the major muscle groups used during the relay races.

Extension

During the static stretching part of the cool-down, review the cues of the field events, and explain how students will be helping others as they practice their self-selected field events next class.

Guiding questions for students:

- What is the importance of cooling down properly?
- What muscle groups should you stretch after running the 4 × 100 and 4 × 400?
- What are the cues for each field event?

Student Choices/Differentiation

Students may modify the stretches, if needed.

What to Look For

- Students are performing the proper cool-down that we practiced in previous lessons.
- Students know how to stretch each muscle group.
- Do students have questions about the field events, and do they know the cues for performing each event?

Formal and Informal Assessments

- Peer evaluation: checklist on critical features of hand-offs
- Exit slip: Explain the rules for relay races in track and field.

Closure

- Review the relay races and how to pass the baton.
- Discuss pacing and how the speed changes for different distances.
- During the stretches, explain how students will be practicing a self-selected field event during the next class to perform during the class track meet.

Reflection

- Were students able to hand off using the hand-offs learned?
- Did students work well together during the relay?
- Do students understand how and why to warm up and cool down?

Homework

- Watch videos of relay races to see how they are done and the types of hand-offs used in high school or beyond.
- Look over the rules and cues of how to perform the field event you will be practicing tomorrow.

Resources

American Sport Education Program. (2008). *Coaching youth track and field*. Champaign, IL: Human Kinetics.

Internet keyword search: "hand-offs," "4 × 100 hand-offs in track"

LESSON 6: EVENT PRACTICE

Grade-Level Outcomes

Primary Outcomes

Individual-performance activities: Demonstrates correct technique for basic skills in 1 self-selected individual-performance activity. (S1.M24.6)

Social interaction: Demonstrates respect for self by asking for help and helping others in various physical activities. (S5.M6.8)

Accepting feedback: Demonstrates self-responsibility by implementing specific corrective feedback to improve performance. (S4.M3.6)

Embedded Outcomes

Self-expression & enjoyment: Identifies why self-selected physical activities create enjoyment. (S5.M4.7)

Movement concepts: Describes and applies mechanical advantage(s) for a variety of movement patterns. (S2.M12.8)

Lesson Objectives

The learner will:

- demonstrate the correct technique for self-selected events by implementing specific corrective feedback.
- ask for help and help others throughout the lesson.

Equipment and Materials

- Clips of each field event at each field event station for students to watch
- Sheets with the correct cues for students to use at each field event station
- Equipment to record and show students' practice
- Equipment and area for each field event
- Quizzes for students to take on the skills they have selected to practice
- Sheets for students to write their names and circle the two running events and which field event they will compete in

Introduction

Will someone please share the critical elements that you saw in your homework assignment? Did anyone see athletes drop the baton? Hand-offs can be very difficult. Keep practicing!

Today, you will practice the events in which you will compete during our class track meet. Your performance will be video-recorded.

You should have watched the video clips and read over the cues as this was your homework. While at your event area, you will practice the skill and focus on the cues to help with proper technique. While you are waiting, you will record your peers and watch your video, comparing what you see to the cues to help you and your peers learn proper technique. Before you begin, go through your dynamic warm-up and dynamic stretching. In the last 5 minutes of your practice time, you will take a knowledge assessment about the cues and basic rules for the event you have chosen to focus on. What questions do you have?

Instructional Task: Field Event Practice Stations (Shot Put, Long Jump, High Jump)

■ **PRACTICE TASK**

Students complete a dynamic warm-up and dynamic stretching.

In groups of two to four, students work together using the cue sheet and recording devices to help and encourage each other while practicing the shot put, long jump, and high jump, focusing on correct technique.

Extension

As you walk around, students show you a recording of a student jumping and explain what the student was doing well and what could be done to improve one of the missed cues.

Refinements

- Shot put: Keep the shot next to the neck and jaw, keeping the elbow up.
- Long jump: Keep eyes up, looking out toward the sky, while arms and legs rotate forward. During the landing, bring your butt toward your heels.
- High jump: Maintain speed at the end of the J. Drive the inside knee up as you jump.

Guiding questions for students:

After each field event:

- What cue were you struggling with, and how were you working to improve it?
- What success did you have? Why do you think you had success, from a mechanical perspective?

EMBEDDED OUTCOME: S2.M12.8. For the cue that was just discussed, have students discuss the mechanical advantages that the cue provides for the movement patterns in the field event.

EMBEDDED OUTCOME: S5.M4.7. Discuss with students why they chose this event and how choosing physical activity leads to more fun and enjoyment.

Remember that when we are talking about others' performances, we are respectful and talk about how they did in relation to the cues. For example: You did a nice job on your J approach. Next time, drive up your inside leg.

Student Choices/Differentiation

According to skill level, students can modify the events or use traditional equipment or boundaries.

What to Look For

- Are students using correct form during field events?
- Are students providing correct feedback?
- Are they using the technology correctly?

Instructional Task: Knowledge Test

■ **PRACTICE TASK**

Students spread out in general space or go to a classroom to take a knowledge assessment.

Student Choices/Differentiation

Modify tests, if needed.

What to Look For

Students demonstrate basic understanding of track and field skills taught in the module.

Formal and Informal Assessments

Knowledge assessment of the cues and rules to perform their events correctly

Closure

- Bring students together to talk specifically about what you observed in each event area. Discuss how students were doing in relation to their events but also how they were working together and giving feedback. Answer any questions students still have about their events.
- Briefly explain what events will be performed the first day of the meet and what students will be doing to prepare. On made-up slips of paper, have students write their names and circle the two races they want to run and the one field event they will compete in.

Reflection

- Are students able to self-evaluate and give meaningful feedback?
- Was I able to help each student at each event so we can move on to the competition the next class session?

Homework

Review the cues and watch video clips of the self-selected field event you are performing in the class track meet.

Resources

American Sport Education Program. (2008). *Coaching youth track and field*. Champaign, IL: Human Kinetics.

LESSON 7: TRACK MEET

Grade-Level Outcomes

Primary Outcome

Individual-performance activities: Demonstrates correct technique for basic skills in 1 self-selected individual-performance activity. (S1.M24.6)

Embedded Outcomes

Working with others: Accepts differences among classmates in physical development, maturation and varying skill levels by providing encouragement and positive feedback. (S4.M4.6)

Personal responsibility: Exhibits responsible social behaviors by cooperating with classmates, demonstrating inclusive behaviors and supporting classmates. (S4.M1.7)

Lesson Objectives

The learner will:

- demonstrate the ability to perform and compete in a variety of track and field events.
- show sportsmanship and proper etiquette while competing and watching classmates.

Equipment and Materials

- Long jump area, rake, and what you will use for measuring jumps
- Track or area for your races and what you will need to mark the distances and starting points
- The pre-determined list of who is in which race and how many races for each distance from the student-selected sheets last class
- Watch or timer for races and a place to record times if needed

Introduction

Today, we will begin our class track meet, which will extend over two class periods.

This is how the meet will work: After the warm-up, we will perform one field event and then our individual track races. Everyone must participate in at least two races and one field event if it is the one you chose to practice. During the field event, you may cheer for your classmates, but you must continue to stay warmed up for your races.

Let students know what the three race distances will be (e.g., 100, 200, 400). Explain the order of the races and field event, your procedures for how students will be grouped, and what you want them to do to be organized (where to be and when).

Instructional Task:
Warm-Up and First Field Event (Long Lump)

■ PRACTICE TASK

As a class, students go through their dynamic warm-up.

Students who have selected to do the long jump report to the long jump area to practice their run-through and get their marks.

Once everyone has their marks they will all perform a set number of jumps.

You may choose to measure or not measure the jumps. To save time, instead of measuring, put markers on the side of the pit showing the longest jumps.

Extension

Conduct a formal assessment for long jump using a checklist or rubric.

Refinement

Make sure students are correctly identifying their marks.

EMBEDDED OUTCOME: S4.M4.6. Discuss with students the importance of accepting differences among classmates. Be sure to discuss physical development, maturation, and varying skill levels and how to provide encouragement and positive feedback to those students who are different from oneself.

Student Choices/Differentiation

Students who are not long-jumping continue to warm up and walk or jog around to prepare for their running races.

What to Look For

Using a checklist or rubric, assess students' form and successful attempts.

Instructional Task: Running Races

■ PRACTICE TASK

Students compete in the two self-selected races against classmates and for time.

Discuss with students pacing and performing their best.

In between races, discuss with students what they observed and discuss what was done well and what can be done to help the racers.

Guiding questions for students:

- Did you feel that you warmed up enough before the race?
- When you finished the race, did you feel that you gave your best effort?

Refinement

Stop races and correct or offer feedback on running form and pacing if needed.

EMBEDDED OUTCOME: S4.M1.7. Discuss with students how to support their classmates during track and field activities. Make sure that students are including everyone and cooperating during the different track and field events.

Student Choices/Differentiation

- Challenge students to improve their times (if using a timing device).
- Students choose their race distances.

What to Look For

- Do students understand pace? Are they speeding up and slowing down?
- Are students encouraging classmates and being supportive and respectful?

Instructional Task: Group Cool-Down

■ PRACTICE TASK

Have students go through a class cool-down of jogging or walking and stretches.

Provide different stretches for areas of the body that could be sore.

Guiding questions for students:

- What are three different stretches for the leg muscles?
- Why is the cool-down important?

Student Choices/Differentiation

Distance for a jog or walk cool-down will vary depending on students.

What to Look For

- Students are cooling down by walking or jogging the intended distance.
- Students are using proper form to stretch.
- Students are performing specific stretches and not just standing or sitting.

Formal and Informal Assessments

Skills assessment as students perform the field events, using a checklist or rubric of critical elements

Closure

- After all races conclude, talk with students about the effort and sportsmanship displayed.
- Provide examples of what you saw that went well in the field events and races as well as what students can do differently the next class to make the final day successful.
- Discuss with students what the next day will look like and how they can help make it successful, as two field events and relay races will occur.

Reflection

- How did the warm-ups go while the long jump was going on?
- What can I do differently to make this smoother for the next class?
- How did the long jump and the assessment of students go?
- How did the races go?
- Did students understand what to do?
- Did the number of students in each race allow the race and recording of times to go smoothly?

Homework

Review critical elements for the skills assessment next class.

Resources

American Sport Education Program. (2008). *Coaching youth track and field*. Champaign, IL: Human Kinetics.

Dougherty, N.J. (Ed.) (2010). Physical activity & sport for the secondary school student. 6th ed. Reston, VA: National Association for Sport and Physical Education.

LESSON 8: FINISHING THE MEET

Grade-Level Outcomes

Primary Outcome

Individual-performance activities: Demonstrates correct technique for basic skills in 1 self-selected individual-performance activity. (S1.M24.6)

Embedded Outcome

Social interaction: Demonstrates the importance of social interactions by helping and encouraging others, avoiding trash talk and providing support to classmates. (S5.M6.7)

Lesson Objectives

The learner will:

- demonstrate correct technique in a variety of track and field events.
- encourage others during a track meet.

Equipment and Materials

- High jump area and mat
- Shot put area and shots or softballs
- Track or area for your races and what you will need to mark the distances and starting points
- List of pre-determined relay teams
- Watch or timer for races and a place to record times if needed
- Batons or what you will use to represent the batons

Introduction

Today is the second day of the track meet.

Discuss with students again what went well in the previous class and what they should be doing during each event, as well as the behaviors you should be seeing. Review the warm-up and explain the order of field events and how the relay races will occur. Answer questions as needed. As students will be assessed, review the cues for each field event.

Instructional Task: Warm-Up and Shot Put

■ PRACTICE TASK

As a class, students go through the dynamic warm-up and stretches.

Students who have selected to do the shot put will report to the shot put area to warm up, practice their throws, and then compete.

If places are being tracked, this can be done quickly in two different ways. The first is like the long jump. A pre-determined number of markers are placed at the site of the farthest throws, and no measurements are taken.

In the second option, the first throw is marked. The student immediately throws again, and the farthest throw is measured.

Extension

Conduct a formal assessment of the shot put, using a rubric or checklist.

Refinements

- Provide feedback as necessary to help students learn from what they have done incorrectly. Try to minimize feedback that might influence the assessment.
- Make sure that students are not sacrificing form for distance in the shot put (injuries may occur).

EMBEDDED OUTCOME: S5.M6.7 Discuss with students the importance of proper social interactions (helping and encouraging others, avoiding trash talk, and providing support to classmates).

Student Choices/Differentiation

- Students who are not performing the shot put warm up and perform dynamic stretching to prepare for the relay races.
- Choice of a shot or softball should be the same for all students, but the selection of which should be pre-determined after lesson 6 based on students' understanding of the cues for ability and safety.

What to Look For

Using a checklist or rubric, assess the critical elements and successful trials of the shot put.

Instructional Task: Relay Races

■ PRACTICE TASK

Discuss with students pacing and performing their best. Review where the hand-offs will take place and how to hand off the baton.

Guiding questions for students:

- Why is it important for the person receiving the baton to be running during the hand-off?
- Why is it important to put the correct hand back when receiving the baton?

In pre-determined teams, students compete in two relay races.

Refinements

- Before the second race, discuss what you saw students doing well and what can be improved for the next race.
- Reinforce the importance of sportsmanship by congratulating and cheering for classmates. Discuss appropriate behaviors when performances go well and when they do not happen the way that students wanted.

Student Choices/Differentiation

- The distances should allow for all students to be successful.
- Distances for each runner can be equal, or each one can have a different distance.

What to Look For

- Are students cheering for their teammates and other classmates? (What are they saying?)
- Are students showing good sportsmanship? (How are they acting during and after each race?)
- Do students understand when and how to hand off the baton?
- Are students pacing themselves? (Are they speeding up and slowing down?)

Instructional Task: High Jump

■ PRACTICE TASK

Students perform the high jump.

Start the bungee or bar at about mat height. Everyone takes one jump at that height. Those students who miss three times at that height are out of the competition but should continue to support classmates who are still competing. Those students who clear that height continue at the next height, which should be 1 or 2 inches (2.5 to 5 cm) higher. Continue this way until only one student has cleared the bar at its highest point.

Extension

Conduct a formal assessment of the high jump.

Guiding questions for students:

Think about the following before jumping:
- Which leg is dominant, and from what side should you start your J approach?
- What should you be doing with your non-dominant leg and body while jumping?

Student Choices/Differentiation

- For safety, use a bungee instead of the bar.
- Students have a choice to try higher levels if they are successful at lower levels.

What to Look For

Using a checklist or rubric, assess the critical elements and successful trials of the high jump.

Formal and Informal Assessments

Formal skills assessment on critical elements and legal jumps and throws

Closure

- Discuss with students what you observed (good and bad) during the track meet.
- Talk about performances, effort, and sportsmanship.
- Ask students what they learned and enjoyed during the unit.

Reflection

- From the two-day meet, what could be changed to help students be successful?
- What went well in how the events were set up, and what could be changed?
- Did students have enough practice trials throughout the module to be successful in the track and field meet?

Homework

Have students watch or read about the next module.

Resources

American Sport Education Program. (2008). *Coaching youth track and field*. Champaign, IL: Human Kinetics.

CHAPTER 10

Applying Students' Skills and Knowledge to Physical Activity Participation

It seems that one cannot turn on the television or radio or go online without hearing or reading about the obesity epidemic that afflicts many parts of the world. At the same time, recent literature in the field shows a decrease in physical activity levels when children move into adolescence (Corbin, Pangrazi, & Le Masurier, 2004; Patnode, et al., 2011; Xu & Liu, 2013). The middle school years, then, appear to be a critical time for supporting students' physical activity and for helping them meet the recommended minimum of 60 minutes of physical activity every day. With that goal in mind, SHAPE America focused Standard 3 on the knowledge and skills needed to attain and maintain health-related fitness and participation in lifelong physical activity (SHAPE America, 2014). This chapter zeros in on Standard 3 in lessons within two modules on physical activity participation: one for grade 6 and one for grade 8. Both modules provide opportunities for students to learn the importance of physical activity, how to pursue it safely, and how to plan and track their physical activity outside of the physical education classroom.

The Physical Activity Participation Module for grade 6 places the emphasis on students' learning how to use physical activity logs (one- or two-day and two-week) and designing fitness plans from the basic fitness activities and testing in the module. The Physical Activity Participation Module for grade 8 emphasizes progressing through the content to develop and implement a cross-training program. Most of the lessons in this module focus on strength and endurance, while the homework incorporates aerobic activities. Note: Many of the lessons in these modules do not include warm-up or cool-down routines, so you should incorporate your own routines.

The Grade-Level Outcomes addressed in both modules target students' participation in physical activity for at least 60 minutes per day. While it might be unrealistic to expect that students will log 60 minutes of physical activity each day solely by participating in a typical middle school physical education program, the goal is for students to participate in different physical activities and to continue them outside of the classroom. In the module for grade 8, for example, depending on the teaching environment and curriculum, you can address many of the outcomes (e.g., S3.M2.8, S3.M3.8, S3.M5.8, and S3.M6.8) in homework assignments.

For easy reference, each module begins with a block plan chart of the Grade-Level Outcomes addressed in each lesson. Each module addresses multiple National Standards, although most of the outcomes addressed directly in the lessons reside under Standard 3. The Physical Activity Participation Module for grade 6 focuses mainly on participating in moderate to vigorous activity (Outcome S3.M6.6) and designing and implementing a program of remediation based on the results of health-related fitness assessment (Outcome S3.M15.6). The lessons also place some emphasis on using fitness equipment correctly (Outcome S4.M7.6) and maintaining a physical activity log for at least two weeks (outcome S3.M16.6).

The main focus in the Physical Activity Participation Module for grade 8 is designing and implementing a cross-training program (Outcome S3.M4.8), with many other outcomes under Standards 3 and 4 addressed as well. All in all, the modules provide great lessons for implementing physical activity and teaching students to plan and prepare for an active lifestyle.

GRADE 6 PHYSICAL ACTIVITY PARTICIPATION MODULE

Lessons in this module were contributed by John Kruse, a middle school physical education teacher with the Los Angeles Unified School District.

Grade-Level Outcomes Addressed, by Lesson	Lessons							
	1	2	3	4	5	6	7	8
Standard 1. The physically literate individual demonstrates competency in a variety of motor skills and movement patterns.								
Catches with a mature pattern from a variety of trajectories using different objects in varying practice tasks. (S1.M3.6)	E							
Throws, while stationary, a leading pass to a moving receiver. (S1.M5.6)	E							
Dribbles with dominant hand using a change of speed and direction in a variety of practice tasks. (S1.M8.6)			P					
Standard 2. The physically literate individual applies knowledge of concepts, principles, strategies and tactics related to movement and performance.								
Standard 3. The physically literate individual demonstrates the knowledge and skills to achieve and maintain a health-enhancing level of physical activity and fitness.								
Participates in moderate to vigorous aerobic physical activity that includes intermittent or continuous aerobic physical activity of both moderate and vigorous intensity for at least 60 minutes per day. (S3.M6.6)	P	P	P		P			
Sets and monitors a self-selected physical-activity goal for aerobic and/or muscle- and bone-strengthening activity based on current fitness level. (S3.M8.6)		E	E					
Employs correct techniques and methods of stretching. (S3.M9.6)						P		
Differentiates between aerobic and anaerobic capacity, and between muscular strength and muscular endurance. (S3.M10.6)					E			
Describes the role of warm-ups and cool-downs before and after physical activities. (S3.M12.6)				E				
Defines resting heart rate and describes its relationship to aerobic fitness and the Borg Rating of Perceived Exertion (RPE) Scale. (S3.M13.6)					P			
Designs and implements a program of remediation for any areas of weakness based on the results of health-related fitness assessment. (S3.M15.6)							P	P	P
Maintains a physical activity log for at least 2 weeks and reflects on activity levels as documented in the log. (S3.M16.6)		P			P			P
Standard 4. The physically literate individual exhibits responsible personal and social behavior that respects self and others.								
Demonstrates self-responsibility by implementing specific corrective feedback to improve performance. (S4.M3.6)								E
Accepts differences among classmates in physical development, maturation and varying skill levels by providing encouragement and positive feedback. (S4.M4.6)				E		E		
Uses physical activity and fitness equipment appropriately and safely, *with the teacher's guidance*. (S4.M7.6)	E					E	E	
Standard 5. The physically literate individual recognizes the value of physical activity for health, enjoyment, challenge, self-expression and/or social interaction.								
Describes how being physically active leads to a healthy body. (S5.M1.6)						E		

P = Primary; E = Embedded

LESSON 1: USING PEDOMETERS WITH THROWING AND CATCHING ACTIVITIES

Grade-Level Outcomes

Primary Outcome

Fitness knowledge: Participates in moderate to vigorous aerobic physical activity that includes intermittent or continuous aerobic physical activity of both moderate and vigorous intensity for at least 60 minutes per day. (S3.M6.6)

Embedded Outcomes

Catching: Catches with a mature pattern from a variety of trajectories using different objects in varying practice tasks. (S1.M3.6)

Passing and receiving: Throws, while stationary, a leading pass to a moving receiver. (S1.M5.6)

Safety: Uses physical activity and fitness equipment appropriately and safely, *with the teacher's guidance.* (S4.M7.6)

Lesson Objectives

The learner will:

- explore moderate to vigorous aerobic physical activity that is intermittent or continuous in nature.
- track pedometer steps to determine whether various activities are of moderate or vigorous intensity.

Equipment and Materials

- Variety of throwing implements (e.g., rag balls, foam footballs, rubber animals), enough for every student
- Pedometers
- Pedometer worksheet
- Pencils (1 per group of 2)
- Clipboards (1 per group of 2)
- Cones
- Grass field
- Stopwatches (1 per small group)

Introduction

Today, we will begin our lessons on physical activity participation. Through throwing and catching, we will explore exercise intensity. Who has used a pedometer before? Who knows what it does? Those who don't will by the end of today's lesson.

Instructional Task:
Explanation of Pedometers and Pedometer Tool

■ PRACTICE TASK

Pass out pedometers, clipboards, pencils, and pedometer worksheets to students.

EMBEDDED OUTCOME: S4.M7.6. Make sure that students are using pedometers appropriately (check for safety, validity, reliability, etc.).

The worksheet will help students calculate steps per minute and determine their physical activity intensity.

Guiding questions for students:

Today, you will use pedometers to count your steps while you practice throwing and catching. That will help you determine your level of physical activity during class.

- How many steps do you think you will take during this class period?
- Do you think you will engage in moderate physical activity or vigorous physical activity?
- What are some numbers that you have come up with from the moderate amounts of activity?
- What about vigorous?
- Why do you think the numbers are different?
- What are some things that you could do to increase or decrease the amounts of activity?

Student Choices/Differentiation

Students may work by themselves or with a partner on this task.

What to Look For

- Students are attaching pedometers in the correct location.
- Students are following along with how the pedometer steps per minute worksheet works.

Instructional Task: Throwing and Catching Warm-Up

■ PRACTICE TASK

Students practice throwing and catching, starting off throwing from a short distance to warm up the major muscles involved in the activity.

Using the worksheet provided, students track their times to determine steps per minute and exercise intensity, so that they can determine proper warm-ups.

Remind students to warm up at a lower intensity than the main activity.

Extension

If time permits, students can increase the distance of their throws as they warm up.

Student Choices/Differentiation

- Students can choose various objects to throw.
- Students can choose various distances to start off the activity.

What to Look For

- Students are catching the object with proper hand positions below the waist, at the waist, or above the waist.
- Students are filling out the worksheet properly.

Instructional Task: Throwing to a Moving Target and Catching While on the Move

■ PRACTICE TASK

Students practice catching with a mature pattern from a variety of trajectories using different objects in varying practice tasks. Students take turns in the roles of thrower and catcher.

Using stopwatches, students time each of their turns at throwing and catching to determine steps per minute and moderate to vigorous physical activity.

Ask students to predict steps per minute and either moderate or vigorous physical activity while throwing and again while catching.

Stationary students throw to partners, who move back and forth in a grid formation.

The purpose of the activity is to provide students with an opportunity to track activity with a pedometer. You also should make sure that students are making accurate lead passes and are catching from a variety of trajectories using different objects. Feedback can focus on both catching and throwing, as well as pedometer use.

Extensions

- Partner fakes one way and then goes the other way.
- Willie Mays catch: Partner catches the object over the shoulder while running away from the thrower.
- The long pass: Ball is thrown as far as possible toward the partner, who catches it on the run (Hichwa, 1998).

Guiding questions for students:

- Is this a constant or varied practice schedule for the throwing person?
- What kind of feedback can you give your partner based on what you saw?

Student Choices/Differentiation

Students can choose which throwing objects to use and at what distances.

What to Look For

- Students are catching the object with proper hand positions below the waist, at the waist, or above the waist.
- Students are using a variety of trajectories and throwing distances.

Formal and Informal Assessments

Please note that all of the assessments for this lesson are formative, because underlying content is being practiced for the standards addressed.

- Pedometer tool worksheet
- Informal throwing and catching
- Exit slip: What is a pedometer? What can we measure while using one?

Closure

Debrief students on the lesson while pedometers and worksheets are being collected.

- How did your steps per minute and exercise intensity compare when you were in the roles of throwing and catching?
- How did your steps per minute and exercise intensity for your throwing warm-up compare with the rest of practice?
- Were today's activities enough to give you 60 minutes of physical activity for the day?
- What can you do to reach 60 minutes of physical activity for the day?
- How could we redesign today's learning experience so that the throwing person gets more steps per minute?

Note: Because this is a convergent guiding discovery, students should realize that their steps per minute should be lower when they are the stationary thrower. Also, students should realize that they could redesign the learning experience so that the thrower is on the move also.

Reflection

- How are students' throwing and catching skills improving over the course of the school year?
- How engaged were students in tracking their physical activity using pedometers?

Homework

Continue practicing throwing and catching at home, during recess, and at lunch. If you can, try tracking this information and figuring out your steps per minute. A number of smart phone apps can track your steps (i.e., turn your phone into a pedometer).

Resources

Hichwa, J. (1998). *Right fielders are people too: An inclusive approach to teaching middle school physical education.* Champaign, IL: Human Kinetics.

Schmidt, R.A., & Wrisberg, C.A. (2008). *Motor learning and performance: A situation-based learning approach.* 4th ed. Champaign, IL: Human Kinetics.

Wickstrom, R.L. (1983). *Fundamental movement patterns.* 3rd ed. Philadelphia: Lea & Febiger.

PEDOMETERS

Some pedometers now track activity time. Some simply measure steps. If your pedometer measures only steps, you will need to use a stopwatch or watch to track your time.

Caution: Beginning exercisers and people who have health issues should not try to reach the 120 to 140 steps per minute range. They should remain patient, working up slowly to a higher exercise intensity over a couple of months.

Steps per minute (SPM)	Intensity	Definition
120-140	Moderate	Activity of an intensity equal to brisk walking
	Vigorous	Movement that expends more energy or is performed at a higher intensity than moderate-intensity activity

Source: Graser, S.V., Vincent, W.J., & Pangrazi, R.P. (2009). Step it up. *Journal of Physical Education, Recreation & Dance, 80*(1), 22-24.

Formula: Determine exercise intensity by dividing number of steps by time.

Step 1: Measure the time of exercise or physical activity. (Time of exercise or physical activity is 30 minutes.)

Step 2: Use the pedometer to track how many steps are taken. (Total number of steps taken is 4,000.)

Step 3: Calculate exercise intensity using this formula: steps taken ÷ minutes of exercise = steps per minute. *Example:* You take 4,000 steps over 30 minutes; so, 4,000 steps ÷ 30 minutes = 133 steps per minute.

Step 4: Calculate your own exercise intensity using the formula, perhaps involving a parent or guardian.

Step 5: Record your steps per minute on your physical activity log.

Instructions

Use the stopwatch to track your time as the thrower and catcher. Also, record your total steps in each role. Clear the pedometer of steps when you switch roles, if possible. Otherwise, track your steps so that you know how many you took for each activity.

Practice Schedule

Warm-up: Stand close to each other and throw your object back and forth while you warm up your throwing muscles.

Practice the following throws randomly, with the thrower choosing which patterns the catcher will take. Attempt each throw about three or four times before trading off with your partner. (Adjust based on allotted class time.) The thrower stays stationary, while the catcher moves.

Throws (Hichwa, 1998):

- Catcher fakes one way and moves the other way.
- Willie Mays catch: Catcher catches the ball on the run and over the shoulder.
- The long pass: Thrower throws the ball as far as possible, and the catcher catches it on the run.

Record the following:

Student 1: Name: _____

Time throwing: _____ Steps taken: _____ Steps per minute: _____ Moderate/Vigorous (circle):   Yes   No

Time catching: _____ Steps taken: _____ Steps per minute: _____ Moderate/Vigorous (circle):   Yes   No

Student 2: Name: _____

Time throwing: _____ Steps taken: _____ Steps per minute: _____ Moderate/Vigorous (circle):   Yes   No

Time catching: _____ Steps taken: _____ Steps per minute: _____ Moderate to vigorous (circle):   Yes   No

From R.J. Doan, L.C. MacDonald, and S. Chepko, eds., 2017, *Lesson planning for middle school physical education* (Reston, VA: SHAPE America; Champaign, IL: Human Kinetics).

LESSON 2: ONE-DAY (WEEKDAY) PHYSICAL ACTIVITY LOG

Grade-Level Outcomes

Primary Outcomes

Fitness knowledge: Participates in moderate to vigorous aerobic physical activity that includes intermittent or continuous aerobic physical activity of both moderate and vigorous intensity for at least 60 minutes per day. (S3.M6.6)

Assessment & program planning: Maintains a physical activity log for at least 2 weeks and reflects on activity levels as documented in the log. (S3.M16.6)

Embedded Outcome

Fitness knowledge: Sets and monitors a self-selected physical-activity goal for aerobic and/or muscle- and bone-strengthening activity based on current fitness level. (S3.M8.6)

Lesson Objectives

The learner will:

- create a one-day physical activity log that will lead eventually to a two-week physical activity log.
- participate in muscle- and bone-strengthening activities.

Equipment and Materials

- 4 cones
- Indoor gym space or classroom
- LCD overhead projector
- Wall or screen to project onto
- Large Wiffle balls (1 per 2 students)
- Pencils
- Clipboards (enough for cooperative groups of 4 to 5 students)
- Copies of 1-day physical activity log (1 per student for homework and a few extra for cooperative groups during class time)

Introduction

Today, you will start to keep track of your physical activity by using a physical activity log. By the end of the school year, you will be keeping track of your physical activity in a two-week physical activity log. This two-week activity log will be part of a portfolio that you will turn in at the end of the year.

Instructional Task: Muscle- and Bone-Strengthening Activities With Wiffle Ball

■ PRACTICE TASK

This task assumes that the class has been working on a variety of muscle- and bone-strengthening activities over the course of the school year.

Students work in pairs on upper-body strengthening exercises such as various planks and push-ups, as well as various abdominal exercises.

Note: Find most of these exercises or variations in Hichwa, 1998.

While in push-up position:

- Students are able to give a low five to a partner. (Students assume a push-up position, each facing a partner. On your command, students touch the partner's wrist with their hand: right hand to partner's left wrist and then left hand to partner's right wrist.)
- Students are able to give a high five to a partner. (Students assume a push-up position, each facing a partner. On your command, students touch the partner's opposite shoulder with their hand: right hand to partner's left shoulder and then left hand to partner's right shoulder.)
- Roll a Wiffle ball back and forth with a partner about 12 feet (3.5 m) apart. (Working in pairs, one student is in a push-up plank position and the other is standing behind the first student's feet. The standing partner rolls a Wiffle ball on the ground to the right of the partner, who stops the ball with the right hand, transfers it to the left hand, and rolls it back to the standing partner.)

While in curl-up position:

Toss a Wiffle ball back and forth with a partner (like a medicine ball). Make sure you are in a curl-up and not a sit-up to avoid injury to the tailbone.

Note: Undertake the previous tasks only if students participated in a scientifically based fitness assessment such as Fitnessgram earlier in the year, so that you have some idea about their fitness levels.

EMBEDDED OUTCOME: S3.M8.6. Students create and monitor a self-selected physical activity goal for aerobic and/or muscle- and bone-strengthening activity based on current fitness levels.

Extension

Students set and monitor self-selected physical activity goals. Each student comes up with at least one goal for upper-body strength.

Student Choices/Differentiation

- Students choose number of repetitions based on fitness level.
- Students choose their own partners.
- Skills can be modified based on students' skill levels.

What to Look For

- Students are participating in the push-up and curl-up exercises in a safe and controlled manner.
- Students are self-selecting exercises based on their perception of current fitness levels.
- Students are choosing exercises that provide a challenge (overload).

Instructional Task:
One-Day (Weekday) Physical Activity Log

■ PRACTICE TASK

Using an overhead projector, demonstrate how to fill out a one-day physical activity log.

Extension

Students volunteer to give examples of physical activity that they pursue, and you write them in the appropriate place in the log.

Student Choices/Differentiation

Provide videos and handouts to help reinforce the material.

What to Look For

Students learn the basic understanding of using a physical activity log.

Instructional Task: Practice Filling Out an Activity Log

■ PRACTICE TASK

In cooperative groups of four or five, students fill out a one-day physical activity log. Students work together to create a hypothetical person and fill out this sample log.

Extension

Students make sure that they include an activity that will address all muscle groups.

Guiding questions for students:

- What technologies can be used to help you track physical activity in your log?
- What other factors should you consider when filling out the log?

Student Choices/Differentiation

- Show students a sample physical activity log that has been completed, if needed.
- Provide a list of activities if students are having a hard time thinking of activities.

What to Look For

- Students are filling out the log in a complete and correct manner.
- Student work will be fairly simple at this point.
- The sophistication of student work will improve as additional content is presented through the course of this module (e.g., exercise intensity, caloric expenditure, rating of perceived exertion, pedometers, use of technology).

Formal and Informal Assessments

Exit slip: List as many muscle- and bone-strengthening activities as you can.

Closure

- What do you think the most important part of the physical activity log is?
- What are strategies that will help you fill out the log?
- Answer any questions that students may have before dismissing the class. Remind students that the homework is due two days from now.

Reflection

Browse through the student work that was completed in cooperative groups. Look for areas of confusion that need to be clarified before students turn in the log (homework assignment) later in the week.

Homework

Remind students that the one-day (weekday) physical activity log is to be turned in two days from now (this gives you time to fix any misunderstandings that are evidenced in the cooperative work that was turned in).

Should a student lose the physical activity log, a copy can be printed from the school website (PDF).

Resources

Hichwa, J. (1998). *Right fielders are people too: An inclusive approach to teaching middle school physical education*. Champaign, IL: Human Kinetics.

Melograno, V.J. (2000). *Portfolio assessment for k-12 physical education*. Reston, VA: National Association for Sport and Physical Education.

WEEKDAY PHYSICAL ACTIVITY LOG

Name: _____ Period (circle):   1   2   3   4   5   6

Date: _____/_____/_____

Day of the week (circle):   M   T   W   Th   F

Part of day	Activities	Time (min)	Easily measurable? (circle)	Calories	Intensity	Comments (technology or app used, how did you feel?, whom did you participate with?, etc.)
Before school			Yes/No			
Nutrition (morning) break			Yes/No			
Lunch break			Yes/No			
In-class physical activity break (If so, list classes)			Yes/No			
Physical education class			Yes/No			
After school			Yes/No			

From R.J. Doan, L.C. MacDonald, and S. Chepko, eds., 2017, *Lesson planning for middle school physical education* (Reston, VA: SHAPE America; Champaign, IL: Human Kinetics).

LESSON 3: ESTIMATING PHYSICAL ACTIVITY AND CALORIES EXPENDED

Grade-Level Outcomes

Primary Outcomes

Fitness knowledge: Participates in moderate to vigorous aerobic physical activity that includes intermittent or continuous aerobic physical activity of both moderate and vigorous intensity for at least 60 minutes per day. (S3.M6.6)

Dribbling/ball control: Dribbles with dominant hand using a change of speed and direction in a variety of practice tasks. (S1.M8.6)

Embedded Outcomes

Fitness knowledge: Describes the role of warm-ups and cool-downs before and after physical activities. (S3.M12.6)

Fitness knowledge: Sets and monitors a self-selected physical-activity goal for aerobic and/or muscle- and bone-strengthening activity based on current fitness level. (S3.M8.6)

Lesson Objectives

The learner will:
- participate in moderate to vigorous basketball activities that are intermittent or continuous in nature.
- dribble with preferred hand using different speeds.
- estimate how much physical activity she performed and how many Calories (kcal) she expended.

Equipment and Materials

- Basketballs of various sizes (1 basketball per 2 students)
- Pedometers
- Pencils
- Clipboards
- Handouts: Calories Used for Activities by Weight Categories
- Cones
- Basketball courts
- Stopwatch (for you to time basketball practice)
- 3 × 5 cards (1 per student)

Introduction

Today we will explore the quantities of physical activity using a table of various physical activities that also takes into consideration your weight. We will do this through practice tasks designed to make you more skilled at dribbling with your preferred hand.

Instructional Task: Dynamic Warm-Up

■ PRACTICE TASK

Place four large cones in a rectangle or square on the basketball courts.

Students perform a variety of dynamic warm-up movements that are based on locomotor movements. You can call out these movements periodically, or you can ask students what movements they think should be performed based on the day's activities.

EMBEDDED OUTCOME: S3.M12.6. This is a great opportunity to teach students the importance of warming up muscles that they will use in the planned activity.

Guiding questions for students:

- What movements do you think would work best for the lesson today? (Answer: Because today's learning experience involves basketball drills with changes in speed and direction, students should choose locomotor skills that will warm up muscles in the legs that they will use to change direction.)
- Describe the role that the warm-up plays before physical activity.
- Is static stretching a warm-up?

Student Choices/Differentiation

- This warm-up can be performed in small groups with a lead student who directs the warm-up.
- Adjust the warm-up space, speed, and equipment according to students' skill levels.

What to Look For

- Students are participating in a dynamic warm-up before physical activity.
- Students are performing fundamental movement patterns.
- Students are maintaining a low center of gravity when sliding on defense.
- Students are engaged in the warm-up and not just "going through the motions."

Instructional Task: Focus on Muscle- and Bone-Strengthening Activities With a Basketball

■ PRACTICE TASK

This task assumes that the class has been working on a variety of muscle- and bone-strengthening activities over the course of the school year.

Students work in pairs on upper-body exercises such as various plank exercises and push-ups. They also work in pairs on various abdominal exercises.

Note: Students should have participated in a scientifically based fitness assessment earlier in the year so that they have some idea of their current fitness levels.

While in push-up position:

- Low-fives. (Students assume a push-up position, each facing a partner. On your command, students touch the partner's wrist with the hand: right hand to partner's left wrist and then left hand to partner's right wrist.)
- Students are able to give a high five to a partner. (Students assume a push-up position, each facing a partner. On your command, students touch the partner's opposite shoulder with the hand: right hand to partner's left shoulder and then left hand to partner's right shoulder.)
- Roll a basketball back and forth with a partner about 12 feet (3.5 m) apart. (Working in pairs, one student is in a push-up plank position and the other is standing behind the first student's feet. The standing partner rolls a basketball to the right of the partner, who stops the ball with the right hand, transfers it to the left hand, and rolls it back to the standing partner.)

While in curl-up position:

Toss a basketball back and forth with a partner (like a medicine ball). Make sure that you are in a curl-up and not a sit-up to avoid injury to the tailbone.

Extension

Have each student come up with at least one goal for muscle- and bone-strengthening activities.

EMBEDDED OUTCOME: S3.M8.6. Students create and monitor a self-selected physical activity goal for aerobic and/or muscle and bone-strengthening activity based on current fitness level.

Student Choices/Differentiation

- Students choose number of repetitions based on fitness level.
- Students choose their own partners.
- Skills can be modified based on students' skill levels.

What to Look For

- Students are participating in the push-up and curl-up exercises in a safe and controlled manner.
- Students are self-selecting exercises based on their perceptions of current fitness level.
- Students are choosing exercises that provide a challenge (overload).

Instructional Task: Basketball Dribbling and Passing

■ PRACTICE TASK

Use a stopwatch for the next three practice tasks. Students practice the tasks for a total of 10, 20, or 30 minutes, depending on class time available.

Basketball Tag

- Students dribble in open space around the courts (determine number of courts based on number on students). Partner follows dribbling partner ready to take a chest pass, overhead pass, or bounce pass when the teacher blows a whistle.
- On the whistle, dribbling partner jump stops, pivots toward partner, and performs the pass. Partner begins to dribble around the courts.
- Rotate again on teacher whistle.

Student Choices/Differentiation

- Students use various types of passes according to skill level.
- Students may choose the size of the basketball and the speed of the activity.

What to Look For

- Students are dribbling with preferred hand.
- Students are changing direction while dribbling to avoid other students.
- Students are changing speed based on other students on the court.
- Students are pivoting toward partner.

Instructional Task: Dribbling Using Change of Speed and Direction

■ PRACTICE TASK

Dribbling While Guarded

- Students form short lines at the baseline of the courts (avoid excessive wait time).
- In pairs, one student dribbles down the court while the other student guards. The guarding partner is to maintain an athletic stance and essentially provide an obstacle.
- The student dribbling can attempt to dribble around the defender, while the defender attempts to stay in front of the student dribbling.
- At the baseline, the student dribbling performs a chest pass to the partner, and they switch roles.
- Defenders should be semi-active.

Extension

Students who can perform Outcome S1.M8.6 (dribbles with dominant hand using a change of speed and direction in a variety of practice tasks) can "level up" to dribbling with the non-dominant hand using change in speed and direction.

Student Choices/Differentiation

- Students choose partners based on who they feel comfortable with (e.g., if they play club basketball, they find someone who plays basketball all the time; if they are just learning, they find someone else who is just starting to learn).
- Students may choose the size of the ball.
- Students create their own rules for a small-sided game.

What to Look For

- Students are changing speed based on movements of the defender.
- Students are changing direction based on movements of the defender.
- Students are changing both speed and direction at the same time.
- Students are maintaining an athletic stance.
- Students are positioning one hand down to guard the ball and the other hand up over the shoulder and to the side to protect against a pass while maintaining a defensive position.
- Students are correctly performing a jump stop.
- Students are performing the chest pass with full extension of the elbows.
- Students are stepping toward the target with one foot while performing the chest pass.

Instructional Task: Frogger Basketball

■ PRACTICE TASK

This is a variation of dribble maze as described in Kleinman (2001, pp. 328-329).

Form groups of students in line at the baseline and sidelines.

Students dribble perpendicular to each other so that they are forced to change speed and direction and look where they are going, not at the ball.

Extensions

- Students dribble with preferred and non-preferred hand using a change of speed and direction in small-sided game play.
- If students are able to demonstrate the skill with both hands, they can level up to a small-sided game and work independently. This allows you to provide more effective feedback and teaching of students who have not demonstrated proficiency yet.

Student Choices/Differentiation

- Students may choose the size of the ball.
- Students create their own rules for a small-sided game.
- If students are unable to perform tasks, they move back to the practice tasks with the rest of the class.

What to Look For

- Students are dribbling the ball around waist height.
- Students are looking toward the intended direction.
- Students are changing direction and speed without a double dribble.

Instructional Task:
Estimating Physical Activity and Calories

■ PRACTICE TASK

Students distribute the clipboards and handouts (Calories Used for Activities by Weight Categories).

- Tell students the length of time they participated in basketball drills.
- Have them estimate how many Calories (kcal) they expended, or "burned," by playing basketball.
- They need to find this estimate based on their weight and time.

Students write the number of Calories used and the exercise time on a 3 × 5 card to take home.

Student Choices/Differentiation

- Provide examples if needed.
- Students can work in pairs or groups if they are having a difficult time.

What to Look For

- Students are using the table by both time and weight.
- Students are recognizing that the table is based on 10 minutes of activity time.
- Students are multiplying Calories (kcal) out to 20 or 30 minutes if they were active for longer than 10 minutes.
- Students are estimating the Calories (kcal) based on the information provided when their exact weight is not listed.

Formal and Informal Assessments

Informal assessment: dribbling skills

Closure

- Think, pair, share—Discuss if you think this table is an accurate estimation of how many Calories (kcal) you burned, or expended, today. (Answers may differ based on whether they were in a game versus being in the basketball drills.)
- Think about the strength and conditioning we did at the beginning of class. Are the push-up and plank exercises easily measured in Calories (kcal)? Are they listed anywhere on the table?
- What is your guess about the quantity of Calories (kcal) used for aerobic-type activities versus muscle- and bone-strengthening activities such as strength training or weightlifting?

Reflection

- How are students progressing in dribbling?
- Are students able to demonstrate the proper use of the table for determining Calories (kcal) expended?

Homework

Students fill out their one-day (weekday) physical activity logs.
Instruct students to include today's physical activity (recorded on their 3 × 5 cards) in their logs.

Resources

Hichwa, J. (1998). *Right fielders are people too: An inclusive approach to teaching middle school physical education.* Champaign, IL: Human Kinetics.

Kleinman, I. (2001). *Complete physical education plans for grades 7-12.* Champaign, IL: Human Kinetics.

Sound Body Sound Mind Foundation. (2014). Sound body sound mind: Teaching the basics of movement and physical activity—high school & middle school curriculum. Los Angeles: Sound Body Sound Mind Foundation.

Calories Used for Activities by Weight Categories

	Body weight in pounds (this has been converted from kilograms)									
	44 lb.	55 lb.	66 lb.	77 lb.	88 lb.	99 lb.	110 lb.	121 lb.	132 lb.	143 lb.
Activity	Calories (kcal) for 10 minutes									
Basketball (game)	35	43	51	60	68	77	85	94	102	110
Calisthenics	13	17	20	23	26	30	33	36	40	43
Cross-country skiing (leisure)	24	30	36	42	48	54	60	66	72	78
Cycling (6 mph; 9.7 km/h)	15	17	20	23	26	29	33	36	39	42
Cycling (9 mph; 14.5 km/h)	22	27	32	36	41	46	50	55	60	65
Field hockey	27	34	40	47	54	60	67	74	80	87
Figure skating	40	50	60	70	80	90	10	110	120	130
Horseback riding -canter	8	11	13	15	17	19	21	23	25	27
-trot	22	28	33	39	44	50	55	61	66	72
-gallop	28	35	41	48	50	62	69	76	83	90
Ice hockey (on-ice time)	52	65	78	91	104	117	130	143	156	168
Judo	39	49	59	69	78	88	98	108	118	127
Running (5 mph; 8.0 km/h)*	37	45	52	60	66	72	78	84	90	95
Running (6 mph; 9.7 km/h)	48	55	64	73	79	85	92	100	107	113
Running (7.5 mph; 12.1 km/h)	—	—	76	83	91	99	107	115	125	130
Running (9 mph; 14.5 km/h)	—	—	—	—	—	113	121	130	140	148
Snowshoeing	35	42	50	58	66	74	82	90	98	107
Soccer (game)	36	45	54	63	72	81	90	99	108	117
Squash	—	—	64	74	85	95	106	117	127	138
Swimming, front crawl (30 m/min)	25	31	37	43	49	56	62	68	74	80
Swimming, breast-stroke (30 m/min)	19	24	29	34	38	43	48	53	58	62
Swimming, back-stroke (30 m/min)	17	21	25	30	34	38	42	47	51	55
Table tennis	22	28	33	39	44	50	55	61	66	72
Tennis	22	28	33	39	44	50	55	61	66	72
Volleyball (game)	20	25	30	35	40	45	50	55	60	65
Walking* (2.5 mph; 3.2 km/h)	17	19	21	23	26	28	30	32	34	36
Walking* (4 mph; 6.4 km/h)	24	26	28	30	32	34	37	40	43	48

*Note: The transition from walking to running occurs between 4 and 5 mph (6.4 and 8.0 km/h). Walking at 2.5 mph (4 km/h) is a slow walk. Walking at 4 mph is a fast walk and is almost running.

From R.J. Doan, L.C. MacDonald, and S. Chepko, eds., 2017, *Lesson planning for middle school physical education* (Reston, VA: SHAPE America; Champaign, IL: Human Kinetics). Adapted from O. Bar-Or and T. Rowland, 2004, *Pediatric exercise medicine: Physiological principles to health care application* (Champaign, IL: Human Kinetics).

LESSON 4: USING SCALES TO MEASURE EXERCISE INTENSITY

Grade-Level Outcomes

Primary Outcome

Fitness knowledge: Defines resting heart rate and describes its relationship to aerobic fitness and the Borg Rating of Perceived Exertion (RPE) Scale. (S3.M13.6)

Embedded Outcomes

Fitness knowledge: Differentiates between aerobic and anaerobic capacity, and between muscular strength and muscular endurance. (S3.M10.6)

Working with others: Accepts differences among classmates in physical development, maturation and varying skill levels by providing encouragement and positive feedback. (S4.M4.6)

Lesson Objectives

The learner will:

- define resting heart rate.
- use a rating of perceived exertion (RPE) scale to estimate exercise intensity.

Equipment and Materials

- OMNI Scale for rating of perceived exertion (with pictures of riding a bike)
- Children's Effort Rating Table (CERT) (1-10)
- OMNI Scale with pictures of walking to running (0-10)
- Borg Rating of Perceived Exertion (RPE) Scale (6-20)
- Fitnessgram PACER cadence or music
- Sound system to play cadence
- Cones to mark off PACER course distances of 15 meters, 17 meters, and 20 meters
- Data collection card for RPE and PACER, with one column for PACER lap and the other column for RPE
- Pencils
- Graph paper
- Clipboards
- Whiteboard easel

Introduction

Today, we will continue our exploration of exercise intensity. Remember, you have a project coming up for which you will need to record your physical activity for two weeks in a log. Part of this log will include recording exercise intensity. Today's learning experience is one example of many ways that exercise intensity can be estimated and recorded.

Who can define heart rate? Yes, we usually measure it in beats per minute. What is resting heart rate? What is the ideal score for resting heart rate? We will explore heart rate and scales for measuring it in today's lesson.

Instructional Task: Introduction of Rating of Perceived Exertion (RPE) Scale (1-10)

■ PRACTICE TASK

Show students two or three RPE scales from 0 to 10 and 1 to 10 and explain how they work. Explain how the scales are used.

Guiding questions for students:

- Let's form a hypothesis. If we were to run the PACER and you could not maintain the pace any longer, at what number do you think you would be?
- How can these scales be used for estimation and for production?
- What do you think these scales represent?

Student Choices/Differentiation

Have examples of various scales available.

What to Look For

Students use vocabulary such as intensity, exercise, increasing.

Instructional Task: PACER Calibration

■ PRACTICE TASK

Students will work in pairs while performing the PACER (Progressive Aerobic Cardiovascular Endurance Run).

The PACER is to be run in two heats. The students performing the PACER tell their partners what number they perceive each time they return. The partners are seated or standing at the end of the course with a pencil, data collection sheet, chosen scale, and clipboard. When the runners approach the data collectors (partners), the partners shows the scale so that the runners can report how they currently feel.

Data is collected every other lap. Students switch roles when everyone has completed the PACER in heat one.

Extension

Provide students graph paper or a spreadsheet on a computer to graph the RPE against PACER laps.

EMBEDDED OUTCOME: S4.M4.6. Students should encourage classmates and accept differences in fitness levels during the PACER test and graphing sessions. Reinforce students who provide encouragement.

EMBEDDED OUTCOME: S3.M10.6. The PACER test provides an opportunity to check students' understanding of aerobic and anaerobic capacity and muscular strength and endurance.

Guiding questions for students:

- Is the PACER test primarily a test of aerobic or anaerobic capacity?
- Why do you think so?
- Is the PACER test primarily a test of muscular strength or muscular endurance? Why?

Student Choices/Differentiation

- Allow students to choose which RPE scale they would like to use (riding bike 0 to 10, walk/run 0 to 10, or CERT 1 to 10 with no pictures). Please note that in some communities, some children may not know what it is like to ride a bike, and some may not know what it is like to ride a bike up a hill. Consequently, the walk/run scale may be more appropriate.
- As an option, PACER courses of different lengths can be set up to provide additional conditioning for students who typically do not perform very many laps. Distances of 15 meters, 17 meters, and 20 meters seem to work well when using the 20-meter distance cadence from Fitnessgram.

What to Look For

- Are students working well together with reporting and recording scores?
- Do students tend to finish the PACER with an RPE of 10?

- Formative assessment: Students/teacher should see that the RPE increases in a linear fashion with the increase in number of PACER laps. They should also see that they were at a level 10 when they could not continue the PACER any longer. If the RPE is not linear, and they stopped the PACER before they were at a 10, there is a calibration issue.

Instructional Task:
Presentation of Two Scales and Debrief

■ PRACTICE TASK

Show depictions of the different children's scales (OMNI and CERT) next to the Borg Rating of Perceived Exertion (RPE) Scale.

Explain the limitations of both scales: overestimation of RPE and subjectivity versus objectivity. The scales are subjective in nature compared with objective feedback that you get from an exercise machine that provides speed, power (watts), and Calories burned, or from a cell phone app that provides speed, distance, Calories burned, and heart rate.

Guiding questions for students:

- Here are two scales (Borg and 0 to 10). Notice how one is from 0 to 10 and the other is from 6 to 20. Both are used to estimate exercise intensity. Why do you think we have both of these?
- Based on the Borg scale, and the fact that you are sitting here at rest listening to me, what number would you choose?
- How accurate do you think these scales are?
- Why would a teacher use them?

Extension

Let students take one or more of the scales home with them. These are options to be used with their upcoming project: a two-week physical activity log.

Student Choices/Differentiation

- Provide many examples of the two scales.
- For the activity log project, allow students to use the RPE scales despite teaching them the more objective options.

What to Look For

- Students understand the difference between subjective and objective assessments.
- Students can answer 6 when at rest and using the Borg scale.
- Students are able to explain the difference between the two scales.

Formal and Informal Assessments

- Modified Fitnessgram PACER
- Recording of PACER laps and course attempted
- Reporting RPE to a partner
- Graphing RPE and PACER laps

Closure

- How do you feel after the PACER test?
- Would you do anything differently if you took it again?
- Do you have any questions about how to use an RPE scale?

Reflection

- Do students seem to understand the use of the RPE scale?
- Does use of the RPE scale seem to result in better engagement in the PACER?

Homework

When participating in various physical activities, think about your exercise intensity. See if you can apply what you learned today to the games you play at recess. This will be important when you eventually record your physical activity for two weeks.

Take home your data collection sheet and finish graphing your PACER and RPE data. A sample of a completed graph is on the school's physical education website.

Continue your physical activity log. Be sure to include today's activities in physical education and activities you do outside of school or during various times throughout the school day.

Resources

Astrand, P.O. (1952). *Experimental studies of physical working capacity in relation to sex and age.* Copenhagen: Munsksgaard.

Astrand, P.O., & Rodahl, K. (1986). *Textbook of work physiology: Physiological bases of exercise.* New York: McGraw-Hill.

Brooks, G.A., Fahey, T.D., White, T.P., & Baldwin, K.M. (2000). *Exercise physiology: Human bioenergetics and its applications.* Columbus, OH: McGraw-Hill Education.

Rowland, T.W., & Bar-Or, O. (2004). *Pediatric exercise medicine: From physiologic principles to health care applications.* Champaign, IL: Human Kinetics.

Internet keyword search: "running scale"

BORG RATING OF PERCEIVED EXERTION SHEET

Directions for Partner Borg Rating of Perceived Exertion (6-20)

You will perform the PACER test. As you know, PACER stands for Progressive Aerobic Cardiovascular Endurance Run. We will use three different-length courses for the PACER: a 15-meter, a 17-meter, and a 20-meter. You may choose the distance based on your current fitness level. Remember, if you typically run 15 to 20 laps, the 15-meter course will keep you in longer, which will help you work on your endurance. This is a form of overload.

I will show you a scale during the PACER each time you run toward me, and I will ask you how hard you are exercising. Please give me a number between 6 and 20 that best describes how you're feeling at that moment. Some of the numbers have words or pictures next to them to help you. You can choose any number between 6 and 20, not only those numbers that have words or numbers next to them.

There is no right or wrong answer. Today, we are just trying to learn how you feel during the exercise.

The Children's Effort Rating Scale (CERT)	
1	Very, very easy
2	Very easy
3	Easy
4	Just feeling a strain
5	Starting to get hard
6	Getting quite hard
7	Hard
8	Very hard
9	Very, very hard
10	So hard I'm going to stop

Reprinted, by permission, from O. Bar-Or and T. Rowland, 2004, *Pediatric exercise medicine: Physiological principles to health care application* (Champaign, IL: Human Kinetics), 360.

Script modified from: O. Bar-Or and T. Rowland, 2004, *Pediatric exercise medicine: Physiological principles to health care application* (Champaign, IL: Human Kinetics).

Directions for the Children's Effort Rating Table (CERT: 1-10)

You are going to perform the PACER. As you know, PACER stands for Progressive Aerobic Cardiovascular Endurance Run. We are using three different-length courses for the PACER. We have 15-meter, 17-meter, and 20-meter courses. You get to choose the distance based on your current fitness level. Remember, if you typically run a lower number of laps such as 15 to 20 laps, the 15-meter distance will keep you in longer and you will be able to work on your endurance. This is a form of overload.

I will show you a scale during the PACER each time you return toward me. I will ask you how hard you are exercising. Please give me a number that best describes your feeling of the exercise at the moment. There may be words or pictures opposite the numbers to help you. You can choose any number between 6 and 20, not only the numbers with words next to them.

There is no right or wrong answer. Today, we are just trying to learn how you feel during the exercise.

Script modified from: O. Bar-Or and T. Rowland, 2004, *Pediatric exercise medicine: Physiological principles to health care application* (Champaign, IL: Human Kinetics).

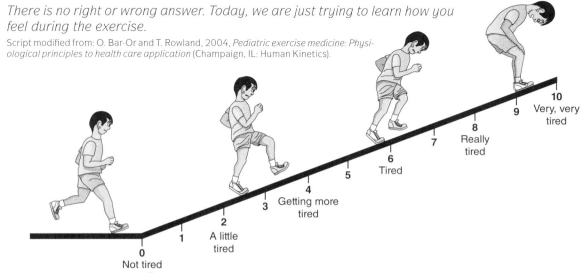

Adapted from R.J. Robertson, 2004, Perceived exertion for practitioners: Rating effort with the OMNI picture system (Champaign, IL: Human Kinetics), 23.

(continued)

(continued)

Directions for the OMNI Rating Scale (OMNI: 0-10)

You are going to perform the PACER. As you know, PACER stands for Progressive Aerobic Cardiovascular Endurance Run. We are using three different-length courses for the PACER. We have 15-meter, 17-meter, and 20-meter courses. You get to choose the distance based on your current fitness level. Remember, if you typically run a lower number of laps such as 15 to 20 laps, the 1- meter distance will keep you in longer and you will be able to work on your endurance. This is a form of overload.

I will show you a scale during the PACER each time you return toward me. I will ask you how hard you are exercising. Please give me a number that best describes your feeling of the exercise at the moment. There may be words or pictures opposite the numbers to help you. You can choose any number between 0 and 10, not only the numbers with words next to them.

There is no right or wrong answer. Today, we are just trying to learn how you feel during the exercise.

Script modified from: O. Bar-Or and T. Rowland, 2004, *Pediatric exercise medicine: Physiological principles to health care application* (Champaign, IL: Human Kinetics).

Directions for the OMNI Rating Scale (CERT: 0-10)

You are going to perform the PACER. As you know, PACER stands for Progressive Aerobic Cardiovascular Endurance Run. We are using three different-length courses for the PACER. We have 15-meter, 17-meter, and 20-meter courses. You get to choose the distance based on your current fitness level. Remember, if you typically run a lower number of laps such as 15 to 20 laps, the 15-meter distance will keep you in longer and you will be able to work on your endurance. This is a form of overload.

I will show you a scale during the PACER each time you return toward me. I will ask you how hard you are exercising. Please give me a number that best describes your feeling of the exercise at the moment. There may be words or pictures opposite the numbers to help you. You can choose any number between 0 and 10, not only the numbers with words next to them.

There is no right or wrong answer. Today, we are just trying to learn how you feel during the exercise.

Script modified from: O. Bar-Or and T. Rowland, 2004, *Pediatric exercise medicine: Physiological principles to health care application* (Champaign, IL: Human Kinetics).

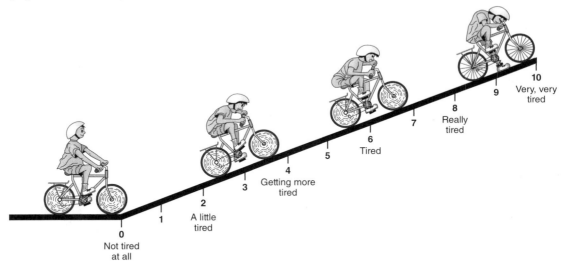

Adapted from R.J. Robertson, 2004, Perceived exertion for practitioners: Rating effort with the OMNI picture system (Champaign, IL: Human Kinetics), 21.

From R.J. Doan, L.C. MacDonald, and S. Chepko, eds., 2017, *Lesson planning for middle school physical education* (Reston, VA: SHAPE America; Champaign, IL: Human Kinetics).

LESSON 5: TWO-DAY (WEEKEND) PHYSICAL ACTIVITY LOGS

Grade-Level Outcomes

Primary Outcomes

Fitness knowledge: Participates in moderate to vigorous aerobic physical activity that includes intermittent or continuous aerobic physical activity of both moderate and vigorous intensity for at least 60 minutes per day. (S3.M6.6)

Assessment & program planning: Maintains a physical activity log for at least 2 weeks and reflects on activity levels as documented in the log. (S3.M16.6)

Fitness knowledge: Employs correct techniques and methods of stretching. (S3.M9.6)

Embedded Outcome

Physical activity knowledge: Describes how being physically active leads to a healthy body. (S5.M1.6)

Lesson Objectives

The learner will:

- use a two-day (weekend) physical activity log independently to record participation in physical activity.
- participate in moderate to vigorous aerobic activity.
- employ correct technique and methods of stretching.

Equipment and Materials

- 4 cones
- Pencils
- Clipboards (enough for cooperative groups of 4 or 5 students)
- Copies of two-day physical activity log (1 per student for homework and a few extra for cooperative groups during class time)

Introduction

Today you will continue to track your physical activity by using a two-day physical activity log. Later in the module you will track one- and two-week physical activity, which will be included in your portfolio.

Instructional Task: Static Stretching

■ **PRACTICE TASK**

After a class warm-up, have the class go through static stretches.

Remind students that it is best to stretch a muscle that is warm and that static stretching is not a warm-up. Instead, it can be used to maintain or improve range of motion around a joint. Improvements in range of motion require repeated micro damage to the muscle.

Guiding questions for students:

- How would you compare dynamic warm-ups to static stretching?
- What is the purpose of each?

Extension

Students use a physical activity measurement and compare stretching output to other activities they have done.

Student Choices/Differentiation
- Students may work in self-selected groups with students leading stretches.
- Students can choose what stretches to do as long as they are not contraindicated.

What to Look For
- Students are holding the stretches long enough to be effective.
- Students are stretching muscles that have been warmed up.

Instructional Task:
Two-Day (Weekend) Physical Activity Log

■ PRACTICE TASK

In pairs, students complete a log for a hypothetical student using activities from previous classes. Point out how the two-day (weekend) log differs from the one-day (weekday) log you have used up to this point.

EMBEDDED OUTCOME: S5.M1.6. This would be a great time to discuss with students how being physically active leads to a healthy body.

Refinements
- Make sure students are using content that was taught in previous lessons (e.g., exercise intensity, Caloric expenditure, RPE, pedometers, use of technology).
- Misunderstandings should be identified and addressed with the whole class to ensure quality of work turned in as homework.

Guiding questions for students:
- What technology can be used to help you fill out your log?
- Are there certain types of activities missing from your log that you might consider adding to your routine?

Student Choices/Differentiation
- Group students by ability.
- Have examples to show students.

What to Look For
- Students are filling out the log in a complete and correct manner.
- Students are using instruments or tools (e.g., exercise intensity, Caloric expenditure, RPE, pedometers, technology) to measure their physical activity.

Formal and Informal Assessments
- Informal teacher observation of the content listed in the right-hand column of the activity log
- Two-day (weekend) physical activity (PA) log completed in cooperative groups (browse through work turned in and adjust instruction, if needed)

Closure
- How will your two-day PA log differ from your one-day PA log?
- When filling out your logs, which was easiest to consider (exercise intensity, Caloric expenditure, RPE, pedometers, use of technology)? Which was the hardest?

Reflection

Browse through the student work that was completed in cooperative groups. Look for areas of confusion that need to be clarified before students turn in the log (homework assignment) the following week (e.g.: if assigned on a Thursday, misunderstanding can be addressed on Friday, before students begin work on the assignment).

Homework

Remind students that the two-day (weekend) physical activity log is to be turned in immediately following the weekend (depending on school schedule).

Should a student lose the physical activity log, a copy can be printed from the school website (PDF).

Resources

Corbin, C.B., Le Masurier, G.C., & Lambdin, D.D. (2007). *Fitness for life: Middle school*. Champaign, IL: Human Kinetics.

Melograno, V.J. (2000). *Portfolio assessment for k-12 physical education*. Reston, VA: National Association for Sport and Physical Education.

Real-World Biomechanics. (2012). To stretch or not to stretch. Available at www.realworldbiomechanics.blogspot.com.

Internet keyword search: "60 minutes of physical activity per day"

WEEKEND PHYSICAL ACTIVITY LOG

Name: _____ Period (circle): 1 2 3 4 5 6

Weekend dates: _____

Saturday

Part of day	Activities	Time (min)	Easy to measure? (circle)	Calories	Intensity	Comments (technology or app used, how did you feel?, with whom did you participate?, etc.)
Morning			Yes/No			
Afternoon			Yes/No			
Evening			Yes/No			

Totals

Total number of activities: _____

Total time (min): _____

How many of the activities were easy to measure? _____

Total number of calories expended: _____

Sunday

Part of day	Activities	Time (min)	Easy to measure? (circle)	Calories	Intensity	Comments (technology or app used, how did you feel?, with whom did you participate?, etc.)
Morning			Yes/No			
Afternoon			Yes/No			
Evening			Yes/No			

Totals

Total number of activities: _____

Total time (min): _____

How many of the activities were easy to measure? _____

Total number of calories expended: _____

Scoring Guide

Criteria for competence:

1. Lists physical activity.
2. Records time for physical activity.
3. Considers if PA was easily measured.
4. Records Calories (kcal) if easily measured.
5. Includes a measure of exercise intensity.
6. Sums the total time spent in the activity.
7. Considers if activity was easily measured.
8. Includes a total for the number of Calories (kcal).

From R.J. Doan, L.C. MacDonald, and S. Chepko, eds., 2017, *Lesson planning for middle school physical education* (Reston, VA: SHAPE America; Champaign, IL: Human Kinetics).

LESSON 6: FITNESSGRAM TESTING

Grade-Level Outcomes

Primary Outcome

Assessment & program planning: Designs and implements a program of remediation for any areas of weakness based on the results of health-related fitness assessment. (S3.M15.6)

Embedded Outcomes

Working with others: Accepts differences among classmates in physical development, maturation and varying skill levels by providing encouragement and positive feedback. (S4.M4.6)

Safety: Uses physical activity and fitness equipment appropriately and safely, *with the teacher's guidance.* (S4.M7.6)

Lesson Objectives

The learner will assess her health-related fitness using a scientifically based fitness assessment such as Fitnessgram.

Note: The instructional tasks will be spread out over a few days. The length of this lesson plan will depend on class size, students' familiarity with the assessments, and how deeply you want to go into the content involved in each assessment.

Equipment and Materials

- Fitnessgram sound system
- Cadences for PACER, curl-up test, push-up test (on CD, iPod, or smartphone)
- Sit-and-reach device (several will save time)
- Modified pull-up bars
- Paperwork for collection of scores (printed on card stock helps)
- Cones for PACER
- Stopwatches for mile run/walk
- Measuring tape or trundle wheel to measure distance of PACER
- Curl-up strips
- Fitnessgram software (for generating student reports)
- Task cards provided by Fitnessgram (includes protocol, look-up tables, and form corrections)
- Stadiometer (to measure height)
- Scale

Other scientifically based health-related fitness assessments include Eurofit (1993).

Introduction

This week we will be focusing on assessment of your health-related fitness. It is anticipated that fitness testing will take a few days. It should go smoothly since we have practiced the various Fitnessgram assessments. We will use the results of the Fitnessgram to identify areas of fitness that you need to work on. Your Fitnessgram report and scores should be part of your end-of-year portfolio for you to reflect on them.

EMBEDDED OUTCOME: S4.M7.6. Students will be using fitness equipment throughout the lesson. Make sure students know the proper and improper ways of using the fitness equipment.

Instructional Task: PACER Assessment

■ PRACTICE TASK

Administer the PACER test for measurement of aerobic capacity. (Decide on 15- or 20-meter distance.) Review protocol briefly.

The following are common procedure points that need to be stressed:

- Single beep means end of lap; turn around and run back to the other line.
- Triple beep means that the test will speed up; turn around and run back to the other line.
- Foot must touch the end line by the time the beep sounds for each lap.
- On first miss, turn around where you are and run to the other line; try to get back on pace.
- On second miss, move to the side and cool down by walking. End of test.
- Partner should note lap number and record the score.

Remind students that the PACER has a built in warm-up.

Go over the academic vocabulary involved with PACER:

Progressive

Aerobic

Cardiovascular

Endurance

Run

Partners record scores.

EMBEDDED OUTCOME: S4.M4.6. This is a good opportunity to teach students about the importance of accepting and supporting each other, since they will be pushing themselves and recording scores for one another.

Extension

Students look up how their aerobic capacity compares to the Healthy Fitness Zone for the Fitnessgram assessment.

Student Choices/Differentiation

Students choose a partner to work with and whether to go first or second.

What to Look For

- Students stay in their lanes.
- Students are following test protocols.

Instructional Task: Push-Up Assessment

■ PRACTICE TASK

Review protocol briefly.

Remind students that the push-up assessment measures upper-body strength and endurance. Having a strong upper body can be an indicator of healthy bone density.

Partners record scores.

Extension

Students look up how their push-up scores compare to the Healthy Fitness Zone for the Fitnessgram assessment.

Student Choices/Differentiation

Students choose a partner to work with and whether to go first or second.

What to Look For

- Back is flat.
- Elbows come down to 90 degrees.
- Students are following the test cadence.

Instructional Task: Curl-Up Assessment

■ PRACTICE TASK

Review protocol briefly. The test is stopped on the second form correction.

Remind students that the curl-up assessment is a measure of abdominal strength and endurance. Strong abdominal muscles help prevent low back problems.

Partners record scores.

Extension

Students look up how their curl-up scores compare to the Healthy Fitness Zone for the Fitnessgram assessment.

Student Choices/Differentiation

Students choose a partner to work with and whether to go first or second.

What to Look For

- Head must return to the ground.
- Fingers go completely across the curl-up strip.
- Heels must stay on the ground.
- Students are following the test cadence.
- Stop test on second form correction.

Based on Meredith and Welk 2010.

Instructional Task: Shoulder Stretch

■ PRACTICE TASK

Review protocol briefly.

1. With right hand, reach up and over shoulder and down back as if pulling up a zipper. Reach up with left hand and touch fingertips.
2. Fingers touch.
3. Switch sides.

Source: Fitnessgram task card.

Remind students that flexibility at the shoulder joint helps prevent shoulder injuries.

Test both sides.

Partners record scores.

Extension

Students look up how their shoulder stretch scores compare to the Healthy Fitness Zone for the Fitnessgram assessment.

Student Choices/Differentiation

Students choose a partner to work with and whether to go first or second.

What to Look For

Students are performing the task correctly.

Instructional Task: Sit and Reach

■ PRACTICE TASK

Review protocol briefly.

Remind students that good flexibility in the lower back and hamstring muscles, as measured by the sit and reach, helps prevent low back problems.

Partners record scores.

Extension

Students look up how their sit-and-reach scores compare to the Healthy Fitness Zone for the Fitnessgram assessment.

Student Choices/Differentiation

Students choose a partner to work with and whether to go first or second.

What to Look For

- Are students stretching slowly and gently or bouncing to get the longest stretch?
- Are they using the box correctly?

Instructional Task: Modified Pull-Up

■ PRACTICE TASK

Review protocol briefly. The test is stopped on the second form correction.

Remind students that this test is a measure of upper-body strength and endurance.

Partners record scores.

Extension

Students look up how their modified pull-up scores compare to the Healthy Fitness Zone for the Fitnessgram assessment.

Student Choices/Differentiation

Students choose a partner to work with and whether to go first or second.

What to Look For

- Shoulders are directly under the bar.
- Palms are facing away.
- Only heels are touching the floor.
- Chest touches the elastic band.
- Students return to starting position with elbows extended.
- Body remains straight.
- Stop test on 2nd form correction.

Source: Fitnessgram task card.

Instructional Task: Body Mass Index

■ PRACTICE TASK

Note: Height and weight should be measured by the teacher and not by students. Safeguards need to be established to protect student privacy.

The class should be engaged in an activity in which you can pull out small groups of students so that one student can be measured for height and weight while the rest of the small group await their turn (with shoes removed and ready to be measured). Keep the scale and stadiometer behind a screen to ensure student privacy while you keep an eye on the rest of the class.

Activities to keep the rest of the class engaged can be fitness based (e.g., jumping rope, walking around a track) or skills based (e.g., striking, passing), or students can start on their homework.

Extension

Use skinfold calipers in place of body mass index, depending on school district policy and your training.

What to Look For

- There is a discrepancy between the way the CDC recommends rounding height and weight and the way that Fitnessgram handles the data.
- If using Fitnessgram, round down on height to the nearest inch.
- Height needs to be measured accurately, since it is squared in the BMI formula.
- When measuring height, the Frankfurt plane needs to be aligned so that the head is level. The head may pull away from the stadiometer for this measurement.

Formal and Informal Assessments

- Homework assignment on academic vocabulary
- Fitnessgram is a formal assessment, but it is not linked to a standard and should not be converted to a grade.

Closure

- Did you feel challenged by any of the fitness assessments today? If so, which ones and why?
- Review how you did on each test, and think about which areas you might need to work on.

Reflection

Browse through student work that was completed to see where misunderstandings occurred.

Homework

Provide students with sample Fitnessgram reports that have been copied in a way that there is no name on the report.

Students read the report and underline any vocabulary that they do not understand.

Students circle any numbers on the report that they do not understand.

Students analyze areas of strength and weakness for the hypothetical student.

Students write down which areas they need to work on and select one for remediation purposes.

Resources

Corbin, C., et al. (2014). Youth physical fitness: Ten key concepts. *Journal of Physical Recreation and Dance, 85*(2), 24-31.

Council of Europe, Committee for the Development of Sport. (1993). *Handbook for the Eurofit tests of physical fitness.* 2nd ed. Strasbourg: Council of Europe Publishing.

Institute of Medicine. (2012). *Fitness measures and health outcomes in youth.* Washington: National Academies of Sciences.

Melograno, V.J. (2000). *Portfolio assessment for k-12 physical education.* Reston, VA: National Association for Sport and Physical Education.

Nihisher, A.J., et al. (2007). Body mass index measurement in schools. *Journal of School Health, 77*(10), 651-671.

The Cooper Institute. (2013). Meredith, M.D., & Welk, G.J. (Eds.). *Fitnessgram & Activitygram test administration manual.* Updated 4th ed. Champaign, IL: Human Kinetics.

LESSON 7: PERSONAL FITNESS PLAN

Grade-Level Outcomes

Primary Outcome

Assessment & program planning: Designs and implements a program of remediation for any areas of weakness based on the results of health-related fitness assessments. (S3.M15.6)

Embedded Outcome

Safety: Uses physical activity and fitness equipment appropriately and safely, *with the teacher's guidance.* (S4.M7.6)

Lesson Objective

The learner will design or revise a fitness plan based on his fitness scores from previous lessons.

Equipment and Materials

- Copies of Designing Health-Related Fitness Flow Chart and Physical Activity Programming worksheet
- Pencils
- Clipboards (1 per student)
- Gym space
- LCD overhead
- Wall or screen to project on
- Personalized Fitnessgram reports (folded over so that only the student name shows to maintain privacy)
- Teacher-created station cards with possible exercises or physical activity listed for each component of fitness
- Equipment to support teacher-created station cards

Introduction

Today, we will begin to design and implement a physical activity or physical fitness program to address areas of weakness that we have identified through our health-related fitness assessments.

Instructional Task:
Seven-Day Physical Activity Log Review

■ PRACTICE TASK

Students need to follow along as you model filling out the log using the overhead projector.

Model how to use a cell phone application, RPE scale, pedometer tool (for determining steps per minute and moderate to vigorous physical activity), and physical activity table.

Modeling both technology and non-technology options is important for reaching every student in the class.

Note: As wearable technology becomes more prevalent, the way that you model it likely will change, and it will vary based on the community in which you teach.

Extension

Students can practice using one of the apps in conjunction with an activity.

Student Choices/Differentiation

- Encourage students to try different ways to determine exercise intensity, including cell phone applications or websites, but only with parental or guardian approval.
- Encourage students to think about exercise equipment (treadmill, elliptical, rowing machine, etc.) that they may have at home or at a gym or health club that they may belong to.

What to Look For

Students volunteer the use of some technology or websites that they use at home (e.g., Nike's chip in the shoe and application, Fitbit).

Instructional Task:
Designing Health-Related Fitness Flow Chart

■ PRACTICE TASK

With students in cooperative groups, distribute a sample of a few Fitnessgram reports to each group (with the names removed). Students go through the reports and use a flow chart to assess personal health for each component of fitness.

Groups rotate from station to station in allotted time intervals (determined by available class time) to look at suggested activities or exercise that can be used to remediate a fitness plan.

Students need to determine what the established health requirement is (shown on Fitnessgram report).

Cooperative groups record training that could be used to maintain or achieve a match between the established health requirement and personal health level.

You can also model how to do this while providing an example using the overhead LCD projector.

Guiding questions for students:

- Where else might you see a flow chart or diagram like this?
- Is a redesign of the established health requirement possible?
- If a redesign of the established health requirement is not possible, what options are you left with?

Student Choices/Differentiation

- Students can choose which sample report to use.
- Cooperative groups can decide what exercise or physical activities can be performed to achieve a match between the personal health of the hypothetical person provided and the established health requirement.

What to Look For

- Students recognize that a redesign of the health requirement is really not an option. Scientists and doctors establish these.
- Students recognize that they need to train for a match to take place between their personal health and established health requirement.
- Student recognize that they might have seen a flow chart or diagram for the rock cycle or water cycle.

Instructional Task: Independent Work
on Remediation of Personal Fitness Plan

■ PRACTICE TASK

Pass out the Designing Health-Related Fitness Flow Chart and Physical Activity Programming worksheet.

Also distribute Fitnessgram reports generated from the Fitnessgram 10.0 software. Reports should be folded so that only the student name shows.

Students begin independent work on their own health-related fitness program of remediation for any areas of weakness based on their health-related fitness assessment results.

Students can again rotate to the various stations in the gym to get ideas for remediation and to try various exercises (e.g., a station with various sand bells and various strengthening exercises for the upper body).

EMBEDDED OUTCOME: S4.M7.6. This is a great opportunity to review safety and appropriate equipment use as students begin to work independently.

Extension

Encourage students to think about activities they do and lifestyle choices they make that may not help their health-related fitness (e.g., excessive screen time, playing video games with poor posture, doing homework with poor posture, poor nutrition choices, doing homework without taking time for physical activity breaks).

Student Choices/Differentiation

Struggling students may be matched with high-achieving students for this task if necessary.

What to Look For

- Students' interpretation of their Fitnessgram reports is correct.
- Students can follow the flow chart for designing a program of remediation.

Formal and Informal Assessments

- Physical Activity Programming Worksheet. When combined with implementation of the program, it will become formal (summative).
- A program of remediation for areas of weakness based on results of health-related fitness assessments should be evidenced in students' two-week physical activity logs (S3.M16.6), to be assigned after students design their programs (Lesson 8).

Closure

- Now that you have started your program in class, you should implement it every day for the next two weeks.
- Do you have any questions about how to work on your remediation area?

Reflection

- Do students seem to understand the idea of how the flow chart works?
- Are they able to come up with activities that will help them achieve a match between the established health-related fitness requirement and their own personal fitness?

Homework

Finish designing the personal health-related fitness program using the information provided in class.

You will need to bring your completed fitness program to the next class to share with other students.

Resources

Kroemer, K.H.E., Kroemer, H.J., & Kroemer-Elbert, K.E. (2010). *Engineering physiology: Bases of human factors engineering/ergonomics*. 4th ed. New York: Springer Science & Business Media.

DESIGNING HEALTH-RELATED FITNESS FLOW CHART

Name: _____ Period (circle):   1   2   3   4   5   6

Weekend dates: _____

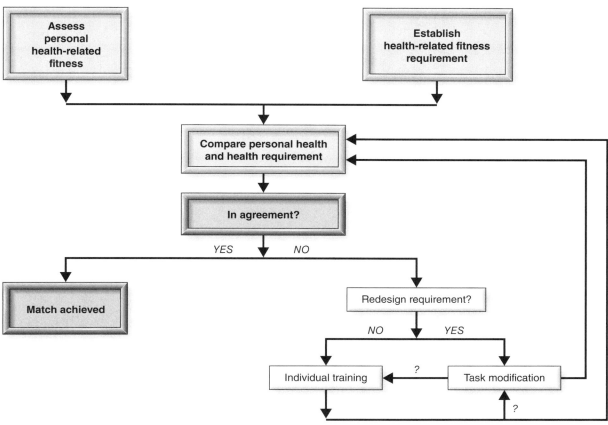

Adapted from Fig. 8.6 found in Kroemer, K.H.E., Hiltrud, J.K., Kroemer-Elbert, K.E. (2010). Engineering physiology: Bases of human factors engineering/ergonomics, 4th ed. (New York, NY: Springer Science-Business Media).

From R.J. Doan, L.C. MacDonald, and S. Chepko, eds., 2017, *Lesson planning for middle school physical education* (Reston, VA: SHAPE America; Champaign, IL: Human Kinetics).

PHYSICAL ACTIVITY PROGRAMMING WORKSHEET

1. Aerobic Capacity

Personal health score: _____ Health requirement: _____

Compare the two above.

In agreement (circle):   Yes   No

Can you change the health requirement (circle)?   Yes   No

Individual training: What training (physical activity) can you do if you need to improve or maintain your level of fitness for **aerobic capacity**?

How many days do you think it will take you to meet the requirement for aerobic capacity? If you already have a match or you are above the requirement, when do you think you should assess you aerobic capacity again?

2. Abdominal Curl-Up

Personal health score: _____ Health requirement: _____

Compare the two above.

In agreement (circle):   Yes   No

Can you change the health requirement (circle)?   Yes   No

Individual training: What training (physical activity) can you do if you need to improve or maintain your level of fitness for **abdominal curl-ups**?

How many days per week will you do this? _____

Explain how you will use the principle of overload?

How many days do you think it will take you to meet the requirement for aerobic capacity? If you already have a match or you are above the requirement, when do you think you should assess your abdominal curl-ups again?

3. Trunk Extension (Trunk Lift)

Personal health score: _____ Health requirement: _____

Compare the two above.

In agreement (circle): Yes No

Can you change the health requirement (circle)?   Yes   No

Individual training: What training (physical activity) can you do if you need to improve or maintain your level of fitness for **trunk extension (trunk lift)**?

How many days per week will you do this? _____

Explain how you will use the overload principle.

How many days do you think it will take you to meet the requirement for aerobic capacity? If you already have a match or you are above the requirement, when do you think you should assess your (trunk extension) trunk lift?

4. Push-Up (Upper Body)

Personal health score: _____ Health requirement: _____

Compare the two above.

In agreement (circle): Yes No

Can you change the health requirement (circle)?   Yes   No

Individual training: What training (physical activity) can you do if you need to improve or maintain your level of fitness for **push-up (upper body)**?

How many days per week will you do this? _____

Explain how you will use the overload principle.

How many days do you think it will take you to meet the requirement for aerobic capacity? If you already have a match or you are above the requirement, when do you think you should assess your (upper-body) push-up?

5. Shoulder Stretch Right and Left (Flexibility)

Personal health score: _____ Health requirement: _____

Compare the two above.

In agreement (circle): Yes No

Can you change the health requirement (circle)?   Yes   No

Individual training: What training (physical activity) can you do if you need to improve or maintain your level of fitness for **shoulder stretch right and left (flexibility)**?

How many days per week will you do this? _____

Explain how you will use the overload principle.

How many days do you think it will take you to meet the requirement for aerobic capacity? If you already have a match or you are above the requirement, when do you think you should assess your (flexibility) shoulder stretch, right and left?

6. Body Mass Index

Personal health score: _____ Health requirement: _____

Compare the two above.

In agreement (circle):   Yes   No

Can you change the health requirement (circle)?   Yes   No

Individual training: What training (physical activity) can you do if you need to improve or maintain your level of fitness for **body mass index**?

How many days per week will you do this? _____

Explain how you will use the overload principle.

How many days do you think it will take you to meet the requirement for aerobic capacity? If you already have a match or you are above the requirement, when do you think you should assess your body mass index?

(continued)

(continued)

7. Power

Personal health score: _____ Health requirement: _____

Compare the two above.

In agreement (circle): Yes No

Can you change the health requirement (circle)?   Yes   No

Individual training: What training (physical activity) can you do if you need to improve or maintain your level of fitness for **power**?

How many days per week will you do this? _____

Explain how you will use the overload principle.

How many days do you think it will take you to meet the requirement for power? If you already have a match or you are above the requirement, when do you think you should assess your **power**?

Criteria for Competence

1. Clearly identifies one the following:
   - a physical job with a fitness need,
   - a physical task,
   - an occupational fitness requirement,
   - a fitness requirement for a sport,
   - a health-related fitness requirement (can be one or more).
2. Clearly assesses current personal abilities, limitations, or fitness.
3. Makes a comparison between #2 and #3.
4. Decides whether or not #2 or #3 are in agreement.
5. Decides whether a match is achieved or a redesign of #1 is possible.
6. Decides on either individual training or redesigning #1.
7. Makes a comparison again at #3 after training or redesign.

Scoring Guide

- Clearly identifies one the following:
   - a physical job with a fitness need,
   - a physical task,
   - an occupational fitness requirement,
   - a fitness requirement for a sport,
   - a health-related fitness requirement.
- Clearly assesses current personal abilities, limitations, or fitness.
- Makes a comparison between #2 and #3.
- Decides whether or not #2 or #3 are in agreement.
- Decides whether a match is achieved or a redesign of #1 is possible.
- Decides on either individual training or to redesign #1.
- Makes a comparison again at #3 after training or redesign.

From R.J. Doan, L.C. MacDonald, and S. Chepko, eds., 2017, *Lesson planning for middle school physical education* (Reston, VA: SHAPE America; Champaign, IL: Human Kinetics).

LESSON 8: DESIGNING AND IMPLEMENTING A TWO-WEEK PHYSICAL ACTIVITY LOG

Grade-Level Outcomes

Primary Outcomes

Assessment & program planning: Maintains a physical activity log for at least 2 weeks and reflects on activity levels as documented in the log. (S3.M16.6)

Assessment & program planning: Designs and implements a program of remediation for any areas of weakness based on the results of health-related fitness assessments. (S3.M15.6)

Embedded Outcome

Accepting feedback: Demonstrates self-responsibility by implementing specific corrective feedback to improve performance. (S4.M3.6)

Lesson Objectives

The learner will:

- implement a program of remediation for areas of weakness based on the results of health-related fitness assessments.

- maintain a physical activity log for at least two weeks (to be included in the learner's portfolio) that tracks the implementation of a program of remediation.

Equipment and Materials

- Copies of two-week physical activity log (Make PDF copies available to students online to cut down on paper distribution.)

- Student portfolios (By now these should include a one-week PA log, a program of remediation [fitness plan], a scoring guide for the portfolio, and a portfolio registry [additions and deletions].)

- Station cards listing each component of health-related fitness

- Various equipment for muscular strength stations (e.g., sand bells, medicine balls, aerobic steps, exercise bands)

Introduction

Today, you will implement your program of fitness remediation. You will do that by beginning work on a two-week physical activity log. This log will help you track how you implement your plan. At the end of two weeks, you will be asked to reflect on your plan. All of this work will be kept in your portfolios.

Instructional Task: Sharing Program of Remediation

■ **PRACTICE TASK**

In small groups, students rotate to stations labeled with individual components of health-related fitness.

Students do the following at each station.

- Cardiorespiratory endurance: Students share what activities they plan on participating in that will either maintain or improve this component.

- Muscular strength and endurance of the upper body: Students demonstrate with available equipment exercise they have listed that will either maintain or improve this component.

- Flexibility: Students demonstrate flexibility exercises that they plan on participating in that will help maintain or improve this component.

- Muscular strength and endurance of the abdominal muscles: Students demonstrate with available equipment exercises they can do to maintain or improve this component.

EMBEDDED OUTCOME: S4.M3.6. Use this task to reinforce self-responsibility as students work independently and use assessment results to make improvements.

Refinement

Students can refine their fitness plans during this activity if they get a new idea or deepen their understanding of how to remediate an area of fitness (e.g., students might discover options other than push-ups for improving upper-body strength and endurance).

Student Choices/Differentiation

Students may pick groups to work in.

What to Look For

Listen to student conversations and observe student demonstrations to check for understanding.

Instructional Task:
Design and Implement Physical Activity log

■ PRACTICE TASK

Distribute sample pages to be used for the physical activity log, and review with students how they are to be used:

- Distribute physical activity log forms and portfolios.
- Students review the programs that they designed.
- Students look at previous work in their portfolios and reflect on it. Provide them with guiding questions to help them.

Students should start creating their two-week physical activity logs. They should also reflect on the process of implementing their programs and the logs.

Extension

Students can practice some of the activities they have planned. This allows you to check for understanding and make sure the activities are aligned with the areas of remediation. It will also provide some moderate to vigorous physical activity if the bone- and muscle-strengthening section is taken out.

Guiding questions for students:

- How can you make the work that you are about to do for the next two weeks better than the work that is already in your portfolio?
- Has your thinking or understanding about physical activity changed at all?

Student Choices/Differentiation

- Students can design their own physical activity logs if they prefer to have their own format. Logs should include the following, at a minimum:
  - Day
  - Date
  - Activity
  - Time
- Students can pair up to review each other's drafts for some simple feedback before trying to implement their plans.

What to Look For

Students are using the physical activity log correctly.

Formal and Informal Assessments

- Observe student demonstrations and listen to student conversations.
- Students' portfolios will provide evidence of standard S3.M16.6.

Closure

- What are two important things to remember as you work on your two-week log?
- How does being physically active affect your well-being?
- Do you have any questions about this assignment?

Reflection

- What assistance will students need during the next two weeks?
- What is the best way to motivate students to keep up with their logs?

Homework

For the next two weeks, you will implement your physical fitness program. While doing so, you will maintain a two-week physical activity log. At the completion of this log, you will be asked to reflect on your activity levels that you documented in the log. Copies of the forms to be used for the log can be found on the school's physical education website. Finally, your two-week log, fitness plan, and reflection will be included in your physical education portfolio.

Resources

Melograno, V.J. (2000). *Portfolio assessment for k-12 physical education.* Reston, VA: National Association for Sport and Physical Education.

GRADE 8 PHYSICAL ACTIVITY PARTICIPATION MODULE

Lessons in this module were contributed by John Kruse, a middle school physical education teacher with the Los Angeles Unified School District.

Grade-Level Outcomes Addressed, by Lesson	Lessons 1	2	3	4	5	6	7	8
Standard 1. The physically literate individual demonstrates competency in a variety of motor skills and movement patterns.								
Standard 2. The physically literate individual applies knowledge of concepts, principles, strategies and tactics related to movement and performance.								
Standard 3. The physically literate individual demonstrates the knowledge and skills to achieve and maintain a health-enhancing level of physical activity and fitness.								
Participates in a variety of self-selected aerobic-fitness activities outside of school such as walking, jogging, biking, skating, dancing and swimming. (S3.M3.8)		E						
Plans and implements a program of cross-training to include aerobic, strength & endurance and flexibility training. (S3.M4.8)	P	P	P	P	P	P	P	P
Participates in moderate to vigorous aerobic and/or muscle- and bone-strengthening physical activity for at least 60 minutes per day at least 5 times a week. (S3.M6.8)	E							E
Compares and contrasts health-related fitness components. (S3.M7.8)						E		
Uses available technology to self-monitor quantity of exercise needed for a minimal health standard and/or optimal functioning based on current fitness level. (S3.M8.8)				E				
Employs a variety of appropriate static stretching techniques for all major muscle groups. (S3.M9.8)				P				
Describes the role of flexibility in injury prevention. (S3.M10.8)				E				
Designs and implements a warm-up/cool-down regimen for a self-selected physical activity. (S3.M12.8)					P			
Defines resting heart rate and describes its relationship to aerobic fitness and the Borg Rating of Perceived Exertion (RPE) scale. (S3.M13.6)						E		
Defines how the RPE Scale can be used to adjust workout intensity during physical activity. (S3.M13.8)							P	
Explains how body systems interact with one another (e.g., blood transports nutrients from the digestive system, oxygen from the respiratory system) during physical activity. (S3.M14.8)			E					
Describes the relationship between poor nutrition and health risk factors. (S3.M17.8)	E							
Demonstrates basic movements used in other stress-reducing activities, such as yoga and tai chi. (S3.M18.8)				E				
Standard 4. The physically literate individual exhibits responsible personal and social behavior that respects self and others.								
Accepts responsibility for improving one's own levels of physical activity and fitness. (S4.M1.8)								E
Provides encouragement and feedback to peers without prompting from the teacher. (S4.M3.8)			E					
Independently uses physical activity and fitness equipment appropriately, and *identifies specific safety concerns* associated with the activity. (S4.M7.8)			E					
Standard 5. The physically literate individual recognizes the value of physical activity for health, enjoyment, challenge, self-expression and/or social interaction.								
Identifies the 5 components of health-related fitness (muscular strength, muscular endurance, flexibility, cardiovascular endurance, body composition) and explains connections between fitness and overall physical and mental health. (S5.M1.8)						P		
Analyzes the empowering consequences of being physically active. (S5.M2.8)				E				
Demonstrates respect for self by asking for help and helping others in various physical activities. (S5.M6.8)							E	

P = Primary; E = Embedded

LESSON 1: MUSCULAR STRENGTH AND ENDURANCE STATIONS

Grade-Level Outcomes

Primary Outcome

Engages in physical activity: Plans and implements a program of cross-training to include aerobic, strength & endurance and flexibility training. (S3.M4.8)

Embedded Outcomes

Nutrition: Describes the relationship between poor nutrition and health risk factors. (S3.M17.8)

Fitness knowledge: Participates in moderate to vigorous aerobic and/or muscle- and bone-strengthening physical activity for at least 60 minutes per day at least 5 times a week. (S3.M6.8)

Lesson Objectives

The learner will:

- reflect on and discuss the importance and benefits of physical activity.
- record aerobic activities in which she participates during the week outside of class.
- compare her activity level to physical activity guidelines for aerobic activity.
- make a basic plan for aerobic activity participation outside of class that meets the physical activity guidelines based on frequency.
- review and practice muscular strength and endurance (MSE) exercises.

Equipment and Materials

- Copies of the Physical Activity Questionnaire for Older Children (PAQ-C, for children 8 to 14 years of age)
- Copies of weekday and weekend physical activity logs
- Clipboards
- Resistance bands
- Sand bells
- Hand weights
- Aerobic steps
- Cones
- Shoulder folders for station cards
- Station cards
- Index cards
- Pencils
- Whiteboard easel
- Video device for peer evaluations

Introduction

Today, we start work on implementing a basic cross-training plan that will include aerobic fitness, muscular strength and muscular endurance, and flexibility training. During class, we'll focus on muscular strength and endurance, but you will need to include the aerobic and flexibility component outside of class. You will track your activities in a log (or by using a device) that you will bring to class every day. The goal is to meet physical activity guidelines in aerobic and muscle- and bone-strengthening activities.

These lessons will challenge you to integrate physical activity into your daily life in a meaningful way.

EMBEDDED OUTCOME: S3.M6.8. During class, focus on muscular strength and endurance. Students will track their activities in a log (or by using a device) that they will bring to class every day.

Instructional Task: Discussion on Importance and Benefits of Physical Activity

■ PRACTICE TASK

Give a PowerPoint presentation on the importance and benefits of physical activity, covering material not mentioned in the class discussion.

Guiding questions for students:

- What is the importance of physical activity?
- What are some benefits of physical activity?
- Why is it important to be physically active as teenagers?

Extension

The discussion can move into recommendations for physical activity.

EMBEDDED OUTCOME: S3.M17.8. Students describe the relationship between poor nutrition and health risk factors (especially with regard to physical activity).

Student Choices/Differentiation

- Students select own partners to discuss with.
- Videos and handouts can reinforce material.

What to Look For

Students' ability to come up with the importance and benefits of physical activity.

Instructional Task: Muscular Strength and Endurance Stations

■ PRACTICE TASK

After a proper warm-up, students rotate through various muscular strength and endurance stations (bench press, standing press, biceps curl, reverse lunge, calf raise, upright row, bent-over row, and abdominal curl-up) focusing on major muscle groups of the body, performing one set of 6 to 15 repetitions.

Extensions

- If time permits, a second set can be included.
- Peers can use a video device and a checklist to assess correct form at each of the stations.

Refinement

Refine any of the skills in the stations as needed.

Student Choices/Differentiation

Students can choose 10 to 20 repetitions. (Note: since there is not consensus in the field as to the optimal number of reps for resistance training with middle school aged children.)

What to Look For

- Students are using proper form.
- Students are following the instructions on the station cards.

Instructional Task: Aerobic Activity Recall

▦ PRACTICE TASK

On the whiteboard easel, write the following guideline for children and adolescents: Aerobic: Most of the 60 minutes or more a day should be either moderate- or vigorous-intensity aerobic physical activity, and should include vigorous-intensity physical activity at least three days a week.

Students write down on an index card the aerobic physical activity they participated in last week. They should include the amount of time for each activity.

Students compare their physical activity to the guideline.

Extension

On the back of the card, students write a basic plan to either maintain or meet the guideline for the upcoming weeks.

Refinement

Make sure students are choosing aerobic activities (moderate or vigorous).

Student Choices/Differentiation

- Students can choose various aerobic physical activities in their basic plans.
- Have examples for students to view if needed.

What to Look For

- Students are identifying aerobic activities of moderate or vigorous intensity.
- Students are writing a realistic plan based on their current fitness level and current participation in physical activity.

Instructional Task: Physical Activity Log

▦ PRACTICE TASK

Distribute and go over the log students will be using to record their physical activity in class and outside of class.

Extensions

Provide a sample log for students to view.

Student Choices/Differentiation

Students can choose to use a device or app as a log instead.

What to Look For

Students are recording all of their in-class physical activity.

Formal and Informal Assessments

- Peer checklist: students' form at activity stations
- Exit slip: What is your definition of aerobic activity?

Closure

Today, our focus was on muscular strength and endurance activities. These types of activities typically do not burn a huge number of Calories, and additional physical activity is necessary outside of class.

- What will you do to make sure that you get enough physical activity today?
- What was your favorite station? Why?
- What was your least favorite station? Why?

Reflection

- Do students have a good understanding of the importance and benefits of physical activity?
- Will students need additional explanations on how to complete the physical activity log?
- Do students have a general understanding of aerobic activities?

Homework

For homework, you will complete a physical activity questionnaire called the PAQ-C. Instructions on how to complete this questionnaire can be found on the school's physical education website.

In addition, you will take home your weekday PA log and add additional activities you have participated in or will participate in. Try to participate in moderate to vigorous aerobic and muscle- and bone-strengthening physical activity for at least 60 minutes per day, at least five times a week.

Resources

Kowalski, K., Crocker, P., & Donen, R. (2004). *The Physical Activity Questionnaire for Older Children (PAQ-C) and Adolescents (PAQ-A) manual.* Saskatoon: University of Saskatchewan College of Kinesiology.

U.S. Department of Health and Human Services. (2008). *Physical activity guidelines for Americans.* Washington, DC: Author. Available at www.health.gov.

SELF-ASSESSMENT OF PHYSICAL ACTIVITY PATTERNS OUTSIDE OF PHYSICAL EDUCATION CLASS

Directions: Review your two-week physical activity log and observe your physical activity patterns. Focus on the physical activity that you participated in outside of physical education class.

1. Did you participate in physical activity three or more time, per week outside of physical education class? Circle: Yes   No

2. If yes, list the types of physical activity you did for the two weeks outside of physical education class.

3. If no, what can you do to increase the number of times you participate in physical activity outside of physical education class?

From R.J. Doan, L.C. MacDonald, and S. Chepko, eds., 2017, *Lesson planning for middle school physical education* (Reston, VA: SHAPE America; Champaign, IL: Human Kinetics).

WEEKDAY PHYSICAL ACTIVITY LOG

Name: _____ Period (circle): 1 2 3 4 5 6

Date: _____/_____/_____

Day of the week (circle): M T W Th F

Part of day	Activities	Time (min)	Easily measurable? (circle)	Calories	Intensity	Comments (technology or app used, how did you feel?, with whom did you partici-pate?, etc.)
Before school			Yes/No			
Nutrition (morning) break			Yes/No			
Lunch break			Yes/No			
In-class physical activity break (If so, list classes)			Yes/No			
Physical education class			Yes/No			
After school			Yes/No			

From R.J. Doan, L.C. MacDonald, and S. Chepko, eds., 2017, *Lesson planning for middle school physical education* (Reston, VA: SHAPE America; Champaign, IL: Human Kinetics).

WEEKEND PHYSICAL ACTIVITY LOG

Name: _____ Period (circle): 1 2 3 4 5 6

Weekend dates: _____

Saturday

Part of day	Activities	Time (min)	Easy to measure? (circle)	Calories	Intensity	Comments (technology or app used, how did you feel?, with whom did you participate?, etc.)
Morning			Yes/No			
Afternoon			Yes/No			
Evening			Yes/No			

Totals

Total number of activities: _____

Total time (min): _____

How many of the activities were easy to measure? _____

Total number of calories expended: _____

Sunday

Part of day	Activities	Time (min)	Easy to measure? (circle)	Calories	Intensity	Comments (technology or app used, how did you feel?, with whom did you participate?, etc.)
Morning			Yes/No			
Afternoon			Yes/No			
Evening			Yes/No			

Totals

Total number of activities: _____

Total time (min): _____

How many of the activities were easy to measure? _____

Total number of calories expended: _____

Scoring Guide

Criteria for competence:

1. Lists physical activity.
2. Records time for physical activity.
3. Considers if PA was easily measured.
4. Records Calories (kcal) if easily measured.
5. Includes a measure of exercise intensity.
6. Sums the total time spent in the activity.
7. Considers if activity was easily measured.
8. Includes a total for the number of Calories (kcal).

From R.J. Doan, L.C. MacDonald, and S. Chepko, eds., 2017, *Lesson planning for middle school physical education* (Reston, VA: SHAPE America; Champaign, IL: Human Kinetics).

SAMPLE STATION CARDS

Bench Press

- Lie down, face up, on a stack of aerobic steps.
- Use either hand weights or sand bells.
- Extend your arms straight up to full extension.

Standing Press

- Standing straight up, lift either hand weights or sand bells straight up (over your head).
- Arms should be extended fully.

Biceps Curl

- Stand with your palms face up and lift either hand weights or sand bells.
- Curl weights up from your thighs to your chest.
- Keep your elbows in next to your body.

Reverse Lunge

- Stand with feet shoulder-width apart.
- Step backward with one foot and bend the knee of the other leg as you lower your body down; the knee of the back leg should almost touch the ground.
- Bring the back foot back up to the starting position and alternate legs. Hold hand weights or sand bells in your hands to increase resistance if needed.

Calf Raise

- Stand on the edge of an aerobic step on the balls of your feet.
- Hold hand weights or sand bells in your hands if needed.
- Lift your body by pointing your toes and contracting your calf muscles.

Upright Row

- Stand and hold hand weights or sand bells at your sides.
- Pull the weights straight up to the height of your chin using your shoulder muscles.

Bent-Over Row

- Stabilize yourself on a stack of aerobic steps (see picture).
- Hold a weight in one hand and lift it all the way up to your chest.
- Switch arms after completing one set.

Abdominal Curl-Up

- Lie on your back and bend your hips and knees.
- Your feet should be about 1 foot (30 cm) away from your buttocks.
- Hold your arms at your sides and curl up (lifting your shoulders and head off the ground).
- Use your abdominal muscles for this motion; do not lift all the way up (no sit-ups) to prevent hurting your tailbone.

From R.J. Doan, L.C. MacDonald, and S. Chepko, eds., 2017, *Lesson planning for middle school physical education* (Reston, VA: SHAPE America; Champaign, IL: Human Kinetics).

LESSON 2: ADDING WEIGHTS TO MUSCULAR STRENGTH AND ENDURANCE STATIONS

Grade-Level Outcomes

Primary Outcome

Engages in physical activity: Plans and implements a program of cross-training to include aerobic, strength & endurance and flexibility training. (S3.M4.8)

Embedded Outcomes

Accepting feedback: Provides encouragement and feedback to peers without prompting from the teacher. (S4.M3.8)

Engages in physical activity: Participates in a variety of self-selected aerobic-fitness activities outside of school such as walking, jogging, biking, skating, dancing and swimming. (S3.M3.8)

Safety: Independently uses physical activity and fitness equipment appropriately, and *identifies specific safety concerns* associated with the activity. (S4.M7.8)

Lesson Objectives

The learner will:

- discuss self-assessment of his current level of physical activity using the physical activity questionnaire (PAQ-C).
- refine his plan for aerobic activity based on data from PAQ-C.
- practice exercises to improve muscular strength and endurance.
- document physical activity in physical education class using log sheets.

Equipment and Materials

- Copies of Weight Training Chart
- Pencils
- Clipboards
- Aerobic steps
- Sand bells
- Medicine balls
- Resistance tubing
- Hand weights
- Cones for stations
- Station cards
- Shoulder folders for station cards
- Completed index cards from Lesson 1 with basic physical activity plan

Introduction

Today, we will continue to explore the importance of physical activity. For homework, you were to complete a physical activity questionnaire called the PAQ-C. You also were to continue logging your physical activity outside of class. I hope these activities made you think about your levels of physical activity and caused you to reflect on how active you are.

Instructional Task: Discussion of PAQ-C

■ PRACTICE TASK

Students share the results of their PAQ-C with partners. Students should discuss the results and share what they learned from filling out the questionnaire.

EMBEDDED OUTCOME: S4.M3.8. Ask students to provide encouragement and feedback to peers without your prompting.

Extension

Students could revise their basic physical activity plans based on PAQ-C results.

Refinement

Go over any activities from the questionnaire that students were not familiar with.

Student Choices/Differentiation

Students may choose their partners.

What to Look For

- Students are having intelligent conversations about the questionnaire.
- Students are encouraging peers without prompting from you.

Instructional Task: Muscular Strength and Endurance Stations

■ PRACTICE TASK

Students rotate through muscular strength and endurance stations. Again, assign 6 to 15 repetitions.

Students use a weight training chart to record the amount of weight they use for each exercise.

Extensions

- Encourage students to attempt various weights in order to reach overload.
- Add a cardio station (stationary bike) and a flexibility station (focus on upper body).

Refinement

Make sure students start with weights that they know they can lift. They can move up in weight if they can handle the lighter weights.

EMBEDDED OUTCOME: S4.M7.8. Ensure that students use the equipment appropriately, without prompting, and identify safety concerns associated with the activity.

Student Choices/Differentiation

Students can choose from a variety of equipment.

What to Look For

- Students are using proper form.
- Students are following the instructions on the station cards.
- Students are attempting various weights.
- Students are identifying specific safety concerns at each station.
- Students are using fitness equipment safely.

Instructional Task: Refine Physical Activity Plans

■ PRACTICE TASK

Distribute index cards from Lesson 1, and ask students to review the basic physical activity plans they created. Now that they have taken the PAQ-C and shared with their partners, encourage them to refine their plans if needed.

Extension

Students can calculate the quantity of physical activity needed based on their weight.

EMBEDDED OUTCOME: S3.M3.8. Encourage students to select and perform a variety of aerobic fitness activities outside of school.

Student Choices/Differentiation

List a variety of aerobic fitness activities that students can perform outside of school.

What to Look For

- Students are putting thought into refining their basic physical activity plans.
- Students are participating in aerobic fitness activities outside of school.

Instructional Task: Document Physical Activity

■ PRACTICE TASK

Students log the physical activity they performed in class in their physical activity logs.

Refinement

Make sure students are using the physical activity logs correctly.

Student Choices/Differentiation

Students can choose to log physical activity electronically if they have an appropriate app.

What to Look For

Students are correctly logging their in-class physical activity.

Formal and Informal Assessments

- PAQ-C
- Basic physical activity plan
- Discussion of PAQ-C

Closure

Today, you were able to discuss the results of your physical activity questionnaire with a classmate and to continue practicing your muscular strength and endurance exercises. Again, keep in mind that the muscular strength and endurance activities typically do not provide enough physical activity. If you were to depend only on what you did in class today, you would fall short on aerobic-type physical activity. You are again encouraged to think of how you will fit in additional physical activity outside of class time.

What obstacles do you face with busy school schedules, and what can you do about it?

Reflection

- Are students performing the muscular strength and endurance exercises properly?
- Are they experimenting with various weights to find overload?
- Did students revise their basic physical activity plans based on the results and discussion of their questionnaires?

Homework

For homework, you will again log your out-of-class physical activity. Keep striving to participate in moderate to vigorous aerobic and muscle- and bone-strengthening physical activity for at least 60 minutes per day, at least five times a week.

Resources

Kowalski, K., Crocker, P., & Donen, R. (2004). *The Physical Activity Questionnaire for Older Children (PAQ-C) and Adolescents (PAQ-A) manual.* Saskatoon: University of Saskatchewan College of Kinesiology.

NASPE. (2005). *Physical best activity guide: Middle and high school levels.* Champaign, IL: Human Kinetics.

LESSON 3: INTRODUCTION TO PORTFOLIOS

Grade-Level Outcomes

Primary Outcome

Engages in physical activity: Plans and implements a program of cross-training to include aerobic, strength & endurance and flexibility training. (S3.M4.8)

Embedded Outcomes

Health: Analyzes the empowering consequences of being physically active. (S5.M2.8)

Fitness knowledge: Explains how body systems interact with one another (e.g., blood transports nutrients from the digestive system, oxygen from the respiratory system) during physical activity. (S3.M14.8)

Lesson Objectives

The learner will:

- practice to improve muscular strength and endurance.
- document physical activity outside of class and in class.
- review the scoring guide for her portfolio.
- develop a list of potential items for her portfolio.

Equipment and Materials

- Copies of scoring guides for portfolios (page 24 in Melograno, 2000).
- Copies of Weight Training Chart (see lesson 7)
- Pencils
- Clipboards
- Crates to store portfolios
- Reflection of physical activity handout
- 3 × 5 cards
- Sand bells
- Hand weights
- Medicine balls
- Aerobic steps
- Station cards
- Shoulder folders for cards
- Cones for each station

Introduction

To continue our lessons on the importance of physical activity, today we will add a portfolio that will allow you to collect work samples of physical activity and fitness. This portfolio will help you collect evidence of how your thinking about physical activity or perhaps even your participation in physical activity has changed.

Instructional Task: Quick Write

■ PRACTICE TASK

Students write a reflection on a 3 × 5 card that answers the questions "What is physical activity, and why is it important to me?"

Note: This is a possible artifact for student portfolios.

Extension

EMBEDDED OUTCOME: S5.M3.8. Students discuss the empowering consequences of being physically active. Encourage students to reflect and write on how it affects them at this stage of their lives.

Student Choices/Differentiation

Provide an example of a good reflection.

What to Look For

- Students provide a good definition for physical activity.
- Students reflect on what physical activity means to them.
- Students analyze the empowering consequences of being physically active.

Instructional Task:
Muscular Strength and Endurance Stations

■ PRACTICE TASK

Students participate in additional practice of muscular strength and endurance stations. Encourage students to pay attention to the number of reps they are performing. If they find they are able to exceed 15 reps, they can increase the weight.

Extensions

- Add a cardio station (jogging around gym) and a flexibility station (focus on lower body).
- Explain how early improvements in muscular strength (e.g., an increase in weight lifted) is the result of the nervous system learning more than actual muscular strength improvements.

EMBEDDED OUTCOME: S3.M14.8. Discuss with students how the body systems interact with one another during physical activity.

Student Choices/Differentiation

Students can choose from a variety of equipment.

What to Look For

- Students are using proper form.
- Students are following the instructions on the station cards.
- Students are attempting various weights.
- Students have a basic understanding of how the body systems interact with each other during physical activity.

Instructional Task: Think, Pair, Share on Scoring Guide

■ PRACTICE TASK

Distribute the weighted scoring guide and folders for portfolios. Students discuss in pairs how the weighted rubric works.

Extension

Students create a list of possible artifacts having to do with physical activity that they will start to collect for their portfolios. Possible artifacts include training logs, fitness tests, basic physical activity plans, and reflections on physical activity.

Student Choices/Differentiation

- Provide various examples of student portfolios that students can choose from.
- Have them look at how the scoring guides were used to assess the student work.

What to Look For

Students understand what should be included in the portfolios.

Formal and Informal Assessments

- Student portfolios
- Exit slip: Explain what happens in your body during physical activity.

Closure

Today, we started our physical activity portfolios. As we continue the module, you should be thinking about what pieces of student work you would like to include in your portfolio to show your understanding or change in understanding about physical activity.

Reflection

- Do students seem to understand how the scoring guide will be used to assess their portfolios?
- Are students giving max effort in the stations?
- Are students filling out physical activity logs correctly?

Homework

Continue to log your physical activity inside and outside of class.

Teach your family about how the body systems interact during physical activity.

Resources

Melograno, V.J. (2000). *Portfolio assessment for k-12 physical education.* Reston, VA: National Association for Sport and Physical Education.

Internet keyword search: "body system interactions," "muscular strength and the nervous system"

LESSON 4: FLEXIBILITY TRAINING PLAN

Grade-Level Outcomes

Primary Outcomes

Engages in physical activity: Plans and implements a program of cross-training to include aerobic, strength & endurance and flexibility training. (S3.M4.8)

Fitness knowledge: Employs a variety of appropriate static stretching techniques for all major muscle groups. (S3.M9.8)

Embedded Outcomes

Fitness knowledge: Describes the role of flexibility in injury prevention. (S3.M10.8)

Fitness knowledge: Uses available technology to self-monitor quantity of exercise needed for a minimal health standard and/or optimal functioning based on current fitness level. (S3.M8.8)

Stress management: Demonstrates basic movements used in other stress-reducing activities, such as yoga and tai chi. (S3.M18.8)

Lesson Objectives

The learner will:

- practice exercises to improve muscular strength and endurance.
- document physical activity outside of class and in class.
- develop a flexibility training plan for outside of class.

Equipment and Materials

- Copies of Weight Training Chart (see lesson 7)
- Pencils
- Clipboards
- Sand bells
- Hand weights
- Medicine balls
- Aerobic steps
- Cones for stations
- Station cards
- Shoulder folders for station cards
- Heart rate monitors

Introduction

Today, you will add an important component to your physical activity plan: flexibility training.

Instructional Task: Class Discussion

■ **PRACTICE TASK**

Ask students these questions using a whiteboard:

- When is the best time to stretch?
- What does stretching help us do?
- Is stretching an appropriate warm-up?
- Is static stretching considered moderate to vigorous physical activity?

Extension

Show video clips of students performing stretches correctly and incorrectly. In groups, have students describe what they see as correct or incorrect.

Student Choices/Differentiation

- Student may choose their groups.
- Pictures or videos can reinforce content.

What to Look For

Students identify proper stretching behaviors.

Instructional Task:
Muscular Strength and Endurance Stations

■ PRACTICE TASK

Students rotate through muscular strength and endurance stations.

Encourage students to try different weights to put them in the range of 6 to 15 reps.

Extension

Add a cardio station (fitness video) or a flexibility station (yoga video).

EMBEDDED OUTCOME: S3.M8.8. Students wear heart rate monitors during the station activities to self-monitor effort during exercise. Students can compare scores to minimal health standards or optimal functioning based on current fitness levels.

Student Choices/Differentiation

Students can choose from a variety of equipment.

What to Look For

- Students are using proper form during the exercises.
- Students are putting forth maximum effort.
- Students are using appropriate weight.

Instructional Task: Static Stretching Stations

■ PRACTICE TASK

Point out that now is the best time to stretch because muscles are warm from working out.

Students rotate through stretching stations that combine stretching movements and stretching-related content.

Refinement

Circulate around the class and provide feedback so that students are holding the stretches using proper form.

Extension

Students discuss the benefits of being flexible in sports and in life.

EMBEDDED OUTCOME: S3.M10.8. Students describe the role of flexibility in preventing injuries.

Student Choices/Differentiation

Students provide a couple of different options for each major muscle group.

What to Look For

- Students are using proper form.
- Students are holding stretches long enough to make improvements.
- Students are reading the content on stretching at various stations.

Instructional Task: Flexibility Training Plan

■ PRACTICE TASK

Provide students with 3 × 5 cards, and ask them to develop a flexibility training plan to be incorporated into their aerobic training plans.

Extension

Students can use computers to research different ways of improving flexibility.

Student Choices/Differentiation

- Provide samples of flexibility plans.
- Students can work in groups.

What to Look For

- Students are able to develop a flexibility training plan.
- Students are able to find exercises to improve flexibility in an Internet search.

Formal and Informal Assessments

- Class discussion
- Exit slip: Describe three ways flexibility is important to overall health.

Closure

Today, we reviewed static stretching and included it as part of your workout following your muscular strength and endurance training. Remember that while stretching is important, it is not considered moderate to vigorous physical activity and should not be considered part of your daily 60 minutes. Keep trying to improve your overall health by participating in at least 60 minutes of physical activity each day!

Reflection

- Do students seem to understand the importance of stretching?
- Do students understand stretching is not moderate to vigorous physical activity?
- Are students performing the stretches correctly?

Homework

For homework, add static stretching to your physical activity plan. Make sure that you record stretching in your log. Remember to include stretching at the end of other activities so you are not stretching cold muscles, and remember that stretching is not a proper warm-up.

EMBEDDED OUTCOME: S3.M18.8. Encourage students to try a stress-reducing activity such as yoga and tai chi for homework. Suggest they go to the local fitness center or yoga studio to take a class, rent or borrow a yoga DVD, or find yoga clips online.

Resources

NASPE. (2005). *Physical best activity guide: Middle and high school levels*. Champaign, IL: Human Kinetics.

Internet keyword search: "flexibility plans," "static stretching"

LESSON 5: MAKING CONNECTIONS BETWEEN HEALTH-RELATED FITNESS AND OVERALL HEALTH

Grade-Level Outcomes

Primary Outcomes

Engages in physical activity: Plans and implements a program of cross-training to include aerobic, strength & endurance and flexibility training. (S3.M4.8)

Physical activity knowledge: Identifies the 5 components of health-related fitness (muscular strength, muscular endurance, flexibility, cardiovascular endurance, body composition) and explains connections between fitness and overall physical and mental health. (S5.M1.8)

Fitness knowledge: Designs and implements a warm-up/cool-down regimen for a self-selected physical activity. (S3.M12.8)

Embedded Outcome

Fitness knowledge: Compares and contrasts health-related fitness components. (S3.M7.8)

Lesson Objectives

The learner will:

- practice exercises to improve muscular strength and endurance.
- document physical activity outside of class and in class.
- identify the components of health-related fitness.
- explain how the components are evident in his physical activity log.
- describe the relationship between health-related fitness and health.

Equipment and Materials

- Red pens
- Portfolios
- Copies of Weight Training Chart (see lesson 7)
- Pencils
- Clipboards
- Crates to store portfolios
- Reflection of physical activity handout
- 3 × 5 cards
- Sand bells
- Hand weights
- Medicine balls
- Aerobic steps
- Station cards
- Shoulder folders for station cards

Introduction

The purpose of today's lesson is to continue practicing our exercise for improving muscular strength and endurance. Also, we will identify the components of health-related fitness and describe the relationship between health-related fitness and health. We also will design warm-up and cool-down activities for our muscular strength and endurance stations.

Instructional Task:
Design Warm-Up and Cool-Down Activities

▥ PRACTICE TASK

Now that you are comfortable with the muscular strength and endurance stations, you will design and perform proper warm-ups and cool-downs for the stations. In groups of three or four, first design a warm-up that will prepare your muscles for muscular strength and endurance activities. When you are finished, design cool-down activities.

Extension

Students evaluate one another's warm-up and cool-down activities.

Refinement

Make sure that students design activities that are specific to muscular strength and endurance.

Student Choices/Differentiation

- Provide examples of proper warm-up and cool-down activities.
- Students may choose their groups.

What to Look For

Students use activities that are specific to muscular strength and endurance activities.

Instructional Task:
Muscular Strength and Endurance Stations

▥ PRACTICE TASK

After students perform their warm-up activities, they continue with muscular strength and endurance stations.

Remind them to pay attention to the number of reps and to increase the amount of weight if necessary.

Refinement

Remind students that initial improvements in strength come from neuromuscular learning and more efficient movement rather than actual strength gains in the muscle.

Extensions

- Students perform their designed cool-down activities.
- Add a cardio station (student choice) and a flexibility station (full body).

Student Choices/Differentiation

Students can choose from a variety of equipment.

What to Look For

- Students are using proper form.
- Students are increasing in amount of weight, resistance, or reps being used.
- Students are using a proper warm-up and cool-down.

Instructional Task:
Identification of Health-Related Fitness

▥ PRACTICE TASK

Students review their physical activity logs from the previous several days.

Using red pens, students write the following abbreviations (listed on whiteboard easel) to identify which one or two components of fitness are most influenced by the activities they have logged (i.e., write the abbreviation in red pen next to the activity).

> AC = aerobic capacity
>
> FL = flexibility
>
> ME = muscular endurance
>
> MS = muscular strength
>
> BC = body composition

Reinforce the idea that some activities influence one or more component of fitness. Students should identify the one or two that are most influenced by the activity (e.g., playing basketball is a good way to improve aerobic capacity and to improve or maintain body composition).

Extension

Students peer-assess others' work if they finish early.

EMBEDDED OUTCOME: S3.M7.8. In small groups, students compare and contrast health-related fitness components.

Student Choices/Differentiation

- If students struggle with this assignment, provide sample logs with components of fitness identified.
- Students can work together on this assignment if needed.

What to Look For

Students list the correct components of fitness next to activities listed in their physical activity logs.

Instructional Task: Portfolio Reflection

■ PRACTICE TASK

Students write a paragraph in their portfolios based on the following prompt: Describe the relationship between health-related fitness and overall health.

Student Choices/Differentiation

Provide students more time if needed.

What to Look For

Students are able to describe the relationship between health-related fitness and overall health.

Formal and Informal Assessments

- Identification of components of fitness in their physical activity logs
- Paragraph on the relationship between health-related fitness and health
- Peer assessment of identification of components of fitness

Closure

Today, we identified the five components of fitness and described the relationship between these components of fitness and health. You should continue to think about these components of fitness and how physical activity influences them as you continue your learning experiences for this module and select work samples to go into your portfolios.

Reflection

- Do students properly identify the components of fitness most influenced by the activities listed in their logs?
- Did students design warm-ups and cool-downs specific to muscular strength and endurance?
- Are students making the connection between health-related fitness and overall health?

Homework

Continue logging your physical activity during class and outside of class.

Resources

NASPE. (2005). *Physical best activity guide: Middle and high school levels.* Champaign, IL: Human Kinetics.

Internet keyword search: "proper warm-up and cool-down for muscular strength and endurance," "health-related fitness"

LESSON 6: USING SCALES IN YOUR FITNESS PLANS

Grade-Level Outcomes

Primary Outcomes

Engages in physical activity: Plans and implements a program of cross-training to include aerobic, strength & endurance and flexibility training. (S3.M4.8)

Fitness knowledge: Defines how the RPE Scale can be used to adjust workout intensity during physical activity. (S3.M13.8)

Embedded Outcome

Fitness knowledge: Defines resting heart rate and describes its relationship to aerobic fitness and the Borg Rating of Perceived Exertion (RPE) scale. (S3.M13.6)

Lesson Objectives

The learner will:

- practice to improve muscular strength and endurance.
- document physical activity outside of class and in class.
- apply rating of perceived exertion (RPE) to adjust intensity level as needed.
- review the concept of RPE.
- use the PACER to calibrate RPE.

Equipment and Materials

- Copies of various RPE scales (1-10 or Borg 6-20)
- PACER cadence
- PACER course
- Cones for PACER
- Sound system
- Sand bells
- Medicine balls
- Hand weights
- Aerobic steps
- Station cards
- Shoulder folders for station cards

Introduction

Today, we will review the concept of ratings of perceived exertion, or RPE. Technology often helps us measure exercise intensity. Sometimes, though, technology is not available, and so we use ratings of perceived exertion instead.

Instructional Task: Think, Pair, Share on Scales

■ PRACTICE TASK

In pairs, students discuss what they remember about ratings of perceived exertion. They should have learned about this concept in grade 6.

EMBEDDED OUTCOME: S3.M13.6 Discuss with students the relationship between heart rate and aerobic fitness with the Borg Rating of Perceived Exertion (RPE) scale.

Guiding questions for students:

- How is heart rate related to rating of perceived exertion, or RPE?
- Is rating of perceived exertion objective or subjective?
- Is RPE typically used in muscular strength and endurance activities?

Refinement

Explain RPE using a Borg scale versus a scale from 1 to 10.

Student Choices/Differentiation

- Students may choose their partners.
- Students may choose which guiding question to focus on.

What to Look For

Students understand that the Borg scale represents a given heart rate. For example, a 16 would mean a heart rate of 160.

Instructional Task: RPE Calibration

■ PRACTICE TASK

Students participate in the PACER (Progressive Aerobic Cardiovascular Endurance Run) so they can calibrate RPE in their heads.

Display RPE scales in shoulder folders on top of cones on each end of the PACER course.

Students should push themselves to exhaustion before dropping out of the PACER, so they should feel like they are at a level 20 on the Borg scale or a 10 on a 1 to 10 scale.

Refinement

Remind students to think about what level they have reached at the completion of each lap.

Extension

Students use heart rate monitors to see how well they perceive their effort when using a Borg scale.

Student Choices/Differentiation

- Students can choose the RPE scale:
  - 1 to 10
  - Borg scale 6 to 20
- Set up different-length PACER courses to provide additional conditioning for students who typically perform few laps. Distances of 15, 17, and 20 meters seem to work well when using the 20-meter-distance cadence from Fitnessgram.

What to Look For

- Students work well together with reporting and recording scores.
- Students tend to finish the PACER with an RPE of 10 or 20.
- Students see that the RPE increases in a linear fashion with the increase in number of PACER laps. They also see that they were at a level 10 or 20 when they could not continue the PACER any longer. If the RPE is not linear, and they stopped the PACER before they were at a 10 or 20, check for a calibration issue.

Instructional Task:
Muscular Strength and Endurance Stations

■ PRACTICE TASK

Students continue their muscular strength and endurance station work.

Guiding questions for students:

- Do you think RPE scales would work for muscular strength and endurance training, or is there a better way to judge your exercise intensity for muscular strength and endurance?
- What is the benefit of using the scales?
- How will this affect your overall fitness plans?

Extensions

- Students combine aerobic activity with flexibility in one station.
- Add a second set to stations, if time permits.
- Students perform the warm-ups and cool-downs that they designed in previous lessons.

Student Choices/Differentiation

Students can choose from a variety of equipment.

What to Look For

Students recognize that keeping track of weight and reps is a more objective measure for muscular strength and endurance training and that RPE is not typically used.

Formal and Informal Assessments

- Think, pair, share on RPE
- RPE calibration
- Exit slip: What are the major differences in the scales we discussed today?

Closure

Today, we reviewed RPE scales and calibrated RPE using the PACER. Keep in mind that RPE can also be used to adjust your exercise intensity. For example, if you have been working out at a level 7 for a while, you can increase your intensity by attempting to work out at a level 8.

Reflection

- Do students seem to grasp the key ideas on RPE, and can they be expected to use this information in their homework?
- Does use of the RPE scale seem to result in better engagement in the activities?

Homework

Continue logging your physical activity for both class time and out-of-class time for homework.

Make sure you study the material posted throughout the module on the school's physical education website. You will be taking a quiz on key terms and concepts taught in the first six lessons.

In addition, you should see if you can log the exercise intensity of your physical activities in the intensity column using ratings of perceived exertion.

Resources

Rowland, T.W., & Bar-Or, O. (2004). *Pediatric exercise medicine: From physiologic principles to health care applications.* Champaign, IL: Human Kinetics.

LESSON 7:
DESIGNING AT-HOME FITNESS PLANS

Grade-Level Outcomes

Primary Outcome

Engages in physical activity: Plans and implements a program of cross-training to include aerobic, strength & endurance and flexibility training. (S3.M4.8)

Embedded Outcome

Social interaction: Demonstrates respect for self by asking for help and helping others in various physical activities. (S5.M6.8)

Lesson Objectives

The learner will:

- practice exercises to improve muscular strength and endurance.
- design a muscular strength and endurance routine that she can implement at home.
- document her physical activity outside of class and in class.
- demonstrate in a quiz her knowledge of terminology and concepts taught throughout the module.

Equipment and Materials

- Copies of Muscles in Action Plan
- Copies of Labeled Muscle Diagram
- Copies of Weight Training Chart
- Clipboards
- Pencils
- Station cards
- Shoulder folders
- Sand bells
- Hand weights
- Medicine balls
- Aerobic steps

Introduction

We have been learning and practicing muscular strength and endurance concepts and routines in this module. The goal is for you to become a physically literate person who can implement these concepts and habits on your own. Today, you will continue working on muscular strength and endurance in class, but you'll also plan and think about how you can continue that on your own at home. You also will take a quiz on the material you have learned in these lessons.

Instructional Task:
Muscular Strength and Endurance Station

▪ PRACTICE TASK

Students participate in another group warm-up and complete the muscular strength and endurance stations.

As students rotate through the stations, they fill in the worksheet Muscles in Action Plan by listing muscular strength and endurance activities that they think they can realistically do at home with the equipment they have. Also, provide them with a copy of the Labeled Muscle Diagram, or have copies at each station for reference.

You might not have strength training equipment at home, but can you think of body-weight exercises that you could do to work the same muscle group?

EMBEDDED OUTCOME: S5.M6.8. Some students might have difficulty answering all the questions on the worksheet or performing the physical activity task. Discuss with the class why it's important to ask for help when needed and to help others in physical activity tasks.

Extensions

- Students can participate in another group's cool-down activities.
- Students may list machine exercises if their parents or guardians have machines at home.

Student Choices/Differentiation

- Students can choose from a variety of exercises.
- Students can choose from a variety of equipment.
- Students can choose equipment at home or body-weight exercises.
- Provide examples of muscular strength and endurance plans for students to look at if needed.

What to Look For

Students are selecting the correct exercises based on muscle groups.

Instructional Task: Physical Activity Quiz

■ PRACTICE TASK

Students take a teacher-created quiz on material covered throughout the module.

Student Choices/Differentiation

Students may be provided any test accommodations that are needed.

What to Look For

Students demonstrate understanding of terminology and concepts used throughout the module.

Formal and Informal Assessments

- Muscles in Action worksheet
- Physical activity quiz

Closure

Today, through assigned worksheets, you designed a muscle strength and endurance plan that you will hopefully be able to implement at home. We are approaching the end of our module, and you hopefully feel equipped to participate in physical activity on your own outside of school.

Reflection

- Did students have enough time to realistically design a muscle strength and endurance program?
- Will they need additional time next class session?

Homework

Continue logging the physical activity you do in class and outside of class time. Your physical activity homework should now include aerobic-type activities, muscular strength and endurance exercises, and flexibility exercises. Be sure to keep up on this assignment since most of you are likely to select this as a major part of your portfolio.

Resources

NASPE. (2005). *Physical best activity guide: Middle and high school levels.* 2nd ed. Champaign, IL: Human Kinetics.

MUSCLES IN ACTION PLAN

List one exercise for each muscle group listed.

Muscle group	Exercise for muscle group
Quadriceps	
Biceps	
Triceps	
Hamstrings	
Pectorals	
Gastrocnemius	
Deltoid	
Trapezius	
Latissimus dorsi	
Obliques	
Rectus abdominis	
Gluteus maximus	

From R.J. Doan, L.C. MacDonald, and S. Chepko, eds., 2017, *Lesson planning for middle school physical education* (Reston, VA: SHAPE America; Champaign, IL: Human Kinetics). From NASPE, 2005, *Physical Best activity guide: Middle and high school levels*, 2nd edition, (Champaign, IL: Human Kinetics).

LABELED MUSCLE DIAGRAM

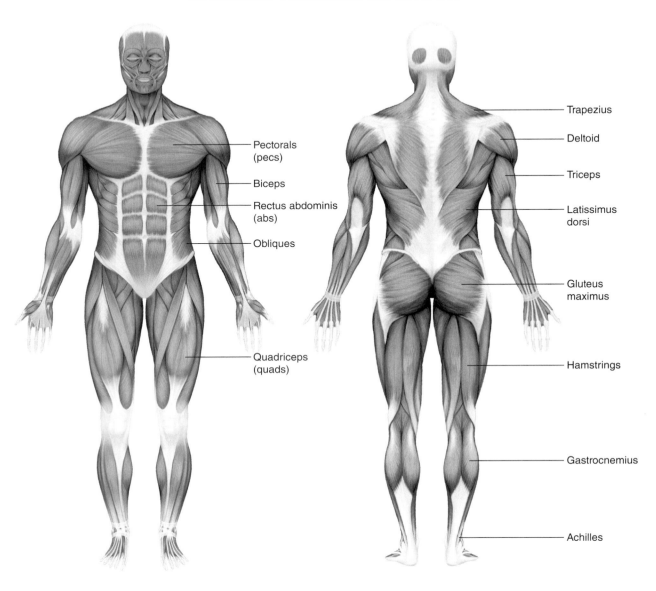

Pectorals
(pecs)

Biceps

Rectus abdominis
(abs)

Obliques

Quadriceps
(quads)

Trapezius

Deltoid

Triceps

Latissimus
dorsi

Gluteus
maximus

Hamstrings

Gastrocnemius

Achilles

WEIGHT-TRAINING CHART

Name: _____ Class: _____ Date: _____

Warm-up weight	Initial 8-12 rep weight	Exercise	Date					
			Set 1		Set 2		Set 3	
			Weight	Reps	Weight	Reps	Weight	Reps

Comments:

From R.J. Doan, L.C. MacDonald, and S. Chepko, eds., 2017, *Lesson planning for middle school physical education* (Reston, VA: SHAPE America; Champaign, IL: Human Kinetics). From NASPE, 2005, *Physical Best activity guide: Middle and high school levels*, 2nd edition, (Champaign, IL: Human Kinetics).

LESSON 8: SHARING MUSCULAR STRENGTH AND ENDURANCE PLANS

Grade-Level Outcomes

Primary Outcome

Engages in physical activity: Plans and implements a program of cross-training to include aerobic, strength & endurance and flexibility training. (S3.M4.8)

Embedded Outcomes

Personal responsibility: Accepts responsibility for improving one's own levels of physical activity and fitness. (S4.M1.8)

Fitness knowledge: Participates in moderate to vigorous aerobic and/or muscle- and bone-strengthening physical activity for at least 60 minutes per day at least 5 times a week. (S3.M6.8)

Lesson Objectives

The learner will:

- evaluate a classmate's muscular strength and endurance routine.
- implement his own muscular strength and endurance routine.
- document his physical activity outside of class and in class.
- assess his current level of physical activity.
- add artifacts to his physical activity portfolio.
- compare his current level of physical activity to the level at which he was participating at the beginning of the year or module.
- reflect on how well he was able to implement the three aspects of cross-training between class and outside of class.

Equipment and Materials

- Copies of the Physical Activity Questionnaire for Older Children (PAQ-C)
- Copies of Weight Training Chart (see lesson 7)
- Pencils
- Clipboards
- Sand bells
- Hand weights
- Medicine balls
- Aerobic steps

Introduction

Today, you will have the opportunity to share the muscular strength and endurance routine that you designed the last time we met. When we share our plans, try to help one another improve the plans. We are all trying to improve our fitness. We also will practice a couple of our muscular strength and endurance routines and add artifacts to our portfolios.

Instructional Task:
Sharing Muscular Strength and Endurance Plans

■ PRACTICE TASK

In small groups, students share and demonstrate the muscular strength and endurance training plans they have developed for home.

Students should evaluate their peers' work critically but also be respectful of peers' feelings.

EMBEDDED OUTCOME: S4.M1.8. Discuss with students the importance of accepting responsibility for improving their own levels of fitness.

Extension

From their partners' feedback, students make changes to their fitness plans. Students write brief summaries of the changes they made and why.

Student Choices/Differentiation

Students may choose their groups.

What to Look For

Students share and demonstrate training exercises that have not been practiced in class.

Instructional Task: Implementation of Muscular Strength and Endurance Plan

■ PRACTICE TASK

For additional feedback by peers and teacher, students select a couple of activities from their plans in which to participate during this task.

Students participate in at least two reps from each activity.

Extension

Students practice other classmates' plans (modified to their skill levels).

Student Choices/Differentiation

Students have their choice of exercises from their muscular strength and endurance plans.

What to Look For

Students demonstrate proper form for the exercises they select.

Instructional Task: Portfolios

■ PRACTICE TASK

Pass out student portfolios and student work. Students choose which artifacts they would like to include in their portfolios.

Help students organize and find a use for the portfolios in their everyday lives.

Student Choices/Differentiation

Students can choose from a variety of their work.

What to Look For

Students choose work that shows a change in thought process or a growth in learning and understanding of the content.

Formal and Informal Assessments

- Student portfolios
- Student demonstrations and sharing of their muscular strength and endurance plans
- Written summary of changes to fitness plans

Closure

This is the end of our module focusing on participation in physical activity. I hope that you feel confident in your ability to combine muscular strength and endurance, aerobic-type activities, and flexibility training into a complete program that you can pursue on your own outside of class.

Reflection

- Were students provided enough time to share and demonstrate their muscular strength and endurance programs in class?
- Based on their demonstrations, do students seem to understand how to design a complete muscular strength and endurance program on their own?

Homework

For homework, you will again take the physical activity questionnaire called the PAQ-C. Compare both results to see if you have increased your participation in physical activity.

In addition, you will finish your portfolio for homework and add a reflection. The reflection is to describe how well you were able to implement the three aspects of cross-training between class and outside of class.

Visit the school's physical education website to review material for the next module.

EMBEDDED OUTCOME: S3.M6.8. Throughout these lessons, you were asked to participate in moderate to vigorous aerobic and muscle- and bone-strengthening physical activity for at least 60 minutes per day and track it in a log. Next class period, please turn in your physical activity logs.

Resources

Melograno, V.J. (2000). *Portfolio assessment for k-12 physical education.* Reston, VA: National Association for Sport and Physical Education.

NASPE. (2005). *Physical best activity guide: Middle and high school levels.* Champaign, IL: Human Kinetics.

CHAPTER 11

Applying Students' Skills and Knowledge to Program Design and Fitness Assessment

This chapter focuses on program design and the assessment of physical activity and fitness. It can be viewed as an extension of the physical activity participation content in Chapter 10, which presented lessons through which students learned to use physical activity logs and fitness test data to design individual fitness plans. This chapter enhances students' experiences by integrating scientific concepts, a greater variety of assessment instruments, and numerous fitness tracking devices into the lessons. Students will enjoy the challenge of developing fitness plans, remediating areas of weaknesses within their plans, and monitoring progress toward their goals.

The three lesson modules contained in this chapter provide opportunities for students to participate in physical activity, assess their fitness levels, and create basic physical activity plans to help ensure that they engage in the recommended amount of daily physical activity. The Fitness Through 5K Program Design Module, for grade 6, teaches exercise science concepts within an aerobic training program in which students train for a 5K fun run. The Physical Activity and Fitness Program Design Module for grade 7 emphasizes using previously learned racket skills for physical activity while students maintain daily and weekly activity logs. Students also design a physical activity program and remediate areas of weakness according to results of the fitness testing. The Monitoring Physical Activity With Technology Module for grade 8 teaches students to use a variety of exercise equipment and technology to plan and implement a physical activity program.

As in Chapter 10, many of the lessons in this chapter do not include warm-ups or cool-downs. It is up to you to choose those most appropriate for the lessons. The modules in this chapter focus on having students learn the five components of health-related fitness and their connections to physical and mental health. Students participate in health-related fitness activities in class and learn to plan a fitness program to use at home. The lessons challenge students to set self-selected fitness and physical activity goals that are appropriate according to their levels of fitness. Because physical education classes alone cannot provide all the physical activity needed to meet the recommended 60 minutes per day of moderate to vigorous physical activity, the modules are designed to foster participation in a wide range of physical activities and to continue them outside of the classroom.

Some teachers feel most comfortable interjecting fitness content into other modules of instruction so that they can teach fitness year-round. We have tried to organize the lessons within the modules in this chapter to allow for that kind of flexibility. For example, while teaching a unit on badminton, you could have students tackle one instructional task from each of the lessons in this chapter for 20 minutes before or after each badminton lesson. Or, you could teach one or two lessons from either of the fitness-related modules in this chapter before your class begins a module on pickleball. If you like addressing fitness one day each week (e.g., Fitness Fridays), you can do that, too. You can place students' physical activity logs and program design worksheets on your school's physical education website so that students can access and update them throughout the year. Of course, you also can simply teach the modules in blocks, as they appear here.

For easy reference, each module begins with a chart of the National Standards and Grade-Level Outcomes addressed within each lesson. The main areas of focus of the Fitness Through 5K Program Design Module for grade 6 are identifying the components of the overload principal (Outcome S3.M11.6) and employing correct techniques and methods of stretching (Outcome S3.M9.6). Students also are expected to accept differences among classmates (Outcome S4.M4.6) and participate in self-selected physical activities outside of physical education class (Outcome S3.M2.6). The main areas of focus in the Physical Activity and Fitness Program Design Module for grade 7 are designing and implementing a program of remediation for two areas of weakness based on the results of health-related fitness assessments (Outcome S3.M15.7) and maintaining a physical activity and nutrition log for at least two weeks (Outcome S3.M16.7). The Monitoring Physical Activity With Technology Module for grade 8 has students using technology to self-monitor the amount of exercise they undertake, with the goal of meeting or exceeding the U.S. Department of Health and Human Services' guideline of 60 minutes of aerobic physical activity each day (2008) and designing and implementing a program of remediation for two areas of weakness based on the results of health-related fitness assessments (Outcome S3.M15.8).

These modules provide excellent examples for implementing physical activity, tracking and assessing fitness levels, and teaching students to design and implement fitness and physical activity plans that will help them stay active for a lifetime.

FITNESS THROUGH 5K PROGRAM DESIGN MODULE (GRADE 6)

Lesson plans in this module were contributed by John Kruse, a middle school physical education teacher with the Los Angeles Unified School District.

Grade-Level Outcomes Addressed, by Lesson	1	2	3	4	5	6	7	8
Standard 1. The physically literate individual demonstrates competency in a variety of motor skills and movement patterns.								
Standard 2. The physically literate individual applies knowledge of concepts, principles, strategies and tactics related to movement and performance.								
Standard 3. The physically literate individual demonstrates the knowledge and skills to achieve and maintain a health-enhancing level of physical activity and fitness.								
Participates in self-selected physical activity outside of physical education class. (S3.M2.6)	E	E	E	E	E	E	E	
Sets and monitors a self-selected physical activity goal for aerobic and/or muscle- and bone-strengthening activity based on current fitness level. (S3.M8.6)	P						E	P
Employs correct techniques and methods of stretching. (S3.M9.6)			P	P	P		P	P
Differentiates between aerobic and anaerobic capacity, and between muscular strength and endurance. (S3.M10.6)					P	P		
Identifies each of the components of the overload principle (FITT formula: frequency, intensity, time, type) for different types of physical activity (aerobic, muscular fitness and flexibility). (S3.M11.6)		P	P	P	P	P	P	P
Describes the role of warm-ups and cool-downs before and after physical activity. (S3.M12.6)			E					
Identifies major muscles used in selected physical activities. (S3.M14.6)						E		
Maintains a physical activity log for at least 2 weeks and reflects on activity levels as documented in the log. (S3.M16.6)	E							E
Standard 4. The physically literate individual exhibits responsible personal and social behavior that respects self and others.								
Accepts differences among classmates in physical development, maturation and varying skill levels by providing encouragement and positive feedback. (S4.M4.6)	E	E		E				
Standard 5. The physically literate individual recognizes the value of physical activity for health, enjoyment, challenge, self-expression and/or social interaction.								
Describes how being physically active leads to a healthy body. (S5.M1.6)		E						
Identifies components of physical activity that provide opportunities for reducing stress and for social interaction. (S5.M2.6)					E			
Describes how moving competently in a physical activity setting creates enjoyment. (S5.M4.6)								E

P = Primary; E = Embedded

LESSON 1: ESTABLISHING A BASELINE

Grade-Level Outcomes

Primary Outcome

Fitness knowledge: Sets and monitors a self-selected physical-activity goal for aerobic and/or muscle- and bone-strengthening activity based on current fitness level. (S3.M8.6)

Embedded Outcomes

Working with others: Accepts differences among classmates in physical development, maturation and varying skill levels by providing encouragement and positive feedback. (S4.M4.6)

Assessment & program planning: Maintains a physical activity log for at least 2 weeks and reflects on activity levels as documented in the log. (S3.M16.6)

Engages in physical activity: Participates in self-selected physical activity outside of physical education class. (S3.M2.6)

Lesson Objectives

The learner will:

- determine his current aerobic fitness level.
- set and monitor a self-selected physical activity goal.

Equipment and Materials

- Beginner's 5K Training Schedule, 1 copy per group of 4 or 5 students (see lesson 2)
- PACER test cadence
- Sound system
- 20-meter PACER course set up with cones
- Stopwatches
- Index cards
- Physical Activity and Nutrition Log templates (weekdays, Saturday, and Sunday), 1 per student (see grade 6 module in Chapter 10, lessons 2 and 5)

Introduction

Today, we will determine our current fitness levels in regard to aerobic fitness. We will discuss the difference between aerobic capacity and cardiorespiratory endurance. After determining a fitness score, each individual will self-select a goal. In the next class, you'll start training to improve your scores.

EMBEDDED OUTCOME: S3.M16.6. Students will create physical activity logs to track and reflect upon their activity levels.

Instructional Task: Aerobic Capacity Assessment

■ PRACTICE TASK

Students choose partners and measure their aerobic fitness. Partners decide whether they want to use the mile run/walk or the PACER test.

Students who choose the mile run/walk should perform a brief warm-up, while the PACER has a built-in warm-up.

Run two heats of both the PACER and the mile run/walk so that each partner has the chance to measure her fitness and to also assist her partner.

Partners should provide encouragement and positive feedback.

EMBEDDED OUTCOME: S4.M4.6. Discuss with students that not all people perform the same. Some people develop earlier and some later. Fitness scores might vary, but we all should encourage one another.

Extension

Discuss how the PACER differs from the mile run/walk and how the PACER is preferred because pacing and motivation are not as much of an issue when compared to participation in the mile.

Student Choices/Differentiation

Students can choose the mile run/walk or the PACER.

What to Look For

- Students keep accurate count of PACER laps.
- Students keep accurate count of laps and mile run/walk times.
- Students encourage partners.

Instructional Task: Goal Setting

■ PRACTICE TASK

On a whiteboard, define *cardiorespiratory endurance* as "the ability to perform large-muscle, whole-body exercise at a moderate to high intensity for extended periods of time."

Explain that cardiorespiratory fitness is important because it provides an indication of a person's ability to perform functional fitness activities of daily life that are dependent on our cardiovascular, respiratory, and muscular systems.

Introduce and explain SMART goals, and have students set a goal to improve on either the number of laps they ran for the PACER or to improve their running time for the mile run/walk.

Extensions

- Explain that the PACER and mile run/walk are designed to measure aerobic capacity. Define *aerobic capacity* on the whiteboard as "the maximal amount of oxygen that the body can take in and use." It is expressed as $\dot{V}O_2$max, in which the $\dot{V}$ stands for volume, the *O2* stands for oxygen, and *max* stands for maximum.
- Discuss how aerobic capacity is a measure of health status rather than functional fitness.

Refinement

Make sure that goals are measurable and achievable.

Student Choices/Differentiation

Students choose SMART goals based on their own fitness levels.

What to Look For

Students set realistic SMART goals for their current fitness levels.

Formal and Informal Assessments

- Baseline aerobic capacity assessment
- Exit slip: Why is cardiorespiratory endurance important?

Journal assignment:

- Are you surprised by your test score today?
- Did you think it would be higher or lower?
- How are you going to make sure that you reach the goal that you set in today's class?

Closure

Review the concept of the healthy fitness zone, and let students know that they will start a 5K run/walk training program to see how they can influence their fitness scores through this type of conditioning program.

EMBEDDED OUTCOME: S3.M2.6 To help them train for the 5K run/walk, instruct students to participate in at least one physical activity of their choice each day outside of physical education class.

Reflection

- What additional help will students with limited technology at home need to complete the homework assignment?
- Do students seem to understand the difference between aerobic capacity and cardiorespiratory endurance?

Homework

Determine your aerobic capacity score. Set a SMART goal for increasing your aerobic capacity.

Start filling in your physical activity and nutrition log.

Resources

The Cooper Institute. (2013). Meredith, M.D., & Welk, G.J. (Eds.). *Fitnessgram & Activitygram test administration manual.* Updated 4th ed. Champaign, IL: Human Kinetics.

Corbin, C.B, Welk, G.J., Richardson, C., Vowell, C., Lambdin, D., & Wikgren, S. (2014). Youth physical fitness: Ten key concepts. *Journal of Physical Education, Recreation & Dance, 85*(2), 22-31.

LESSON 2: BEGIN TRAINING FOR A 5K

Grade-Level Outcomes

Primary Outcome

Fitness knowledge: Identifies each of the components of the overload principle (FITT formula: frequency, intensity, time, type) for different types of physical activity (aerobic, muscular fitness and flexibility). (S3.M11.6)

Embedded Outcomes

Physical activity knowledge: Describes how being physically active leads to a healthy body. (S5.M1.6)

Working with others: Accepts differences among classmates in physical development, maturation and varying skill levels by providing encouragement and positive feedback. (S4.M4.6)

Engages in physical activity: Participates in self-selected physical activity outside of physical education class. (S3.M2.6)

Lesson Objectives

The learner will:

- begin to experience the progressive overload principle through a walk/run progression.
- discuss and list benefits of being physically active.

Equipment and Materials

- Beginner's 5K Training Schedule handout, 1 per group of 4 or 5 students
- Stopwatches, 1 per group of 4 or 5 students
- Whiteboard easel on casters
- Index cards
- Pencils

Introduction

Today, you will start a walk/run program so that you can explore an important concept in program design called the overload principle. This program will take several weeks, and we will incorporate it into our remaining units of instruction. We will incorporate this program to make improvements and to follow the principle of progressive overload. In addition, we will look at how this walk/run program influences your aerobic capacity, which you measured recently through either the PACER or the mile run/walk. Keep in mind that incorporating structured exercise two times per week typically maintains fitness, and incorporating it three or more times per week typically improves fitness.

Instructional Task: Warm-Up

■ PRACTICE TASK

Have students complete a brisk 5-minute walk in small groups of four or five, with one person in each group keeping time.

EMBEDDED OUTCOME: S5.M1.6. While students are completing this walk, have them discuss and come up with a list of the benefits of being physically active.

Student Choices/Differentiation

- Music can be played.
- Students walk at the pace of their choice (encourage a brisk walk).

BEGINNER'S 5K TRAINING SCHEDULE

Week 1		
Workout 1	**Workout 2**	**Workout 3**
1. Walk 5 minutes 2. Jog 1 minute 3. Walk 90 seconds Alternate #2 and #3 for 20 minutes.	Repeat Week 1, Workout 1.	Repeat Week 1, Workout 1.

Week 2		
Workout 1	**Workout 2**	**Workout 3**
1. Walk 5 minutes 2. Jog 90 seconds 3. Walk 2 minutes Alternate #2 and #3 for 20 minutes.	Repeat Week 2, Workout 1.	Repeat Week 2, Workout 1.

Week 3		
Workout 1	**Workout 2**	**Workout 3**
1. Walk 5 minutes 2. Jog 90 seconds 3. Walk 90 seconds 4. Jog 3 minutes 5. Walk 3 minutes Do #2–#5 twice.	Repeat Week 3, Workout 1.	Repeat Week 3, Workout 1.

Week 4		
Workout 1	**Workout 2**	**Workout 3**
1. Walk 5 minutes 2. Jog 3 minutes 3. Walk 90 seconds 4. Jog 5 minutes 5. Walk 2.5 minutes 6. Jog 3 minutes 7. Walk 90 seconds 8. Jog 5 minutes	Repeat Week 4, Workout 1.	Repeat Week 4, Workout 1.

Week 5		
Workout 1	**Workout 2**	**Workout 3**
1. Walk 5 minutes 2. Jog 5 minutes 3. Walk 3 minutes 4. Jog 5 minutes 5. Walk 3 minutes 6. Jog 5 minutes	1. Walk 5 minutes 2. Jog 8 minutes 3. Walk 5 minutes 4. Jog 8 minutes	1. Walk 5 minutes 2. Jog 20 minutes

Week 6		
Workout 1	**Workout 2**	**Workout 3**
1. Walk 5 minutes 2. Jog 5 minutes 3. Walk 3 minutes 4. Jog 8 minutes 5. Walk 3 minutes 6. Jog 5 minutes	1. Walk 5 minutes 2. Jog 10 minutes 3. Walk 3 minutes 4. Jog 10 minutes	1. Walk 5 minutes 2. Jog 22 minutes

Week 7		
Workout 1	**Workout 2**	**Workout 3**
1. Walk 5 minutes 2. Jog 25 minutes	Repeat Week 7, Workout 1.	Repeat Week 7, Workout 1.
Week 8		
Workout 1	**Workout 2**	**Workout 3**
1. Walk 5 minutes 2. Jog 28 minutes	Repeat Week 8, Workout 1.	Repeat Week 8, Workout 1.
Week 9		
Workout 1	**Workout 2**	**Workout 3**
1. Walk 5 minutes 2. Jog 30 minutes	Repeat Week 9, Workout 1.	Repeat Week 9, Workout 1.

Adapted from Couch to 5K® Training Schedule, www.coolrunning.com/engine/2/2_3/181.shtml.

For the full Couch to 5K® training plan, with distances, visit www.coolrunning.com.

What to Look For

- Students are walking briskly.
- Students are discussing as a group the benefits of being physically active.
- Group leaders are precisely timing the 5-minute warm-up.

Instructional Task: Training (Week 1, Workout 1)

■ PRACTICE TASK

Have students alternate 60 seconds of jogging and 90 seconds of walking for a total of 20 minutes.

Leaders in each small group time the 60- and 90-second intervals; you keep track of the 20-minute duration.

EMBEDDED OUTCOME: S4.M4.6 No matter the skill level, have students encourage each other within their small groups.

Refinement

An explanation of forefoot or midfoot running will help students understand how the mechanics of this type of running can help reduce impact forces on the body.

- Run with a slight forward lean.
- Land on the ball of the foot and not the heel.
- Landing on the heel causes impact forces to travel up the leg.
- Landing on the forefoot causes a slight bend in the knee and helps reduce the impact force (it is like landing a jump with knees bent versus knees straight).

Student Choices/Differentiation

- Student leaders can rotate.
- If students struggle with jogging, let them power walk.

Note: You can modify the Beginner's 5K Training Schedule to fit various school and class schedules (e.g., block schedule, shorter or longer class periods).

What to Look For

- Are students following the alternating routine of 60 seconds of jogging and 90 seconds of walking?
- Are students handling the activity fairly easily or are they struggling?
- Are the leaders keeping everyone on task?

Instructional Task: Review of Training Program

■ PRACTICE TASK

Display the definition of *progressive overload* on a portable whiteboard.

Distribute the Beginner's 5K Training Schedule handout to small groups, and have students examine it, looking for evidence of progressive overload.

Have students list on an index card where they see evidence of progressive overload.

Guiding questions for students:

- Can you think of how you could apply the principle of progressive overload to an exercise such as push-ups?
- How would you identify a baseline for push-ups so you can monitor progress?

Extension

Pass out multiple workout designs with progressions. In groups, students identify the overloads in the workouts.

Student Choices/Differentiation

Help students by providing videos and handouts on the overload principle.

What to Look For

- Students are examining the Beginner's 5K Training Schedule handout closely in cooperative groups.
- Students are listing evidence of progressive overload found in the running schedule.
- Students are discussing how the walk/jog program progresses.

Formal and Informal Assessments

Exit slip: Turn in your index cards showing evidence of progressive overload.

Journal assignment:

- After day 1 of training, how do you feel?
- Were peers helpful during the first day of training?
- How are you planning to improve fitness outside of class?

EMBEDDED OUTCOME: S3.M2.6 *To increase overall fitness, try to participate in at least one physical activity outside of physical education class.*

Closure

Have each group share one piece of evidence from their index cards (with the class) and then hand them in as an exit slip.

Reflection

- Examine the exit slips to determine where students are at in their thinking about progressive overload.
- What challenges are likely to present themselves as students experience additional days of this running program and they are introduced to the content of the FITT formula?

Homework

Share with a family member or friend the 5K running plan we are using. Ask if that person would like to partici-pate in the program with you.

Participate in physical activity outside of class, and record the activity and how long you participated in your physical activity log.

Finish your journal assignment.

Resources

Couch to 5K® Running Program: www.coolrunning.com

Internet keyword search: "5K running plans," "training programs," "overload principle"

LESSON 3: TRAINING FOR A 5K, DAY 2

Grade-Level Outcomes

Primary Outcomes

Fitness knowledge: Identifies each of the components of the overload principle (FITT formula: frequency, intensity, time, type) for different types of physical activity (aerobic, muscular fitness and flexibility). (S3.M11.6)

Fitness knowledge: Employs correct techniques and methods of stretching. (S3.M9.6)

Embedded Outcomes

Fitness knowledge: Describes the role of warm-ups and cool-downs before and after physical activity. (S3.M12.6)

Engages in physical activity: Participates in self-selected physical activity outside of physical education class. (S3.M2.6)

Lesson Objectives

The learner will:

- continue his experience of the progressive overload principle through a walk/run progression.
- discuss and list benefits of being physically active.
- perform correct techniques and methods of stretching after participating in a walk/run progression.

Equipment and Materials

- Stopwatches (1 per group of 4 or 5 students)
- Whiteboard easel on casters
- Index cards
- Pencils
- Beginner's 5K Training Schedule, 1 copy per group of 4 or 5 students (see lesson 2)
- Index cards listing the major research findings on the health benefits of physical activity

Introduction

For homework, you were supposed to ask a friend or family member to participate in our 5K running program. Did anyone have success in recruiting?

Today, we will continue our walk/run progression so you can continue to experience the progressive overload principle.

Instructional Task: Warm-Up

■ PRACTICE TASK

Have students complete a brisk 5-minute walk in small groups of four or five, with one person in each group keeping time.

EMBEDDED OUTCOME: S3.M12.6. During the warm-up, have students discuss the role of warm-ups and cool-downs before and after physical activity and place their answers on index cards. Make sure that students are making connections to specific warm-ups and cool-downs for specific activities.

Collect these index cards at the end of the warm-up.

Student Choices/Differentiation

- Student leaders can rotate.
- Students walk at their own pace.

What to Look For

- Students are walking briskly.
- Students are listing as a group the role of warm-ups and cool-downs before and after physical activity.
- Group leaders are timing the 5-minute warm-up precisely.

Instructional Task: Training (Week 1, Workout 2)

■ PRACTICE TASK

Distribute teacher-generated index cards that list the health benefits of physical activity based on major research findings.

Have students alternate 60 seconds of jogging and 90 seconds of walking for a total of 20 minutes.

Leaders in each small group time the 60- and 90-second intervals; you keep track of the 20-minute duration.

During the periods of walking, have students alternate reading and discussing the health benefits of physical activity listed on the index cards.

Note: You can modify the Beginner's 5K Training Schedule to fit various school and class schedules (e.g., block schedule, shorter or longer class periods).

Refinement

Make sure students know to land on their forefoot or midfoot when running.

Guiding questions for students:

- Did any of the benefits on the index cards match the ones you generated in your groups?
- If you have heard these benefits before, where did you learn them?
- Were you surprised by any of the benefits?

Student Choices/Differentiation

- Student leaders can rotate.
- Students can be grouped by pace.
- Students can walk at a pace comfortable for reading and talking instead of brisk walking.

What to Look For

- Are students following the routine of alternating 60 seconds of jogging with 90 seconds of walking?
- Are they discussing and reading aloud the benefits of physical activity from the index cards?
- Are students landing on the forefoot or midfoot when running instead of heel striking?

Instructional Task: Review of Training Program

■ PRACTICE TASK

Define *progressive overload* and *frequency* on the portable whiteboard.

Guiding questions for students:

- How many times each week do you need to train to maintain fitness?
- How many times each week do you need to train to improve fitness?

- An inactive person decides to start an exercise program. She decides to use the progressive overload principle. As a result, what is this person likely to avoid?
- Why is overload necessary to improve fitness?

Student Choices/Differentiation

Have handouts or videos available for students to use if needed.

What to Look For

- Students recognize that training two days per week typically helps to *maintain* fitness, and training three or more times per week typically helps to *improve* fitness.
- Students are able to answer questions and give examples.

Instructional Task: Stretching

▥ PRACTICE TASK

Demonstrate proper stretching of the major leg muscles.

Have students perform these stretches while you provide feedback.

Remind students that stretching is best performed at the end of training when muscles are really warm and that there is no scientific evidence that stretching before physical activity is beneficial or prevents injury. The only exception might be in sports such as gymnastics and certain types of dance, in which pre-activity stretching helps increase range of motion.

Extensions

- Discuss the concept of range of motion and how flexibility and stretching can help maintain or improve range of motion.
- Discuss how flexible hamstring and hip flexor muscles can help prevent low back pain when combined with strong abdominal muscles.

Refinement

Make sure that students are moving slowly to stretch (without bouncing).

Student Choices/Differentiation

- Model various stretches for the same muscle or muscle group.
- Provide a list of modified stretches, if needed.

What to Look For

- Are students holding the stretch long enough to make improvements in range of motion or to maintain range of motion?
- Are they holding the stretch and not bouncing?

Formal and Informal Assessments

- Informal assessments
- Warm-up index cards

Closure

Journal assignment:

- Was running and walking today easier or more difficult than in previous lessons?
- Where does frequency fall into the goal you set in Lesson 1?
- What are some critical elements of stretching?

EMBEDDED OUTCOME: S3.M2.6. To help students in their training, encourage them to participate in at least one self-physical activity of their choice outside of class each day.

Reflection

- Examine the index cards that students completed during the warm-up.
- Do students' answers differ significantly from the content presented later in class?
- Is it likely that the content provided during the walk/run on the teacher-provided index cards will change their thinking about how being physically active leads to a healthy body?
- Are faster students being supportive of slower students within groups?
- Are students working together to learn the content during the walking portion of the walk/jog?

Homework

Share with your parents or guardians what you learned in physical education today about the benefits of being physically active.

If this lesson on walk/run progression interests you, you might want to look into downloading an app with a parent's or guardian's permission. If you download an app, you may use it in class with your smartphone. Your parents also might be interested in this app. In fact, many adults have a difficult time starting an exercise program, and an app can help with that.

Participate in physical activity outside of class, and record the activity and how long you participated in your physical activity log.

Finish your journal assignment.

Resources

Couch to 5K® Running Program: www.coolrunning.com

Internet keyword search: "5K running plans," "safety in stretching," "benefits of physical activity"

LESSON 4:
INTENSITY AND TRAINING FOR A 5K, DAY 3

Grade-Level Outcomes

Primary Outcomes

Fitness knowledge: Identifies each of the components of the overload principle (FITT formula: frequency, intensity, time, type) for different types of physical activity (aerobic, muscular fitness and flexibility). (S3.M11.6)

Fitness knowledge: Employs correct techniques and methods of stretching. (S3.M9.6)

Embedded Outcomes

Working with others: Accepts differences among classmates in physical development, maturation and varying skill levels by providing encouragement and positive feedback. (S4.M4.6)

Engages in physical activity: Participates in self-selected physical activity outside of physical education class. (S3.M2.6)

Lesson Objectives

The learner will:

- continue her experience of the progressive overload principle through a walk/run progression.
- discuss and list benefits of being physically active.
- discuss intensity and why it is important in a workout.
- perform correct stretching techniques after participating in a walk/run progression.

Equipment and Materials

- Stopwatches (1 per group of 4 or 5 students)
- Whiteboard easel on casters
- Index cards
- Pencils
- Pedometers
- Beginner's 5K Training Schedule, 1 copy per group of 4 or 5 students (see lesson 2)

Introduction

Today, we will continue our walk/run progression so you can continue to experience the progressive overload principle. Today's major topic is intensity and where we find intensity in our walk/jog progression.

Instructional Task: Warm-Up

■ PRACTICE TASK

Have students complete a brisk 5-minute walk in small groups of four or five, with one person in each group keeping time.

Have students again discuss the benefits of being physically active.

Guiding questions for students:

- Did your discussions change after using the provided index cards in the last lesson? In what ways?
- Did knowing the additional benefits of physical activity motivate you to walk a little faster today?
- If you were going to explain the benefits to a sibling or parent, what would you say?

Student Choices/Differentiation

Students can use a running program they have downloaded to their smartphones.

What to Look For

- Students are walking briskly enough to elevate heart rate.
- Students' discussion of the benefits of physical activity is more sophisticated.
- Group leaders are precisely timing the 5-minute warm-up.

Instructional Task: Training (Week 1, Workout 3)

■ PRACTICE TASK

Provide some or all students with pedometers depending on class size and available equipment.

Have students alternate 60 seconds of jogging and 90 seconds of walking for a total of 20 minutes.

Leaders in each small group time the 60- and 90-second intervals; you keep track of the 20-minute duration.

Have students keep track of the distance traveled during the 20-minute walk/jog (e.g., How many laps did they cover during that time? How many steps?).

Refinement

Students should focus on a relaxed arm swing while running.

EMBEDDED OUTCOME: S4.M4.6 Discuss with students that not all classmates perform at the same fitness level as themselves. Teach students how to accept differences among classmates and to provide encouragement and positive feedback.

Student Choices/Differentiation

Students can choose to run with a peer with the same running ability.

Note: You can modify the Beginner's 5K Training Schedule to fit various school and class schedules (e.g., block schedule, shorter or longer class periods).

What to Look For

- Students are alternating the 60 seconds of jogging with 90 seconds of walking.
- Students are keeping track of distance traveled (e.g., laps around the school, field, track).

Instructional Task: Review of Training Program

■ PRACTICE TASK

Define *progressive overload*, *frequency*, and *intensity* on the portable whiteboard.

Ask students how far they traveled today during the 20-minute walk/jog.

In week 2 of our walk/jog training program, we will step it up to 90 seconds of jogging and 2 minutes of walking for a total of 20 minutes. This week, we alternated 60 seconds of jogging with 90 seconds of walking.

Guiding questions for students:

- Form a hypothesis about the distance you will travel next week. If we increase the amount of running to 90 seconds rather than 60 seconds and increase the walking to 2 minutes rather than 90 seconds, what do you think your distance traveled might be?
- If you see an increase in the distance traveled, does this tell you something about the intensity of your workout?

Extension

Provide the following example: A group of students were able to perform two to four Fitnessgram push-ups at the beginning of the school year. As a result, the teacher suggested that these students perform 10 modified push-ups with the rest of the class, who were performing 10 traditional push-ups for a few weeks as part of their physical education class. After a few weeks, the teacher suggested that the first group of students attempt 10 traditional push-ups for training.

Guiding questions for students:

- What component of the overload principle is this?
- How did you come up with that answer?

Student Choices/Differentiation

- Provide videos or handouts for lower-skilled students.
- More advanced students can draw a visual representation (graph) of what the training program will look like over a span of weeks in addition to identifying *intensity* as the answer.

What to Look For

- Students recognize that, with an increase in running time, they should see an increase in the distance traveled even though they are increasing the walking time, as well.
- Students recognize that if they don't see an increase in the distance traveled next week, they are likely to see an increase the following week because the progression continues.

Instructional Task: Stretching

▪ PRACTICE TASK

Demonstrate for students the proper way to stretch the major muscles of the legs after walking and jogging.

Have students perform these stretches while you provide feedback.

On the whiteboard, write *contract-relax-antagonist-contract* (CRAC) and the definition for *PNF* (proprioceptive neuromuscular facilitation).

Explain what PNF is and how the CRAC sequence works for PNF.

Demonstrate how they can do this individually or in pairs.

Extensions

- Depending on class time, conduct a more in-depth discussion of how PNF stretching works.
- Have students stretch the same muscle or muscle group multiple times. Ask if they see an improvement in the range of motion each time.

Student Choices/Differentiation

- Students can perform PNF stretching in pairs or individually.
- Student volunteers can lead small groups of students.

What to Look For

- Students are holding the stretch long enough to make improvements in range of motion or to maintain range of motion.
- Students are following the sequence for PNF stretching.

Formal and Informal Assessments

- Index cards (identifying *intensity* as the component of overload being manipulated)
- Informal assessment on stretching
- Exit slip: What is the difference between PNF and static stretching?

Closure

- Have the walk/jog groups share something new that they learned today.
- How does PNF compare to static stretching?
- Explain in your own words how progressive overload works.

EMBEDDED OUTCOME: S3.M2.6 *To increase overall fitness, try to participate in at least one physical activity outside of physical education class.*

Journal assignment:

- How do you plan to use intensity to achieve your goal?
- Do you find stretching to be enjoyable or not? Why?

Reflection

- Are students interested in this new concept of PNF stretching?
- Do students seem to understand that as the distance increases in the 20-minute walk/jog, the intensity of the workout has also increased?

Homework

Demonstrate for you parent or guardian how PNF stretching works. Make sure everyone's muscles are warmed up before doing this.

Participate in physical activity outside of class, and record the activity and how long you participated in your physical activity log.

Finish your journal assignment.

Resources

Corbin, C.B., & Lindsay, R. (2007). *Fitness for life.* Updated 5th ed. Champaign, IL: Human Kinetics.

Couch to 5K® Running Program: www.coolrunning.com

Internet keyword search: "5K running plans"

LESSON 5:
AEROBIC VERSUS ANAEROBIC ACTIVITY

Grade-Level Outcomes

Primary Outcomes

Fitness knowledge: Identifies each of the components of the overload principle (FITT formula: frequency, intensity, time, type) for different types of physical activity (aerobic, muscular fitness and flexibility). (S3.M11.6)

Fitness knowledge: Differentiates between aerobic and anaerobic capacity, and between muscular strength and endurance. (S3.M10.6)

Fitness knowledge: Employs correct techniques and methods of stretching. (S3.M9.6)

Embedded Outcomes

Health: Identifies components of physical activity that provide opportunities for reducing stress and for social interaction. (S5.M2.6)

Engages in physical activity: Participates in self-selected physical activity outside of physical education class. (S3.M2.6)

Lesson Objectives

The learner will:

- continue his experience of the progressive overload principle through a walk/run progression.
- participate in correct stretching techniques after participating in a walk/run progression.
- differentiate between aerobic and anaerobic activities.

Equipment and Materials

- Beginner's 5K Training Schedule, 1 copy per group of 4 or 5 students (see lesson 2)
- Stopwatches (1 per group of 4 or 5 students)
- Whiteboard easel on casters
- Index cards
- Pencils
- Pedometers

Introduction

Today we will continue our walk/run progression so you can continue to experience the progressive overload principle. Today, the key concepts you will be learning are intensity and aerobic versus anaerobic fitness.

Instructional Task: Warm-Up

■ PRACTICE TASK

Have students complete a brisk 5-minute walk in small groups of four or five, with one person in each group keeping time.

EMBEDDED OUTCOME: S5.M4.6. Many people walk with a friend or small group for exercise. Discuss with students how this might increase enjoyment or reduce stress for people who might not be motivated to exercise.

Student Choices/Differentiation

- Student leaders can rotate.
- Students can rotate groups or choose to walk with new peers.

What to Look For

- Students are walking briskly.
- Students' discussion of using physical activity for enjoyment is more sophisticated.
- Group leaders are precisely timing the 5-minute warm-up.

Instructional Task: Training (Week 2, Workout 1)

■ PRACTICE TASK

Have students alternate 90 seconds of jogging and 2 minutes of walking for a total of 20 minutes.

Provide pedometers to some or all students, depending on class size and available equipment.

Leaders in each small group time the 90-second and 2-minute intervals; you keep track of the 20-minute duration.

Have students keep track of the distance traveled during the 20-minute walk/jog (e.g., How many laps did they cover during that time?).

Students with pedometers can also keep track of how many steps were taken during this time.

Refinements

- Efficient runners do not bounce up and down very much when they run. Have students attempt to run without bouncing. Students can assess each other by watching a classmate run next to a wall or fence. Using the fence or wall as a reference point, students should see minimal bouncing up and down.
- Encourage students to use a slight forward lean when running. This makes it easier for the foot to land under the center of gravity rather than having the heel strike out in front of the center of gravity. Heel striking makes it difficult for the body to reduce impact forces.

Student Choices/Differentiation

- Rotate student leaders.
- Students can choose their groups.
- Students can use a pedometer or a running plan app on their smartphones.
- Students can watch video clips of good running form.
- Let students take breaks if they need them.
- Students can listen to music for motivation (as long as they can keep up with the changing pace commands).

Note: You can modify the Beginner's 5K Training Schedule to fit various school and class schedules (e.g., block schedule, shorter or longer class periods).

What to Look For

- Students are alternating 90 seconds of jogging with 2 minutes of walking.
- Students are keeping track of distance traveled (e.g., laps around the school, field, track).
- Students are maintaining good running and walking form while doing the training program.

Instructional Task: Review of Training Program

■ PRACTICE TASK

Define *progressive overload*, *frequency*, *intensity*, and *time* on the portable whiteboard.

Guiding questions for students:

- How far did you travel today using the 20-minute walk/jog?
- How many steps did you take today?
- Was your hypothesis from last week correct?

Point out that an increase in distance means that they have increased their intensity.

If you covered the same distance, then you definitely will see an increase in week 3 when we increase the amount of jogging again. What other data did we collect in class that would indicate an increase in intensity?

Student Choices/Differentiation

Students may use visual aids defining terminology to help them remember the concepts.

What to Look For

- Students recognize that progressive overload will result in an increase in intensity.
- Students are able to apply the overload concepts when answering questions.

Instructional Task: Stretching

■ PRACTICE TASK

Practice and reinforce PNF and static stretching after the physical activity.

Extension

Depending on class time, conduct a more in-depth discussion of how PNF stretching works.

Student Choices/Differentiation

- Students may do PNF stretching in pairs or individually.
- Students may do static stretching.

What to Look For

- Students are holding the stretch long enough to make improvements in range of motion or to maintain range of motion.
- Students are following the sequence for PNF stretching.

Instructional Task: Aerobic Versus Anaerobic

■ PRACTICE TASK

Define *aerobic* and *anaerobic* on the portable whiteboard as follows:

Aerobic = slow energy conversion

Anaerobic = quick energy conversion

Explain how the body converts energy that we take in (food = chemical energy) into human movement and that our bodies have different energy systems that allow us to convert that energy.

One system does this slowly and requires oxygen to do so. This is our aerobic energy system, and this system is utilized when the body has time to take in and use oxygen for energy.

The other system is very quick. It allows us to produce movement quickly and does not require oxygen. This is our anaerobic system. The letters an in front of aerobic mean "without oxygen."

Point out that it is fairly simple to differentiate between activities that are aerobic and anaerobic if we think about it this way.

Extension

Pass out a worksheet listing various activities and exercises. Have students check off whether the activities are aerobic or anaerobic in nature.

Guiding questions for students:

- Do you think today's walk/jog was aerobic or anaerobic?
- To derive the most health benefits for your cardiorespiratory system, would you choose activities that are aerobic or anaerobic?

Student Choices/Differentiation

- Have videos or handouts available.
- Allow students to do worksheets in partners.

What to Look For

- Students recognize that activities that are performed quickly (like sprinting) will use the anaerobic system since the body does not have time to take in and use oxygen to produce the movement.
- Students recognize that activities that are performed slowly (like walking or jogging) are aerobic since the body has time to take in and use the oxygen.
- Students recognize that today's activity was aerobic in nature.

Formal and Informal Assessments

- Worksheet on aerobic versus anaerobic
- Class discussion on aerobic versus anaerobic

Closure

- Have the walk/jog groups share something new that they learned today.
- Define *aerobic* and *anaerobic* in your own words.
- Can you provide an example of a sport or activity that is largely aerobic or anaerobic?
- What two pieces of data would suggest that you had an increase in intensity today? (Answer: an increase in distance covered in 20 minutes; an increase in the number of steps taken in 20 minutes)

EMBEDDED OUTCOME: S3.M2.6. *To increase overall fitness, try to participate in at least one physical activity outside of physical education class. Try to have a good mix of aerobic and anaerobic activities.*

Journal assignment:

- Is the training getting easier?
- Which do you prefer, aerobic or anaerobic activities? Why?
- Which do you think your parents prefer, aerobic or anaerobic activities? Do you think this influences you at all?

Reflection

- Do students seem to understand the difference between aerobic and anaerobic?
- Does simplifying the terms to "aerobic = slow" and "anaerobic = quick" help sixth graders better understand a concept that can be very difficult?

Homework

Think about the difference between muscular strength and endurance. See if you can find good definitions for these terms on the Internet, and bring them to class next time.

Participate in physical activity outside of class, and record the activity and how long you participated in your physical activity log.

Finish your journal assignment.

Resources

Brooks, G.A., Fahey, T.D., & Baldwin, K. (2004). *Exercise physiology: Human bioenergetics and its applications.* 4th ed. New York: McGraw-Hill Education.

Corbin, C.B., & Lindsay, R. (2007). *Fitness for life.* Updated 5th ed. Champaign, IL: Human Kinetics.

Internet keyword search: "5K running plans"

LESSON 6:
MUSCULAR STRENGTH AND ENDURANCE

Grade-Level Outcomes

Primary Outcomes

Fitness knowledge: Identifies each of the components of the overload principle (FITT formula: frequency, intensity, time, type) for different types of physical activity (aerobic, muscular fitness and flexibility). (S3.M11.6)

Fitness knowledge: Differentiates between aerobic and anaerobic capacity, and between muscular strength and endurance. (S3.M10.6)

Embedded Outcomes

Fitness knowledge: Identifies major muscles used in selected physical activities. (S3.M14.6)

Engages in physical activity: Participates in self-selected physical activity outside of physical education class. (S3.M2.6)

Lesson Objectives

The learner will:

- continue her experience of the progressive overload principle through a walk/run progression.
- differentiate between muscular strength and muscular endurance.

Equipment and Materials

- Beginner's 5K Training Schedule, 1 copy per group of 4 or 5 students (see lesson 2)
- Stopwatches (1 per group of 4 or 5 students)
- Whiteboard easel on casters
- Index cards
- Pencils
- Pedometers

Introduction

Today, we will continue our walk/run progression so that you can continue to experience the progressive overload principle. In addition, we will discuss the difference between muscular strength and muscular endurance.

Instructional Task: Warm-Up

■ PRACTICE TASK

Have students complete a brisk 5-minute walk in small groups of four or five, with one student in each group keeping time.

Have students discuss their understanding of the differences between aerobic and anaerobic.

Guiding questions for students:

- Which of these is quick-converting energy and which is slow-converting energy?
- What types of activities can we call aerobic and anaerobic?
- Are all activities purely aerobic or anaerobic? Is it possible that some are a combination of the two?

Student Choices/Differentiation

Students can choose a dynamic warm-up as an alternative.

What to Look For

- Students walk briskly.
- Student groups time their 5-minute warm-ups precisely.
- Students know the basic differences between aerobic and anaerobic fitness.

Instructional Task: Training (Week 2, Workout 2)

■ PRACTICE TASK

Have students alternate 90 seconds of jogging and 2 minutes of walking for a total of 20 minutes.

Leaders in each small group time the 90-second and 2-minute intervals; you keep track of the 20-minute duration.

Have students keep track of the distance traveled (e.g., how many laps they cover, how many steps they take) during the 20-minute walk/jog.

Have students use pedometers to track total number of steps taken.

Student Choices/Differentiation

- Students can use pedometers or a running plan app.
- Allow students to take water breaks if needed.

Note: You can modify the Beginner's 5K Training Schedule to fit various school and class schedules (e.g., block schedule, shorter or longer class periods).

What to Look For

- Students alternate 90 seconds of jogging with 2 minutes of walking.
- Students track distance traveled (e.g., laps around the school, field, track).

Instructional Task: Review of Training Program

■ PRACTICE TASK

Define *progressive overload*, *frequency*, *intensity*, *time*, and *type* on the whiteboard.

Ask students how far they traveled today during the 20-minute walk/jog.

We have been building our vocabulary on the whiteboard each day. Let's look closer at frequency, intensity, time, and type.

Lead a class discussion on the FITT formula. Point out that it is often confused as a principle of exercise, but it simply is a formula that some people use to help them design structured exercise programs and to better use the principle of progressive overload. Progressive overload is the principle of exercise that students really need to understand.

Guiding questions for students:

- How often (Frequency) do you think you need to exercise or participate in exercise or physical activity each week to make improvements in fitness?
- How often (Frequency) for maintaining fitness?
- What principle of exercise can you use to gradually increase the Intensity of exercise over time?
- How long (Time) would you need to spend on aerobic-type activities to see significant health benefits?
- Can you think of various activities (Type) that you could use as aerobic activities to see significant improvements or maintenance in health-related fitness?

Student Choices/Differentiation

Let students review videos or handouts on material.

What to Look For

- Students recognize that the FITT formula is not a principle of exercise.
- Students recognize that the FITT formula can help some people design an appropriate exercise program.
- Students are actively engaged in the discussion.

Instructional Task:
Muscular Strength Versus Muscular Endurance

■ PRACTICE TASK

Define *muscular strength* and *muscular endurance* on the portable whiteboard.

Lead a class discussion about the differences between these two components of fitness.

Guiding questions for students:

- Do you think the walk/jog program contributes more to muscular strength or to muscular endurance?
- Can you identify the major muscles used in the walk/jog program?
- What are other activities that you could undertake to improve the endurance in these muscles?

EMBEDDED OUTCOME: S3.M14.6. Use the guiding questions to help students identify and understand the functions of muscles in the lower body.

Extensions

- List several activities on the whiteboard and see if students can differentiate between activities that improve or maintain muscular strength or muscular endurance.
- Conduct an in-depth conversation about the relationship between muscular strength and endurance.

Guiding questions for students:

- What are some fitness assessments that are commonly used in physical education to measure muscular strength and endurance?
- Which one (muscular strength or endurance) do you think is most important for your favorite sport?

Student Choices/Differentiation

Let students review videos or handouts on material.

What to Look For

- Students recognize that the walk/jog program is working primarily on their muscular endurance because, by definition, muscular strength is the maximum force that a muscle or group of muscles can produce one time.
- Students recognize that the walk/jog program is specific to running and walking more efficiently and that if they want to increase muscular strength, they would have to use resistance training instead.
- Students differentiate between activities that are specific to improving muscular strength and improving muscular endurance.

Instructional Task: Pop Quiz

This is a formative assessment meant as a tool for feedback on students learning the material.

▪ PRACTICE TASK

Administer a short pop quiz on the concepts previously taught to this point of the module.

Student Choices/Differentiation

Provide any testing accommodations needed.

What to Look For

Students demonstrate knowledge of material taught to this point of the module (FITT and progressive overload).

Formal and Informal Assessments

- Class discussions around muscular strength and muscular endurance concepts
- Teacher-created pop quiz

Journal assignment:

- Which do you enjoy more, muscle-strengthening or muscle-endurance activities?
- Do you feel that you are growing stronger in this module, even if you are not using resistance training?

Closure

- Discuss the answers of the pop quiz.
- Ask students to separate into small groups of four or five. Ask groups to volunteer something they learned today about muscular strength or muscular endurance. Dismiss groups as they provide sufficient answers.

EMBEDDED OUTCOME: S3.M2.6 *To increase overall fitness, try to participate in at least one physical activity outside of physical education class. Try to complete both muscle-strengthening and muscle-endurance activities.*

Reflection

- Do students seem to understand the difference between muscular strength and muscular endurance?
- Are students showing appropriate motivation during the training portion of the lesson?
- Are students working well in groups?

Homework

Participate in physical activity outside of class, and record in your physical activity log the physical activity and how long you participated in it.

Finish your journal assignment.

Resources

Corbin, C.B., & Lindsay, R. (2007). *Fitness for life*. Updated 5th ed. Champaign, IL: Human Kinetics.

Internet keyword search: "5K running plans"

LESSON 7: BONE-STRENGTHENING VERSUS MUSCLE-STRENGTHENING ACTIVITIES

Grade-Level Outcomes

Primary Outcomes

Fitness knowledge: Identifies each of the components of the overload principle (FITT formula: frequency, intensity, time, type) for different types of physical activity (aerobic, muscular fitness and flexibility). (S3.M11.6)

Fitness knowledge: Employs correct techniques and methods of stretching. (S3.M9.6)

Embedded Outcomes

Fitness knowledge: Sets and monitors a self-selected physical-activity goal for aerobic and/or muscle- and bone-strengthening activity based on current fitness level. (S3.M8.6)

Engages in physical activity: Participates in self-selected physical activity outside of physical education class. (S3.M2.6)

Lesson Objectives

The learner will:

- continue his experience of the progressive overload principle through a walk/run progression.
- display correct stretching techniques after participating in a walk/run progression.
- differentiate between muscle-strengthening and bone-strengthening physical activities.

Equipment and Materials

- Stopwatches (1 per group of four or five students)
- Whiteboard easel on casters
- Index cards
- Pencils
- Index cards with definitions and examples of bone-strengthening and muscle-strengthening activities
- Small whiteboards (about 8 1/2 × 11 inches; 22 × 28 cm), 1 per small group
- Dry-erase markers (1 per small group)
- Beginner's 5K Training Schedule, 1 copy per group of 4 or 5 students (see lesson 2)

Introduction

Today, we will continue our walk/run progression so that you can continue to experience the progressive overload principle. In addition, we will review the difference between muscle-strengthening and bone-strengthening physical activities and also learn about aerobic conditioning.

Instructional Task: Warm-Up

■ PRACTICE TASK

Have students complete a brisk 5-minute walk in small groups of four or five, with one person in each group keeping time.

Have students discuss in their small groups the differences between bone-strengthening and muscle-strengthening exercises and what activities contribute to each.

Student Choices/Differentiation

Student leaders can rotate.

What to Look For

- Students walk briskly.
- Student groups time their 5-minute warm-ups precisely.

Instructional Task: Training (Week 3, Workout 1)

■ PRACTICE TASK

While students perform the walking portion of their walk/jog activity, they read and discuss the teacher-provided index cards that include definitions and examples of muscle-strengthening and bone-strengthening exercises and aerobic conditioning.

Have students do two repetitions of the following:

1. Jog for 90 seconds.
2. Walk for 90 seconds.
3. Jog for 3 minutes.
4. Walk for 3 minutes.

Group leaders use stopwatches to monitor their groups. Provide each group with a laminated index card specifying the progression.

Have students track distance traveled.

Have students encourage one another within their small groups.

Note: You can modify the Beginner's 5K Training Schedule to fit various school and class schedules (e.g., block schedule, shorter or longer class periods).

Student Choices/Differentiation

- Student leaders can rotate.
- Students can choose their own groups.
- Students can walk at a pace comfortable for reading and talking instead of brisk walking.

What to Look For

- Students alternate jogging and walking.
- Students keep track of distance traveled (e.g., laps around the school, field, track).
- Students read about and discuss muscle-strengthening and bone-strengthening activities during the walking portion of the activity.

Instructional Task: Review of Training Program

■ PRACTICE TASK

Define *progressive overload*, *frequency*, *intensity*, *time*, and *type* on the whiteboard.

Guiding questions for students:

- How far did you travel today during your 20-minute walk/jog?
- Are you seeing a trend in the distance you're covering?
- What are you seeing in regard to intensity?

Briefly review the concept of the FITT formula.

Extension

Challenge students to apply the FITT formula to another activity besides walking and jogging (e.g., swimming or cycling).

Student Choices/Differentiation

Have examples to help students use the FITT formula.

What to Look For

- Students recognize that the FITT formula is not a principle of exercise.
- Students recognize that FITT is a formula that can help some people better design an exercise program.
- Students recognize that the distance they cover and the overall intensity of the activity are increasing.

Instructional Task: Stretching

■ PRACTICE TASK

Have students perform stretches for the major muscle groups of the legs.

Extension

Peer assessment: Have students video-record peers performing stretches. Have peers use a teacher-generated checklist to make sure that students perform the stretches appropriately.

Student Choices/Differentiation

- Students can do PNF stretching in pairs or individually.
- Students can do static stretching.

What to Look For

- Students hold the stretch long enough to maintain or improve range of motion.
- Students follow the sequence for PNF stretching.

Instructional Task: Bone-Strengthening Versus Muscle-Strengthening Activities

■ PRACTICE TASK

Define *bone-strengthening activities* and *muscle-strengthening activities* on the portable whiteboard.

Provide each small group with a small whiteboard and dry-erase marker.

Ask students based on what they have learned today whether the walk/run is a muscle-strengthening or bone-strengthening exercise. Have them explain their answers on the whiteboard.

On the word "Go!" each group holds up its whiteboard to reveal its answer. Have each group explain its answer.

Extension

EMBEDDED OUTCOME: S3.M8.6. Have students evaluate their daily activities and determine a goal for either bone-strengthening or muscle-strengthening exercise.

Student Choices/Differentiation

Students can choose groups.

What to Look For

- Students recognize that the walk/jog program is primarily bone strengthening since there is an impact with the ground.
- Students recognize that the walk/jog program is not really muscle strengthening since this would require resistance training instead.

Formal and Informal Assessments

- Whiteboard activity and class discussion
- Peer assessment: teacher-created checklist on the critical elements of stretching
- Exit slip: Set a goal for either bone-strengthening or muscle-strengthening exercise.

Journal assignment:

- What is the major difference between bone-strengthening and muscle-strengthening activities?
- With regard to how you feel during your training, are you improving fitness?
- Using your vocabulary words, please explain why you are becoming more successful in your training.

Closure

EMBEDDED OUTCOME: S3.M2.6. *To increase overall fitness, try to participate in at least one physical activity outside of physical education class.*

Reflection

- Do students seem to understand the difference between bone strengthening and muscle strengthening?
- Do students recognize that activities can be both aerobic conditioning and bone strengthening?
- Were students able to justify their answers?

Homework

We are going to start planning a 5K fun run next class. See if you can come up with materials to help in the planning process.

We will have our end-of-module quiz. Make sure you review material you learned on the school's physical education website.

Make sure you have your physical activity log filled out completely and ready to be turned in next class. Write a brief reflection on your activity levels and any patterns you see.

Finish your journal assignment.

Resources

U.S. Department of Health and Human Services. (2008). *Physical activity guidelines for Americans*. Washington, DC: Author. Available at www.health.gov.

Internet keyword search: "5K running plans"

LESSON 8: ASSESSMENT DAY

Grade-Level Outcomes

Primary Outcomes

Fitness knowledge: Identifies each of the components of the overload principle (FITT formula: frequency, intensity, time, type) for different types of physical activity (aerobic, muscular fitness and flexibility). (S3.M11.6)

Fitness knowledge: Sets and monitors a self-selected physical-activity goal for aerobic and/or muscle- and bone-strengthening activity based on current fitness level. (S3.M8.6)

Fitness knowledge: Employs correct techniques and methods of stretching. (S3.M9.6)

Embedded Outcomes

Self-expression & enjoyment: Describes how moving competently in a physical activity setting creates enjoyment. (S5.M4.6)

Assessment & program planning: Maintains a physical activity log for at least 2 weeks and reflects on activity levels as documented in the log. (S3.M16.6)

Lesson Objectives

The learner will:

- determine her current aerobic fitness level and compare it to her score from Lesson 1.
- demonstrate her knowledge of the overload principle.
- monitor a self-selected physical activity goal.
- plan a 5K fun run.

Equipment and Materials

- Stopwatches (1 per group of 4 or 5 students)
- Whiteboard easel on casters
- Index cards
- Pencils
- Index cards with definitions of aerobic conditioning, bone-strengthening activities, and muscle-strengthening activities
- Beginner's 5K Training Schedule, 1 copy per group of 4 or 5 students (see lesson 2)

Introduction

EMBEDDED OUTCOME: S3.M16.6. Maintains a physical activity log for at least 2 weeks and reflects on activity levels as documented in the log.

Turn in your physical activity logs for outside of physical education class. Was anyone able to fill in each day of the log? What was your favorite activity? What FITT principle did you improve most with your activity log?

We did not make it through the beginner's 5K training program in class, but I think you all improved fitness. Today, you will perform the same aerobic capacity assessment from lesson 1. Please try your hardest, and let's see whether your scores improve!

You also will take the end-of-module quiz.

Instructional Task:
Aerobic Capacity Assessment Post-Test

■ PRACTICE TASK

Students choose partners and measure their aerobic fitness.

Students must choose the same test that they performed earlier in the module (mile run/walk or the PACER).

Please note that students who choose the mile run/walk will need to perform a brief warm-up; however, the PACER has a built-in warm-up.

Run two heats of both the PACER and mile run/walk so that each partner has a chance to measure his fitness and also to assist his partner.

Partners should provide encouragement and positive feedback.

EMBEDDED OUTCOME: S5.M4.6 Through class discussion, help students make a connection between moving competently in a physical activity setting and enjoyment.

Guiding questions for students:

- How does it feel to take the test a second time?
- Did you reach your goal?
- How does it feel to set a goal and achieve it?
- Do you think you could do this with other physical activities? Which ones?

What to Look For

- Students are keeping accurate count of PACER laps.
- Students are keeping accurate count of laps and mile run/walk time.
- Students are encouraging their partners.

Instructional Task: Stretching

■ PRACTICE TASK

Have students perform stretches for the major muscle groups of the legs.

Refinement

Have students focus on the critical elements that they need to improve according to the peer assessment from Lesson 7.

Student Choices/Differentiation

- Students can do PNF stretching in pairs or individually.
- Students can do static stretching.

What to Look For

- Students hold the stretch long enough to maintain or improve range of motion.
- Students follow the sequence for PNF stretching.

Instructional Task:
Progressive Overload and FITT Formula Quiz

■ PRACTICE TASK

Give each student an index card and pencil.

On the whiteboard, provide the following prompts:

1. What is the *frequency* of the 5K training schedule that you followed?
2. Where have you seen evidence of an increase in *intensity* in the schedule?
3. Where is there evidence of *time* in the schedule?
4. What is the *type* of activity in the schedule?
5. What is the exercise principle that we have been using while we trained for the PACER or 5K run/walk?

Student Choices/Differentiation

Provide any test accommodations needed.

What to Look For

Students recognize the frequency, intensity, time, and type found within the 5K training schedule that they followed.

Instructional Task: Physical Education 5K Fun Run

■ PRACTICE TASK

With our remaining time, we will start planning our 5K fun run. Our goal is to involve the community.
Determine the following:

- Fund-raising ideas
- To whom the funds will be given (e.g., school, athletics, community, American Heart Association)
- When and where
- Design for fliers and posters

Extension

Include parents, school administrations, and stakeholders from the community.

Student Choices/Differentiation

- Students may use the Internet for help.
- Students may review examples of previous 5K fun runs.
- Students may work in partners or small groups.

What to Look For

- Students include everyone and work together.
- Students plan the basics of a 5K fun run.

Formal and Informal Assessments

- Progressive overload and FITT formula quiz
- Physical activity logs for outside of physical education

Journal assignment:

- Did you improve? If so, why? If not, why?
- Did setting goals help?
- In what area of FITT do you feel that you improved the most? Least? Why?
- How does it feel to have completed a 5K training program?

Closure

Besides the 5K fun run, this wraps up our Fitness Through 5K Program Design Module. During the next three Fridays we will make time to work on and monitor our progress in the planning and organization stages of the project. Keep promoting and encouraging others to participate!

Reflection

- Review student quizzes. Do students provide enough evidence for them to move on? Or do these concepts need to be re-taught?
- This is the end of the Fitness Through 5K Program Design Module. Has students' experience with the 5K training schedule provided them with the knowledge and skills to understand the progressive overload principle and to identify the components of the FITT formula as they pertain to aerobic fitness and conditioning?
- Is it worth continuing the 5K training, or will continuing to help students train for distance running infringe on other curriculum demands?

Homework

Finish your journal assignment for homework.

Work on planning and organizing the 5K fun run.

Review the materials on our website for the next module.

Resources

U.S. Department of Health and Human Services. (2008). *Physical activity guidelines for Americans.* Washington, DC: Author. Available at www.health.gov.

Couch to 5K® Running Program: www.coolrunning.com

Internet keyword search: "planning a fun run," "planning a 5K"

SAMPLE QUIZ ON IDENTIFYING
THE FITT AND OVERLOAD FORMULAS

Instructions to students: Here is a sample student fitness training log for an after-school fitness club. All of the efforts were best efforts that included a warm-up for the first few minutes. Examine the data and answer the questions that follow.

Training day	Day	Machine	Level	Total Calories (kcal) burned	Time
1	Mon	Elliptical	4	135	20
2	Wed	Elliptical	5	150	20
3	Fri	Elliptical	6	173	20
4	Mon	Elliptical	7	180	20
5	Wed	Elliptical	8	201	20
6	Fri	Elliptical	9	190	20
7	Mon	Elliptical	9	195	20
8	Wed	Elliptical	9	205	20
9	Fri	Elliptical	10	195	20
10	Mon	Elliptical	10	205	20
11	Wed	Elliptical	10	210	20
12	Fri	Elliptical	11	200	20

Identifying Frequency, Intensity, Time, and Type

1. According to the FITT formula, what is the Frequency for this person's training?

2. According to the FITT formula, what evidence of increasing Intensity do you see?

3. If this person is following the FITT formula, what is the Time?

4. According to the FITT formula, what is the Type?

5. On what training days do you see evidence of overload?

From R.J. Doan, L.C. MacDonald, and S. Chepko, eds., 2017, *Lesson planning for middle school physical education* (Reston, VA: SHAPE America; Champaign, IL: Human Kinetics).

PHYSICAL ACTIVITY AND FITNESS PROGRAM DESIGN MODULE (GRADE 7)

Lesson plans in this module contributed by John Kruse, a middle school physical education teacher with the Los Angeles Unified School District.

Grade-Level Outcomes Addressed, by Lesson	Lessons							
	1	2	3	4	5	6	7	8
Standard 1. The physically literate individual demonstrates competency in a variety of motor skills and movement patterns.								
Demonstrates the mature form of the forehand and backhand strokes with a short-handled implement in net games such as paddle ball, pickleball or short-handled racket tennis. (S1.M14.6)	E	E		E		E	E	
Demonstrates the mature form of forehand strokes with a short- or long-handled implement with power and accuracy in net games such as pickleball, tennis, badminton or paddle ball. (S1.M14.8)						E	E	
Forehand- and backhand-volleys with a mature form and control using a short-handled implement. (S1.M16.7)				E		E	E	
Standard 2. The physically literate individual applies knowledge of concepts, principles, strategies and tactics related to movement and performance.								
Standard 3. The physically literate individual demonstrates the knowledge and skills to achieve and maintain a health-enhancing level of physical activity and fitness.								
Identifies barriers related to maintaining a physically active lifestyle and seeks solutions for eliminating those barriers. (S3.M1.7)		E						
Participates in a variety of strength- and endurance-fitness activities such as Pilates, resistance training, body-weight training and light free-weight training. (S3.M3.7)						P		
Participates in a variety of strength- and endurance-fitness activities such as weight training or resistance training (S3.M4.7)						P		
Participates in a variety of lifetime dual and individual sports, martial arts or aquatic activities. (S3.M5.7)								E
Adjusts physical activity based on quantity of exercise needed for a minimal health standard and/or optimal functioning based on current fitness level. (S3.M8.7)					P		E	E	P
Designs and implements a program of remediation for 2 areas of weakness based on the results of health-related fitness assessment. (S3.M15.7)			P			P	P	P
Maintains a physical activity and nutrition log for at least 2 weeks and reflects on activity levels and nutrition as documented in the log. (S3.M16.7)	P	P		P				
Standard 4. The physically literate individual exhibits responsible personal and social behavior that respects self and others.								
Exhibits responsible social behaviors by cooperating with classmates, demonstrating inclusive behaviors and supporting classmates. (S4.M1.7)			E					
Provides corrective feedback to a peer, using teacher-generated guidelines, and incorporating appropriate tone and other communication skills. (S4.M3.7)	E		E					P
Independently uses physical activity and exercise equipment appropriately and safely. (S4.M7.7)						E		
Standard 5. The physically literate individual recognizes the value of physical activity for health, enjoyment, challenge, self-expression and/or social interaction.								

P = Primary; E = Embedded

LESSON 1: LEARNING TO TRACK ACTIVITY AND NUTRITION

Grade-Level Outcomes

Primary Outcome

Assessment & program planning: Maintains a physical activity and nutrition log for at least 2 weeks and reflects on activity levels and nutrition as documented in the log. (S3.M16.7)

Embedded Outcomes

Forehand & backhand: Demonstrates the mature form of the forehand and backhand strokes with a short-handled implement in net games such as paddle ball, pickleball or short-handled racket tennis. (S1.M14.6)

Accepting feedback: Provides corrective feedback to a peer, using teacher-generated guidelines, and incorporating appropriate tone and other communication skills. (S4.M3.7)

Lesson Objective

The learner will start a two-week physical activity and nutrition log.

Equipment and Materials

- Weekday and weekend physical activity and nutrition logs, 2 per student (see handouts)
- LCD overhead projector
- Calories Used for Activities by Weight Categories handout, 1 per student (see handout)
- Physical Activity Log templates, 1 per student (see grade 6 module in Chapter 10, lessons 2 and 5)
- Portable tennis nets
- Plastic pickleballs
- Plastic paddles
- Tennis rackets
- Low-compression tennis balls
- Foam tennis balls
- Exercise or physical activity app (e.g., MapMyRun, Endomondo, MapMyHike, MapMyRide)

Introduction

Today, you begin work on a physical activity and nutrition log for two weeks. After completing your log, you will reflect on various components of the log and use it and your reflection to make adjustments to your physical activity, if needed. You also will use this log and reflection to design a program of remediation for two areas of weakness on your fitness assessment, if needed. To start off your physical activity and nutrition log, we will review how to determine the number of Calories that you expend through a short game of pickleball or tennis.

Instructional Task: Rallying Drills

■ PRACTICE TASK

Have students engage in 15 minutes of rallying drills through the sport of pickleball.

EMBEDDED OUTCOME: S1.M14.7 The purpose of the activity is to provide physical activity to measure and log in the lesson. Make sure that students are using a mature form of forehand and backhand strokes for pickleball.

Follow the progression found in *Right Fielders Are People, Too*, by John Hichwa.

- Forehand volleys 10×
- Forehand to backhand 10×
- Backhand to forehand 10×
- Backhand to backhand 10×
- Rallying (How many consecutive hits can you have with a partner?)

Extension

If students are proficient at rallying, let them play a modified game (simplified rules, modified boundaries).

EMBEDDED OUTCOME: S4.M3.7 Have students provide feedback on partners' pickleball skills using teacher-generated guidelines.

Student Choices/Differentiation

- Students can use pickleball paddles with plastic pickleballs.
- Students can use tennis rackets with spongy tennis balls.
- Students can use tennis rackets with low-compression tennis balls.
- Students can use racquetball rackets.

What to Look For

- Students use the appropriate grips for forehand and backhand.
- Students use the ready position.
- Students turn the body as the feet pivot.
- Students rotate the hips and shoulders.
- Students meet the ball in front of the feet.
- Students swing low to high.
- Students use a follow-through.
- Students use the backhand and forehand appropriately.
- Students judge the ball's trajectory and speed.

Instructional Task: Recording Calorie Expenditure

▓ PRACTICE TASK

Review how to record Caloric expenditure. Distribute the physical activity logs and the Calories Used for Activities by Weight Categories handout.

Tell students to imagine that they just played 15 minutes of either pickleball or tennis. Based on the Calories Used for Activities by Weight Categories handout, have students determine how many Calories they expended for the 15 minutes.

Note: Calorie, with capital *c,* denotes kilocalories, that is, 1,000 calories.

Extension

How does today's activity compare to other activities in which you participate outside of school? Fill out the handout with other activities you engage in regularly.

CALORIES USED FOR ACTIVITIES BY WEIGHT CATEGORIES

	Body weight in pounds (this has been converted from kilograms)									
Activity	44 lb.	55 lb.	66 lb.	77 lb.	88 lb.	99 lb.	110 lb.	121 lb.	132 lb.	143 lb.
	Calories (kcal) for 10 minutes									
Basketball (game)	35	43	51	60	68	77	85	94	102	110
Calisthenics	13	17	20	23	26	30	33	36	40	43
Cross-country skiing (leisure)	24	30	36	42	48	54	60	66	72	78
Cycling (6 mph; 9.7 km/h)	15	17	20	23	26	29	33	36	39	42
Cycling (9 mph; 14.5 km/h)	22	27	32	36	41	46	50	55	60	65
Field hockey	27	34	40	47	54	60	67	74	80	87
Figure skating	40	50	60	70	80	90	10	110	120	130
Horseback riding -canter	8	11	13	15	17	19	21	23	25	27
-trot	22	28	33	39	44	50	55	61	66	72
-gallop	28	35	41	48	50	62	69	76	83	90
Ice hockey (on-ice time)	52	65	78	91	104	117	130	143	156	168
Judo	39	49	59	69	78	88	98	108	118	127
Running (5 mph; 8.0 km/h)*	37	45	52	60	66	72	78	84	90	95
Running (6 mph; 9.7 km/h)	48	55	64	73	79	85	92	100	107	113
Running (7.5 mph; 12.1 km/h)	—	—	76	83	91	99	107	115	125	130
Running (9 mph; 14.5 km/h)	—	—	—	—	—	113	121	130	140	148
Snowshoeing	35	42	50	58	66	74	82	90	98	107
Soccer (game)	36	45	54	63	72	81	90	99	108	117
Squash	—	—	64	74	85	95	106	117	127	138
Swimming, front crawl (30 m/min)	25	31	37	43	49	56	62	68	74	80
Swimming, breaststroke (30 m/min)	19	24	29	34	38	43	48	53	58	62
Swimming, backstroke (30 m/min)	17	21	25	30	34	38	42	47	51	55
Table tennis	22	28	33	39	44	50	55	61	66	72
Tennis	22	28	33	39	44	50	55	61	66	72
Volleyball (game)	20	25	30	35	40	45	50	55	60	65
Walking* (2.5 mph; 3.2 km/h)	17	19	21	23	26	28	30	32	34	36
Walking* (4 mph; 6.4 km/h)	24	26	28	30	32	34	37	40	43	48

*Note: The transition from walking to running occurs between 4 & 5 miles per hour (mph). Walking at 2.5 mph is a slow walk. Walking at 4 mph is a fast walk and is almost running.

Reprinted, by permission, from O. Bar-Or and T. Rowland, 2004, *Pediatric exercise medicine: Physiological principles to health care application* (Champaign, IL: Human Kinetics), 381.

PHYSICAL ACTIVITY LOG

Weekday Physical Activity Log

Day of the week (circle): M   T   W   Th   F

Part of day	Activities	Time (min)	Easy to measure? (circle)	Calories	Intensity	Comments (technology or app used, how did you feel?, whom did you participate with?, etc.)
Before school			Yes/No			
Nutrition (morning) break			Yes/No			
Lunch break			Yes/No			
In-class physical activity break (If so, list classes)			Yes/No			
Physical education class			Yes/No			
After school			Yes/No			

Weekend Physical Activity Log

Day of the week (circle): M   T   W   Th   F

Saturday (Date: _____)

Part of day	Activities	Time (min)	Easy to measure? (circle)	Calories	Intensity	Comments (technology or app used, how did you feel?, whom did you participate with?, etc.)
Morning			Yes/No			
Afternoon			Yes/No			
Evening			Yes/No			

Sunday (Date: _____)

Part of day	Activities	Time (min)	Easy to measure? (circle)	Calories	Intensity	Comments (technology or app used, how did you feel?, whom did you participate with?, etc.)
Morning			Yes/No			
Afternoon			Yes/No			
Evening			Yes/No			

From R.J. Doan, L.C. MacDonald, and S. Chepko, eds., 2017, *Lesson planning for middle school physical education* (Reston, VA: SHAPE America; Champaign, IL: Human Kinetics).

Student Choices/Differentiation

- Students can choose various methods to determine Caloric expenditure because the table is based on 10 minutes of physical activity:
  - Determine unit rate per minute so that the total number of minutes can simply be multiplied by this number.
  - Take half of the number for 10 minutes and add it to the original number to get a 15-minute expenditure.
  - Multiply the 10-minute expenditure by 1.5 to get a 15-minute Caloric expenditure.
- Have students work in pairs if they have difficulty with the number sense.

What to Look For

- Students determine how many Calories (kcal) are expended while playing tennis.
- Students use the proper weight column on the sheet.
- Students multiply the Calories expended by 2 since the table provides information for 10 minutes.
- Students estimate their Caloric expenditure based on the information provided in the caloric expenditure handout if their exact weight is not listed.

Instructional Task: Use of Log

■ PRACTICE TASK

Have students fill in today's physical activity based on the table.

- Ask students if today's activity is easily measured.
- Explain that some activities may not be easily quantified (e.g., their activities outside of school may not be listed on the table or they may not be easily found in books or on the Internet).
- Review with students some ways we can describe and determine the exercise intensity of various physical activities or exercise. (Examples: Is walking to school considered vigorous or moderate intensity? What types of objective measures can we get from an exercise app that can be used to measure intensity? What kind of feedback do we get from exercise machines such as an elliptical, treadmill, or stationary bike that can indicate exercise intensity?)

Extension

Ask students to categorize the various measures of exercise intensity as either subjective or objective.

Guiding questions for students:

- How can you use these measures of intensity?
- Do you prefer objective measures or subjective measures?
- What are some possible benefits of tracking exercise intensity for an older person especially?

Student Choices/Differentiation

- Students can work in pairs if they are having difficulty with the log.
- Have sample logs for students to view.

What to Look For

- Students recognize the following ways to measure or estimate exercise intensity:
  - Ratings of perceived exertion
  - Average speed (walking, running, riding a bike)
  - Watts (rate of performing work on a treadmill, elliptical, or exercise bike)
  - Moderate or vigorous (perception)
  - Steps per minute
  - Pace (e.g., 18-minute mile when hiking)

- Calories per minute (from a treadmill, elliptical, or exercise bike)
- Heart rate
- Students recognize that measures of intensity can be used with the progressive overload principle.

Instructional Task: Model Use of Physical Activity Log

▪ PRACTICE TASK

Model the use of the activity log using several examples of various physical activities on the overhead LCD projector.

Extensions

- Demonstrate under the overhead LCD how a cellphone app can be used to collect data for various physical activities.
- Point out how these apps can provide useful information on exercise intensity, Caloric expenditure, time, etc.
- Also point out that while these apps provide good information, they are also rough estimates of energy expenditure since the equations they use are based off of the average person (i.e., it is not a perfect science).

Student Choices/Differentiation

- Have videos and handouts ready for students to use if they have difficulties with the content.
- Allow time for think, pair, shares, if needed.

What to Look For

Students have a basic understanding of using various physical activities and technology in the activity log.

Instructional Task: Model Use of Nutrition Log

▪ PRACTICE TASK

Model the use of the nutrition log using the LCD overhead projector. Point out that it is a simple log and that it need not contain detailed nutrition content. This is a homework assignment that accompanies students' two-week physical activity log.

Extension

Have students recall what they had for breakfast or a snack, and include it in their logs.

Student Choices/Differentiation

Students can create their own nutrition logs or journals to provide more specifics as to the nutritional content of the foods they choose to eat.

What to Look For

Students use the physical activity and nutrition log.

Formal and Informal Assessments

Physical Activity and Nutrition Log Self-Assessment

Closure

Today, we reviewed energy expenditure and exercise intensity so that you can complete a two-week physical activity and nutrition log. Being able to complete a two-week log is important so that you can reflect on physical activity and nutrition patterns and their relationship to your health and fitness.

What can you expect to learn when you reflect on these logs in two weeks?

Reflection

- Do students seem to understand what is being asked of them over the next two weeks?
- What additional teaching or review will need to occur over the next two weeks to make this assignment successful?

Homework

Complete your physical activity and nutrition logs over the next two weeks. I will remind you to continue working on this, and we will continue to estimate caloric expenditure and exercise intensity in class. You can print additional logs from the physical education website. If you can't print these at home, you can use a paper, ruler, and pen or pencil to create the forms.

Resources

Bar-Or, O., & Rowland, T. (2004). *Pediatric exercise medicine: From physiological principles to health care application.* Champaign, IL: Human Kinetics.

Hichwa, J. (1998). *Right fielders are people, too: An inclusive approach to teaching middle school physical education.* Champaign, IL: Human Kinetics.

LESSON 2: REFLECTING ON ACTIVITY LOGS; MUSCLE- AND BONE-STRENGTHENING ACTIVITIES

Grade-Level Outcomes

Primary Outcome

Assessment & program planning: Maintains a physical activity and nutrition log for at least 2 weeks and reflects on activity levels and nutrition as documented in the log. (S3.M16.7)

Embedded Outcomes

Physical activity knowledge: Identifies barriers related to maintaining a physically active lifestyle and seeks solutions for eliminating those barriers. (S3.M1.7)

Forehand & backhand: Demonstrates the mature form of the forehand and backhand strokes with a short-handled implement in net games such as paddle ball, pickleball or short-handled racket tennis. (S1.M14.6)

Lesson Objectives

The learner will:

- reflect on his completed physical activity log as it pertains to muscle-strengthening and bone-strengthening physical activity after experiencing these two types of activities in class.
- participate in various muscle- and bone-strengthening physical activities.

Equipment and Materials

- Portable tennis nets
- Plastic pickleballs
- Plastic paddles
- Tennis rackets
- Low-compression tennis balls
- Foam tennis balls
- Resistance bands (variety of resistances)
- Sand bells (variety of weights)
- Agility ladders
- Station cards for muscle-strengthening resistance training and bone-strengthening physical activities (see handout)
- Self-Assessment of Muscle Strengthening and Bone Strengthening Recorded in Physical Activity and Nutrition Log (see handout)

Introduction

Today, you will reflect on your completed two-week physical activity logs after you have experienced examples of muscle-strengthening and bone-strengthening physical activities.

Instructional Task: Stations for Muscle-Strengthening and Bone-Strengthening Physical Activities

■ PRACTICE TASK

In groups of two, students rotate around stations, spending about 3 to 4 minutes at each station.

Students read each station card, which contains definitions and examples.

Students perform the task at each station and rotate on your signal.

STATION CARDS FOR MUSCLE-STRENGTHENING RESISTANCE TRAINING AND BONE-STRENGTHENING PHYSICAL ACTIVITIES

Activity 1

Jog around the perimeter of our area until you hear the signal to go to the next station.

Guidelines, Definitions, and Benefits

Children and adolescents should engage in 60 minutes or more of physical activity daily. Most of those 60 minutes should consist of either moderate- or vigorous-intensity aerobic physical activity and should include 60 minutes of vigorous-intensity physical activity at least three days a week.

Benefit: Aerobic activities *improve* cardiorespiratory endurance.

Activity 2

Volley with your partner until you hear the signal to rotate. Choose either pickleball or tennis.

Guidelines, Definitions, and Examples

As part of their 60 minutes of daily physical activity, children and adolescents should include muscle-strengthening physical activity on at least three days of the week.
Muscle-strengthening activities make muscles do more work than they do during normal activities of daily life.
Muscle-strengthening activities can be unstructured or structured.

Examples of unstructured activities:
• Using a climbing wall
• Games such as tug-of-war

Examples of structured activities:
• Curl-ups or crunches
• Resistance exercises with exercise bands, weight machines, or weights
• Push-ups and pull-ups

Activity 3

See how many push-ups and curl-ups you can complete before you hear the signal to rotate. Take turns with your partner, and have your partner count for you.

Guidelines, Definitions, and Examples

As part of their 60 minutes of daily physical activity, children and adolescents should include muscle-strengthening physical activity at least three days a week.
Muscle-strengthening activities make muscles do more work than they do during normal activities of daily life.
Making muscles do more work than usual is called the overload principle.

Activity 4

Determine a baseline for your muscles for a biceps curl. Choose an exercise band that makes your muscles fail after about 10 repetitions. Once you have determined what resistance band will max out your biceps at about 10 repetitions, use a resistance band that is one step more difficult. This is called overload, and you should not be able to perform 10 repetitions with that band until your muscles get stronger.

Guidelines, Definitions, and Examples

As part of their 60 minutes of daily physical activity, children and adolescents should include bone-strengthening physical activity on at least three days of the week.
Bone-strengthening activities produce a force on the bones that promotes growth and strength.
Activities that cause these forces typically involve impact with the ground.

Examples: Hopping, skipping, jumping, jumping rope, running, gymnastics, basketball, volleyball, and tennis

Activity 5

Jump rope with your partner, and encourage each other until you hear the signal to rotate.

Guidelines, Definitions, and Examples

As part of their 60 minutes of daily physical activity, children and adolescents should include bone-strengthening physical activity on at least three days of the week.
You might notice that bone-strengthening activities can also be muscle-strengthening and aerobic activities.

Activity 6

With your partner, practice a pickleball or tennis forehand volley. Take 10 turns each tossing a ball to your partner's forehand.

Guidelines, Definitions, and Examples

As part of their 60 minutes of daily physical activity, children and adolescents should include muscle-strengthening physical activity at least three days a week.
Muscle-strengthening activities make muscles do more work than they do during normal activities of daily life.
Making muscles do more work than usual is called the overload principle.

Activity 7

Determine a baseline for your muscles for an upright row. Choose an exercise band that makes your muscles fail after about 10 repetitions. Once you have determined which resistance maxes out your muscles at about 10 repetitions, use a resistance band that is one step more difficult. This is called overload, and you should not be able to perform 10 repetitions with that band until your muscles get stronger.

Guidelines, Definitions, and Examples

As part of their 60 minutes of daily physical activity, children and adolescents should include muscle-strengthening physical activity on at least three days of the week.
Muscle-strengthening activities do more work than they do during normal activities of daily life.
Making muscles do more work than usual is called the overload principle.

Activity 8

Determine a baseline for your muscles for a seated row. Choose an exercise band that makes your muscles fail after about 10 repetitions. Once you have determined what resistance band will max out your muscles at about 10 repetitions, use a resistance band that is one step more difficult. This is called overload, and you should not be able to perform 10 repetitions with that band until your muscles get stronger.

Guidelines, Definitions, and Examples

As part of their 60 minutes of daily physical activity, children and adolescents should include muscle-strengthening physical activity on at least three days of the week.
Muscle-strengthening activities do more work than they do during normal activities of daily life.
Making muscles do more work than usual is called the overload principle.

Activity 9

Determine a baseline for your muscles for a triceps extension. Choose sand bells that make your muscles fail after about 10 repetitions. Once you have determined which sand bells max out your triceps at about 10 repetitions, use a sand bells that are one step more difficult. This is called overload, and you should not be able to perform 10 repetitions with that band until your muscles get stronger.

Guidelines, Definitions, and Examples

As part of their 60 minutes of daily physical activity, children and adolescents should include bone-strengthening physical activity on at least three days of the week.
Bone-strengthening activities produce a force on the bones that promotes growth and strength.
Activities that cause these forces typically involve impact with the ground.
Examples: hopping, skipping, jumping

Activity 10

Perform various agility ladder drills until you hear the signal to rotate. Choose from the following ladder drills:
- Two-foot hops: Hop with both feet between each ladder rung.
- One-foot hops: Hop with one foot, jog back, and hop with the other foot.
- Hopscotch: Hop with both feet in and both feet out (advance one rung after each hop.)

Guidelines, Definitions, and Examples

As part of their 60 minutes of daily physical activity, children and adolescents should include bone-strengthening physical activity on at least three days of the week.
Bone-strengthening activities produce a force on the bones that promotes growth and strength.
Activities that cause these forces typically involve impact with the ground.

Examples: Hopping, skipping, jumping

Activity 11

Perform various agility ladder drills until you hear the signal to rotate. Choose from the following ladder drills:
- Carioca, as demonstrated by teacher
- Icky shuffle, as demonstrated by teacher

Guidelines, Definitions, and Examples

As part of their 60 minutes of daily physical activity, children and adolescents should include bone-strengthening physical activity on at least three days of the week.
You might notice that bone-strengthening activities can also be muscle-strengthening and aerobic activities.

Activity 12

Practice your pickleball or tennis backhand volley with a partner. Take 10 turns each tossing a ball to your partner's backhand.

From R.J. Doan, L.C. MacDonald, and S. Chepko, eds., 2017, *Lesson planning for middle school physical education* (Reston, VA: SHAPE America; Champaign, IL: Human Kinetics).

Refinement

Stop the task, if needed, to remind students to focus and work hard during the short amount of time they are on each task.

Student Choices/Differentiation

Provide videos and handouts, if needed, to explain the different stations.

What to Look For

- Students use fundamental movement patterns.
- Students use equipment safely.
- Students follow directions on station cards.

Instructional Task: Station 1

■ PRACTICE TASK

Students read the guidelines for physical activity and examples of aerobic activity.

Students jog around the perimeter of the teaching area until you signal for them to go to the next station.

Refinement

Encourage students to run with a forefoot or midfoot strike.

Student Choices/Differentiation

- Students can choose jogging speed.
- Students can jog with a partner.

What to Look For

- Students read the definitions and guidelines.
- Students jog at an appropriate pace.

Instructional Task: Station 2

■ PRACTICE TASK

Students read the guidelines for physical activity, examples for aerobic activity, and the benefit of aerobic activity.

Students rally with a partner across a portable tennis net.

EMBEDDED OUTCOME: S1.M14.6. See that students use correct forehand and backhand techniques and that they follow through with their hits while participating in the practice task.

Extension

Challenge students to hit the ball across the net in a manner that makes their partners run to meet the ball, causing an increase in heart rate.

Student Choices/Differentiation

- Students can use a pickleball.
- Students can use a low-compression tennis ball.
- Students can use a foam tennis ball.

What to Look For

- Students read the definitions, guidelines, and examples.
- Students use forehand and backhand strokes.
- Students volley the chosen ball back and forth with a partner.

Instructional Task: Station 3

■ PRACTICE TASK

Students read the guidelines for muscle strengthening and the provided examples.

Students perform as many push-ups and curl-ups as they can until they hear the signal to rotate.

Students take turns with their partners, counting for each other.

Extension

Students provide feedback to one another on the form of their push-ups and curl-ups.

Student Choices/Differentiation

- Students can do a traditional push-up.
- Students can do a modified push-up (against a wall or with knees on the ground).

What to Look For

- Students read the station cards.
- Partners provide corrective feedback on push-ups and curl-ups.

Instructional Task: Station 4

■ PRACTICE TASK

Students read the guidelines, definitions, and examples for muscle strengthening.

Students read the definition for the principle of overload.

Students determine a baseline for a biceps curl by using resistance tubing that causes the muscle to fail after approximately 10 repetitions.

After determining a baseline for 10 repetitions, students attempt a resistance band that is one step more difficult (overload).

Extension

Students provide feedback to each other on correct form for the biceps curl.

Student Choices/Differentiation

Provide a selection of resistance bands to determine baseline.

What to Look For

Students experiment with the resistance tubing until they find the level that leads to a 10-repetition max.

Instructional Task: Station 5

■ PRACTICE TASK

Student read the guidelines, definitions, and examples for bone strengthening.

Students jump rope with a partner and encourage each other.

Extension

Partners provide feedback on jump rope technique.

Student Choices/Differentiation

Students can use various jump rope patterns.

What to Look For

- Students read the station cards.
- Students jump rope at a rate that allows them to be engaged for the length of the station interval.

Instructional Task: Station 6

■ PRACTICE TASK

Students read the guidelines, definitions, and examples for bone strengthening.

Students practice the forehand, taking turns tossing the ball to their partners' forehand.

Extension

Challenge students to toss the ball in such a way as to force the hitters to move to the ball so that they create an impact force with the ground (bone-strengthening exercise).

Refinement

Make sure students are making proper tosses to partners.

Student Choices/Differentiation

- Students can use a pickleball or tennis ball.
- Students can use a low-compression tennis ball.
- Students can use a foam tennis ball.

What to Look For

- Students read the station cards.
- Students move to the ball and position their feet to allow for rotation of hips and shoulder girdle when performing the forehand.

Instructional Task: Station 7

■ PRACTICE TASK

Students read the guidelines, definitions, and examples for muscle strengthening.

Students determine a baseline for an upright row with resistance tubing for approximately 10 repetitions.

Students attempt the next level up to experience overload (fewer than 10 repetitions).

Extension

Students provide feedback to each other on technique of the upright row.

Student Choices/Differentiation

Provide a variety of resistance tubing to determine baseline.

What to Look For

- Students execute the upright row properly.
- Students experiment with a variety of resistance bands to find approximately a 10-repetition max load.

Instructional Task: Station 8

■ PRACTICE TASK

Students read the guidelines, definitions, and examples for muscle strengthening.

Students determine a baseline for a seated row with resistance tubing for approximately 10 repetitions.

Students attempt the next level up to experience overload (fewer than 10 repetitions).

Extension

Students provide feedback to each other on technique of the seated row.

Student Choices/Differentiation

Provide a variety of resistance tubing to determine baseline.

What to Look For

- Students execute the seated row properly.
- Students experiment with a variety of resistance bands to find approximately a 10-repetition max load.

Instructional Task: Station 9

■ PRACTICE TASK

Students read the guidelines, definitions, and examples for muscle strengthening.

Students determine a baseline for a triceps extension with a sand bell for approximately 10 repetitions.

Students attempt the next level up to experience overload (fewer than 10 repetitions).

Extension

Students provide feedback to each other on technique of the triceps extension.

Student Choices/Differentiation

Provide a variety of sand bells to determine baseline.

What to Look For

- Students execute the triceps extension properly.
- Students experiment with a variety of resistance bands to find approximately a 10-repetition max load.

Instructional Task: Station 10

■ PRACTICE TASK

Students read the guidelines, definitions, and examples for bone strengthening.

Students perform a variety of agility ladder drills.

Extension

Students can create their own agility ladder drill if they are proficient at the choices presented.

Student Choices/Differentiation

- Students can choose from a variety of agility ladder drills.
- Students can choose their speed during drills.

What to Look For

Students follow the description for the agility ladder drills.

Instructional Task: Station 11

■ PRACTICE TASK

Students read the guidelines, definitions, and examples for bone strengthening.

Students perform various agility ladder drills (more advanced than Station 10).

Extension

Students help coach each other on the drills listed on the station card.

Student Choices/Differentiation

- Students can do the carioca (beginning/intermediate).
- Students can do the icky shuffle (advanced).

What to Look For

Students perform the carioca or icky shuffle on the agility ladders.

Instructional Task: Station 12

■ PRACTICE TASK

Students read the guidelines, definitions, and examples for bone strengthening.

With a partner, students practice their backhand by tossing a ball to the partner's backhand.

Extension

Encourage partners to toss the ball in such a way as to force the hitter to move to the ball so that an impact force with the ground is created (bone-strengthening exercise).

Student Choices/Differentiation

- Students can use a pickleball or tennis ball.
- Students can use a low-compression tennis ball.
- Students can use a foam tennis ball.

What to Look For

Students move to the ball and position their feet to allow for rotation of hips and shoulder girdle when performing the backhand.

Instructional Task: Reflecting on Two-Week Physical Activity and Nutrition Log

■ PRACTICE TASK

Distribute completed two-week physical activity logs.

Have students review their logs using the Self-Assessment of Muscle Strengthening and Bone Strengthening Recorded in Physical Activity and Nutrition Log.

Guiding questions for students:

- Based on your self-assessment, can you identify any areas of physical activity that you need to address in order to meet suggested guidelines?
- Upon reflecting on your physical activity log, what barriers exist that may prevent you from being as active as you may like? What are some possible solutions?
- How has your understanding of health benefits for the activities you engage in changed?

Student Choices/Differentiation

Students may choose to complete the assessment with a partner with whom they feel comfortable.

What to Look For

Students use the self-assessment tool to reflect on their two-week physical activity and nutrition logs.

SELF-ASSESSMENT OF MUSCLE STRENGTHENING AND BONE STRENGTHENING RECORDED IN PHYSICAL ACTIVITY AND NUTRITION LOG

Directions: Read the definitions below. Examine and reflect on the physical activity that you recorded in your Physical Activity and Nutrition Log.

Guidelines: According to the U.S. Department of Health and Human Services, children and adolescents should engage in a minimum of 60 minutes of physical activity daily.

Guidelines	Definitions	Examples
Aerobic: Most of the recommended minimum 60 minutes or more a day of physical activity should be either moderate- or vigorous-intensity aerobic physical activity, and should include vigorous-intensity physical activity at least three days a week.	**Aerobic activities** involve rhythmic movements of the large muscles. This type of activity increases cardiorespiratory fitness.	• Running • Hopping • Skipping • Jumping rope • Swimming • Dancing • Bicycling
Muscle strengthening: As part of their recommended 60 minutes or more of daily physical activity, children and adolescents should include muscle-strengthening physical activity on at least three days of the week.	**Muscle-strengthening activities** make muscles do more work than they usually do in daily life. They use the overload principle and make muscles stronger.	• Games such as tug-of-war • Push-ups and pull-ups • Resistance exercises with exercise bands, weight machines, handheld weights • Climbing wall • Curl-ups and crunches
Bone strengthening: As part of their 60 or more minutes of daily physical activity, children and adolescents should include bone-strengthening physical activity on at least three days of the week.	**Bone-strengthening activities** produce a force on the bones that promotes bone growth and strength. These activities typically involve impacts with the ground.	• Hopping, skipping, jumping • Jumping rope • Running • Sports such as gymnastics, basketball, volleyball, tennis

1. Aerobic physical activity: Did you participate in 60 minutes or more of moderate- to vigorous-intensity physical activity? Circle: Yes   No

2. Muscle-strengthening activity: As part of your physical activity, on how many days of the week did you participate in muscle strengthening?

    Week 1: _____ days

    Week 2: _____ days

3. Bone-strengthening activity: As part of your physical activity, on how many days of the week did you participate in bone strengthening activities?

    Week 1: _____ days

    Week 2: _____ days

4. Barriers to physical activity: Now that you can reflect on your two-week log, identify (by listing in the space below) some barriers related to maintaining a physically active lifestyle (i.e., what might have prevented you from being as active as you wanted to be?). _____

_____

_____

_____

From U.S. Department of Health and Human Services, 2008.

From R.J. Doan, L.C. MacDonald, and S. Chepko, eds., 2017, *Lesson planning for middle school physical education* (Reston, VA: SHAPE America; Champaign, IL: Human Kinetics).

Formal and Informal Assessments

- Physical activity and nutrition log (for two weeks)
- Peer assessment: formal and informal feedback at stations
- Self-assessment of muscle-strengthening and bone-strengthening activities
- Sticker assessment on student understanding of new concepts (see Closure)

Closure

Have red, green, and yellow stickers ready for students. Ask them to place stickers on their self-assessments and reflections using the following color codes:

- Red = "I'm confused; I really need the concepts of muscle strengthening and bone strengthening to be retaught."
- Yellow = "I need you to slow down. I think I understand most of what was taught, but I need some review."
- Green = "I understand everything. I'm ready to move on to new concepts and ideas!"

Reflection

- What are the percentage breakdowns of red, yellow, and green stickers on the student self-assessments?
- Is the class ready to move on? Do the concepts need to be re-taught?

Homework

EMBEDDED OUTCOME: S3.M1.7. What kind of barriers do we face to participating in physical activity? Discuss some of these barriers with your parents or guardians, and try to find some ways to eliminate or work around the barriers that you identify.

Resources

Hichwa, J. (1998). *Right fielders are people, too: An inclusive approach to teaching middle school physical education.* Champaign, IL: Human Kinetics.

Sound Body Sound Mind Foundation. (2014). Sound body sound mind: Teaching the basics of movement and physical activity—high school & middle school curriculum. Los Angeles: Sound Body Sound Mind Foundation.

U.S. Department of Health and Human Services. (2008). *Physical activity guidelines for Americans.* Available at www.health.gov/paguidelines.

LESSON 3: FITNESS ASSESSMENT DAY

Grade-Level Outcomes

Primary Outcome

Assessment & program planning: Designs and implements a program of remediation for 2 areas of weakness based on the results of health-related fitness assessment. (S3.M15.7)

Embedded Outcomes

Personal responsibility: Exhibits responsible social behaviors by cooperating with classmates, demonstrating inclusive behaviors and supporting classmates. (S4.M1.7)

Accepting feedback: Provides corrective feedback to a peer, using teacher-generated guidelines, and incorporating appropriate tone and other communication skills. (S4.M3.7)

Lesson Objectives

The learner will:

- assess her own health-related fitness using a scientifically based fitness assessment such as Fitnessgram in order to design a program of remediation for two areas of weakness based on the results.
- identify barriers related to maintaining a physically active lifestyle.

Note: Spread out the instructional tasks over a few class periods. The length of this lesson will depend on class size, students' familiarity with the assessments, and how deeply you would like to go into the content involved in each assessment.

Equipment and Materials

Fitnessgram assessment materials:

- Sound system
- Cadences for PACER, curl-up test, push-up test (on CD, iPod, or smartphone)
- Sit-and-reach devices (several will save time)
- Modified pull-up bars
- Paperwork for collecting students' scores (printed on card stock helps)
- Cones for PACER
- Stopwatches for mile run/walk
- Measuring tape or trundle wheel to measure distance for PACER
- Curl-up strips
- Fitnessgram software (for generating student reports)
- Task cards provided by Fitnessgram (includes protocol, look-up tables, and form corrections)
- Stadiometer (to measure height)
- Scale

Introduction

For homework, you were to think about and research barriers to participating in physical activity. Please share with a friend a couple of barriers that you found. Does anyone have any interesting ones to share with the class?

This week, we will focus on assessment of your health-related fitness. It is anticipated that fitness testing will take a few days. It should go smoothly because you have practiced the various Fitnessgram assessments. You will use the results of the Fitnessgram to identify areas of fitness that you need to work on. Your Fitnessgram report and scores should be part of your end portfolio so that you can reflect on them during the school year.

Instructional Task: PACER Assessment

Decide on the 15- or 20-meter distance.

■ PRACTICE TASK

Administer the PACER test for measurement of aerobic capacity.

Review protocol, briefly reminding students that the PACER has a built in warm-up.

Go over the academic vocabulary involved with PACER.

- **P**rogressive
- **A**erobic
- **C**ardiovascular
- **E**ndurance
- **R**un

Partners record scores.

Partners should support each other by providing encouragement.

Discuss protocols for the test. The following are common areas to stress to students.

- Single beep means end of lap; turn around and run back to the other line.
- Triple beep means that the test will speed up; turn around and run back to the other line.
- Foot must touch the end line by the time the beep sounds for each lap.
- On first miss, turn around where you are and run to the other line; try to get back on pace.
- On second miss, move to the side and cool down by walking. End of test.
- Partner should note lap number and record the score.

Extension

Have students look up how their aerobic capacity compares to the Healthy Fitness Zone for the Fitnessgram assessment.

Refinement

Encourage runners to pace themselves during the test (especially in the beginning).

Student Choices/Differentiation

- Students choose a partner to work with and decide who will go first or second.
- Students should perform to their own abilities and not compare themselves to others.

What to Look For

Students are following test protocols.

Instructional Task: Push-Up Assessment

■ PRACTICE TASK

Review protocol briefly. Remind students that the push-up assessment measures upper-body strength and endurance. Upper body strength is an indicator of healthy bone density.

EMBEDDED OUTCOME: S4.M1.7 Push-ups can be difficult. Encourage partners to support each other by providing encouragement to their classmates.

Extension

Have students look up how their push-up scores compare to the Healthy Fitness Zone for the Fitnessgram assessment.

Refinement

Make sure students have a flat back and go to 90 degrees for the down position.

Student Choices/Differentiation

Students choose a partner to work with and decide who will go first or second.

What to Look For

- Students have a flat back.
- Students' hands are shoulder-width apart.
- Students follow the push-up cadence.

Instructional Task: Curl-Up Assessment

▨ PRACTICE TASK

Review protocol briefly. Remind students that the curl-up assessment is a measure of abdominal strength and endurance. Strong abdominal muscles help prevent low back problems.

Partners should support each other by providing encouragement.

Partners should provide corrective feedback by keeping track of form corrections and stopping partners on the second form correction.

Extension

Have students compare their curl-up scores to the Healthy Fitness Zone for the Fitnessgram assessment.

EMBEDDED OUTCOME: S4.M3.7 Partners should provide corrective feedback by keeping track of form corrections and stopping partners on the second form correction.

Student Choices/Differentiation

Students choose a partner to work with and decide who will go first or second.

What to Look For

- Heads return to the ground.
- Fingers go completely across the curl-up strip.
- Heels stay on the ground.
- Students follow the cadence.

Source: Fitnessgram task card.

Instructional Task: Shoulder Stretch

▨ PRACTICE TASK

Review protocol briefly. Remind students that flexibility at the shoulder joint helps prevent shoulder injuries.

Review the following key points:

- With right hand, reach up and over shoulder and down back as if pulling up a zipper. Reach up with left hand and touch fingertips.
- Fingers touch.
- Test both sides.
- Partners should support each other by providing encouragement.

Extensions

- Have students look up how their shoulder stretch scores compare to the Healthy Fitness Zone for the Fitnessgram assessment.
- Have students compare their scores for both sides and if different, hypothesize about why.

Student Choices/Differentiation

Students choose a partner to work with and decide who will go first or second.

What to Look For

- Students are doing protocol correctly.
- Students don't pull on their partners' arms to assist them.

Source: Fitnessgram task card.

Instructional Task: Sit and Reach

■ PRACTICE TASK

Review protocol briefly. Remind students that flexibility in the lower back and hamstring muscles, as measured by the sit and reach, helps prevent lower-back problems.

Partners should support each other by providing encouragement.

Partners should provide corrective feedback to make sure the stretching students do not pass 12 inches (30 cm) and do not bounce.

Extension

Have students look up how their sit-and-reach scores compare to the Healthy Fitness Zone for the Fitnessgram assessment.

Refinement

Make sure students do not bounce during activity.

Student Choices/Differentiation

Students choose a partner to work with and decide who will go first or second.

What to Look For

- Legs are fully extended, with back of knees touching the ground.
- Heel of foot not being tested is one fist-width away from the knee of the leg being tested.
- Students are not bouncing or overstretching.

Instructional Task: Modified Pull-Up

■ PRACTICE TASK

Review protocol briefly. Remind students that the modified pull-up is a measure of upper-body strength and endurance.

Partners should support each other by providing encouragement.

Partners should provide corrective feedback, keep track of form corrections, and stop students on the second form correction.

Extension

Have students look up how their modified pull-up scores compare to the Healthy Fitness Zone for the Fitnessgram assessment.

Student Choices/Differentiation

Students choose a partner to work with and decide who will go first or second.

What to Look For

- Shoulders are directly under the bar.
- Palms are facing away.
- Only heels are touching the floor.
- Chest touches the elastic band.
- Students return to starting position with elbows extended.
- Body remains straight.

Source: Fitnessgram task card.

Instructional Task: Body Mass Index

■ PRACTICE TASK

Review protocol briefly.

Note: Height and weight should be measured by the teacher and not by students. Safeguards need to be established to protect student privacy.

The class should be engaged in an activity where the teacher can pull out small groups of students so that one student can be measured for height and weight while the small group awaits their turn (with shoes removed and ready to be measured). Keep the scale and stadiometer behind a screen to ensure student privacy while you keep an eye on the rest of the class.

Extension

While height and weight are being measured, students can work on the following assignment:

- Provide students with sample Fitnessgram reports that have been copied in a way that there is no name on the report.
- Have students read the reports and underline any vocabulary that they do not understand.
- Have students circle any numbers on the reports that they do not understand.

Student Choices/Differentiation

Have videos and handouts available for students to help in learning the activity.

What to Look For

- There is a discrepancy between the way the CDC recommends rounding height and weight and the way that Fitnessgram handles the data.
- If using Fitnessgram, round down on height to the nearest inch.
- Height needs to be measured accurately, since it is squared in the BMI formula.
- When measuring height, the Frankfurt plane needs to be aligned so that the head is level. The head may pull away from the stadiometer for this measurement.

Formal and Informal Assessments

Fitnessgram is a formal assessment but is not a measure of standards-based outcomes. Therefore, Fitnessgram assessment scores should not be used as a grade.

Closure

- Did you feel challenged by the fitness assessments today? If so, by which ones and why?
- Review how you did on each fitness test, and think about which areas you might need to work on.

Reflection

Browse through student work to uncover possible misunderstandings.

Homework

Have students write down areas they think they may need to work on and then select two for remediation. Students will compare them to their computer-generated Fitnessgram reports in the future.

Resources

The Cooper Institute. (2013). Meredith, M.D., & Welk, G.J. (Eds.). *Fitnessgram & Activitygram test administration manual.* Updated 4th ed. Champaign, IL: Human Kinetics.

Corbin, C., et al. (2014). Youth physical fitness: Ten key concepts. *Journal of Physical Education, Recreation & Dance, 85*(2), 24-31.

Council of Europe, Committee for the development of Sport. (1993). *Eurofit tests of physical fitness.* 2nd ed. Strasbourg: Council of Europe Publishing

Institute of Medicine of the National Academies. (2012). *Fitness measures and health outcomes in youth.* Washington, DC: National Academies of Sciences.

Melograno, V.J. (2000). *Portfolio assessment for k-12 physical education.* Reston, VA: National Association for Sport and Physical Education.

Nihisher, A.J., et al. (2007). Body mass index measurement in schools. *Journal of School Health, 77*(10), 651-671.

LESSON 4:
HEALTHY AND OPTIMAL FITNESS ZONES

Grade-Level Outcomes

Primary Outcomes

Assessment & program planning: Maintains a physical activity and nutrition log for at least 2 weeks and reflects on activity levels and nutrition as documented in the log. (S3.M16.7)

Fitness knowledge: Adjusts physical activity based on quantity of exercise needed for a minimal health standard and/or optimal functioning based on current fitness level. (S3.M8.7)

Embedded Outcomes

Volley: Forehand- and backhand-volleys with a mature form and control using a short-handled implement. (S1.M16.7)

Forehand & backhand: Demonstrates the mature form of the forehand and backhand strokes with a short-handled implement in net games such as paddle ball, pickleball or short-handled racket tennis. (S1.M14.6)

Lesson Objective

The learner will reflect on his completed physical activity log as it pertains to the amount of physical activity needed to meet a minimal health standard or optimal functioning level.

Equipment and Materials

- Portable tennis nets
- Plastic pickleballs
- Plastic paddles
- Tennis rackets
- Low-compression tennis balls
- Foam tennis balls
- Determining Physical Activity Goals for Adolescents handout, 1 copy per student
- Healthy Eating for an Active Lifestyle handout, 1 copy per student
- Calories Used for Activities by Weight Categories handout (from Lesson 1)

Introduction

Review homework:

Does anyone feel comfortable sharing his or her remediations from the Fitnessgram data? Which helped in this process more: the generated score reports or actually participating in the assessments (how you felt during the exercises)?

Today, you will determine how much physical activity you need to be healthy. You will determine two zones. One zone will be for a minimal health standard, and the second zone will be for optimal functioning or wellness. You will compare these quantities of physical activity with the paddle and racket sports you practice today. You will remember you determined the number of Calories you expended (or used) as an example before you started your two-week log.

Instructional Task: Calorie Think, Pair, Share

■ **PRACTICE TASK**

Review what a Calorie is.

In pairs, have students discuss what they think a Calorie or kilocalorie is.

When students share, they are likely to think that a Calorie is something that makes you fat.

Discuss how Calories (kcal) are simply a unit of energy and that we get energy from the foods we eat. Calories as a unit of energy can also be used to express energy expenditure—in other words, how much energy we use when we move, perform physical activity, or exercise.

Guiding questions for students:

- How do we quantify the amount of energy we take in or the amount of energy we expend (through human movement)?
- What have you learned in your science classes about energy and Calories?
- What kind of energy do we get from the food we eat?
- When we watch human movement, what kind of energy are we observing?

Student Choices/Differentiation

- This discussion may be as simple as "a unit of energy" for some students.
- More advanced students may discuss how a Calorie is the amount of energy required to heat up a gram of water 1 degree Celsius.

What to Look For

Do students know that:

- A Calorie (with a capital *C*) is equal to 1 kilocalorie?
- A kilocalorie is equal to 1,000 calories (with a lowercase *c*)?
- A Calorie is equal to 1,000 calories?
- In everyday language and nutrition books, calorie or cal has become the same as Calorie?
- Some cellphone fitness apps use "CALORIES (kcals)"?

Instructional Task:
Forehand and Backhand Strike in Grids

■ PRACTICE TASK

Teaching in grids, assign tasks from the controlled environment, moving toward an uncontrolled environment.

EMBEDDED OUTCOME: S1.M14.7 The purpose of the activity is to provide physical activity to measure and log in the lesson. Make sure students are using a mature form of forehand and backhand strokes for pickleball during the activity.

Call out commands. The students practice the task five times and then switch so their partners can perform the same command.

Partners must cooperate by making good tosses. Partners should also encourage one another.

1. Toss the pickleball to the middle section of your partner's forehand side for five hits. Same task with backhand.
2. Toss the pickleball so your partner has to take a quick step to the forearm side to hit the ball. Same task with backhand (step toward backhand side).
3. Toss the pickleball so your partner has to take a quick step forward and hit a forehand shot. Same task with backhand.
4. Toss the pickleball so your partner has to take a quick step back while still hitting a forehand shot. Same task with backhand.

Extensions

We are now going to move into a more game-like, or uncontrolled, setting. The partner tossing should now toss the ball using any of the previous commands.

Switch after five tosses. Repeat this extension until many have had success.

Refinement

Make sure you are still tossing at the midsection and are still using only the forehand or backhand shot.

Student Choices/Differentiation

- Students can play pickleball or tennis.
- For tennis, students can use a foam ball or low-compression ball.

What to Look For

- The biggest concern in this exercise is students' not having a full movement pattern. They cut the hit short to hit the ball back to their partners instead of using a full motor pattern, hitting the ball as hard as they can.
- Make sure students are hitting the balls as hard as they can and completing the full movement pattern with a follow-through.
- If students are swinging and missing, make sure they are tracking the ball all the way to the target.

Instructional Task: Practice Volleying With a Partner

■ PRACTICE TASK

Have students (in groups of two) practice volleying with both backhand and forehand striking patterns. Students should start a short distance apart.

EMBEDDED OUTCOME: S1.M16.6. The purpose of the activity is to provide physical activity to measure and log in the lesson. Make sure students are moving and using both the forehand and backhand strokes to volley.

Extension

Have students take four or five steps back if they are having success with the shorter distances.

Refinement

Focus on keeping the wrist firm and crossing over (turning sideways to target).

Student Choices/Differentiation

- Students can play pickleball or tennis.
- For tennis, students can use a foam ball or low-compression ball.

What to Look For

Students are moving side to side, forward, and backward to successfully volley with their partners (i.e., they should not be standing in one place expecting the ball to come to them).

Instructional Task:
Determine Appropriate Amounts of Physical Activity

■ PRACTICE TASK

Have students read and complete the worksheet Determining Physical Activity Goals for Adolescents.

Extension

Students complete steps 8 to 13 on the worksheet.

Guiding questions for students:

- Based on your current fitness level, what is an appropriate goal for you?
- Should you set a goal based on the minimal health standard or optimal health benefits standard?

Student Choices/Differentiation

- Have examples for students to view if they are having difficulty with the assignment.
- Students may work with partners or in small groups.

What to Look For

Students follow each step on the worksheet and perform the math correctly.

Instructional Task:
Comparison of Physical Activity to Amount Needed

■ PRACTICE TASK

Have students estimate the number of Calories (kcal) they expended in today's sports practice by using the Calories Used for Activities by Weight Categories handout from Lesson 1.

Extension

Ask students what can be concluded about the amount of physical activity that can be obtained in a typical physical education class.

Guiding questions for students:

- Based on the amount of physical activity you determined from the worksheet and the number of Calories expended through today's physical activity, what adjustments can you make to make sure you get enough physical activity?
- Where in the day can you fit in additional physical activity?

Student Choices/Differentiation

- Have examples for students to view if they are having difficulty with the assignment.
- Students may work with partners or in small groups.

What to Look For

- Students estimate Calories (kcal) expended based on time and weight.
- Students use that estimation for tennis since pickleball is very similar to tennis.
- Students recognize that physical education is not likely to be enough. Additional physical activity must occur outside of class.

Formal and Informal Assessments

- Think, pair, share (students recognize that physical education typically does not provide enough physical activity and that additional physical activity outside of class is necessary)
- Self-assessment: comparing their two-week physical activity logs to appropriate amount of physical activity determined from worksheet

Closure

If we look at statistics for overweight and obesity, we learn that 69 percent of adults age 20 and older in the United States are overweight or obese.

- Why is this a problem?
- What have you learned today that could help fix this problem?

Reflection

- Reflect on students' self-assessments.
- Is the class ready to move on?
- Do the concepts need to be re-taught?

Homework

Take your completed physical activity logs home and compare the quantities of physical activity you acquired for those two weeks to the quantities you determined from today's worksheet.

In addition, you will take home the Healthy Eating for an Active Lifestyle handout. You will read it and then reflect on the two-week nutrition part of your log. Your reflection should be about a half page long.

Resources

Corbin, C.B., Masurier, G.C., & Lambdin, D.D. (2007). *Fitness for life: Middle school*. Champaign, IL: Human Kinetics.

Corbin, C., Pangrazi, R., & Welk. G. (1994). Toward an understanding of appropriate physical activity levels for youth. *Physical Activity and Fitness Research Digest, 1*(8), 1-8.

Hichwa, J. (1998). *Right fielders are people, too: An inclusive approach to teaching middle school physical education*. Champaign, IL: Human Kinetics.

Choose My Plate: www.choosemyplate.gov

10 tips
Nutrition Education Series

healthy eating for an active lifestyle

ChooseMyPlate.gov

10 tips for combining good nutrition and physical activity

For youth and adults engaging in physical activity and sports, healthy eating is essential for optimizing performance. Combining good nutrition with physical activity can lead to a healthier lifestyle.

1 maximize with nutrient-packed foods
Give your body the nutrients it needs by eating a variety of nutrient-packed food, including whole grains, lean protein, fruits and vegetables, and low-fat or fat-free dairy. Eat less food high in solid fats, added sugars, and sodium (salt).

2 energize with grains
Your body's quickest energy source comes from foods such as bread, pasta, oatmeal, cereals, and tortillas. Be sure to make at least half of your grain food choices whole-grain foods like whole-wheat bread or pasta and brown rice.

3 power up with protein
Protein is essential for building and repairing muscle. Choose lean or low-fat cuts of beef or pork, and skinless chicken or turkey. Get your protein from seafood twice a week. Quality protein sources come from plant-based foods, too.

4 mix it up with plant protein foods
Variety is great! Choose beans and peas (kidney, pinto, black, or white beans; split peas; chickpeas; hummus), soy products (tofu, tempeh, veggie burgers), and unsalted nuts and seeds.

5 vary your fruits and vegetables
Get the nutrients your body needs by eating a variety of colors, in various ways. Try blue, red, or black berries; red and yellow peppers; and dark greens like spinach and kale. Choose fresh, frozen, low-sodium canned, dried, or 100 percent juice options.

6 don't forget dairy
Foods like fat-free and low-fat milk, cheese, yogurt, and fortified soy beverages (soymilk) help to build and maintain strong bones needed for everyday activities.

7 balance your meals
Use MyPlate as a reminder to include all food groups each day. Learn more at www.ChooseMyPlate.gov.

8 drink water
Stay hydrated by drinking water instead of sugary drinks. Keep a reusable water bottle with you to always have water on hand.

9 know how much to eat
Get personalized nutrition information based on your age, gender, height, weight, current physical activity level, and other factors. Use SuperTracker to determine your calorie needs, plan a diet that's right for you, and track progress toward your goals. Lean more at www.SuperTracker.usda.gov.

10 reach your goals
Earn Presidential recognition for reaching your healthy eating and physical activity goals. Log on to www.presidentschallenge.org to sign up for the Presidential Active Lifestyle Award (PALA+).

Go to www.ChooseMyPlate.gov and www.Fitness.gov for more information.

DG TipSheet No. 25
March 2013
Center for Nutrition Policy and Promotion
USDA is an equal opportunity provider and employer.

LESSON 5: RESISTANCE, BODY-WEIGHT & LIGHT FREE-WEIGHT STATIONS

Grade-Level Outcomes

Primary Outcomes

Engages in physical activity: Participates in a variety of strength- and endurance-fitness activities such as Pilates, resistance training, body-weight training and light free-weight training. (S3.M3.7)

Engages in physical activity: Participates in a variety of strength- and endurance-fitness activities such as weight training or resistance training. (S3.M4.7)

Embedded Outcome

Safety: *Independently* uses physical activity and exercise equipment appropriately and safely. (S4.M7.7)

Lesson Objective

The learner will participate in a variety of strength- and endurance-fitness activities and identify whether the activities are resistance training, body-weight training, or light free-weight training.

Equipment and Materials

- Portable tennis nets
- Plastic pickleballs
- Plastic paddles
- Tennis rackets
- Low-compression tennis balls
- Foam tennis balls
- Resistance bands (variety of resistances)
- Sand bells (variety of weights)
- Agility ladders
- Station cards for muscle-strengthening resistance training (with definitions and examples)
- Station cards for muscle-strengthening resistance training and bone-strengthening physical activities (see handout from Lesson 2)
- What Is It? assessment (see handout)
- Clipboards
- Pencils

Introduction

You will remember in a previous lesson, we explored and experienced aerobic physical activity, muscle-strengthening physical activity, and bone-strengthening physical activity. Today, we will go into greater depth by identifying exercises that involve resistance training, body-weight training, and light free-weight training.

Instructional Task: Stations

■ PRACTICE TASK

Students rotate through the stations used in Lesson 2. This time, they carry the What Is It? assessment with a clipboard and pencil.

WHAT IS IT?

Directions: Check all boxes that apply for each activity. Choose the best answers, meaning the ones that make the most sense. **Hint**: There can be more than one answer for each activity.

Activity 1: Jog around the perimeter of our area.

Aerobic training	Strength and endurance training	Resistance training	Body weight training	Light free-weight training	Muscle-strengthening training	Bone-strengthening training
☐	☐	☐	☐	☐	☐	☐

Activity 2: Volley with your partner.

Aerobic training	Strength and endurance training	Resistance training	Body weight training	Light free-weight training	Muscle-strengthening training	Bone-strengthening training
☐	☐	☐	☐	☐	☐	☐

Activity 3: See how many push-ups and curl-ups you can do.

Aerobic training	Strength and endurance training	Resistance training	Body weight training	Light free-weight training	Muscle-strengthening training	Bone-strengthening training
☐	☐	☐	☐	☐	☐	☐

Activity 4: Determine a baseline for your muscle for a biceps curl.

Aerobic training	Strength and endurance training	Resistance training	Body weight training	Light free-weight training	Muscle-strengthening training	Bone-strengthening training
☐	☐	☐	☐	☐	☐	☐

Activity 5: Jump rope with your partner.

Aerobic training	Strength and endurance training	Resistance training	Body weight training	Light free-weight training	Muscle-strengthening training	Bone-strengthening training
☐	☐	☐	☐	☐	☐	☐

Activity 6: Practice your forehand volley.

Aerobic training	Strength and endurance training	Resistance training	Body weight training	Light free-weight training	Muscle-strengthening training	Bone-strengthening training
☐	☐	☐	☐	☐	☐	☐

Activity 7: Determine a baseline for your muscles for an upright row.

Aerobic training	Strength and endurance training	Resistance training	Body weight training	Light free-weight training	Muscle-strengthening training	Bone-strengthening training
☐	☐	☐	☐	☐	☐	☐

Activity 8: Determine a baseline for your muscles for a seated row.

Aerobic training	Strength and endurance training	Resistance training	Body weight training	Light free-weight training	Muscle-strengthening training	Bone-strengthening training
☐	☐	☐	☐	☐	☐	☐

Activity 9: Determine a baseline for your muscles for a triceps extension.

Aerobic training	Strength and endurance training	Resistance training	Body weight training	Light free-weight training	Muscle-strengthening training	Bone-strengthening training
☐	☐	☐	☐	☐	☐	☐

Activity 10: Perform various agility ladder drills.

Aerobic training	Strength and endurance training	Resistance training	Body weight training	Light free-weight training	Muscle-strengthening training	Bone-strengthening training
☐	☐	☐	☐	☐	☐	☐

Activity 11: Perform various agility ladder drills.

Aerobic training	Strength and endurance training	Resistance training	Body weight training	Light free-weight training	Muscle-strengthening training	Bone-strengthening training
☐	☐	☐	☐	☐	☐	☐

Activity 12: Practice your backhand volley.

Aerobic training	Strength and endurance training	Resistance training	Body weight training	Light free-weight training	Muscle-strengthening training	Bone-strengthening training
☐	☐	☐	☐	☐	☐	☐

From R.J. Doan, L.C. MacDonald, and S. Chepko, eds., 2017, *Lesson planning for middle school physical education* (Reston, VA: SHAPE America; Champaign, IL: Human Kinetics).

Ask students to identify if the activities at each station are:

- Aerobic training
- Strength and endurance training
- Resistance training
- Body-weight training
- Light free-weight training
- Muscle strengthening
- Bone strengthening

Students should select the best answers. More than one box can be checked for each activity.

Stations (from lesson 2):

1. Jog around the perimeter of the teaching area.
2. Volley with a partner across a portable tennis net.
3. Perform as many push-ups and curl-ups as you can.
4. Determine your 10-repetition max for biceps curls and try one level up (overload).
5. Jump rope with a partner and encourage each other.
6. Practice your forehand (take turns tossing a ball to your partner's forehand).
7. Determine your 10-repetition max for the upright row and try one level up (overload).
8. Determine your 10-repetition max for the seated row and try one level up (overload).
9. Determine your 10-repetition max for triceps extensions and try one level up (overload).
10. Perform agility ladder drills.
11. Perform more advanced agility ladder drills.
12. Practice your backhand (take turns tossing a ball to your partner's backhand).

Extension

As you observe the stations, initiate discussions about various activities and how there may or may not be more than one answer.

EMBEDDED OUTCOME: S4.M7.7 Students use various pieces of exercise equipment in the lesson. Make sure students know and use equipment in appropriate ways. Students also should provide corrective feedback with regard to safety, as appropriate.

Student Choices/Differentiation

- Students choose from various weights and resistance bands.
- Students can play tennis or pickleball.
- Students have their choice of equipment.

What to Look for

Students properly identify the physical activity types for each station.

1. Aerobic training and bone strengthening
2. Aerobic training and bone strengthening
3. Muscle strengthening, resistance training, and body-weight training
4. Muscle strengthening, resistance training, and light free-weight training
5. Aerobic training and bone-strengthening
6. Aerobic training and bone-strengthening
7. Muscle strengthening, resistance training, and light free-weight training

8. Muscle strengthening, resistance training, and light free-weight training
9. Muscle strengthening, resistance training, and light free-weight training
10. Aerobic training and bone strengthening
11. Aerobic training and bone strengthening
12. Aerobic training and bone-strengthening

Formal and Informal Assessments

What Is It? (formative assessment)

Closure

At the end of class, debrief the lesson by having students share their responses. Go over each activity and the answers that should have been selected.

Reflection

- Based on the What Is It? formative assessment (see handout) and debriefing at end of class, do students seem to grasp the differences among various types of physical activities?
- Are students ready to tackle Outcome S3.M15.7: Designs and implements a program of remediation for 2 areas of weakness based on the results of health-related fitness assessment?

Homework

Reflect on the following:

What types of physical activities can you choose to do, and how do they influence your Fitnessgram scores?

How much physical activity do you need if you were to quantify this through expending Calories (kcal)?

What barriers prevent you from being as physically active as you can be?

Resources

U.S. Department of Health and Human Services. (2008). *Physical activity guidelines for Americans.* Washington, DC: Author. Available at www.health.gov.

LESSON 6: REMEDIATION OF HEALTH-RELATED FITNESS (PRACTICE)

Grade-Level Outcomes

Primary Outcome

Assessment & program planning: Designs and implements a program of remediation for 2 areas of weakness based on the results of health-related fitness assessment. (S3.M15.7)

Embedded Outcomes

Fitness knowledge: Adjusts physical activity based on quantity of exercise needed for a minimal health standard and/or optimal functioning based on current fitness level. (S3.M8.7)

Forehand & backhand: Demonstrates the mature form of the forehand and backhand strokes with a short-handled implement in net games such as paddle ball, pickleball or short-handled racket tennis. (S1.M14.6)

Volley: Forehand- and backhand-volleys with a mature form and control using a short-handled implement. (S1.16.7)

Forehand & backhand: Demonstrates the mature form of forehand strokes with a short- or long-handled implement with power and accuracy in net games such as pickleball, tennis, badminton or paddle ball. (S1.M14.8)

Lesson Objectives

The learner will:

- work cooperatively to design a program of remediation for two areas of weakness based on the results of health-related fitness assessment.
- execute forehand and backhand strokes for power, accuracy, and form for pickleball or tennis.

Note: Students likely will need more than one class period to complete this lesson objective.

Equipment and Materials

- Portable tennis nets
- Plastic pickleballs
- Plastic paddles
- Tennis rackets
- Low-compression tennis balls
- Foam tennis balls
- Clipboards
- Pencils
- A few Fitnessgram reports (enough for cooperative groups—two areas of weakness should be apparent on these samples)
- A few physical activity logs (enough for cooperative groups)
- Physical Activity Remediation Plan Template, in packets of 14, 1 packet per member of each cooperative group (see handout)
- Scoring Guide for Your Physical Activity Remediation Plan handout, 1 per student

Introduction

Share with a peer your homework from last class. Who wants to share with the group what you came up with for the three questions?

Today, in addition to practicing your backhand and forehand in tennis and pickleball, you will apply your knowledge of fitness to design a health-enhancing program of physical activity. We'll split into two groups today. One group will practice the forehand and backhand, while the other group will work on designing a physical activity remediation plan. Halfway through the class period, we will rotate so that everyone has a chance to work on both the striking skill and the program-design skill.

Instructional Task: Small-Sided Games Practice

■ PRACTICE TASK

Create three practice tasks. Students may choose one of the following to participate in.
1. Practice a mature form of the forehand and backhand in a net game using cross-court and down-the-line shots. Score an extra point if one of these shots ends the rally.

EMBEDDED OUTCOME: S1.M14.6. Make sure students are using mature forehand and backhand shots while hitting cross court and down the line.

1. Forehand- and backhand-volleys with a mature form and control at the net. Have students keep the volleys going by seeing how many they can hit in a row.

EMBEDDED OUTCOME: S1.M16.7. Make sure students are using proper technique when performing volleys with a partner.

1. Practice a mature from of forehand and backhand strokes with power. Students are awarded for hitting targets placed along the baseline.

EMBEDDED OUTCOME: S1.M14.8. Make sure students are not sacrificing striking pattern for power.

Rotate with the other group at the midpoint of the class period.

Encourage students to think about their current skill level and choose the station they need to work on.

Extension

Set up one court with a video-recording device. Have students review their technique.

Student Choices/Differentiation

- Students can play pickleball or tennis (with low-compression ball).
- Students can choose station 1, 2, or 3.
- Students can rotate to the next station.

What to Look For

- Station 1: Students are progressing to where they can start volleying the ball back and forth.
- Station 2: Students are progressing to where they can start to play a competitive game.
- Station 3: Students are demonstrating proficient use of the forehand and backhand and starting to demonstrate control and power.

Instructional Task: Program Design

■ PRACTICE TASK

Create cooperative groups of four or five students who will work together to design a hypothetical program based on a sample Fitnessgram report where two areas of remediation are needed.

In addition, provide sample physical activity and nutrition logs to students.

Students also should use the Scoring Guide for Your Physical Activity Remediation Plan to guide their work.

Tell students that this is their opportunity to work cooperatively and learn from each other. This is practice for the real thing. Soon, they will receive their own Fitnessgram reports and their own Physical Activity Remediation Plan Template to design their own programs.

Rotate with the other group at the midpoint of the class period.

PHYSICAL ACTIVITY REMEDIATION PLAN TEMPLATE

Day: _____

Time of day	Amount of time you will spend performing this activity	Activity	Fitness component addressed	Why are you doing this?	Intensity level	Calories (kcal) expended

Total Calories (kcal) for the day: _____

Total physical activity time: _____

From R.J. Doan, L.C. MacDonald, and S. Chepko, eds., 2017, *Lesson planning for middle school physical education* (Reston, VA: SHAPE America; Champaign, IL: Human Kinetics).

SCORING GUIDE
FOR YOUR PHYSICAL ACTIVITY REMEDIATION PLAN

Directions: Design a two-week program of remediation for two areas of weakness based on the results of your health-related fitness assessment (Fitnessgram report). This plan provides your teacher with evidence that you have the knowledge and ability to apply many of the concepts we have learned as a class this year in an effort to attain and maintain a health-enhancing level of physical activity, which applies to National Standard 3.

Implementation: Important! You are expected to implement this plan and keep track of what you do in a log. Make sure that you choose activities that you will actually do.

You can use the template provided to help you design your plan. You will need to make 13 additional copies in order to have enough for a two-week plan. A PDF version is available on the school website. If you do not want to make copies, you can simply use notebook paper, a ruler, and a pen or pencil to create the form.

Use the following scoring guide. It is a simple yes/no self-assessment of your work. Using this scoring guide will help you turn in high-quality work.

1	Yes	No	Evidence of a proper warm-up for the chosen activities or sports
2	Yes	No	Evidence that you took the Fitnessgram report into consideration and that you are working on improving two areas of weakness
3	Yes	No	Lists the time of day when you plan to undertake to activities
4	Yes	No	Lists the approximate amount of time you plan to spend on the activities
5	Yes	No	Considers the amount of physical activity that is needed for attaining an optimal functioning standard of fitness or a minimal health standard of fitness
6	Yes	No	Includes aerobic activities
7	Yes	No	Includes muscle-strengthening activities that are either structured or unstructured
8	Yes	No	Includes bone-strengthening activities
9	Yes	No	Includes some estimate of measure of exercise intensity (e.g., moderate or vigorous; Calories per minute; RPE; heart rate; steps per minute; watts; pace)
10	Yes	No	Tracks total number of minutes engaged in activity and Calories (kcal) expended per day

From R.J. Doan, L.C. MacDonald, and S. Chepko, eds., 2017, *Lesson planning for middle school physical education* (Reston, VA: SHAPE America; Champaign, IL: Human Kinetics).

Extension

Students can share their findings with classmates.

EMBEDDED OUTCOME: S3.M8.7 As part of the activity, students suggest adjustments to physical activity based on the hypothetical log and physical activity guidelines.

Student Choices/Differentiation

- Provide various samples of Fitnessgram reports that students can choose from.
- Provide a couple of samples of two-week physical activity and nutrition logs that students can choose from.

What to Look For

- Students examine the Fitnessgram reports for two needed areas of remediation.
- Students determine quantities of needed physical activity for a minimal health standard and optimal functioning.
- Students fill out the remediation plan templates to include everything listed on the scoring guide.

Formal and Informal Assessments

Scoring Guide for Your Physical Activity Remediation Plan

Closure

You just practiced designing a program of remediation for two areas of weakness based on health-related fitness assessment results. This was a good opportunity to learn from each other and to practice on a hypothetical person. Soon, you will do this for yourself using the results of your own fitness assessment. If you feel that you are ready to do it on your own, give me a thumb up. If you need more practice, give me a thumb in the middle. If you feel that you are completely lost and we need to review, give me a thumb down.

Reflection

- How much additional time will students need to complete this assignment?
- What misunderstandings will need to be cleared up before assigning this to be completed individually with their own reports and data?
- What additional clarifications need to be made?
- Are there any important concepts that need to retaught before moving forward?

Homework

Think and write about how much physical activity is recommended to be healthy. What adjustments can you make to your physical activity and busy lives to fit in the recommended amounts?

Resources

Corbin, C., Pangrazi, R., & Welk, G. (1994). Towards an understanding of appropriate physical activity levels for youth. *Physical Activity and Fitness Research Digest, 1*(8), 1-8.

U.S. Department of Health and Human Services. (2008). *Physical activity guidelines for Americans.* Washington, DC: Author. Available at www.health.gov.

LESSON 7:
CREATING A FITNESS PROGRAM DESIGN

Grade-Level Outcomes

Primary Outcome

Assessment & program planning: Designs and implements a program of remediation for 2 areas of weakness based on the results of health-related fitness assessment. (S3.M15.7)

Embedded Outcomes

Forehand & backhand: Demonstrates the mature form of the forehand and backhand strokes with a short-handled implement in net games such as paddle ball, pickleball or short-handled racket tennis. (S1.M14.6)

Volley: Forehand- and backhand-volleys with a mature form and control using a short-handled implement. (S1.16.7)

Forehand & backhand: Demonstrates the mature form of forehand and backhand strokes with a short- or long-handled implement with power and accuracy in net games such as pickleball, tennis, badminton or paddle ball. (S1.M14.8)

Fitness knowledge: Adjusts physical activity based on quantity of exercise needed for a minimal health standard and/or optimal functioning based on current fitness level. (S3.M8.7)

Lesson Objectives

The learner will:

- design a program of remediation for two areas of weakness based on the results of her Fitness-gram report.
- include as part of the program physical activity that results in attaining either a minimum health standard or an optimal functioning level.
- implement the program once it has been designed.

Equipment and Materials

- Portable tennis nets
- Plastic pickleballs
- Plastic paddles
- Tennis rackets
- Low-compression tennis balls
- Foam tennis balls
- Clipboards
- Pencils
- Student Fitnessgram reports generated from Fitnessgram software
- Completed physical activity logs
- Physical Activity Remediation Plan Template, 1 per student (see handout from Lesson 6)
- Scoring Guide for Your Physical Activity Remediation Plan, 1 per student (see handout from Lesson 6)
- Calories Used for Activities by Weight Categories, 1 per student (see handout from Lesson 1)

Introduction

Review homework.

Today, you will continue practicing your backhand and forehand. Again, we will split the class in two. This means that you will spend half of your time today practicing your backhand and forehand, and will spend the other half on designing a physical activity program.

Instructional Task: Small-Sided Games Practice

■ PRACTICE TASK

Students participate in a pickleball station.

Station 1. Sharpshooters

Place poly spots throughout the court.

Students use the forehand and backhand to place pickleballs in specified points on the court.

Extension

Students return a shot from a peer and try to hit the target.

EMBEDDED OUTCOME: S1.M14.6. Make sure students are using mature forehand and backhand shots while striking for accuracy.

Station 2. Modified game

Students rally back and forth scoring points.

Extensions

- Students start with the serve.
- Students play by all rules.

EMBEDDED OUTCOME: S1.M14.8. Make sure students are not sacrificing striking pattern during game play.

Station 3: Rally for points

Students rally with a partner to see how many hits they can make in a row.

Extension

Students can perform the same task but volley for points.

EMBEDDED OUTCOME: S1.M16.7. Make sure students are using proper technique when performing volleys with a partner.

Student Choices/Differentiation

- Students can play pickleball or tennis (with low-compression ball).
- Students can choose a station.
- Students can rotate stations if they would like or stay at a particular station longer if more practice is needed.

What to Look For

- Station 1: Students are using a mature form and improving accuracy.
- Station 2: Students are playing the game with success.
- Station 3: Students are rallying with a high number of contacts.

Instructional Task: Program Design

■ PRACTICE TASK

Distribute the following:

- Fitnessgram reports
- Physical Activity/Fitness Plan Worksheet
- Scoring Guide for Two-Week Physical Activity Plan
- Physical Activity/Fitness Plan Template
- Students should use the Physical Activity Remediation Plan Template and Scoring Guide for Your Physical Activity Remediation Plan to help them design their plans.

PHYSICAL ACTIVITY REMEDIATION PROGRAM DESIGN

Directions: You will design a two-week program of remediation for two areas of weakness based on the results of health-related fitness assessment. In addition, you will adjust physical activity (if needed) based on quantities of exercise needed for a minimal health standard or optimal functioning based on current fitness levels.

1. Examine the Fitnessgram report that you have been provided. List two areas on your Fitnessgram report that need a program of remediation. If your report does not show two areas in need of remediation, list two areas that you would like to improve.

   _____

   _____

2. List some physical activities that you could include in this program to address the two areas identified above. Remember to consider activities that are aerobic, muscle strengthening, and bone strengthening.

3. Previously, you determined the amount of physical activity necessary for attaining a minimal health standard of fitness and an optimal functioning standard of fitness. That allowed you to determine zones for each of those levels. List the zones of Calorie (kcal) expenditure needed to attain these two zones.

Minimal Health Standard of Fitness

Calories (kcal) per day: _____ to _____ Calories (kcal)

Calories (kcal) per week: _____ to _____ Calories (kcal)

Optimal Functioning Standard of Fitness

Calories (kcal) per day: _____ to _____ Calories (kcal)

Calories (kcal) per week: _____ to _____ Calories (kcal)

4. Examine your two-week physical activity log. Based on the Calorie (kcal) estimates you listed, did you meet the minimal health standard or optimal health standard? Or, were you unable to determine this because you were not able to easily determine your physical activity expenditure?

5. Place a check next to the statement that is true.
   - ❏ I met the minimal health standard by expending _____ Calories (kcal) for the week.
   - ❏ I met the optimal functioning standard by expending _____ Calories (kcal) for the week.
   - ❏ I was unable to determine this since I had difficulty estimating my Calorie (kcal) expenditure.

6. If you were unable to estimate your Calorie expenditure, were you able to determine if you met the general rule of thumb of 60 minutes of moderate to vigorous physical activity each day?
   - Circle: Yes   No

7. Design a program of physical activity that will address your two areas of weakness based on your Fitnessgram report (step 1) and the quantity of physical activity needed. Remember the following guidelines for children and adolescents. You should also use the Calories Used for Activities by Weight Categories table and review the self-assessment of your Physical Activity and Nutrition Log for muscle-strengthening and bone-strengthening activity.

(continued)

(continued)

Guidelines	Definitions	Examples
Aerobic: Most of the recommended minimum 60 minutes or more a day of physical activity should be either moderate- or vigorous-intensity aerobic physical activity, and should include vigorous-intensity physical activity at least three days a week.	**Aerobic activities** involve rhythmic movements of the large muscles. This type of activity increases cardiorespiratory fitness.	• Running • Hopping • Skipping • Jumping rope • Swimming • Dancing • Bicycling
Muscle strengthening: As part of their recommended 60 minutes or more of daily physical activity, children and adolescents should include muscle-strengthening physical activity on at least three days of the week.	**Muscle-strengthening activities** make muscles do more work than they usually do in daily life. They use the overload principle and make muscles stronger.	• Games such as tug-of-war • Push-ups and pull-ups • Resistance exercises with exercise bands, weight machines, handheld weights • Climbing wall • Curl-ups and crunches
Bone strengthening: As part of their 60 or more minutes of daily physical activity, children and adolescents should include bone-strengthening physical activity on at least three days of the week.	**Bone-strengthening activities** produce a force on the bones that promotes bone growth and strength. These activities typically involve impacts with the ground.	• Hopping, skipping, jumping • Jumping rope • Running • Sports such as gymnastics, basketball, volleyball, tennis

From U.S. Department of Health and Human Services 2008.

From R.J. Doan, L.C. MacDonald, and S. Chepko, eds., 2017, *Lesson planning for middle school physical education* (Reston, VA: SHAPE America; Champaign, IL: Human Kinetics).

Have students begin work on their programs to remediate two areas of weakness.

EMBEDDED OUTCOME: S3.M8.7. Students' programs should also include enough physical activity to reach a minimum health standard of fitness or an optimal functioning standard of fitness. That means students might need to adjust their plans.

Because physical activity in physical education class is typically out of students' control, let them know what is most likely to occur during the upcoming weeks (e.g., a unit that will involve practicing fundamental basketball skills and small-sided games of basketball).

Rotate with the other group at the midpoint of class. Note: The first group of students need to store their papers safely until the end of class. Portfolios or folders in crates can be used.

Refinements

- Have students focus their attention on self-selected physical activities that will occur outside of physical education class.
- Remind students that they will need to implement this plan after they have finished it. They will again be keeping track of their physical activity in a log for two weeks.

Guiding questions for students:

- What technology might help you get an idea of what physical activities burn more Calories than others?
- If you don't have areas in need of remediation, what two areas would you like to improve?

Student Choices/Differentiation

- Students can choose a quantity of exercise based on their current fitness level (i.e., current fitness levels or quantities of physical activity may not allow for an optimal level of physical activity unless the quantity is gradually increased—the principle of progressive overload).
- Students who are not in need of two areas of remediation may choose areas they are interested in improving.
- Use of technology: Students can list technology that may help them quantify physical activity. For example, Fitbit activity monitors generate reports with total number of Calories (kcal) expended and also provide a graph of how many Calories are expended per minute.

What to Look For

- Students examine their Fitnessgram reports for two areas of remediation.
- Students determine quantities of needed physical activity for a minimal health standard and optimal functioning.
- Students fill out the remediation plan templates to include everything listed on the scoring guide.

Formal and Informal Assessments

- Physical Activity/Fitness Plan Worksheet
- Scoring Guide for Two-Week Physical Activity Plan (self-assessment)

Closure

Today you began work on your two-week physical activity plan to remediate two areas of need on your Fitnessgram reports.

- Why is it important to be able to design a program like this?
- How will you know that you have learned this important skill?

Reflection

- What additional assistance will students need as they complete this assignment for homework over the next couple of days?
- What misunderstandings will need to be addressed?

Homework

You will complete your two-week plan for homework. After turning in your two-week plan, you will be expected to follow your two-week plan. That means you should make sure that your plan is realistic.

Resources

Corbin, C., Pangrazi, R., & Welk, G. (1994). Towards an understanding of appropriate physical activity levels for youth. *Physical Activity and Fitness Research Digest, 1*(8), 1-8.

U.S. Department of Health and Human Services. (2008). *Physical activity guidelines for Americans.* Washington, DC: Author. Available at www.health.gov.

LESSON 8: IMPLEMENTING REMEDIATION TO PROGRAM DESIGN

Grade-Level Outcomes

Primary Outcomes

Fitness knowledge: Adjusts physical activity based on quantity of exercise needed for a minimal health standard and/or optimal functioning based on current fitness level. (S3.M8.7)

Assessment & program planning: Designs and implements a program of remediation for 2 areas of weakness based on the results of health-related fitness assessment. (S3.M15.7)

Accepting feedback: Provides corrective feedback to a peer, using teacher-generated guidelines, and incorporating appropriate tone and other communication skills. (S4.M3.7)

Embedded Outcome

Engages in physical activity: Participates in a variety of lifetime dual and individual sports, martial arts or aquatic activities. (S3.M5.7)

Lesson Objectives

The learner will:

- prepare to implement his program of remediation for two areas of weakness based on the results of his Fitnessgram report.
- prepare to adjust his level of physical activity by implementing the physical activity plan.
- provide corrective feedback to a peer using teacher-generated guidelines.

Equipment and Materials

- Portable tennis nets
- Plastic pickleballs
- Plastic paddles
- Tennis rackets
- Low-compression tennis balls
- Foam tennis balls
- Clipboards
- Pencils
- Pedometers

Introduction

Today, you will continue practicing your backhand and forehand. Again, we will split the class in two. This means that you will spend half of your time today practicing your backhand and forehand, and will spend the other half on sharing feedback with a partner on the physical activity plan that you just completed. Remember that you are expected to implement your plan. Today's lesson will provide you with an opportunity to seek feedback from a classmate before implementing your plan. That will allow you to adjust the plan, as needed, before you start.

Instructional Task: Small-Sided Games Practice

■ PRACTICE TASK

King of the court: Have multiple courts set up throughout the gym, with numbers marked with a cone.

Play an 8- to 10-minute game of pickleball, either singles or doubles. At the end of time, instruct the high scores to move to the lower-numbered court (e.g., if they won on court 4, then they move to court 3), and have the player or team with the fewest points move up a court (e.g., if they did not win on court 4, then they will move to court 5). Keep the rotation for the remainder of class.

Students are expected to self-officiate.

If the class is playing doubles, switch partners after a couple of rotations.

EMBEDDED OUTCOME: S3.M5.7 Even though the focus is to increase heat rate and physical activity, students should have fun participating in a lifetime activity.

Extension

After each game, check your pedometers to see how many steps were taken during the game.

Guiding questions for students:

- Did you have higher or lower step counts if you won?
- Why do you think this is?
- Did it change when you played with a different partner?

Student Choices/Differentiation

If students are struggling, give them an opportunity to practice their pickleball skills off the court.

What to Look For

Students are moving and playing students of similar ability levels.

Instructional Task: Peer Assessment

■ PRACTICE TASK

Have students select a partner they feel comfortable with.

Partners will review each other's two-week physical activity plans using a teacher-created peer-assessment form and provide feedback.

Have partners discuss with each other the two areas of remediation they selected from their Fitnessgram reports.

Have partners examine previous physical activity logs and compare current physical activity plans. They should determine if the amount of physical activity that was logged fits into a minimal health standard (3 to 4 kcal per kilogram of body weight per day) or if it provides enough physical activity for optimal functioning (6 to 8 kcal per kilogram of body weight per day). Students should decide if adjustments need to be made and make comparisons to the new physical activity plan.

Extension

Have students use their partners' self-assessment scoring guide to peer-assess their fitness plans. Have them determine if they agree with their partners' self-assessment of their plans.

Refinements

- Students can refine their physical activity plans based on their partners' feedback.
- Students should refrain from sarcasm and should be respectful of their partners' fitness scores and personal information.
- Students should focus on helping each other with their feedback.

Student Choices/Differentiation

- Students may choose their partners.
- Model an example of how to give feedback.

What to Look For

- Students discuss two areas of remediation from the Fitnessgram reports.
- Students determine the amount of physical activity needed for a minimal health standard or optimal functioning.

- Students examine previous physical activity logs for the quantity of physical activity obtained (if it was not quantified by Calories, time could be used instead).
- Students use their partners' self-assessment as a peer assessment (teacher-generated guidelines).
- Students use appropriate tone and communication skills when providing feedback.

Formal and Informal Assessments

Physical activity and fitness portfolios, including the following:

- Completed two-week physical activity plan
- Completed two-week physical activity log (from Lesson 1)
- Student Fitnessgram report generated from Fitnessgram software
- Completed self-assessment of Calories expended over the two-week plan
- Physical Activity Remediation Plan Worksheet
- Scoring Guide for Your Physical Activity Remediation Plan (used as peer-assessment)

Closure

Today, you finished your two-week physical activity plan to remediate two areas of need in your fitness.

- What were the most difficult parts of the plan?
- How will this module help you in the future?

Reflection

- Were students able to provide useful corrective feedback using appropriate tone and communication skills?
- Did students design a program they could actually use?

Homework

It's now time to implement your physical activity remediation plans. This is an opportunity to adjust your physical activity levels. If you need to adjust your level of physical activity, do it carefully. You should not make huge jumps in your physical activity level. Remember to use the progressive overload principle so that you don't hurt yourself.

Resources

Corbin, C., Pangrazi, R., & Welk, G. (1994). Toward an understanding of appropriate physical activity levels for youth. *Physical Activity and Fitness Research Digest, 1*(8), 1-8.

U.S. Department of Health and Human Services. (2008). *Physical activity guidelines for Americans.* Washington, DC: Author. Available at www.health.gov.

MONITORING PHYSICAL ACTIVITY WITH TECHNOLOGY MODULE (GRADE 8)

Lesson plans in this module contributed by John Kruse, a middle school physical education teacher with the Los Angeles Unified School District.

Grade-Level Outcomes Addressed, by Lesson	Lessons							
	1	2	3	4	5	6	7	8
Standard 1. The physically literate individual demonstrates competency in a variety of motor skills and movement patterns.								
Standard 2. The physically literate individual applies knowledge of concepts, principles, strategies and tactics related to movement and performance.								
Standard 3. The physically literate individual demonstrates the knowledge and skills to achieve and maintain a health-enhancing level of physical activity and fitness.								
Identifies the 5 components of health-related fitness (muscular strength, muscular endurance, flexibility, cardiovascular endurance, body composition) and explains the connections between fitness and overall physical and mental health. (S5.M1.8)								P
Participates in a self-selected lifetime sport, dance, aquatic or outdoor activity outside of the school day. (S3.M5.8)					E			
Uses available technology to self-monitor quantity of exercise needed for a minimal health standard and/or optimal functioning based on current fitness level. (S3.M8.8)	P	P	P	P	P	E	P	P
Uses the overload principle (FITT formula) in preparing a personal workout. (S3.M11.8)			P	P				
Designs and implements a warm-up/cool-down regimen for a self-selected physical activity. (S3.M12.8)			E					
Designs and implements a program of remediation for 3 areas of weakness based on the results of health-related fitness assessment. (S3.M15.8)						P	P	P
Standard 4. The physically literate individual exhibits responsible personal and social behavior that respects self and others.								
Accepts responsibility for improving one's own levels of physical activity and fitness. (S4.M1.8)				E				
Uses effective self-monitoring skills to incorporate opportunities for physical activity in and outside of school. (S4.M2.8)		E						
Provides encouragement and feedback to peers without prompting from the teacher. (S4.M3.8)		E					E	
Applies rules and etiquette by acting as an official for modified physical activities and games and creating dance routines within a given set of parameters. (S4.M6.8)	E							
Standard 5. The physically literate individual recognizes the value of physical activity for health, enjoyment, challenge, self-expression and/or social interaction.								
Identifies the 5 components of health-related fitness (muscular strength, muscular endurance, flexibility, cardiovascular endurance, body composition) and explains the connections between fitness and overall physical and mental health. (S5.M1.8)								P
Discusses how enjoyment could be increased in self-selected physical activities. (S5.M4.8)							E	
Identifies and participates in an enjoyable activity that prompts individual self-expression. (S5.M5.8)								E

P = Primary; E = Embedded

LESSON 1: SETTING A FITNESS BASELINE

Grade-Level Outcomes

Primary Outcome

Fitness knowledge: Uses available technology to self-monitor quantity of exercise needed for a minimal health standard and/or optimal functioning based on current fitness level. (S3.M8.8)

Embedded Outcome

Rules & Etiquette: Applies rules and etiquette by acting as an official for modified physical activities and games and creating dance routines within a given set of parameters. (S4.M6.8)

Lesson Objective

The learner will determine the amount of exercise needed to attain a minimal health standard and/or optimal functioning level, based on her current fitness level.

Equipment and Materials

- Determining Physical Activity Goals for Adolescents handout, 1 per student (see handout)
- Pencils
- Clipboards
- Exercise Physiologist Worksheet handout (see handout)
- Ellipticals for one-quarter of class (with electronic readouts)
- Stationary cycles for one-quarter of class (with electronic readouts)

Introduction

Today, we will start a unit of study on using available technology to monitor how much physical activity you participate in. In doing so, you will use this technology to get an idea of how fit you are and determine how much physical activity you need. Eventually, you will use this knowledge and technology to self-monitor the amount of exercise you undertake and to make adjustments.

Instructional Task: Cycle or Elliptical

■ PRACTICE TASK

Students work in pairs for today's class. One partner will ride either a stationary cycle or an elliptical for 20 minutes. The other partner will record the exercising student's data as she performs her workout.

Your partner will serve as your exercise physiologist today, and you are the client.

Partners switch roles after 20 minutes.

EMBEDDED OUTCOME: S4.M6.8. Use the exercise physiologist role to teach students about the proper way to monitor activity for someone else. Remind students to be non-judgmental, accurate in recording, and encouraging of others.

Every 2 minutes, the partner will record the following:

- Speed
- Distance
- Level
- Calories
- RPMs
- Watts
- Heart rate

All information should come from the electronic display. Since the machines you are using measure work (watts), they are known as ergometers. Ergo = work, and meter = measure.

Be sure to use the manual setting and demonstrate that you can give yourself a proper warm-up (it should show in your data).

Extension

Students can graph the data collected. A line graph of the speed and watts should show a warm-up.

Refinement

Make sure students know the different measurements before starting the activity.

Student Choices/Differentiation

- Students select either a cycle or an elliptical.
- Students can choose to manipulate the following variables in order to use the principle of overload:
  - Keep the resistance level the same and attempt to maintain a slightly higher average speed.
  - Increase the resistance level and either expect to see a lower average speed or attempt to keep the average speed the same.
  - Attempt to maintain a higher average heart rate.
  - Attempt to maintain a higher average power (watts) by manipulating speed and resistance.

What to Look For

- "Exercise physiologists" are collecting data every 2 minutes.
- In examining the data, you should see students start off at lower levels and speeds in order to give themselves a proper warm-up.

Instructional Task: Demonstration on Determining Quantities of Exercise Needed

■ PRACTICE TASK

On a whiteboard, perform an example and the mathematics required to complete the handout Determining Physical Activity Goals for Adolescents.

Example: Determine the amount of exercise needed for a 60 kg person for a minimal health standard and optimal functioning. (Answer: 60 kg × 3-4 kcal and 60 kg × 6-8 kcal)

DETERMINING PHYSICAL ACTIVITY GOALS FOR ADOLESCENTS

Name: _____ Date: _____

Introduction: Over the years, various fitness and health guidelines have been promoted. Many of these guidelines are general rules of thumb designed for the general public. You might see these guideline promoted in public service announcements (PSAs). Today, we often hear about 60 minutes of physical activity on television. A good example is the NFL Play 60 campaign.

Another general rule of thumb is to expend, at a minimum, 200 kilocalories from physical activity every day (or 1,000 to 1,400 kilocalories per week). Keep in mind, this is only a minimum.

For optimal health benefits and wellness, a person should expend 2,000 to 3,500 kilocalories per week. This rule of thumb is based on a person who weighs about 150 pounds (68 kg).

Many adults hire personal trainers at great expense to design these fitness programs for them. Because you are in a physical education class, you are developing the skills and knowledge to be a participant in physical activity for a lifetime. This means that you should be able to design a fitness program for yourself based on your needs, not a general rule of thumb. Also, if you acquire these skills and knowledge, it is likely that you won't need to hire a personal trainer to design a fitness program for you. So let's determine just how much physical activity you need.

Determining Physical Activity Levels

HEALTH STANDARD: A MINIMUM ACTIVITY STANDARD

Frequency	Daily. Frequent activity sessions (three or more) each day.
Intensity	Moderate. Alternating bouts of activity with rest periods as needed or moderate activity such as walking or riding a bike to school.
Time	Duration of activity necessary to expend 3 to 4 kcal per kilogram of body weight per day. Equal to Calorie expenditure in 30 minutes or more of active play or moderate sustained activity, which may be distributed over three or more activity sessions.

OPTIMAL FUNCTIONING STANDARD: A GOAL FOR ALL CHILDREN

Frequency	Daily. Frequent activity session (three or more) each day.
Intensity	Moderate to vigorous. Alternating bouts of activity with rest periods as needed or moderate activity such as walking or riding a bike to school.
Time	Duration of activity necessary to expend 6 to 8 kcal per kilogram of body weight per day. Equal to Calorie expenditure in 60 minutes or more of active play or moderate to sustained activity, which may be distributed over three or more activity sessions.

Directions: Follow the numbered steps below to determine the amount of physical activity that you need.

Step 1: Locate and circle your weight in pounds on the table below.

Pounds	Kilograms	Pounds	Kilograms	Pounds	Kilograms	Pounds	Kilograms	Pounds	Kilograms
40	18	95	43	150	68	205	92	260	117
45	20	100	45	155	70	210	95	265	120
50	22	105	47	160	72	215	97	270	122
55	24	110	49	165	74	220	99	275	124
60	27	115	52	170	77	225	102	280	127
65	29	120	54	175	79	230	104	285	129
70	31	125	56	180	81	235	106	290	131
75	34	130	58	185	83	240	108	295	133
80	36	135	61	190	86	245	111	300	136
85	38	140	63	195	88	250	113	305	138
90	40	145	56	200	90	255	115		

(continued)

(continued)

Step 2: Now, convert your weight in pounds to kilograms by looking at the adjacent number on the table. If you are concerned about others knowing your weight, you can fold your paper in half to keep this information private. My weight in kilograms is: _____.

Determining the Health Standard: A Minimum Activity Standard

Step 3: Multiply your weight in kilograms by 3. My weight in kilograms × 3 is _____.

Step 4: Multiply your weight in kilograms by 4. My weight in kilograms × 4 is _____.

Determining an Optimal Functioning Standard: A Goal for All Children

Step 5: Multiply your weight in kilograms by 6. My weight in kilograms × 6 is _____.

Step 6: Multiply your weight in kilograms by 8. My weight in kilograms × 8 is _____.

Based on your physical activity log, are you able to determine the total number of kilocalories that you expended during the two weeks that you recorded? Circle: Yes   No

If you answered no, what are some choices you could make that would help you better estimate this amount of exercise in the future?

What available technology options can help you determine how much physical activity you are getting?

What technology do you have at home that could help you determine how much physical activity you are getting?

Discuss how you could use that technology to better estimate the amount of exercise you engage in.

Reprinted from C.B. Corbin and R.P Pangrazi, 1994, "Toward an understanding of appropriate physical activity for youth," *President's Council on Physical Fitness and Sports Series* 1(8).

From R.J. Doan, L.C. MacDonald, and S. Chepko, eds., 2017, *Lesson planning for middle school physical education* (Reston, VA: SHAPE America; Champaign, IL: Human Kinetics).

Extension

Ask for a student to volunteer his Exercise Physiologist Worksheet handout and show how a comparison can be made between these numbers and the data collected from the machines by comparing how many Calories were actually burned during the workout.

Student Choices/Differentiation

- Provide examples of the handout for students to view.
- Students can work in partners.

What to Look For

Students are filling out their worksheets correctly.

Formal and Informal Assessments

Exercise Physiologist Worksheet handout

Closure

Today, you used ellipticals and stationary bikes to monitor your quantity of exercise. These types of machines are commonly found in fitness centers, health clubs, hotels, people's homes, and sporting goods stores. You have now seen an example of how you can use these machines to monitor your quantities of exercise and get objective data from them. Combining this skill with the knowledge of how much exercise a person needs to be healthy can be a very powerful tool for your overall health and well-being. Throughout the module we will be exploring ways to increase and track physical activity with technology.

Reflection

- Are students able to work effectively together to collect the data from the machines?
- Do students seem to be better engaged in the activity due to the technology and feedback?

Homework

Complete the Determining Physical Activity Goals for Adolescents handout. You will compare how much exercise you obtained from this workout with the amount of exercise you determined you need from the worksheet.

Resources

Corbin, C., Pangrazi, R., & Welk, G. (1994). Toward an understanding of appropriate physical activity levels for youth. *Physical Activity and Fitness Research Digest, 1*(8), 1-8.

EXERCISE PHYSIOLOGIST WORKSHEET

Client: _____

Exercise physiologist: _____

Date: _____

Period (circle):   1   2   3   4   5   6

Type of ergometer (circle):   Cycle   Elliptical

Vocabulary:

ergo = work
meter = to measure
An **erg** is a unit of measuring work.
A **meter** is the SI unit of length.

Selected program (circle one):

Manual	Interval training
Random	Heart rate
Rolling hills	Fat burn
Fitness test	Constant watts

Instructions: Fill in the data table below. Record data every 2 minutes. Note: The Select button will let you change the displayed data.

Time (min)	Speed (kph)	Distance (km)	Level	Calories (kcal)	RPM	Watts	Heart rate (bpm)
2							
4							
6							
8							
10							
12							
14							
16							
18							
20							

From R.J. Doan, L.C. MacDonald, and S. Chepko, eds., 2017, *Lesson planning for middle school physical education* (Reston, VA: SHAPE America; Champaign, IL: Human Kinetics).

LESSON 2: FITNESS CIRCUIT TRAINING

Grade-Level Outcomes

Primary Outcome

Fitness knowledge: Uses available technology to self-monitor quantity of exercise needed for a minimal health standard and/or optimal functioning based on current fitness level. (S3.M8.8)

Embedded Outcomes

Personal responsibility: Uses effective self-monitoring skills to incorporate opportunities for physical activity in and outside of school. (S4.M2.8)

Accepting feedback: Provides encouragement and feedback to peers without prompting from the teacher. (S4.M3.8)

Lesson Objectives

The learner will:

- use a heart rate monitor to self-monitor the amount of exercise in which she participates.
- create fitness circuits with a range of fitness activities.

Equipment and Materials

- IHT heart rate monitors that estimate Calories (kcal) burned
- Fitness center:
  - Agility ladders
  - Sand bells
  - Aerobic steps
  - Weighted bars
  - Jump ropes
  - Medicine balls

Introduction

Today, we are continuing our module of studying where you can use available technology to self-monitor the quantity of exercise needed for a minimal standard and for optimal functioning. For homework you determined this quantity by multiplying your weight in kilograms by 3 and 4 Calories to determine a minimal standard and by 6 and 8 Calories to determine how much you would need for optimal functioning. Today, you will use heart rate monitors that estimate the number of Calories you burn during your workout.

Instructional Task:
Calories and Heart Rate Monitors Discussion

▮ PRACTICE TASK

Guiding questions for students:

- What ways have heart rate monitors been traditionally used? (e.g., measure exercise intensity, heart rate)
- Can we judge the effectiveness of heart rate monitors by how much physical activity we are getting? (yes)

That is what you are doing today. You are tracking how many Calories are being burned during circuit training.

Remind students that you can quantify the amount of exercise a person gets more accurately if you track Calories rather than just time. This is because Calories tell us how much energy is being used.

Guiding questions for students:

- Who can remember what Calories are?
- Where do we get them from?

Remember, food energy is chemical energy, and human movement is mechanical work or mechanical energy. This is what allows us to quantify how much exercise we are getting.

Student Choices/Differentiation

Handouts or videos will help students learn the content.

What to Look For

Students have an understanding of Calories and why we would use heart rate monitors.

Instructional Task: Circuit Training

■ PRACTICE TASK

Divide the class into six groups. Each group will receive one of the following pieces of equipment to start.

- Agility ladders
- Sand bells
- Aerobic steps
- Weighted bars
- Jump ropes
- Medicine balls

Students create their own fitness circuit training stations using their piece of equipment. After 4 or 5 minutes, groups will rotate to the next piece of equipment and design a new fitness circuit training station.

Cycle continues until all groups have three different circuit training stations (rotate the rest of the way in Lesson 4).

Encourage students to design the routine with various levels at each station so that students of various ability levels can be challenged (e.g., beginning, intermediate, and advanced agility ladder drills).

Refinement

Make sure students are designing a circuit that will keep their group moving and provide a significant workout.

Extension

Have students put heart rate monitors on and lead each other through their stations.

EMBEDDED OUTCOME: S4.M3.8. Encourage students to provide encouragement and feedback to peers without prompting from the teacher.

Student Choices/Differentiation

- Students design various levels at each station.
- Students may choose their groups.
- If students need ideas, provide a handout with suggested activities they can choose from.

What to Look For

- Students properly execute the exercises at each station.
- Students fully participate in the circuit training workout.
- Students encourage others without being prompted.

Instructional Task: Comparing Energy Expenditure

■ PRACTICE TASK

This practice task prepares students for their homework.

Provide students with a sample heart rate graph and data. Inform students this is the type of graph they will be looking at for homework. They will receive an e-mail with the data from their heart rate monitor later today.

In cooperative groups, have students calculate a minimal health standard and optimal functioning standard for a 185-pound (84 kg) person. Use these numbers to make a comparison with the sample graph and data provided.

Refinement

Review calculating the minimal health standard and optimal functioning standard if needed.

Guiding questions for students:

- How do you convert 185 pounds to kilograms?
- What is the minimal health standard for our 185-pound person?
- What is the optimal functioning health standard for this 185-pound person?
- What is the difference between the quantities of exercise this sample person obtained and the minimal standard and optimal functioning standard you calculated?
- What would this person need to do outside of physical education class to obtain one or both of these recommendations?
- Identify some times during the day that are available for people your age to get additional physical activity.

Student Choices/Differentiation

- Students can choose from several graphs with data from various activities or sports.
- Students can work in pairs.

What to Look For

- Students correctly convert to kilograms for a 185-pound person.
- Students correctly determine the ranges for a minimal health standard and optimal functioning standard.
- Students compare the Calories burned in the sample data to the ranges that were determined.

Formal and Informal Assessments

- Calculations for sample 185-pound person
- Homework reflection submitted via e-mail and cloud storage

Closure

Today, you used technology to track how much physical activity you were able to obtain in a typical physical education class. Based on the data you collected and the amount of physical activity you determined in the previous lesson, what can you conclude?

- Students should conclude that we need additional physical activity outside of physical education if we want to be healthy (i.e., a typical physical education class does not provide enough time to get enough physical activity).
- Ask students if their use of technology provided them with additional motivation.

Reflection

- Does the use of technology seem to enhance engagement in the lesson?
- Did students plan appropriate circuit stations?
- Did students provide maximal effort during the lesson?
- Were students able to use heart rate monitors correctly?

Homework

Your heart rate data are being stored in the cloud by the company that manufactures the heart rate monitors we used today.

Later today, you will receive an e-mail with a link to look at the data. For homework, reflect on the quantity of exercise you obtained in class today and tell me how this compares to the minimal health standard and optimal functioning standard that you have calculated for yourself based on your weight. To do this, you simply need to reply to the e-mail message, and I will be able to see your reflection after you have submitted it.

Embedded outcome: S4.M2.8. If you fell short of the recommended quantity of your choosing (either minimal or optimal functioning), I want you to tell me how you are going to incorporate additional physical activity opportunities outside of school to obtain this recommendation.

Resources

Interactive Health Technologies Spirit System (heart rate monitor supplier and cloud management system)

LESSON 3: COMPARING AND REVIEWING DATA

Grade-Level Outcomes

Primary Outcomes

Fitness knowledge: Uses available technology to self-monitor quantity of exercise needed for a minimal health standard and/or optimal functioning based on current fitness level. (S3.M8.8)

Fitness knowledge: Uses the overload principle (FITT formula) in preparing a personal workout. (S3.M11.8)

Embedded Outcome

Fitness knowledge: Designs and implements a warm-up/cool-down regimen for a self-selected physical activity. (S3.M12.8)

Lesson Objectives

The learner will:

- use available technology to self-monitor the amount of physical activity needed for attaining a minimal health standard and/or level of optimal functioning.
- use the overload principle with available technology to increase his amount of exercise.

Equipment and Materials

- Pencils
- Clipboards
- Exercise Physiologist Worksheet handout, 1 per student (see handout from lesson 1)
- Completed Exercise Physiologist Worksheet handouts from Lesson 1
- Fitness center:
    - Ellipticals (with electronic readouts) for one-quarter of class
    - Stationary cycles (with electronic readouts) for one-quarter of class

Introduction

Today, you will use the overload principle to increase the quantity of exercise you can undertake. To do that, you will use technology and also examine the data you collected the other day when you used either an elliptical or stationary cycle. You will remember that these machines are called ergometers. Ergo means "work" and meter means "to measure." In other words, ergometers are work-measuring machines. We can use these to our advantage because they provide objective data and because we can control the resistance on them. Once again, we will use "exercise physiologist" and "client."

Instructional Task: Cycle or Elliptical

■ PRACTICE TASK

Provide students with their Exercise Physiologist Worksheet handouts from Lesson 1. Have students examine their data.

Guiding questions for students:

- What columns of data on your sheet give you an idea of the intensity you were working at last time?
- To increase the total number of Calories (kcal) you burn, what principle of exercise can you use?
- What variable can you manipulate to effectively use the principle of overload and to increase the number of Calories (kcal)?

One partner ("client") will ride either a stationary cycle or an elliptical for 20 minutes. The other partner ("exercise physiologist") will record the exercising student's data as she performs her workout.

Note: Since you are comparing scores across lessons, students should use the same piece of exercise equipment (stationary cycle or elliptical) they used from Lesson 1.

Since we are trying to increase the work you perform today, you will need to decide if you are going to increase the resistance or the speed to create your overload.

Every 2 minutes, have partners record the following:

- Speed
- Distance
- Level
- Calories
- RPMs
- Watts
- Heart rate

All information should come from the electronic display.

Note: Because the machines you are using measure work (Watts), they are known as ergometers (ergo = work; meter = measure).

EMBEDDED OUTCOME: S3.M12.8. Be sure to use the manual setting and demonstrate that you can give yourself a proper warm-up (it should show in your data) by starting off easy and gradually increasing the intensity.

Extension

Students can graph the data collected. A line graph of the speed and watts should show a warm-up.

Refinement

Make sure students know the different measurements before starting the activity.

Student Choices/Differentiation

- Students select either a cycle or an elliptical.
- Students can choose to manipulate the following variables in order to use the principle of overload:
    - Keep the resistance level the same and attempt to maintain a slightly higher average speed.
    - Increase the resistance level and either expect to see a lower average speed or attempt to keep the average speed the same.
    - Attempt to maintain a higher average heart rate.
    - Attempt to maintain a higher average power (watts) by manipulating speed and resistance.

What to Look For

- "Exercise physiologists" are collecting data every 2 minutes.
- In examining the data, you should see students start off at lower levels and speeds in order to give themselves a proper warm-up.

Instructional Task: Review of Data

■ **PRACTICE TASK**

Have students compare their two sets of data (Lessons 1 and 3).

Guiding questions for students:

- Is there evidence of a warm-up that consisted of a lower intensity at the start?
- Is there evidence that the principle of overload was effectively used to obtain a higher number of Calories expended?

Extension

Students can graph the two sets of data to create a visual comparison.

Student Choices/Differentiation

Students can review similar data for an example.

What to Look For

- Students recognize that a gradual increase in the intensity of the exercise provides a good warm-up.
- Students recognize that manipulation of any combination of speed, level, watts, and heart rate will result in a higher number of Calories burned.

Formal and Informal Assessments

- Exercise Physiologist Worksheet handout (evidence of a warm-up)
- Exercise Physiologist Worksheet handout (evidence of overload principle being used)

Closure

You have now seen an example of how you can use these machines to monitor your quantities of exercise and get objective data from them. In addition, you have now seen how you can use these machines to your advantage since you can precisely control the resistance level to help you use the principle of exercise called overload. The principle of overload is also known as progressive overload. Imagine how fit you could get if you were able to progressively overload your training like this several times per week.

- Could you use this principle of exercise to efficiently obtain the quantities of exercise you need for optimal functioning?
- Could you do this ever so gradually, letting the body get gradually stronger while preventing injury?

Reflection

- Based on the student data collected, are students able to effectively use the principle of overload?
- Are students warming up and cooling down correctly?
- Are students correctly performing the roles of clients and exercise physiologists?

Homework

Finish graphing your two sets of data so you can see a good visual of how you successfully used the overload principle. If you were unable to accomplish more Calories burned, look for where you made a mistake or reasons why and think about what you could do differently next time. For example, perhaps you went too hard by setting the level too high. Or perhaps you did not eat properly this morning or you have a cold.

Resources

Corbin, C., Pangrazi, R., & Welk, G. (1994). Toward an understanding of appropriate physical activity levels for youth. *Physical Activity and Fitness Research Digest, 1*(8), 1-8.

LESSON 4: FINISH CIRCUIT TRAINING

Grade-Level Outcomes

Primary Outcomes

Fitness knowledge: Uses available technology to self-monitor quantity of exercise needed for a minimal health standard and/or optimal functioning based on current fitness level. (S3.M8.8)

Fitness knowledge: Uses the overload principle (FITT formula) in preparing a personal workout. (S3.M11.8)

Embedded Outcome

Personal responsibility: Accepts responsibility for improving one's own levels of physical activity and fitness. (S4.M1.8)

Lesson Objectives

The learner will:

- use a heart rate monitor to self-monitor the amount of exercise in which she participates.
- use the overload principle with available technology to increase the amount of exercise in which she participates.
- create fitness circuits with a range of fitness activities.
- reflect on own task cards and review others.

Equipment and Materials

- IHT heart rate monitors that estimate Calories (kcal) burned
- Fitness center:
  - Agility ladders
  - Sand bells
  - Aerobic steps
  - Weighted bars
  - Jump ropes
  - Medicine balls

Introduction

Today, you will continue using available technology to self-monitor the amount of exercise you need to attain a minimal standard of health and for optimal functioning. In Lesson 2 you designed a circuit training workout and reflected on the total number of Calories you burned. This time, you will finish designing the circuit training workout and review other groups' material to see whether we all are using the principle of overload to burn a higher number of Calories.

Instructional Task: Circuit Training

■ PRACTICE TASK

In the same groups from Lesson 2, have students finish rotating through the following pieces of equipment:

- Agility ladders
- Sand bells
- Aerobic steps
- Weighted bars
- Jump ropes
- Medicine balls

Remind students to create their own fitness circuit training stations using their piece of equipment. After 4 or 5 minutes, groups will rotate to the next piece of equipment and design a new fitness circuit training station.

Cycle continues until all groups have completed six different circuit training stations (three of the circuits should come from Lesson 2).

Encourage students to design the routine with various levels at each station so that students of various ability levels can be challenged (e.g., beginning, intermediate, and advanced agility ladder drills).

Refinements

- Make sure students are designing a circuit that will keep their group moving and provide a significant workout.
- Remember, you're trying to create an overload, so think about ways to increase the intensity for your station.

Extension

Have students put heart rate monitors on and lead each other through their stations. Note: Keep track of the total time of the workout so that it is the same amount of time as in Lesson 2.

EMBEDDED OUTCOME: S4.M1.8. It is each student's responsibility to improve levels of fitness. Remind students they should be working hard during the activities to improve their fitness levels.

Student Choices/Differentiation

- Students design various levels at each station.
- Students create their own circuits.

What to Look For

- Students properly execute the exercises at each station.
- Students fully participate in the circuit training workout.

Instructional Task: Circuit Training Share

■ PRACTICE TASK

For each piece of equipment, have each group leave the circuit training task card they created.

Students should explore each piece of equipment with the different groups' task cards (no heart rate monitors since this would throw off the data for the homework assignment).

In groups, students should answer the following questions.

Guiding questions for students:

- Please provide evidence of the overload principle using other groups' circuit training task cards.
- Which task card for each station is the best? Justify your answer.
- If you could make modifications to your task cards, what would they be? Why?

Student Choices/Differentiation

- Students can work at their own pace.
- Students can choose their groups or work alone for this activity.

What to Look For

- Students are exploring other groups' circuit training task cards.
- Students are evaluating their own and other groups' circuit training task cards.
- Students are using class-related terminology when answering the questions.

Formal and Informal Assessments

Homework reflection submitted via e-mail and cloud storage

Closure

Today, you used technology to track how much physical activity you were able to obtain in a typical physical education class. Based on the data you collected and the amount of physical activity you determined necessary, what can you conclude?

- Students should conclude that we need additional physical activity outside of physical education if we want to be healthy (i.e., a typical physical education class does not provide enough time to get enough physical activity).
- Ask students if their use of technology provided them with additional motivation.

Reflection

- Does the use of technology seem to enhance engagement in the lesson?
- Are students applying the overload principle successfully?
- Are students working hard at each station?
- Are students reflecting on their own work after viewing their classmates' task cards?

Homework

Later today, you will receive an e-mail with a link to look at the data. For homework, compare the total number of Calories you expended today with the total number you expended for the previous circuit training workout (Lesson 2). Reply to the e-mail and answer the following questions:

- Did you successfully burn more Calories today?
- What kind of workout provided you with more objective data: using an ergometer (elliptical or stationary cycle) or circuit training?
- Which type of workout made it easier to use the principle of overload: using an ergometer (elliptical or stationary cycle) or circuit training?
- Which type of workout was more fun?

In addition, for those of you with smartphones, please remember to bring them to class next time. If you have a smartphone, also download a free physical activity tracker such as Endomondo or MapMyRun. Be sure to get your parent's or guardian's permission before doing so. We will use smartphone technology the next time we meet to track our physical activity.

Resources

Corbin, C., Pangrazi, R., & Welk, G. (1994). Toward an understanding of appropriate physical activity levels for youth. *Physical Activity and Fitness Research Digest, 1*(8), 1-8.

Interactive Health Technologies Spirit System (heart rate monitor supplier and cloud management system)

LESSON 5:
CELL PHONE APPS AND MILE RUN/WALK

Grade-Level Outcomes

Primary Outcome

Fitness knowledge: Uses available technology to self-monitor quantity of exercise needed for a minimal health standard and/or optimal functioning based on current fitness level. (S3.M8.8)

Embedded Outcome

Engages in physical activity: Participates in a self-selected lifetime sport, dance, aquatic or outdoor activity outside of the school day. (S3.M5.8)

Lesson Objectives

The learner will:

- use a heart rate monitor to self-monitor the amount of exercise in which he participates.
- use a smartphone application to self-monitor the amount of exercise in which he participates.
- participate in a mile run/walk.

Equipment and Materials

- Overhead LCD projector
- Students' smartphones (depending on school policy)
- IHT heart rate monitors that estimate Calories (kcal) burned (for students without smartphones)

Introduction

Today, we are continuing our module of study where you will use available technology to self-monitor the quantity of exercise needed for a minimal standard and for optimal functioning. This time, you will use a smartphone app to monitor the quantity of exercise you do during class today.

Instructional Task: Cell Phone App Demonstration

■ PRACTICE TASK

With an overhead LCD projector, demonstrate the features of a fitness or physical activity tracker.

Make sure to demonstrate how to locate the number of Calories (kcal) that are expended. Other features to point out include:

- Distance traveled
- Speed
- Map

Students can follow along with their own cell phone app and share with others in the class.

Extensions

- A number of students can share apps that you may not be familiar with and the features they like most about them.
- Hand out a data sheet from someone's workout using one or two of the apps. Have students point out the important pieces of data on the data sheet.
- Introduce other physical activity tracking devices (e.g., Fitbits) as well.

Student Choices/Differentiation

- Students can use various smartphone apps.
- Provide examples of data printouts from workouts using the apps.
- Students can work in groups when analyzing the reports.

What to Look For

Make sure that students can locate the features of the app they are using, specifically the total number of Calories.

Instructional Task: Mile Run/Walk

■ PRACTICE TASK

Have students wear heart rate monitors if they do not have a cell phone app.

Students who have cell phone apps should turn them on and select running.

Using the physical activity tracker of choice, have students track their fitness on a mile run/walk.

Extension

Discuss the purpose of the mile/run walk.

Refinement

Make sure students know how to use the technology before starting the mile run/walk.

Student Choices/Differentiation

- Students can run, walk, or do both.
- Students without a cell phone app can pair up with a partner who runs or walks at their approximate speed.

What to Look For

Students should use their cell phone apps to keep track of their running distance.

Formal and Informal Assessments

Mile run/walk homework

Closure

Today, you used technology to track how much physical activity you were able to obtain in a typical physical education class. Based on the data you collected and the amount of physical activity you determined necessary, what can you conclude? Do you think the data was the same even though you used a different device?

- Students should conclude that we need additional physical activity outside of physical education if we want to be healthy (i.e., a typical physical education class does not provide enough time to get enough physical activity).
- Ask students if their use of technology provided them with additional motivation.

Reflection

- Based on the data collected, does it appear as though any students are having issues with putting on the heart rate monitor correctly?
- Do students seem to be more engaged when they are able to use their own smartphone technology and app?

Homework

Compare the quantity of exercise you obtained today during the mile/run walk with the guidelines you calculated the other day.

EMBEDDED OUTCOME: S3.M5.8. Participate in a self-selected activity that will allow you to obtain the guideline of your choice (either a minimal standard or optimal functioning standard).

Resources

Corbin, C., Pangrazi, R., & Welk, G. (1994). Toward an understanding of appropriate physical activity levels for youth. *Physical Activity and Fitness Research Digest, 1*(8), 1-8.

Interactive Health Technologies Spirit System (heart rate monitor supplier and cloud management system)

LESSON 6: PROGRAM DESIGN

Grade-Level Outcomes

Primary Outcome

Assessment & program planning: Designs and implements a program of remediation for 3 areas of weakness based on the results of health-related fitness assessment. (S3.M15.8)

Embedded Outcome

Fitness knowledge: Uses available technology to self-monitor quantity of exercise needed for a minimal health standard and/or optimal functioning based on current fitness level. (S3.M8.8)

Lesson Objectives

The learner will:

- design and implement a program of remediation for three areas of weakness based on the results of her health-related fitness assessment.

- use available technology to self-monitor the amount of exercise in which she participates as part of her program of remediation.

Equipment and Materials

- Clipboards
- Pencils
- Student Fitnessgram reports generated from Fitnessgram software
- Completed physical activity logs from Physical Activity and Fitness Program Design Module
- Physical Activity Remediation Program Design handout, 1 per student (see handout in grade 7 module, lesson 7)
- Scoring Guide for Your Physical Activity Remediation Plan, 1 per student (see handout in grade 7 module, lesson 6)
- Physical Activity Remediation Plan Template, packets of 14, enough packets for cooperative groups (see handout in grade 7 module, lesson 6)

Introduction

Today, you will design your own program of remediation for three areas of health-related fitness. If you do not have three areas of weakness, you can choose three you want to improve or a combination of the two (remediation and improvement). You will receive Fitnessgram reports from fitness testing that you performed earlier in the school year.

For a sample Fitnessgram lesson, see Lesson 1 in the Fitness Through 5K Program Design Module.

Instructional Task: Program Design

■ PRACTICE TASK

Distribute student Fitnessgram reports, completed physical activity logs, physical activity and fitness plan worksheet, scoring guide, and physical activity and fitness plan template.

Review the various handouts with students, and have them start to design their physical activity programs.

Explain that they are expected to use technology to track their physical activity. However, activities such as static stretching are not expected to be measured.

Assist students with questions they may have, and clarify any concepts that they are expected to apply for this assignment.

EMBEDDED OUTCOME: S3.M8.8. Have students think about what technology they will use to help them implement and monitor their plans.

Extension

Encourage students to think about activities and lifestyle choices they do that may not help their health-related fitness (e.g., excessive screen time, playing video games with poor posture, doing homework with poor posture, poor nutrition choices, doing homework without taking time for physical activity breaks).

Refinement

Make sure students are focusing on remediation of three areas of health-related fitness.

Student Choices/Differentiation

- Students can work with a partner to help with program design.
- Provide examples of different technology devices students can use.

What to Look For

- Students are correctly interpreting their Fitnessgram reports.
- Students are reviewing their physical activity logs.
- Students are determining how much physical activity is needed.
- Students are identifying health-related fitness items in need of remediation or desired improvement.
- Students are planning physical activity.
- Students are deciding what technology to use to track physical activity.

Formal and Informal Assessments

Self-assessment scoring guide

Closure

This assignment is meant to help you gain the skills and knowledge to be active for a lifetime, but it is not necessary to design programs like these for the rest of your life. However, thinking about it on occasion can be beneficial. Being able to design your own program can help prevent or fix a number of medical problems. Imagine how much money people spend on personal trainers. As a physically literate person, you should not have to do this if you know how to design your own program.

Reflection

- Are students ready to complete this assignment for homework? Or will students require additional support in class before finishing this for homework?
- Are students finding ways to use technology in their plans?

Homework

Finish your remediation program and bring it back to class for review. After we have reviewed your plan, you will have the opportunity to implement your plan during class and outside of school.

Resources

The Cooper Institute. (2013). Meredith, M.D., & Welk, G.J. (Eds.). *Fitnessgram & Activitygram test administration manual.* Updated 4th ed. Champaign, IL: Human Kinetics.

Corbin, C., Pangrazi, R., & Welk, G. (1994). Toward an understanding of appropriate physical activity levels for youth. *Physical Activity and Fitness Research Digest, 1*(8), 1-8.

LESSON 7: IMPLEMENTING THE FITNESS PLAN USING TECHNOLOGY, PART 1

Grade-Level Outcomes

Primary Outcomes

Assessment & program planning: Designs and implements a program of remediation for 3 areas of weakness based on the results of health-related fitness assessment. (S3.M15.8)

Fitness knowledge: Uses available technology to self-monitor quantity of exercise needed for a minimal health standard and/or optimal functioning based on current fitness level. (S3.M8.8)

Embedded Outcomes

Self-expression and enjoyment: Discusses how enjoyment could be increased in self-selected physical activities. (S5.M4.8)

Accepting feedback: Provides encouragement and feedback to peers without prompting from the teacher. (S4.M3.8)

Lesson Objectives

The learner will:

- implement a program of remediation for three areas of weakness based on the results of his health-related fitness assessment.
- use available technology to self-monitor the amount of exercise in which he participates as part of his program of remediation.

Equipment and Materials

- Physical Activity Remediation Program Design handout, 1 per student (see handout in grade 7 module, lesson 7)
- Scoring Guide for Your Physical Activity Remediation Plan, 1 per student (see handout in grade 7 module, lesson 6)
- Physical Activity Remediation Plan Template, 1 per student (see handout in grade 7 module, lesson 6)
- IHT heart rate monitors
- Students' smartphones and apps
- Fitness center (with middle school appropriate equipment):
  - Sand bells
  - Medicine balls
  - Resistance bars
  - Resistance bands
  - Agility ladders
  - Spinning bikes
  - Ellipticals
  - Stationary bikes
  - Aerobic steps
  - Jump ropes

Introduction

The last time we met you designed a program of remediation for three areas of weakness based on the results of your personal health-related fitness assessment. Today, you will have the opportunity to begin implementing your plan by using the equipment we have available in our fitness center.

Instructional Task: Review of Remediation Plan

▪ PRACTICE TASK

Have students select a partner they feel comfortable with.

Partners will review each other's personal fitness plans.

Students should use the self-assessment scoring guide as evidence to show their partners how they have included everything.

Have partners discuss with each other the three areas of remediation they selected from their Fitnessgram reports.

Extension

Have students use their partners' self-assessment scoring guide to peer-assess their fitness plans. Have them determine if they agree with their partners' self-assessment of their plans.

EMBEDDED OUTCOME: S4.M3.8. Students should ask for constructive feedback from their partners on their fitness plans.

Refinements

- Students can refine their physical activity plans based on their partners' feedback.
- Students should focus on helping each other with their feedback.

Student Choices/Differentiation

- Students can select a partner they feel comfortable with.
- Model an example of how to give feedback.

What to Look For

- Students are providing feedback to their partners without prompting from the teacher.
- Students are using the self-assessment scoring guide when reviewing their plans with their partners.

Instructional Task: Implementation of Plan

▪ PRACTICE TASK

After students have refined their plans, allow them to work either independently or in small groups to implement their plans.

Instruct students to focus on two or three of the areas they identified in their plans.

Students self-select fitness activities and equipment in the fitness center. They should work respectfully with each other by sharing equipment.

Students also need to select appropriate technology to help monitor their quantities of exercise. This can include:

- Teacher-provided heart rate monitors
- Electronic feedback from an elliptical or stationary bike
- Their own smartphones and apps
- Fitbits

Refinements

- Students can continue to refine their plans if they discover the need for refinements as they begin to implement their programs. For example, they may discover a baseline number of reps for a strengthening exercise, or they may discover at what level they feel most comfortable as a starting point on a stationary bike or elliptical.
- Students should log their physical activity at the end of or during their workouts.

Student Choices/Differentiation

- Students can choose from various equipment.
- Students can choose from various exercises.
- Students can choose from various technologies to monitor exercise.

What to Look For

- Students select exercises and equipment that are appropriate for the area of remediation they are working on.
- Students are using equipment safely.
- Students are sharing equipment.

Formal and Informal Assessments

Self-assessment scoring guide

Closure

Today, you were able to begin the implementation of your fitness program meant to remediate three areas of need based on your health-related fitness results. Before I dismiss the class, you are going to participate in a think, pair, share. Discuss with a partner how your enjoyment today may have increased as a result of your ability to self-select your physical activities.

Call on a few students to share their partners' thoughts after they have had about 1 minute to discuss the topic.

Reflection

- How well did students do at selecting physical activities and equipment that addressed their remediation needs?
- Did students encourage each other and provide feedback without prompting?
- Did students use the fitness center equipment safely and respectfully?
- Did they seem to enjoy themselves as a result of being able to self-select activities rather than being directed by the teacher?

Homework

Continue to implement your programs of remediation and log your activities. In the last lesson of the module you will have an opportunity to implement your programs further.

EMBEDDED OUTCOME: S5.M4.8. Please write a short narrative for how self-selecting physical activities can increase enjoyment and hopefully increasing fitness levels. Be creative!

Resources

The Cooper Institute. (2013). Meredith, M.D., & Welk, G.J. (Eds.). *Fitnessgram & Activitygram test administration manual.* Updated 4th ed. Champaign, IL: Human Kinetics.

Corbin, C., Pangrazi, R., & Welk, G. (1994). Toward an understanding of appropriate physical activity levels for youth. *Physical Activity and Fitness Research Digest, 1*(8), 1-8.

LESSON 8: IMPLEMENTING THE FITNESS PLAN USING TECHNOLOGY, PART 2

Grade-Level Outcomes

Primary Outcomes

Assessment & program planning: Designs and implements a program of remediation for 3 areas of weakness based on the results of health-related fitness assessment. (S3.M15.8)

Fitness knowledge: Uses available technology to self-monitor quantity of exercise needed for a minimal health standard and/or optimal functioning based on current fitness level. (S3.M8.8)

Physical activity knowledge: Identifies the 5 components of health-related fitness (muscular strength, muscular endurance, flexibility, cardiovascular endurance, body composition) and explains the connections between fitness and overall physical and mental health. (S3.M1.8)

Embedded Outcome

Self-expression & enjoyment: Identifies and participates in an enjoyable activity that prompts individual self-expression. (S5.M5.8)

Lesson Objectives

The learner will:

- continue to implement a program of remediation for two or three areas of weakness based on the results of her health-related fitness assessment.
- use available technology to self-monitor quantity of exercise as part of the implemented program of remediation.
- explain the connections between fitness and overall physical and mental health.

Equipment and Materials

- Physical Activity/Fitness Plan Worksheet, 1 per student
- Scoring Guide for Two-Week Physical Activity Plan, 1 per student
- Physical Activity/Fitness Plan Template, 1 per student
- Physical Activity Remediation Program Design handout, copies for cooperative groups (see handout in grade 7 module, lesson 7)
- Scoring Guide for Your Physical Activity Remedial Plan, 1 per student (see handout in grade 7 module, lesson 6)
- Physical Activity Remediation Plan Template, packets of 14 and enough packets for cooperative groups (see handout in grade 7 module, lesson 6)
- IHT heart rate monitors
- Students' smartphones and apps
- Fitness center (with middle school appropriate equipment):
  - Sand bells
  - Medicine balls
  - Resistance bars
  - Resistance bands
  - Agility ladders
  - Spinning bikes
  - Ellipticals
  - Stationary bikes
  - Aerobic steps
  - Jump ropes

Introduction

Does anyone want to share their homework narrative? It is important we find enjoyment in physical activities. I look forward to viewing what you wrote. The last time we met you were able to start the implementation of your program of remediation based on health-related fitness results. This time, you will focus on the one or two remaining areas of remediation that you did not work on before. Today, you are going to continue that implementation and also explain the connection between fitness and overall physical and mental health.

Instructional Task: Continued Implementation of Plan

■ PRACTICE TASK

After students have refined their plans, allow them to work either independently or in small groups to implement their plans.

Instruct students to focus on one or two of the areas remaining in their plans.

Students self-select fitness activities and equipment in the fitness center. They should work respectfully with each other by sharing equipment.

Students also need to select appropriate technology to help monitor their quantities of exercise. This can include:

- Teacher-provided heart rate monitors
- Electronic feedback from an elliptical or stationary bike
- Their own smartphones and apps
- Fitbits

Refinements

- Students can continue to refine their plans if they discover the need for refinements as they begin to implement their programs.
- Students should log their physical activity at the end of or during their workouts.

Student Choices/Differentiation

- Students can choose from various equipment.
- Students can choose from various exercises.
- Students can choose from various technologies to monitor exercise.

What to Look For

- Students select exercises and equipment that are appropriate for the area of remediation they are working on.
- Students are specifically working on areas they did not get to last time. This will allow you to monitor and make sure students are doing activity correctly (for the future).
- Students are using equipment safely.
- Students are sharing equipment.

Instructional Task: Module Review (Big Picture)

■ PRACTICE TASK

Today, you continued the implementation of your program of remediation. Your plans are based on fitness testing of the five components of fitness.

Guiding questions for students:

- Can anyone describe the five components of health-related fitness?
- Can you match the activities you performed in the module with the five components of health-related fitness?

Discuss the connections between fitness and overall physical and mental health.

Guiding questions for students:

- What is the connection between fitness and overall physical health?
- Can you provide examples to strengthen your case?
- What is the connection between fitness and overall mental health?
- Can you provide examples to strengthen your case?

Extension

Students can research fitness and overall physical and mental health for a mini research project. Project ideas include the following:

- PowerPoint: Identify the benefits of fitness for overall health.
- Brochure: Create a brochure to hand out in the community on the benefits of fitness and overall health.
- Research paper
- Debate: Half the class debates that fitness is more beneficial to physical health, while the other half debates that it is more important to mental health.

Student Choices/Differentiation

Show video clips or use handouts to help make connections for students.

What to Look For

- Students identify and describe the components of health-related fitness.
- Students understand the basic connections between fitness and overall physical and mental health.

Formal and Informal Assessments

Self-assessment scoring guide

Closure

- What is the most difficult area to remediate in your plan? Is it difficult because of the work you must do, or do you not enjoy that area of fitness?
- What is your favorite technology tool you used in the module? Why?
- Keep tracking your fitness using technology. If you come upon anything new, please share with me so I can post the new technology tool to the school's physical education website.

Reflection

- Based on Big Picture activities, how well do students understand the connections between fitness and overall physical and mental health?
- Do you need to review these concepts, or are students ready for a summative assessment?

Homework

Continue to implement your program of remediation and log your activities. Keep track of your physical activity. You will turn in a two-week physical activity log that shows how you continued to implement your plan after we start a new unit.

EMBEDDED OUTCOME: S5.M5.8. Throughout these lessons, you have been making choices with the use of technology to improve your fitness. Choose one aspect of your fitness plan and try to participate in an enjoyable activity (e.g., Dance Dance Revolution, creative dance, martial arts) that prompts individual self-expression.

Resources

The Cooper Institute. (2013). Meredith, M.D., & Welk, G.J. (Eds.). *Fitnessgram & Activitygram test administration manual*. Updated 4th ed. Champaign, IL: Human Kinetics.

Corbin, C., Pangrazi, R., & Welk, G. (1994). Toward an understanding of appropriate physical activity levels for youth. *Physical Activity and Fitness Research Digest, 1*(8), 1-8.

Glossary

applying—A level of competency at which learners can demonstrate the critical elements of the motor skills or knowledge components of the Grade-Level Outcomes in a variety of physical activity environments.

assessment—The gathering of evidence about student learning and making inferences about student progress and growth based on that evidence (SHAPE America, 2014, p. 90).

competency—Sufficient ability, skill, and knowledge to meet the demands of a specific task or activity. In this book, competency is defined as the ability for individuals to participate at the recreational level with skill and ability in self-selected activities (SHAPE America, 2014, p. 115).

deliberate practice—A highly structured activity, the explicit goal of which is to improve performance. Tasks are invented to overcome the learner's weaknesses, and performance is monitored carefully to provide cues for ways to improve further (Ericsson et al., 1993, p. 368).

differentiated instruction—Instruction that is varied to address the needs of students and their various levels of skill or knowledge.

embedded outcomes—Grade-Level Outcomes that are related to the primary content of a lesson and that give students opportunities to meet more than one outcome during the learning or practice task (Holt/Hale & Hall, 2016, p. 18; SHAPE America, 2014, p. 41).

emerging—A level of competency at which learners are in the beginning stages of acquiring motor skills and knowledge. Mastery of the skills and knowledge is emerging through deliberate practice tasks, and, at this stage, learners are developing competency.

etiquette—Expectations regarding behavior and social norms associated with specific games or activities; rules of behavior that define and provide parameters for the appropriate participation in the activity or game (SHAPE America, 2014, p.116).

fielding and striking games—Games such as baseball, softball, and cricket in which one team occupies positions throughout the space (field) and the other team attempts to score by batting or striking an object into open space in the field, providing enough time for the hitter to run between bases (or wickets) (Haibach et al., 2011, p. 365; Mitchell, Oslin, & Griffin, 2006, p. 21).

fitness activities—Activities with a focus on improving or maintaining fitness, which might include yoga, Pilates, resistance training, spinning, running, fitness walking, fitness swimming, kickboxing, cardio-kick, Zumba and exergaming (SHAPE America, 2014, p. 116).

FITT—An acronym that stands for frequency, intensity, time, and type of exercise, each of which can be manipulated to create an overload on the body to force it to adapt, or become more fit (see *overload principle*) (Shape America, 2014, p. 116).

formative assessment—Assessment that is ongoing during instruction, allowing teachers to track student progress and adapt instruction (SHAPE America, 2014, p. 90).

fundamental motor skills—The locomotor, non-locomotor or stability, and manipulative skills that provide the foundation for the more complex movement patterns of games and sports, gymnastics, and dance (Shape America, 2014, p. 116).

games and sports—Includes the following game categories: invasion, net and wall, target, and fielding and striking (Shape America, 2014, p. 116).

grid activities—Activities conducted within squares or rectangles in which learners participate in modified game play using pre-determined tactics or skills (Shape America, 2014, p. 116).

individual interest—Interest that is influenced by one's experiences and personal preferences.

individual-performance activities—Activities that one can perform alone. Examples include gymnastics, figure skating, track and field, multi-sport events, in-line skating, wrestling, self-defense, and skateboarding (Shape America, 2014, p. 116).

invasion games—Games in which "teams score by moving a ball (or a projectile) into another team's territory and either shooting into a fixed target (a goal or a basket) or moving the projectile across an open-ended target (a line). To prevent scoring, one team must stop the other from bringing the ball into its territory and attempting to score" (Mitchell et al., 2006).

learning domains—Classifications of learning that involve three domains: the cognitive domain (thinking), the affective domain (emotions), and the psychomotor domain (physical or kinesthetic) (Bloom, Engelhart, Furst, Hill, and Krathwohl, 1956).

level 1 outcomes—Grade-Level Outcomes for high school students that reflect the minimum fitness knowledge and skills that students must acquire and attain by the time they graduate to be considered prepared to maintain a healthy fitness level in college or in a career (SHAPE America, 2014, p. 116).

level 2 outcomes—Grade-Level Outcomes for high school students that build on Level 1 competencies by augmenting the fitness knowledge and skills considered desirable for college or career readiness (SHAPE America, 2014, p. 117).

lifetime activities—Activities that are suitable for participation across the life span and that one can pursue alone or with a partner, as opposed to only with a team. As used in this book, lifetime activities include the categories of outdoor pursuits, selected individual-performance activities, aquatics, net and wall games, and target games (SHAPE America, 2014, p. 117).

maturing—A level of competency at which learners demonstrate the critical elements of the motor skills and knowledge components of the Grade-Level Outcomes, which will continue to be refined with practice. As the environmental context varies, a maturing pattern might fluctuate, reflecting more maturity in familiar contexts and less maturity in unfamiliar or new contexts, thus the term *maturing* (SHAPE America, 2014, p. 117).

modified games—Small-sided games in which the rules have been modified to emphasize the skills taught in class (e.g., creating a penalty for dribbling to emphasize teaching students to pass rather than dribble) (SHAPE America, 2014, p. 117).

movement concepts—Concepts related to the skillful performance of movement and fitness activities, including spatial awareness, effort, tactics, strategies, and principles related to movement efficiency and health-enhancing fitness (SHAPE America, 2014, p. 117).

net and wall games—Games in which "teams or individual players score by hitting a ball into a court space with sufficient accuracy and power so that opponents cannot hit it back before it bounces once (as in badminton or volleyball) or twice (as in tennis or racquetball) (Mitchell et al., 2006, p. 21).

outcomes—Statements that specify what learners should know or be able to do as the result of a learning experience (SHAPE America, 2014, p. 117).

outdoor pursuits—Activities that are pursued in the outdoors, including recreational boating (e.g., kayaking, canoeing, sailing, rowing), hiking, backpacking, fishing, orienteering and geocaching, ice skating, skateboarding, snow or water skiing, snowboarding, snowshoeing, surfing, bouldering/traversing/climbing, mountain biking, adventure activities, and ropes courses. Selecting outdoor pursuits often depends on the environmental opportunities within one's geographical region (SHAPE America, 2014, p. 117).

overload principle—The principle of placing progressively greater stress or demands on the body during exercise to cause it to adapt (become more fit). This is done by manipulating the frequency, intensity, time (duration), and type (FITT) of activity (SHAPE America, 2014, p. 117).

physically literate individuals—Those who have learned the skills and acquired the knowledge necessary to participate in a variety of physical activities. A physically literate individual knows the implications and the benefits of involvement in various types of physical activities, participates regularly in physical activity, is physically fit, and values physical activity and its contributions to a healthy lifestyle (SHAPE America, 2014, p. 11).

relatedness—A sense of being connected or supported by others (Zhang et al., 2011, p. 53).

situational interest—Temporary interest that arises spontaneously and is influenced by the learning environment and other environmental factors.

small-sided games—Organized games in which the number of players involved is reduced from the conventional competitive version of the sport (e.g., 2 v 2 basketball, 3 v 3 volleyball, 6 v 6 lacrosse) (SHAPE America, 2014, p. 117).

summative assessment—Assessment that occurs at the close of a unit of instructional sequence, providing teachers with a comprehensive summary of each student's progress and growth (SHAPE America, 2014, p. 90).

target games—Games in which "players score by throwing or striking an object to a target" (Mitchell et al., 2006, p. 21). Accuracy is a primary focus of the activity, and competitors make no physical contact with one another (Haibach et al., 2011, p. 369). Strategies and tactics are based on movement accuracy and consistency.

technology—Software, websites, devices, and applications used in a physical education setting to enhance teaching and learning (SHAPE America, 2014, p. 118).

References

Preface

Gallahue, D.L., Ozmun, J., & Goodway, J. (2012). *Understanding motor development: Infants, children, adolescents, adults.* New York: McGraw Hill.

SHAPE America – Society of Health and Physical Educators. (2014). *National Standards & Grade-Level Outcomes for k-12 physical education.* Champaign, IL; Human Kinetics.

Chapter 1

Barnett, L.M., van Beurden, E., Morgan, P.J., Brooks, L.O., & Beard, J.R. (2008a). Childhood motor skill proficiency as a predictor of adolescent physical activity. *Journal of Adolescent Health, 44,* 252-259.

Barnett, L.M., van Beurden, E., Morgan, P.J., Brooks, L.O., & Beard, J.R. (2008b). Does childhood motor skill proficiency predict adolescent fitness? *Medicine & Science in Sports & Exercise, 40,* 2137-2144.

Bernstein, E., Phillips, S.R., & Silverman, S. (2011). Attitudes and perceptions of middle school students toward competitive activities in physical education. *Journal of Teaching in Physical Education, 30,* 69-83.

Bryan, C., Sims, S., Hester, D., & Dunaway, D. (2013). Fifteen years after the Surgeon General's report: Challenges, changes, and future directions in physical education. *Quest, 65,* 139-150.

Chen, A., & Darst, P.W. (2001). Situational interest in physical education: A function of learning task design. *Research Quarterly for Exercise and Sport, 72*(2), 150-164.

Couturier, L.E., Chepko, S., & Coughlin, M. (2007). Whose gym is it? Gendered perspectives on middle and secondary school physical education. *The Physical Educator, 64*(3), 152-157.

Duckworth, A., Peterson, C., Matthews, M., & Kelly, D. (2007). Grit: Perseverance and passion for long-term goals. *Journal of Personality and Social Psychology, 92*(6), 1087-1101.

Ennis, C. (2011). Physical education curriculum priorities: Evidence for education and skillfulness. *Quest, 63,* 5-18.

Ericsson, K. (2006). The influence of experience and deliberate practice on the development of superior performance. In K. Ericsson, N. Chamness, P. Feltovich, & R. Hoffman (Eds.), *The Cambridge handbook of expertise and expert performance* (pp. 685-705). Cambridge, UK: Cambridge University Press.

Garn, A.C., Cothran, D.J., & Jenkins, J.M. (2011). A qualitative analysis of individual interest in middle school physical education: Perspective of early adolescents. *Physical Education & Sport Pedagogy, 16*(3), 223-236.

Garn, A.C., Ware, D.R., & Solmon, M.A. (2011). Student engagement in high school physical education: Do social motivation orientations matter? *Journal of Teaching in Physical Education, 30,* 84-98.

Grieser, M., Vu, M.B., Bedimo-Rung, A.L., Neumark-Sztainer, D., Moody, J., Young, D.R., & Moe, S.G. (2006). Physical activities attitudes, preferences, and practices in African American, Hispanic, and Caucasian girls. *Health Education & Behavior, 33*(1), 40-51.

Hannon, J.C., & Ratcliffe, T. (2005). Physical activity levels in coeducational and single-gender high school physical education settings. *Journal of Teaching in Physical Education, 24,* 149-164.

Hill, G., & Hannon, J.C. (2008). An analysis of middle school students' physical education physical activity preferences. *The Physical Educator, 65*(4), 180-194.

Kambas, A., Michalopoulou, M., Fatouros, I., Christoforidis, C., Manthou, E., Giannakidou, D., Venetsanou, F., Haberer, E., Chatzinikolaou, A., Gourgoulis, V., & Zimmer, R. (2012). The relationship between motor proficiency and pedometer-determined physical activity in young children. *Pediatric Exercise Science, 24,* 34-44.

Ntoumanis, N., Pensgaard, A., Martin, C., & Pipe, K. (2004). An idiographic analysis of amotivation in compulsory school physical education. *Journal of Sport & Exercise Science, 26,* 197-214.

Ommundsen, Y. (2006). Pupils' self-regulation in physical education: The role of motivational climates and differential achievement goals. *European Physical Education Review, 12*(3), 289-315.

Placek, J.H. (1983). Conceptions of success in teaching: Busy, happy, and good? In T. Templin, & J. Olsen (Eds.), *Teaching in physical education* (pp. 46-56). Champaign, IL: Human Kinetics.

SHAPE America – Society of Health and Physical Educators. (2014). *National Standards & Grade-Level Outcomes for k-12 physical education.* Champaign, IL; Human Kinetics.

Smith, M.A., & St. Pierre, P. (2009). Secondary students' perceptions of enjoyment in physical education: An American and English perspective. *The Physical Educator, 66*(4), 209-221.

Stodden, D.F., Goodway, J.L., Langendorfer, S.J., Roberton, M., Rudisill, M.E., Garcia, C., & Garcia, L.E. (2008). A developmental perspective on the role of motor skill competence in physical activity: An emergent relationship. *Quest, 60,* 290-306.

Stodden, D., Langendorfer, S., & Roberton, M. (2009). The association between motor skill competence and physical fitness in young adults. *Research Quarterly for Exercise and Sport, 80*(2), 223-229.

Strong, W.B., Malina, R.M., Blimkie, C.J., Daniels, S.R., Dishman, R.K., Gutin, B., Hergenroeder, A.C., Must, A., Nixon, P., Pivarnik, J.M., Rowland, T., Trost, S., & Trudeau, F. (2005). Evidence based physical activity for school-age youth. *Journal of Pediatrics, 146,* 732-737.

Stuart, J.H., Biddle, S.H., O'Donovan, T.M., & Nevill, M.E. (2005). Correlates of participation in physical activity for adolescent girls: A systematic review of recent literature. *Journal of Physical Activity and Health, 2,* 423-434.

Subramaniam, P.R. (2009). Motivational effects of interest on student engagement and learning in physical education. *International Journal of Physical Education, 46*(2), 11-19.

Xu, F., & Liu, W. (2013). A review of middle school students' attitudes toward physical activity. In L.E. Ciccomascolo, & E.C. Sullivan (Eds.), *The dimensions of physical education* (pp. 286-295). Burlington, MA: Jones & Bartlett Learning.

Zhang, T., Solmon, M., Kosma, M., Carson, R.L., & Gu, X. (2011). Need support, need satisfaction, intrinsic motivation, and physical activity participation among middle school students. *Journal of Teaching in Physical Education, 30,* 51-68.

Chapter 2

Holt/Hale, S., & Hall, T. (2016). *Lesson planning for elementary physical education: Meeting the national standards & grade-level outcomes.* Champaign, IL: Human Kinetics.

SHAPE America – Society of Health and Physical Educators. (2014). *National Standards & Grade-Level Outcomes for k-12 physical education.* Champaign, IL; Human Kinetics.

Chapter 3

Couturier, L.E., Chepko, S., & Coughlin, M. (2007). Whose gym is it? Gendered perspectives on middle and secondary school physical education. *The Physical Educator, 64*(3), 152-157.

Derry, J.A. (2002). Single-sex and coeducation physical education: Perspectives of adolescent girls and female physical education teachers. *Melpomene Journal, 21*(3), 21-27.

Eime, R., Harvey, J., Sawyer, N., Craike, M., Symons, C., Polman, R., & Payne, W. (2013). Understand-

ing contexts of adolescent female participation in sport and physical activity. *Research Quarterly for Exercise and Sport, 84,* 157-166.

Gallahue, D.L., Ozmun, J., & Goodway, J. (2012). *Understanding motor development: Infants, children, adolescents, adults.* New York: McGraw-Hill.

Haibach, P.S., Reid, G., & Collier, D.J. (2011). *Motor learning and development.* Champaign, IL: Human Kinetics.

Hill, G., & Hannon, J.C. (2008). An analysis of middle school students' physical education physical activity preferences. *The Physical Educator, 65*(4), 180-194.

SHAPE America – Society of Health and Physical Educators. (2014). *National Standards & Grade-Level Outcomes for k-12 physical education.* Champaign, IL; Human Kinetics.

Yli-Piipari, S., Leskinen, E., Jaakkola, T., & Liukkonen, J. (2012). Predictive role of physical education motivation: The developmental trajectories of physical activity during grades 7-9. *Research Quarterly for Exercise and Sport, 83*(4), 560-569.

Chapter 4

Graham, G., Holt/Hale, S.A., & Parker, M. (2010). *Children moving: A reflective approach to teaching physical education.* New York: McGraw Hill.

SHAPE America – Society of Health and Physical Educators. (2014). *National Standards & Grade-Level Outcomes for k-12 physical education.* Champaign, IL; Human Kinetics.

Chapter 5

Chepko, S., & Doan, R. (2015). Teaching for skill mastery. *Journal of Physical Education, Recreation & Dance, 86,* 9-13.

SHAPE America – Society of Health and Physical Educators. (2014). *National Standards & Grade-Level Outcomes for k-12 physical education.* Champaign, IL; Human Kinetics.

Chapter 6

SHAPE America – Society of Health and Physical Educators. (2014). *National Standards & Grade-Level Outcomes for k-12 physical education.* Champaign, IL; Human Kinetics.

Chapter 7

SHAPE America – Society of Health and Physical Educators. (2014). *National Standards & Grade-Level Outcomes for k-12 physical education.* Champaign, IL; Human Kinetics.

Chapter 8

Gilbertson, K., Bates, T., McLaughlin, T., & Ewert, A. (2006). *Outdoor education: Methods and strategies.* Champaign, IL: Human Kinetics.

Miles, J., & Priest, S. (Eds.). (1999). *Adventure programming*. State College, PA: Venture.

Ntoumanis, N., Pensgaard, A., Martin, C., & Pipe, K. (2004). An idiographic analysis of amotivation in compulsory school physical education. *Journal of Sport & Exercise Science, 26,* 197-214.

Rohnke, K., & Butler, S. (1995). *Quicksilver*. Dubuque, IA: Kendall/Hunt.

SHAPE America – Society of Health and Physical Educators. (2014). *National Standards & Grade-Level Outcomes for k-12 physical education*. Champaign, IL; Human Kinetics.

Chapter 9

Hill, G., & Hannon, J.C. (2008). An analysis of middle school students' physical education physical activity preferences. *The Physical Educator, 65*(4), 180-194.

SHAPE America – Society of Health and Physical Educators. (2014). *National Standards & Grade-Level Outcomes for k-12 physical education*. Champaign, IL; Human Kinetics.

Treasure, D.C, & Roberts, G.C. (2001). Students' perceptions of the motivational climate, achievement beliefs, and satisfaction in physical education. *Research Quarterly for Exercise and Sport, 72*(2), 165-175.

Chapter 10

Corbin, C., Pangrazi, R., & Le Masurier, G. (2004). Physical activity for children: Current patterns and guidelines. *Journal of Physical Activity and Health, 1,* 281.

Patnode, C.D., Lytle, L.A., Erickson, D.J., Sirard, J.R., Barr-Anderson, D.J., & Story, M. (2011). Physical activity and sedentary activity patterns among children and adolescents: A latent class analysis approach. *Journal of Physical Activity and Health, 8*, 457-467.

SHAPE America – Society of Health and Physical Educators. (2014). *National Standards & Grade-Level Outcomes for k-12 physical education*. Champaign, IL; Human Kinetics.

Xu, F., & Liu, W. (2013). A review of middle school students' attitudes toward physical activity. In L.E. Ciccomascolo, & E.C. Sullivan (Eds.), *The dimensions of physical education* (pp. 286-295). Burlington, MA: Jones & Bartlett Learning.

Chapter 11

U.S. Department of Health and Human Services. (2008). *Physical activity guidelines for Americans*. Washington, DC: Author. Available at www.health.gov.

Glossary

Bloom, B.S., Engelhart, M.D., Furst, E.J., Hill, W.H., Krathwohl, D.R. (1956). Taxonomy of educational objectives: The classification of educational goals. Handbook I: Cognitive domain. New York: David McKay Company.

Haibach, P.S., Reid, G., & Collier, D.J. (2011). *Motor learning and development*. Champaign, IL: Human Kinetics.

Mitchell, S., Oslin, J., & Griffin, L. (2006). *Teaching sport concepts and skills: A tactical games approach*. Champaign, IL: Human Kinetics.

SHAPE America – Society of Health and Physical Educators. (2014). *National Standards & Grade-Level Outcomes for k-12 physical education*. Champaign, IL; Human Kinetics.

Zhang, T., Solmon, M., Kosma, M., Carson, R.L., & Gu, X. (2011). Need support, need satisfaction, intrinsic motivation, and physical activity participation among middle school students. *Journal of Teaching in Physical Education, 30,* 51-68.

Suggested Readings

Having the Skills to Succeed

Barnett, L. M., van Beurden, E., Morgan, P. J., Brooks, L. O., & Beard, J. R. (2008). Childhood motor skill proficiency as a predictor of adolescent physical activity. *Journal of Adolescent Health*, *44*, 252-259.

Barnett, L. M., van Beurden, E., Morgan, P. J., Brooks, L. O., & Beard, J. R. (2008). Does childhood motor skill proficiency predict adolescent fitness? *Medicine & Science in Sports & Exercise*, *40*, 2137-2144.

Bernstein, E., Phillips, S. R., & Silverman, S. (2011). Attitudes and perceptions of middle school students toward competitive activities in physical education. *Journal of Teaching in Physical Education*, *30*, 69-83.

Bevans, K., Fitzpatrick, L., Sanchez, B., & Forest, C. B. (2010). Individual and instructional determinants of student engagement in physical education. *Journal of Teaching in Physical Education*, *29*, 399-416.

Castelli, D. M., & Valley, J. A. (2007). Chapter three: The relationship of physical fitness and motor competence to physical activity. *Journal of Teaching in Physical Education*, *26*, 358-374.

Duckworth, A., Peterson, C., Matthews, M., & Kelly, D. (2007). Grit: Perseverance and passion for long-term goals. *Journal of Personality and Social Psychology*, *92* (6), 1087-1101.

Faigenbaum, A., Lloyd, R., Sheehan, D., & Myer, G. (2013). The role of the pediatric exercise specialist in treating exercise deficit disorder in youth. *Strength & Conditioning Journal*, *35* (3), 34-38.

Hamilton, K., & White, K. M. (2008). Extending the theory of planned behavior: The role of self and social influences in predicting adolescent regular moderate-to-vigorous physical activity. *Journal of Sport & Exercise Science*, *30*, 56-74.

Hands, B., Larkin, D., Parker, H., Straker, L., & Perry, M. (2009). The relationship among physical activity, motor competence and health-related fitness in 14-year-old adolescents. *Scandinavian Journal of Medicine & Science in Sports*, *19*, 655-663.

Hardy, L., Reinten-Reynolds, T., Espinel, P., Zask, A., & Okely, A. (2012). Prevalence and correlates of low fundamental movement skill competency in children. *Pediatrics*, *130* (2), e390-e398.

Kambas, A., Michalopoulou, M., Fatouros, I., Christoforidis, C., Manthou, E., Giannakidou, D., Venetsanou, F., Haberer, E., Chatzinikolaou, A.,

Gourgoulis, V., & Zimmer, R. (2012). The relationship between motor proficiency and pedometer-determined physical activity in young children. *Pediatric Exercise Science*, *24*, 34-44.

Luban, D., Morgan, P., Cliff, D., Barnett, L., & Okely, A. (2010). Fundamental movement skills in children and adolescents. *Sports Medicine*, *40* (12), 1019-1035.

Standage, M., Duda, J., & Ntoumanis, N. (2003). Predicting motivational regulations in physical education: The interplay between dispositional goal orientations, motivational climate, and perceived competence. *Journal of Sport Sciences*, *21*, 631-647.

Stodden, D. F., Goodway, J. L., Langendorfer, S. J., Roberton, M., Rudisill, M. E., Garcia, C., & Garcia, L. E. (2008). A developmental perspective on the role of motor skill competence in physical activity: An emergent relationship. *Quest*, *60*, 290-306.

Stodden, D., Langendorfer, S., & Roberton, M. (2009). The association between motor skill competence and physical fitness in young adults. *Research Quarterly for Exercise and Sport*, *80* (2), 223-229.

van Beurden, E., Barnett, L. M., Zask, A., Dietrich, U. C., Brooks, L.O., & Beard, J. (2003). Can we skill and activate children through primary school physical education lessons? "Move It Groove It"—a collaborative health promotion intervention. *Preventive Medicine*, *36*, 493-501.

The Learning Activity Is Interesting

Bryan, C., Sims, S., Hester, D., & Dunaway, D. (2013). Fifteen years after the Surgeon General's report: Challenges, changes, and future directions in physical education. *Quest*, *65*, 139-150.

Chen, S., Chen, A., & Zhu, X. (2012). Are K-12 learners motivated in physical education? A meta-analysis. *Research Quarterly for Exercise and Sport*, *83* (1), 36-48.

Chen, A., & Darst, P. W. (2001). Situational interest in physical education: A function of learning task design. *Research Quarterly for Exercise and Sport*, *72* (2), 150-164.

Gao, Z., Lee, A. M., Ping, X., & Kosam, M. (2011). Effect of learning activity on students' motivation, physical activity levels and effort/persistence. *ICHPER-SD Journal of Research in Health, Physical Education, Recreation, Sport & Dance*, *6* (1), 27-33.

Prusak, K. A., Treasure, D. C., Darst, P. W., & Pangrazi, R. (2004). The effects of choice on the motivation of adolescent girls in physical education. *Journal of Teaching in Physical Education, 23*, 19-29.

Smith, M.A., & St. Pierre, P. (2009). Secondary students' perceptions of enjoyment in physical education: An American and English perspective. *The Physical Educator, 66* (4), 209-221.

Stuart, J. H., Biddle, S. H., O'Donovan, T. M., & Nevill, M. E. (2005). Correlates of participation in physical activity for adolescent girls: A systematic review of recent literature. *Journal of Physical Activity and Health, 2*, 423-434.

Subramaniam, P. R. (2009). Motivational effects of interest on student engagement and learning in physical education. *International Journal of Physical Education, 46* (2), 11-19.

Treasure, D. C., & Roberts, G. C. (2001). Students' perceptions of the motivational climate, achievement beliefs, and satisfaction in physical education. *Research Quarterly for Exercise and Sport, 72* (2), 165-175.

Wilkinson, C., & Bretzing, R. (2011). High school girls' perceptions of selected physical activities. *The Physical Educator, 68* (2), 58-65.

Zhang, T., Solmon, M., Kosma, M., Carson, R. L., & Gu, X. (2011). Need support, need satisfaction, intrinsic motivation, and physical activity participation among middle school students. *Journal of Teaching in Physical Education, 30*, 51-68.

The Learning Experience Provides a Socially Supportive and Inclusive Climate

Cockburn, C. (2001). Year 9 girls and physical education: A survey of pupil perception. *The Bulletin of Physical Education, 37* (1), 5-24.

Cockburn, C., & Clarke, G. (2002). "Everybody's looking at you!": Girls negotiating the "femininity deficit" they incur in physical education. *Women's Studies Forum, 25* (6), 651-665.

Couturier, L. E., Chepko, S., & Coughlin, M. (2007). Whose gym is it? Gendered perspectives on middle and secondary school physical education. *The Physical Educator, 64* (3), 152-157.

Eime, R., Harvey, J., Sawyer, N., Craike, M., Symons, C., Polman, R., & Payne, W. (2013). Understanding contexts of adolescent female participation in sport and physical activity. *Research Quarterly for Exercise and Sport, 84*, 157-166.

Fagrell, B., Larsson, H., & Redelus, K. (2012). The game with the game: Girls' position in physical education. *Gender and Education, 24* (1), 101-118.

Garn, A. C., Cothran, D. J., & Jenkins, J. M. (2011). A qualitative analysis of individual interest in middle school physical education: Perspective of early adolescents. *Physical Education & Sport Pedagogy, 16* (3), 223-236.

Garn, A. C., Ware, D. R., & Solmon, M. A. (2011). Student engagement in high school physical education: Do social motivation orientations matter? *Journal of Teaching in Physical Education, 30*, 84-98.

Grieser, M., Vu, M. B., Bedimo-Rung, A. L., Neumark-Sztainer, D., Moody, J., Young, D. R., & Moe, S. G. (2006). Physical activities attitudes, preferences, and practices in African American, Hispanic, and Caucasian girls. *Health Education & Behavior, 33* (1), 40-51.

Haerens, L., Kirk, D., Cardon, G., De Bourdeauhuij, I., & Vansteenkiste, M. (2010). Motivation profiles for secondary school physical education and its relationship to the adoption of a physically active lifestyle among university students. *European Physical Education Review, 16* (2), 117-139.

Hannon, J. C., & Ratcliffe, T. (2005). Physical activity levels in coeducational and single-gender high school physical education settings. *Journal of Teaching in Physical Education, 24*, 149-164.

Hill, G., & Hannon, J. C. (2008). An analysis of middle school students' physical education physical activity preferences. *The Physical Educator, 65* (4), 180-194.

Hills, L. (2006). Playing the field(s): An exploration of change, conformity and conflict in girls' understandings of gendered physicality in physical education. *Gender and Education, 18* (5), 539-556.

Kahan, D., & Graham, K. (2013). Quantitative analysis of students' reasons for nonsuiting and support of policy change at one middle school. *Research Quarterly for Exercise and Sport, 84*, 512-521.

McKenzie, T. L., Prochaska, J. J., Sallis, J. F., & LaMaster, K. J. (2004). Coeducational and single-sex physical education in middle schools: Impact on physical activity. *Research Quarterly for Exercise and Sport, 75* (4), 446-449.

Ntoumanis, N., Pensgaard, A., Martin, C., & Pipe, K. (2004). An idiographic analysis of amotivation in compulsory school physical education. *Journal of Sport & Exercise Science, 26*, 197-214.

Ommundsen, Y. (2006). Pupils' self-regulation in physical education: The role of motivational climates and differential achievement goals. *European Physical Education Review, 12* (3), 289-315.

O'Neill, J. R., Pate, R. R., & Liese, A. D. (2011). Descriptive epidemiology of dance participation in adolescents. *Research Quarterly for Exercise and Sport, 82* (3), 373-380.

Patnode, C. D., Lytle, L.A., Erickson, D. J., Sirard, J. R., Barr-Anderson, D. J., & Story, M. (2011). Physical activity and sedentary activity patterns among children and adolescents: A latent class analysis approach. *Journal of Physical Activity and Health, 8*, 457-467.

Portman, P. (2003). Are physical education classes encouraging students to be physically active?: Experiences of ninth graders in their last semester of required physical education. *The Physical Educator, 63* (3), 150-161.

Taylor, W., Yancey, A., Leslie, J., Murray, N., Cummings, S., Sharkey, S., Wert, C., James, J., Miles, O., & McCarthy, W. (1999). Physical activity among African American and Latino middle school girls: Consistent beliefs, expectations, and experience across two sites. *Women & Health, 30* (2), 67-82.

Velija, P., & Kumar, G. (2009). GCSE physical education and the embodiment of gender. *Sport, Education and Society, 14* (4), 383-399.

Xu, F., & Liu, W. (2013). A review of middle school students' attitudes toward physical activity. In L. E. Ciccomascolo & E. C. Sullivan (Eds.), *The dimensions of physical education* (pp. 286-295). Burlington, MA: Jones & Bartlett Learning.

Yli-Piipari, S., Leskinen, E., Jaakkola, T., & Liukkonen, J. (2012). Predictive role of physical education motivation: The developmental trajectories of physical activity during grades 7-9. *Research Quarterly for Exercise and Sport, 83* (4), 560-569.

Gender Differences in Middle School

Couturier, L. E., Chepko, S., & Coughlin, M. (2005). Student voices: What middle and high school students have to say about physical education. *The Physical Educator, 63* (4), 170-177.

Couturier, L. E., Chepko, S., & Coughlin, M. (2007). Whose gym is it? Gendered perspectives on middle and secondary school physical education. *The Physical Educator, 64* (3), 152-157.

Grieser, M., Vu, M. B., Bedimo-Rung, A. L., Neumark-Sztainer, D., Moody, J., Young, D. R., & Moe, S. G. (2006). Physical activities attitudes, preferences, and practices in African American, Hispanic, and Caucasian girls. *Health Education & Behavior, 33* (1), 40-51.

Hill, G., & Hannon, J. C. (2008). An analysis of middle school students' physical education physical activity preferences. *The Physical Educator, 65* (4), 180-194.

Kahan, D., & Graham, K. (2013). Quantitative analysis of students' reasons for nonsuiting and support of policy change at one middle school. *Research Quarterly for Exercise and Sport, 84*, 512-521.

O'Neill, J. R., Pate, R. R., & Liese, A. D. (2011). Descriptive epidemiology of dance participation in adolescents. *Research Quarterly for Exercise and Sport, 82* (3), 373-380.

Prusak, K. A., & Darst, P. W. (2002). Effects of types of walking activities on actual choices by adolescent female physical education students. *Journal of Teaching in Physical Education, 21*, 230-241.

Shen, B., Chen, A., Tolley, H., and Srabis, K. (2003). Gender and interest-based motivation in learning dance. *Journal of Teaching in Physical Education, 22*, 396-409.

Xu, F., & Liu, W. (2013). A review of middle school students' attitudes toward physical activity. In L. E. Ciccomascolo & E. C. Sullivan (Eds.), *The dimensions of physical education* (pp. 286-295). Burlington, MA: Jones & Bartlett Learning.

Single-Sex Environments

Derry, J. A. (2002). Single-sex and coeducation physical education: Perspectives of adolescent girls and female physical education teachers. *Melpomene Journal, 21* (3), 21-27.

McKenzie, T. L., Prochaska, J. J., Sallis, J. F., & LaMaster, K. J. (2004). Coeducational and single-sex physical education in middle schools: Impact on physical activity. *Research Quarterly for Exercise and Sport, 75* (4), 446-449.

Treanor, L., Graber, K., Housner, L., & Weigand, R. (1998). Middle school students' perceptions of coeducational and same-sex physical education classes. *Journal of Teaching in Physical Education, 18*, 43-56.

Physical Activity Levels

Bradley, C. B., McMurray, R. G., Harrell, J. S., & Deng, S. (2000). Changes in common activities of 3rd through 10th graders: The CHIC Study. *Medicine & Science in Sports & Exercise, 32* (12), 2071-2078.

Eime, R., Harvey, J., Sawyer, N., Craike, M., Symons, C., Polman, R., & Payne, W. (2013). Understanding contexts of adolescent female participation in sport and physical activity. *Research Quarterly for Exercise and Sport, 84*, 157-166.

Patnode, C. D., Lytle, L.A., Erickson, D. J., Sirard, J. R., Barr-Anderson, D. J., & Story, M. (2011). Physical activity and sedentary activity patterns among children and adolescents: A latent class analysis approach. *Journal of Physical Activity and Health, 8*, 457-467.

Yli-Piipari, S., Leskinen, E., Jaakkola, T., & Liukkonen, J. (2012). Predictive role of physical education motivation: The developmental trajectories of physical activity during grades 7-9. *Research Quarterly for Exercise and Sport, 83* (4), 560-569.

Student Engagement and Motivation

Bernstein, E., Phillips, S. R., & Silverman, S. (2011). Attitudes and perceptions of middle school students toward competitive activities in physical education. *Journal of Teaching in Physical Education, 30*, 69-83.

Bevans, K., Fitzpatrick, L., Sanchez, B., & Forest, C. B. (2010). Individual and instructional determinants of student engagement in physical education. *Journal of Teaching in Physical Education*, *29*, 399-416.

Chen, A., & Darst, P. W. (2001). Situational interest in physical education: A function of learning task design. *Research Quarterly for Exercise and Sport*, *72* (2), 150-164.

Gao, Z., Lee, A. M., Ping, X., & Kosma, M. (2011). Effect of learning activity on students' motivation, physical activity levels and effort/persistence. *ICHPER-SD Journal of Research in Health, Physical Education, Recreation, Sport & Dance*, 6 (1), 27-33.

Gao, Z., Lee, A. M., Solmon, M. A., & Zhang, T. (2009). Changes in middle school students' motivation toward physical education over one school year. *Journal of Teaching in Physical Education*, *28*, 378-399.

Garn, A. C., Cothran, D. J., & Jenkins, J. M. (2011). A qualitative analysis of individual interest in middle school physical education: Perspective of early adolescents. *Physical Education & Sport Pedagogy*, *16* (3), 223-236.

Prusak, K. A., Treasure, D. C., Darst, P. W., & Pangrazi, R. (2004). The effects of choice on the motivation of adolescent girls in physical education. *Journal of Teaching in Physical Education*, *23,* 19-29.

Taylor, W., Yancey, A., Leslie, J., Murray, N., Cummings, S., Sharkey, S., Wert, C., James, J., Miles, O., & McCarthy, W. (1999). Physical activity among African American and Latino middle school girls: Consistent beliefs, expectations, and experience across two sites. *Women & Health*, *30* (2), 67-82.

Ward, J., Wilkinson, C., Graser, S. V., & Prusak, K. A. (2008). Effects of choice on student motivation and physical activity behavior in physical education. *Journal of Teaching in Physical Education*, *27*, 385-398.

Zhang, T., Solmon, M., Kosma, M., Carson, R. L., & Gu, X. (2011). Need support, need satisfaction, intrinsic motivation, and physical activity participation among middle school students. *Journal of Teaching in Physical Education*, *30*, 51-68.

About the Editors

Photo courtesy of University of Southern Mississippi.

Robert J. Doan, PhD, is an assistant professor of physical education in the University of Southern Mississippi's School of Kinesiology. Previously, he taught physical education in elementary school. Dr. Doan serves as a board member for the Mississippi Association for Health, Physical Education, Recreation and Dance, a SHAPE America state affiliate organization. He also serves as a physical education teacher education program reviewer for SHAPE America and as an article reviewer for two of SHAPE America's professional journals: *Strategies* and *Journal of Physical Education, Recreation & Dance*. Dr. Doan has conducted research on a variety of physical education topics and has presented at multiple conferences at the state, regional, and national levels. Dr. Doan earned his undergraduate degree from Grand Valley State University, attended Winthrop University for his master's degree, and completed his PhD in physical education with emphasis in curriculum and assessment at the University of South Carolina.

Photo courtesy of SUNY.

Lynn Couturier MacDonald, DPE, is a professor and chair of the physical education department at State University of New York College at Cortland (SUNY Cortland) and a former president of the National Association for Sport and Physical Education (NASPE). She chaired NASPE's Curriculum Framework & K-12 Standards Revision Task Force, which revised the National Standards for K-12 Physical Education and developed SHAPE America's Grade-Level Outcomes for K-12 Physical Education. Dr. MacDonald also served as a member of the SHAPE America task force that revised the National Standards for Initial Physical Education Teacher Education in 2016 and has served in numerous capacities for NASPE, the American Alliance for Health, Physical Education, Recreation and Dance (AAHPERD), and the National Council for the Accreditation of Coaching Education. She has published in several peer-reviewed journals in the areas of physical education pedagogy and women's sport history. Dr. MacDonald earned her BS and DPE degrees in physical education from Springfield College and her MS in biomechanics from the University of Illinois at Champaign-Urbana. Her postdoctoral study includes earning a graduate certificate in advanced feminist studies from the University of Massachusetts–Amherst and an MA in American studies from Trinity College in Connecticut. In 2016, she was inducted as a fellow in the North American Society for Health, Physical Education, Recreation, Sport and Dance, and in 2014, she received the AAHPERD Honor Award in recognition of her service to the physical education profession.

Photo courtesy of Winthrop University.

Stevie Chepko, EdD, is an independent consultant and researcher. Dr. Chepko is a former senior vice president of accreditation for the Council for the Accreditation of Educator Preparation. She is a well-respected authority on performance-based standards, teaching for mastery, and assessment in physical education. A hallmark of Dr. Chepko's professional service has been the development of materials that engage practitioners and that reflect best practices in the field. She served as the chair of the National Association for Sport and Physical Education (NASPE) task force named in 2006 to revise the National Standards for Initial Physical Education Teacher Education and served on the NASPE Curriculum Framework Task Force that developed SHAPE America's National Standards and Grade-Level Outcomes for K-12 Physical Education. Dr. Chepko's commitment to the profession has been recognized with many honors, including the American Alliance for Health, Physical Education, Recreation and Dance Honor Award; Eastern District Association (EDA), Vermont, Massachusetts and South Carolina Honor Awards; NASPE's Joy of Effort Award; selection as an inaugural fellow in the North American Society for Health, Physical Education, Recreation, Sport and Dance; and EDA Memorial Lecturer. She is a member of the West Virginia University Physical Education Hall of Fame and the Castleton State College Athletic Hall of Fame. Dr. Chepko earned her undergraduate degree from West Virginia University, attended the University of North Carolina at Greensboro for further graduate work, and completed her EdD in curriculum and instruction and sport history at Temple University.

About the Contributors

Photo courtesy of SUNY Cortland.

JoEllen Bailey, PhD, joined the faculty of State University of New York at Cortland (SUNY Cortland) in 2002 after teaching and coaching in higher education and public schools in both Minnesota and Wisconsin. She teaches courses at both the undergraduate and graduate levels at SUNY Cortland and coordinates the physical education study abroad program for student teaching in Australia. Her scholarly activity centers on teaching pedagogy; in particular, how to improve teacher education in physical education and the student teaching experience.

Photo courtesy of Herve Pelletier.

Matthew Bristol, BS, is a PreK-8 physical education teacher at Putney Central School in Putney, VT. Matt earned his BS in physical education at the University of Vermont, where he was awarded the Outstanding Physical Education Award from the university's College of Education. Matt has implemented many new programs at Putney Central, including a unique bicycle education program, on which he has presented at SHAPE America's Annual Convention & Expo and at the annual conference of the Vermont Association of Health, Physical Education, Recreation and Dance (VTAHPERD). In 2014, Matt received VTAHPERD's Rising Star Award. In his free time, Matt enjoys coaching, golfing, mountain biking, playing basketball, and spending time with friends.

Photo courtesy of DigiPrO Photography.

Colleen Buchanan started performing in musicals and plays when she was 7 years old. Later, she earned a BA in speech and theatre from Wagner College, a BSE in physical education, and an MS in recreation and outdoor pursuits from State University of New York at Cortland (SUNY Cortland). Buchanan was a competitive Scottish Highland Dancer for more than 15 years and has been the dance competition organizer for the Central New York Scottish Games for more than 20 years. She has been a member of the PECentral.com Dance Advisory Board since 2010, and in 2014 she was named Dance Education Teacher of the Year from the New York State Association for Health, Physical Education, Recreation and Dance. As a lecturer at SUNY Cortland for 21 years, Buchanan teaches a variety of dance, activity, and pedagogy courses.

Photo courtesy of Swofford Career Center, Inman, SC.

Erin Curran is assistant principal at Swofford Career Center in Inman, SC. She is a graduate of Winthrop University in Rock Hill, SC, where she earned a BS in physical education teacher certification and an MS in athletic administration. She also has an MEd in administration and supervision from Converse College in Spartanburg, SC. Before serving as assistant principal at Swofford Career Center, Erin facilitated a successful low ropes challenge course at the school for six years and has worked in the adventure education field for 12 years. She loves the idea of bringing tough concepts to life through activities and challenges, believing that adventure education develops character and teaches students how to become responsible citizens.

©Robyn Davis

Robyn Davis is a physical educator and coach in Charlotte, VT. She has worked to integrate physical education across the curriculum, bringing the joy of movement to students and the community. Robyn has been active in state, regional, and national associations, presenting and coordinating workshops and conferences. She is passionate

about physical education and wellness and their impact on developing lifelong habits for a healthy lifestyle.

Photo courtesy of Jeska Bailey Photography.

Evelyn J. Gordon, **PhD,** is an assistant professor of sport coaching education at the University of Southern Mississippi, where she teaches undergraduate courses in pedagogy. Her research interests include new teacher induction programs, informal and formal mentoring, and sport team cohesion.

Aaron Hart is director of educational programs for US Games and is a lecturer at State University of New at Cortland (SUNY Cortland). In 2015, Hart launched Online Physical Education Network (OPEN) at OPENPhysEd.org as a public service of US Games. He also has co-written several other curriculum projects, including the SPARK Middle School and High School projects. Hart travels throughout the United States to provide professional development, conference presentations, and curriculum support to physical educators and the school communities in which they work.

Photo courtesy of Isabelle Hart.

John Kruse is a middle school physical education teacher with the Los Angeles Unified School District. He is certified in physical education by the National Board for Profession Teaching Standards and also holds a master's degree in special education. In addition to teaching, Kruse has been highly involved in professional development as a teacher leader and co-site director of a California Health-Physical Education Subject Matter Project. Kruse has presented at state, regional, and national conferences and has obtained several grants to support quality physical education at his school. He recently received the 2016 Middle School Teacher of the Year award from the California Association for Health, Physical Education, Recreation and Dance, a state affiliate organization of SHAPE America's.

Photo courtesy of Jay Berkowitz, Los Angeles World Airports.

Brad Rettig has taught middle school physical education in Lincoln Public Schools in Nebraska for 10 years. He has helped develop physical education curricula for the school district and served on the National Association for Sport and Physical Education task force that developed SHAPE America's National Standards and Grade-Level Outcomes for K-12 Physical Education.

©Brad Rettig

Lori Secrist, EdS, is a National Board Certified Teacher in Early Middle Childhood Physical Education and has taught elementary school physical education for 17 years. She is currently serving as the assistant principal at the Center for Innovative Learning at Pinecrest, an alternative education program, and as an adjunct professor teaching undergraduate courses for the School of Education at the University of South Carolina - Aiken. Her focus is adding professional development training for her staff to increase movement opportunities into the daily curriculum of the students she currently serves.

Photo courtesy of Listas Photography.

About SHAPE America

SHAPE America – Society of Health and Physical Educators is committed to ensuring that all children have the opportunity to lead healthy, physically active lives. As the nation's largest membership organization of health and physical education professionals, SHAPE America works with its 50 state affiliates and is a founding partner of national initiatives including the Presidential Youth Fitness Program, *Let's Move!* Active Schools, and the Jump Rope For Heart and Hoops For Heart programs.

Since its founding in 1885, the organization has defined excellence in physical education, most recently creating *National Standards & Grade-Level Outcomes for K-12 Physical Education* (2014), National Standards & Guidelines for Physical Education Teacher Education (2009), and *National Standards for Sport Coaches* (2006), and participating as a member of the Joint Committee on National Health Education Standards, which published *National Health Education Standards, Second Edition: Achieving Excellence* (2007). Our programs, products and services provide the leadership, professional development and advocacy that support health and physical educators at every level, from preschool through university graduate programs.

The SHAPE America website, www.shapeamerica.org, holds a treasure trove of free resources for health and physical educators, adapted physical education teachers, teacher trainers, and coaches, including activity calendars, curriculum resources, tools and templates, assessments, and more. Visit www.shapeamerica.org and search for Teacher's Toolbox.

Every spring, SHAPE America hosts its National Convention & Expo, the premier national professional-development event for health and physical educators.

Advocacy is an essential element in the fulfillment of our mission. By speaking out for the school health and physical education professions, SHAPE America strives to make an impact on the national policy landscape.

Our Vision: Healthy People—Physically Educated and Physically Active!

Our Mission: To advance professional practice and promote research related to health and physical education, physical activity, dance and sport.

SHAPE AMERICA'S COMMITMENT: 50 MILLION STRONG BY 2029

Approximately 50 million students are enrolled currently in America's elementary and secondary schools (grades preK through 12). SHAPE America is leading the effort to ensure that by the time today's youngest students graduate from high school in 2029, all of America's young people are empowered to lead healthy and active lives through effective health and physical education programs. To learn more about 50 Million Strong by 2029, visit www.shapeamerica.org.

One step can start a national movement.

Membership does more than advance your career—it's also your first step in a national movement to help all children become healthy, physically educated adults.

Joining SHAPE America Is Your First Step Toward:

- **Improving your instructional practices.** Membership is your direct connection to the books and other classroom resources, webinars, workshops, and professional development you need. **Members save up to 30%!**

- **Staying current on trends in education.** We will deliver the news to you through our weekly e-newsletter *Et Cetera,* our quarterly member newsletter *Momentum,* and peer-reviewed journals like *Strategies: A Journal for Physical and Sport Educators,* the *American Journal of Health Education, Journal of Physical Education, Recreation & Dance,* and *Research Quarterly for Exercise and Sport.*

- **Earning recognition for you and your program.** Showcase your school's achievements and gain funding through grant and award opportunities.

- **Growing your professional network.** Whether it's a face-to-face event or online through the member-exclusive community—Exchange—you'll gain access to a diverse group of peers who can help you respond to daily challenges.

Join Today. www.shapeamerica.org/membership

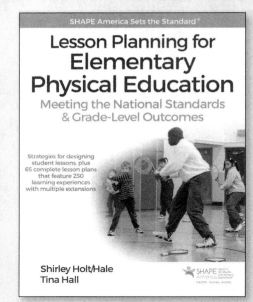

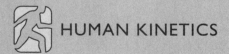